JEWISH EMANCIPATION

Jewish Emancipation

A HISTORY ACROSS FIVE CENTURIES

David Sorkin

PRINCETON UNIVERSITY PRESS

PRINCETON & OXFORD

Copyright © 2019 by Princeton University Press

Published by Princeton University Press
41 William Street, Princeton, New Jersey 08540
6 Oxford Street, Woodstock, Oxfordshire OX20 1TR

press.princeton.edu

All Rights Reserved

LCCN 2019936032
ISBN 9780691164946

British Library Cataloging-in-Publication Data is available

Editorial: Eric Crahan and Pamela Weidman
Production Editorial: Debbie Tegarden
Jacket Design: C. Alvarez-Gaffin
Jacket Credit: *Baruch Eschwege as a Volunteer Fusilier*, ca. 1817–18. Painted by Moritz
Daniel Oppenheim (1800–82). Historisches Museum, Frankfurt / akg-images
Production: Merli Guerra
Publicity: Kate Farquhar-Thomson

This book has been composed in Classic Miller

Printed on acid-free paper. ∞

Printed in the United States of America

10 9 8 7 6 5 4 3 2 1

For Daphne, Netta, Maxima, and Ramona

CONTENTS

Maps

Halftones

JEWISH EMANCIPATION

Ambiguous and Interminable Emancipation

ON NOVEMBER 13, 1934, NAHUM GOLDMANN, a diplomat representing three prominent Jewish organizations, met with Benito Mussolini, Italy's Fascist dictator, to request his assistance to avert some of the looming threats to Jews across Europe. At the end of the conversation Mussolini, a truculent opponent of democracy, asked Goldmann a pointed question: "Why have Jews everywhere always been such dogged supporters of formal democracy?"[1] Acutely aware that this was "a very delicate point," Goldmann thoughtfully answered: "Democracy brought the Jews emancipation and civil rights, and they are naturally thankful to it."[2]

This book is a history of the Jews' "emancipation and civil rights." It analyzes the complex and multidirectional process whereby Jews acquired civil and political rights and came to exercise citizenship's prerogatives. The book is primarily concerned with Europe yet also examines North Africa and the Middle East, the United States and Israel. It assesses the transition from late medieval institutions and the ways in which rights were acquired; the limitations of rights as well as continuing forms of state and non-state discrimination; and, in some cases, the revocation and subsequent restoration of rights. The book is primarily a legal and political history focused on the process of gaining, exercising, retaining, and, where lost, recovering rights, as well as the tensions between laws and their implementation.

The term "emancipation" has been historically polysemous, denoting the inclusion of the excluded and the elevation of the oppressed. It has been applied to the manumission of slaves, the liberation of serfs, the equalization of workers and women, and the release from persecution or disabilities of adherents of dissenting religions. The emancipation of Jews has affinities to all those acceptations, but it is directly linked to the last. The very term "emancipation" came to be widely applied to Jews after "Catholic emancipation" in England (1829). For the purposes of this book, "Jewish emancipation" concerns first and foremost the Jews' inclusion, elevation, or equalization as a distinct religious group. European polities had engaged in destructive wars and systematic persecution over religion for centuries; to endeavor to erect multiconfessional societies, first through various forms of toleration, then through equality, was a historic achievement. Only in the twentieth century did emancipation come to designate alterations in the Jews' status as a "nation" or a "race."[3]

Emancipation included civil and political rights. Civil rights comprised residence and occupation, property ownership, and freedom of worship, as well as serving as a witness in court, swearing an oath, and having juridical standing to bring a lawsuit. Political rights denoted appointment to the civil service, holding elected office, and exercising the franchise.

For the purposes of this book emancipation designates the acquisition, loss, or recovery of any of those rights. In some cases, the full range of civil and political rights was at stake; in others exclusively political rights; in still others only one right. Equality requires the ability to exercise all rights; inequality results from the deprivation of even one right. I use "emancipation" as an elastic term to delineate a protracted and variegated process whose myriad installments ranged from the maximal to the minimal.

My aim in writing a study of emancipation is to redirect the focus of modern Jewish history. I want to point the camera lens to this neglected yet foundational event of the past four and a half centuries. The two colossal events of the mid-twentieth century, the Holocaust and the State of Israel's foundation, have obstructed our field of vision and overwhelmed our cognitive capacities. We have largely lost sight and comprehension of the *longue durée* of modern Jewish history, the contours of the last half millennium.

The murder of six million Jews and the establishment of a Jewish state were events of monumental importance. They deserve the libraries of books and mountains of articles devoted to them, as well as those yet to come. Yet a narrative of Jewish history that focuses on or concludes in 1933–45 or 1948, whether it construes those events as accidental or inevitable, is fundamentally problematic. We are now in the twenty-first century; history has not ceased. Those two events mark neither the consummation nor the culmination of modern Jewish history. In fact, both are part and parcel of the long history of Jewish emancipation. They were reactions to, indeed developments from, emancipation. In philosophical parlance, they were epiphenomena. Emancipation was, and remains, the principal event.

If emancipation is so consequential, why have scholars and writers not addressed it? Many scholars have acknowledged emancipation's undeniable centrality. Salo Baron, the first historian of the Jews appointed at a major American university, wrote in the opening lines of his classic article, "Ghetto and Emancipation" (1928): "The history of the Jews in the last century and a half has turned about one central fact: that of Emancipation."[4] Or as David Vital, then at Tel-Aviv University, wrote more recently:

> The principal engine of change in the modern history of the Jews of Europe was the revolutionary idea that it might after all be right and proper for them to enjoy full and equal civil and political rights with all other subjects of the several realms they inhabited. All turned, therefore, in the final analysis on the matter of emancipation. . . . No other factor operating upon them in modern times would serve so powerfully to precipitate such revolutionary changes in their mores, their culture, their internal social structure, and, more generally and loosely, their private and collective concerns and expectations.[5]

Despite such pronouncements, much of the attention emancipation receives is limited in scope and implication. Most scholarship focuses on individual cities, regions, or countries; it is neither comparative nor transnational. The scholarship therefore does not impinge upon, let alone substantively alter, received interpretations. The accepted views largely remain what they were almost half a century ago, before a bourgeoning scholarship began to reshape the understanding of modern Jewish history.[6]

The reasons for this relative neglect are obvious. As the symbol of modernity, separating the medieval from the modern world, "tradition" from "modernity," emancipation is more likely to be extolled or excoriated than rigorously studied: it is overdetermined by the Jewish world's ideological divisions. Those divisions have produced two formidable obstacles to rigorous scholarship.

The first obstacle is that emancipation is held responsible for the dissolution of the communal autonomy or self-government that for millennia had provided diaspora Jewry with a coherent framework for cohesive collective life. From early in the emancipation process Jewish integrationists or emancipationists had celebrated the end of this communal structure and emancipation's supposedly unqualified benefits. They portrayed emancipation as a form of providential progress from the dark night of persecution and subjugation to the blazing sunlight of toleration and equality.[7]

In marked contrast, Jewish self-segregationists or nationalists held emancipation culpable not only for the end of communal autonomy and self-government but also for its odious result, "assimilation," a concept they invented and propagated. Zionists, Bundists, and Autonomists regarded emancipation as the cause of all modern Jewry's agonies and tragedies. They thought emancipation had either coerced or, worse still, seduced Jews to renounce their language, culture, religion, and, ultimately, national life. They cultivated the characteristic fin-de-siècle nationalist invention of a pure essentialist world that had been lost.[8]

The second and even more forbidding obstacle is the supposedly negative verdict of history. For many Jews, the Holocaust unequivocally proclaimed not just emancipation's calamitous failure in fact but its ineluctable failure in principle. Many Jews wittingly or unwittingly espoused a determinist teleology.[9] In their eyes emancipation engendered the Jews' assimilation, which in turn awakened Christian animus and provoked a new enmity, political and racial anti-Semitism. In a Europe in the grip of aggressive irredentism, ultranationalism, and racism, the old animus and the new enmity joined to produce the Holocaust.

The lesson many Jews and historians of modern Jewry derived from the Holocaust was to repudiate emancipation by making it either culpable for, or complicit in, the Holocaust: they considered Nazism solely vis-à-vis the Jews.[10] That parochial view led them to forget the implications of Nahum Goldmann's answer to Mussolini: democracy was the cause of emancipation, its destruction the essential precondition of emancipation's demolition. Nazi Germany's first step toward racist legislation, persecution, deportation, and mass murder was to raze democracy.[11]

For many this teleology has one additional station, the founding of the State of Israel. There tragedy gave way to triumph, destruction to salvation. Zionism emerged in response to the dual threat of assimilation within and anti-Semitism without. The Jewish state alone rescued European Jewry's surviving remnants. It alone offered all Jews everywhere refuge from the Diaspora (Galut), most immediately those from North Africa (Maghreb) and the Middle East (Mashreq). Israel restored the Jews' national life and pride. For some it opened the path to messianic redemption.[12]

This book aims neither to celebrate nor to censure emancipation. I neither idealize emancipation as the pinnacle of progress nor denigrate it as the nadir of egregious error. I offer neither a narrative of triumph nor a chronicle of tragedy. Rather, I endeavor to capture emancipation's inherent ambiguities, its triumph and its tragedy. The triumphs and tragedies were interlocking; each implied the other. There could not have been triumphs without vicissitudes, tragedies without striking successes. Yet even more, I try to capture quotidian and complex political processes that defy hyperbole.

This book emphasizes the "how" of emancipation: it analyzes emancipation as a process. This is a political and legal history that tries to study emancipation's unfolding to describe and define its highly diverse permutations. First and foremost, we need to know precisely what emancipation was.[13] We can only achieve this understanding if we investigate emancipation as part of the larger history of citizenship. The Jews' emancipation cannot be studied in isolation. To cast it as a parochial issue is to misconceive it from the start. We must locate it in its multiple and varied contexts, namely, the individual states in which it developed as well as the transnational patterns that emerged. Furthermore, emancipation was, and remains, an interminable project. It was not a neatly circumscribed or clearly bounded event; it has continued for over five centuries. We must study it from its origins to its recent manifestations.

Chronology

Emancipation was recurring and interminable. Jews began to gain rights neither with the Enlightenment's advocacy of a common humanity nor with the French Revolution's promulgation of citizenship. It did not end with the achievement of emancipation across western and central Europe (England, 1858; Austria-Hungary, 1867; Italy, 1870; Germany, 1870) or eastern Europe (Russia, 1917).[14] Emancipation was neither a one-time, chronologically discrete event nor a linear one.

In Italy Jews gained emancipation five times (1796–99, 1801, 1848, 1870, 1944) and lost it four times (1800, 1813–15, 1848, 1938). In France Jews gained emancipation six times (1790, 1791, 1818, 1870, 1944, 1961) and lost it twice (1808, 1940). In the German states, they attained rights four times (1800–1813, 1848, 1870, 1945) and lost them three times (1815, 1848, 1933–41). In Russia Catherine granted privileges in the 1780s that she and her successors rescinded from the 1790s; Alexander III and Nicholas II restricted or overturned (1881–1914) privileges Alexander II had extended in the 1850s to 1870s; and in the 1920s the Bolsheviks disenfranchised many of the Jews the February 1917 revolution had enfranchised. In the United States Jews struggled to gain political rights in some states in the nineteenth century. In the 1940s to 1960s they campaigned to regain the civil rights they had lost in the first half of the twentieth century.

A chronology of emancipation that starts from 1750 or 1789, and ends in 1870 or 1917, is erroneous. Emancipation started earlier and, significantly, extended later. Indeed, emancipation continues to the present.

In the abstract there is a clear divide between privileges in corporate society and rights in civil society. In a corporate or estate society privileges were group specific. Groups held specific privileges through legislated charters that granted them a defined legal status, for example, nobles, priests, burghers. In contrast, the American and French revolutions introduced universal rights predicated on the liberty and equality of the individual. Civil society emerged when group-specific privileges gave way to uniform rights guaranteeing individual equality.[15]

Whereas privileges in corporate society are conceptually distinct from rights in civil society, historically they were not. Citizenship in civil society emerged from citizenship in corporate society; parity of privileges in corporate society could lead to equality in civil society.

From 1550 Jews in eastern (Polish-Lithuanian Commonwealth) and western Europe (Italian city-states; Bordeaux) began to gain extensive privileges bordering on parity with Christian burghers and merchants. In some cases, there was a direct transition from privileges to rights. From the 1590s Jews in western Europe began to gain civil rights in nascent civil societies (Amsterdam, London).

The ancien régime persisted and informed the new one in other ways as well. Corporate structures and the confessional state, that is, a state defined by the embrace of one religion, survived well into the nineteenth century, sometimes longer. They became a locus of institutional and ideological opposition to emancipation.

There was no single legal status that characterized Jews across Europe let alone other continents prior to emancipation. In fact, there were multiple points of departure. To posit the existence of a single entity such as the "autonomous community" as characteristic of Jewish life everywhere is to reify the pre-emancipation past.[16] Similarly, one cannot speak of the "ghetto" as representative of that pre-emancipation Jewish life. "Ghetto" versus "emancipation" is an evocative yet false binary. Actual ghettos were the exception rather than the rule. This book has no single background chapter describing the Jews' status prior to emancipation. Instead, I describe the situation place by place, region by region, polity by polity.

We cannot define emancipation without including the developments of the sixteenth to the eighteenth centuries. They were not precursors or harbingers but integral elements (chapters 1–6).[17]

Emancipation did not end in 1870 or 1917. Although the Minority Rights Treaties (1919–24) that emerged from the wreckage of World War I guaranteed Jews citizenship in the successor states to the Austro-Hungarian Dual Monarchy, the states infringed those rights. Hungary was the first, enacting a numerus clausus in education (1920). Until 1931, Poland used legislation of the former partitioning powers to impose restrictions. Austria employed a racial definition to prevent former Galician Jews from gaining rights. Romania enacted laws that denied Jews rights in its newly acquired territories. After a decade of acting as the "incubator of nations," the Soviet government brutally dismantled the institutions that supported Jews as an extraterritorial minority (chapter 22).

The Nazis put the abrogation of emancipation front and center. They abolished German Jews' political rights in 1933–35 and systematically deprived them of remaining rights until stripping them of state membership at the time of deportation (1941). Nazi Germany's example encouraged its allied and client states. Poland endeavored to exclude Jews from the economy and educational institutions. Hungary enacted its "First Jew Law" in 1938 aiming to reduce their participation in the economy and followed with more. Romania began to restrict the Jews' rights from 1934. As part of its "second" Fascist revolution (1938), Italy adopted racial laws excluding Jews from the economy and relegating them to an inferior form of citizenship. Vichy France's "national revolution" did much the same (chapter 23).

Regaining citizenship in Europe after World War II entailed the restoration of rights, the restitution of property, and the negotiation of reparations. Some issues of property and reparations are still being addressed (chapter 24). The new state of Israel faced the challenge of shaping citizenship for a heterogeneous population: Jews from various countries as well as Arabs, Bedouins, and Druze (chapter 26). In the United States Jews campaigned for civil equality (employment, housing, university admissions) for almost two decades (1948–64) (chapter 27).

Equality and the exercise of citizenship were and are, always and everywhere, fragile, subject to substantial infringement if not outright abrogation. The process of emancipation continues into the twenty-first century. Jews everywhere live in the era of Emancipation.

Citizenship

Extending the chronology backward to the sixteenth century reveals something fundamental about the nature of citizenship. Jews were not seeking admission to states possessing fully formed concepts of citizenship. Rather, the states were in formation and defining citizenship and equality. Moreover, they did so largely in relationship to religion.

In Europe religion defined the boundaries of belonging to a polity into the nineteenth and twentieth centuries. Indeed, putatively ethnic or national divisions in the nineteenth and twentieth centuries were often, at bottom, religious ones.[18] Consequently, the formation of citizenship frequently entailed a procession of hierarchically arranged religions. Confessional states first created citizenship for members of the established, public, or dominant religion. Next came dissident or dissenting Christians. Jews were necessarily the problematic last group. In Anglican England Jews followed Protestant dissenters (non-Anglicans) and Catholics. In the Catholic Habsburg Empire, they followed the Eastern Orthodox and Protestants, in Catholic France Protestants (Huguenots). In the "Protestant pluralism" of the thirteen colonies and the United States, Jews and Catholics followed minority Protestants. The Ottoman Empire introduced equality primarily for Christian minorities; Jews were collateral beneficiaries.[19]

The Jews' status vis-à-vis other religions appeared in the built environment: Christian Europe had an ecclesiastical building code. "Public worship" (*exercitium religionis publicum*) was usually reserved for the established or dominant faith. It permitted an ecclesiastical building distinguished by a spire and bells that stood in a visible public space: a street or boulevard, a square, or a piazza. Its adherents could mount public observance such as processions. "Private worship" (*exercitium religionis privatum*) was assigned to a dissenting or inferior confession. It prescribed an ecclesiastical building hidden from the public view: bereft of spire and bells, the building stood in a lane or behind other buildings in a courtyard. Its adherents had to avoid gathering in public view; they were prohibited from mounting public observance. Domestic worship (*devotio domestica*) was granted to the least tolerated of faiths: small groups could worship in an adherent's home. Synagogues followed this code; I attempt to trace the synagogue's shifting status.[20]

As Jews gained rights Judaism's status came into play. What was Judaism's status vis-à-vis the established/dominant and dissenting/minority religions? Did it enjoy the same perquisites as other religions? Was it a public organization or a private association? Was it tax exempt? If the state subsidized other religions did it subsidize Judaism? If the state paid pastors' and priests' salaries did it also pay those of rabbis? The equality of Judaism was integral to the Jews' equality. Emancipating the Jews entailed emancipating Judaism.

Two states in Europe created models of citizenship abstracted from birth and religion: the Habsburg Empire did so by reform, France by revolution.[21] Significantly, and not surprisingly, these two states provided the models for legislation emancipating Jews as well. Other states then adapted that legislation to their own political structures.

The Habsburg Joseph II created the model of conditional or incremental emancipation, meaning partial rights given in reward for utility to the state. Joseph II's legislation was inherently ambiguous: it both admitted Jews to existing estates ("into" estates) and deprived them of estate or quasi-estate status ("out of" estates). He gave some Jews rights by admitting them to guilds, that is, they gained estate-specific privileges ("into" estates). He also gave Jews rights by dismantling or reducing the corporate Jewish community's privileges ("out of" estates). In practice, partial emancipation persisted until 1867 when the new Dual Monarchy resolved the fundamental ambiguity of "into" and "out of" estates in favor of the latter (chapters 4, 11, 12, 13, 14).

France created the model of unconditional emancipation, meaning immediate full and equal rights gained through extraction "out of" estates. This legislation was in keeping with the Revolution's general dissolution of estates and corporate bodies, for example, nobility, clergy. France's practice of emancipation was, however, decidedly ambiguous. Sephardic Jews gained rights through the confirmation of their privileges (1790); there was an early reversion to conditional rights (Napoleon, 1808); forms of inequality lingered into the 1830s and 1840s; and the entire process recapitulated itself in Algeria (1830–70), although the Mzabi Saharan Jews did not receive citizenship until 1961 (chapters 7, 9, 17).

Unconditional emancipation or outright abrogation came with seismic events such as revolutions, unifications, wars, and the collapse of democracy that thoroughly transformed the political landscape. Those events were, however, always linked to long-term developments. German unification, for example, completed an ongoing emancipation of almost a century. As is usually the case, a prolonged concatenation of events prepared the way for the seemingly dramatic rupture.

Citizenship in Europe involved two legal traditions. States granted citizenship by residence (jus soli) and by descent (jus sanguinis). States rarely used exclusively one law. France, for example, oscillated between the two for centuries.[22] To understand the nature of citizenship and the Jews' status, it is imperative to know which legal tradition a state employed and precisely how the state defined and deployed it.

The Three Regions

An "east" versus "west" binary has become a commonplace in writing about European Jewish history. Since the fin de siècle, Jews of all persuasions and many historians of modern Jewry contrasted the emancipated "west," threatened by "assimilation" and the new political and racial anti-Semitism, with the unemancipated "east," subject to persecution and discrimination, endemic poverty and pogroms. This distinction possessed more verisimilitude than veracity; it was ideological rather than analytical.[23]

We should instead divide Europe into three regions. A tripartite scheme allows us to discern the regions' distinct political practices and legislative policies as well as the interaction between the regions. This book posits that no one region let alone country can be treated as normative. The venerable tendency of historians to make German Jewry the model for emancipation—an intense and torturous emancipation formative for "modernity"—is untenable.[24] Emancipation comprised a "complex variegated family of instances": gaining equal rights across Europe's three regions was fundamentally similar, yet the differences between regions, and the variations among countries, were also fundamental.[25]

WESTERN EUROPE (HOLLAND, ENGLAND, FRANCE) (CHAPTERS 1, 5, 7, 8, 9, 17, 23, 24)

In southern France, the Netherlands, and England Jews gained civil rights through the circumstances of settlement (chapter 1). The scope of the struggle for rights was therefore narrow: Jews had to mobilize only for political rights. This pattern also applied, mutatis mutandis, to the Dutch and British colonies and to Jamaica, Canada, and the United States (chapter 18). The duration of the struggle for rights was, albeit intense, relatively brief.

Emancipation's sticking point in France was Alsace. Since France had definitively acquired the entire region only in the seventeenth century, Jews had corporate privileges and an occupational structure characteristic of the Holy Roman Empire that was in tension with their neighbors and France's laws (chapters 5, 7, 9).

CENTRAL EUROPE (GERMAN STATES, HABSBURG EMPIRE) (CHAPTERS 3, 4, 8, 11, 12, 13, 14, 22, 23, 24).

From the sixteenth to eighteenth centuries polities had enacted "Jewry laws" that imposed an inferior legal status, relegating Jews to the margins of corporate society and differentiating among them according to their ascribed utility. Some prominent individuals ("Court Jews") gained extensive privileges. The struggle for rights was broad in scope, encompassing both civil and political rights, and prolonged, lasting for most of a century. Central European states granted conditional or partial emancipation, making additional rights contingent upon "regeneration," that is, the restructuring of occupations, education, and communal and religious life to promote utility to the state.[26] The state legislated and supervised that regeneration. States granted rights by moving Jews both "into" and "out of" estates. A definitive policy of "out of" estates came only with the seismic events of restructuring (Dual Monarchy, 1867) or unification (Germany, 1870).

A complication peculiar to central Europe was the dualism of local/municipal citizenship (*Stadtsbürgerschaft*; *Heimatrecht*) versus state citizenship (*Staatsbürgerschaft*; *Staatsangehörigkeit*). That dualism was due to the persistence of corporate institutions and informed the emancipation process throughout, assuming ever newer forms. A further complication was the territories that Prussia (Posen) and the Habsburg Empire (Galicia) seized from Poland: these backwaters became testing grounds for legislation (chapters 6, 10).

EASTERN EUROPE (POLISH-LITHUANIAN COMMONWEALTH, RUSSIA, CONGRESS POLAND) (CHAPTERS 2, 6, 10, 15, 16, 22, 23, 24)

Tsarist Russia found itself in conflict with the structure of the territories it seized in the partitions of Poland (1772, 1793–95), including the Jews' privileges and the private market town (shtetl). As in central Europe, the struggle for rights was broad in scope, encompassing both civil and political rights, and prolonged, lasting for over a century. It also involved far more Jews: sheer numbers became a significant factor.

Russian legislation followed central European models of conditional emancipation that made rights contingent upon regeneration. In adopting central European models, Russia emphasized coercion ("sticks") over incentives ("carrots"). Moreover, Russian legislation adhered to the policy of moving Jews as individuals "into" estates, in large part because of the estates' nature. The estates were not direct descendants of medieval or early modern institutions that were independent of, and potentially resistant to, state authority. Rather, the tsarist monarchy devised the estates in the eighteenth century to serve its interests. Finally, in contrast to western and central Europe, where civil rights came first, Jews first gained political rights (Congress Poland, 1861; Russia, 1905) and then civil rights (Congress Poland, 1862; Russia, 1917).

The Ottoman Empire constituted a fourth region of emancipation. An Islamic polity intent on preserving the integrity of religious groups, it shaped its own version of emancipation. By abolishing the centuries-old status of a tribute-paying inferior (*dhimmi*), the empire granted legal equality to Christians, Jews, and members of other religions (1839, 1856). At the same time, the Ottoman Empire accorded the restructured religious communities (*millets*) authority over education and jurisdiction over personal status, for example, marriage, divorce, burial (chapter 21). The State of Israel inherited Ottoman personal status laws: it rejected civil marriage and gave rabbinic courts control of marriage and divorce (chapter 26).

Politics

Emancipation mobilized Jews politically, consistently and continuously, from its inception until today. Jews were actively engaged in gaining parity and equality from the start. They were tirelessly engaged in defending rights once gained. They were, then, active agents at every stage. A distinct emancipation politics emerged over five centuries.

At least two positions have militated against the proper recognition of emancipation politics. First, many historians emphasized that emancipation was "as much a historic necessity for the modern state as it was for the Jews."[27] They therefore regarded rulers, bureaucrats, and parliaments as the principal actors. In this interpretation, Jews were either supporting actors or passive beneficiaries.[28]

More influentially, Jewish nationalists and nationalist historians denied the very possibility of diaspora Jewish politics. They asserted that their own movements initiated Jewish politics in modern Europe. Nahum Goldmann claimed, for example, that Chaim Weizmann had "created" Jewish diplomacy.[29] For nationalists "emancipation politics" was not just a solecism but a true oxymoron, a logical and historical impossibility.[30] They coined the term "auto-emancipation" to characterize their agency on behalf of nationalist projects in contrast to the Jews' putative passivity vis-à-vis "emancipation."[31]

I have tried to note Jews' political engagement wherever I found it. Since my emphasis is on the larger process of emancipation it has not been possible to offer a full analysis of emancipation politics let alone a general anatomy of modern Jewish politics. Similarly, I have noted, yet not tried to offer, a detailed account of emancipation's opponents. I have pointed to the main positions and ideas, but I have not tried to assess persons, parties, or movements. Emancipation politics and emancipation's opponents are appropriate subjects for another book.

It is important to state explicitly what else this book is not: it is neither a survey of modern Jewish history nor a study of the Jews' "modernization." To be sure, as David Vital's long passage attests, emancipation was the "engine" of momentous changes in every aspect of Jewish life. For my purposes, it is essential to disaggregate emancipation from its consequences, yet also from its causes. I defer consideration of consequences just as I eschew a detailed examination of emancipation's causes. I offer neither a grand theory of origins nor a sweeping account of ramified results.[32] Emancipation is immense; it invites voluminous treatment; it risks an unreadable tome. To counteract that tendency, I adhere to the counsel I have offered for over three decades to students embarking on research: "choose a broad topic narrowly defined."

Conclusion

Some readers may find this book's conclusions disturbing. Once we realize that emancipation is an interminable process that is an integral aspect of Jews' contemporary experience, we are forced to acknowledge that there are in fact no settled answers to the most pressing political and indeed existential issues of Jewish life. Neither the establishment of the State of Israel nor the flourishing of American Jewry let alone the rebuilding of Jewish life in Europe has definitively answered emancipation's challenges. The larger struggle for political equality and the full exercise of citizenship, for Jews, by Jews, and for other groups, remains pressing. The only thing we can confidently assert is that this struggle is inherently protean: it will be populated by ever new issues and causes, by proponents and opponents whose appearance and actions we cannot predict.

PART I

The Three Regions Emerge

MAP I. Sixteenth- and seventeenth-century port cities in Italy (Ancona, Ferrara, Venice, Livorno) and on the Atlantic seaboard (Bordeaux, Hamburg, Amsterdam, London). Cox Cartographic.

MAP II. Holy Roman Empire and the Polish-Lithuanian Commonwealth circa 1648.
Cox Cartographic.

CHAPTER ONE

Merchant Colonies

EMANCIPATION EMERGED FROM A NEW ERA in European and Jewish history. The sixteenth century witnessed the end of two and a half centuries of expulsions (England 1290, France 1394) that had culminated in the exile from Spain (1492) and from central European towns and cities in the first half of the sixteenth century. Those expulsions had virtually emptied western Europe and most of urban central Europe of Jewish settlement.

Yet within half a century or so, numerous rulers were inviting Jewish merchants into their cities on exceptionally propitious terms. These terms ranged from minimal rights of settlement, residence, trade, and worship to forms of near parity or parity of privileges in civil matters. To be sure, the most favorable of these privileges were not unprecedented: Jews had possessed citizenship in various towns or cities during the Middle Ages.[1] Yet after the prolonged period of expulsions such privileges were unquestionably novel.

Why this new municipal status? Why the award of some combination of civil privileges, for example, freedom of settlement, residence, property ownership, occupations, and worship, though decidedly not political privileges, that one historian has termed "civil inclusion"?[2]

The Jews' new status resulted from an ensemble of factors. Mercantilism was an early modern form of state or city-state economic policy that aimed to maximize state revenues by giving precedence to economic considerations. This policy of state aggrandizement, or state-driven capitalism, included: developing trade and especially exports but also trade-related manufacturing and population increase through various forms of colonization. The premise was that the larger and wealthier the populace, the greater the state's revenues.

Acting on these ideas commercial cities, and especially port cities, endeavored to create the physical and legal conditions that would attract foreign merchants, and, if possible, stimulate native merchants, to bring the trade and wealth that could fill state or city-state coffers.[3]

Foreign merchant colonies in European cities were founded on chartered privileges of settlement and trade. Generally known as "nations," such colonies dated from as early as the twelfth century yet proliferated in the fifteenth and sixteenth centuries. These "nations" had a common geographic origin and prior to the Reformation often shared a local or regional version of Catholic practice. After the Reformation they often shared a distinct religion in contrast to, and sometimes in conflict with, that of the larger society.[4] Venetians, Genoese, Portuguese, and Germans flocked to seaports like Bruges and Antwerp; Florentines, Milanese, Genoese, Germans, and Portuguese gathered in commercial centers like Lyon.[5]

Such merchant colonies were characterized by self-government and immunity from local law.[6] The home government generally appointed a consul who governed the merchant colony. He exercised jurisdiction over legal disputes among its members; apportioned and collected dues or taxes; and meted out punishment. Those who went to local courts were subject to fines. The consul also negotiated with the local authorities, trying to gain or retain exemption from any special taxation beyond normal tariffs or the obligation to serve as, or quarter, soldiers.[7]

The members of a merchant colony often prayed in a consular chapel or a designated area of a local church. "Community life found its most visual expression in religious ceremonies."[8] In some cities individual merchants obtained municipal citizenship.

However commercially successful, the colony was always legally precarious: its all-important privileges rested on a charter that was revocable and usually required periodic renewal.

The Jewish merchants who congregated in some of those same cities formed variations on the merchant colony. Their political status was comparable to that of the other merchant colonies or "nations." They were granted charters that delineated their privileges. The charters had a specified duration that entailed periodic renewal.

There were usually significant differences between the Jews' charters and those of the other merchant colonies. Sometimes Jews gained greater religious freedom than other groups, that is, the privilege of private worship (designated building that was not visibly a synagogue) or even public worship (a recognizably sacred building) rather than mere domestic worship. Salient emblems of this status were the public synagogues of Livorno (1595) and Amsterdam (Esnoga; 1675) and the private synagogue in London (Bevis Marks; 1701).

Sometimes self-government had a broader scope because of the nature of Jewish law. Jews sometimes had inferior economic privileges, that is, they were excluded from guilds or other established occupations to prevent competition with native groups. Usually the charters granted some combination of civil privileges (residence, occupations, property ownership, worship) but not political ones (civil service, political office, military commissions).

There was also a fundamental distinction between the corporate parity of chartered communities, such as Ancona, Venice, Livorno, Bordeaux, and Hamburg, and the civil parity of those without charters, such as Amsterdam and London. In the latter Jews gained rights on an ad hoc basis in an emerging civil society. In the cases of Amsterdam and London, we should additionally consider the relationship between the Jews' status at home and in the colonies: mercantilist policy was often at its most magnanimous in the distant colonies. The overwhelming need to implant white colonists resulted in more generous privileges or even more extensive forms of parity.

The Jewish merchants who inhabited these communities were active agents in their creation. They sought out likely cities, submitted petitions and projects, negotiated privileges, and even wrote tracts in the vernacular defending their participation in commerce. However critical these merchants were to the foundation of new settlements, they were, as affluent leaders, a small percentage of the Jewish population. The majority did not seek or receive grants of extensive privileges: they at best sought the privilege of residence and the accompanying hope for gainful employment or a modicum of charity. Not surprisingly, the wealthy who founded new settlements erected oligarchical, lay-dominated community structures.[9]

The cities that housed these diverse merchant communities constituted the sites of the "port Jews"—those Jews of Sephardi and Italian extraction whose experience of the early modern period was distinguished from their Ashkenazi counterparts by a favorable legal status, residence in cities that valued maritime commerce, and acculturation to some version of European culture.[10]

Those same cities belonged to what geographers and economists call the "urban column." These were the cities "arching upwards from Northern Italy, through Switzerland and South Germany, into the Rhineland and Southern Netherlands, onwards through the United Provinces and then curving across the North Sea, through London, to end in the industrialised West Midlands of England . . . a pattern of cities . . . which in turn dominated European commerce and manufacturing from the Late Middle Ages onwards . . . [and which revealed a] gradual shift of commercial and industrial hegemony from south to north-west Europe."[11] These cities functioned as major agents of change, being at the forefront of not only commerce and industry but also the "growth of literacy," "the production of arts," and, significantly, "religious toleration."[12] It was within the "urban column's" port cities during the period of overseas expansion that Jews became one highly valued merchant group alongside others.

Mercantilism promoted the development of a Sephardi merchant network across the Mediterranean after the Spanish expulsion. Unlike their Ashkenazi coreligionists who had largely been forced into pawnbroking and usury, Jews in Spain had vigorously pursued commerce. They had the double advantage of possessing capital and knowledge of markets. After the expulsion, they fully exploited those advantages.

The rise of Ottoman power, marked by the fall of Constantinople (1453) and the conquest of Syria and Egypt (1516–17), benefited Jewish merchants in numerous ways. Unlike the former Byzantine-Mamluke rulers, the Ottomans not only permitted Jews to engage in trade but may well have propelled them in that direction by forcefully transplanting large numbers from places like the Balkans, where many had been artisans, to urban centers such as Istanbul, where it was easier to find a commercial niche.

The newly empowered Ottoman Empire concomitantly made it increasingly difficult for Venetian merchants to maintain the lucrative Levant trade. After the Ottoman-Venetian war of 1463–79 the sultan insisted on a reciprocal trade agreement.[13] The Ottomans imposed more stringent trade regulations than had their Byzantine-Mamluke predecessors. They ended the Venetian monopoly and required customs duties from foreigners, which also encouraged indigenous merchants, including Jews, to enter trade.

The Papal State in Ancona and the Grand Duchy of Tuscany in Livorno took decisive steps to reap the financial rewards of that trade. The preferred means was to grant trading and residential privileges to Jews, Greeks, and Armenians who possessed firsthand knowledge of Ottoman and European markets. Raison d'état thus came to prevail over religious considerations.[14]

Ancona

The turning point came in the papal enclave of Ancona. The authorities first allowed Greek, Muslim, and Jewish merchants to trade in the city (1514, 1518). At the request of some Jewish merchants, the authorities then specifically authorized "Jews, Turks, Greeks and all other merchants of the Levantine nations" to reside in the city and trade with the Levant while also granting generous concessions (1544).[15]

The charter granted Levantine Jews freedom of trade and movement; exemption from local jurisdiction and taxes; amnesty for crimes committed elsewhere (treating them "as if born into the world only today"); and the right to build a synagogue. The charter set no limits on the period of residence, creating the basis for the permanent community that the Jewish "Levantine" merchants sought.[16]

In response to further requests from Jewish merchants, and with Pope Paul III's authorization, Ancona in 1547 offered New Christians immunity as well by applying the privileges already vouchsafed to Levantine Jews to those "from Portugal or Spain": "even if they are of the group of Jews called New Christians . . . or otherwise tracing their origin to the Hebrew nation." The pope boldly pioneered in extending immunity to crimes against Christianity by shielding them from inquisitorial prosecution.[17] Except for political privileges, they were to be treated as citizens of Ancona.

This was a radical "precedent according to which an individual's religious behavior could be ignored by the state." It was a major achievement in the *conversos*' search for "safe havens all over Europe." It was a policy that would be widely imitated in Italy and potentially across Catholic Europe.[18]

Less than a decade later Pope Paul IV, formerly the head of the Roman Inquisition, rescinded his predecessor's order and mercilessly burned some two dozen Ancona Jews at the stake (1555). Nevertheless, Paul III's audacious act remained potent: Ferrara (1550), Savoy (1572), and Florence (1549) adopted it; Henry II of France (1550) adapted it (Bordeaux); and Venice (1573) cautiously followed.[19]

Venice

The city first allowed "Levantine" merchants temporary residence (at first four months, later two years) and built a new ghetto to house them (Ghetto Vecchio; 1541). Daniel Rodriga (d. 1603), a Portuguese *converso*, submitted petitions and plans to further Jewish settlement in Venice for thirty years. He was truly "the inaugurator of the charter system of the Jewish merchants of Venice."[20] He similarly proposed establishing a free trading station in Spalato (1577) that gave Venetian merchants access to Romania and, through escorted convoys, guaranteed merchant vessels safe passage against pirates.[21]

Venice appropriated from Rodriga the companion category of "Ponentine" merchants to allow former *conversos* who had remained in Europe to trade there as well.[22] Moreover, Venice acknowledged Rodriga as "consul of the Ponentine Jews" (1573).[23] Venice offered them a ten-year charter and immunity from prosecution for religious infractions committed elsewhere (1589). In the ghetto, they could openly revert to Judaism, indeed were required to do so, and could build a synagogue.[24]

These freedoms speedily made Venice the "mother city" of the Sephardi diaspora. They also demonstrated the Jews' special status. First, Jews enjoyed a religious freedom denied to other groups, albeit one limited to private worship. Protestant merchants were first allowed to hold private services from 1657; Turks could not gain permission to erect a mosque. The ghettos housed eight synagogues: while some had lavishly decorated interiors, all were built in existing structures so that none were publicly recognizable. The most visible from the street was the Scuola Grande Tedesca, which had five arched windows and an outward projecting niche that contained the ark recess.[25]

Second, the charter granted them the immediate and unprecedented privilege to trade with the Levant as Venetian subjects. The usual requirement was twenty-five years of residence. This privilege was unmatched: the Senate denied the application of a group of Christian merchants for a similar privilege. Jews were also granted complete freedom of movement to and from Venice.

The charter stipulated that Jews were to live in the ghetto and to wear a distinctive yellow head-covering.[26]

Jews exercised extensive self-government, although juridical jurisdiction was sharply limited. They elected their own leaders and, in conjunction with the government, controlled admission of members. They organized an elaborate system for allocating taxation through an "assessment committee" that interviewed taxpayers annually. It was "the most feared and probably most loathed organ of Venetian Jewish self-government."[27]

The community was oligarchical, membership in the "Large Assembly" being restricted to those (10–11%) who paid a considerable amount (12 ducats) in annual tax.[28] The community was also divided along the "ethnic" lines that were manifest in separate charters and the ghetto's eight synagogues. The "Tedeschi" or Italian and German Jews, who held five-year charters for pawn-broking and moneylending, were pitted against the Levantine and Spanish Jews, whose ten-year charters enabled them to trade with the Levant (in 1634 the Tedeschi were permitted to engage in the Levant trade as well).[29] In the ghetto's "ethnic power balance" the Levantine and Spanish eventually came to share power with the Tedeschi.[30]

The Venetian Senate renewed the ten-year charter numerous times. In 1633 a third residential area, the "Newest Ghetto" (Ghetto Nuovissimo), was set aside for Jewish merchants. In 1638 Simone Luzzatto (1583–1663), a Venetian rabbi, wrote a tract in Italian to defend renewal of the charter in which he offered the first extended justification of the new Jewish commerce of port cities.[31]

Livorno

Although based on Venice's charter, the "Livornina" of 1593 exceeded it in introducing parity of privileges in multiple realms while also recognizing Jews as Tuscan "subjects."

The Duke of Tuscany could take such pioneering steps because Livorno was a new creation (in 1606 it received city status). Built on the site of a former fishing village, Livorno epitomized the era's social experimentation in attempting to lure a new population to a frontier city that was a virtual tabula rasa without guilds, a patriciate, or a court. It exemplified Renaissance architecture in its star-shaped perimeter defenses and perpendicularly aligned streets. This experiment was remarkably successful: by 1650 Livorno had supplanted Venice as the center of Mediterranean trade.[32]

Livorno granted Jews "all of the privileges, rights and favors which Our merchants, Florentine and Pisan citizens and Christians, enjoy." It allowed them to engage in all trades, including retail; exempted them from wearing any special clothing or sign; and permitted the purchase of real estate.

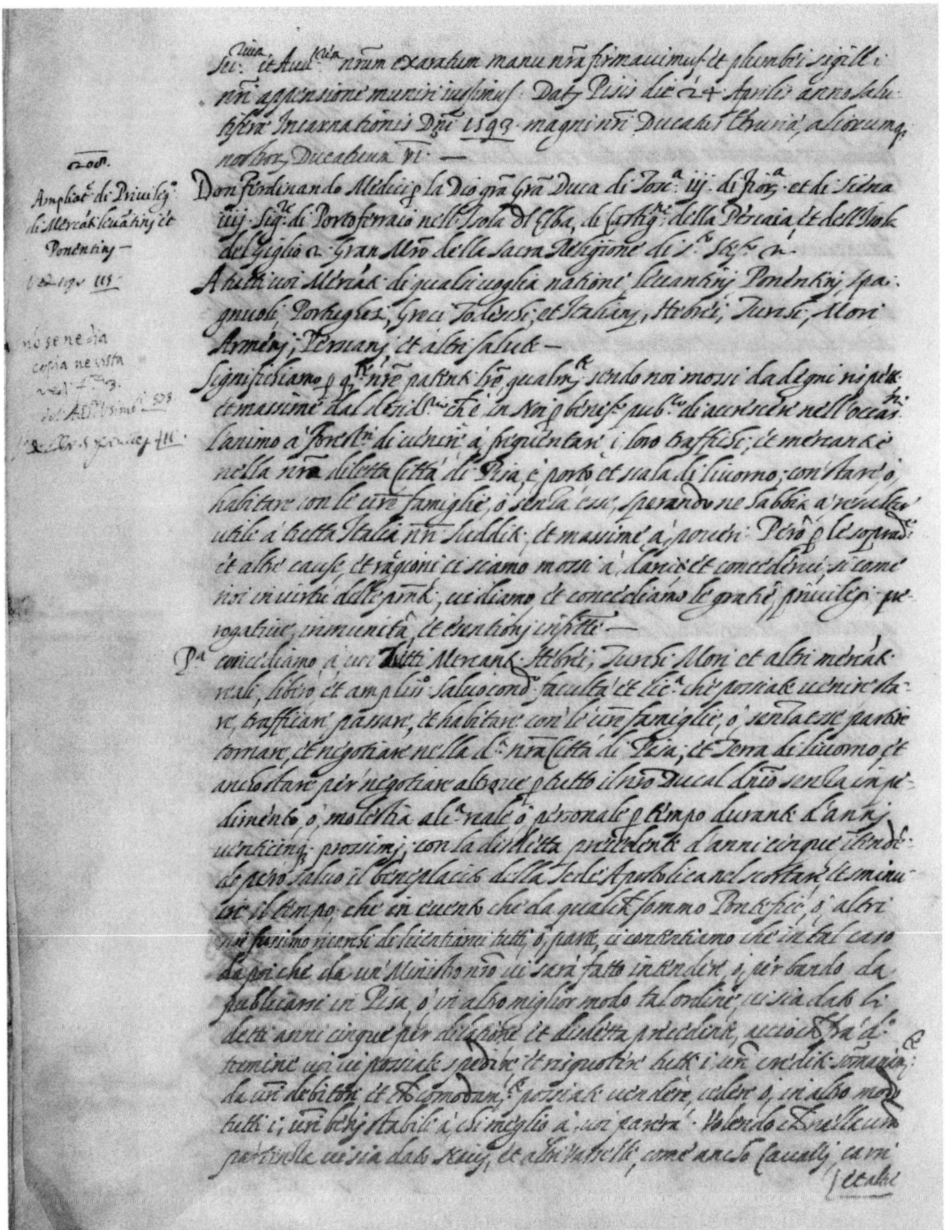

FIGURE 1. First page of Livornina (Charter, 1593); Archivio di Stato di Firenze, *Pratica segreta*, 189, c 196v.

In Livorno Jews were one *nazione* alongside others: English, French, Flemish, Dutch, Genoese, Swedish, Armenian, Ragusean, and Greek merchant colonies. Yet there were two significant differences. The Jews alone were "subjects" (*suddita nazione*), forming an autonomous body (*corpo politico*) exempt from direct taxation under Tuscany's protection. The other nations were classified as foreigners (*nazioni estere*) governed by consuls.[33] Accordingly, the *nazione ebrea* also held the power of naturalization (from 1614). Admission to the *nazione* by secret ballot (*ballotazione*) brought the right of residence and, with the approval of the authorities, the status of a Tuscan subject. The corporate body controlled naturalization; the state did not grant it directly to the individual Jew.[34]

As a corollary of the naturalization privilege, Jews were required to be permanent residents; in return, they were exempted from taxation. This situation was emphasized in 1694 when the Neapolitan-Sardinian navy seized a ship filled with goods owned by Livornese Jews. The Grand Duke intervened on their behalf, with the result that the Spanish king recognized them "as subjects of a friendly prince."[35]

The second difference from the other nations was size: the Jewish *nazione* was exponentially larger than the others, constituting some 10 percent of Livorno's population.[36]

Like the other merchant communities, Jews had considerable communal autonomy. Perhaps the distinguishing feature of the merchant colony's autonomy was lay control. "Consuls" headed the other "nations." Jews had five lay leaders (*massari*, stewards) whom the Grand Duke appointed from a list of nominees. Each nation had an assembly. The Jews' assembly, called "the sixty," submitted the list of nominees for *massari* to the Grand Duke.[37]

The lay leaders adjudicated civil and minor criminal cases between its members according to *halakha* and imposed disciplinary action: it had "the right to act in place of the secular authorities."[38] Self-government was highly oligarchical with some offices (*congresso dell nazione*) being heritable for three generations (revoked under Habsburg rule in 1769–80).[39] The *nazione ebrea*, as already mentioned, also held the power of naturalization (from 1614). Jews gained the right of public worship, erecting a purpose-built synagogue in 1595, prior to the other nations (Uniates, 1606; Anglican services, 1707; Armenians, 1714; Greek Orthodox, 1757).[40]

The wide-ranging powers of the *nazione ebrea* were an enhanced version of those of the other merchant communities. Many contemporaries considered Livorno a model of toleration. The Livornina, which remained in effect through most of the Grand Duchy's subsequent history (to 1836), became a template for other rulers.[41]

It should be noted that the Italian cities that favored Jews with such privileges were exceptional. Elsewhere the situation was substantially different. In 1555 the Papal States under Paul IV began to propagate a policy of Counter-

Reformation intolerance (Cum Nimis Absurdum) and Inquisition that was to last some three centuries.[42] One immediate result was ghettoization. Tuscany forced its other (non-Sephardic) Jews into ghettos in Florence and Siena: for the now ghettoized Jews (from 1570) in Florence, "real estate ownership was a rare privilege," though a considerable number managed to live outside the ghetto.[43] In 1567 Genoa expelled Jews from all of its territories.[44] In 1569 Pope Pius V expelled Jews from all of the Papal States with the exception of Rome and Ancona.[45] Savoy issued a charter (1572) to attract New Christian merchants to Nice by permitting them to revert to Judaism; it rescinded the charter under the pope and emperor's combined pressure.[46] Under similar pressure from the papacy, Duke Alfonso of Este destroyed the Jewish community of former *conversos* at Ferrara in 1583, sending at least three to Rome to be burned at the stake.[47] The Duchy of Milan expelled its Jews in 1591.[48]

The precedents in Ancona, Venice, and Livorno migrated northward to the new Atlantic and new world colonial economy, shaping Jewish settlements in such places as Bordeaux, Antwerp, Hamburg, and Amsterdam, and eastward to Trieste.[49] Jews admitted to Bordeaux (1550), Antwerp (1564), and Amsterdam (1590s) came under the guise of Portuguese Christians. How transparent was the ruse? Did the authorities simply prefer to turn a blind eye? The answer varied from place to place; what did not vary was that rulers viewed the *conversos*/Jews as a "merchant colony."

Bordeaux

In Bordeaux, a locus of France's mercantilist policy, the *conversos* enjoyed extensive privileges yet their religious identity remained ambiguous for almost a century and a half. Bordeaux was a thriving port decimated by the English departure after their defeat (1453). Louis XI tried to repopulate it and stimulate commerce by attracting foreign merchants: he issued two ordinances (1472, 1474) that permitted them to trade without letters of naturalization and exempted them from the law of escheat (*droit d'aubaine*).

Aware of Bordeaux's potential, *converso* merchants settled there and then requested official recognition. They chose a well-known professor and commercial liaison to speak on their behalf.[50] Henry II chose to ignore that these *marchands portugais* were *conversos* and issued *lettres patentes* (1550) that granted "parity" with privileged Frenchmen: freedom of movement, commerce, property ownership, and writing wills.[51]

For the first three decades these *marchands portugais* enjoyed these privileges on the king's authority alone since the local authority, the Bordeaux Parlement, did not register the privileges until 1580. Gradually the local authorities came to recognize the Portuguese merchants' utility, albeit not without reluctance. In 1615 the Portuguese were permitted to apply for citizenship in Bordeaux (at the cost of three hundred francs); this became a requirement for those who wished to engage in retail trade. All lived as observant Catholics; some were clandestine Jews.

By the late seventeenth century the local authorities had begun to refer to the Portuguese "naturalized strangers" (*étrangers naturalisés*) as Jews. In 1684 Bordeaux's Council expelled ninety-three poor Jewish families deemed of no utility to the local economy.

The revocation of the Edict of Nantes (1685), which expelled Protestants, aroused true consternation among the Portuguese. Louis XIV opted for extortion over expulsion. He levied a new tax in contravention of the *lettres patentes*; the community was in no position to protest.

The merchants subsequently began to play a pivotal role in Bordeaux's finances. They thrice advanced loans to the city (1709, 1712, 1721) to purchase wheat. They became major supporters of the regional winegrowers by loaning significant sums as well.

In the 1690s, the arrival of recent émigrés from Portugal who were perhaps more eager to observe Jewish practices (in 1683 Don Pedro had expelled all "New Christians" condemned by the Inquisition) reinforced their religious commitments. They first ceased baptizing their children. After the turn of the century they ceased to marry in church. They merely announced their marriages to the parish priest, who duly registered them.

In 1723 Louis XV officially recognized their religion: in exchange for a sizable gift (100,000 livres), he issued *lettres patentes* that confirmed their former privileges while recognizing them officially as Jews. They retained their original status, enjoying the same privileges and fiscal obligations as other merchant or corporate groups including the ability to control their commercial and financial operations. They were, however, excluded from the Chamber of Commerce and the guilds. In the eighteenth century they maintained a paid representative in Paris to negotiate on their behalf.[52]

The members of the *nation* established the rudiments of a community structure through the creation of a welfare society, the *Sedaca* (1693). Adding other associations under its auspices, including hiring a rabbi, the *Sedaca* and its wealthy lay syndics exercised control over Jewish life. The community never exercised civil jurisdiction.

The *nation* comprised a privileged merchant corporation that fit the structure of Bordeaux. From the end of the seventeenth century Bordeaux had organized "nations" of foreign merchants. These possessed the requisite privileges to engage in commerce and finance and the authority to regulate their members.[53]

The *nation* was a predominantly bourgeois group that paid a collective tax like other corporations, though its was substantially higher. It maintained a cemetery and cared for its own sick and poor, although as the numbers grew, it restricted itself to supporting ninety Sephardi families.

In 1760 the king approved an ordinance (*Règlement de la nation des Juifs Portugais de Bordeaux*) that gave the *nation* the ability to expel a member by a two-thirds vote. The community promptly expelled 152 poor Jews, mostly from Avignon. The king issued a further ordinance in 1766 confirming the oligarchical composition of the *nation's* leadership.

Hamburg

With northern Europe's commerce thriving at the end of the sixteenth century, Hamburg's Senate welcomed a bevy of foreign merchants (Walloons, Flemish, Italians, French, Dutch, English). Sephardi *conversos* began to settle in Hamburg in the 1590s as the "Portuguese nation [*natio lusitana*]." As early as 1603 there was official mention of them as Jews. The seven families of 1606 became some one hundred families by 1648, by 1663 some one hundred twenty, totaling about 600 persons.

The Senate understood the Portuguese merchants' importance for Hamburg's otherwise declining trade with Spain and Portugal; it defended them against Lutheran pastors' animus. One means to offset the local clergy was to solicit a University Theological Faculty's expert opinion. For example, the Frankfurt on the Oder faculty (August 29, 1611) asserted: "it has been paternal and Christian to have tolerated the Portuguese Jews until now, and it is equally paternal and Christian to continue to tolerate them."[54]

In 1612 the Portuguese negotiated a first five-year contract with the Senate. It accorded them a status similar to the Dutch (from 1605) and English (from 1611) merchant colonies (the Dutch and English were designated *Schutzverwandte*, the Jews *Schutzjuden*), although their potential occupations were more restricted. In exchange for an annual contribution (1,000 marks) they were given the privilege of settlement and residence and "equality with our citizens and other residents in upright, honest commercial dealings." In civil and criminal matters they were subject to the Hamburg courts. They had no privilege of religious worship except for purchasing a burial plot; circumcision was expressly prohibited. They were neither to defame Christianity nor to proselytize Christians.[55] The Portuguese initially conducted religious services in three separate domestic locations, to which the authorities turned a blind eye.

The 1617 renewal of the contract doubled the tax, brought some loosening of occupational privileges, and permitted the importation of kosher meat. Ownership of real estate was allowed exclusively to one celebrated doctor; numerous Portuguese apparently found ways to evade this restriction.[56] The contract of 1623 guaranteed their personal safety.

In response to complaints about the Jews' effrontery in publicly observing Jewish holidays and trading on Sundays, the Senate solicited an expert opinion from the universities of Jena and Altdorf that led to the promulgation of a new *Reglement* on July 8, 1650. This legislation delineated the restrictions on their religious life, granting exclusively "domestic worship" of up to fifteen persons in a private home so long as only small groups entered or exited together. It reiterated the prohibition on owning real estate and encouraged residence in one quarter of the city (*Neustadt*).

This first Jewry law (*Judenordnung*) subjected them to the same sumptuary laws as other citizens.[57] Two years later (September 1652) the community reorganized itself by unifying the three existing places of worship. It also bought land on which to build a synagogue yet, facing insurmountable government opposition, sold the plot.[58]

Embroiled in a wide-ranging confrontation with the burghers over many issues including taxation, the Senate in 1697 decided on a 20,000 mark special exaction plus an annual tax of 6,000 marks combined with further restrictions on religious life. The Senate asked the far less wealthy Ashkenazi Jews for a special exaction of 30,000 marks. These decisions led many Sephardim to emigrate, especially to Amsterdam.[59] From that point the Sephardic community declined. The 1710 *Judenreglement*, which included both Sephardim and Ashkenazim, continued to permit only domestic services. When the community did finally obtain permission to build a euphemistically designated "meeting house," it stood behind another building so that it was not visible from the street.[60] In 1746 the community demolished a half-finished synagogue in response to the clergy's adamant opposition.

The Portuguese brought to Hamburg trade in unrefined sugar, wine, oil, tobacco, pepper, and other spices. They opened sugar refineries. They also participated in the Hamburg Bank, founded in 1619; by 1623 they held forty-three accounts. They also obtained a legislated number of positions as brokers: from four of the total (1653), the number rose to twenty Portuguese and one hundred Christians (1692). Yet by 1732, with the community's decline, Jews filled only five of these positions.[61]

Beyond Charters

We have now reached a historic divide. The Jews in Ancona, Venice, Livorno, Bordeaux, and Hamburg procured charters. They formed recognized merchant communities with a clearly defined corporate status, with Livorno and Bordeaux being notable for "corporate parity."

In marked contrast, the Jews in Amsterdam and London were subject neither to charters nor to specific Jewry laws. In these cities, in which merchant colonies functioned without charters, Jews attained parity through the mechanisms of an emerging civil society.[62] The Jews' rights resulted from the ambiguity of their legal status that they tested on an ad hoc basis, whether in the courts or the legislature.

Jews entered and lived as individuals. The Jewish community was a voluntary society, though it arrogated to itself virtually all the powers of an autonomous community or Kehillah. In the cases of Amsterdam and London, moreover, the new world colonies played a significant role in the attainment of improved legal statuses and the exploration of new economic and occupational opportunities, though paradoxically through charters.

Amsterdam

The Esnoga, the magnificent public synagogue built in 1671–75, rose high above the neighborhood and seated some two thousand. It symbolized Amsterdam Jewry's affluence and status.[63] What other Jewish community in western Europe had the means, security, and legal privilege to erect such an imposing edifice?

The Esnoga rested, however, on ambiguous foundations. Jews, unlike Catholics, Mennonites, and Lutherans, could presume to erect a public ecclesiastical building because they were legally foreigners who had not been explicitly denied that right. That very ambiguity was, then, the novelty and strength of the Sephardi Jews' position in Amsterdam.

In Amsterdam the Sephardi Jews or former *conversos* constituted a "voluntary religious association governed, in part, as a mercantile community."[64] Amsterdam did not issue a charter, even though other Dutch cities did; it did not carefully define the Jews' status. It did not issue charters to other merchant communities.[65] Rather, the Jews' status emerged over time in response to changing circumstances.

The state decided not to issue a Jewry law and instead to delegate responsibility to the municipalities (1619).[66] The most the Amsterdam authorities elaborated were three regulations (1616) concerning religious and social behavior: "not to speak or write . . . anything that may, in any way, tend to the disdain of our Christian religion"; "not to attempt to seduce any Christian person from our Christian religion nor to circumcise one"; "not to have any carnal conversation, whether in or out of wedlock, with Christian women or maidens, not even when such are of ill repute."[67]

The Sephardi merchants who began to settle in Amsterdam in the 1590s were permitted to procure municipal citizenship; the first did so in 1597. Yet this was municipal citizenship with a difference. While Jews were subject neither to special supervision and taxes nor to residential restrictions, their citizenship was not heritable. They remained "permanent first generation immigrants." They were not admitted to the guilds and had no access to administrative, legal, or military posts.[68] Their burgher membership was less than that of the majority Calvinists. It was equal or superior to those of Catholics and some other Protestant dissenters who were restricted to private worship but inferior in that they were not excluded from the guilds.[69]

FIGURE 2. Amsterdam Esnoga. Sketch of the Amsterdam synagogue by Jan
Spaan, 1765. Courtesy of the Amsterdam City Archives (010097010639).

Freedom of worship was attained de facto and not de jure, and was restricted at first (1614): the community had to resort to the legal fiction of the
synagogue being "owned" by a member of the City Council. The Estates General in 1654 and 1657 admitted Jews to "minor citizenship" to protect former
Iberian Jews' ships from seizure by Spain.[70]

The Jews possessed "synagogal" autonomy but not "judicial autonomy": the
municipal authorities treated the Jews' organization as the "Jews' church"
(*Jodenkerck*).[71] Jews paid their taxes to the municipality and state directly
as individuals, not collectively through the kahal.[72] Moreover, there was a
form of "civil" marriage: newlyweds had to register the marriage with the city
authorities.[73]

The kahal arrogated to itself a vast array of powers based on its fundamentally ambiguous status: the municipality neither deputed nor disputed those
powers. The first clause of the kahal's regulations stated: "The Mahamad will
have authority and superiority over everything."[74] The kahal supervised "synagogue worship, education, charity and . . . censorship."[75] Amsterdam's Mahamad knew that the Jews' position was as precarious as it was privileged. It
accordingly attempted to impose various forms of discretion; it exercised the
autocratic powers of a merchant colony. It imposed the minor ban of excommunication for a variety of offenses.[76]

Poor relief came to define the community's role in Amsterdam's mosaic of
hierarchically arranged religious groups.[77] From 1622 the Mahamad collected
a tax on imports and exports (*imposta*), characteristic of a merchant colony, to
fund its operations, especially charity.[78] The Mahamad chose various methods
to deal with the poor: at first re-emigration, then an elaborate system of sup-

port in Amsterdam itself, and finally, from the mid-seventeenth century, shipment to the colonies.

The Dutch West India Company encouraged colonization through a general policy of toleration. While recognizing the Reformed Church as the "sole and exclusive public church," the company guaranteed freedom of private worship to attract Jews, and especially *converso* merchants, to Dutch Brazil.[79] After the Portuguese planters had revolted the colony sorely needed capital and technical knowledge of sugar refining. The Estates General accordingly issued the "Honorable Patent" (Patenta Onrossa; December 7, 1645) that recognized Jews as equal "to our native-born."[80]

In Surinam's privilege of 1665 Jews were "considered as English-born" and possessed "every privilege and liberty possessed by and granted to the citizens and inhabitants of this colony."[81] In the Caribbean colonies Jews gained equality in the 1650s in Nova Zeelandia or Essequibo ("Jews shall be accepted as burghers"; 1657) and Cayenne ("they shall enjoy all Liberties and Exemptions of our other colonists as long as they remain there"; 1659).[82] The Dutch colonies, unlike Amsterdam, had charters that explicitly defined privileges.

We should not fail to mention that Amsterdam was an exception. Other provinces in the Republic either prohibited Jews altogether or restricted their numbers. Many Dutch cities refused to admit Jews: Groningen not until 1711, Utrecht in 1789, Deventer the 1790s.[83]

London

The readmission of the Jews to England yielded extensive privileges but no formal edict or Jewry law. Amsterdam's Jews lobbied for access to England to find additional outlets for a growing Sephardi immigrant population, especially the indigent, and to circumvent England's Navigation Acts that now challenged Dutch mercantile supremacy. Residence in London would give Sephardi merchants access to English shipping, markets, and colonial goods, and especially guarantee the flow of sugar central to the entire Sephardi trade network.[84]

Menasseh Ben Israel (1604–57), a rabbi and renowned author of books on Judaism, went to London as the Amsterdam Mahamad's unofficial representative to negotiate the readmission. Menasseh published two brief tracts in English to promote the cause.[85]

Cromwell convened a conference at Whitehall (December 1655) to consider readmitting the Jews. He adjourned the conference without reaching a decision, or perhaps precisely to avoid a negative decision, with the result that wealthy Jewish merchants were allowed to settle de facto.[86] From the outset, the tiny Jewish population was without a charter or Jewry laws. It was organized as a voluntary synagogue-based community.

Its most prominent members were "endenizened," that is, through royal *lettres patentes* they gained access to the colonial trade, though they paid higher duties on goods (91 from 1665 to 1680).[87] Endenization was an inferior status to being "native born," as the latter enjoyed basic rights of commerce, residence, and property ownership.[88]

In this "statutory vacuum" Jews tested the limits of their rights empirically.[89] One right Jews were denied, because of their inability to take the requisite oath that contained the phrase "on the faith of a Christian," was to become freemen of the City of London, which gave the right to operate retail businesses there. In practice, the authorities probably permitted some Jews to do so.[90]

The first Jew was admitted to be a broker in 1657; in 1697 the number was set at twelve alongside one hundred English brokers.[91] Of 107 proprietors of the Bank of England in 1701 twelve were of Spanish and Portuguese origin.[92] In the 1660–1680s Jews gained judicial standing, that is, the right to bring cases and to serve as witnesses.[93] Charles II (1674) and James II (1685) employed "the dispensing powers of the Crown" to confirm the Jews' religious freedom that was twice challenged under the Conventicle Act. A court case (1718) confirmed the Jews' right to own property.[94]

The community similarly took advantage of the "statutory vacuum," and Amsterdam's model, to extend its authority and impose strict discipline. The Mahamad claimed "authority and supremacy over everything," instituted a tax on imports and exports (*imposta*), and declared a monopoly on religious life, prohibiting the establishment of rival synagogues.[95] The Mahamad further followed Amsterdam's practice in supporting its own poor: in the 1670s one-quarter of households received some relief.[96]

Jews had prayed at Creechurch lane since 1657 and remodeled the space in 1674. Bevis Marks (1699–1701), the first purpose-built synagogue, was located on a lane rather than a public street. Designed by a Quaker, Bevis Marks's façade resembled a modest dissenting chapel; it signaled Judaism's inferior place of private worship in the religious hierarchy.[97] Similarly, the Ashkenazi "Great Synagogue" (1722), whose façade resembled Bevis Marks ("tho' it is built after the same Model, is not half so big"), was hidden from public view in the Duke's Place Courtyard.[98]

The English colonies either followed the Dutch precedent or adopted the very privileges the Dutch had extended to Jews. Here as well, unlike in England itself, there were charters, in large measure because the colonies were founded on charters. In Surinam (1665), where Jews were considered to be "as English born," the English copied the wording of the Dutch charter at Essequibo (1658).[99] In New York Jews continued to enjoy the economic privileges they had gained under the Dutch: by 1700 they no longer suffered any economic disabilities and additionally acquired the rights of freemanship (1688) and naturalization (from 1718). Jews appear to have voted for office in the first half of the eighteenth century as well.[100] The Plantation or Naturalization Act (1740) aimed primarily at Jews in the Caribbean islands (chapter 5).[101]

Conclusion

These merchant colonies constituted the west European region of emancipation. Raison d'état and shifting trade patterns induced governments in such cities as Ancona, Livorno, and Venice to grant Jews extensive privileges of residence and trade, worship and communal autonomy. In Bordeaux Jews originally gained privileges as New Christians; over time they emerged as Jews and received confirmation of those privileges. In Livorno and Bordeaux those privileges entailed virtual parity with Christian merchants. Hamburg's Senate first attracted a Jewish merchant colony by extending privileges but later, by imposing heavy taxes, drove it away.

In Amsterdam and London, which had ceased granting charters to foreign merchant colonies, Jews found themselves in the novel and ambiguous situation of functioning without a charter. They therefore gained rights on an ad hoc basis, becoming members of an emerging civil society.

The Jews of Bordeaux, Amsterdam, and London were to make virtually seamless transitions from corporate or civic parity to equal citizenship. In Livorno corporate parity persisted and became an obstacle to individual rights until the mid-nineteenth century.

CHAPTER TWO

Burgher Estate

OBSERVANT TRAVELERS IN THE EARLY MODERN PERIOD noticed that Jews had attained an enviable political position in the Polish-Lithuanian Commonwealth. Antonio Maria Gratiani, a papal diplomat in Poland in 1595, unexpectedly found himself reporting:

> In these principalities one still comes upon masses of Jews who are not disdained as much as in some other lands. They do not live here under pitiful conditions and do not engage in lowly pursuits. . . . Rather, they possess land, engage in commerce, and devote themselves to study, especially medicine and astrology. . . . They possess considerable wealth and they are not only among the respectable citizens, but occasionally even dominate them. They wear no special marks to distinguish them from Christians and are even permitted to wear the sword and to go about armed. In general they enjoy equal rights.[1]

An English traveler, William Coxe, wrote that "this people date their introduction into Poland about the time of Kazimierz the Great, and . . . they enjoy privileges which they scarcely possess in any other country except England and Holland."[2]

In the Polish-Lithuanian Commonwealth the Jews' commercial utility made them highly prized. In contrast to the Italian city-states, where they were commissioned to bolster a polity's position in an already functioning yet constantly shifting trading network, here the Polish Crown and magnates invited them to create new patterns of trade and production. This was even more the case in the Ukrainian territories that Poland acquired and began to colonize in the sixteenth century.

Magnates founded market towns on their private estates to which they invited Jewish colonists. The Jews who accepted these invitations negotiated collective privileges that often endowed them with parity or virtual parity with the Christian burghers in civil matters, for example, residence and property ownership, occupational and religious freedom. These charters gained in importance as the numbers of Jews in the Polish-Lithuanian Commonwealth grew, and especially as the proportion living in the new southeastern territories increased dramatically.

Jews had first come to the Kingdom of Poland in the tenth century, and emigration from central and western Europe began in the twelfth century. Small numbers of Italian and Sephardi Jews arrived in the sixteenth and seventeenth centuries. By the mid-seventeenth century there were perhaps 150,000 Jews in a total population of eleven million. Historians estimate that by 1720 the Jewish population had reached 375,000, by 1764 750,000.[3]

Following the template of an influential Austrian charter, King Boleslav V granted Jews their first privileges in 1264.[4] Boleslav's charter served as the model for many subsequent Polish charters from the fourteenth through the sixteenth centuries. Jewish leaders submitted drafts of the charters for negotiation and approval. The charters thus reflected their hierarchy of concerns: subjection to the king's and their own law rather than municipal jurisdiction; economic rights and security; and religious freedom including the oath to be sworn in court proceedings involving non-Jews (Poland had no equivalent to the humiliating *more judaïco* that German-speaking central Europe increasingly used from the thirteenth century). Municipalities had power over Jews only in matters touching their own real estate.[5]

Jews also negotiated charters with individual towns. Here the crucial factor was the Christian burghers: the greater their strength, the less favorable the privileges, since they regarded the Jews as direct competitors. As one historian has put it: "in larger, older, crown cities residential segregation tended to be stricter, competition more intense and animosities more dangerous."[6] In royal towns in which the burghers wielded considerable power, Jews aimed to negotiate the right of residence and ownership of real estate in perpetuity, the right to buy and sell goods like the burghers, and exemption from municipal jurisdiction.[7]

Jews were not the only group functioning as merchants under urban charters. Scots and Armenians, Dutch and Italians also belonged to the "urban ethnic heterogeneity" that was "one of the striking features of the Polish commonwealth."[8] They organized themselves in similar ways, forming brotherhoods with their own courts, tax collection, and sanctions. A veritable "ethnic division of commodities" existed: various groups specialized in, or indeed monopolized, commerce in particular goods.[9]

Yet the Jews diverged significantly from these other groups in sheer numbers. In the middle of the seventeenth century there were perhaps 8,000 Scots and 2,000–3,000 Italians; there were 150,000 or more Jews.[10] Jews comprised a high percentage of urban dwellers in a predominantly agricultural society.[11] In the eighteenth century, Jews constituted half of the urban population and in large areas of the country an even higher percentage.[12] This quantitative difference became a qualitative one. The sheer magnitude of Jewish population entailed a political position of another order: the other groups did not have royal charters that afforded protection at the highest level. Instead, they relied entirely on local charters.

In the sixteenth century the king's power declined and the magnates' rose, turning the Commonwealth into a "Republic of Nobles" or a "magnate oligarchy." With the ensuing "decentralization of the socio-political structure of the Polish Commonwealth," local privileges gained in importance.[13] This shift fundamentally altered the situation of ever larger segments of the Jewish population. In 1539 the Sejm passed legislation giving the owners of private towns, which comprised over half of Poland's towns at the time, exclusive jurisdiction over their Jews. This was crucial to the process by which the magnates expanded dominion over village dwellers.[14]

In 1569, with the Union of Lublin creating the Polish-Lithuanian Commonwealth, the Kingdom of Lithuania transferred control of the Ukraine to the Polish Crown. The Crown awarded Polish nobles vast Ukrainian latifundia. After 1569 the Crown introduced Polish privileges into the Ukrainian territories; these royal privileges in fact had little practical effect.[15]

Jews were initially invited to Poland to serve as bankers and moneylenders. Some served as "royal factors," administering royal assets and organizing loans. Others engaged in tax farming and the leasing of toll stations. These activities awakened Jewish leaders' apprehension because of the potential to arouse the local populace's resentment.[16] Indeed, the first regulation of the organized Jewish community (Council of the Lands) was to prohibit individual Jews from administering large estates and customs houses or collecting taxes on salt and liquors.[17] In the long term the decline of royal power and the structure of the Polish-Lithuanian Commonwealth combined to direct Jews to a different range of occupations.

Jews, alongside other ethnic commercial groups, filled the economic interstice between the nobility and the serfs.[18] This situation gave rise to a wide-ranging and enduring Jewish-magnate alliance or "marriage of convenience." One of its central features was the "arenda" or leasing system.[19] Dating from as early as the fourteenth century, a Jew would lease for a fixed sum a monopoly on an estate's natural products (timber, grain, hides), which the lessee then sold locally, regionally, or by export. Or he would lease a monopoly on the distillation and sale of liquor, which also utilized estate products (grains, beet sugar).[20] Leases on entire estates were more common in the sixteenth century. Later leases tended to be restricted. Jewish monopolies on liquor were especially important in the east and the Ukraine.[21]

The Jews' main occupation was, however, commerce. Germans, Dutch, Italians, and Scots tended to be the large-scale first-order merchants. Jews were in the main "second-order" merchants who supplied raw materials, distributed imported goods, and rented excess space on the rafts headed to Danzig that the first-order merchants organized. They were "the link between the big import-export trade and local markets." Jews also played a major role in the overland trade to fairs in the German states, especially Leipzig, as well as in fairs in the Polish towns and in local trade generally. Jewish artisans were concentrated in clothing, food, and precious metals.[22]

To generate a steady source of revenue, magnates invited Jews to develop the economies of their estates' private towns. "By the end of the seventeenth century, private towns accounted for 64 percent of the total number of towns in Poland and 75 percent of those in Lithuania."[23] The magnates had complete freedom in populating, and organizing the economy of, their private towns. The guilds and burghers who wielded true power in royal towns, where their insistent complaints about the unfair competition of Jewish merchants and artisans had considerable impact, exercised little if any leverage over the magnates. The Christian burghers' impotence redounded to the Jews' benefit. The magnates broadened dramatically the scope of the Jews' economic activity.

Opatów, for example, a private town located in "Little Poland," was first inhabited by Jews after 1518 when it passed from the Church to the hands of a nobleman. By 1765 it had a Jewish population of over 2,000. Between one-third and two-fifths of the Jews were engaged in commerce, about one-third in artisanry.[24] Jewish artisans (butchers, furriers, hat makers) had their own guilds; by the 1750s they appeared to dominate their trades. Jews similarly predominated in commerce, with the notable exception of the wine trade, from which the "ethnic division of commodities" excluded them, and were especially active in long-distance trade. Jews monopolized the manufacture and distribution of alcoholic beverages.[25]

The colonization of the Ukraine reinforced the Jewish-magnate alliance, while also bringing new dangers. The Jews' middleman function, already politically fraught, became explosive in this religiously charged colonial setting in which Catholic Polish nobles, aided by missionizing Catholic priests, employed Jewish agents to rule Greek Orthodox Ukrainian peasants.[26]

In contrast to the newly immigrated Jews of the Italian and North Atlantic ports, then, most Jews in the eastern territories of Polish-Lithuanian Commonwealth were internal migrants. There may also have been some exiles from Moravia and the Germanies who had escaped the ravages of the Thirty Years War.[27] The Jews who heeded the call to colonize the Ukraine negotiated collective privileges with the magnates. Such local privileges began to supersede royal privileges in importance since the disposition of justice, which depended on the "actual balance of power," was usually in the local magnate's hands.[28]

In general Jews negotiated for, and magnates granted, a new legal status in the charters they issued for their private towns. Jews enjoyed the same civil privileges as the Christian burghers ruled by Magdeburg law, the urban legal system that had migrated eastward in the twelfth and thirteenth centuries. They possessed parity with respect to trade and economy, residence and property rights. They also bore equal obligations for municipal taxes and civic duties such as the night watch and maintaining the cleanliness of public spaces. They did not enjoy similar political privileges, since in most cases they were excluded from municipal government. There were some exceptions, in which Jews participated collectively through their community administration (kahal), electing a specified number of representatives.[29] That Jews shared an equal civic status with other burghers meant that they came to constitute a sort of second burgher estate that functioned in relationship to, and in significant ways cooperated and competed with, yet in general paralleled, that of the Polish burghers.[30]

To return to the example of Opatów: the Jews' privileges, dating from 1545 and intermittently renewed (1571, 1595, 1633), gave them parity with Christian residents in their "fiscal obligations to the town owner" and in their "full commercial freedom."[31] They possessed the right to a synagogue and a cemetery, a school and a poorhouse. The charter recognized the competence of their courts; they were removed from municipal jurisdiction.[32] They participated indirectly in municipal elections: a representative of the kahal assisted the guild-masters in choosing officials.[33]

An example in the Ukraine was the small town of Jampol (1765: 293 Jews). Prince Janusz Wiśniowiecki, the magnate owner, issued a charter in 1711 that Michał Kazimierz Radziwiłł reissued in its entirety in 1753. Wiśniowiecki explicitly aimed to rebuild his town after "the afflictions of the last thirty years," mentioning the "tiresome Turkish war and frequent Tatar incursions, and now the daily trial of the Swedish and Muscovite armies." He awarded his Jewish residents "freedom to engage in all forms of trade," and craftsmen, "Christian and Jews," the privilege to "settle in this city and conduct free trade with each other." He allowed the construction of a synagogue, for which "wood from our hereditary and leased forests" would be made available. He empowered the kahal with jurisdiction over Jews in Jampol as well as over lessees on his estates. He required the kahal to devote days of labor to maintaining the urban fabric. Exceptionally, he permitted Jews to participate in the municipal council by electing a representative to deliberate alongside the one from the "castle" and the two the burghers chose.[34]

The Jews' status as a parallel burgher estate materialized in synagogue construction. The sixteenth to eighteenth centuries saw the erection of great wooden synagogues: these were conspicuous public buildings that followed the design of wooden churches and manor houses. In addition, there were the square synagogues with a central lectern (*bimah*) surrounded by four pillars (Lublin, 1567; Premyśl, 1592–95) that utilized the designs Italian architects had introduced.[35] Significantly, synagogues appeared in etched panoramas of Polish cities from as early as 1537: as prominent public buildings they constituted a recognized piece of the urban landscape.[36]

г. Мстиславль Могилевской губ. № 8.
Синагога.

FIGURE 3. Wooden synagogue in Mstislavl built in the first half of the seventeenth century. YIVO Record ID 940, Collection R1, cat. no. MSTISLA1 Frame 46232.

The Jews' privileges that put them on equal footing with the burghers had an unforeseen consequence. During the eighteenth century, magnates increasingly integrated the Jews' communal institutions into the town's or estate's administrative structures. The magnates imposed themselves with force and frequency in Jewish community affairs to ensure control and an undiminished share of revenue.

> In general in this period, Polish authorities, and the magnate latifundium owners in particular, tried to preempt the prerogatives of the *kehalim* in matters both large and small. Whether it was imposing taxes on members, granting settlement rights, regulating economic competition, granting publishing or *arenda* licenses, regulating weights and measures, contracting debts, settling disputes, or even punishing religious transgressions and organizing synagogue life, the tendency in the eighteenth century was for the non-Jewish authorities to intrude more and more.[37]

Even rabbinical appointments became just one more opportunity for magnates to exercise patronage and generate revenue.[38]

The Jews' parity in local charters sheds interesting light on the Council of the Lands (1580–1764), the vaunted organ of self-government. Originating as a fiscal agency to apportion and collect a capitation tax, which was speedily translated into a global tax of a fixed sum owed to the monarch, the Council functioned as a sort of early modern parliament. It was a "bicameral institution" whose "(lay) parliament" performed the charge of political representation through hired intercessors (*shtadlanim*) and "rabbinical tribunal" presided over other aspects of self-government. The Council had to accept that many Jews were exempt from its jurisdiction, especially those granted special titles and individual privileges ("factor," "serwitor," "sekretarz") in recognition of service to the magnates. The Council was not a chartered institution: its authority derived from the individual community charters.[39]

The Jews' parity in local charters served as the basis for alliances with the burghers in contracts known as "ugody." Despite the "Jewish-magnate" marriage of convenience, Jews and burghers sometimes cooperated to oppose the magnate: to preclude a magnate or prince from purchasing a particular property or forbidding recourse to the nobility on a specific issue or range of issues.[40] In one apparently extreme case Jews and burghers joined together to attack and destroy a local noble's home.[41] In entering into these agreements, Jews acted as free agents. These were voluntary arrangements; they often carried multiple signatures showing that a "wide range of community members" gave "assent to the provisions."[42]

Significant numbers of Jews enjoyed parity of privileges in magnate-owned private towns. Historians estimate that by the eighteenth century, 70 percent of Jews lived in the eastern half of the Polish Commonwealth, and between one-half and three-quarters of all Jews lived in magnate-owned cities, towns, and villages.[43] The wars of the early eighteenth century encouraged this trend, as Jews were able to recover more quickly from the upheaval and spoliation of the Russian and Swedish armies than the general urban population. Magnates encouraged them with tax exemptions and other enticements to repopulate and rebuild shattered towns and town economies.[44]

Nevertheless, we should not forget the areas that excluded Jews. The decline of town economies combined with the Counter-Reformation effort at re-Catholicization to disseminate animus against Jewish merchants and commerce: the privilege of excluding Jews (*de non tolerandis Judaeis*) proliferated in the sixteenth and seventeenth centuries, with some new instances even in the eighteenth century.[45] Kiev's burghers, for example, secured such an edict in 1619.[46] Yet there was also considerable ambiguity about the consequences of these laws. In some cases Jews could live in a suburb or area exempt from municipal jurisdiction while in other cases they were allowed visits of a few days to conduct business in towns that prohibited their permanent residence.[47]

Conclusion

The Jews of the Polish-Lithuanian Commonwealth constituted the eastern region of emancipation. Jews enjoyed royal privileges in Poland from the thirteenth century. From the sixteenth century local magnate-issued privileges replaced these as the Polish-Lithuanian Commonwealth increasingly became a decentralized nobles' republic. Through an alliance with the magnates, Jews gained collective privileges in private market towns that gave them parity with Christian burghers. The number of Jews who enjoyed such privileges, and thereby constituted a parallel burgher estate, grew dramatically in the seventeenth and eighteenth centuries, especially in the Ukraine.

The brutal partitioning of the Polish-Lithuanian Commonwealth at the end of the eighteenth century would disrupt efforts at reform and complicate the transition from parity of privileges to rights.

CHAPTER THREE

Juridical Equality

THE POLITICAL STATUS OF JEWS in central Europe was linked to the Holy Roman Empire of the German Nation (HRE). The self-proclaimed western heir of the Roman Empire, and its sole heir after the fall of the Byzantine Empire (1453), this elusive and enigmatic entity covered an immense and varied territory, extending from Alsace and the Netherlands in the west to Bohemia in the east, from parts of Italy in the south to parts of Denmark in the north. The Holy Roman Empire was a decentralized constitutional polity consisting of a "dual system" of emperor and estates, perhaps most similar to the Dutch or Polish commonwealth.[1]

The elected emperor's task was to maintain the integrity of the empire against external enemies and peace among its multifarious constituent parts, especially preventing stronger members from preying on weaker ones.[2] Yet the emperor usually lacked the machinery to enforce his will beyond an importunate moment of impending crisis, if then. He was dependent on the "estates" for an army and revenue; the estates regularly rejected, or haughtily reduced, his requests for both. The agreement of 1452, by which the emperor was always the ruler of the Habsburg Empire, further compromised his position, since he was located on the HRE's southeastern periphery rather than at its geographical center.

The estates were the myriad individual polities: 405 in the "diet" (*Reichstag*) of 1521, 314 in 1780, though there were many more without representation. The polities included secular principalities and archbishoprics, bishoprics and abbeys, free and imperial cities, imperial knights and imperial counts. Their rulers, no matter how powerful, remained "vassals of the emperor"; they were not sovereigns but overlords in a feudal nexus of personal fealties. Their subjects could appeal to the emperor and to imperial institutions to defend their freedom, whether to resist oppressive urban oligarchies or encroaching territorial absolutisms. This constantly shifting dual system of emperor and estates defined political status within the empire, the Jews' included.[3]

Jews settled in central Europe as early as the Carolingian Empire (800 AD). They first congregated in urban areas along such rivers as the Rhine (Bonn, Cologne, Mainz, Speyer, Worms), the Moselle (Metz, Trier), and the Moldau (Prague), where they engaged in local and international trade.[4]

Two significant legislative acts of the thirteenth century were emblematic of the dual system of the imperial and the local characteristic of the late medieval and early modern Holy Roman Empire. During the Crusades, local privileges had failed to protect the Jews. In consequence, Emperor Frederick II (1236) placed the Jews under his direct jurisdiction, designating them as "serfs of the treasury" (*servi camerae*), which may also have translated Pope Gregory IX's canon law notion of the Jews' servitude (1234) into practical terms.[5] In so doing the emperor elevated their status by making them direct royal dependents. They were enabled to appeal directly to him for assistance; they were freed from the customary obligations of other subjects. This protection functioned throughout the late Middle Ages and well into the early modern period, especially when emperors prevented expulsions, for example, Worms (1487/88) and Kurmainz (1516). Nevertheless, the protection's effectiveness diminished from the fourteenth century.[6]

The conferral of this status transformed the Jews into a vulnerable group since, outside the estate system, they were an immediate source of exploitable income. The emperor could sell his "imperial right" to the Jews' revenue (*Judenregal*) to the highest bidder or trade it for some other advantage.

Such practices appeared in the fourteenth century when Emperors Heinrich VII and Ludwig the Bavarian vouchsafed the *Judenregal* for particular towns and areas to various rulers and when Charles IV (1346) sold his claim to the Jews' taxation to various towns.[7] This approach became increasingly apparent first with the "commercialization" and "territorialization" of the fourteenth and fifteenth centuries, and then against the background of the Reformation. Territorial rulers transmuted the emperor's former "protection" of the Jews (*Schutzverhältnis*) into a primarily "pecuniary" relationship (*Steuerverhältnis*). They exploited the Jews as a source of funding for the treasury. As the emperor's protection was hollowed out, the Jews became increasingly dependent on the local ruler.[8]

The role of local legislation began a decade after Emperor Frederick II's imperial decree. Duke Frederick of Austria (1244) issued a privilege that was notably generous in protecting the Jews' ability to lend money and to trade in specific goods. The privilege freed them from the jurisdiction of municipal courts, and especially the Magdeburg law that soon came to dominate urban life across central and eastern Europe. This privilege, as mentioned in the chapter on eastern Europe, became a template for charters across central and eastern Europe.[9]

As the imperial protection (*Judenregal*) lost its effectiveness, the privilege (*Schutzbrief; Schutz und Schirm*) that the local ruler issued for an individual and his family took its place. Valid for short time spans (three to six years) and limiting conditions for trading and moneylending, these privileges promoted the Jews' insecurity by preventing them from having permanent domicile. The Reich's political fragmentation reinforced that situation by encouraging constant migration between neighboring territories.[10]

The dependence on local privileges coalesced with events in the late medieval and early modern period to cause a major demographic shift: whereas the Jews had first settled in riparian cities and towns, they were now propelled into rural areas. With the chaos and persecutions during the Black Death of the fourteenth century, including the levying of exorbitant taxes in the cities, Jews migrated south to Italy and eastward to towns, villages, and minor polities, as well as to Lithuania and Poland. The few continuous urban settlements that remained were Frankfurt am Main and Friedberg, Prague and Worms.[11] The largely "urban and popular" expulsions of the pre-Reformation era, and the largely "princely and ecclesiastical" expulsions of the Reformation and Counter-Reformation eras, reinforced this pattern of rural concentration.[12]

The reforms that the estates introduced at the Reichstag at Worms (1495) and at Augsburg (1500) established the Reich as a "new kind of polity." It renewed the Jews' connection to imperial institutions.[13] The Imperial Court Chamber (*Reichskammergericht*) was independent of the royal court and was intended to "maintain the public peace and adjudicate in disputes between the emperor's vassals." It promoted the acceptance of Roman law throughout the empire's legal system. Within a few decades of its founding all the court's members were required to have formal legal training. The estates further succeeded in limiting imperial power by demoting the emperor from the position of a sovereign to that of a "referee in the legal system."[14] In 1507 the court secured its own revenue stream through a special tax (*Kammerzieler*), something the emperor never succeeded in gaining for his military ventures.[15]

Characteristically for the Holy Roman Empire, Worms and Augsburg yielded a "stalemate between Emperor and Estates." To prevent the estates-initiated court from gaining dominance, the emperor further developed his own court (*Reichshofrat*; Imperial Aulic Council). Together, the two courts promoted the steady adoption of Roman law that transformed the Holy Roman Empire's social relations through "juridification."

In these imperial institutions Jews found a means to defend themselves: they had now attained the significant political status of juridical parity. The introduction of Roman law revived the legal concept of Jews as citizens (*cives Romani*) with recognized legal standing.[16] As the famous scholar Johannes Reuchlin wrote (1510): "the members of both sects [Judaism and Christianity] belong to the Holy Empire as citizens of the Empire. . . . Therefore, the Imperial Law is equally binding for Christians and Jews."[17]

With the accompanying standardization of legal procedures, they gained the right to be plaintiffs, defendants, and witnesses. They could swear an oath in court on the Torah. Like other subjects, Jews turned to the courts to defend their privileges. They followed standard legal procedure which, symptomatic of the Holy Roman Empire, was exasperatingly protracted and prohibitively expensive. One had to file a complaint with a territorial sovereign; negotiate with a Territorial Commission; supplicate to the Reichstag; and, finally, file suit with the Imperial Court.[18]

Jewish communities successfully used this procedure to prevent urban expulsions prior to the Thirty Years War.[19] In a suit against the city of Colmar (1544–48) at the Imperial Court Chamber, Josel of Rosheim (d. 1594), the famous intercessor, appealed to the Jews' status as "cives Romani."[20] Thus the juridical parity that derived from the empire's "juridification" of social relations provided significant imperial protection.[21]

Beginning in the sixteenth century the Jews' legal status in the empire was determined in at least three ways. Emperors continued to issue imperial decrees—though with decreasing impact. Territories began to enact uniform legislation (*Judenordnungen*) that divided Jews into categories. Cities and territories bestowed privileges on individual Jews or groups of individuals.[22]

In keeping with his general revival of imperial traditions to stem the tide of Protestant expansion, Emperor Charles V confirmed the Jews' "long standing rights and privileges." At Speyer in 1544 he issued a generous charter for the Jews of the empire. More significantly, he continued the process of including Jews in the general turn to constitutional law.[23] In 1577 Rudolf II as Habsburg emperor issued a new charter for the Jews of Bohemia, guaranteeing perpetual settlement, albeit without contesting their exclusion from some Crown cities. This charter resulted in a rapid increase in the number of Jews in Prague as well as throughout Bohemia.[24]

Bohemia and Moravia were, indeed, something of an exception in central Europe. Prague was the largest center of urban Jewish life in early modern Europe: from 1623 Jews possessed extensive privileges of trade and commerce. The remaining Jews in Bohemia resembled their brethren in the Polish-Lithuanian Commonwealth: they lived in small and medium-sized towns on noble estates. During the eighteenth century they dispersed into the countryside to escape the impact of the 1724 *Familiantengesetz* (familiants law) that capped the number of families. The Jews of Moravia also lived in small to medium-sized towns on noble estates and, in contrast to Bohemia, created a cohesive supracommunal council in the seventeenth century.[25]

Territorial princes began to issue Jewry laws (*Judenordnungen*) from the beginning of the sixteenth century that specified privileges in considerable detail. The laws exhibited striking uniformity across territories: they were the work of nascent bureaucracies that, in communication with one another, were attempting to standardize territorial state laws.[26]

Princes had considerable self-interest at stake in this legislation: Jews were a source of direct revenue that did not need the approval of estates or other rival entities. Jews had equally much at stake: these Jewry laws not only defined their legal status but also were the ground on which to appeal to the Imperial Chamber Court or the Imperial Aulic Council if the ruler or another party violated them.[27] Nevertheless, it is in this period that, in respect to legal status, they gradually became less "Jews of the Empire [*Reichsjuden*]" and more "Jews of the territorial state [*Territorialjuden*]."[28]

The year 1603 was a critical juncture in defining the nature of organized life for the approximately 12,000 Jews living in the Holy Roman Empire. Jewish leaders convened a synod during the Frankfurt fair to establish an empire-wide system of courts and taxation. Two powerful rulers (the electors of Cologne and Mainz), who were jealous of their powers and revenues, denounced this effort as politically subversive (*lèse-majesté*) and demanded that an Imperial Commission investigate.

Emperor Rudolf II, preoccupied with the Turkish wars and desperate for funds, either could not or would not resist the two electors and the estates to defend the Jews, so the Imperial Commission began its proceedings in 1606. The result was that the synod failed, the Jews paid a clearly extortionate indemnity to the elector of Cologne, and the presence of the Imperial Commissions in Frankfurt and Worms may have undermined the Jews' political position and thereby contributed to their expulsions from those two cities (Frankfurt 1614, Worms 1615), although they were speedily restored under imperial aegis.[29]

Unlike the Jews of Poland who created the Council of the Lands in 1580, then, the Jews of the empire failed to establish a centralized organization. Instead, they devised regional forms of self-government, the so-called "Jewish regional diets" (*Judenlandtage*) or "rural Jewish corporations" (*Landjuden-schaften*), that aggregated the widely dispersed and atomized rural settlements of an individual family or a few families in order to provide rabbis, courts, and a mechanism for tax collection.[30] The failure of the Frankfurt Synod and the growth of regional self-government attested to the fact that local and territorial governments, rather than the empire, with the significant exception of the imperial courts, were now the arbiters of the Jews' political status.[31]

The Jews' resettlement of central Europe began in the 1570s and visibly accelerated during the Thirty Years War. That resettlement rested on privileges that Jews negotiated as individuals with territorial princes and imperial cities; these contrasted with the collective privileges Jews negotiated with Italian and Atlantic seaboard cities and magnates in the Polish-Lithuanian Commonwealth.[32]

With this resettlement Jews also began to diversify economically, making the transition from moneylending to various types of commerce.[33] Of the 272 heads of household in Frankfurt in 1694, 163 were engaged in retailing especially of textiles, while only 109 still loaned money and dealt in old clothes.[34]

In the Duchy of Kleve the last complaints about Jews engaging in usury were heard in 1737.[35]

Court Jews (*Hoffaktoren*), who served rulers as army contractors and minters, bankers and purveyors of luxury goods, exemplified such individual privileges. These privileges often included residence in an otherwise prohibited city, especially a capital; permission to buy real estate and erect a residence; and freedom of travel, including exemption from tolls.[36] A Court Jew's letter of privilege routinely allowed for the settlement of his family and retinue (slaughterer, tutors, bookkeepers, domestic servants). The Court Jew's privilege in many instances laid the foundation for a new Jewish community.[37]

In Kleve, as in many other locations after the Thirty Years War, rulers competed to recruit Jews who would generate revenue for the treasury and stimulate the economy. The community in Kleve was organized by, and for the benefit of, one Court Jew, Berend Levi of Bonn.[38] Jews were permitted into Duisburg (1720) in consequence of the territorial ruler's growing dominance over the estates, which had strenuously resisted admitting Jews in the past. The courts guaranteed them equal treatment in their commercial transactions.[39]

These individual privileges could be combined into a collective general privilege for individuals, as was the case in Halle. Two Court Jews, Jakob Levin and Bernd Wolff from Halberstadt, petitioned the elector of Brandenburg in 1691 for permission to settle in Halle and subsequently received the status of "protected Jews" (*vergleitete Schutzjuden*). Three years later another Court Jew, Assur Marx (Marcus), also received permission to settle and conduct business in Halle. Finally, in response to a petition from the nine Court Jews now resident in Halle, the government bundled the existing individual privileges into a "General Privilege" and expressly prohibited additional settlement.[40]

Another form of individual privilege occurred at fairs and in Jewry laws in the differentiation of individuals based on capital. Breslau had a privilege not to tolerate Jews after it expelled them in 1455. The Breslau fair, however, attracted Jews from across the Habsburg Empire and particularly the Polish-Lithuanian Commonwealth, with the latter as an especially important constituency, transacting as much as two-thirds of the trade with Poland.[41] In 1537 Ferdinand I issued an edict that welcomed merchants regardless of religion and specifically mentioned Jews.[42] From 1635 to 1702 Jews had permission to visit the fair and to remain a few days before and after. In 1697 a privilege was granted differentiating between five different groups based on the amount of goods or cash they brought and the proposed duration of stay.[43]

The Jews' resettlement of Breslau, despite the city's privilege of exclusion, resulted from the fair and the Habsburg imperial mint. To conduct the business that remained after each fair, recognized Jewish regional and municipal organizations negotiated permission to appoint an agent, who was the equivalent of a resident consul, to transact business until the next fair. In 1696 ten such agents lived in Breslau.[44] Court Jews in the service of the Habsburg emperor began to administer the imperial mint in Breslau as early as 1546. They obtained permission to rent houses in the city.[45] These two groups of Jews who initially resettled Breslau had individual privileges.[46]

Prussia maintained individual statuses within the framework of collective privileges or, after 1730, state laws. In May 1671 the Great Elector admitted to Berlin by royal decree, for a period of twenty years, fifty named families who had been expelled from Vienna. No other Jews were permitted to settle.[47]

The Great Elector was attempting to populate his thinly settled territories and stimulate commerce. In 1685, he invited Huguenots expelled from France. The General Privilege (*Generalprivilegium*) of 1730, Prussia's first state law for the Jews, attested to the emerging absolutist territorial state. Its bureaucracy created special departments (*Judenkommissionen*) to administer Jewry laws because of the important revenues they generated.[48] Under Frederick II, Prussia's Jewry law (*Judenreglement*) of 1750 established six distinct individual statuses.

> The first, smallest and wealthiest class was that of the *Generalprivili-gierte* or the "generally privileged." These persons were permitted to settle in the area set aside for Jews without a special permit and could purchase houses and land. As merchants they enjoyed the same rights as Christians and, in exceptional cases, they were allowed to acquire citizenship and were able to pass these rights on to their children. The second class consisted of *Ordentliche Schutzjuden* or "privileged protected Jews." They did not have the right of free choice of residence and their status could only be passed on to one of their children. *Außerordentliche Schutzjuden* or "unprivileged protected Jews," made up the third class. They were permitted to take up residence only by virtue of the useful professions they practiced as physicians, opticians, painters, engravers and the like. A father from this class could "place" one of his children—that is, include the child in his right of residence—but only if the child had assets of at least one thousand thalers. The fourth class consisted of community employees, including the rabbis. Class five was made up of the "tolerated," that is, "unprotected" Jews, who required the patronage of a "protected Jew" in order to stay in Berlin. They were only permitted to marry if their intended spouse was from the two highest classes. This fifth class also contained the children of those "privileged protected Jews" who could not inherit their father's status, along with the children of the "unprivileged protected Jews" and the employees of the community. The servants and domestics employed in the homes and commercial enterprises of the *Generalpriviligierte* comprised the sixth class. Their stay in Berlin was dependent on the duration of their employment.[49]

Das III. Capitel.
Von
Juden-Sachen.

No. I. Edict wegen der Pohlnischen Juden Arretirung auff denen Jahrmärckten ꝛc. Vom 20. August. 1650.

Nachdem Sr. Churfürstl. Durchl. zu Brandenburg, zu Magdeburg, in Preussen, zu Jülich, Cleve, Berge, Stettin, Pommern ꝛc. Hertzog ꝛc. Unser gnädigster Herr, uff einkommene vornehme Intercessionales, und dan auch auff ihr demüthiges Bitten, den Juden in Pohlen, das hiebevor wegen des handels in der Chur-Brandenburg gehabte Privilegium, wiederumb auff die nechstfolgende Sieben Jahr in Gnaden ertheilet, und darnegst befreyet, daß, vermöge der pacten zwischen der Crohn Pohlen und der Chur-Brandenburg, Sie, die Pohlnische Juden, uff den Jahrmärckten und in Städten, wegen der Ausländischen, so sie zu besprechen haben mögen, nicht arrestabell seyn sollen, vielmehr aber einer den andern für seiner ordentli-

chen Obrigkeit zu belangen. Alß wird allen Magistraten in der Chur Brandenburg hiedurch befohlen, sich hiernach zu achten und solchem nach zukommen. Nichtes weniger werden auch alle Churfürstl. Zöllner und Geleidts Leute ernstlich beschliget, keine ungewöhnliche Zölle von den Juden zu fodern, noch sie sonsten mit einiger Newerung zu beschweren, sondern wann sie das, was die Zoll Rollen besagen, erlegen, unaufgehalten passiren zu lassen, damit deshalb keine Klage einkomme, Urkundlichen unter Sr. Churfürstl. Durchl. Subscription und Pettschafft gedrucktem Secret, Geben zu Cölln an der Spree, am 20. August. 1650.

Fr. Wilhelm.

(L. S.)

No. II. Edict wegen auffgenommenen 50. Familien Schutz-Juden, jedoch daß sie keine Synagogen halten. Vom 21. May 1671.

Wir Friderich Wilhelm, von GOttes Gnaden, Marggraff zu Brandenburg, des Heil. Röm. Reichs Ertz Cammerer und Churfürst, ꝛc. Bekennen hiermit öffentlich, und geben einem jeden dem es nöthig, in Gnaden zuwissen, wie daß Wir aus sonderbaren Ursachen, und auff Unterthänigstes Anhalten, Hirschel Lazarus, Benedict Veit, und Abraham Ries, Juden, bevorab zu Beforderung Handels und Wandels bewogen worden, einige von andern Orten sich weggebende Jüdische Familien, und zwar funfftzig derselben, in Unser Lande der Chur-und Marck Brandenburg, und in Unseren sonderbaren Schutz gnädigst auf- und anzunehmen, thun auch solches hiemit und Krafft dieses auff folgende Conditiones :

1. Wollen wir ermeldten funfftzig Jüdischen Familien, derer Namen, und Anzahl von Personen, auch an was Ort jede sich niedergelassen, uns forderlichst durch eine richtige Specification kund gethan werden soll, in gedachte Unsere Lande der Chur- und Marck Brandenburg, auch in Unser Hertzogthum Crossen und incorporirte Landen hiemit auffgenommen haben, dergestalt und also, daß ihnen Macht gegeben seyn sol, in denen Oertern und Städten, wo es ihnen

am gelegensten ist, sich niederzulassen, allda Stuben, oder gantze Häuser, Wohnungen und Commodität vor sich zu miethen, zu erkauffen oder zu erbauen, doch in der Masse, daß, was sie Kauffweise an sich bringen, Widerkäufflich geschehe, und was sie erbauen, auch nach Verfliessung gewisser Jahre an die Christen wieder verlassen werden müsse, jedoch, daß ihnen die Unkosten davor restituiret werden.

2. Sol diesen Jüdischen Familien vergönnet seyn, ihren Handel und Wandel im gantzen Lande dieser Unser Chur- und Marck Brandenburg, Hertzogthumb Crossen und incorporirten Oertern, Unsern edicten gemäß zu treiben, wobey wir ihnen noch ausdrücklich nachgeben, offene Krahme und Buden zu huben, Tücher und dergleichen Wahren, in stücken zuverkauffen oder auch Ellenweise außzumessen, groß und klein Gewichte zu halten (doch daß sie dadurch keine Vervortheilung im Kauff oder Verkauff) noch auch denen Rahts-Wagen, oder wo der Magistrat das grosse Gewichte hat, etwas abgehe, mit Neuen und Alten Kleidern zu handeln, ferner in ihren Häusern zu schlachten, und was sie zu ihrer Nohtdurfft und ihrem Gesetze nach von dem geschlachteten nicht bedürffig, solches zu verkauf-

V. Th. V. Abtheil.   Q   fen

FIGURE 4. Prussian edict of May 21, 1671, allowing settlement of fifty Jewish families in Berlin though without a synagogue. Christian Otto Mylius, *Corpus Constitutionum Marchicarum* (Berlin and Halle, 1737–55), part 5, sec. 5, chapter III, no. II, p. 121. Leo Baeck Institute.

The predominance of individual privileges or statuses based on the individual's ability to generate revenue resulted in the immiseration of the mass of Jews. Lacking privileges, they were excluded from fixed residence and occupation. The Jewish population of the empire increased considerably in the first half of the eighteenth century, in part naturally and in part by migration from Poland: from some 25,000 in 1700 to 60,000 to 70,000 in 1750. The Jews' economic situation deteriorated: as their numbers and tax levies rose, economic opportunities declined. In 1750 50 to 66 percent of the Jews subsisted below the level of the corporate guild burghers and perhaps as few as 10 percent, or as many as 50 percent, lived a marginal existence of petty trade and begging, community odd jobs and domestic service, theft and prostitution. This diverse group came to be designated as "pauper Jews" (*Betteljuden*) and appeared more regularly in police files than on community tax rolls.[50]

Expulsions and wars, restrictive legislation and exorbitant taxation, as well as the predominance of community oligarchies, contributed to this situation. In 1670 Habsburg emperor Leopold I expelled the Jews from Vienna and Lower Austria, though he revoked the expulsion order in 1683. In 1744 Empress Maria Theresa expelled the Jews from Prague, although she also later revoked that order. In 1726 Habsburg emperor Charles VI introduced the infamous *Familiantengesetz*, which limited the number of families in Bohemia (8,541), Moravia (5,106), and Silesia (119) and allowed only the family's eldest son to marry. The wealthy leaders of Jewish communities generally endeavored both to minimize the number of impecunious Jews who could not pay their share of taxes and to ensure that other non-taxpayers were refused admission.[51]

The preponderance of individual privileges manifested itself in the character of the synagogue building. Jews gained the privilege of domestic or in some cases private worship, and the synagogue was constructed according to the norms of vernacular or sometimes court architecture.[52] In Fürth, for example, the synagogue (1692) was a vernacular building that was not identifiable from the exterior.[53] Berlin's first community synagogue, the Heidereuther Gasse synagogue (1712–14), whose design was influenced by court architecture, was built in a courtyard so it would not be visible from the street.[54] Following Amsterdam's lead, many of these synagogues did contain better accommodations for women.[55]

Unlike the synagogues in Livorno, Amsterdam, or many towns and cities of the Polish-Lithuanian Commonwealth, the synagogue in the Holy Roman Empire exhibited the status of private worship. It was not a publicly recognizable ecclesiastical building.

Conclusion

The Jews of the Holy Roman Empire constituted the central European region of emancipation. Some historians would contend that the Holy Roman Em-

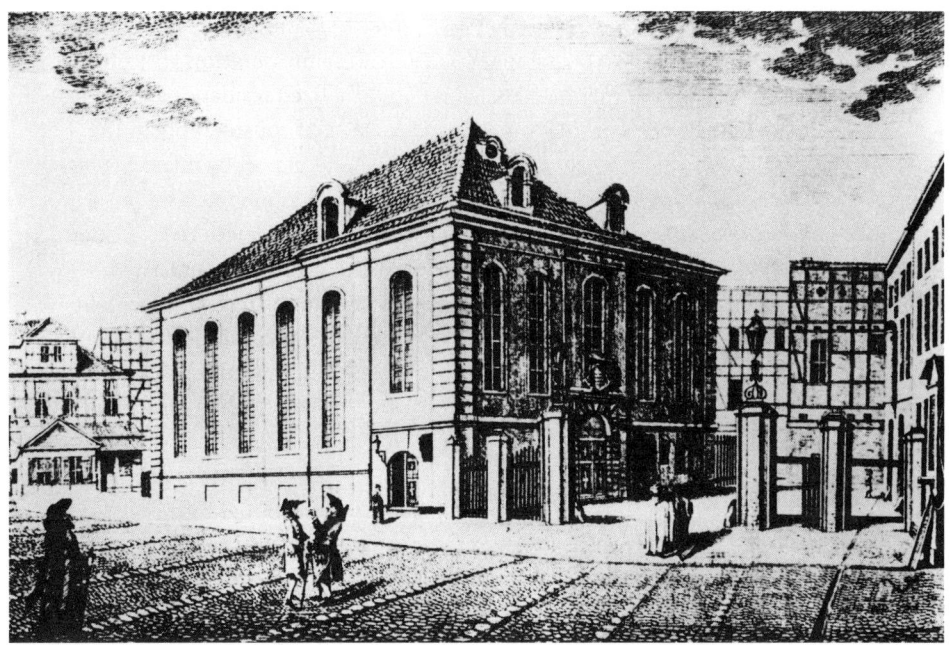

FIGURE 5. Berlin Heidereutergasse, 1795 etching. Shows synagogue in a courtyard
hidden from public view. Art Resource, 303265.

pire's "archaic, traditionalist constitution . . . created a society that tolerated
religious and ethnic differences to a far greater degree than the more centralized states of Western Europe"; in other words, "early modern central Europe
was a pluralistic, complex society more tolerant of differences than England,
France or Spain."[56]

Whether this observation is accurate or not, it concerns toleration, not parity. Jews in the Holy Roman Empire fell behind Jews to the east and west in
their political status. They gained neither collective corporate privileges nor
the civic rights of emerging civil societies. To be sure, their juridical equality in
the courts of the Holy Roman Empire marked a significant elevation in status.
The Court Jews' extensive individual privileges were also an elevation in status,
yet only for a miniscule elite. In sum, Jews in the Holy Roman Empire did not
keep pace with their brethren east and west, thus making the transition to
emancipation, when it came, a painful rupture.

PART II

The Two
Legislative Models

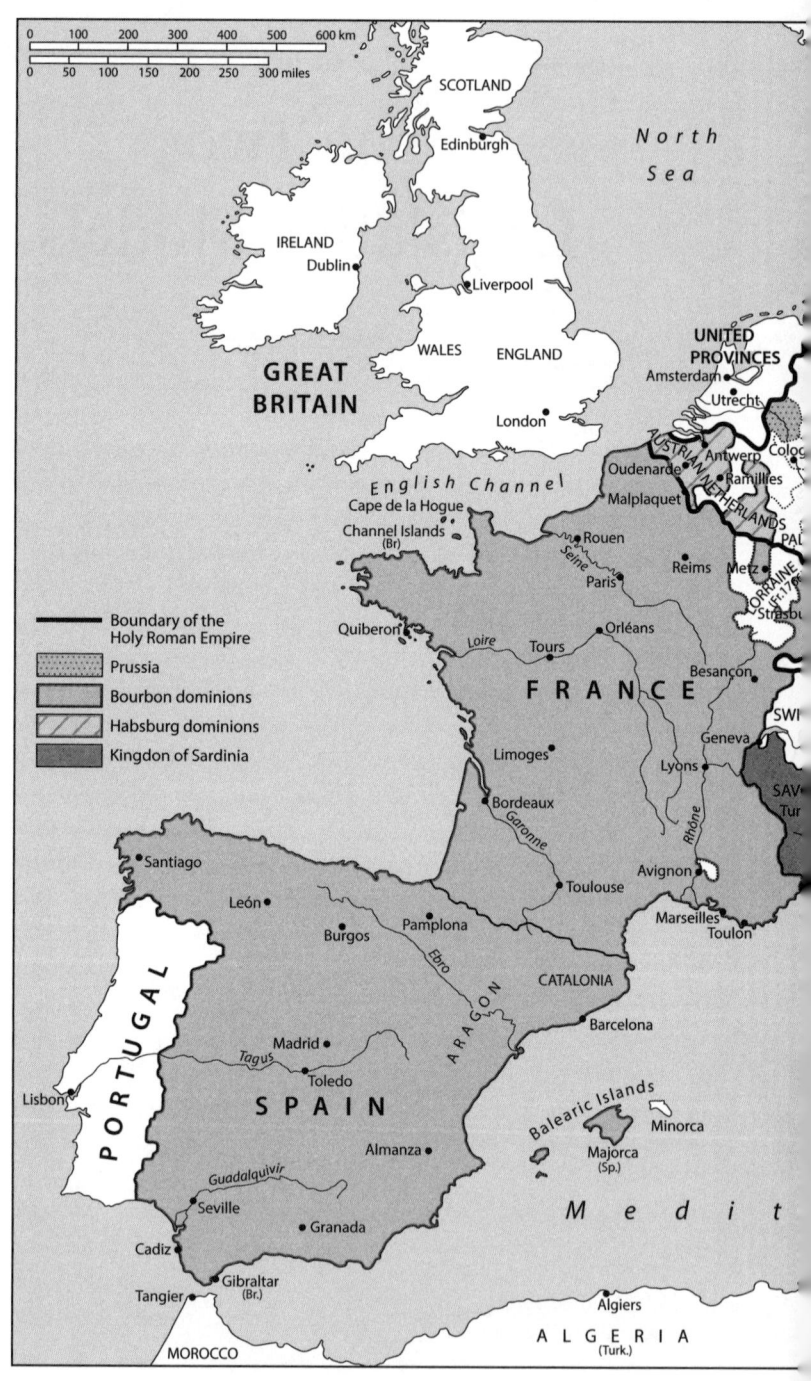

MAP III. Europe around 1740/1750. Cox Cartographic.

MAP IV. Partitions of Poland (1772, 1793, 1795) identifying the territories each of the partitioning powers seized. Cox Cartographic.

MAP V. Napoleonic Europe, 1810. Cox Cartographic.

CHAPTER FOUR

Bureaucrat, Laboratory, Emperor

BETWEEN 1740 AND 1789 GOVERNMENTS ACROSS EUROPE began to enact legislation to ameliorate the inferior status of members of prohibited and persecuted religions. These governments were motivated by two distinct yet complementary sets of ideas. On one side, they followed raison d'état: enhancement of state power through centralization, increased revenue, re-population, conquest, and/or colonial expansion. On the other side, they espoused Enlightenment ideas: toleration, natural rights, and a belief in progress through reform.[1]

That Jews figured in this legislation was significant: governments created a semblance of comparability in treating them alongside other religious groups. Yet the differences were also significant. Legislation for Christians had priority; legislation for Jews always followed that for the relevant Christian groups. In addition, the legislation for Jews usually diverged in substantive ways.

The legislation predominantly concerned civic rights (residence, occupations, property, worship), though some also included political rights. Some of this legislation went the furthest of any in the ancien régime in creating parity in a corporate society (Bordeaux, 1774; Russia, 1785; Galicia, 1789) or equality in an emerging civil society, especially in the colonies (Plantation Act, 1740). Some legislation maintained or even increased discriminatory and oppressive regulations (Prussia, 1750; Alsace, 1784). There was also some truly breathtaking legislation that was only partially implemented (Russia, 1785) (chapter 6). While there was local and municipal legislation in this period as well, the balance began to shift toward territorial, state, or empire-wide laws.

Two central European figures produced the ideas and legislation that would play a leading role from the 1780s until the mid-nineteenth century. In 1781–82 a Prussian journalist and bureaucrat, Christian Wilhelm von Dohm (1751–1820), published the single most influential book in favor of emancipation. By literally recasting the terms of the debate, he had a direct impact on legislation across Europe until 1848. In the Habsburg Empire Joseph II issued a spate of edicts from 1782 to 1789 that aimed to transform the Jews' status. His edicts not only remained in force in some of the Habsburg lands until 1848 but also served as models for emancipation legislation throughout Europe. The initial laboratory for many of these policies was the Habsburg's Italian territories of Lombardy and Tuscany.

At first glance Dohm and Joseph II would seem to have offered two competing versions of emancipation. Dohm's argument for "civic amelioration" (*bürgerliche Verbesserung*) constituted a form of unconditional emancipation: full rights were the sine qua non for the Jews' regeneration and integration. Joseph II's "toleration" presented a form of conditional emancipation: he granted some rights while maintaining numerous restrictions. Joseph aimed to legislate from above the Jews' improvement, increasing their utility for, and better integrating them into, the state.

In practice Dohm's prescriptions and Joseph II's legislation often converged. Since Joseph and Dohm spoke the same language of utility and regeneration, bureaucrats and legislators frequently invoked Dohm while following Joseph II. In tandem, Dohm's advocacy and Joseph II's legislation constituted a potent model of state-directed conditional emancipation.

Prussia

Christian Wilhelm von Dohm was a representative figure of the Prussian Enlightenment's (*Aufklärung*) politicization.[2] Moses Mendelssohn (1729–86), an experienced intercessor on behalf of Jewish communities, invited him to write his tract to address the situation of Alsatian Jewry (chapter 5).[3] Dohm formulated an argument for the Jews' equality in an entirely political framework. To be sure, previous advocates had voiced many of the individual arguments. He was the first, however, to articulate the complete constellation of ideas of populationism, "environmentalism," and Enlightenment perfectibility in a sustained and systematic manner with "luminous impartiality."[4] Moreover, in proposing unconditional emancipation, his book provoked other writers to articulate the other major positions: conditional emancipation and the categorical denial of emancipation.[5]

Dohm asked "if and by what means the Jews can become morally and politically better than they are now."[6] He replied that the two answers were inseparable since he understood emancipation as a moral issue within a political framework. The Jews' disabilities and juridically enforced concentration in trade and moneylending were "the true source of their corruption." He asserted that "the moral character of the Jews, as that of all men, is capable of the most complete development and the most unfortunate degradation."[7] At bottom, "the Jew is more a man than a Jew."[8] Dohm deemed corrupting the petty commerce and itinerant hawking of the poorest Jews; he did not demean large-scale trade and its wealthy practitioners (chapter 3).

Dohm had unquestioned faith in the ennobling power of freedom and equality ("environmentalism"): "When the oppression which he experienced for centuries has made him morally corrupt, then a more equitable treatment will again restore him."[9] He appealed to a populationist version of raison d'état: since the state's wealth derives from a large and growing population, the state should fully utilize all its residents. He advocated that the Jews gain the full rights of citizens, that they educate their children to develop "their moral and political character," and that they abandon petty commerce for agriculture and artisanry. The last required the weakening or abolition of the guilds; here emancipation was associated with a movement "out of" estates.[10]

Dohm's unconditional emancipation came with some qualifications. He would not immediately admit Jews to civil service appointments: he would give preference to members of the "more numerous nation."[11] He thought Jews should be subject to conscription: since their present physical inadequacies would prevent them from serving as soldiers for several generations, they could in the meantime pay for surrogates.[12] At the same time, he would allow Jewish communities to retain a crucial aspect of their former communal autonomy, namely, separate courts for cases among themselves.[13]

Dohm's impact was "epoch-making" for legislation as well as for the public debate.[14] One prominent example is Baden in 1809. An internal government memorandum of 1797 that prepared the ground for legislation resounded with Dohm's language and argumentation. The 1809 edict did the same.[15] The edict granted the partial rights of conditional emancipation.

The Laboratory of Lombardy and Tuscany

In the second half of the eighteenth century, Habsburg rulers used Tuscany and Lombardy as the testing ground for policies later introduced elsewhere in the empire. These far-reaching absolutist reforms aimed to replace the two polities' "city-state order" with a centralized state of uniform law and administration.[16] The reforms strove to recognize individual rights within extant corporate structures. Such reforms generally applied to Jews and necessarily improved their political status.

In Lombardy's "laboratory for Habsburg administration," Vienna aimed to increase revenues by introducing (1740–1750s) taxation on landownership.[17] An associated goal was to create a tax-generating rural bourgeoisie as a political counterweight to the predominant patricians. In 1755 the government created a new communal administration based in an assembly (*convocato*) of landholders; each had one vote. In 1760 the state used a recently completed cadastral land survey (*censimento*) to introduce property taxation designed to end patricians' tax exemptions.[18] In 1770 the government instituted direct taxation in place of tax farming (*Ferma generale*).

After a 1769 visit to Lombardy, Joseph II proposed new centralized institutions that "transformed everything from the foundations" by separating administrative from judicial functions, dissolving the old patrician magistracies, and employing foreigners. Through their control of the Senate, the patricians continued to thwart Vienna's goals.[19]

During his decade of sole rule Joseph II visited Lombardy twice (February/March 1784; June/July 1785). He introduced a still more radical reform of the administration in 1786, especially a merger with the Duchy of Mantua, the dissolution of the Senate—the patricians' power base—and a restructuring of local administration that aimed to eliminate privilege and autonomy.[20]

By integrating Jews as taxpayers and landowners, these far-reaching reforms made Lombardy a "testing place" for Habsburg Jewry policy. In 1765 the government abolished the separate administration of Jews (*comissario degli ebrei*); in 1772 permitted them to borrow money from the municipal loan bank (Monte di Pietà); and in 1779 abolished the Inquisition. That same year the government permitted the purchase of real estate and entry to a range of new occupations: "to engage in arts and manufactures even outside the Ghetto, to deal in foodstuffs, to practice as physicians, and to frequent the public academies for training." The government also abolished communal accountability for delinquent individuals.[21]

In Tuscany, Peter Leopold's reforms (1765–90) aimed to replace the paternal state with a social contract between a "community of landowners" and a limited monarchy. He introduced free trade in grain and suppressed internal barriers (1781). Over the course of a generation or more patricians disappeared from the ranks of the bureaucracy, giving place to new nobles and provincial notables.[22] His Penal Code of 1786 instituted a fundamental reform of justice in abolishing capital punishment and discrimination according to birth or social condition. Nevertheless, many older laws remained in force.[23]

As part of his municipal reform (1772–86; *riforma delle comunità*), Peter Leopold aimed to dismantle the Jews' segregation by granting them rights on par with those of other citizens.[24] His administration granted them religious freedom, freedom of property and trade, and admission to Tuscan universities and literary and scientific societies. Jews who purchased urban and rural real estate qualified to participate in municipal government, a form of municipal citizenship.[25] This policy appears not to have been fully implemented. For example, in Florence in 1779–80 Jews bought houses in the ghetto. If a Jew's name was drawn to hold office he was replaced by a Catholic.[26]

The situation differed in some rural areas. In a town such as Pitigliano in the Lower Province of Sienna, which contained about 222 Jews in the mid-1780s (10% of the population), Jews had been allowed to own property since the sixteenth century and bought more in Peter Leopold's sales of national property (1780s). In 1783 Peter Leopold abrogated three ancient taxes to encourage the Jews' equality. In the 1780s and 1790s Jews did indeed hold lower municipal offices for which they were eligible. Only Catholics had access to higher offices.[27]

Habsburg Empire

In his autocratic frenzy of sole rule in the 1780s, Joseph II produced the most influential legislation in shaping emancipation across continental Europe until 1848. His enactment of a range of forms of conditional emancipation under the aegis of the state, a mixture of rights and restrictions that aimed to heighten the Jews' state-defined utility, provided templates for governments across the continent. It even gained mention in the National Assembly during the French Revolution.

The French Revolution offered a rival conception of immediate unconditional emancipation (1790–91). Yet Joseph's influence touched even the competition: in 1808 Napoleon reverted to conditional emancipation relying on Joseph's legislation (chapter 9). Joseph II's model predominated among governments engaged in incremental reform, the dominant model on the continent except for brief interludes of revolution. Of course, the 1780s' pioneering legislation grew increasingly conservative when applied in the nineteenth century.

Joseph II famously promulgated edicts of toleration for all the larger minority religions in the Habsburg Empire: first Protestants and Greek Orthodox, then Jews (he did not hesitate to persecute or exile dissenting Protestant sects).[28] While his Edict of Toleration (1782) maintained the supremacy of the Catholic Church, Joseph for the first time granted legal recognition to Protestants and the Greek Orthodox by bestowing civic status: the purchase of homes and property, membership in towns and guilds, entrance to universities and the civil service.

The edict upheld Catholic supremacy by restricting Protestants and the Eastern Orthodox to domestic worship (prayer at home) or, if the numbers warranted (five hundred individuals), private worship (a church without bells, a tower, or a public entrance on the street). In mixed marriages with a Catholic father all children were to be raised Catholic; in mixed marriages with a Protestant father, the children were to follow the parent's religion by sex.[29]

Joseph had multiple reasons for issuing the Edict of Toleration. He wanted to deprive foreign powers of any pretext to interfere in Habsburg affairs (Prussia for Protestants, Russia for the Greek Orthodox).[30] He wanted the Protestants and Greek Orthodox to contribute to their fullest capacity, and give their undivided loyalty, to the state. He genuinely embraced "a true Christian toleration" that allowed each subject to find his own means of salvation. He thought his reforms of the Catholic Church would attract Protestants and others to

Catholicism: increasing the number of parishes, enhancing pastoral care, improving the clergy's education.[31] Finally, following Maria Theresa's initiative, he endeavored to create an abstract and general notion of citizenship that would unify the Habsburg's disparate territories. In this regard Habsburg absolutism preceded, and offered an alternative to, France's revolution.[32]

Joseph considered including the Jews in his initial toleration edicts; his advisors convinced him this would insult the Christians.[33] Legislating for the Jews was complex. He could not promulgate one blanket edict since they had different statuses in the monarchy's many territories and were excluded from others. Joseph therefore issued separate legislation for each of the relevant provinces. That was an arduous and prolonged process that, involving negotiation with each territorial administration, extended virtually throughout the decade of his sole rule (1781 to 1789).[34] His legislation manifestly radicalized over the course of the decade.

Based on the Habsburg experience in Lombardy and Tuscany, Joseph aimed to integrate the Jews into the monarchy in two ways. First, he wanted to increase their economic productivity to help fill the monarchy's perennially depleted coffers. He therefore opened a range of previously prohibited occupations (transport, handicrafts, arts) and encouraged them to become farmers. He allowed wealthy Jews to establish factories in hitherto vacant areas (though not in Hungary, which was to remain largely agricultural). He opened the schools and universities (until its abolition in 1782, the requirement to assert belief in the Immaculate Conception had excluded Protestants and Jews).[35] He even permitted students to reside in towns otherwise closed to Jews to attend high school.

Second, he aimed to absorb the Jews into the monarchy's administration by requiring that they adopt German as the official language of business within two years. He required Jewish children to attend primary schools to learn German, either in Jewish schools funded by the community or in existing non-Jewish schools. He required that Jews take German personal and family names (July 23, 1787).

Over the course of the 1780s he extended the meaning of integration; this was in keeping with his radical turn around 1785.[36] In his edicts for Lower Austria (January 1782) and Moravia (February 1782) Joseph made the Jews "nearly equal" to "foreigners of other religions." In contrast, when he imposed compulsory military conscription on December 18, 1788, he spoke of the Jews as "fellow citizens." In his 1789 edict for Galicia he made the Jews equal "in rights as well as in duties" to other "subjects."[37] Joseph's general policy was to incorporate Jews "into" the existing estates that he was systematically depriving of power.[38]

While extending privileges to the point of equality, Joseph also retained a range of restrictions, many draconian. He aimed to maintain the Jews' current numbers through the "family laws" (*Familiantengesetz*) in place since the 1720s, which established a maximum number of families (Bohemia, Lower Austria) and allowed only the eldest son to marry, and then only after the father's death. He did not permit immigration or natural increase. Thinly populated Hungary was the exception since a general "populationist" policy prevailed there. He also did not abrogate the restrictions that historically had kept certain regions or cities closed to Jews. His one concession was to abolish the demeaning "body tax" (*Leibmauth*).

Joseph's promulgation of privileges and restrictions was deliberate; he understood the two as being complementary and not contradictory. His amalgam of carrots and sticks, the essence of absolutist reform, subsequently became the legislative model for conditional emancipation across Europe.

BOHEMIA

Until the partition of Poland, Bohemia and Moravia contained the "largest, most consolidated and economically and culturally the most important Jewish community" (approximately 60,000–80,000) in the Habsburg lands.[39] The edict of October 18, 1781, for Bohemia established the major characteristics of the edicts that followed. The most significant changes concerned the Jews' "improved education and enlightenment [*besseren Bildung und Aufklärung*]." The edict required German language instruction either through the founding of Jewish schools or, if student numbers were too low to warrant a separate school, attendance of Christian schools. Poor Jews were encouraged to become farmers and were also allowed to work as itinerant peddlers. Jews in general were permitted to engage in transport and artisanship, the arts and manufacture without hindrance from the guilds. The edict especially encouraged the founding of new industry.

The regime's stringent restrictions remained in place: the legislated number of families (since 1726; 8,600 under Joseph II); the right of marriage for only the eldest son; and areas historically closed to Jews (with 1724 the zero hour). Similarly, the Jews' judicial and communal autonomy stayed intact.[40]

SILESIA

Prussia seized the bulk of Silesia in 1740. The edict of December 15, 1781, for the remnant of Jews inhabiting the rump border district, left in place the same harsh restrictions on numbers and marriage as in Bohemia. Only the body tax was abolished. Jewish children were to attend Christian schools since their numbers were insufficient to establish separate Jewish schools. The edict introduced the same economic measures encouraging artisanship, the arts, and industry.[41]

LOWER AUSTRIA

The "Patent of Toleration" for Lower Austria (January 2, 1782) intended to grant the Jews privileges "in respect to . . . means of livelihood and the enjoyment of civil and domestic conveniences" that made them "nearly equal [*beynahe gleichsetzen*] to members of other foreign religions" and, in so doing, rendered them "more useful and useable for the state." Overall the patent gave little and withheld much, piling on restrictions and prohibitions taken from the 1764 Jewry Law (*Judenordnung*).[42] It maintained the existing number of Jews and prohibited public worship and a public synagogue. It validated the existing prohibitions on Jewish settlement. It limited the privileges it granted: especially notable was that the Jews could undertake all forms of artisanship, "yet without the right of citizenship and mastership"—a stipulation that deprived them of the all-crucial local citizenship (*Heimatrecht*). It did repeal the odious "body tax" (*Leibmauth*). Education was central, though the Jews were to bear the costs of new schools. The few wealthy Jews allowed to live in Vienna lacked the status of a legal community; the mass of poor Jews was denied entry.[43] The few wealthy Jews were no longer required to have beards and could carry swords.

MORAVIA

The decree for Moravia (February 3, 1782) aimed to reconcile "a freedom in accordance with law," without reference to "nation or religion," with the extant discriminatory laws. The edict neither permitted an increase in the number of Jews (5,400 families in 52 communities) nor admitted them to areas from which they had previously been banned. The sole exception was for those Jews who wished to establish factories in hitherto vacant areas.

In trying to "make the Jews more useful and serviceable to the state," it made them "nearly equal" to members of "other foreign religions." It prescribed the founding of schools, at the Jews' expense, opened the universities to talented Jewish students, and permitted Jewish students to attend high schools in towns that otherwise prohibited Jews. Jews were encouraged to undertake farming using their own labor. All handicrafts and artisanry were opened to them. The edict abolished the "body tax" (*Leibmauth*) and all distinctions of outward appearance, for example, clothing and beards. It permitted dignitaries to carry a sword.[44]

HUNGARY

The patent for the Jews of Hungary (75,000, 1781/82; March 31, 1783) followed the model of the other patents yet, having taken two years to negotiate, was more complex.[45] It legislated three permissible languages for official documents (German, Hungarian, Latin), with a two-year transition period. Unlike the other patents, it threatened sanctions for violations. It required the founding of Jewish schools; in areas with a sizable Jewish population it stipulated the creation of a "central school," for which Prague's Jewish school was to serve as a model. It permitted Jewish students to attend Christian schools, for which Vienna's arrangements were to serve as a model. The patent included numerous provisions about the hiring and training of teachers, religious instruction, the inspection of schools, and the prohibition of private tutors. Jews were encouraged to attend the universities aside from the theological faculty. The patent opened various occupations as in other provinces, including the guilds, though, as in Vienna, "masterships" were forbidden to them. Jews were now permitted to lease peasant farms (Joseph forbade this in Bohemia and Moravia) if the owner or other Jews performed the labor. They were released from wearing distinguishing clothing but required to shave their beards (Joseph relented in response to petitions from Jewish leaders).[46]

The major difference from the other provinces was that the edict for Hungary did not limit numbers. No equivalent to the "family laws" (*Familianteng-esetz*) had been legislated for Jews in Hungary in the past. Joseph chose not to discourage immigration to a province in which half the arable land was uncultivated and the population was notably sparse.[47] He may also have realized that no legislation would stanch the constant flow of immigrants.[48]

CONSCRIPTION

Joseph's program to integrate the Jews reached its apogee in his edict (June 4, 1788) requiring conscription throughout the empire. Joseph considered military service the ultimate act of state integration. So long as the Habsburg state treated the Jews as tolerated aliens, they were not required to serve in the army, although in some provinces, for example, Hungary, they paid a tax for that privilege. For the Jew to become a "fellow citizen" (*Mitbürger*), as Joseph put it in a subsequent resolution (August 19, 1788), "he will perform the same service that everyone else is obligated to do." The corollary was that Joseph expressly permitted Jewish soldiers to be promoted through the ranks, even becoming officers commanding Christian soldiers, something that had been available to Protestants in the army prior to 1782.[49]

Joseph's multiple edicts offered forms of conditional emancipation "into" estates ranging from "nearly equal" (Moravia, Lower Austria) to fully equal (Galicia; chapter 6). His legislation centered on occupational freedom—especially admission to the guilds, access to education, administrative integration (language, names), and, finally, conscription. Joseph's legacy to reforming absolutist states was a menu of options from which sovereigns and bureaucrats could select a suitable mix.

His legislation was formative. In the 1780s he first inspired his brother-in-law Louis XVI's privilege for the Jews of Alsace (1784), then his Edict of Toleration for the Protestants and finally his initiation of a similar process for the Jews (chapter 5). In the revolutionary National Assembly the Abbé Grégoire ("Motion"; August 3, 1789) and the Count Clermont-Tonnerre (December 23, 1789) cited him (chapter 7).[50] Joseph had a direct impact on later legislation: Prussia in 1797, Russia in 1804, and France in 1808, to name only the most immediate examples.[51] Joseph truly deserved the sobriquet, albeit originally derisory, "emperor of the Jews."[52]

Free Ports

Joseph II's policies directly affected Jews in the free ports of Livorno and Trieste. Since their extensive corporate privileges vouchsafed them parity of civic rights, Joseph's major impact was on political rights.

In Livorno since 1614 Jews alone among the "nations" had the privilege of naturalization through the community (contingent upon the government's approval; chapter 1). With the reforms of the 1780s they acquired the right to participate in the new municipal councils. Here was an opportunity for Jews to function as "active subject-citizen-proprietors." Decrees of 1774 and 1779 excluded Jews from such offices by requiring that if a Jew were chosen by ballot he was to defer to a Catholic substitute. Jewish community leaders (*massari*) negotiated with the government to alter this unsatisfactory situation, reaching a compromise (1780) in which one seat would be reserved for a Jewish deputy whom the Grand Duke would select. This was a breakthrough in political status in enabling Jews to exercise public authority through corporate representation. It did not involve individual rights.

In 1784 the Austrian authorities named a Livornese Jew to serve as "imperial vice-consul" in Aleppo. A French consul protested the appointment, but the ambassador defended it as being in keeping with Joseph II having given "the Jews of his state a social and political existence."[53]

The Habsburgs modeled on the Livornina the founding patents (1719, 1725) of Trieste, the empire's warm-water free port.[54] Some Jews had resided in Trieste before the establishment of the free port through individual privileges. Trieste's Jews therefore held three sorts of privileges: individual (or Court Jew) privileges, free port patents, and the corporate privileges of a *nazione*.

Maria Theresa authorized the Jews as the first corporate body in 1746 and permitted a public synagogue (by the 1790s there were three). In 1771 Maria Theresa's "Privilege and Statute" accorded them "all the Prerogatives and Liberties suitable to a Nation to which we have assured . . . Our Sovereign Protection." She thus granted parity with Habsburg subjects as individuals.[55]

Joseph II's toleration edict had four significant results in Trieste. The ghetto was legally abolished, though its boundaries had long been porous. The community school became a "state-supervised normal school." Jewish courts (1782–85) lost jurisdiction over civil matters yet continued to adjudicate ritual ones. Finally, Jews had been members of the Chamber of Commerce (Borsa) since its inception in the 1740/1750s; they were now deemed eligible to serve on its Executive.[56] For Trieste's Jewish merchants, participating in the Borsa's Executive was tantamount to exercising political rights though, it should be noted, in a decidedly corporate structure.[57]

The Habsburg codification of law in the 1780s brought a further legal change by introducing jus soli: after ten years of residence foreigners could apply to be naturalized. Foreign-born Jews were now entitled to apply for naturalization as individuals with community officials providing attestations.[58]

Conclusion

Dohm advocated unconditional emancipation, presenting all the major arguments in a political framework. In contrast, Joseph II promulgated conditional emancipation drawing on the experience of state centralization in Lombardy and Tuscany. Joseph's edicts for Jews followed those for Protestants and the Greek Orthodox. He aimed to promote the Jews' economic productivity and administrative integration within a corporate framework. His edicts during the 1780s became ever more radical, at first giving Jews parity with other minority religions, later treating them as "fellow citizens" (1788).

Since Dohm's tract and Joseph II's edicts spoke the same language of utility and regeneration, they were subsequently understood to provide the theory and practice for legislating conditional emancipation. Although the French Revolution would introduce a stirring ideal of immediate unconditional emancipation (chapter 7), it was the central European model of conditional emancipation that was to dominate until the middle of the nineteenth century.

CHAPTER FIVE

Civil Rights in Western Europe

WESTERN EUROPEAN STATES introduced limited changes to the Jews' status in the eighteenth century. England introduced a policy of naturalization for Jews in its colonies in part to compete with Holland's successful free port (St. Eustatius). It failed to ease naturalization at home. France awarded corporate parity to the Jews of Bordeaux and Bayonne. In Alsace, France's first colony and largest concentration of Jews, the monarchy removed one humiliating tax but otherwise failed to alter the structure of debilitating laws.

England

In England legislation turned on the issue of naturalization for the truly affluent. Eighteenth-century England and her colonies had a threefold hierarchy of subjecthood: natural-born subjects, naturalized subjects, and denizens. "Naturalization" was an expensive and cumbersome process that required an Act of Parliament. It permitted access to the colonial trade and granted secure property rights. Endenization was more readily obtained through royal *lettres patentes*. It also allowed access to the colonial trade, yet the "denizen" had to pay "alien duties" and did not possess secure property rights. Denizens were not permitted to own or will freehold real estate. At death their property was liable to Crown confiscation (escheat).[1]

The Plantation Act ("An Act for Naturalising Such Foreign Protestants, and Others, Therein Mentioned, As Are Settled, or Shall Settle, in Any of His Majesty's Colonies in America"; 1740) was intended to break new ground in naturalization policy. It enabled colonists who resided for seven continuous years, and took the appropriate oaths, to become "his Majesty's natural born subjects." It specifically allowed Jews to omit the words "on the true faith of a Christian" to be able to swear the required oaths. It permitted Quakers merely to affirm the oath's contents.[2]

The Plantation Act's sponsors were willing to overlook religious differences to develop the colonies. Parliament endeavored to keep its religious conflicts at home: unless expressly stated, legislation on religious matters, where Anglicans were the majority, did not apply to the colonies, where Anglicans were in the minority.[3]

In passing the Act, Parliament tried to assert its authority over the colonies, which theretofore had adopted their own naturalization policies.[4] Parliament wanted England to be able to compete commercially with the Dutch, and especially the highly successful free port of St. Eustatius, which had lured numerous Jewish merchants with the award of full civil and political equality (see next section).[5] Parliament disguised the fact that the Act aimed specifically at Jews. The title read "Foreign Protestants and Others"; Jews were mentioned only in the Act's body.

In fact, the Plantation Act supplemented rather than supplanted existing practices. Each colony continued to grant its own naturalizations; the local and the imperial forms existed side by side. Authorities in London deemed this situation so intolerable that after 1760 they began to question the legality of local naturalization; they prohibited it altogether in 1773. The issue consequently figured among the colonists' grievances in the Declaration of Independence.[6]

Jews attained naturalization in both ways. Of the 185 Jews who took advantage of the Plantation Act between 1740 and 1753, the majority resided in Jamaica (150), the rest in the thirteen colonies (New York, 24; Pennsylvania, 8 or 9; Maryland, 1 or 2; South Carolina, 1).[7] Jews obtained "local" naturalization in at least two colonies, New York and Massachusetts, though there may have been cases in Maryland and Virginia.[8] Such naturalization brought Jews enhanced if not complete civic rights.

Jews did not gain political rights, though there may have been individual exceptions. In Jamaica, which accounted for approximately 80 percent of the imperial naturalizations, the Assembly subjected Jews to extraordinary taxation and prohibited them from voting and holding office (1711 and 1750).[9] In New York Jews gained full political rights in 1777 (when New York imposed a Test Act that excluded Catholics until 1806).[10]

Local naturalization was exclusively local: it was not transportable to another colony let alone to England.[11] In contrast, imperial naturalization was valid "in all the dominions of the King."[12] Although Jews naturalized under the Plantation Act were recognized in England as "his Majesty's natural born subjects," they were nevertheless deprived of political rights. They were prohibited from administrative appointments ("offices or places of trust") and, under the disabilities imposed on all non-Anglicans, were excluded from voting or holding elected office.[13]

Whereas Parliament apparently acted on its own initiative in proposing the Plantation Act, the "Jew Bill" of 1753 resulted from the Jewish merchant elite's political action. Headed by Joseph Salvador (1716–86), a coral and diamond merchant who later served the government as financial expert and underwriter, the "committee of deputies" of the Spanish and Portuguese Synagogue approached the government to alter the naturalization laws.[14]

The committee wanted Parliament to make naturalization convenient for their prosperous foreign-born brethren already resident in London. The "Jew Bill" was expressly designed to alleviate the disabilities of a handful of wealthy merchants: "many persons of considerable substance professing the Jewish religion are prevented from being naturalized."[15] Naturalization by Parliament would exempt wealthy merchants from the "alien duties" exacted from "denizens" as well as secure the right to own and will property.[16]

The bill became embroiled in a recurring dispute over immigration and naturalization between inclusive Whigs and exclusionist Tories (1693–94, 1709–10, 1747, 1751). Tories drew on the anti-immigration sentiment of the County faction and City merchants. They incited religious antagonism by vociferously objecting to increasing the ranks of non-Anglicans ("foreign Protestants"); they raised the old rallying cry of "the Church in danger."[17] The "Jew Bill" became the spark of anti-ministerial agitation which, with an approaching election, became so dangerously heated that the Whigs repealed it themselves.[18]

The same Parliament that repealed the "Jew Bill" refused a week later to repeal the Plantation Act.[19] Those who opposed the former contended either that it threatened to inundate England with Jewry's flotsam and jetsam or that the Jews would dominate England's trade and purchase its best estates. Those who championed the latter claimed that it contributed to the empire's "wealth and strength."[20] The Lord Chancellor (Hardwicke) argued that to repeal

> would be of such fatal consequence to our plantations, and such a breach of public faith, that I am sure no man who has any regard to the happiness, the credit or the character of the country would desire it. . . . Even with respect to the Jews, the discouraging of them to go and settle in our American colonies, would be a great loss, if not the ruin of, the trade of every one of them.[21]

Holland

Legislation altering the Jews' political status did not come at home, since Jews enjoyed civic rights in those places that granted them residence, but rather in the colonies, notably St. Eustatius.[22]

From the late seventeenth century Jews were present on the island of St. Eustatius, which had the advantage of proximity to the English, French, and Spanish islands. In 1730–31 Jews received a pledge of equal status with their Christian neighbors: "freedom of religion and trade and that no difference whatsoever be shown between Christians and those of the aforementioned nation."[23] A free port from 1756, St. Eustatius prospered as an entrepôt for the transshipment of goods—Edmund Burke called it "a magazine for all the nations of the earth"—including contraband.[24] It especially thrived by selling munitions and other supplies to the revolutionaries during the American War of Independence. Indeed, the Dutch authorities there were the first to recognize the colonies' independence by offering an eleven-gun salute to a visiting American frigate (November 1776). The British took revenge by invading and plundering the island in 1781. Admiral Rodney first expropriated and then exiled all the Jewish merchants without their families.

France

Louis XVI's reign (from 1774) opened a window on reform in France—in which the potent model of Joseph II, Louis's brother-in-law, was ubiquitous—including new legislation concerning the Jews' civic rights.[25] The Jews of Bordeaux achieved the consummation of their corporate privileges. The Jews of Alsace succeeded in removing one humiliating and extortionate law; they failed, however, to widen their civic privileges. Louis's ministers issued a toleration edict for Protestants (1787) and commenced work on one for Jews.

The syndics of Bordeaux Jewry took advantage of Jacques Turgot's reformist ministry (1774–76) to press the case for an extension of their residential and occupational privileges. Bordeaux Jewry's paid agent in Paris, Jacob Rodrigues Péreire (1715–80), the famous educator of the deaf, persuaded Turgot (1727–81), an advocate of free trade and religious toleration, to have Louis XVI issue *lettres patentes* (June 1776) granting Bordeaux Jews residential and commercial freedom throughout the kingdom. The decree recognized them, on grounds of their commercial contributions, "as loyal subjects" to be treated like "our other subjects."[26] This privilege represented the consummation of their corporate parity. The Bordeaux Parlement registered the privilege in March 1777, the Parlement for the island colonies (Conseil du Cap) in 1782. In contrast, the Paris Parlement repeatedly refused to register it, leaving the Bordeaux Sephardim in Paris in an uncertain status.[27]

The Jews of Alsace and Metz, the largest in France (approximately 20,000–25,000), were less successful in improving their civic status. These Jews, alongside the equally problematic Protestant populace—predominantly Lutherans with a sprinkling of Calvinists, Anabaptists, and Mennonites—came under France's jurisdiction as a consequence of imperial aggrandizement.[28] France began to acquire territories in Alsace, a "stubborn congeries of fiefs, free cities and ecclesiastical holdings," in piecemeal fashion in the sixteenth and seventeenth centuries and especially after the 1648 Peace of Westphalia.[29] Jews first fell under French administration in the 1560s.[30]

In the very years Louis XIV used brutal means to render France exclusively Catholic, for example, *dragonnades*, commutation to the galleys, and the Revocation of the Edict of Nantes (1685), and renewed the prohibition on Jews, he paradoxically acquired a substantial Protestant and Jewish population through his conquests in the northeast. The experience of Alsace's Jews adumbrated that of the Jews who were to come under Bavarian administration during the Napoleonic period or Russian administration after the partitions of the Polish-Lithuanian Kingdom.

Russia, Bavaria, and France had expressly prohibited public Jewish settlement for centuries, while turning a blind eye to the advantageous settlement of a few Jews. Through territorial annexation they inadvertently acquired a large Jewish populace. In the eyes of the tsarist, Bavarian, and Bourbon governments, their respective Jewries posed a tenacious administrative problem. In the early eighteenth century, some high-ranking members of the French administration even broached the idea of ridding Alsace of either recent Jewish immigrants or, indeed, all Jews.[31]

The experience of Alsatian Jewry also adumbrated that of Galicia's Jews insofar as a border region passing between two powers resulted in a fundamental incongruity. In Galicia, a Jewish economy of market towns and leases (*arenda*) linked to the Polish gentry would be brought under a reformist central European regime (chapters 6 and 10). In Alsace Jews held privileges from a "seigneurial territorial system," which, rooted in the Holy Roman Empire and governed by the Peace of Westphalia, "collided" with France's "centralizing authority."[32]

Alsace had the status of a colony. The secretary of state for war had primary responsibility for the area; Louis XIV offered Catholic colonists incentives of land and cash; and Colbert's tariff system categorized the area as effectively foreign soil.[33] Alsace was a "bewildering patchwork" of laws in general yet especially for the Jews. In 1784 Jews resided in some 182 villages; some 900 towns and villages excluded them entirely while some permitted only restricted numbers.[34]

Whereas Alsace's Jews were problematic for the monarchy from the moment of acquisition, they would remain so because of the endemic tensions with their neighbors. Excluded from the guilds, Jew were legally limited to peddling, moneylending, and trade in cattle, horses, and old clothes.[35] These occupations condemned most of them to near poverty while inciting ill will among the Christian populace. Peasants needed loans because of the heavy burden of taxation, which they often had to pay in cash: during the century Christian lenders assumed the bulk of business.[36] In the course of the eighteenth century Jewish leaders in Alsace petitioned numerous times for permission to practice a broader range of occupations. Since any loosening of restrictions infringed on guild privileges, the requests failed.[37]

Synagogue buildings displayed the Jews' tenuous status. In the seventeenth and eighteenth centuries in general, Jews prayed privately in Alsace. They had a designated building that resembled a vernacular residential structure (often half-timbered); it was not a publicly visible ecclesiastical building. There were, however, two exceptions. In Haguenau, a synagogue dating from the fourteenth century had been rebuilt in 1683 after a fire; in Bergheim, a synagogue in service from 1551 functioned throughout the period.[38]

In 1777–79 the notorious "Affair of Counterfeit Receipts" roiled the province: some Alsatians, including officials, counterfeited reams of receipts signed in Hebrew so that debtors, mostly peasants, could claim to have repaid Jewish lenders. The affair emphasized the pervasive tensions arising from moneylending, making it imperative in leaders' eyes that Alsace's poor Jews acquire other forms of employment.

In response, Cerf Berr (1726–94), the self-appointed leader of Alsatian Jewry, submitted a memorandum to the government requesting various improvements in the Jews' status. In addition, as we saw in the previous chapter, he contacted Moses Mendelssohn to write a tract to promote a new government policy toward poor Jews.[39] Mendelssohn enlisted Christian Wilhelm Dohm, who produced his famous *On the Civic Amelioration of the Jews* (1781–82). Dohm printed Cerf Berr's memorandum to the French government as an appendix to his tract.[40]

Cerf Berr (1779 or 1780) implicitly referred to Bordeaux Jewry's 1776 privilege. Asserting that the Jews were a "corporation" (*corps*) under the king's protection since 1657, Cerf Berr requested release from the current "status of oppression": the double vise of onerous taxes and restricted occupations squeezed the Jews into a life of penury if not crime. If the government would permit the "freedom" to live anywhere in the province and to pursue "legal" occupations, especially "freedom of commerce," the Jews would, like their brethren in "Nancy, Metz, Bordeaux and Bayonne," turn their aptitude for commerce into "utility for the state."[41]

Cerf Berr especially pleaded for "the abolition of a toll as onerous as it is humiliating," the body or transit tax (*péage corporel*) otherwise applicable only to foreigners. This tax especially hampered the Jews at Strasbourg, the area's commercial center: they had to pay exorbitant daily admission fees.[42]

Cerf Berr petitioned for the strengthening of self-government. Rabbis and Jewish courts should have jurisdiction over civil and police cases between Jews; such cases should not be subject to appeal to French courts. Furthermore, the rabbis and *parnassim* should have the right to maintain discipline and order within the community through scrupulous use of the ban.[43] Foreign Jews should not be admitted without the government's express permission.[44]

Louis XVI responded to Cerf Berr's petition with two privileges in 1784. The first (January 1784) abolished the body tax. In doing so it significantly, albeit obliquely and perhaps inadvertently, for the first and only time under the ancien régime designated the Jews of Alsace as subjects:

> the Jews are subjected to a body tax that treats them like animals; and since this is repugnant to the consideration that we have for all

our subjects, to allow it to subsist, in regard to any of them, a tax that appears to demean humanity, we believe ourselves obligated to abolish it.[45]

The government retreated from that formulation in the second privilege (July 10, 1784): it used the locution "Jews of Our province of Alsace" and carefully distinguished "Jews" from "our subjects."

The July privilege started on an ominous note: the first five of twenty-one paragraphs addressed the problem of foreign Jews. Those without legal rights were to be expelled; those on business who presented proper documentation would be allowed a three-month stay; and those who lacked proper credentials would be treated like vagabonds.

The privilege extended new advantages to the wealthy. They were permitted to engage in banking, large-scale business, and commerce and to open factories for textiles, iron, glass, and pottery. They were required to keep their accounts in the vernacular (en langue vulgaire).

The privilege imposed harsh restrictions on middling and poor Jews. Contracts on cattle and grain were to be recorded with a notary or in the presence of two community officials; otherwise the contract was voided and the person subject to expulsion. Receipts in Hebrew were null and void; only those in French or "the vernacular used in Alsace" were valid (these strictures on official languages echo Joseph II's edicts). Ownership of real estate was permitted only for one's own residence and the contiguous grounds that were to be "proportional to the status and needs of the owner."

Jews could turn to the courts solely for individual matters; syndics alone could represent Jews collectively. The privilege recapitulated at least two aspects of Joseph II's edicts: it imposed restrictions on marriages (as in Bohemia and Lower Austria) and ordered a census.[46]

During the century, a separate legal category for a handful of wealthy Jews emerged as well: these were the fifteen or so Jews who received individual naturalization. Such naturalization was available to foreigners, including Protestants and, perhaps inadvertently, Jews. The fifteen were prominent individuals, including Cerf Berr, who had rendered service to the Crown or were so wealthy as to be a fiscal asset.[47] These individuals did not establish a precedent for a more general grant of rights. They were active agents seeking privileges for themselves. Some of them, notably Cerf Berr, also actively advocated on behalf of their fellow Jews.[48]

Louis XVI reached the apogee of his reforms with his 1787 Edict of Toleration for Protestants, which echoed Joseph II's edict. He aimed to redress the legal complications resulting from the revocation of the Edict of Nantes and Louis XIV's subsequent enactment (March 8, 1715) that declared Protestant life in France illegal. The edict granted "non-Catholics" civil standing (état civil): the rights of marriage, inheritance, and property ownership. Yet it granted no more than that. The edict expressly denied public worship, legal standing for the clergy, and political rights. Political rights included royal patronage, judicial and municipal office, teaching appointments, and master craftsmanships.[49]

After the edict's promulgation everyone, including its authors, assumed that, since it addressed "non-Catholics," it also applied to the Jews. Louis XVI's government definitively declared that it did not, however, when the Parlement of Metz otherwise refused to register it.[50] Louis XVI then charged Chrétien-Guillaume de Lamoignon de Malesherbes (1721–94), the veteran administrator who had headed the commission that drafted the edict for the Protestants, with undertaking the same for Jews. Louis is reported to have told him, "You have made yourself a Protestant, now I will make you a Jew."[51]

Malesherbes convened a commission with various Jewish representatives from Bordeaux, Alsace, Avignon, and Paris. Apparently unable to reconcile the conflicting points of view necessary to reach definitive conclusions, Malesherbes resigned before his commission had submitted a specific recommendation. The king subsequently lost interest.[52]

Conclusion

In England Jews continued to gain specific civic rights in a piecemeal manner. Only the wealthy could aspire to naturalization. The merchant elite's effort to gain easier naturalization with the "Jew Bill" (1753) failed when it became embroiled in the general Whig-Tory conflict. The government eased the path to naturalization in the colonies, where increasing the white population was deemed critical (Plantation Act; 1740).

In France the Jews of Bordeaux reached the acme of corporate privileges by gaining residential and commercial freedom throughout the kingdom (1776). In contrast, Alsatian Jewry continued to suffer from major restrictions. The privileges it brought from the Holy Roman Empire were at odds with a centralizing French administration. Moreover, occupational and residential restrictions that forced Alsace's Jews into moneylending and petty trade created enduring tensions with the surrounding populace. Louis XVI's patents (1784) removed one demeaning law but otherwise imposed harsher laws on most Jews while further privileging the wealthy. Since Louis XVI's Edict of Toleration for Protestants ("non-Catholics") did not apply to Jews, his government attempted, but failed, to produce legislation for Jews modeled on Joseph II's.

To this point the discourse of "utility" and "regeneration" held sway. The Revolution would introduce an alternative discourse of rights that would compete for dominance throughout the long nineteenth century (1789–1917).

CHAPTER SIX

Partition and Parity

CALLED "THE HORROR OF OUR AGE," the partitions of Poland (1772, 1793, 1795) were as momentous as the French Revolution in upending Europe's ancien régime. Russia, Prussia, and the Habsburg Empire's dismembering of Poland consummated the eighteenth century's new international relations: for the first time three powers violated the integrity of a neighboring state solely for their own aggrandizement. The partitions sealed Russia's and Prussia's claims to being great powers; guaranteed the three autocratic powers' dominance of eastern Europe, including the suppression of democratic reform; and established borders that would hold, despite incessant and increasingly violent local conflicts, until 1914. The partitions resulted in the commonplace of a Europe divided between a liberal west and a neo-feudal east.[1]

The partitions, which one historian has deemed "the commencement of the modern era in Jewish history," determined the conditions of most of Europe's Jews during the long nineteenth century.[2] The bulk of European Jewry ceased to inhabit one polity. Now divided between three, each Jewry gradually went its own way, becoming Russian, Habsburg/Galician, and Prussian. The three experienced different versions of emancipation. Jews in Posen and Galicia were subject to the central European pattern of incremental rights both "into" and "out of" estates; in Russia Jews underwent the east European pattern of incremental rights "into" estates or deferred rights. Nevertheless, strong similarities persisted because of the shared socioeconomic structure among the three Jewries residing in the backwaters of their respective empires.

First Partition (1772)

The second half of the eighteenth century was a fatefully tumultuous period for the Polish-Lithuanian Commonwealth. The Commonwealth was beset by seemingly insuperable challenges within and predatory neighbors without who shamelessly intervened. In 1764 King Stanisław Augustus Poniatowski

(1732–98) came to the throne and struggled to maintain and reform the Commonwealth.[3]

In the discussions of major constitutional reforms to strengthen the Commonwealth, altering the Jews' position was linked to, or dependent upon, the status of other non-Catholics. Foreign sponsors exploited these groups (Prussia the Protestants, Russia the Orthodox) as a pretext to intervene in the Commonwealth's affairs.[4] Some reforms were adopted for non-Catholic Christian burghers: first freedom of religious practice and the right to contract mixed marriages (1768), then to hold municipal citizenship (1775) and to join guilds and confraternities. In Lithuania burghers were given the right to buy land (1775).[5]

The Sejm introduced only one major piece of legislation for the Jews: in 1764 it abolished the Council of Four Lands. Organized in 1580 for fiscal purposes, the Council had in general represented the Jews to the Commonwealth. Many Polish officials eager to streamline financial administration believed that the Council was an obstacle to the efficient collection of taxes and urged its abolition. Continuing that same effort, the Sejm restructured the poll tax (1764), from a lump sum to a per capita charge, significantly raising the Jews' assessment. The Sejm raised the assessment again in 1775.[6] The local Kehillot were responsible for collecting the enhanced tax.[7] In the Commonwealth reform stagnated after the so-called "Partition Parliament" (1772–75), as the various factions fought to a standstill.[8]

The three partitioning powers shared the experience of trying to govern a territory whose structure was at odds with their own. The territories of the Polish-Lithuanian Commonwealth were a semifeudal magnate-dominated estate society dotted with magnate-owned private towns. These territories now came under the rule of the Habsburg Empire and Prussia, which were autocratic states ruling estate societies, whereas Russia was an autocratic state in the process of introducing its own version of estates.[9] For all three partitioning powers privately owned towns were an alien phenomenon. Posen, Galicia, and, ultimately, the western borderlands or Pale of Settlement would become, respectively, the impoverished backwaters of their respective polities.

Beyond this shared experience there was a major distinction among the partitioning powers. Prussia and the Habsburg Empire already had Jewish subjects and Jewry laws. Like Bourbon France vis-à-vis Alsace in the previous century, tsarist Russia did not have a publicly recognized Jewish populace. It had to invent policies for its newly acquired Jews.[10]

Unlike the Polish-Lithuanian Commonwealth, some of the partitioning powers did enact significant legislation. Despite the tumult of the Commonwealth's decline and the first partition, Jews in eastern Europe remained at the forefront in gaining new political statuses—at least on paper. In the 1780s Jews under tsarist and Habsburg rule were the first in Europe to gain state-sanctioned parity with their Christian neighbors; in both cases the legislation was only imperfectly implemented. This was a parity gained through integration "into" estates, a policy that tsarist Russia would continue to utilize throughout the nineteenth century. The French Revolution's dismantling of estate society would offer an alternative policy of emancipation "out of" estates that ultimately prevailed (chapter 7).

Prussia

Prussia aimed to put the newly acquired area of Royal Prussia and the Netze district, with a population just under 600,000, "on a Prussian footing." This meant applying the Prussian systems of administration (taxation, judiciary, conscription) and co-opting the Polish nobility through recruitment to the bureaucracy. It also included filling the province with German settlers and purchasing estates from bankrupt nobility or those who preferred to migrate eastward to Warsaw and the Commonwealth.[11]

Prussia did not enact significant legislation for the 10,000 to 25,000 Jews, mostly in the Netze district, that it gained in the first partition (1772). It did attempt to absorb them into its fiscal and administrative system. This meant fitting the Polish estate system of commerce dispersed across the countryside and private market towns into the centralized Prussian system of commerce concentrated in a few towns.[12]

Prussia continued its cameralist policy, enshrined in the Jewry Law of 1750, of admitting only those Jews who contributed to the economy (especially those who possessed a minimum of 1,000 thalers). Prussia therefore expelled some 7,000 Jews, including artisans, into Poland-Lithuania and attempted to replace them with Christian settlers. The Prussian administration's more ambitious plans for large-scale expulsions of Jewish merchants and artisans failed because local guilds and magistrates protested. They feared serious disruption of local economies and the potential loss to creditors. Jewish communities, hard put to meet their tax assessments in the Commonwealth, had borrowed heavily from local institutions such as churches and monasteries. The Prussian state had inherited the debts owed to Jesuit institutions disbanded in 1773.[13]

Habsburg Empire

That the Habsburg monarchy imposed a new name ("Galicia and Ludomeria") on the areas it expropriated from Poland was not accidental. The co-regents Maria Theresa and Joseph II claimed that the transfer of power invalidated the extant legal and political system, allowing them to reinvent the region. They not only applied their policies of state centralization but in fact endeavored to mold a model province.

Galicia became the "core land of the Josephinian reforms."[14] Only in Galicia, which he toured five times (1773, 1780, 1783, 1786, and 1787), did Joseph attempt to restructure a magnate-dominated estate society and semifeudal economy as well as alter fundamentally the Jews' role.[15] Joseph wanted to break the nobles' power and elevate and empower the serfs and the burghers. He wanted to "regenerate" (*regenerieren*) the Jews by directing them away from "usury" and "vagrancy." He wanted all these groups to generate greater revenue for his cash-starved treasury. Joseph II's edicts for the Jews in Galicia were consequently more radical than those elsewhere. They were also in keeping with his truly radical reform of land taxes and serfdom throughout the monarchy in the second half of his decade of sole rule.[16] According to the official census of 1773, which most historians agree was inaccurately low, Galicia included 224,981 Jews among 2,307,973 inhabitants.[17] Maria Theresa's Jewish Ordinance (*Judenordnung*) of July 16, 1776, contained a fundamental tension between centralization and financial need. On one side, the ordinance aimed at legal uniformity by dissolving numerous and especially debt-ridden communal structures (kahal). It reorganized the community according to the recently imposed six regional districts. It limited the rabbinical courts' jurisdiction and created a General Directory responsible for all fiscal matters. On the other side, the ordinance introduced a host of special taxes, for example, Sabbath candles and kosher meat, marriage and "toleration," that, in addition to being onerous, maintained the Jews' legal distinctiveness.[18]

The Habsburg administration lacked the personnel and the resources, which it had hoped to raise from Galicia itself, to implement much of its reform program from 1772 to 1779, until the installation of the new administration appointed in 1779 (Graf Brigido).[19] In 1781–72 the local authorities expelled over a thousand indigent Jews to Poland while beginning to settle reliable German colonists in the area.[20]

In preparation for future legislation, Joseph's law of May 27, 1785, abolished all autonomous Jewish institutions, including self-government and the judiciary.[21] It encouraged Jews to become farmers and artisans; required that they keep their account books in German or the "vernacular" (Joseph promoted German as the monarchy's administrative language); prohibited itinerant peddling; and left the marriage tax in place while exempting Jewish farmers. Only in Galicia were Jews allowed to purchase arable land without converting.[22]

The Jewish ordinance of May 7, 1789, went the furthest of all Joseph's toleration edicts in trying to reshape the Jews by offering a conditional emancipation (general equality) "into" estates within a program of state-supervised regeneration (incentives and restrictions).

We, Joseph II etc., in consideration of the provisional measures instituted for the Jews [*Judenschaft*], find it consonant with the accepted principles of sufferance [*Duldung*] and conducive to the general weal, to abolish the difference that legislation has enforced between Christian and Jewish subjects [*christliche und jüdische Untertanen*], and to confer on the Jews domiciled in Galicia all the benefits and rights that our other subjects enjoy.

In general, then, Galician Jewry [*Judenschaft*] will henceforth be regarded in all rights and all duties entirely like other subjects.[23]

The edict placed Jews under the jurisdiction of the local authority alongside Christians: "every Jewish resident as a subject belongs to the same local authority as the rest of the local residents, be they Christians or Jews" (#16). It abolished restrictions on the number of families in each locale and the marriage tax (#24). Jews were directed to use the ordinary courts (#41, 46). Because the state now regarded Jews "as equals to the rest of the subjects," they were not to distinguish themselves by their dress, except for the rabbis (#47).

The edict reduced the Jewish community to the status of a "guild" (*Innung*) restricted to religious activities (#16). Contributions to the community's expenses were organized according to "three professional ranks" (*Gewerbeklasse*): employees (farmers, manual laborers, and service workers); community functionaries (rabbis, doctors, cantors); and employers or the self-employed in industry and trade (#22). Rabbis were again deprived of all punitive and judicial authority (none had survived the 1785 ordinance) (#44).

The edict imposed two new duties of language and conscription. Every community was required to establish a primary school that would teach German (#11). Knowledge of German was, moreover, a prerequisite for studying Talmud and for contracting a marriage (#12, 13). The community was to conduct its affairs solely in German (#19). Second, "Jewish subjects like the Christian" were liable to conscription (#49) and would serve in transportation divisions with provisions for kosher food and religious observance. The army would conduct a "census," "in the same way that it is taken of Christian subjects" (#23).

The edict aimed to expunge Jews from the rural economy as innkeepers and distillers while encouraging them to remain as traders or, better still, farmers.[24] To that end it granted Jews occupational freedom (#31) but qualified it both positively and negatively. The positive qualification was that Jews were encouraged to become farmers: the community was to provide special aid so that a certain number could settle on the land (#37). As an incentive, farmers were exempted from the imperial protection tax (*Kaiser-Gulden*) (#51).

The negative qualification was that Jews were to be excluded from the rural areas in which, through the distillation and sale of liquor, they were thought to corrupt the peasantry: "an absolute restriction on renting inns to Jews either in villages or towns will remain" (#32). The edict restricted the leasing system (*arenda*) by excluding "flour mills," "markets stall franchises," and "building plots belonging to those paying mortgage taxes" (#34).

Joseph issued the edict a year before his death. The governor he had appointed for Galicia (Brigido) opposed it, as did the nobles who stood to lose considerable revenues. Most provisions were not implemented.[25] Many towns continued to restrict Jews to a specific quarter; others maintained an outright ban on Jews' settlement. Many towns excluded Jews from municipal politics; many occupations remained closed.[26] Jews themselves divided over the reforms.

Despite its manifest failure on the ground, the edict for Galicia was inordinately influential. It served as a template for tutelary states aiming to regenerate the Jews through a conditional emancipation "into" estates that combined carrots (rights, incentives) and sticks (duties, restrictions, punishments). Clermont-Tonnerre would note it during his speech of December 23, 1789, in the National Assembly. It became the model for Prussia's 1797 legislation for Posen (*General-Juden-Reglement für Süd- und Neuostpreussen*) and for Russia's first effort at comprehensive legislation (1804). Habsburg emperor Francis I echoed its language of parity in his edict of 1797 systematizing legislation for the Jews of Bohemia.[27] It influenced subsequent Russian legislation as well. The central and east European regimes that adapted the edict tended to realign its balance by favoring sticks over carrots.[28]

Tsarist Russia

The western borderlands of Belorussia, the area Russia seized in the first partition, served Catherine as the laboratory for her general administrative reforms, beginning with the introduction of the poll tax (1773) and the Provincial Reform of 1775 (1778).[29] In implementing these reforms her administrators exhibited a striking ambivalence toward Jews that predated the first partition.

For centuries Russia had deliberately excluded Jews from its territories, with Catherine II renewing the ban as late as 1762. To stimulate commerce and generate revenue, however, Catherine surreptitiously permitted a handful of Jews into Riga, "New Russia" (areas on the Black Sea's north shore acquired from the Ottomans in the 1730s), and even St. Petersburg.[30]

As had been the case with France in Alsace, Russia acquired a sizable Jewish population—also a Catholic population, Roman and Uniate—as an unintended consequence of imperial aggrandizement. The rapacious first partition brought over 50,000 Jews from Poland's former Belorussian territories under tsarist administration.[31] Catherine's policymakers and administrators lacked exact knowledge of the Polish territories as well as of their Jews. Utilizing abstractions built on partial information, they oscillated between two extreme images and policies.[32]

On one side, Russian administrators devised a sympathetic image of Jews as industrious revenue-producing merchants and artisans. As individuals, they could be integrated into the existing estate system. Integration into Russian society from this point onward would occur by inscribing individual Jews "into" estates.

These estate categories (*sosloviia*) were new structures the autocratic state had imposed (1775 and 1785) that aimed to streamline administration and stimulate the economy.[33] Unlike estates in western and central Europe that were "a repository of organized rights, prerogatives and privileges" developed over centuries, Russia's were "a vehicle for exploitation by the state."[34]

Assignment to these estates removed Jews from the jurisdiction of their own autonomous institutions (kahal), which, inherited from the Polish-Lithuanian Commonwealth, were gradually reduced in scope and ultimately reconfigured (1844).[35] Popular resistance to undermine these efforts at equality within estates could take the form of refusing to admit Jews as residents or excluding Jews from voting or holding office through various forms of electoral chicanery.

On the other side, Russian officials conceived a hostile image of Jews as deceitful commercial competitors and, above all, malicious corrupters of the peasantry through the distillation and sale of liquor.[36] Such an image entailed removing Jews from the countryside by quarantining them in the towns and according them a separate collective legal status.[37] The popular hostility of such direct competitors as merchants and the landless Polish gentry encouraged this policy of separation.

In the initial years of Russian rule (1772–80), the administration, out of a combination of convenience and ignorance, tended to confirm the legal arrangements inherited from the Polish Commonwealth. Decrees of 1772, 1776, and 1779, for example, preserved the Jews' separate corporate status; they "assessed all tax-paying Jews at one standard rate regardless of occupation or social status."[38]

In the next decade (1781–90), in response to the Pugachev uprising's devastation of the southeast (1773–74), Catherine attempted to strengthen urban and commercial life and provincial administration. She tried to integrate the Jews as individuals by making them members of the new legal "estates" (city residents, *meshchanstvo*; merchants, *kupechestvo*) she had begun to introduce in 1775. In consequence, the 1780s were the historic high point of integration.

Catherine assented to the petition of a group of Jews to join the merchant estate in Belorussia in 1778–79.[39] In March 1781 individual merchants, exempted from the head tax imposed on all Jews, gained permission to pay the same tax rate as their Christian counterparts. Moreover, they paid the urban magistrate directly rather than via the kahal.[40] Soon thereafter most Jews were inscribed as townsmen even if they resided in villages.[41]

Catherine's "Charter for the Towns" (1785) aimed to build urban life by allowing members of all religious groups to pursue commerce and participate in urban self-government. Catherine decided at the outset that Jews were to be treated on equal terms. Full implementation of the charter would have given

Jews parity in their estates in civic (occupation, residence, taxation) and political (judiciary or "Magistracy," municipal government) matters. This would have been the most favorable legal status Jews had anywhere in Europe at the time.[42] Indeed, in the municipal elections of the 1780s, Jews triumphed in eight mayoral elections (seven in Mogilev Province, one in Polotsk). This was unprecedented.[43] Nevertheless, local officials prohibited the successful Jewish candidates from swearing the Christian oath required to take office.[44]

On the other side, in 1782 a local decree that restricted merchants and town dwellers to residence in towns was extended to the entire empire. Another decree limited the privilege to sell spirits to the government and the nobility. Although these decrees originally concerned other groups, the administration applied them to the Jews as well, causing considerable damage. Russian officials drove thousands of Jews from the countryside into towns and forced thousands out of their occupations as distillers and tavern keepers.[45]

In response to these expulsions and the ambiguities surrounding the charter's implementation, including the elections, Jews in Belorussia sent a delegation to St. Petersburg. Headed by the merchant leader Lavka Faybishovich, the delegation submitted petitions from eighteen communities (1784) seeking redress of grievances.[46]

Catherine sent these petitions to the Senate, which, in response, issued the "Charter" of May 7, 1786 ("Concerning the Protection of the Rights of Jews in Russia in Respect to Their Legal Responsibility, Trade and Industry"). It guaranteed Jews equality with other members of their estate regardless of religion while also according them two special rights: residence in the countryside, even while being registered as "townsmen," by precluding "premature" resettlement, and the distillation and sale of spirits if they held valid leases.[47] Historic though it was, this charter was never enforced because of the Belorussian population's stiff opposition.[48]

Jews in eastern Europe continued to experience pioneering political statuses even with the first partition, indeed, precisely because of it. This situation belies what might be called the "lachrymose theory of pre-partition woe," namely, the view that east European Jewry was an oppressed, persecuted, and impoverished group in the early modern period.[49] Many Jews in eastern Europe gained one version of parity in the seventeenth and eighteenth centuries and were in line to receive yet another version from the partitioning powers.

Four-Year Sejm

The first partition in 1772 had propelled the Polish elites to adopt reforms. The Sejm established a central administration consisting of a Permanent Council supported by five commissions. These measures led to increased tax revenues, a more efficient organization of the army, and the reassertion of central control over the towns.[50] In May 1791 the Sejm enacted a new constitution

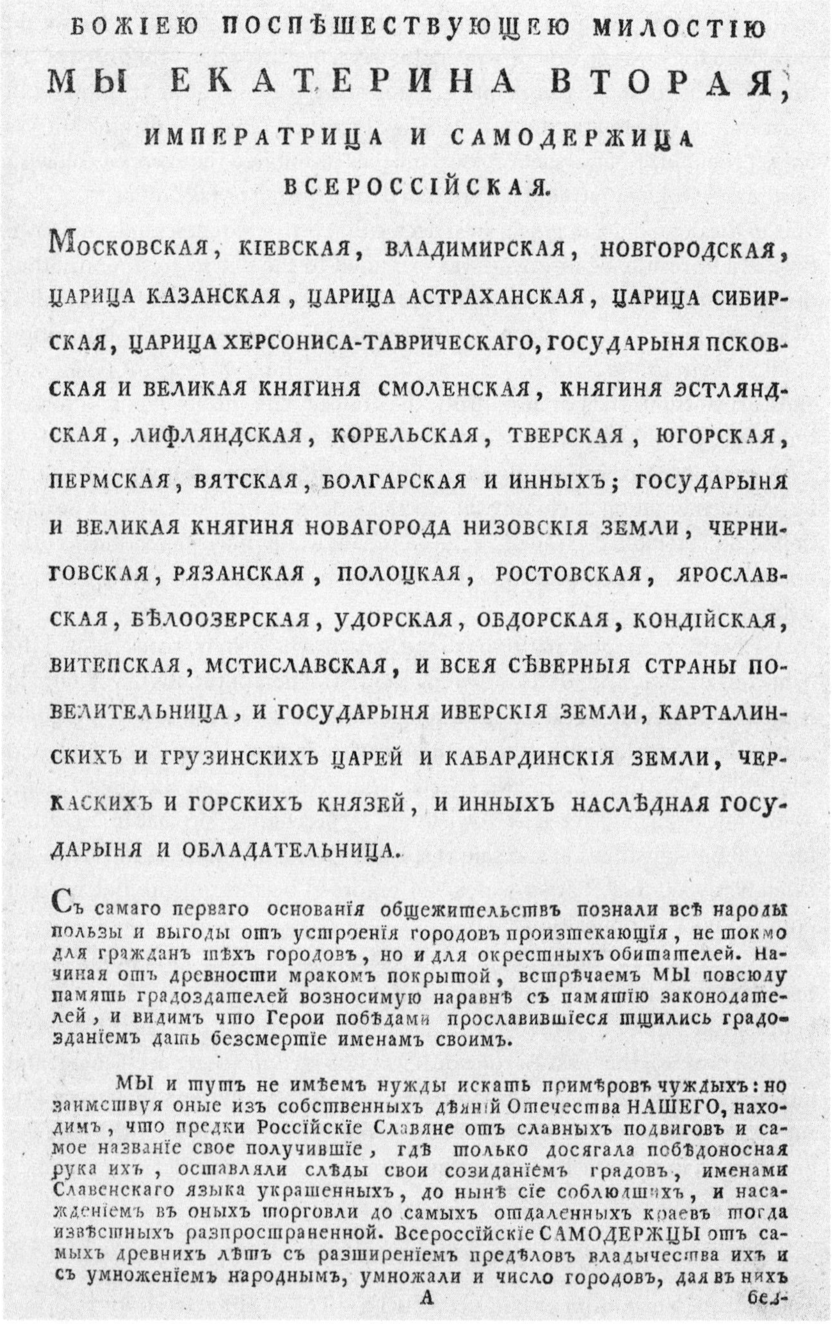

БОЖІЕЮ ПОСПѢШЕСТВУЮЩЕЮ МИЛОСТІЮ

МЫ ЕКАТЕРИНА ВТОРАЯ,

ИМПЕРАТРИЦА И САМОДЕРЖИЦА

ВСЕРОССІЙСКАЯ.

МОСКОВСКАЯ, КІЕВСКАЯ, ВЛАДИМИРСКАЯ, НОВГОРОДСКАЯ, ЦАРИЦА КАЗАНСКАЯ, ЦАРИЦА АСТРАХАНСКАЯ, ЦАРИЦА СИБИРСКАЯ, ЦАРИЦА ХЕРСОНИСА-ТАВРИЧЕСКАГО, ГОСУДАРЫНЯ ПСКОВСКАЯ И ВЕЛИКАЯ КНЯГИНЯ СМОЛЕНСКАЯ, КНЯГИНЯ ЭСТЛЯНДСКАЯ, ЛИФЛЯНДСКАЯ, КОРЕЛЬСКАЯ, ТВЕРСКАЯ, ЮГОРСКАЯ, ПЕРМСКАЯ, ВЯТСКАЯ, БОЛГАРСКАЯ И ИННЫХЪ; ГОСУДАРЫНЯ И ВЕЛИКАЯ КНЯГИНЯ НОВАГОРОДА НИЗОВСКІЯ ЗЕМЛИ, ЧЕРНИГОВСКАЯ, РЯЗАНСКАЯ, ПОЛОЦКАЯ, РОСТОВСКАЯ, ЯРОСЛАВСКАЯ, БѢЛООЗЕРСКАЯ, УДОРСКАЯ, ОБДОРСКАЯ, КОНДІЙСКАЯ, ВИТЕПСКАЯ, МСТИСЛАВСКАЯ, И ВСЕЯ СѢВЕРНЫЯ СТРАНЫ ПОВЕЛИТЕЛЬНИЦА, И ГОСУДАРЫНЯ ИВЕРСКІЯ ЗЕМЛИ, КАРТАЛИНСКИХЪ И ГРУЗИНСКИХЪ ЦАРЕЙ И КАБАРДИНСКІЯ ЗЕМЛИ, ЧЕРКАСКИХЪ И ГОРСКИХЪ КНЯЗЕЙ, И ИННЫХЪ НАСЛѢДНАЯ ГОСУДАРЫНЯ И ОБЛАДАТЕЛЬНИЦА.

Съ самаго перваго основанія общежительствъ познали всѣ народы пользы и выгоды отъ устроенія городовъ проистекающія, не токмо для гражданъ тѣхъ городовъ, но и для окрестныхъ обитателей. Начиная отъ древности мракомъ покрытой, встрѣчаемъ МЫ повсюду память градоздателей возносимую наравнѣ съ памятію законодателей, и видимъ что Герои побѣдами прославившіеся тщились градозданіемъ дать безсмертіе именамъ своимъ.

МЫ и тутъ не имѣемъ нужды искать примѣровъ чуждыхъ: но занимствуя оные изъ собственныхъ дѣяній Отечества НАШЕГО, находимъ, что предки Россійскіе Славяне отъ славныхъ подвиговъ и самое названіе свое получившіе, гдѣ только досягала побѣдоносная рука ихъ, оставляли слѣды свои созиданіемъ градовъ, именами Славенскаго языка украшенныхъ, до нынѣ сіе соблюдшихъ, и насажденіемъ въ оныхъ торговли до самыхъ отдаленныхъ краевъ тогда извѣстныхъ разпространенной. Всероссійскіе САМОДЕРЖЦЫ отъ самыхъ древнихъ лѣтъ съ разширеніемъ предѣловъ владычества ихъ и съ умноженіемъ народнымъ, умножали и число городовъ, дая въ нихъ

А

бед-

FIGURE 6. Catherine II's 1785 Charter for the Towns. *Gorodove Polozhenie* (2007 + 75), Beinecke Library, Yale University.

that aimed to ratify the governmental reforms of the previous two decades. The constitution left the estate structure largely intact, including serfdom and corvée labor.

In the 1760s and 1770s the Jews' status was linked to that of other non-Catholics; in the constitutional overhaul of the 1790s their relationship to the burgher estate was paramount. Yet the new constitution significantly failed to "integrate" or to "equalize" the burgher and noble estates. Burghers received disappointingly limited political participation. The failed reform of the burgher estate, and the burghers' unabated opposition to granting Jews parity through municipal citizenship, doomed all proposals for reform of the Jews' status.[51]

Dohm's tract and Joseph II's legislation for Galicia were the chief influences on the public discussion of the Jews' situation and the Sejm's deliberations.[52] The key issue in the public discussion was granting Jews parity with burghers by admitting them to municipal citizenship. Following the contours of the Dohm debate, the familiar threefold division emerged between proponents of immediate unconditional rights, advocates of conditional rights contingent upon regeneration, and the outright opponents of granting rights.[53]

In the proposed legislation, for example, the "Law on Towns" (April 18, 1791) restricted civic rights to "free Christians." The constitution declared "all honest foreigners and craftsmen of all Christian denominations" eligible for municipal citizenship, thus excluding Jews.[54] Further plans for reforms never reached the floor of the Sejm: the delegates debated neither the "Reform of the Jews" (1792) nor the "Arrangement for the Jewish People throughout the Polish Nation" (1792). The latter would have limited settlement to towns in which Jews already resided and granted solely civic rights. The Jews would have remained a separate estate under a revamped system of courts and councils. The "Arrangement" exhibited Joseph II's influence in requiring the adoption of Polish costume and surnames and creating nationally supervised schools offering a secular curriculum.[55]

Since Jewish leaders were acutely aware of what was at stake in the convocation of what became the Four-Year Sejm (1788–92), they mobilized in an unprecedented manner. The Jews had had no formal national representation since the Sejm dissolved the Council of the Lands in 1764.[56] After its dissolution Jews had been able to represent their interests solely in local councils. With the convocation of the Sejm Jews held elections and chose 120 representatives.[57] These representatives addressed major issues: freedom of domicile and occupation in royal cities; an end to a separate estate status; and especially parity with Christian burghers through municipal citizenship.[58]

The representatives lobbied the Sejm and submitted memoranda and petitions. Even before the election of representatives, Jewish leaders had submitted a "Humble Request" in autumn 1789 to permit small groups to settle in the two hundred royal towns that still banned Jews. Two years later the Jews

("Jews' Demands"; June 4, 1791) claimed parity with burghers, including freedom of residence and occupations in all towns and municipal citizenship for
Jewish property owners.[59] Following established practice, the representatives
also offered to repay community debts as well as to make large contributions
to the king, the Exchequer, and the army.[60]

Most proposals separated the Jews' status in private and ecclesiastical
towns from royal towns because of the substantive differences. In private
towns, there was the question of nobles' rights, including ownership and jurisdiction, for which they would have to be compensated. Nobles vigorously opposed emancipating Jews in private estate towns.[61] No one offered an accept-
able solution to these objections.

The obstacles to a successful reform of the Jews' status were probably insurmountable. The towns' representatives lobbied vociferously in opposition
to the Jews' proposals. The Jewish representatives were divided on substance
and strategy among themselves; they were similarly divided from the proponents of reform in the Sejm. Moreover, the failure to reform the burgher estate
and to create a standard of common citizenship presented an insuperable barrier to reforming the Jews' status.

Conclusion

In the 1760s the Polish-Lithuanian Commonwealth failed to enact reform
for its Jews aside from abolishing the Council of the Lands. Jews mobilized
to an unprecedented extent to face the challenges of the Four-Year Sejm
(1788–92).

With the first partition the three autocratic powers began to divide the
Commonwealth's Jews. For all three powers the privately owned magnate town
was an alien phenomenon: what had been the source of many Jews' extensive
privileges now started to become a long-term liability.

The first partition did yield legislation that, if implemented, would have
conferred some of the best political statuses in Europe. Joseph II introduced
equality with other subjects for Galicia's Jews, though he hedged it with formidable restrictions. Catherine II tried to make Jews full-fledged members
of towns.

Joseph's and Catherine's legislation belonged to the 1780s' acme of Enlightened absolutist reform. Subsequent partitions would occur at a less propitious
moment.

CHAPTER SEVEN

Revolution

THE REVOLUTION IN FRANCE fashioned a new political culture informed with the ideals of natural rights and equality (the "Declaration of the Rights of Man and Citizen"). In principle, the Revolution should have introduced the ideal of equality for Jews by legislating immediate, full citizenship. That was not to be the case. The legislation of unconditional rights had a troubled career from the start.[1] In response to those difficulties, moreover, various and competing delegations of Jews, representing the multiple communities and their respective interests, actively engaged in the process of gaining rights at every point.

The National Assembly's first piece of legislation (January 1790), for the Sephardic Jews of Bordeaux and Bayonne, did grant equal rights but through an extension of ancien régime privilege. It was revolutionary in content but not in form. The Assembly's second piece of legislation, for the Ashkenazic Jews of Alsace, initially provoked heated debate and was deferred for eighteen months. It was ultimately passed in a manner and at a time that diminished, but did not entirely efface, its revolutionary significance (September 1791). The next day, however, the National Assembly qualified it with additional legislation.

In general, the revolutionary ideal of full equality only triumphed in moments of seismic upheaval—major wars, revolutions, national unifications—which, by shattering the established rules of political life, enabled the institution of a new, albeit sometimes evanescent, order. For the balance of the time Joseph II's model of conditional reform held sway across the continent. Yet the seemingly insurmountable problem for the legislators who followed Joseph II was that, in repeated demonstrations of Zeno's paradox, they continuously reduced the distance to equality without ever reaching the final goal.

Estates General

The monarchy convened the Estates General, for the first time since 1614, to avert bankruptcy. The process involved organizing electoral assemblies according to the three orders (nobility, clergy, Third Estate), selecting deputies, and then drafting instructions or "grievances" (*cahiers de doléances*) to guide the deputies once in Paris. Both issues affected the Jews. First, were the Jews natives (*régnicoles*) eligible to participate in the electoral assemblies? Second, how would the electoral assemblies envision the Jews' future status? How would the Jews envision their status?

After some initial hesitation, the Jews in Bordeaux were admitted to the various corporate assemblies. In Alsace, in contrast, the corporations adamantly refused admission. In response, Cerf Berr proposed that the Jews choose their own deputies and write their own "grievances," a compromise that the central administration (*intendants*) accepted. By the time Alsace's Jewish deputies convened (May 1789), the Estates General had been in session for ten days.[2]

Among the hundreds of "grievances" (*cahiers de doléances*), three assemblies, the nobilities of Paris and Toul and the third estate in Metz, notably announced their support for extending rights to the Jews. Some assemblies in Alsace and Lorraine wanted to maintain or even increase restrictions, especially limiting the size of the Jewish population. The majority of the 307 "grievances" that mentioned the Jews were preoccupied with the larger issues of "usury, commercial competition and the shortage of currency." The majority that addressed usury were concerned with Christians as well as Jews.[3]

The six deputies selected to represent the Jews of Alsace and Lorraine—the oligarchical communities did not hold elections—requested freedom of occupations, residence, marriage, and property ownership as well as the abrogation of special taxes. The Lorraine deputies proposed limiting new residency permits to wealthy Jews. The Alsace deputies requested the continuation of corporate privileges through the retention of communal (syndics) and juridical autonomy.[4] They concluded their "grievance" with a ringing endorsement of the ideals of regeneration and utility: the "Jewish nation present in Alsace strives to regenerate [*régénérer*] itself absolutely and in a manner that will render it useful [*utile*] for the state."[5]

National Assembly: December 23, 1789

As the National Assembly struggled to define the nation and citizenship, the Jews' status defied an easy solution. The Assembly introduced two types of citizenship. "Passive" citizenship denoted civic rights based on the "Declaration of the Rights of Man and Citizen" and the right of residence (jus soli).[6] "Active" citizenship denoted political rights, which were on a scale according to taxation.[7] Both forms of citizenship were in question for the Jews of the northeast, and at crucial moments the deputies blurred the distinction between them. For the Jews of Bordeaux, because of their historic privileges, the debate concerned only active citizenship.

The Estates General's metamorphosis into the National Assembly in June 1789 loosened the monarchy's grip. Rioters in Alsace looted manor houses and endeavored to destroy seigneurial registers; rioters also attacked Jews and tried to destroy loan registers. On August 3, 1789, the Abbé Grégoire (1750–1831) requested royal protection for the Jews.[8] He highlighted the pitfalls of conditional equality as exemplified by the unduly autocratic Joseph II.

> Education and legislation never attain their goal unless one adopts a gradual course regulated by circumstances. The goal is frequently missed, because the methods and the laws are not adapted to the national character [*génie National*] or because one does not prepare the national character to receive them and the edict of Joseph II was defective in failing to take the [necessary] intermediate measures.[9]

The king extended protection to the Jews on August 26, yet his actions did not quell the violence.

That very day the National Assembly passed the "Declaration of the Rights of Man and Citizen" (August 26, 1789). The Jews of Paris immediately petitioned the Assembly to announce that the Declaration applied to Jews without qualification, giving them passive or "civil rights" (*état civil*), since "the title of man guarantees us that of citizen; and the title of citizen gives us all the rights of the city."[10] At the same time the petitioners renounced all claims to corporate autonomy, announcing their desire to "submit like all the French to the same law, the same order, the same courts."[11] The National Assembly did not respond to this request.[12]

In the face of continuing violence, on September 27, 1789, two members of the Jewish delegation from Alsace, David Sintzheim (1745–1812) and Théodore Cerf Berr, again requested the National Assembly's protection. On September 28, 1789, the Count Stanislas de Clermont-Tonnerre (1757–92) supported that request: "even though a person is not a citizen his throat cannot be cut with impunity." Clermont-Tonnerre explained the popular hatred of the Jews as the consequence of the common people's inability to comprehend complex causality.

> This is the effect of oppression and opprobrium: the oppressed person becomes unjust and the demeaned person becomes base. The people are unable to follow the series of truths; its view stops with what injures it. [The people] does not inquire whether the person of whom it is a victim is himself a victim of others, and if the immediate cause of its harm is not itself the effect of another cause, a remote cause that is no less insistent.[13]

The Assembly passed a motion that "Monsieur the President . . . write to the public officials of Alsace that the Jews are under the safeguard of the law and require of the King the protection they need."[14]

The now famous debate of December 23, 1789, on the Jews' status occurred accidentally. On December 21 the deputies addressed the question of whether the "Declaration of the Rights of Man and Citizen" applied to Protestants. They then debated whether the Declaration applied to such proscribed professions as actors and executioners. The deputies blundered onto the Jews' status. In response to Brunet de Latuque's (1757–1824) motion that no one be excluded from active citizenship by religion or profession, a delegate from Colmar, Jean-François-Reubell (1747–1807), queried whether the motion included Jews. The Count Clermont-Tonnerre answered bluntly, "Yes."[15]

In accordance with the motion, the debate of December 23, 1789, officially addressed political rights: "the admission of non-Catholics to all municipal and provincial offices, and all civil and military appointments, like all other citizens."[16] Clermont-Tonnerre seemed to adhere to this narrow agenda in his opening speech. He argued from principle: the "Declaration of the Rights of Man and Citizen" established the criteria of citizenship. Neither profession nor religion could render someone ineligible for active citizenship. The executioner acts according to the law; the actor has royal sponsorship. As for religion, "the state's law" is indifferent to it. Judaism is not an obstacle; the Jews are perfectly capable of being citizens. "The most serious accusations [against them] are unjust; the others are specious." The Jews must renounce their corporate privileges and submit to France's one law—just as the Paris delegation had proposed on August 26.

> But they say to me the Jews have their own judges and laws. I respond that that is your fault and you should not allow it. We must refuse everything to the Jews as a nation and accord everything to Jews as individuals. We must withdraw recognition from their judges; they should only have our judges. We must refuse legal protection to the maintenance of the so-called laws of their Judaic organization; they should not be allowed to form in the state either a political body or an order. They must be citizens individually. But, some will say to me, they do not want to be citizens. Well then! If they do not want to be citizens, they should say so, and then, we should banish them. . . . In short, Sirs, the presumed status of every man resident in a country is to be a citizen.[17]

In affirming the Jews' eligibility, Clermont-Tonnerre extended the motion on the floor to include "passive" citizenship: by discussing "judges" and "laws," he slipped, perhaps unwittingly, into the arena of civic rights. Moreover, he pointed to Joseph II's legislation, presumably for Galicia, as a model:

> In the Emperor's states the Jews enjoy not just the rights of citizen but in addition the possibility of attaining those honorific distinctions that we have destroyed but which there retain their vigor.[18]

In contrast to Clermont-Tonnerre, the deputies who opposed the motion deliberately erased the distinction between "active" and "passive" citizenship: they denied the Jews either form of citizenship. The Abbé Jean Siffrein Maury (1746–1817) gainsaid citizenship to executioners because they "assassinate in cold blood," actors since, removed from paternal authority, they are immoral. As a separate nation, the Jews merit toleration and protection but are incapable of being citizens.

> the word *Jew* is not the name of a sect but of a nation that has laws which it has always followed and still wishes to follow. Calling Jews citizens would be like saying that without letters of naturalization and without ceasing to be English and Danish, the English and Danish could become French. . . .
>
> They should not be persecuted: they are men. They are our brothers; and a curse on whomever would speak of intolerance! No one can be disturbed for his religious opinions; you have recognized this, and from that moment on you have assured Jews the most extended protection. Let them be protected therefore as individuals and not as French for they cannot be citizens.[19]

Protestants, in contrast, qualify for citizenship through the edict of 1787.

> It should not be concluded from what I have said about the Jews that I confuse the Protestants with them. Protestants have the same religion and the same laws as us, but they do not have the same creed. However, since they already enjoy the same rights, I see no reason to deliberate on the section that concerns them in the proposed motion.[20]

Adrien Duport's (1759–98) attempt to bring an alternative motion on December 23, 1789, to grant active and passive rights to all Frenchmen, Jews included, failed to pass by five votes. On December 24 the deputies resumed consideration of Brunet de Latuque's original motion.[21] The Assembly passed that motion, yet significantly added an amendment specifying that it did not apply to the Jews ("without intending to prejudge anything concerning the Jews on whose fate the Assembly would decree"). Jews were, then, explicitly excluded from political rights until some future deliberation. What about civic rights? At best, that status remained unresolved, with the advocates (Mirabeau, Grégoire, Clermont-Tonnerre) convinced that, in the face of such vehement opposition, it was better to postpone the issue. At worst, the adversaries in Alsace rejected all claims to citizenship.[22]

National Assembly: January 28, 1790

The Assembly's failure to determine the Jews' status propelled the various Jewish delegations into concerted action. On January 4, 1790, three delegates from Bordeaux arrived in Paris, five more were on their way, and immediately met with Cerf Berr and the delegation from the northeast. The eight delegates met numerous times with their Ashkenazi brethren yet only in late January found their positions to be irreconcilable. The Alsatians wanted economic equality and juridical autonomy; they were willing to forego "active" citizenship. The Bordelais wanted full citizenship by virtue of their corporate privileges.[23] The deputations were aware of the perils of breaking ranks yet also of the manifest advantage that one community's attaining citizenship would bring to the other.[24]

The Bordelais mounted a campaign on their own behalf among the deputies in Paris. They published an address on January 17 distancing themselves from their brethren. The delegates accused the Jews of Alsace of "religious zeal" in wanting to live "under a separate regime" in which they would be "a class of citizens separate from all the others." They argued that Bordeaux's Jews were "naturalized Frenchmen," enjoying "all the rights of citizens [*Régnicoles*]" since 1550. They neither lived under a separate regime ("neither laws, nor courts, nor separate officers") nor behaved any differently than their fellow citizens. They had participated fully in the political life of Bordeaux, including serving in the militia. Why should they be "the only citizens" denied their "civil and political rights"?[25]

The Bordeaux delegates' lobbying succeeded. By January 27 Talleyrand, the Bishop of Autun (1754–1838), who headed the National Assembly's Constitutional Committee, was prepared to bring a motion on their behalf. Cerf Berr's strenuous objection to a separate motion for Bordeaux Jewry failed.

The Bordeaux deputies emphasized their privileges and the fact that they had been "renewed by reign after reign." They thereby established the terms of the National Assembly's debate and motion.[26] Speaking on behalf of the Constitutional Committee on January 28, 1790, Talleyrand recapitulated the arguments the Bordeaux deputies had presented. He stressed that they were already citizens "by virtue of their *lettres patentes*, legally, registered and renewed from reign to reign."[27] He moved that their citizenship be confirmed and they be made "active citizens." His original motion read:

> That the Jews for whom the ancient laws accorded the quality of citizen, as well as those who have an immemorial possession of enjoying them, preserve [the status of citizen], and in consequence are active citizens so long as they possess the other qualification required by the Assembly's decrees.[28]

The Abbé Maury objected to the motion: once passed, it would be extended to the Jews of Alsace and Lorraine. He proposed that the Jews of Bordeaux simply be confirmed in the rights they enjoy by virtue of their *lettres patentes*.[29] Clermont-Tonnerre attacked the Assembly's action as a violation of principle, transgressing the uniformity of liberty by establishing two standards: "are your decrees founded on eternal and immutable principles or on privileges to be obtained by some group . . . ?"[30] He nevertheless hoped for principle's ultimate triumph: "the Jews of Alsace will be citizens since they are men and French [*hommes et Français*] and because you have decreed that every Frenchman (*homme Français*) is a citizen when he swears the civic oath and fulfills the conditions of the law."[31]

Some deputies asked that the motion be deferred because of the late hour. Amid the general clamor, other deputies proposed amendments, causing much confusion. Those in favor prevailed and the motion was passed by 374 votes to 224 votes.

> The National Assembly decrees that all of the Jews known in France under the name of Portuguese, Spanish, and Avignonese Jews, shall continue to enjoy the rights they have hitherto enjoyed, and which have been granted to them by *lettres patentes*. In consequence thereof, they shall enjoy the rights of active citizens, if they possess the other qualifications required by the decrees of the National Assembly.[32]

This was in form decidedly not a revolutionary decree: it was a renewal and extension of corporate privileges. That was the reason for Clermont-Tonnerre's vehement objection. In the ancien régime corporations approached each new monarch to request the renewal of existing privileges and the extension of new ones. The Bordeaux deputies had noted that practice in their *Adress* ("renewed by reign after reign"). The National Assembly opted to follow it, proceeding as if it were a new sovereign renewing and extending privileges. As a renewal of existing privileges, the Assembly confirmed civic rights or passive citizenship. As the extension of a new privilege, it granted political rights or active citizenship.[33]

The Jews of Bordeaux, Bayonne, and Avignon had attained rights at a moment of revolutionary upheaval although not through a revolutionary act. The Jews of the southwest thus experienced a seamless transition from their extensive privileges, which had been virtually tantamount to civic rights, to political rights and full citizenship. Such a pacific transition, rather than a jarring rupture, constituted a key feature of the west European pattern of emancipation. In southwest France, England, and Holland, Jews attained most civic rights as part of the process of settlement or resettlement. They attained political rights by campaigning on their own behalf. That effort and the attainment of political rights did not, however, disrupt their basic legal situation. Moreover, the Sephardic Jews understood themselves as paving the way for citizenship for all Jews. The Abbé Maury had good reason to be apprehensive.[34]

National Assembly: September 28, 1791

The eighteen months that elapsed before the Jews of the northeast gained full citizenship were filled with frenzied advocacy in Paris, the headquarters of the

Revolution. Indeed, on January 28, 1790, prior to the vote in the National Assembly, Jacques Godard, a lawyer and member of the Commune, and Zalkind Hourwitz (1751–1812), a Polish Jewish émigré and Royal Librarian, wearing his uniform as a guardsman, visited the Paris Commune to present the case for equality.[35] The next day the Paris Commune voted unanimously in favor of "active citizenship" for the Jews of Paris and sent that decision to the other Parisian districts and the National Assembly.[36]

Godard, Hourwitz, and others spent most of February visiting the Paris districts. The result was that all districts that reported, save one, supported admission of the Jews to citizenship. On February 25, a deputation from the Commune visited the National Assembly. Despite this successful lobbying, the National Assembly again deferred the issue. That was a fateful decision, since subsequently the Assembly would be far more divided and preoccupied.[37]

The legal limbo of the Jews of Paris and the northeast threatened them with the ominous persistence of their ancien régime status. With each session that the National Assembly chose not to vote, and each new election in which the Jews did not participate, the Jews' position as an excluded group solidified. In the reorganization of the Paris Police (January 1791), for example, the same administrator responsible for "vagabonds, crooks, beggars, foreigners" was assigned to supervise the Jews. Representatives of Parisian Jewry and individuals such as Zalkind Hourwitz vociferously protested. Within a few days the municipality removed the Jews from the list of groups requiring police supervision.[38]

The Jews of Paris continued to send requests to the National Assembly and the Commune of Paris insistently intervened with the National Assembly. Deputies in the National Assembly raised the question almost monthly only to have the Abbé Maury, Reubell, and other opponents stymie it. Despite these repeated setbacks, the Paris Commune's tenacious lobbying played a critical role in ultimately obtaining the National Assembly's affirmative vote.[39]

It was under a set of entirely changed circumstances that the National Assembly finally voted on rights for the Jews of Paris and the northeast. The conflict over the Civil Constitution of the Clergy (July 12, 1790) had radicalized the Revolution by introducing an irreconcilable conflict over the Church's status. The National Assembly had dissolved the remaining corporate structures, including titles of hereditary nobility (June 19, 1790) and guilds, masterships, and privileged manufactures (March 2, 1791), and had abolished a specifically onerous tax, also a form of privilege, on the Jews of Metz ("Brancas tax"; July 20, 1790). Moreover, the National Assembly had concluded its major business in approving the new constitution on September 3, 1791. It was set to adjourn so that on October 1, 1791, the new Legislative Assembly could convene.[40]

With his motion of September 27, 1791, Adrien Duport aimed to induce a lame-duck legislature to complete a piece of unfinished business. The new constitution had definitively established the criteria for citizenship. How could one continue to defer a decision on the Jews?

> I believe that liberty of religion no longer permits any distinction about the political rights of citizens by reason of their belief. The question of political existence has been adjourned; therefore, Turks, Muslims, men of all sects, are admitted to political rights in France. I request that the postponement [of the Jews' rights] be revoked, and in consequence it be decreed that the Jews in France enjoy active political rights.[41]

Reubell, a deputy from Alsace, immediately opposed the motion. Regnault's defense of Duport's motion clinched the matter. Regnault answered: "I request that all those who speak against this motion be called to order since they are attacking the Constitution itself."[42]

Duport and Regnault thus succeeded in casting the issue as a question of the constitution's integrity. This was in stark contrast to the debate on December 23, 1789: the deputies then failed to make it a vote about the integrity of the "Declaration of the Rights of Man and Citizen."

The motion's significance was evident in its tortured wording.

> The National Assembly, considering that the constitution establishes the conditions requisite to be a French citizen and to become an active citizen, and that every man who, being duly qualified, swears the civic oath and engages to fulfill all the duties the constitution prescribes, has a right to all the advantages it insures.
>
> [This motion] annuls all postponements, restrictions and exceptions contained in the preceding decrees, affecting individual Jews who shall take the civic oath, which will be regarded as a renunciation of all privileges and exceptions previously introduced in their favor.[43]

The first paragraph addressed the fundamental ambiguity of the Jews of the northeast's status by admitting them to "passive" and "active" citizenship. The second paragraph abrogated all prior privileges the ancien régime had granted. This motion thus constituted a radical break with the past. In contrast to the Jews of Bordeaux's seamless transition, here was a true rupture, the repeal of a century or more of legislation. The concatenation of events that led the National Assembly to vote in favor of rights, and the very wording of the motion, constituted a new pattern of emancipation "out of" estates. Equality rested on the abrogation of corporations and privileges and the incorporation of Jews into the state. September 28, 1791, thus represented an alternative to Joseph II's legislation of the previous decade of a partial emancipation "into" estates. Here instead was a full emancipation "out of" estates. From this point onward, the two models would rule continental Europe's corridors of power. In central Europe "out of" estates would vie with Joseph's conditional

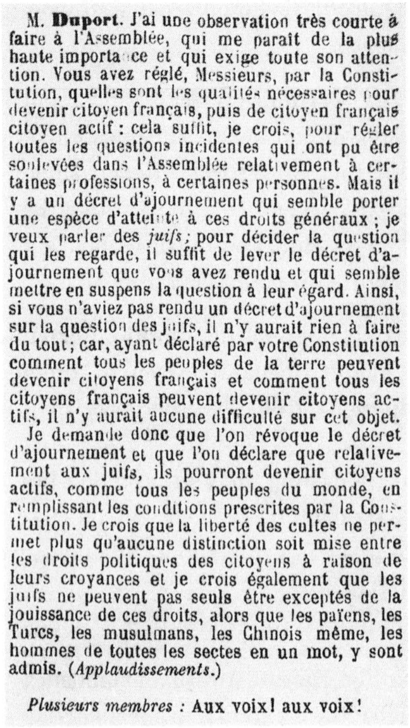

M. **Duport**. J'ai une observation très courte à faire à l'Assemblée, qui me paraît de la plus haute importance et qui exige toute son attention. Vous avez réglé, Messieurs, par la Constitution, quelles sont les qualités nécessaires pour devenir citoyen français, puis de citoyen français citoyen actif : cela suffit, je crois, pour régler toutes les questions incidentes qui ont pu être soulevées dans l'Assemblée relativement à certaines professions, à certaines personnes. Mais il y a un décret d'ajournement qui semble porter une espèce d'atteinte à ces droits généraux ; je veux parler des *juifs ;* pour décider la question qui les regarde, il suffit de lever le décret d'ajournement que vous avez rendu et qui semble mettre en suspens la question à leur égard. Ainsi, si vous n'aviez pas rendu un décret d'ajournement sur la question des juifs, il n'y aurait rien à faire du tout ; car, ayant déclaré par votre Constitution comment tous les peuples de la terre peuvent devenir citoyens français et comment tous les citoyens français peuvent devenir citoyens actifs, il n'y aurait aucune difficulté sur cet objet.

Je demande donc que l'on révoque le décret d'ajournement et que l'on déclare que relativement aux juifs, ils pourront devenir citoyens actifs, comme tous les peuples du monde, en remplissant les conditions prescrites par la Constitution. Je crois que la liberté des cultes ne permet plus qu'aucune distinction soit mise entre les droits politiques des citoyens à raison de leurs croyances et je crois également que les juifs ne peuvent pas seuls être exceptés de la jouissance de ces droits, alors que les païens, les Turcs, les musulmans, les Chinois même, les hommes de toutes les sectes en un mot, y sont admis. (*Applaudissements.*)

Plusieurs membres : Aux voix! aux voix!

FIGURE 6A. Adrien Duport's speech in the National Assembly (September 27, 1791) arguing that granting the Jews rights is a constitutional issue. *Archives Parlementaires de 1787 à 1860*, 62 vols. (Paris, 1862–79), 31:372, Sterling Library, Yale University.

emancipation "into" estates. In tsarist Russia "into" estates would, following Catherine the Great, remain the preferred model.

The twenty-one-month delay in granting citizenship to the Jews of Paris and the northeast fundamentally redefined its meaning. Had the National Assembly voted Jews citizenship in December 1789 alongside Protestants, actors, and executioners it would have been an enthusiastic ratification of the ideals of equality and humanity. Instead, the votes on September 27–28, 1791, which awarded Jews, free Blacks, and mulattos in France equality, highlighted constitutional coherence as the decisive factor: withholding rights threatened to vitiate the constitution at its core. The debate enunciated the extent to which granting Jews equality was, in fact, a "necessity for the state."[44]

Yet Duport's motion did not end the matter. The next day (September 28, 1791) Reubell, the relentless and wily adversary, proposed a motion to address the dangers the Jews' citizenship posed to Alsace. He requested legislation that would ensure the equitable resolution of debts owed to Jewish creditors. The legislation required that within one month Jews provide the government with detailed lists of their loans. Government officials would then determine fair terms of repayment.[45]

This legislation fundamentally compromised the Jews' equality. It imputed guilt without proof. It regarded the Jews as a singular group engaged in exploitative behavior; on those grounds, it subjected them to special government supervision. Here the Jews' involuntary economic role, and specifically the image of the rapacious Jewish usurer, enabled Reubell to open a window to state supervision. This qualification of citizenship, although it remained a dead letter, boded ill for the future. Napoleon would enact harsher legislation to address the same issue in 1808.

The National Assembly mitigated the revolutionary content of September 27 with the state supervision of September 28. In fact, the National Assembly again perpetuated ancien régime policy: it treated the Jews of Alsace as inhabitants of a border region that required special tutelary if not punitive legislation. Such ongoing state supervision of Jewish economic behavior was in fact to be a salient feature of the central European pattern of emancipation.

Conclusion

The French Revolution's alteration of the Jews' political status was truly fundamental and ambiguous. The National Assembly's legislation did not have an unalloyed revolutionary pedigree. The ancien régime persisted in the legislation of January 1790 that granted political rights to the Jews of Bordeaux as an extension of privilege. Rights for the Jews of Alsace were deferred for twenty-one months until September 1791 when a lame-duck Assembly finally resolved the issue as a matter of constitutional integrity.

Despite these ambiguities, the Revolution introduced the pattern of unconditional emancipation "out of" estates, which became a potent model for polities aiming to create a civil or bourgeois society. Through conquest and occupation over the next quarter century, France would export that model to the rest of Europe.

The Revolution polarized Europe. Full emancipation or equal rights irrevocably became associated with the ideas of 1789. When and where those ideas triumphed, so did Jewish emancipation. When and where opponents triumphed, Jewish emancipation suffered either abridgment or outright abrogation.

CHAPTER EIGHT

War

THE FRENCH ARMIES that occupied large swaths of Europe, including Italy, Holland, and the German states, brought emancipation in their baggage trains. Those same baggage trains disgorged an oppressive occupation: autocratic government, exorbitant taxation, huge levies of men, and secularizing policies.[1] Not surprisingly, the French occupations, and rights for Jews, were highly divisive.

Like France itself, the occupied countries split between adherents of the Revolution and the ancien régime, with the latter often in the majority. In the case of Italy, the French came (1796–99), went, and came again (1800), leading to multiple changes in government within a few years. In the case of the Netherlands and German states (Rhineland, Frankfurt am Main, Hamburg), French occupation yielded full emancipation. In contrast, alliance with France resulted in partial emancipation (Bavaria, Baden). Partial emancipation also came indirectly, with military defeat and competition with France's administrative model (Prussia).

In all cases emancipation came with the ancien régime's collapse or reform, which was sometimes superficial and quickly reversible. The enduring result was that emancipation became inextricably associated with the revolutionary ideas of 1789 and the introduction of a new politics and economy.

Italy

The Habsburg reforms had begun to remake Lombardy and Tuscany (chapter 4). There the French armies encountered transformed ancien régime polities. In contrast, the Papal State, the Duchies of Parma and Modena, and the Kingdom of Naples were largely untouched. There the French invaders introduced the policies of administrative centralization and uniformity.[2] Indeed, in those latter polities the Counter-Reformation policy of ghettoization had continued during the eighteenth century; the tally of ghettos rose from twenty-eight to forty-one.[3]

The three years of French rule (1796–99), known as the "Jacobin triennium," brought a first emancipation in a "piecemeal process, contingent on the success of the French army."[4] French armies conquered primarily the Po valley and the northern Papal States. The "French Directory" regarded the invasion as a "financial operation": the army lived off the land and Napoleon levied excessive taxes.[5] The French found allies in Italian "moderates" who favored the French constitution of 1795 (legal equality, private property, freedom of commerce and religion). The French did not support Italian Jacobins enamored of the more radical policies found in the French constitution of 1793.[6]

For Jews, the symbol of change was the ghetto's demise, often enacted by burning the ghetto's gates. Accompanying the symbolic change were substantive legal ones. In central Italy, the short-lived Cispadane Republic's constitution of March 27, 1797 (Article 4), declared the polity's fidelity to Catholicism and instituted a hierarchy of religious observance by prohibiting the public exercise of other religions, with the significant exception of Judaism. At the same time, the constitution provided every citizen protection for religious opinions "so long as he is obedient to the laws."[7]

The Cisalpine Republic in northern Italy, which lasted twenty-two months and had 3.5 million inhabitants drawn from five different states, had a constitution based on the French Directorial constitution of 1795 that guaranteed equality of religions and public observance (Article 455; July 9, 1797).[8] The new government announced that "every man is born and remains free and should fully enjoy all rights. The Jews are citizens and must be recognized as such in society." The government invited the Jews to send delegates to the Constituent Assembly.[9] In Livorno the Jewish leadership preferred to retain its corporate privileges that, pursuant to Peter Leopold's reforms, included one representative on the municipal council. The only substantive legal change was admission to the National Guard.[10] In Florence the French proclaimed equality of Jews and Christians on March 25, 1799.[11]

The pendulum swings between regimes could be truly vertiginous. The French dismantled Rome's ghetto in February 1798, for example, only to see the Neapolitan army restore it in October. The next month (November 1798) the French dismantled the ghetto again. The armies of the coalition that expelled the French the following spring (1799) again returned Jews to the ghetto.[12]

Jews appeared to be among the most visible beneficiaries of a French occupation that failed to abolish the feudal order yet threatened the Catholic Church.[13] After Napoleon had departed for Egypt, Austrian and Russian troops had invaded northern Italy (February to September 1799) to restore the ancien régime. Violent "Viva Maria" or "throne and altar" insurgencies, often supported if not led by priests, erupted in the name of religion and counter-revolution. The insurgents targeted Jews alongside Jacobins and other French supporters. There were unprecedented massacres at Senigallia (June 18, 1799) and Siena (June 28, 1799). In contrast, citizens in Pitigliano successfully fought the rebels to defend the local Jews.[14]

Napoleon brought a second emancipation to Italy when he returned in 1800 as First Consul of the Republic and defeated the Austrians at Marengo (Peace of Luneville; February 1801).[15] In Tuscany Leopold's laws remained in place until 1808 (chapter 4). When Napoleon incorporated Tuscany into his empire in 1808, the Code Napoléon extended equality to the Jews of Livorno and Florence. Yet March 17 also brought application of the *décret infâme* (chapter 9). The Jews of Livorno and Piedmont immediately submitted petitions and gained exemption from the laws aimed at the Jews of Alsace.[16] In 1809 Napoleon restored the Duchy of Tuscany and placed his sister, Elisa Baciocchi, on the throne. She had previously extended equality to the Jews of Lucca and Piombino.[17] The French reoccupation of Trieste in 1809–13 admitted Jews to the civil service and gave them the right to election to the new municipal council.[18]

Netherlands

The Netherlands, alongside Bordeaux and England, constituted the west European region of emancipation. There civic rights were already largely in place; emancipation turned on political rights. In none of the three was the abrogation of corporate privilege a prerequisite for the granting of rights. Amsterdam, it will be recalled, was a nascent civil society that did not issue corporate privileges: the Jews had the status of a "church" and their self-arrogated community "autonomy" rested on ambiguous legal foundations (chapter 1).

Across western Europe Jews fully participated in the process of gaining political rights. A small group initiated the process in the Batavian Republic by submitting a petition aimed to secure "active" citizenship.

The French occupation and the founding of the Batavian Republic were another installment in the continuing conflict within the Dutch Republic. In the eighteenth century "Patriots" who desired greater civic freedom clashed repeatedly with the oligarchic Regents and the monarchical House of Orange. In 1787 a Patriot revolt unseated William V only to have a Prussian invasion return him to power.[19] "From 1789 the Patriot Revolution became inextricably linked . . . to the French Revolution."[20] French troops conquered the southern Netherlands between 1792 and 1794; France formally annexed the area in October 1795. French troops advanced north over the frozen rivers in December 1794 to the welcome of Patriot Committees. The Batavian Republic (January 1795) resumed the failed Patriot revolt of 1787; for many it represented the republic's restoration.[21]

Led by the wealthy, most Jews rejected the Patriot-inspired Batavian Republic. Jews had strong historic links to the House of Orange that had given them refuge and religious freedom.[22] Prominent Jewish merchants and bankers had close ties to the stadtholder and his household.

In 1795 leaders of the Sephardic and Ashkenazic communities, for example, first suppressed a revolutionary decree proclaiming freedom of religion—because of its alleged threat to Judaism. Then they refused to circulate the republic's subsequent decree criticizing them for that act of suppression. Moreover, they announced a prohibition on Jews bearing arms on the Sabbath to prevent enlistment in the civil guard.[23]

The very party that in principle supported the Jews' active citizenship included formidable opponents.[24] Patriot clubs enrolled large numbers of shopkeepers and craftsmen who, wedded to the guild system for their livelihood in a declining economy, considered Jewish peddlers and petty merchants dangerous competitors.[25] The Patriot Clubs in Amsterdam, for example, refused to admit Jews. In response, some Jews established a club of their own (Felix Libertate, February 6, 1795) that also accepted non-Jews.[26] The civil guards in some cities admitted Jews, for example, Amersfoort, Groningen, and Hague, but Amsterdam's adamantly refused.[27]

Jewish property owners voted in the republic's first elections (1796). Six members of Felix Libertate subsequently submitted a petition requesting confirmation of the political rights they had just exercised. In the ensuing debate, theological topics were front and center: the Jews saw themselves, and were seen, as one religious group among others.[28] The Jewish Patriots' petition carefully refuted a catalogue of accusations about messianism and chosen-ness, misanthropy and moral character. The petitioners further discussed the Jews' allegiance to the House of Orange and the alleged pernicious consequences of admitting them to rights.[29]

The National Assembly responded by commissioning the "Report on the Equalization of Jewish with All Other Batavian Citizens," which, presented on August 1, 1796, not only presumed the Jews' citizenship but commenced with an unsettling assertion: if the Jews' votes were illegitimate, then so was the Assembly itself![30]

The report conceived of the Jews as one confession in a multiconfessional state.[31] The report endorsed full citizenship on three grounds. Common humanity: "that the Jews are also men and can be good citizens." The Revolution's basic principles: "natural and complete equality of the rights of man." And confessional parity: "the Jews can so little be excluded as the Quakers, the Calvinists or the Catholics, who in fact are not excluded; they are integrated members of the sovereignty and the original assembly."[32]

The report analyzed the Jews' dietary laws and marriage practices, concluding that Jews were no more exclusive than Catholics or Mennonites. The report also affirmed the Jews' ability to perform military service by pointing to their presence in the Habsburg and French armies and, closer to home, the Dutch fleet and National Guard.[33]

Unlike the debates on the Jews' status in France, which lasted only a few hours, the Batavian Assembly's debate continued for eight days (August 22–31, 1796).[34]

The Assembly questioned the Jews' eligibility for citizenship in general even though only political rights were on the table. Opponents asserted the Jews were a nation defined by belief in a messianic national restoration and separated by a distinct code of civil law. In addition, many considered citizenship a new privilege that the provinces and municipalities, not the Assembly, should grant. In contrast, proponents understood equality to be a matter of principle and an inclusive right for which the Jews were perfectly eligible since they were one confession among others. Finally, the debate established the crucial point that Jews were to be given rights not as a collective but as individuals who desired, and met the criteria for, citizenship.[35]

The Assembly was in general divided between three groups. "Federalists" aimed to preserve the rights of the provinces and municipalities. "Unitarists" aspired to centralized power and far-reaching democratization. "Moderates" wanted some centralization but with limited democratization. The vote on the Jews' emancipation did not fall strictly along party lines. More "Unitarists" voted in favor and most "Federalists" were opposed, but significant numbers broke ranks.

On August 30, 1796, the National Assembly voted in favor of the report (45 to 24) and two days later, under pressure from the French ambassador, unanimously adopted the decree.[36] Only a week after the Assembly's vote the "Constitutional Committee" resumed discussing the matter as if Jews were not eligible for active rights and then proceeded to devise a voter register that did not automatically include Amsterdam's Jews.[37]

Nevertheless, in the elections of August 1, 1797, two Jews won seats in the Second National Assembly (H. L. Bromet; H. de H. Lemon) and one a seat in the Amsterdam City Council (M. Moresco). Highlighting the internal political divisions, the Jewish opponents of Felix Libertate exited the Ashkenazic synagogue en masse to vote against the Jewish candidates.[38]

This was the first election of Jews to national office in Europe (Jews were elected to municipal office in Russian-occupied Poland after 1785 but were generally prevented from taking office; Jews were also elected to municipal office in parts of Italy). Indeed, Bromet and Lemon tried to use their offices to promote the cause of equal rights for Jews in the German states at the abortive Congress of Rastatt (1798).[39]

The three representatives served only briefly: they lost their seats with the coup d'état of June 12, 1798, that ousted the entire "Radical" party to which they belonged. Jewish candidates were not subsequently elected for some time.

The Netherlands was a case in which de jure rights had mostly symbolic value. The Netherlands' economy had been contracting throughout the second half of the eighteenth century. Access to the guilds, from which Jews had been excluded since settling in the country, and which remained closed, had more value than the franchise. Moreover, after initially electing some officials, both Jews and Catholics were largely ostracized from political life.[40]

German States

The Holy Roman Empire was not a "terminal anachronism" "inevitably" destined to disappear. Francis II's 1806 order of dissolution was an unexpected event that shocked, and shook the foundations of, central Europe.[41] The Reich's demise followed from the partitions of Poland. The jurist and bureaucrat Friedrich Carl von Moser (1723–98) had observed of the Holy Roman Empire: "Once Poland has been fully partitioned we'll be next on the menu."[42] Here the culprit was Napoleon: his territorial aggrandizement, by flouting the sovereignty of polities, whetted the German princes' appetites.

The Reich's internal reform, the "Principal Conclusions of the Extraordinary Imperial Commission" (1803), ostensibly aimed to compensate rulers for war expenses and territories lost to France. In fact, it led to an unprecedented seizure of territory at the weakest polities' expense.[43] The Reich's reform expropriated the Catholic Church by dissolving monasteries, closing dioceses, shuttering universities, and secularizing much of the Church's land.[44] The reform altered the Holy Roman Empire's religious balance by giving Protestants a majority in the Reichstag and in the College of Princes. The emperor, a Catholic, refused to ratify that drastic shift.[45]

France's policy was to create a "third Germany" of medium states, the Confédération du Rhin, to vie with the two major powers, Austria and Prussia. The policy provoked a crisis when the Confederation withdrew from the Reich on August 1, 1806.[46] Napoleon's ultimatum (July 22, 1806) forced Francis's hand. Finding himself unable to fulfill his oaths as emperor, and hoping to extract the best possible outcome for Austria by unifying the Habsburg's Reich territories with the Austrian monarchy, he abdicated the Crown and, surprisingly and illegally, dissolved the Reich itself.[47]

Like the Polish partitions, the Reich's collapse fundamentally altered the framework of politics and the Jews' status. The end of the Holy Roman Empire's limited monarchy unleashed the individual states, now larger in size and reduced in number, to pursue their independent policies. One consequence was that in the nineteenth century nationalism came to overshadow dynastic politics.[48] In this respect the collapse of the Holy Roman Empire was a nineteenth-century rehearsal for the next century's demise of Austria-Hungary and the emergence of the radically nationalist successor states (chapter 22).

With the collapse of the Reich's courts, Jews lost the juridical equality that had given them legal recourse since the early sixteenth century. They would try to pursue the same strategies in the German Confederation that succeeded in the Holy Roman Empire. Whether there was the possibility of an empire-wide improvement in their legal status remained an open question.

In this new geopolitical landscape, German polities divided in three vis-à-vis the Jews' status. The French authorities occupying Hamburg, Frankfurt am Main, and the states on the left bank of the Rhine extended full rights. As France's allies and beneficiaries, Baden and Bavaria enacted general constitutional reforms, struggling to implement the Code Napoléon. As part of those reforms they promulgated partial emancipation, mixing "into" estates with "out of" estates.[49] In competition with the French model, Prussia offered civic rights as part of a general reform "out of" estates.[50]

A distinct central European pattern of emancipation consequently emerged. Drawing on the combined influence of Joseph II and Dohm, these states fashioned a state-supervised conditional emancipation in which further rights were contingent upon improvement. Improvement was cast in terms of education and moral formation understood through the ideal of *Bildung*. Emancipatory legislation aiming to educate the Jews and elevate their moral stature combined incentives and restrictions, sometimes extremely harsh. Emancipation thus became a quid pro quo of regeneration for rights under the tutelary state's aegis.

The net result was that in the tessellated German states the competing emancipation policies existed side by side: unconditional and conditional rights, "into" estates (Joseph II) and "out of" estates (France). Moreover, the persistence of estate society gave rise to another peculiar feature of central Europe emancipation: the separation of local citizenship (a locale or commune, *Ortsbürgerrecht, Heimatrecht*; or municipality, *Stadtsbürgerrecht*) from state citizenship (*Staatsbürgerrecht*). In some states that separation would complicate the process of emancipation as Jews attained one form of citizenship but not the other.[51]

West German States; French Regimes

Reforms began with the French occupation and the Peace of Campo Formio that awarded the region to France. In 1797 the French Republic incorporated Cologne, the Rhineland's major commercial entrepôt, abrogating its municipal constitution that had excluded Jews for some four hundred years. The first Jewish family took up residence in April 1798; by 1815 the Jewish population numbered over two hundred.[52] In Mainz the municipal government ordered the ghetto gates burned in 1798.[53]

WESTPHALIA

The Kingdom of Westphalia (1807–13) was designed to be the alternative "third Germany's" model state. It was the first polity that Napoleon's Grand Empire integrated through the Napoleonic code. The code was an instrument of state centralization and authority: it imposed rationally justified positive law in opposition to customary law, legal equality and uniformity in opposition to estates and corporations.[54] Accordingly, Westphalia was the exemplary experiment in Jewish emancipation in a French-ruled German state.[55]

A series of constitutional acts between November 15 and December 7, 1807, constituted the kingdom, with Article 45 introducing the civil code. The imposition of this post-revolutionary code on an estate society produced fierce opposition and, as importantly, administrative chaos.[56]

King Jerôme (1784–1860), Napoleon's brother, emancipated the kingdom's 15,000 Jews on November 15, 1807, by declaring their equality with Christians.[57] Just as his brother had convened Jews in Paris, Jerôme assembled a delegation in Kassel (February 1808) to ensure integration in, and fidelity to, the kingdom (chapter 9). He also empowered the Jews (March 31, 1808) to organize a Consistory, with Israel Jacobson at its helm (March 31, 1808).[58]

To prove the Jews' worthiness for equality, Jacobson turned Westphalia into a showcase for reforms in education and worship. The synagogue he built in Seesen embodied these changes: it had a bell tower outside and an organ inside, a raised pulpit for sermons, and a reader's platform (*bimah*) near the ark.[59] In defiance of his brother, Jerôme exempted Westphalia's Jews from the punitive "Infamous Decree" of 1808.[60]

FRANKFURT

In 1806 Napoleon designated Frankfurt as the capital of the Confederation of the Rhine. The new law of December 27, 1806, recognized members of the "three Christian confessions" as citizens eligible to hold office; it extended equality to Calvinists and Catholics who had hitherto been denied public worship and other privileges. Carl von Dalberg, the city's ruler, appointed a committee to investigate the Jews' status, which heard merchants and artisans' vociferous complaints.[61]

Dalberg consequently embraced the idea of incremental emancipation in the spirit of Joseph II: reformist legislation (1808) would govern the Jews until they were moral equals (*Bildung*) of their Christian neighbors. Like Joseph II's legislation for Austria, he maintained the quota of permitted Jewish families, restricted the number of marriages, and imposed strict educational requirements for the bride and groom, for example, knowledge of German and arithmetic. He required rabbis to have studied at a university. He significantly raised the annual tax assessment. His one concession was to enlarge the ghetto slightly.[62]

Frankfurt Jewry mounted a campaign to oppose the new law. Dalberg was so inundated with memoranda and letters, and the city so agitated, that he declared a moratorium on the public discussion of the legislation.[63]

Circumstances changed in 1810. Napoleon elevated Frankfurt to the status of a Grand Duchy under Dalberg's rule and insisted that the Code Napoléon

FIGURE 7. Seesen synagogue (Westphalian Consistory). Located in a public space, the synagogue had features of a church (spire, bell). Leo Baeck Institute, F 3197.

become law.[64] Dalberg issued an edict on August 16, 1810, that declared "the equality of all subjects before the law." Nevertheless, he equivocated in implementing the code, preferring to preserve clerical and aristocratic privileges and to keep "denizens" (*Beisassen*) without rights and subject to toleration taxes.[65]

He similarly equivocated in extending equality to the Jews. Only the city's dire finances changed his mind. He struck a deal in which the Jews would gain equality in exchange for an enormous one-time payment equivalent to twenty years of the annual "toleration tax." On December 28, 1811, after the community had made the payment by taking a loan, Jews were proclaimed equal in their rights and duties to Christian citizens; 645 Jews took the oath of citizenship in 1812.

This equality, gained by purchase rather than principle, was to last all of seven hundred days (chapter 11). In contrast, it took the community over half a century (until 1863) to retire the loan.[66]

HAMBURG

Hamburg contained the largest urban Jewry in the German states (1800: 6,430). The Jews constituted a merchant colony or corporation governed by the 1710 Jewry Law (*Reglement*) (chapter 1). Deprived of access to the guilds, Jews engaged in various commercial occupations, for example, trading in used clothing, colonial wares, and some foodstuffs. A few grew rich; most struggled to subsist.[67]

Jews became citizens with Hamburg's incorporation into the French Empire (December 10, 1810): that put into effect the emancipation decree of September 1791. The Napoleonic decrees of 1808 (*décret infâme*) also came into effect; a Jewish delegation submitted a memorandum that succeeded in averting its implementation (chapter 9).[68]

Subsequently two Jews were elected to the thirty-person municipal council; two Jews were sworn in among twenty notaries; and one Jew was elected to the four-person commercial court. At the same time, Jews contributed to the enormous levies the French imposed on Hamburg's wealthiest citizens.[69] In general England's continental blockade caused commerce to decline under French rule.[70]

France's Allies

Napoleon's policy of creating counterweights to Prussia and Austria led him to expand and elevate the status of some German polities, especially Baden and Bavaria. Influenced by the example of Napoleon's Civil Code, these states attempted to unify their new territories through constitutional reform. As part of that reform they also introduced versions of emancipation for their substantially enlarged Jewish populations.

BADEN

France's first German ally to introduce emancipatory legislation, Baden promulgated a state-supervised conditional emancipation relying on Joseph II and Dohm.[71] This compromise position was in keeping with its acceptance of Napoleon's Civil Code. Baden adopted the Civil Code but qualified it with a mass of laws that largely preserved corporate social relations.[72]

Napoleon granted Baden sovereignty and elevated its ruler to a Grand Duke. Baden (1803–6) grew fivefold in territory and over sixfold in its Jewish population (1802: 2,265; 1808: 14,200).[73]

Baden's government undertook to integrate its new territories under a uniform constitution (1807). Baden granted citizenship to all law-abiding persons, regardless of religion (para. 1; March 14, 1807), and recognized Judaism as a "constitutionally tolerated" religion alongside Christianity. The constitutional edict of June 14, 1808, recognized Jews as "state citizens" but not as "local citizens" (para. 19) until they had an occupation and livelihood equivalent to those of Christians. Jews therefore lacked the all-important right of residence. Similarly, the edict prohibited residence in areas that hitherto had excluded Jews.[74] Baden was, then, a significant example of a state that, still in thrall to its estates, granted state citizenship without local citizenship.

The edict of January 13, 1809, affirmed the equality of Jews and Judaism.[75] To ensure that the Jews in fact deserved that status by attaining the desired *Bildung*, the edict introduced measures for their improvement along the lines of Joseph II's: a new communal structure, compulsory primary education, vocational training including access to all forms of artisanship, the adoption of family names, and the use of German for business matters.[76] In 1815 all toleration fees (*Schutzgeld*) were abolished and the first Jew was admitted to the civil service as a teacher in Karlsruhe.[77]

BAVARIA

A beneficiary of Napoleon's patronage, Bavaria became a kingdom (1806) possessing considerable new territory. In the first decade of the nineteenth century, King Maximilian Joseph and his enterprising minister, Joseph Montgelas, began to transform Bavaria into a centralized state by introducing Enlightenment-inspired reforms that included religious toleration and the secularization of marriage.[78]

Like France and Russia, Bavaria had largely excluded Jews, aside from Court Jews in Munich. It inadvertently gained a Jewish population (from 3,000 in 1800 to 30,000 in 1813) as the result of territorial aggrandizement (Franconia, Swabia, and various ecclesiastical and noble polities). By doubling in size from 1801 to 1803, Bavaria acquired a significant Protestant population as well.[79]

Bavaria looked to the precedents of Catholic powers to deal with its Jewish population: it consistently emulated the more punitive aspects of French enactments of the 1780s as well as Joseph II's legislation. A January 26, 1801, memorandum claimed that the "Jews are obviously injurious [*schädlich*] to the state" because of their occupations; the state must endeavor to render them "useful [*nützlich*]" through new occupations.

Like France's edict of 1787, a toleration edict of August 26, 1801, applied exclusively to Protestants. Like the 1784 *lettres patentes* for Alsace, a March 25, 1802, law that abolished the infamous transit tax (*Leibzoll*) maintained residential restrictions: areas previously closed remained so, whereas those that were open had strict quotas. The legislation encouraged education and non-guild crafts, forbade peddling, and imposed conscription. In reforming the army according to a canton system, the state (August 20, 1804) authorized Jews and Mennonites to hire proxies in lieu of service.[80]

The Munich "Jewish Regulation" (*Judenregulativ*) of June 17, 1805, granted new privileges of residence throughout the city and the purchase of real estate. It also imposed a "register" (*Matrikel*) that restricted the Jews' numbers, limited residence to one offspring, and set strict monetary qualifications (1,000 reichsthaler) for marriages. It permitted factories and manufacture and, in the spirit of ancien régime mercantilist legislation, for example, Prussia's 1750 *Judenreglement*, provided a detailed list of the goods Jews were allowed to trade.[81]

The edict of June 10, 1813, similarly emulated Joseph II's harshest legislation in its effort to control numbers and redirect occupations by admitting Jews "into" estates. In this regard, it was also in keeping with Bavaria's general retreat from the Napoleonic Code. The government's ambitions to implement the code reached a high point in 1808; they declined in the face of unyielding aristocratic opposition.[82]

The edict aimed to limit the size of the Jewish population by allowing only Jews who already possessed a local "right of residence" (*Indigenat*) to acquire "civic rights and privileges." Moreover, the numbers of Jews in local communities were to remain static or, ominously, be reduced (Article 12). No immigration was permitted (Article 11).[83] The Article (22) that made Jews members of the community (*Gemeinde*) in which they resided thus applied only to those who already held such a residence right. Here was a salient case of local rights limiting state rights.[84]

Moreover, the most draconian provision limited permission to marry to the quota set by each community's "Jewish list" (*Judenmatrikel*). In the first half of the nineteenth century this quota would propel thousands of Jews, especially single males, to emigrate, especially to the United States.[85]

Again echoing Josephinian legislation, only Jews meeting three criteria could exceed the existing quotas or settle in new areas: those "establishing factories and large commercial enterprises," "master craftsmen," or farmers who purchased land (Article 13). Petty trade (*Schacherhandel*) was forbidden (Article 20), and Jews engaged in petty trade would not be permitted to marry (Article 14).

The edict opened all occupations to Jews, including the guilds (Articles 15, 18), thus transferring them "into" estates, and granted freedom to acquire property (Article 16). It required Jewish children to attend public schools or parents to found Jewish schools (Articles 32, 33). It required heads of family to take proper family names (Articles 4–9).

Finally, the edict established the Jews as a religious group by guaranteeing freedom of worship and according Judaism the inferior status of a "private" rather than a public "Church society" (Article 23). It dissolved all Jewish corporations (Article 21) and distributed their debts; deprived rabbis of any juridical authority (Article 30); and established the structure of Jewish communities and the qualifications for rabbis (Articles 23, 24, 25–29). In this regard Bavaria dissolved the Jews' corporate community, moving them "out of" estates.

Competing with France

With his stunning victories at the battles of Jena and Auerstedt, Napoleon brought the Prussian state to its knees (1806–7). He deprived Prussia of over half its territory and population and imposed crippling reparations. Prussia consequently undertook a series of reforms that aimed to recast its relationship to its subjects; it "deregulated the economy, redrew the ground rules of rural society and reformulated the relationship between the state and civil society." Unlike Baden and Bavaria, which promulgated new constitutions, Prussia's reforms were "more radical and consistent" with respect to economic issues, especially "deregulation of commerce, of manufacture, of the labor market, or internal trade." Most telling, "the Napoleonic shock was the catalyst, not the cause" for these reforms; government ministers had considered almost all of them years before the defeat.[86]

The same was true for the edict on the Jews. In three prior bursts of activity (1787–93, 1795–98, 1800–1801) Jewish community leaders and notables had interceded with the Prussian government. They convened meetings and submitted petitions and memoranda cataloguing in minute detail the laws that hampered, and the taxes that squelched, their economic enterprises. They negotiated directly with Prussian bureaucrats for full economic and residential freedom and equality with Christians.[87] For example, David Friedländer (1750–1834), scion of a wealthy merchant family and Moses Mendelssohn's self-appointed disciple, petitioned the Prussian state over a period of five years (1787–92) to improve the Jews' political status. Embracing Dohm's criterion of utility yet without his overarching political framework, Friedländer appealed to the Prussian state's beneficence.[88]

After Prussia's collapse and the transfer of government (1807) first to Memel and then Königsberg, the Jews of the latter city negotiated directly with the Prussian government. Berlin Jews subsequently pointed to the need for comprehensive reform in the face of the diminution and impoverishment of their community. The Jews of Breslau met with Karl August von Hardenberg (1750–1822) when he visited that city and later sent a delegation to Berlin. Israel Jacobson (1768–1828), a banker and president of the Westphalian Consistory, intervened directly with Hardenberg, whom he had known for over twenty-five years, on behalf of a new law (1807).[89] David Friedländer even participated in the intramural government debate in 1811.[90] Moreover, Prussian officials knew it was imperative to act: Jews to the east and west were gaining rights.[91]

Piecemeal reforms had accumulated in the interim. The Prussian government abolished the odious "body tax" (*Leibzoll*) in 1787–88.[92] Berlin's new Commercial Exchange (1803) gave Jews as many seats as Christians. Berlin's new Stock Exchange (1805) included Jews as members and board members.[93] The November 1808 Municipal Ordinance (*Städteordnung*), which based political participation on property ownership, applied to "protected property-owning Jews," allowing them to vote and hold municipal office. As a result, notable Jews, including David Friedländer, were elected to municipal office in Berlin and Königsberg.[94] Jews gained admission to the civil guard in Berlin and other cities (1809).[95]

In keeping with the general reforms' economic emphasis, the March 11, 1812, "Edict Concerning the Civil Conditions of the Jews in the Prussian State," was primarily concerned with economic freedom.[96] Its thirty-nine paragraphs addressed residential (#10) and occupational freedom (#11–13) and property ownership (#12). In exchange, it required that Jews take German family names (#2, 3), use German in all contracts and accounting (#2), and assume the same "civic obligations" as Christians, including conscription (#16). Foreign Jews were excluded from residence (#31) and employment (#34). Citizenship attached to males: a foreign Jewess acquired citizenship by marrying a Prussian Jewish citizen but not vice versa (#18, 19). Jews were in general guaranteed "equal civil rights and freedoms" with Christians (#7) and relief from all special taxes and levies (#15). School and community offices were accessible by merit (#8).

The partial and conditional nature of the Jews' new status was evident, following Dohm: the edict deferred a decision on access to state offices (#9).[97] Similarly, a concluding paragraph announced that in the future there would be decisions on Judaism's status (*kirchlichen Zustandes*) and on the "improvement of instruction for Jews," for which knowledgeable and respected Jewish leaders would be consulted (#39).[98]

What was the significance of Prussia's legislation? The occupational and residential freedom did not exceed Joseph II's legislation of the early 1780s.

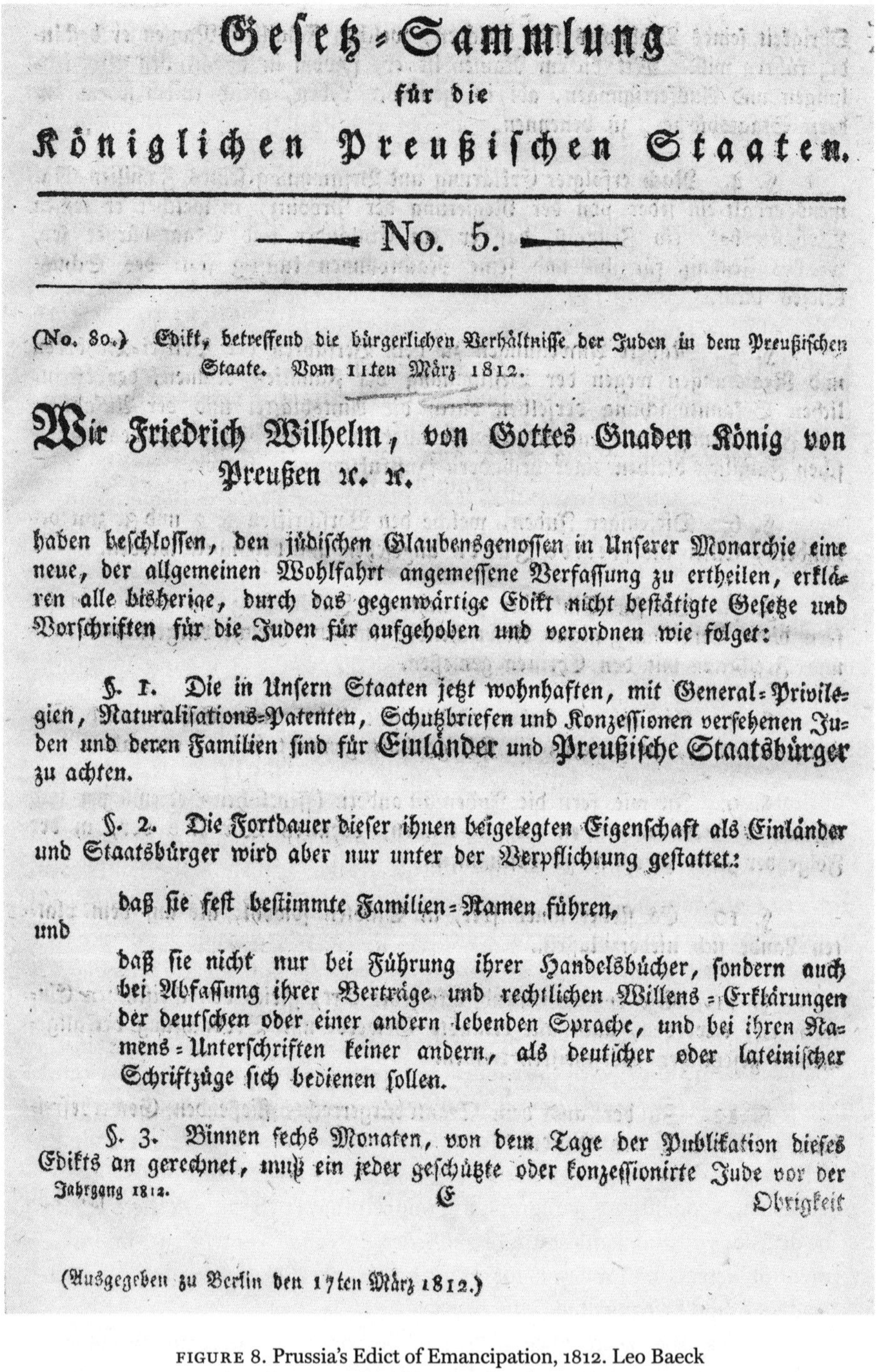

Geseß-Sammlung

für die

Königlichen Preußischen Staaten.

━━ No. 5. ━━

(No. 80.) Edikt, betreffend die bürgerlichen Verhältnisse der Juden in dem Preußischen Staate. Vom 11ten März 1812.

Wir Friedrich Wilhelm, von Gottes Gnaden König von Preußen ꝛc. ꝛc.

haben beschlossen, den jüdischen Glaubensgenossen in Unserer Monarchie eine neue, der allgemeinen Wohlfahrt angemessene Verfassung zu ertheilen, erklären alle bisherige, durch das gegenwärtige Edikt nicht bestätigte Gesetze und Vorschriften für die Juden für aufgehoben und verordnen wie folgt:

§. 1. Die in Unsern Staaten jetzt wohnhaften, mit General=Privilegien, Naturalisations=Patenten, Schutzbriefen und Konzessionen versehenen Juden und deren Familien sind für **Einländer** und **Preußische Staatsbürger** zu achten.

§. 2. Die Fortdauer dieser ihnen beigelegten Eigenschaft als Einländer und Staatsbürger wird aber nur unter der Verpflichtung gestattet:

daß sie fest bestimmte Familien=Namen führen, und

daß sie nicht nur bei Führung ihrer Handelsbücher, sondern auch bei Abfassung ihrer Verträge und rechtlichen Willens=Erklärungen der deutschen oder einer andern lebenden Sprache, und bei ihren Namens=Unterschriften keiner andern, als deutscher oder lateinischer Schriftzüge sich bedienen sollen.

§. 3. Binnen sechs Monaten, von dem Tage der Publikation dieses Edikts an gerechnet, muß ein jeder geschützte oder konzessionirte Jude vor der

(Ausgegeben zu Berlin den 17ten März 1812.)

FIGURE 8. Prussia's Edict of Emancipation, 1812. Leo Baeck
Institute, Joseph Goldman Collection, AR25802.

The abrogation of all extant legislation and the grant of equality with Christian "burghers" resembled Joseph's 1789 legislation for Galicia. In deliberate contrast to France's revolutionary model, the 1812 edict did not invoke a principle of equality: it was a "concession of status rather than the recognition of rights."[99]

Nevertheless, the Prussian edict was pioneering in emancipating Jews "out of" estates as part of the reform program that abolished guilds and serfdom (October 1807) and introduced municipal self-government. It was "legalistic in form and revolutionary in content"; it began to constitute aspects of civil society.[100] Moreover, Prussia essentially dissolved the tension between "town" and "state" citizenship by introducing occupational and residential freedom.[101]

Conclusion

The French Revolution and Napoleon constituted seismic events, as formative for Jewish emancipation outside France as in it. France's victories and occupations resulted in varied forms of emancipation.

In Italy equal rights came (1796–99) and went and came again (1800) with Napoleon's occupations. Under pressure from the French occupation, the Batavian Republic's Assembly engaged in a comprehensive eight-day debate before voting to grant Jews political rights (1796).

The characteristically fragmented German states divided into three groups over the issue of Jews' rights. In the territories France occupied, the government granted full rights, for example, in the Kingdom of Westphalia and Hamburg. Allied states such as Baden and Bavaria struggled to reconcile French law with corporate structures. They granted partial rights by moving Jews "into" estates; they legislated regeneration, imposing a state-supervised quid pro quo. Baden granted state but not local citizenship. Bavaria imposed harsh quotas on residence and moved Jews "out of" estates by dismantling the corporate Jewish community. In competition with France, Prussia granted basic civil rights by shifting Jews "out of" estates (1812). It withheld the political right of state service and kept Judaism in an inferior status.

Jews' rights in the Italian and German states remained partial and precarious. It would take two additional seismic events to bring formal equality.

CHAPTER NINE

Sanhedrin

AFTER THE REVOLUTION'S YEARS OF TUMULT, Napoleon set out to stabilize France to establish his autocratic and, ultimately, imperial rule. Napoleon in general aspired, as he put it, to "finish with the romance of the Revolution . . . and see what is realistic and possible in its principles."[1] One part of that effort was to resolve the Revolution's conflicts over religion: he accomplished that through the Concordat with the papacy (1801) and the institution of the Protestant *Consistoire* (1802). Another part was to impose a uniform law code for civil society, which he attained with the promulgation of the Civil Code (1804), later renamed the Napoleonic Code (1807). In respect to the Jews, Napoleon merged these two efforts by convening an Assembly of Jewish Notables (1806) and then, in his typically grandiose manner, a Sanhedrin (1808), named for the ancient tribunal.[2]

Napoleon considered full and unconditional emancipation for the Jews of Alsace, as one his advisors formulated it, an act of "unwise generosity" that demanded reconsideration.[3] Passing through Strasbourg in January 1806, Napoleon heard bitter complaints about the Jews' usury, greed, and creeping domination. Without bothering to hear from the Jews themselves, he told his ministers in the Council of State (*Conseil d'État*) three months later that the Jews were a "nation within a nation" whose numbers should be limited and commercial activities restricted. In consequence, Napoleon ordered a one-year suspension of Jewish loans (May 30, 1806).[4] Yet he wanted the Jews themselves to agree to, and give him legal justification for, more far-reaching discriminatory legislation, an intention he of course kept secret.[5]

As a further piece of business left by the Revolution, Napoleon wanted to resolve the Jewish communities' unpaid debts. The revolutionary assemblies had in general nationalized the debts of dissolved religious corporations, yet had not done so for the Jews. There was, then, the lingering question of responsibility for those debts.

Napoleon's Civil Code played a critical role in his effort to make France stable and governable. The revolutionaries had tried to replace the ancien régime's corporate structure with the cohesion of the egalitarian family. Revolutionary law had diminished parental authority, given women juridical equality in some realms, and introduced liberal conditions for divorce. The family, conceived as a legal contract between equals or virtual equals, was to serve as "both legal matrix and social cement, bonding each individual to the new nation."[6]

Napoleon's code replaced the Revolution's egalitarian vision with a "domestic monarchy." The code envisaged a "new alliance of the state, father and conjugal family." The male head of household alone was the "juridical individual," the wife was subordinate to her husband through the revived ancien régime notion of marriage as a relationship of "duties and rights," and divorce was rendered virtually unobtainable.[7] The state was this patriarchal family writ large: in Napoleon's words, as "the head of the family is absolutely at the disposition of the Government, so is the family absolutely at the disposition of its head."[8]

Napoleon's Civil Code redefined the criteria of citizenship in keeping with the patriarchal family. The Revolution had continued the ancien régime practice of citizenship by birthplace or residence (jus soli). The laws of April 30–May 2, 1790, for example, stipulated five years of continuous residence as a condition of citizenship. The Revolution had abolished harsh laws of inheritance (escheat; August 6, 1790) for foreigners and eased naturalization. To be French was to be "a man or woman who was born in France and continues to live there."

The Civil Code introduced the principle of descent (jus sanguinis). To be French was to be "a child born to a French father."[9] The law posited the nation "as the sole source of the quality of being French." The nation was a family that transmitted its name through parentage. This revival of Roman law "inaugurated the era of modern nationality law in France and throughout Europe." Napoleon exported the code under his soldiers' bayonets.[10]

Napoleon convened an Assembly of Notables comprised of 111 delegates, laymen, and rabbis drawn from France and the Kingdom of Italy. His ministers posed twelve questions that aimed to ascertain far more than whether Jews could live in conformity with the letter of the law of the new Civil Code. The Civil Code had changed the rules of the game. Napoleon's ministers asked whether Jews could now claim a place in that game. Did Jews who had gained citizenship under the revolutionary law of birthplace and residence (jus soli) deserve to retain it under the law of descent (jus sanguinis)? Could Jews, whom Napoleon regarded as a "nation with a nation," be citizens of a France defined by the patriarchal family and understood as a family writ large?

The very language in which Napoleon conceived of the Assembly unmistakably signaled this situation. He understood himself to be convening the

"Estates General of the Jews," that is, the ancien régime corporate body that predated the Revolution. To his mind the Jews' citizenship had effectively been annulled.[11]

Napoleon's commissioners (July 29, 1806) set a threatening tone for the Assembly. Acknowledging the complaints that had reached the throne, Louis-Matthieu Molé emphasized Napoleon's paternal good will in convening such an assembly that "has no precedent in the annals of Christianity." Yet he also bared the emperor's fist:

> The wish of His Majesty is, that you should be Frenchmen; it remains with you to accept of the proffered title, without forgetting that, to prove unworthy of it, would be renouncing it altogether.[12]

The commissioners presented the delegates with twelve questions. The first three addressed the foundational issue of whether Jews could be members of the "family" that the Civil Code made the basic cell of Napoleon's France.

1. Is it lawful for Jews to marry more than one wife?
2. Is divorce allowed by the Jewish religion? Is divorce valid, although not pronounced by courts of Justice, and by virtue of laws in contradiction with the French code?
3. Can a Jewess marry a Christian, or a Jew a Christian woman? Or has the law ordered that the Jews should only intermarry among themselves?[13]

The first question was crucial for the patriarchal family's success. That family was predicated on monogamy. Polygamy violated society's legal framework and morality. Indeed, later in the century French colonial authorities would raise the same questions about Jews (1840) and cite polygamy as a cause to deny citizenship in Algeria to all Muslims and Mzabi Saharan Jews.[14]

The second question aimed to defend the Civil Code's drastic reduction of divorce. Revolutionary legislation (September 20, 1792) had introduced divorce and made it accessible by admitting a variety of causes: abuse or cruelty, insanity or criminal behavior, mutual consent or incompatibility, desertion and emigration. The Civil Code ended those liberties by so heavily restricting the permissible causes for divorce, and especially the wife's ability to file, that divorce became virtually unobtainable.[15] In order to integrate Jews into the patriarchal family, Napoleon's ministers had to determine that Jews would not allow divorce "in contradiction with the French code."

The third question linked the crucial issues of marriage and citizenship. The ministers asked whether Jews were willing to join the nation defined by descent (jus sanguinis) through marriage into the "French" family. If the delegates rejected intermarriage either in principle or in practice, then they were refusing to become part of the French "family" of blood. Napoleon not merely refused to countenance compromise on this issue. He also contemplated enacting coercive legislation requiring that every third marriage be an intermarriage. Napoleon was adamant that Jews cease to be a "nation within a nation" and join the French "family."[16]

In formulating answers to the first three questions, the Assembly of Notables became a working body in which, to the commissioners' surprise and perhaps the delegates' as well, the rabbis played a critical role. Napoleon's prefects had chosen the delegates. The majority were lay notables, namely, "landholders and other distinguished Jews." Some fifteen of the delegates were rabbis.[17] The delegates had elected as president Abraham Furtado (1756–1817), a wealthy Bordelais with extensive experience in Jewish and municipal politics.[18]

After Furtado fulsomely recognized the emperor's plan, in calling the Assembly, to "hasten" the "regeneration of some of our brethren" and "to completely reform habits occasioned by a long state of oppression," he appointed a Committee of Twelve to draft answers. The committee included four rabbis, most notably David Sintzheim (1745–1812) of Strasbourg.[19] The commissioners discerned a division in the Assembly between a "philosophic" camp, with Furtado at its head, and a "rabbinic" one, whose leadership Sintzheim quickly assumed. It was to be Sintzheim's enduring achievement to forge a consensus between the camps.

Sintzheim was uniquely positioned to achieve that consensus. As Cerf Berr's brother-in-law and successor, he ranked among the notables. He had served as one of two Jewish delegates from Alsace to the Estates General and coauthored petitions to the National Assembly. In addition, he directed a yeshiva in Strasbourg and was a celebrated authority on Jewish law respected throughout Europe.[20] It was the crucial third question that made him the leading voice on Jewish law.[21]

On August 4 the Committee of Twelve presented its answers to the first three questions. The committee offered a general preface in which it declared that, according to Jewish law, the delegates recognized the supremacy of civil over religious law. The delegates asserted that according to the *halakhic* dictum, "the law of the land is law" (*dina de-malkhuta dina*),

> it is their duty to consider the law of the prince as the supreme law in civil and political matters; . . . should their religious code . . . contain civil or political commands, at variance with those of the French code, those commands would of course cease to influence and govern them, since they must, above all, acknowledge and obey the laws of the prince.[22]

The committee thus announced its allegiance to both Jewish law and Napoleon's Civil Code as well as its thorough conviction that the two were compatible. To be sure, the delegates innovated by extending the dictum's application from fiscal matters, its purview in previous centuries, to civil law and family law. The rabbis understood this as a permissible adjustment to new circumstances.[23] This reconciliation of civil and Jewish law was to be foundational for the Jews' status as citizens: the "ideology of the Sanhedrin" became integral to the claim to, and attainment of, citizenship in France and across the continent.

The committee's answers to the first two questions were relatively straightforward. Jews would conform to the Civil Code and the new "patriarchal family." Mosaic Law is ambiguous about polygamy, neither commanding nor forbidding it. Jews in the east, especially wealthy ones, had taken multiple wives. In the west, a synod forbade it in the eleventh century and that practice has since prevailed.[24] Similarly, the Civil Code's restrictions on divorce would not pose a problem. Jewish law allows a husband to pursue divorce, but this was rarely practiced. "Since the revolution" Jews have conformed to French law. Religious divorce requires prior civil divorce. Civil and religious divorce combined break all bonds between husband and wife.[25]

The controversial question of intermarriage elicited separate answers from the lay delegates and rabbis. These were reconciled through juxtaposition. The lay delegates emphasized the permissibility of marriages with Christians: biblical law prohibited marriages with "nations in idolatry," not with fellow monotheists.

The rabbis, in contrast, insisted that they could not sanctify a mixed marriage, claiming agreement with Catholic priests.

> Such is the opinion of the Rabbis, members of this Assembly. In general they would be no more inclined to bless the union of a Jewess with a Christian, or of a Jew with a Christian woman, than Catholic priests themselves would be disposed to sanction unions of this kind.[26]

Nevertheless, the rabbis reiterated the supremacy of civil law. They recognized that a "civil" marriage was binding. Moreover, a Jew who engaged in such a marriage did not on that account cease to be a Jew.

Here was a boldly candid answer to whether Jews could join a France defined by family and blood (jus sanguinis). The rabbis stubbornly resisted formidable pressure.[27] As a result, the commissioners began to take the rabbis seriously, realizing that they would answer any question that touched on Jewish law (*halakha*).[28] In contrast, Napoleon retained his secret plan to require that one marriage in three be an intermarriage.

Questions four to six directly addressed citizenship.

4. In the eyes of Jews are Frenchmen considered as brethren or as strangers?
5. In either case what conduct does their law prescribe toward Frenchmen not of their religion?
6. Do the Jews born in France, and treated by the law as French citizens,

acknowledge France as their country? Are they bound to defend it?
Are they bound to obey the laws, and to follow the directions of the
civil code?

Four and five asked whether Jews considered themselves to be members of
the nation as a family writ large. Did they maintain different ethical standards
for Jews and Frenchmen? Question six asked whether Jews admitted to citizenship under the defunct laws of jus soli ("Do the Jews born in France, and
treated by the law as French citizens") in fact deserve that status? Do they regard France as their country and accept the requisite duties? Will they abide
by the new Civil Code?

The Assembly's answer to question four did not satisfy the commissioners. The answer quoted biblical passages about the treatment of the stranger
and Talmudic passages enjoining love for "our brethren . . . who observe the
Noachides." The Assembly again scrupulously excluded Christians from
the class of idolaters. The delegates then acknowledged their "tie of grati-
tude" for "toleration" that "irrevocably linked" their fate with "the common
fate of all Frenchmen."[29] The commissioners declared that the Assembly had
not addressed how the Jews regarded themselves: Were they "a family, a tribe
or a specific people"?[30] The Assembly had either chosen not to respond to or
not comprehended the Civil Code's new definition of what it meant to
be French.

In answering question five the Assembly attempted to rectify its answer to
the previous question. After declaring that Jews treat Frenchmen no differently
than fellow Jews, the Assembly asserted:

> At the present time, when the Jews no longer form a separate people,
> but enjoy the advantage of being incorporated with the Great Nation
> (which privilege they consider as a kind of political redemption) it is
> impossible that a Jew should treat a Frenchman, not of his religion, in
> any other manner than he would treat one of his Israelitish brethren.[31]

The Assembly abjured being "a separate people." They also gave their claim to
citizenship in France the weight of a quasi-messianic formulation ("political
redemption").

The answer to the next question continued that line of argument in aver-
ring that loyalty to France made them strangers to Jews elsewhere: "a French
Jew considers himself, in England, as among strangers, although he may be
among Jews; and the case is the same with English Jews in France." To accen
tuate this point, the delegates asserted that Jews serving in the French army
had been seen "fighting desperately against other Jews, the subjects of countries then at war with France."[32]

The seventh through ninth questions concerned the powers and jurisdiction of the rabbis. Napoleon had integrated Catholics and Protestants into his

centralized state. Would he be able to do the same with the Jews? Do the rabbis possess authority that infringes on the state's?

7. Who elects the Rabbis?
8. What kind of Police-jurisdiction have the Rabbis among the Jews? What judicial power do they exercise among them?
9. Are the forms of the elections of the Rabbis and their police-jurisdiction, regulated by the law, or are they only sanctioned by custom?

In answering question seven the Assembly explained that since the Revolution the election of rabbis had been irregular. To the eighth question the Assembly responded that whereas Jews had jurisdiction in their own land in antiquity, since their dispersion their "tribunals"

> always depended on the will of governments under which the Jews have lived, and on the degree of tolerance they have enjoyed. Since the revolution those rabbinical tribunals are totally suppressed in France and in Italy. The Jews, raised to the rank of citizens, have conformed in everything to the laws of the state; and, accordingly, the functions of the rabbis, wherever they are established, are limited to preaching morality in the temples, blessing marriages, and pronouncing divorces.[33]

The answer to question eight rendered nine moot.

The three final questions concerned Jewish commercial practices.

10. Are there professions from which the Jews are excluded by their law?
11. Does the law forbid the Jews from taking usury from their brethren?
12. Does it forbid or does it allow usury towards strangers?

The answer to the tenth question was a simple negative. Jews could practice all professions and fathers were enjoined to teach their sons a profession. In contrast, the eleventh and twelfth questions elicited sustained answers to the rebarbative and inflated allegations of usury in Alsace.

The delegates answered that Moses envisaged a "nation of husbandmen" in which there would be little trade beyond simple barter. Moreover, such laws as the Sabbatical and Jubilee years aimed to encourage "equality of property" by restraining the accumulation of private property. The Bible conceived of lending as a "principle of charity, and not . . . a commercial regulation." The Bible accordingly had only one word for "interest" and no separate notion of "usury." The delegates thus concluded that "the law of Moses . . . forbids all manner of interest on loan . . . between a Jew and his countryman, without distinction of religion."[34]

The delegates acknowledged that these laws applied to Jews who inhabited their own state. In the qualitatively different circumstances of the diaspora,

Jews "lent money on interest to trading Jews, as well as to men of different persuasions."

The answer to question twelve expanded this view. There were no equivalents among Jews to the rebellions against rapacious creditors that punctuated the histories of ancient Greece and Rome. Taking "interest from the stranger" was only allowed, according to the Talmud, "in commercial intercourse," that is, in "commercial speculation" where the lender shares in the borrower's profit.

> It is an incontrovertible point, according to the Talmud, that interest, even among Israelites, is lawful in commercial operations, where the lender, running some of the risk of the borrower, becomes a sharer in his profits. This is the opinion of all Jewish doctors.[35]

If a few Jews engage in the "nefarious traffic" of usury, then that is no reason to impute this evil to all Jews. "Would it not be deemed an injustice to lay the same imputation on all Christians because some of them are guilty of usury?"[36]

Napoleon and his commissioners were sufficiently satisfied with these answers to want to make them binding. In their meetings with the Assembly's rabbis, the commissioners realized that the Assembly lacked legal standing because of its mixed composition. A body composed primarily of rabbis, on the model of the ancient "Sanhedrin," could transform the answers into legal rulings. Napoleon therefore decided to create a modern Sanhedrin: rabbis would be forty-five of its seventy members.[37]

Napoleon and his commissioners carefully orchestrated the Sanhedrin (February 4–March 9, 1807) to ensure its dignity and to prevent dissent. A Committee of Nine, which Sintzheim headed, drafted the rulings. Two representatives then presented the rulings to the full Sanhedrin. The plenary meetings permitted no discussion. The Sanhedrin considered nine questions, omitting the three concerning the rabbinate (7–9). The Assembly of Notables had emphasized the supremacy of civil over religious law. The Sanhedrin stressed the distinction in Jewish law between eternally binding religious laws and time-bound political decrees that had lost their validity in the diaspora.[38] In separate speeches to the Sanhedrin, Furtado and Sintzheim condemned usury and, by identifying persecution as its root cause, endeavored to exonerate their fellow Jews. In a concluding address in Hebrew Sintzheim defended the Sanhedrin's rulings as arising solely from Jewish law.[39]

With the Sanhedrin's conclusion, the Assembly resumed its meetings. Napoleon wanted to implement the two remaining items on his agenda. He planned to introduce an institutional structure which, modeled on the *Consistoire* he had imposed upon Protestants, would integrate the Jews into the centralized state.[40] In many of its features this plan followed one that Jewish notables had submitted on their own initiative at the end of 1805 or early in 1806.[41]

Napoleon's organization gave power to lay elites, especially those in Paris. It turned the rabbi into a state functionary: rabbis had to sign a declaration to abide by the Sanhedrin's decisions and to provide names of eligible conscripts for the army.[42] By means of the *Consistoire* the French state was to make Judaism equal to Protestantism through a recognized legal status and the payment of rabbis' salaries. Napoleon's government in the end refused to assume responsibility for those salaries.

Napoleon additionally wanted the Assembly to provide justification for punitive laws for Alsace. Napoleon showed no compromise in his vituperative instructions. He wanted "disciplinary measures." He thought "some departments," namely Alsace, had become "vassals to the Jews": the "Jews' suzerainty spread unceasingly through usury and mortgages." He therefore aimed "to weaken if not to destroy, the Jewish peoples' inclination to such a great number of practices which are contrary to civilization." He wanted legislation that for a ten-year period would limit the Jews' ability to lend money and engage in commerce. Moreover, he aimed to achieve that end by requiring that one marriage in three be an intermarriage so that "the Jews' blood will lose its particular character," since "a mass of vitiated blood can be improved only through time."[43] Napoleon's commissioners implemented his instructions with the notable exception of the required intermarriages.

The commissioners pressured Furtado, as president, to propose a motion in which the Assembly asked the government to cure the habits of usurers. Many of the delegates objected to any legislation that differentiated between Jews and other Frenchmen. The commissioners reassured them that the emperor had no such intention. After Furtado delivered a speech highlighting the need to draw a line between usurers and other Jews, the Assembly passed the motion. Napoleon now had the legitimation he desired, albeit at the cost of deceiving Furtado and the Assembly.[44]

Two of the three measures promulgated on March 17, 1808, concerned the establishment of the Consistory and its administration. The third decree addressed the suspension of payments of debts already in force for two years. It outlined strict provisions that favored the debtors. It stipulated government supervision for the Jews' business dealings for ten years. It introduced restrictions on residence to prevent further immigration. Finally, the decree required Jews to serve in person in the army, barring them from hiring replacements, an option available to all other citizens.

The decree exempted the Portuguese Jews of the southwest from all these provisions. The Jews of Paris later gained exemption as well.[45]

Some issues remain unresolved. No provision had been made to retire community debts (Alsace, Metz, Comtat). Jewish leaders in the relevant regions therefore established special organizations to ensure repayment. The state did not assume the payment of rabbis' salaries; that issue would not be resolved until 1830. The special oath for Jews serving as witnesses in courts was not abolished. The Court of Colmar codified it (February 10, 1809) (chapter 17).[46]

Conclusion

Napoleon's measures repudiated the unconditional emancipation of September 27, 1791. Napoleon reverted to a conditional emancipation reminiscent of Reubell's punitive legislation of September 28, 1791. He drew on ancien régime precedents. The questions his commissioners drafted echoed those of the Malesherbes Commission (1787).[47] The third article of the legislation of March 17, 1808, that came to be known as the Infamous Decree (*décret infâme*) resembled Louis XVI's 1784 *lettres patentes* for the Jews of Alsace. In preparing the third article Napoleon's ministers in fact consulted Joseph II's edicts.[48]

It had been no accident, then, that Napoleon said he was convening an "Estates General" for the Jews: for the Jews of Alsace, he had effaced the Revolution's "romance," turning the clock back to May 1789 to treat them as foreigners. In fact, the administrative location of the new *Consistoire* embodied this indeterminate status. If the Jews were a religious group, they should have been under the jurisdiction of the Minister of Cults, if a foreign group, then under the Ministry of the Interior. The legislation placed them under both ministries. The ambiguity of emancipation could not have been more manifest.[49]

CHAPTER TEN

Partitions

THE SECOND AND THIRD PARTITIONS of Poland (1793, 1795) rivaled the French Revolution in destroying the ancien régime. They were also directly connected to it. The Revolution was so all-consuming that France did not intervene to defend the Polish Commonwealth and its own interests in the continental balance of power. The partitioning powers disingenuously claimed that they were preventing the spread of France's revolutionary ideas to Poland as well as indemnifying themselves for the costs of their wars against France.[1]

The first partition had resulted in radical reforms introducing versions of parity, at least on paper: Catherine's "Charter for the Towns" (1785) and Joseph II's edict for Galicia (1789). Catherine and Joseph had introduced their legislation in the heyday of absolutist reform; the number of Jews involved was relatively small (chapter 6).

In stark contrast, the partitions of 1793–95 occurred in a Europe averse to reform. France's revolution frightened the autocratic partitioning powers into conservative, often repressive domestic politics that they swiftly extended to their newly acquired territories. In addition, the expropriated territories, and the numbers of Jews they contained, were so vast that, especially after the Poles' failed insurrection under Kościuszko (1794), the partitioning powers' highest priority was control. At the same time, the three powers' failure to implement their legislation demonstrated the limits of absolutist government.

The Jews' marriage of convenience with the Polish nobility had given rise to their status as a second burgher estate in the Polish-Lithuanian Commonwealth (chapter 2). That relationship now became a liability as each of the three powers in its own way tried to undermine the Polish nobility and its private market towns. The tsarist government aimed to suppress the Polish nobility after the 1794 insurrection; additional insurrections in the nineteenth century would only fortify that goal.[2] The centralizing Habsburg state similarly endeavored to break the Polish nobility's economic and political power in Galicia. Prussian authorities were committed to ending the gentry-leaseholder alliance by transferring Posen's commerce, and its Jews, from the countryside to towns and cities to fit its own pattern of commerce and taxation.[3]

In central Europe, the Jews' peddling and petty commerce was the legislative focal point. In eastern Europe, in contrast, it was the Jews' preponderant role in the liquor trade. Brewing and distilling, innkeeping and extending loans to peasant imbibers, all hinged on the Jews' relationship to the gentry. In fact, the Russian authorities tried to subvert the Polish gentry, who derived a large percentage of their revenue from alcohol, by banishing Jews who leased taverns.[4] Small-scale commerce was a related but subordinate concern.[5]

In the second partition (1793) Russia and Prussia had colluded to seize Polish territory without including the Habsburg monarchy.[6] In the third partition all three powers participated: none wanted the other to gain a strategic advantage.

Prussia

With the second and third partitions Prussia initially applied the inordinately repressive 1750 *Judenreglement* to the new territories of South Prussia (1793) and New-East Prussia (1795) that contained some 125,000–150,000 Jews.[7] The administration first promulgated new legislation on April 11, 1797, the "General Statute for Jews of South and New-East Prussia" (*General-Juden-Reglement für Süd- und Neuostpreussen*).

The 1797 legislation took Joseph II's edicts as a model. It aimed to render the Jews useful to the state through access to occupations and education combined with administrative integration. The legislation further followed Joseph II's in combining privileges with restrictions.[8] Also akin to Joseph's legislation, the 1797 law placed the Jews in an ambiguous legal status. While the law repeatedly integrated Jews "into" estates by dismantling their communal autonomy, the law did not specify the extent to which they were to be integrated into the towns and cities in which they resided or were being required to reside.

The law encouraged Jews to become artisans, farmers, and factory operators (III, #9–15). Jews were to farm unused arable land, to employ Christian labor for only the first three years, and to receive the same incentives (loans, tax exemptions) as Christian colonists (III, #16). Merchants were to restrict themselves to selling staples; trade in luxuries was prohibited (III, #8). They were to conduct trade exclusively in cities (III, #4); they were not to peddle house to house (III, #7). While Jews were generally prohibited from trade in the countryside, the lord of the manor could invite them to trade on his estate (III, #8). Jewish artisans were permitted to have apprentices, although only authorized "native" (*einländlisch*) Jews (III, #12). Disinterested (*unparteiisch*) Christian masters were to judge the masterworks of aspiring Jewish artisans (III, #11).

The schools were opened to Jewish students; alternatively, Jews were permitted to establish schools of their own that taught German, Polish, and arithmetic in addition to religious subjects. If qualified Jewish teachers were not available to teach the secular subjects, Christian ones could be employed or Jewish students could attend Christian schools for those subjects. The state was to pay the salaries of the Jewish teachers (IV, #13).

The state was to integrate Jews through a detailed census and the issuing of identification letters (*Schutzbriefe*). To facilitate the census individuals were to take permanent family names (I, #12). Jews were further required to keep account books in German (III, #8). Rabbis had to be conversant with both German and Polish (IV, #2) to announce laws in the synagogue (I, #11).

The most significant restrictions aimed to limit undesirables such as beggars, foreigners, and those without authorization (I, #2), as well as the odious itinerant peddlers and usurers (II, #3). Jews were not free to choose their residence and occupation: they required permission from the authorities (II, #1). Jews were not to sell liquor, to peddle in the countryside, or to extend loans (III, #2). Towns had the right to limit Jews to residence in designated quarters (*Revier*; II, #7). To marry, men had to be twenty-five years of age, have a guaranteed income, obtain a costly certificate from the authorities (I, #15), and pay special taxes and contributions (V, #9–10). The Prussian authorities thereby reinstated marriage requirements they had lifted in 1795 in the face of protests.[9] These were the only special taxes Jews were to pay aside from funding a surrogate for military duty (V, #1–2, 9–10).[10]

The legislation repeatedly accorded Jews parity with Christians by estates on specific matters (the recurring phrase is "just as for the Christians" [*gleich den Christen*]). Such parity applied to agricultural colonists (III, #5), master artisans (III, #12), tax burdens (III, #17), rebuilding homes after fires (II, #5), appointment of leaders (IV, #12), funding of schools (IV, #13), imposts (V, #1), state funding of schools and synagogues (V, #7), and the schools' secular curriculum (IV, #13). There was, however, no general grant of parity "into" estates.

The legislation effectively ended communal self-government. It abolished Jewish courts, subjecting Jews to the new municipal courts (IV, #3). To neutralize the power of rabbis and the communal organization, the legislation reduced the number of synagogues (IV, #1) and limited the number of religious functionaries (IV, #8). Rabbis were stripped of all coercive power: private religious offenses were exempted from punishment, while Christian courts were to try public religious offenses, albeit in consultation with a rabbi (IV, #4). As with Christian municipal representatives, the magistrate was to choose the Jews' leaders (IV, #11). Finally, to prevent avaricious leaders from exploiting the poor, Jews were to pay taxes directly to the authorities rather than through the community (V, #8).

The legislation placed the Jews in the legal limbo of partial or conditional emancipation. They were deprived of communal autonomy yet were still treated as a community with leaders. They had parity by estate on specific issues but not in general.

Despite the fundamental ambiguity, the 1797 law put Posen's Jews in a legally advantageous position in comparison to their brethren elsewhere in Prussia, who remained under the oppressive 1750 *Judenreglement*. Nevertheless, the Posen leaders convened a council (August 30, 1797; at Kleczewo) to respond to the new law. Such political mobilization recalled efforts only a few years earlier during the Four-Year Sejm. It testified to the Jews' self-confident assertiveness vis-à-vis the new government.

The delegates' memorandum of October 2 raised objections to four aspects of the legislation: marriage restrictions, quotas on the numbers of merchants, having only Christian masters judge the "masterwork" of Jewish artisans (III, #11), and the lack of Jewish courts for civil and religious affairs, especially those involving small sums. The government (November 20, 1797) offered redress to the first three issues. The request regarding courts fell on deaf ears.[11]

This successful petition led the way to a series of administrative decrees that repealed the 1797 law's most restrictive aspects. On February 6, 1802, the administration repealed the right of guilds and towns (*de non tolerandis iudaeis*) to exclude Jews. The government did not enforce the restrictions on the number of Jewish functionaries and synagogues. Jewish communities, rather than magistrates, chose their leaders.[12]

Thus the 1797 law either was substantially revised or went unimplemented. The provisions for education (new schools, qualified teachers, a teachers' seminary), for example, were not realized as the extant educational system remained intact.[13] The extent to which relevant local authorities were familiar with the law reinforced lack of compliance. The Count of Wollowicz, who owned the town of Witkowo, which included 620 Jews, wrote on September 16, 1799: "I have had no knowledge of this edict [*Reglement*] until now."[14]

Russia

The second and third partitions' addition of some 300,000 Jews made the tsarist administration acutely aware of the need for systematic legislation. In general Alexander I concentrated his early reforms in the provinces where the political risks were lowest; legislating for Jews in the newly acquired territories fit this broader policy.[15]

The administration's first step was to gather information from magnates and nobles.[16] It then commissioned the poet, senator, and later justice minister Gavriil Derzhavin (1743–1816) to submit a report. Derzhavin's "Opinion Regarding the Prevention of Famine in White Russia and the Organization of the Way of Life of the Jews" (1800) went to the Committee for the Organization of Jewish Life (appointed November 9, 1802).[17] Alongside Russian bureaucrats, that committee included former members of the Polish Four-Year Sejm.

Derzhavin's "Opinion," informed by Prussia's 1797 law, was far more ambitious than the ensuing legislation. Derzhavin envisaged a total reengineering of Jewish life that would render them "socially organized and morally educated like cultured and enlightened nations."[18] He advocated major population transfers, reeducation as artisans and resettlement as farmers, abrogation of the kahal, and a new organization of Judaism that would undermine the rabbis' powers and eliminate fanaticism. A specially appointed state "protector" was to oversee this multifaceted process.

His specific recommendations that directly influenced the 1804 legislation were removal of Jews from the liquor trade; cancellation of the voting rights Catherine had granted in the "Charter for the Towns"; and prohibition of settlement in Russia proper.[19]

The Jewish notables' suggestions, especially Nota Notkin's, which was perhaps the "first contribution by a Jew to political debate on the Jewish question in Russia," influenced the plan to create workshops and manufacturing in each Jewish settlement and to send Jews as agricultural colonists to the southern provinces.[20]

The members of the committee were fully cognizant of legislation for the Jews elsewhere; they considered their own "more moderate and more indulgent."[21] The main external influence was Joseph II's edicts, either directly or indirectly through Prussia's 1797 legislation.[22] The 1804 legislation abandoned Catherine's ideal of civic and political integration in favor of legal and economic conformity, namely, a conditional emancipation of incentives hedged by restrictions.[23]

The emphasis on education converged with Alexander's legislation (1803) introducing a comprehensive educational structure ranging from village schools to universities.[24] The legislation (Articles 1–6) made Jews eligible to attend all institutions and to take degrees. It required them to wear the appropriate German or Polish attire (Articles 3, 4).

One-fifth of the Articles (15, 16, 33–41) aimed to distance Jews from the liquor trade by prohibiting participation in all its aspects. Here the primary concern was the Jews' alleged baneful impact on the peasants.[25] To protect the peasants the legislation aimed to shift Jews into artisanship, manufacture, and agriculture. In keeping with Russia's general populationist policy, especially in the southern provinces, Jews were treated as prospective agricultural colonists who qualified for cash incentives (loans) and exemptions from taxation (ten years) (Articles 18, 19). The law encouraged Jews to establish factories that supplied military needs (cloth, linen, leather); to this end it made available government loans (Article 21). Jews were free to undertake any trades not banned by law and to enroll in a guild so long as no law prohibited it (Article 23).

Administrative integration took the form first and foremost of Jews being enrolled in the existing estates (Article 30). The legislation integrated Jews into four estates (farmers, manufacturers/artisans, merchants, burghers)—though without granting parity of rights and duties of the respective estate. They were required to use a vernacular language for business purposes (Articles 6, 8), to wear the attire of the respective estate (Article 9), and to adopt family names (Article 31).

The legislation adopted Joseph II's ideal of parity by estate (Article 29) as a distant promise. Once the Jews had proven through education and occupational change that they were deserving, they would be subject to equal taxation. In the tsarist order, equal taxation was the decisive criterion of estate membership.[26]

Despite the long-term goal of integrating Jews "into" estates, the legislation failed to abolish Jewish self-government as a corporate apparatus. Whereas the committee members were fully aware that legislation in Prussia, the Habsburg Empire, and France had achieved this, the 1804 law did the opposite. It empowered the kahal as a tax-collecting agency (Article 54), a function an earlier decree (May 3, 1795) had purportedly abolished.[27]

Finally, by stipulating specific geographical areas in which Jews could trade and practice crafts (Articles 13, 17), the edict began to restrict residence to the western borderlands. This practice would later harden into the Pale of Settlement (1835).

The tsarist government implemented little of the 1804 edict. Opening Christian primary schools to Jewish students, for example, was a dead letter from the start: few schools existed, and where they did, few Jewish students attended.[28] Napoleon's invasion interrupted the transfer of Jews from countryside to towns to remove them from the liquor trade. The government then indefinitely deferred the project, having realized the towns had neither the jobs nor the housing to absorb additional population. The government failed to settle Jews as farmers: it refused to provide the support that the legislation promised.[29] There were also instances in which the government acted contrary to legislation: for example, double taxation largely ceased by 1807.[30]

Habsburg

Joseph II had made Galicia the testing ground for Habsburg policy. Francis I continued that practice in February 1797 when he promulgated the Western Galician Law Code (*Westgalizisches Gesetzbuch*; WGGB).[31] Maria Theresa had initiated work on a uniform law code in 1753 as a mean to unify the empire's heterogeneous collection of dominions.[32] Work on the code extended for nearly six decades; the final product was the General Civil Code (*Allgemeines Bürgerliches Gesetzbuch*; ABGB), introduced in 1811.[33]

The new code Francis pioneered in western Galicia (WGGB) consisted of the General Code's first part. The government precipitately introduced this partial code because of the urgent need to subject the territories newly acquired from Poland to some version of Habsburg law. In September 1797, the code was extended to eastern Galicia as well.[34]

The new law code did not abrogate, but rather accreted to, the earlier legislation, resulting in multiple strata of competing law for Galicia's Jews: Maria Theresa's ordinance of July 16, 1776; Joseph II's edicts of May 27, 1785, and May 7, 1789; and some edicts during Francis's reign. The consequence was fundamental ambiguity in Galician Jewry's status, which, increasingly emphasizing restrictions rather than incentives, undermined Joseph II's ideal of parity.[35]

The 1797 law in general accorded "equal rights acquired at birth . . . irrespective of sex, station and religion." It stipulated the process of attaining citizenship but did not define citizenship itself—because of the strong Habsburg populationist policy encouraging immigration.[36] The criteria for citizenship were ten years of residence or a business, evidence of income or an occupation, and good moral character. Descent or religion was not a factor.[37]

For Galicia's Jews, in contrast, the government endeavored to limit overall numbers and to exclude foreigners, especially the indigent.[38] In 1804–5 Lemberg, the capital, expelled Jews from two neighborhoods outside the city proper, restricting them to residence in the other two, and limited them to conducting business in certain city streets. Foreign Jews, as well as marriage to foreign Jews, were prohibited altogether. Lemberg exempted from these restrictions only Jews possessing large capital sums and conducting large-scale commerce.[39]

Unlike Bohemia and Moravia, Galicia had no fixed quota of permissible marriages. The authorities did require prospective couples to obtain a license, which included an examination on morality and Judaism.[40] This system encouraged growing numbers of young couples to contract illegal marriages.[41] For purposes of taxation and conscription each family was required to maintain a "family book" with the names of its members. The "family book" also presupposed the possession of a proper family name.[42]

As for municipal citizenship, three decrees (February 16, 1789, September 2, 1792, October 22, 1807) appeared to permit Jews to obtain that status. Nevertheless, the local authorities construed the decrees to require explicit permission from the "highest authority" (höchste Bewilligung) for the municipal government to act. Since the "highest authority" had not expressly issued such a decree, the legal consensus was that the Jews of Galicia at present were ineligible for municipal citizenship.[43]

The issue of state citizenship was subordinated to that of commerce.[44] Habsburg law no longer treated Galicia's Jews as "protected subjects" (Schutz-unterthan). It classified them instead according to the location in which they conducted commerce, that is, city or countryside. Joseph II's edict had permitted Jews to buy real estate and hold leases. Francis promulgated a decree in 1793 that strictly forbid Jews to purchase real estate that involved jurisdiction over peasants or burghers. The decree also limited leases that involved the production or distribution of liquor.[45] A decree of 1811 prohibited the purchase of city houses that had not previously belonged to a Jew.[46] Decrees of 1798 and 1804 excluded Jews from the mining industry, including attending annual fairs in mining cities.[47] Despite Joseph's 1789 decree that had opened the guilds to Jews, guild privileges continued to exclude them.[48]

The authorities dealt a blow to the secular education of Jews in Galicia in 1806 when they closed the Jewish schools, including Lemberg's seminary for teachers. These had been erected in accordance with Joseph II's 1789 decree. By 1806 over 4,000 students attended some 107 primary schools. Herz Homberg (1749–1841), the founder and inspector of the German schools for Jews in Galicia, had published a pamphlet opposing Napoleon's Sanhedrin. Misunderstanding Homberg's intention, the government proscribed the pamphlet and closed the schools with which he had been associated.[49]

Duchy of Warsaw

Napoleon created the Duchy of Warsaw first from territories taken from Prussia's share of the partitions (1807), which he then augmented with some of Austria's (Treaty of Schönbrunn, 1809). The duchy was smaller than the territories left by the second partition. Nevertheless, Napoleon required it to raise an unprecedentedly large army (115,000) that entailed enormous taxation.[50]

The king of Saxony nominally ruled the duchy under Napoleon's protection. The duchy enacted a constitution on July 22, 1807. Contrary to the Governing Committee's early attempts to draw on the 1791 Polish constitution, the duchy adopted the Code Napoléon, which established equality before the law, a uniform concept of state citizenship, and active political rights based on property qualification. Nevertheless, the predominant nobility, which controlled the legislature and the most important administrative posts, actively blocked the code's implementation. While burghers did receive the right to purchase estates, access to state positions, and state and municipal citizenship, they were in no position to contest the nobility's grip on power. Like Westphalia, here was a Napoleonic vassal-state in which an intact estate society distorted a constitution's uniformity and equality based on the Code Napoléon.[51]

Contrary to the Code Napoléon, the government denied the Jews municipal rights and eagerly exploited Napoleon's Infamous Decree (*décret infâme*). The government used it as a pretext to have the king sign edicts to deprive Jews first of electoral rights (September 7, 1808), because of impending elections, and then, for a ten-year period, civic and political rights (October 17, 1808).[52] The revocation of state and municipal citizenship excluded Jews from all civil service posts, including scientific and educational institutions, from practicing law, and from craft guilds and merchant confraternities. The government imposed a special tax on kosher meat and further required conscription.

A decree of November 19, 1808, deprived Jews of the right to purchase real estate. The government further restricted the Jews' residential freedom by establishing Jewish quarters (*Revir*) in towns (March 16, 1809). An effort to remove Jews from villages crystallized in a decree (October 30, 1812) prohibiting Jews from producing or selling liquor or living in taverns and inns.

Conclusion

The partitioning powers' conservative reaction to the French Revolution and Napoleon brought to the fore the tensions of partial or conditional emancipation. Although Joseph II's 1789 legislation remained the dominant influence, the partitioning powers introduced multiple restrictions that neutralized its ideal of parity.

Prussia's 1797 legislation of conditional emancipation left Posen's Jews in limbo. It stripped them of communal autonomy yet still treated them as a community. They had parity by estate on specific issues—"into" estates—but not in general. In response to Jewish leaders' protests, the Prussian authorities lifted the worst restrictions.

Russia's 1804 legislation aimed to shift Jews out of the liquor trade and into education, artisan crafts, and farming. It integrated them "into" estates, albeit without parity of taxation. The legislation dismantled the organized community (kahal) yet empowered it as a tax-collecting agency. The legislation introduced the idea of restricting Jews' residence to the western provinces. Most of the legislation remained a dead letter.

Francis I's Western Galician Law Code (1797) aimed to introduce uniform law to the area; instead, it became one among multiple layers. Although de jure entitled to municipal citizenship, Jews were de facto excluded. They were also denied entry to many occupations Joseph II had opened.

The nobles who dominated the Duchy of Warsaw in general blocked the implementation of the Code Napoléon. In keeping, they exploited Napoleon's Infamous Decree to deprive Jews of civil and political rights, which also excluded them from a range of occupations, that is, education, law, and crafts. The duchy imposed new taxation and residential restrictions and attempted to remove Jews from the liquor trade.

In the first half of the nineteenth century the three partitioning powers would continue to monitor each other and enact related legislation for the Jews.

PART III

The Three Regions in the Nineteenth Century

MAP VI. Europe, 1815 and 1871. Cox Cartographic.

MAP VII. "Pale of Settlement" of Jews in tsarist Russia, 1835. Cox Cartographic.

CHAPTER ELEVEN

Restoration

THE CONGRESS OF VIENNA redrew Europe's map for the following century: despite incessant local wars of increasing duration and destruction, the basic diplomatic settlement held until 1914. In establishing Europe's boundaries, the Congress also ratified emancipation's division into the three regions of western, central, and eastern Europe.

When he came to power Napoleon had to decide how much to retain of the Revolution. The victorious powers, in turn, had to determine what to maintain of Napoleon's reshaping of Europe. The initial peace treaty that Russia, Prussia, Austria, and Britain signed with the restored Bourbon monarch (May 30, 1814) left major territorial questions unanswered. The Congress had to resolve the futures of Poland, Saxony, Belgium, Switzerland, and the German states.

In western Europe emancipation remained intact. In eastern Europe the partitioning powers, despite territorial adjustments, did not tamper with extant legal arrangements. In marked contrast, major changes occurred in the German and Italian states.

Western Europe

Louis XVIII reinstated the Code Napoléon and recognized the transfer of Church property. The 1814 Charter restored Bourbon rule and took a deliberately ambiguous stance on Catholicism. It tried to reconcile two conflicting positions: it declared religious freedom in Article 5 yet recognized the Catholic religion as the "religion of the State" in Article 6. Article 7 stipulated that only Catholic and Christian ministers would receive salaries from the state treasury. Louis XVIII upheld the principle of civic equality for all Frenchmen, questioning neither the Jews' emancipation nor Napoleon's Infamous Decree, which remained in force in Alsace until 1818 (chapter 16).[1]

The Netherlands maintained the emancipation decree of September 2, 1796, in its new constitution that affirmed equality for members of all religions;

indeed, the government officials who had implemented the original decree were still in office. The conflict in the Netherlands turned on the Consistory.

The French administration had introduced a centralized community structure that empowered new leaders favorable to the Batavian Republic. They displaced the former oligarchy (*parnassim*). Government authorities fully recognized their dilemma. Reinstating the former community structure would question the Jews' eligibility for citizenship by subverting their status as a confession; retaining the Consistory would appear to continue the despotic French occupation. The Hague Jewish community's secretary proposed a middle way that the government adopted: it abolished the Consistory and restored existing synagogues yet introduced a central administration (Supreme Committee for Israelite Affairs), which the new "enlightened" leaders controlled.[2]

The treaty establishing Belgium (July 21, 1814) as part of a joint kingdom of the Netherlands announced equality for members of all religions (Article 2), tacitly including Jews. While the Belgian States General rejected the Articles on religious liberty (190–93) and voted against the constitution or "fundamental law," King William I promulgated it (August 24, 1815).[3]

The diplomats thus introduced a pioneering precedent in European diplomacy: as new states emerged, the great powers required equality for members of all religions—even if the great powers themselves did not adhere to this standard. This practice would eventually gain Jews rights in Greece and, on paper, Romania. It was the antecedent of the post–World War I Minority Rights Treaties (chapter 22).

Eastern Europe

Any changes introduced to the partitions of Poland would affect the bulk of European Jewry. In fact, the Congress largely respected the partitions. Russia did not gain full control of Poland as Tsar Alexander I hoped but did increase its dominance. The Congress turned Napoleon's Duchy of Warsaw into Congress Poland, which, nominally autonomous, was under the tsar's sovereignty through a personal union.[4] The Habsburgs recovered most of Galicia.[5] Prussia recovered the western portions of the former Duchy of Warsaw, now renamed the Grand Duchy of Poznan, as well as the southern portions of the Netze district.[6]

The Congress's concluding declarations (Article I; June 9, 1815) recognized the claims of Poland to "nationality." This was a historic yet hollow pronouncement since implementation was left to the partitioning powers.[7]

Central Europe

Napoleon had radically refashioned central Europe. He had destroyed the Holy Roman Empire and drastically reduced the number of polities by creating the Confederation of the Rhine, the Kingdom of Westphalia, and a few enlarged states, for example, Bavaria and Baden (chapter 8). Napoleon's fall therefore raised fundamental questions about central Europe. Would Napoleon's territorial adjustments stand? What would replace the Holy Roman Empire and the Confederation of the Rhine? How much would remain of the Revolution's legal legacy (*Code Napoléon*)? Would corporate society be restored?

The Congress allowed most of Napoleon's territorial adjustments to stand, for example, enlarged and elevated Bavaria, Baden, and Württemberg. Scores of rulers who had lost their territories did not recover them. As a victor, Prussia obtained 40 percent of Saxony's population and 60 percent of its area as well as territories to the west carved from the former Kingdom of Westphalia (Rhineland) to compensate for the loss of land in the east. Prussia's population doubled to ten million.[8]

For central Europe, the Congress was a constitutional convention as well as a peace conference.[9] The Congress replaced the Holy Roman Empire with a new organization, the German Confederation, composed of thirty-nine states. Prussia wanted a federation with a strong executive that would empower it and Austria to dominate the smaller states. The Habsburgs, fearing Prussia, aimed for a looser association. The smaller states resisted unification and both Habsburg and Prussian domination.[10]

Prussia's representatives—Karl August von Hardenberg (1750–1822) and Wilhelm von Humboldt (1767–1835)—wanted uniform legislation that would extend the equivalent of Prussia's 1812 edict to all the German states. The Jews' equality thus became linked to German unification. Although the Jews' status was not officially on the agenda of the German Committee (*Deutsche Comité*), Hardenberg and Humboldt tried to pass such an agreement in the first six weeks of negotiations. Those weeks (October 14–November 24, 1814) were the most opportune. Only the five leading German states participated ("Five Kingdoms": Austria, Prussia, Bavaria, Württemberg, and Hannover); Hardenberg's influence was at its height; and Metternich supported him.

Nevertheless, Bavaria and Württemberg, Napoleon's former allies, truculently opposed unification. They insisted on state sovereignty in internal affairs, including the right to maintain the status quo for Jews.[11] Moreover, as the negotiations proceeded, the bitter conflict over Poland's and Saxony's fate divided Austria and Prussia.[12]

The German Committee's inability to resolve the question of the Jews' status meant the issue devolved to the Congress. Jewish diplomacy ensured that the issue became an official item of business.[13] Since Frankfurt am Main, Hamburg, Bremen, and Lübeck had already begun to rescind the rights Jews had gained under the French, Jewish leaders in those cities sent representatives to plead their case.

Jewish leaders in the three Hanseatic cities (Hamburg, Bremen, and Lübeck) hired a Christian lawyer, Carl August Buchholz (1785–1843), a liberal, as their advocate. Buchholz published a tract in which he extended Dohm's ideas using subsequent debates and the actual experience of rights.[14] He argued that the state should be indifferent to its citizens' religion.[15] He echoed Wilhelm von Humboldt's view that the state was a legal and not an educational institution; it should grant equal rights immediately to enable the Jews to regenerate themselves.[16] One law applied to all the German states could best accomplish this, that is, the Prussian edict of 1812.[17] Buchholz also composed shorter memoranda that influenced the Prussian delegates.[18]

The Jewish banking elite of Vienna, for example, Bernhard Eskeles (1753–1839), Nathan Arnstein (1743–1838), and their wives, who had been holding salons for decades, lavishly entertained members of the Congress and tried to influence their opinions. On behalf of their brethren in the Habsburg lands, they submitted a petition to Emperor Francis requesting civil equality, especially in commercial matters ("rights of purchase, of trade and of possession").[19] They also served as intermediaries: they helped Buchholz gain entry to Habsburg ministers.[20]

Napoleon's return from Elba (March–June 1815) introduced new urgency: the allies needed all states cooperating on the battlefield. The German Committee of five gave way to a larger one consisting of the Hanseatic cities, Frankfurt, and a dozen smaller states, for example, Hessen-Darmstadt, Saxony, Baden, and Holstein. That enlarged committee bolstered the cause of state sovereignty. In eleven meetings spread over twenty days (May 23–June 10, 1815) the committee succeeded in drafting the articles of the German Confederation, a compromise document repeatedly revised. Article 16 on religion epitomized such compromise.[21]

Article 16's first sentence guaranteed the status of individuals belonging to the three recognized Christian sects.

> The difference among Christian religious factions cannot establish any distinction in the enjoyment of civil and political rights [*bürgerlichen und politischen Rechte*] in the states and territories of the German Confederation.

The Article followed the Peace of Westphalia (1648) in recognizing only the three major Christian creeds (Catholic, Lutheran, and Calvinist); it exceeded Westphalia in declaring the civil and political equality of the three creeds' members. This declaration seemingly established a deep divide between Christians with rights and Jews without.

The reality was more complex: the Article had little practical effect, and the territorial changes left many Catholics in an inferior status in Protestant polities.[22] The reconfiguration of states, especially along the Rhine, had created considerable Catholic minorities whose status varied according to the same factors as the Jews', for example, state sovereignty and a restored corporate order. A few states awarded Catholics equal rights; a few granted rights with some restrictions.[23] Others abrogated rights gained under French occupation

(Holstein-Oldenburg, 1811; Braunschweig, 1818). The Protestant Hansa cities rescinded the equality the French had granted Catholics yet improved the status quo ante. Lübeck admitted them to citizenship. Bremen and Hamburg enlarged the scope of Catholic observance to include public worship and the use of vacant church buildings.[24]

In the remainder of Article 16 the victory of the proponents of state sovereignty was most evident. Two late, compromise changes subverted the Jews' rights through sleight of hand.

> The Confederation's Diet shall take under advisement the means of effecting, in the most uniform manner, an amelioration in the civil status of adherents of the Jewish faith in Germany, as well as the means for providing and guaranteeing for the same in the Confederated States the enjoyment of civil rights [*bürgerlichen Rechte*] in exchange for the assumption of all citizenship duties [*Bürgerpflichten*]. Until then, however, the rights granted by the individual Confederated States shall be maintained for the adherents of this creed.[25]

In the original draft, the second sentence's conclusion read: "the enjoyment of citizenship rights in exchange for the assumption of all citizenship duties." "Citizenship duties" (*Bürgerpflichten*) and "citizenship rights" (*Bürgerrechte*) were matching terms that highlighted a true exchange: full rights for full duties. The Hanseatic representatives' modification, from "citizenship rights" (*Bürgerrechte*) to "civil rights" (*bürgerlichen Rechte*), posited an unequal exchange by excluding political rights. Now the performance of equal duties gained merely "civil rights."

Those same representatives also notoriously modified a preposition in the final sentence. By substituting "by [*von*] the states" for "in [*in*] the states," they liberated the Hanseatic cities and the small states from the French administrations' laws. The change allowed them to claim that those laws had been promulgated "in" but not "by" the sovereign polities. They were therefore illicit.[26] It remains an open question whether Hardenberg and Metternich were deceived by this emendation or understood its significance.[27]

State particularism's success in resisting unification and uniform legislation for Jews resulted in the revocation of rights. Hamburg returned its Jews to their ancien régime status. The Senate did make one concession: individuals who had started manufacturing businesses were able to continue them during their lifetime.[28] Lübeck issued an expulsion order in 1816 and in 1819 prohibited Jews from entering the city to trade.[29] The French had first admitted Jews to Bremen, so the city excluded them in 1816, allowing them a six-year grace period to shutter businesses and sell residences.[30] Frankfurt am Main first excluded Jews from municipal offices and representation and then rescinded civil rights. Metternich and Hardenberg interceded in vain. Frankfurt's Jews appealed to the Confederation's Court through Article 16. The case dragged on until 1824, when the Court affirmed the Jews' civil rights insofar as there were no restrictions. The city had in fact adopted restrictions: a quota on marriages, a prohibition on purchasing real estate, and limits on commerce. The affirmation of civil rights was a pyrrhic victory.[31]

Among the states Mecklenburg not only rescinded its emancipation edict of 1813, modeled on Prussia's, but deprived Jews of civil rights as well by invoking a 1755 law.[32] More ominously, Prussia retreated from advocating uniform rights and instead came to mirror within its borders the lack of uniformity among the states. In tension with its own state-building aspirations, the Prussian government refused to extend the 1812 edict to its newly acquired territories. In consequence, some twenty-two different laws for Jews were in effect across its scattered domains.[33]

Particularism's triumph also perpetuated a central European peculiarity: the distinction between state and local citizenship. Had Prussia's 1812 edict been adopted as a model, especially alongside its 1808 municipal law, Jews would have automatically gained both state and local citizenship. Instead, in many of the states that had been allied with Napoleon and maintained or subsequently restored corporate society, local citizenship belonged to a bundle of privileges contingent upon guild or commune membership. In those polities, state citizenship did not entail the right of local residence. State and local citizenship remained separate and distinct.[34] The persistence of corporate structures meant that emancipation in central Europe would continue to be an amalgam of "into" and "out of" estates.

Metternich championed rights for Jews at the Congress and interceded on their behalf with various polities. Yet the Habsburg lands did not introduce substantive legal change. Joseph II's multiple edicts (Lower Austria, Bohemia, Moravia, Hungary) and Leopold's reforms (Tuscany) remained in place. Even the adoption of the General Civil Code (*Allgemeines Bürgerliches Gesetzbuch* [ABGB]; January 1, 1812) did not alter the situation. The code did not apply to Jews.[35]

The situation in Italy resembled that in the German states in at least two important respects. Multiple sovereign states continued to exist and the majority restored the ancien régime. Habsburg rule predominated in Italy beginning with the annexation of Venice's former territories, and Habsburg relatives ruled in Parma, Modena, and Tuscany.[36]

In two polities Jews retained civil although not political rights. In Tuscany, the status quo ante meant a return to Leopold's reforms. In Parma, the Code Napoléon remained in force.

The Papal States, the Duchy of Modena, and the Kingdom of the two Sicilies were restored. The old rulers brought the old laws. In the Kingdom of Sardinia Victor Emanuel I's royal edict (April 21, 1814) reimposed all the former restrictive Jewish laws, for example, the ghetto, special taxes, exclusion from the professions and educational institutions, and the prohibition on owning real estate. Francesco IV of Modena reintroduced the harsh code of 1771 with similar provisions. Most egregious were the Papal States, where Pope Pius VII restored the eighteenth-century laws in every detail, including obligatory attendance at conversion sermons (in general domestic matters Cardinal Consalvi retained some of the bureaucratic and administrative features of Napoleonic rule).[37]

Conclusion

The Congress affected the status of Jews in western Europe only in bringing equality to the Jews in Belgium. In eastern Europe, the Congress brought territorial adjustments; the larger legal arrangements remained in place. In contrast, in central Europe the Congress failed to bring unification and a uniform law for Jews. The German states became a mosaic of disparate laws. Many polities revived the ancien régime. Moreover, the dualism of "state" versus "local" or municipal rights began to emerge. Italy offered a similar profile of multiple states, disparate legal statuses, and in many states a resuscitated ancien régime.

CHAPTER TWELVE

Central Europe, 1815–1847

IN CENTRAL EUROPE emancipation was at its most intense from 1815 to 1847 where it was one aspect of the German states' twin foundational struggle: between the ancien régime and civil society, between monarchical absolutism and representative government.[1] The institutions of estate society persisted in some north and central German states; the free cities restored the status quo ante.[2] The former Napoleonic client states, especially Baden and Bavaria, issued royal decrees introducing constitutions with limited parliamentary government organized by corporations. Prussia and the Habsburg Empire refused to issue constitutions. In 1822 Prussia introduced provincial assemblies organized by corporations (*Stände*).[3]

The nature of government complicated the struggle. Bureaucracies metamorphosed "from an instrument of the ruler's will into an independent agent of the state."[4] Nevertheless, the states lacked sufficient personnel to govern their territories and therefore enlisted the aid of such corporate elites as noble landowners, hometown governments, and guilds. The states thereby reinforced the ancien régime.[5]

The central state's struggle with the local estates engendered the peculiar central European dualism of local (*Stadtsbürgerrecht*) versus state (*Staatsbürgerrecht*) rights, which came to fruition in this period.[6] Individuals could possess one kind of citizenship but not the other. In many instances, local corporations continued to control access to domicile, which could even be distinct from local citizenship. In some cases, state citizenship was an extension of local or municipal citizenship. In other cases, state citizenship was primary.[7]

This battle over the nature of citizenship manifested in nomenclature. Some older terms for "domicile" (*Indigenat*; *Heimat*) associated the right of local residence with corporations, especially guilds and communes. Most German states in fact attached rights to birth or residence in a locale (jus soli).[8] In contrast, relatively new terms such as "state citizen" (*Staatsbürger*) and "state member" (*Staatsangehörige*) denoted an unmediated and uniform relationship to the state.[9] In some cases interstate treaties governing the poor, the homeless, and the stateless, a major concern in the period, gave rise to the notion of "state membership." In these treaties, the category of "state member" gradually supplanted that of "subject."[10]

The states retained their confessional character. The ancien régime's persistence meant that despite the German Confederation's guarantee of equality to individuals of the three Christian denominations (Article 16), Protestant states discriminated against dissident Protestants, Catholics, and Jews, while Catholic states discriminated against Protestants and Jews.[11]

A nascent civil society embodied countervailing trends. The period witnessed the explosive growth of secondary associations (*Vereine*).[12] The burgeoning of the press and other publications strengthened the public sphere. Local, municipal, and state representative institutions, however limited, provided an arena for politics.

The scope of the emancipation process was comprehensive: all rights, civil and political, were on the table. Moreover, the meaning of emancipation was ambiguous. In granting various freedoms—residential, fiscal—most laws transferred Jews "out of" estates. Other laws, such as those granting access to guilds, sent them "into" estates.

The German states contained a farrago of legal statuses; the "multitude of parallel developments" magnified the pressure.[13] Some polities had not extended rights (Saxony); others had extended and rescinded them (Frankfurt, Hamburg). Some states had extended some rights and begun to erode them (Prussia); other states had granted partial rights or conditional emancipation (following Joseph II) and now legislated regeneration in exhaustive detail (Baden). In some states that acquired territory after 1815, multiple laws prevailed (Prussia, Bavaria). Emancipation was a "haphazard affair . . . of one-off concessions that could be delayed, reversed or reinterpreted" and resulted from "momentary calculations, local conditions and shifting balances of social and political power."[14]

Frequent public debates in journals and pamphlets, parliaments and newspapers, resulted in a mass of publications: some 2,500 titles from 1815 to 1850.[15] In the initial debates opponents recapitulated the old argument that the Jews' immutable character deprived them of economic utility. Those opponents demanded everything from religious reform to conversion. Some of these same opponents propounded the new argument that, without conversion, Jews had no place among the German people (*Volk*) constituted as a Christian state.[16] The Romantic ideal of a Christian state defended corporate institutions.

Most proponents embraced a notion of conditional or incremental emancipation: in the tradition of Joseph II, the tutelary state was to educate Jews to become worthy of citizenship by transforming their occupations and endowing them with true moral character through education (*Bildung*).[17] In their own public sphere of sermons, journals, and associations, Jewish leaders, especially preachers and rabbis, endlessly reiterated this ideology of emancipation consisting of the quid pro quo of rights for regeneration (*Bildung*)—which included occupations, religious reform, and the acquisition of German language and culture.[18]

Gabriel Riesser (1806–63) altered the terms of debate in the 1830s when he categorically rejected conditional emancipation. A lawyer and self-appointed advocate for rights, Riesser argued that emancipation was a legal issue of equal rights in exchange for equal duties. He accused the German states of acting inconsistently and illegally. Moreover, he denounced the states for establishing "an entrance fee of deceit" (*Eingangszoll der Lüge*) by offering rights in exchange for conversion.[19]

The political journalist and satirist Ludwig Börne (1786–1837) expressed a similar sentiment.

> It is hypocrisy and foolishness to claim that a people must first be educated [*gebildet*] in order to be capable of freedom; freedom must precede education [*Bildung*], she is its mother and teacher.[20]

Prussia

At the Congress of Vienna Hardenberg and Humboldt had unsuccessfully endeavored to extend Prussia's 1812 law to all the German states (chapter 11). After 1815 Prussia retreated from that commitment in its own territories. In 1816 and 1818 Frederick William III (r. 1797–1840), who eschewed both a constitution and a parliament, refused to extend the 1812 law to the new territories Prussia had acquired. The 1812 edict applied to some 68,000 Jews in 1816. The other 58,000 lived under twenty or more different laws.[21] Moreover, on March 3, 1818, Prussia indefinitely prolonged the validity of Napoleon's Infamous Decree in its territories on the Rhine's left bank (chapter 9).[22]

In 1823 Prussia created corporate-based provincial diets. Dominated by the nobility, these were purely advisory bodies charged with some supervision of public institutions. Prussia thereby unwittingly activated countervailing trends. In the provincial diets, for example, the status of "nobility" derived from ownership of an estate rather than birth. The number of commoners who owned estates rose dramatically during the period (Jewish estate owners were required to select a Christian proxy).[23] Moreover, the diets began to serve as a political forum for a wide range of subjects, including greater freedom and even a constitution.

Similarly, the 1808 Municipal Law had called local self-government into being (chapter 8). Combined with the formation of associations, towns and cities became the sites of a growing, predominantly middle-class civil society.

Prussia's conservatism regarding religion aroused considerable ferment. The state sponsored the union of Lutheranism and Calvinism (1817), dissident "Old Lutherans" rejected that union, and a Pietist revival gripped large numbers across the social spectrum. Prussia's attempt to impose its conservatism in its new Rhineland territories fomented conflict with Catholics, especially over offspring's religion in interfaith marriages.[24] In general Prussia's conservative policies in the Rhineland faltered in the face of sustained resistance from the Catholic and Protestant middle classes.[25]

Frederick William regarded the Jews' status as a religious rather than a political issue: his preferred solution was conversion. The Prussian state actively promoted conversion through the Berlin Society for the Propagation of Christianity and missionary schools, especially in Poznań.[26]

Frederick William's government eroded the 1812 edict. In 1815 government ministers deemed Jews who had won the Iron Cross medal during the Wars of Liberation ineligible for civil service positions, claiming that temporary bravery was no substitute for true character.[27] A series of decrees in response to individual cases prohibited Jews from serving as land surveyors (January 1820), army officers (June 1822), and academics (August 1822). Prussia barred Jews from the civil service in its territories on the left bank of the Rhine (January 1823). A March 1831 law reserved the office of mayor for Christians. Jewish religious institutions had the inferior status of private organizations.[28]

Municipal government was a counterweight to Prussia's conservative state policies. As Moritz Veit (1806–64), a Berlin bookseller, community leader, and later city councillor, put it at midcentury: "equality as municipal citizens and in the chamber of commerce have until now been the Jews' shield and protector."[29] Cities and towns produced diverse experiences.

In cities such as Berlin and Breslau the artisan guilds dominated municipal government. There only a handful of the most prominent Jewish upper bourgeoisie gained municipal appointments from 1808 to 1840. When the balance of power started to shift to the new commercial and professional bourgeoisie in the 1840s, a larger number and broader selection of Jews gained office.[30]

Silesian towns, in contrast, lacked a developed structure of artisan guilds. Moreover, among Polish-speaking peasants and artisans the Jews largely comprised the aspiring German-speaking bourgeoisie. Jews therefore played an outsized role in Silesia's municipal politics throughout the first half of the nineteenth century.[31]

In these towns Jews served both the Jewish and general community. Indeed, businessmen and professionals brought their experience in Jewish communal institutions to local organizations and municipal government. A type of local notable emerged who, as a leader in Jewish and general community affairs, and integrated in local associations, won positions, usually honorary, in municipal government.[32] Here rights, albeit partial, gave rise to political alliances. In these towns Jews epitomized the new bourgeoisie.[33]

Posen

Posen, the territories Prussia seized in the partitions of Poland, illustrates another legal status in Prussia's territories. After 1815 the Prussian government left the legal status of the area's 37,000 Jews unresolved, refusing to rule whether the 1797 Prussian General Statute or the Napoleonic laws, including the Duchy of Warsaw's adoption of the Infamous Decree, were in force. Local authorities generally appealed to the 1797 General Statute.[34]

From 1822 the criteria for citizenship were a version of jus soli: continuous residence in the province (since 1815), a proper occupation, a considerable capital sum, a proper German name, and the ability to use the German language. Under these terms only a thin stratum of the upper bourgeoisie qualified for citizenship and participated in municipal politics.[35]

The Prussian state and the Poznań government generally considered the provinces' Jews to require regeneration. From as early as 1822 Berlin planned to issue a separate edict for Poznań. The Prussian authorities considered the numerous tavern keepers and house-to-house peddlers to be both a menace to the local populace and inferior to the Jews in the older provinces. They did not merit the 1812 edict.[36] Similarly, in 1827 the newly convened gentry-dominated Poznań Diet (*Landtag*) rejected the idea of introducing the 1812 edict. The Diet recommended a ten-year probationary period that would include the adoption of religious reforms. The government did not enact this proposal.[37]

The Prussian government instead began to consider a two-class system analogous to the one it had devised in 1823 for peasant landowners (former serfs).[38] The minority of Jews who possessed capital (*Besitz*) or education (*Bildung*) would be eligible for limited rights. The 1797 edict would continue to govern the majority who would live on sufferance (*Schutzjuden*) until regenerated.[39]

The Ordinance for the Grand Duchy of Poznań of June 1, 1833, was a concession of selective emancipation to individuals.[40] Its thirty articles introduced a hierarchy of ancien régime categories based on utility to the state: "naturalization," "toleration," and expulsion ("those to be returned to their domicile [*Heimat*])."[41]

Jewish men and single or widowed women were eligible for "naturalization" if, in addition to an irreproachable police record, command of German, possession of a proper family name (Article 17), and proof of residence since June 1, 1815, s/he met one of five criteria: practiced a recognized art or profession, possessed and worked arable land, had a solvent urban business, possessed a city property (2,000 thalers), or had significant capital (5,000 thalers) (Article 18).[42] Naturalization brought residential freedom (urban or rural), occupational freedom, and "equality with Christians" before the law (Article 20). Although naturalization entailed municipal and state citizenship, it did not include full political rights: naturalized Jews were excluded from appointment to representative state institutions (Article 20).[43]

"Tolerated Jews" (*geduldete Juden*) were required to register with the authorities, to update that registration annually, and to show proof of residence since June 1, 1815 (Articles 21–23). They were not allowed to marry before the age of twenty-four. They could live in towns; the ordinance abolished restricted Jewish quarters (*Revier*). They were not municipal citizens. They could not engage in retail trade, sell liquor, or peddle; had to be active farmers to live in rural areas; were not allowed to run taverns or have Christian servants, employees, or apprentices; and could not sell drinks on credit (Article 25).[44]

The 1833 ordinance built on Prussia's 1797 General Statute, which had followed Joseph II in providing access to education and the trades. Jewish children (boys and girls) between the ages of seven and fourteen were required to attend either the Christian or an approved Jewish school, whose language of instruction was German (Articles 9–11). For the first time anywhere in its territories, Prussia accorded these schools the status of "public" (*öffentlich*) institutions eligible for state funding.[45] Students were subsequently to be trained in a productive occupation, whether as artisans, farmers, or professionals; none were to engage in peddling (Article 13). The restrictions on the liquor trade and peddling also recapitulated those in the 1797 General Statute.

The ordinance followed the 1797 statute in continuing to integrate the Jews into existing legal structures. The legislation accorded the Jewish community the inferior status of a private "tolerated religious society"; it was recognized as a public "corporation" equal to the Christian denominations only for fiscal purposes (Articles 1–4). The legislation also established rules for self-governance (Articles 5–8).[46] The ordinance made the community responsible for the education and professional training of children.[47] Young men had to either serve in the army or pay for a surrogate (Article 14). Aside from the lengthy list of onerous restrictions, "tolerated" Jews were equal (Article 27) to Christians.

Like Prussia's 1823 edict for peasants, the 1833 ordinance improved the situation of the small favored group (naturalized) at the expense of the rest (tolerated). Naturalization was an ongoing process; the percentage of the naturalized increased over time. The naturalized had the right to move to the older Prussian territories. Poznań's Jews were the first from the former Polish-Lithuanian Kingdom to attain rights; they did so in considerable numbers.[48]

The Prussian authorities inflicted severe hardships in trying to regenerate the "tolerated" through artisanship and farming. The tolerated were hampered in obtaining credit. Some had difficulty carrying on their businesses without Christian employees and servants. Moreover, because Russia had closed its border to imports from Poznań, artisans, especially tailors, lost their markets. As much as half of the Jewish population was impoverished.[49]

Many of the tolerated fought the various restrictions by petitioning for exemptions. Others, especially unattached sons of the poor, opted to emigrate: the majority went to the United States, but some went to Australia and France.[50] The categorization also corroded solidarity: some Jewish associations in the 1840s admitted only the naturalized.[51]

Jews' participation in municipal self-government in Poznań resembled that in the towns of Upper Silesia but with a three-decade lag.[52] As noted, from 1822 until 1833 only the upper bourgeoisie gained citizenship and then participated in municipal politics.[53] Nevertheless, the Jews' place in local politics was so conspicuous that the Prussian governor saw fit to limit it to one-third of offices.[54]

After the 1833 ordinance in practice admitted the "naturalized" to municipal citizenship (approximately 45 percent in 1843), Jews in the city of Posen, for example, allied with the German middle classes in opposition to local Polish nobles and notables. With the government's encouragement, that "German" alliance dominated municipal government from the 1840s until almost the end of the century.[55]

Frederick William IV

Frederick William IV (1795–1861), who acceded to the throne in 1840, brought the conflict between corporations and civil society to a head. An advocate of the Christian state "steeped in the corporatist ideology of the romantic counter-enlightenment," he attempted to reverse the 1812 edict in a cabinet order of 1841.[56] He envisioned Jewish corporations (*Judenschaften*) that would elect delegates to local authorities. He wanted to release Jews from obligatory military service.[57]

This attempt to revert to an ancien régime structure and undermine all claims to citizenship aroused vociferous opposition from his ministers and local administrations.[58] Jewish leaders submitted petitions that appealed to the 1812 edict, their contribution in the Wars of Liberation, and their growing social integration. Some Jewish communities in the Rhineland requested complete equality, as did the Rhenisch Diet (1843).[59] Frederick William's order was not implemented.[60]

In the meantime, an 1845 law (*Allgemeine Gewerbeordnung*) that introduced economic freedom eased the situation of the "tolerated" in Poznań. To protect the "Christian state," the law excluded Jews from state or communal offices. A further law of December 1845 that introduced general conscription prohibited Jews from receiving officer's commissions. It limited twelve-year veterans, who otherwise would have qualified for all state positions, to "subaltern" appointments.[61]

Despite the serious opposition, Frederick William IV persevered with his corporatist project: he brought it to fruition in an 1847 draft law submitted to the newly convened Prussian Diet—itself organized according to estates.[62] The law envisaged the creation of compulsory "Jewish corporations" (*Juden-schaften*): Jews would no longer function as individual members of society but, as the outraged Moritz Veit wrote, as "a medieval corporation separated from the political community in which it resides."[63] The corporation would take responsibility for training young men in trades and represent its members in municipal self-government. While the law did preserve pieces of the 1812 edict by granting economic and residential freedom, it deliberately excluded them from the "Christian state" by avoiding any mention of citizenship.[64] Eighty Jewish communities signed a petition in opposition.[65]

The law the Diet approved on July 23, 1847, did not create "Jewish corporations": rather, it contained provisions for religious life. It accorded Judaism the clearly inferior status of a "private association"; Protestant and Catholic churches were recognized public corporations (Article 37). It required equal duties of Jews but allowed extant laws to limit equal rights (Article 1). It excluded Jews from all state positions involving "judicial, policing or executive authority" (Article 2). It permitted them to teach technical subjects, for example, medicine, mathematics, and natural science, at all ranks at universities and technical schools. They were prohibited from posts in all culturally sensitive subjects (Article 2). For the first time, it accorded Jewish elementary schools outside of Poznań the coveted status of public institutions (*öffentlich*) eligible for state funding, including buildings as well as teachers' salaries and pensions.[66]

The law contained special provisions for Jews in Poznań. Naturalized Jews were made equal to Jews elsewhere in Prussia; their rights became heritable (Article 26). Tolerated Jews remained subject to numerous restrictions, except those the 1845 law had lifted. They did not have freedom of residence, marriage, or migration to other provinces; they were not municipal citizens (Articles 31–34).[67]

Frederick William IV's commitment to the "Christian state" triumphed over the imperative of administrative integration. Keeping Poznań's Jews (37.8 percent of Prussia's Jews) under special laws trumped the state's need for legal uniformity.[68]

Cologne

This center of Rhineland commerce presents an example of the Jews' situation in Prussia's recalcitrant, heavily Catholic western territories. Cologne first admitted Jews with the French occupation in 1798; predominantly wealthy Jews began to settle in the city.[69] Under French law Jews enjoyed full emancipation until the promulgation of the Infamous Decree. A Prussian commission (1818) declared the Jews unprepared for full rights and renewed the Infamous Decree indefinitely.[70]

With Napoleon's fall Cologne required Jews to apply for individual settlement patents (1814–26). The city authorities denied most of these, especially for petty traders, signaling defiance of Prussian control. Individual Jews vehemently protested these rejections. After 1826 the Prussian administration confirmed virtually all applications.[71]

Cologne's politics began to change dramatically with the growth of a new business elite whose economic interests converged with Jewish merchants'. This new elite derived its wealth from trade (grain, iron, coal) and transport on the new railroads and steamships. It was composed largely of newcomers to Cologne, many Protestant. In the 1840s as "class took precedence over religion," Cologne and other Rhenish urban liberals began to favor emancipation for Jews.[72] Jewish leaders, and especially the Oppenheim family, whose bank played a major role in promoting local commerce, advocated unceasingly for equality. An alliance of shared economic interests promoted equality.[73]

Baden

Baden continued to grant state citizenship, albeit significantly restricted, but not local citizenship. It thereby limited Jews' ability to find or transfer residence. The new 1818 constitution, in accord with the German Confederation (Article 16), confirmed equality for citizens (Article 7) of the three Christian denominations (Article 9), aside from "explicit exceptions"—which excluded Jews from political rights, state offices, and election to the Lower Chamber.[74] An ordinance of 1820 (Article 12) barred Jews from all those communes (*Gemeinden*) in which they did not already possess the right of residence, while also prohibiting them (Articles 24, 27, 54) from serving in local government. The ordinance concentrated them in specific areas (173 of 1,555 communes). Such concentration impeded the very changes deemed prerequisites for rights, for example, new occupations and social integration.[75]

A year after Grand Duke Leopold's (1790–1852) succession to the throne, new communal legislation (1831) demoted the Jews by default. The law endowed some 80,000 Baden residents with rights by removing the distinction between local citizens (*Ortsbürger*) and tolerated non-citizens (*Schutzbürger*). Since the legislation did not apply to Jews, they were left as the only tolerated non-citizens (*Schutzbürger*). The law thus introduced an invidious distinction between Christian local citizens and tolerated Jews.[76] Moreover, the legislation (Article 13) made election to the council and office of mayor contingent upon a profession of Christian faith, thus excluding from local government those Jews who already held local citizenship.[77] Baden's Jews protested these provisions in numerous petitions and memoranda throughout the 1830s and 1840s.[78]

In the same period Baden introduced three circumscribed forms of equality. In 1828 the Lower Chamber voted unanimously to abrogate the last special tax for Jews. In 1833 the Jewish community began to receive a state subsidy comparable to that of other religions. An 1835 school ordinance granted Jewish teachers equality with Christian teachers, including salary.[79]

Throughout the period the Baden Lower Chamber made wide-ranging demands for regeneration. In the debates of 1819–20 and 1822–23, the majority declared that regeneration must precede rights. Regeneration was to include religious reforms (Sunday Sabbath, German liturgy), abolition of exclusivist national practices (dietary laws, circumcision), and occupational change. The Diet did not debate the issue again for a decade but then did so at all its subsequent sessions (1833, 1835, 1837, 1840, 1842, 1845). The majority, including many liberals, reiterated that the Jews had not sufficiently regenerated to warrant rights or to overcome popular objections. Jews petitioned repeatedly, emphasizing the urgent need for local rights.[80]

In 1846 two-thirds of the Lower Chamber voted in favor of emancipation. The radicals had gained strength in the most recent elections while the appearance of the dissenting German Catholic movement (*Deutschkatholiken*) had raised the issue of religious freedom by pointing to the contradiction in denying equality on religious grounds.[81] The vote crucially put equality on liberalism's agenda. On February 14, 1848, a motion for full equality was put to the Lower Chamber.

Bavaria

Bavaria's government first had to decide whether to extend its 1813 edict to its territories gained between 1814 and 1816, which had increased its Jewish population from 30,000 to 53,400. The government applied the 1813 edict to Würzburg and Aschaffenburg (1816) but not the Rheinpfalz, where French law (1791) had first emancipated the Jews and then subjected them to the Infamous Decree.[82]

Bavaria subsequently debated the implementation of various aspects of the 1813 decree. For example, paragraph 12 had raised the possibility of any locale reducing the number of Jews permitted by the "Jewish list" (*Matrikel*). Jews vigorously fought the application of that paragraph, while local officials, lacking clear instructions, acted arbitrarily. A May 17, 1818, ruling confirmed the local communities' authority to decide whether Jews should be granted the right of residence. In contrast, in some instances the state approved the settlement of Jewish businessmen whom local communities opposed. There were instances of the state coercing guilds to accept Jewish apprentices by withholding routine approval of Christian applicants.[83] Jews who became local community (*Gemeinde*) members were, however, deemed ineligible to hold office.[84]

Bavaria's new constitution (1818) provided for an Assembly organized according to corporations and granted equality to members of the three Christian denominations (IV, #9) in keeping with the German Confederation's Article 16. Bavaria discriminated against Protestants, preventing the establishment of new communities.[85] Non-Christians would enjoy freedom of conscience but possess state rights only as specified in additional edicts (IV, #9). Moreover, state rights depended upon local rights (*Indigenat*; IV, #1).[86]

The Assembly debated the Jews' status and the implementation of the 1813 edict. The 1818–19 deliberations confirmed the 1813 edict, yet the disparate laws in Bavaria's various territories complicated the edict's application.[87] Jewish leaders lobbied the Bavarian Assembly in 1819 for full rights.[88] A local rabbi, Samson Rosenfeld, submitted a memorandum to the Assembly emphasizing conditional emancipation's baneful consequences: "the restrictions on [the Jews'] civil rights, and the resulting disdain of their fellow citizens, is the root of all evil."[89] He highlighted Bavaria's legal inconsistency: "In respect to duties we are full citizens, in respect to rights only half citizens."[90]

The Chamber of Delegates voted in favor of revising the law; the king and his government promised a new law.[91] The "Hep Hep" riots, heated protests against emancipation that turned violent, swept across numerous German states in 1819–22. The riots derailed Bavaria's promises.[92] In response to the riots, the Assembly voted in 1821 to curtail the Jews' rights; in contrast, government bureaucrats wanted to extend them.[93] Significantly, districts that already contained Jews favored full rights, whereas districts that did not, and apparently feared an influx of Jews, were opposed.[94]

Over the next two and a half decades Bavaria's Assembly and bureaucracy repeatedly considered revising the Jews' status. A stalemate resulted from a liberal Lower House facing a conservative monarch (Ludwig I; 1825–48) and Upper House.[95] Jewish leaders actively promoted their cause to the king and Assembly through deputations and petitions.[96]

Incomplete emancipation entailed a high degree of surveillance: the government monitored the Jews' numbers and occupations. Moreover, incomplete emancipation yielded demands for religious reform. Representatives, bureaucrats, and writers demanded that Jews make Judaism more compatible with Christian society, for example, Sunday Sabbath and abolition of the dietary laws.[97]

In response to numerous Jewish petitions, the Assembly took up the question of the Jews' status (1831–32), recognizing that the *Matrikel* was the primary problem: even those with preferred occupations were often unable to obtain the elusive right of residence. Considerable numbers of Jews emigrated, both individuals and families, especially to the United States. Both chambers of the Assembly endorsed a revision of restrictions; the king did not proceed. This was the first Bavarian Parliament to favor a grant of additional rights.[98] In part in response to continuing Jewish petitions, the Assembly debated the issue twice in 1846, deciding to undertake reform within three years.[99] For example, Lazarus Adler, rabbi in Kissingen, argued in a memorandum to the Bavarian Assembly (1846) that it was not the Jews but Judaism that was at issue: since conversion brought full rights, religion alone was the obstacle to full freedom.[100] Proponents of the Christian state who rejected rights alleging Judaism's intolerance were themselves intolerant since they would exclude not only Jews but also the Christian confessions whose truth they disputed.[101] He requested full rights or, failing that, the abolition of the *Matrikel*.[102]

Habsburg Empire

Metternich retreated from his initial stand at the Congress of Vienna where, alongside Hardenberg and Humboldt, he had championed the extension of Prussia's 1812 edict throughout the German states (chapter 11). Metternich generally rejected change: he did not reform the peasants' semifeudal condition, continued to accord Protestants the inferior status of Joseph II's toleration edict, and deemed all constitutions seditious—in the Habsburg case as antithetical to the dynastic loyalty that unified the empire. Accordingly, he eschewed altering the Jews' status. The period 1815–47 thus brought a mix of minor modifications, while the 1840s increasingly heard calls for full equality.[103]

Vienna

Since readmission to the imperial capital in 1693, settlement had been limited to those the government deemed useful: an elite of bankers, army purveyors, and manufacturers who paid a hefty tax for their privilege. In 1820 the 135 tolerated individuals and their households comprised about 1,000 individuals.[104] They were allowed neither an organized community nor a proper synagogue. Instead, they prayed in private homes or, later, in a prayer room (from 1817). Announcing that the existing building was unsafe, Jewish leaders had the prayer room demolished and commissioned a new building.

The elegant neo-classical Seitenstettingasse synagogue (1826) had a large rotunda surmounted by a dome, ionic columns, and lattice work for the women's gallery. It was built in a courtyard to conform to the status of private worship—the same inferior status as Protestants.[105]

Bohemia

The 1720s law limiting the number of families (*Familiantengesetz*; 8,600 families) remained the salient feature of Bohemian Jewry's legal status and the focus of their protests. This law allowed a family with residence rights to settle the firstborn son alone, yet only after the father's death. It was the first law in

a legal handbook for Bohemian Jewry. The only additions after 1815 were ordinances and administrative rulings governing the law's application. An 1818
ordinance required that marriage applicants have a minimum capital (300
florins; 500 in Prague). An 1833 ordinance regarded the administration of the
Jewish morality test required for a marriage license.[106]

Moravia

The draconian law limiting the number of families (*Familiantengesetz*; 5,400
families) was also the salient feature in Moravia next to the ambiguity of multiple strata of law. For example, a June 1833 law clarifying the procedure for
awarding the right of settlement (*Familiantenstelle*) "did not explicitly abolish
the relevant extant laws," making it necessary to consult them as well.[107]
Women notably had no legal standing vis-à-vis settlement rights.

> If the deceased holder of a settlement permit [*Familiant*] left only
> daughters, then this family is considered to be extinguished; the daugh-
> ters are at liberty to marry at home or abroad.[108]

The fundamental ambiguity was egregious: since 1792 Jews were under
general law except for explicit exceptions, yet under multiple edicts (1798, 1799,
1803) they were not treated as full "subjects."[109] There were multiple measures
of their inequality. They paid a raft of special taxes: an edict of 1798 established
most of these, while edicts of 1828 and 1830–31 consolidated their administration in one government department.[110] Certain cities (Brünn, Olmütz) continued to prohibit permanent residence.[111] Prohibitions (since 1725) on leasing
estates remained in force, as did those on employing Christian servants.[112] The
legality of emigration to Hungary attracted special mention.[113]

Galicia

As in Moravia, ambiguity prevailed in Galicia in consequence of the multiple
layers of law: Maria Theresa's 1776 edict; Joseph II's edicts; the 1797 Western
Galician Law Code; Francis's legislation; and subsequent ordinances. New
laws or administrative ordinances generally continued to undermine Joseph
II's ideal of parity.[114] Numerous towns prohibited Jews from settlement; burghers in many towns excluded Jews from artisan and merchant guilds.[115]
Marriage laws progressed from "formal" equality under Joseph II to "real"
functional equality in the Vormärz by incorporating relevant Jewish law. In
practice, the high marriage taxes and the test for Jewish morality continued to
promote illegal marriages (*wilde Ehen*).[116] Endemic poverty resulted in specific sanitation ordinances governing housing, especially unhygienic overcrowding, and trade in used clothing. Poverty also encouraged emigration,
especially to Hungary.[117]

Hungary

In consequence of the general political stalemate (state versus estates) in Hungary, in which the numerous nobility predominated, the Jews' situation barely changed. The Diet of 1790–91 had qualified Joseph II's toleration decrees by requiring Jews to obtain residence and work permits from local authorities. The fifty or so royal or privileged cities retained the right to exclude Jews. Jews largely remained "under aristocratic aegis" in private towns, with the corresponding range of occupations: lessees, innkeepers, and millers. Jewish efforts in 1807 and 1811 to improve their legal situation failed.[118] Hungary remained a destination for Jewish emigrants from Bohemia, Moravia, and Galicia.

Limited change came in 1840 when the Diet both voted in favor of equality and adopted a new Commercial Code that gave Hungary's approximately 250,000 Jews residential mobility (Law 29), especially entrance to royal cities. The foremost Hungarian advocate of rights was Jozsef Eötvös (1813–71). His speech in the Lower House helped win the day by carefully and evocatively dismissing all the standard arguments against equality.[119] Although fully aware of the resolution's limited effect, one Jewish author excitedly exclaimed:

> the Enlightenment celebrated a true triumph in the midst of a great people [*Volk*], and God's spirit fluttered through its representatives' Assembly.[120]

Conclusion

Partial emancipation in the German states and Habsburg lands yielded varied and inconsistent statuses. Restrictions on population and residential rights were the basic holdover from the ancien régime: Baden's denial of local citizenship, Bavaria's *Matrikel*, Bohemia's and Moravia's *Familiantengesetz*. Posen's two-tier system—"naturalized" and "tolerated"—echoed the ancien régime.

These restrictions were the chief objects of the Jews' protests; they were also the chief impetus for emigration (poverty, especially in Galicia, ran a close second). Partial rights also inspired public discussions of the Jews' regeneration in which Judaism was front and center.

Although a vehement liberal opposition to emancipation was conspicuous, the tide began to turn in the 1830s and 1840s (Bavaria, 1831–32; Baden, 1846). Some liberals abandoned the policy of conditional emancipation or regeneration for rights; they instead embraced unconditional emancipation based on the principle of equality. This change was reminiscent of the French National Assembly's shift from the debate of December 23, 1789, to the law of September 28, 1791. The revolution of 1848 would further place that principle on liberalism's agenda, yet again neither unambiguously nor irrevocably.

CHAPTER THIRTEEN

Revolution

THE REVOLUTION THAT FAILED, 1848, also failed to emancipate central Europe's Jews. Although the revolution shook the continent, it did not significantly impact Jewish rights in western or eastern Europe. It affected the legal status solely of central Europe's Jews.[1] Central Europe's approximately 1.4 million Jews (German states, Habsburg lands, Italy) won rights only to see them vanish: they lost equal rights in the Habsburg Empire for the first time, in some German states for the second time, and in some Italian states for the third time.[2]

The revolution established equality before the law as liberalism's sine qua non despite many liberals' ambivalence if not outright hostility.[3] Even conservative governments felt the Jews' equality was indispensable to restore order and appease public opinion. Prussia and Austria's counterrevolution enacted equality: the former then opted to erode it, the latter to rescind it. The counterrevolution dismantled one of the confessional state's central pillars only to reerect it. Bavaria's resurgent conservative government promoted the Jews' equality.[4]

Origins

The revolution irrupted after a three-year crisis (1845–48) of crop failure, credit shortage, and commercial downturn.[5] In provincial and capital cities political mobilization against the existing order took many forms: the licit means of banquets, parades, carnivals, songs, and newspapers—albeit highly censored—and the illicit means of secret societies. In Prussia (1847) a "United Diet" clashed with the king, in the Papal States a Consultative Assembly challenged Pius IX.

The liberal cantons' triumph in Switzerland's Civil War (1847) together with Palermo's uprising (January 12, 1848) ignited the fire. In Paris banquets produced barricades, King Louis Philippe abdicated, and, under pressure from the crowds that invaded Parliament and massed before city hall, politicians proclaimed the Republic (February 24, 1848). Insurrections followed in Munich, Vienna, Budapest, Venice, Cracow, Milan, and Berlin.[6] With the exception of Paris, the insurrectionists "stopped at the foot of the throne," limiting their demands to constitutional monarchy.

Prussia

In 1847 King Frederick William IV called a "United Diet" composed of all the provincial diets to address the state's fiscal needs, especially funding for railroads in the east, which he considered a military imperative.[7] After the king categorically refused a constitution and the deputies refused to approve new loans, he dissolved the Diet (June 26, 1847). In Berlin demonstrations that began on March 9 turned violent on March 18. The king dismissed his conservative ministers, appointed liberal replacements, and convened a Second United Diet that called elections for a Prussian National Assembly (May 1848).[8]

The king and the National Assembly wrangled over a constitution for half a year. In November, the government staged a coup first by adjourning the National Assembly and transferring it to the city of Brandenburg (November 9) and then by dismissing it altogether (December 5). The government promulgated a new constitution that very day.[9]

The National Assembly's draft "Decree on the Foundations of the Future Constitution" (April 1848) had introduced "the exercise of civic rights . . . independent of religious faith." The king's imposed constitution of December 5, 1848, similarly affirmed (Article 11) that "citizens enjoy local and state rights independent of religious faith."[10]

Whereas Prussia's revolution had in principle succeeded in introducing unconditional equality, the reactionary government gradually eroded it, much as Frederick William III's government had the 1812 edict. The constitution of January 31, 1850, affirmed equality regardless of religion (Article 12) yet effectively negated it by recognizing Christianity as the state religion (Article 14).[11] Subsequent administrative rulings upheld crucial provisions of the 1847 law and excluded Jews from state offices.[12]

Posen

The revolution improved the Jews' status in Posen. The constitutions of December 5, 1848, and of January 31, 1850, in proclaiming the equality of subjects, abrogated the June 1, 1833, ordinance's category of "tolerated" Jews and elevated them to the status of "naturalized."[13]

Baden

In early March citizens gathered in Karlsruhe and presented petitions to the Diet. A moderate majority empowered a committee to set to work on a new constitution; the Grand Duke appointed a liberal ministry and acceded to constitutional reform.[14] At the same time peasants in the countryside revolted against their oppressors: nobles and land registries, rent offices and Jewish creditors.[15]

On February 14, 1848, a liberal delegate, Lorenz Brentano (1813–91), introduced a motion in the Lower House to grant Jews full political and civic rights. Interrupted by revolutionary events, the Lower House first approved the motion on May 13 with one dissenting vote. In collusion with the government, the Upper House deliberately deferred the bill. The Upper House finally passed a law (February 13, 1849) that granted full political rights in state and local government but withheld communal rights, including residence and access to communal goods.[16] Baden's dualism of state and local rights survived the revolution.

Bavaria

The revolution forced the disgraced Ludwig I to abdicate. The new government under Maximilian II enacted a package of liberal laws (June 1848) that introduced freedom of the press, ministerial responsibility, and an enlarged franchise and abolished most feudal obligations.[17]

The Assembly's 1846 mandate to reconsider the Jews' status within three years had propelled the government to begin gathering information in 1847. In July 1848, the governor of Upper Bavaria submitted a report endorsing complete equality, including abolition of the notorious residence quota (*Matrikel*). The report cited the Bavarian Parliament's decision of June 4 to grant equal voting rights to members of all religions and the Frankfurt Parliament's expected decision in favor of equality.[18]

In March and April Maximilian turned against the revolution, disavowing the Frankfurt Parliament's Constitution and Declaration of Basic Rights and replacing many of his liberal ministers with conservatives. He devised a bundle of reformist legislation, including equality for Jews, intended to appease moderates and liberals. Maximilian II's government submitted a bill in May 1849.

Lower House committees considered the bill in October and it reached the Lower House floor for debate on December 10, 1849. Elected in July, this House was more conservative than its predecessor, creating a novel situation. With the government supporting the bill, conservative opponents were "challenging the state and attacking Jews rather than defending the state and Christianity against challenges from Jews and Liberals."[19] The debate extended for five days. Many deputies on both sides acknowledged that "press" opinion firmly backed the legislation whereas public opinion opposed it. Many deputies fought the bill because it abolished local rights, especially the community's prerogative to determine residence. The dualism of state and local rights played a critical role.[20] In the end ninety-one deputies voted for, forty against.

Newspapers covered the five-day debate; the final vote attracted extensive coverage. Opposition papers organized a successful petition campaign.[21]

Because of the Upper House's conflict with the government—the committee that presented the bill debate (February 15, 1850) opposed it—it was a foregone conclusion that that House would defeat the bill (29–7).[22] Thus the infamous residence quota (*Matrikel*) remained in place.

Frankfurt Assembly

The Frankfurt Assembly tried to rectify the Congress of Vienna's mistakes: it aimed to unify the German states with a new constitution recognizing equality of adherents of all religions, including Jews. Representatives from a number of states met in Heidelberg (March 1848) and issued an appeal for elections to a constituent national assembly.[23] Elections were held in May and the Frankfurt National Assembly convened later that month.[24]

The delegates took up the issue of the Jews' rights in regard to Article III, #13: "Religious confession will neither condition nor limit the enjoyment of civic and state rights [*bürgerlichen und Staatsbürgerlichen Rechte*]. [Religious confession] cannot be prejudicial to duties to the state."[25] The delegates to the Constitutional Committee immediately recognized that granting "equality before the law" was "tantamount to granting full emancipation to the Jews."[26] Most of the delegates assumed that the measure would not be popular, and one asserted that it would "have an adverse effect on practical conditions." Despite their reservations, the delegates voted unanimously to affirm the principle.[27]

The National Assembly's debate of the "Basic Rights of the German People," like that of the Constitutional Committee, turned on the constitution and the principle of equality. As delegate Beseler put it: the "Jews' legal situation . . . cannot be handled from the perspective of expediency; it has become a matter of necessity."[28] Justus von Linde asserted that any qualification of rights because of religion vitiated "freedom of conscience." In contrast to the German Confederation, which had extended equality only to the three Christian confessions, this constitution embraces "the principle of the free exercise of religion and of equality in state law" for all religions.[29]

Two delegates tried to inject particularist issues. Moritz Mohl (1802–88), representing Stuttgart, requested exceptional laws for Jews since, as an irreversibly "alien element," they engage in exploitative practices that are "pernicious to the [German] people."[30] Rheinwald wanted to ban the Jesuit order since it promoted despotism and injured Catholicism.[31]

Gabriel Riesser, elected from the Duchy of Lauenberg and then chosen as vice president of the Assembly, answered Mohl by accentuating equality. The Assembly had already agreed to equality for non-German speakers: Should Jews be disadvantaged because they speak German? Diets in Prussia and Bavaria had already voted for equality. He appealed to the law:

> Trust the power of justice [*Recht*], the power of uniform law [*Gesetz*] and Germany's great destiny. Do not believe that there can be exceptional laws without perniciously rending the entire system of freedom, without planting in it the seed of destruction.[32]

The delegates deferred Rheinwald's particularist amendment. They voted to close discussion and accept the Article.

Delegates who held negative images of Jews did not suddenly renounce them; those who felt ambivalent did not spontaneously become unequivocally positive. Rather, the revolution created that rare moment of constitution making in which the delegates addressed issues from the perspective of general principles. They conversed abstractly about citizenship as a political concept and the equality of all faiths as a matter of law. As Riesser indicated, the delegates had already agreed that, since "citizenship" was a political concept, non-German speakers, for example, Italians, Poles, and Danes, would also enjoy equality. The delegates similarly transcended the issue of communal rights so that the dualism of state versus local rights did not appear.[33]

The Frankfurt Parliament thus engaged in true constitution making. It followed the French National Assembly in making the conceptual leap from empirical particulars to political principles: whereas the National Assembly's debate on December 23, 1789, turned on the Jews, the truncated debate of September 27–28, 1791, addressed the constitution. Most of the Vormärz German state diet debates specifically addressed the Jews. In contrast, the Frankfurt Parliament's debate turned on equality before the law and the political concept of citizenship.

The "Basic Rights of the German People" became law on December 27, 1848. After the revolution's collapse, the Confederation Diet repealed it (August 23, 1851).[34] As one perceptive observer put it, "The Jew stands and falls with democracy."[35]

Italy

From Sicily (January 1848) uprisings spread across the peninsula. They first brought preemptive constitutions in Tuscany (February), then in Piedmont, the Papal States, and Parma (March). A new government emerged in Lombardy-Venetia as Venice and Milan expelled Habsburg troops.[36]

The new order incorporated changes in public opinion and legislation toward the peninsula's approximately 31,000 Jews. Since 1830 liberal writers, drawing on the debates in France, England, and the German states, had published numerous tracts in favor of removing disabilities.[37] Some Jewish writers had advocated conditional emancipation accompanied by regeneration; others claimed unconditional emancipation on grounds of justice and the rights of man.[38] Jews actively pursued "regeneration" (*rigenerazione*) through education, occupational change, and migration to polities, such as Lombardy-Venetia and Tuscany, that offered more favorable conditions.[39]

Pius IX introduced some minor improvements in the Jews' legal status in the Papal States in 1846 when he declared an end to compulsory conversion sermons and the humiliating carnival tribute and allowed a few Jews to live outside Rome's ghetto.[40] In 1845 Tuscany admitted non-Catholics to municipal office; in 1847, it permitted Jews to compete for university bursaries and enroll in the National Guard. In Piedmont liberals such as Count Roberto d'Azeglio led a campaign for rights while Jews sent deputations to meet with the king.[41]

The revolution swiftly ushered in equality. Tuscany enacted full religious freedom on February 17, Venice on March 22, and Modena on April 10.[42] Piedmont adopted a new constitution for Catholics (February 8, 1848) and ten days later extended parity to Protestants (Waldenses). Six weeks later (March 29, 1848), after Jewish leaders intervened to argue that the government needed to harmonize Lombard's liberal and Piedmont's repressive laws, the king applied the new freedoms to Jews as well. The government subsequently admitted Jews to the university and military service.[43]

Habsburg troops in the north and French troops in the south suppressed the revolution; it collapsed by the summer of 1849 and reversed the rush to rights. Tuscany rescinded its liberal constitution and canceled religious equality. Modena and Mantua abrogated rights and imposed fines. Papal Rome restored the ghetto and harsh rule. The significant exception was Piedmont: it became Italy's model for constitutional rule and religious equality.[44] In the Italian as in the German states, the revolution made Jewish equality integral to the attainment of constitutional government.

Habsburg

Protests enveloped the Habsburg Empire's urban centers. In the Pressburg Hungarian Diet (March 3, 1848), a forum of political activism since 1825, Lajos Kossuth (1802–94) demanded a constitutional Hungary. In Prague, a bilingual meeting first requested unifying the Czech lands and then a separate ministry resembling Hungary's. On March 13, 1848, demonstrators in Vienna demanded Metternich's resignation, while confrontations with the army turned bloody and riots erupted in the suburbs. The emperor promised freedom of the press and a constitution; Metternich resigned and went into exile.[45]

On March 31, the government abolished compulsory peasant labor (*robota*) in Bohemia.[46] On April 25, 1848, the emperor promulgated a constitution for

Austria and Bohemia that, modeled on those of Baden and Belgium, guaranteed freedom of religion and equality before the law (Articles 17–31). Yet it left to a future Parliament (Article 27) the issue of the many special laws governing the Jews' civil and political rights as well as the right to own land throughout the empire.[47] Once convened, the new Parliament would have a mandate to amend the constitution.[48]

The counterrevolution began with Prince Windisch-Graetz's assault on Prague in June 1848; it continued with his assault on Vienna in October 1848.[49] After crushing the revolution, Francis Joseph I issued a new constitution on March 4, 1849, that introduced uniform citizenship laws throughout the Habsburg lands based on jus soli.[50] This constitution granted to members of all faiths, including Jews, citizenship, freedom of occupation, freedom to buy real estate, freedom of residence (*Freizügigkeit*) that superseded local laws (*Heimatrecht*), and access to state offices, including the judiciary.[51] The government recognized the need to codify the new laws so that local authorities could implement them, yet failed to do so.[52]

Franz Joseph issued an order on October 4, 1851, for a new commission to revise the constitution. He personally deleted the passage guaranteeing equality to members of all religions.[53] His ruling left the bureaucracy and judiciary in a quandary. Which law was in force? The status quo ante? The constitution of 1848? Or the constitution of 1849?

On December 31, 1851, the emperor issued two laws that further confused the legal situation. One law abrogated the constitution (*Reichsverfassung*), the other the Basic Law (*Grundrechte*), including equality before the law for members of all faiths. Yet the constitution applied throughout the empire, the Basic Law only to the German Crown lands. Moreover, the abrogation laws contained a final qualifying sentence: the current laws remained in force until additional directives were issued.[54]

Which were the current laws? Administrators and judges pondered the issue. The emperor provided some direction when he ruled (October 2, 1853) that, in respect to the right of property ownership, the laws in place prior to the revolution were valid. He thus opened the door to further restrictions.[55]

After December 31, 1851, state citizenship remained dependent upon local residence rights (*Heimatrecht*).[56] As in Baden and Bavaria, the dualism of local and state rights remained intact.

Hungary

The Hungarian Diet (1848) delayed deciding on the Jews' status, in part for fear of fomenting urban violence. In Pressburg (April 23, 1848), a riot of apprentices forced Jews who after 1840 had settled outside the restricted Jewish area to return to it.[57] With Jewish representatives gathered to press their cause, the Diet passed two emancipation laws: one for the nationalities and a separate one for Jews (July 1849).[58] The counterrevolution imposed a special tax on Jews as an indemnity for their role in the revolution. After some negotiation, the government reduced the sum and agreed to commute it into an endowment for Jewish schools, a teacher's training college, and a rabbinical seminary.[59]

Galicia

Peasants disrupted a long planned noble-led Polish rebellion against Austrian rule in 1846 when they began to murder their noble landlords and burn manor houses. The Habsburg authorities applauded the peasants for subverting the insurrection; they punished the rebels by incorporating Krakow into Austria and fining the Jewish community for some Jews' participation.[60]

The failed rebellion restrained Galicia's 1848 revolution, which included peasant concerns alongside demands for representative government and national self-determination. A Lemberg delegation presented the imperial authorities with a petition for wide-ranging autonomy (March 19, 1848). To forestall peasant unrest, the Galician governor abolished compulsory peasant labor (*robot*) as well as patrimonial jurisdiction.[61]

At first the revolution brought Galician Jews relief from specific disabilities. On October 5, 1848, Parliament voted to abolish all special taxes, including those specific to Jews: the kosher meat tax (since 1784) and the candle tax (since 1794). This legislation, effective November 1, 1848, endured.[62] On February 25, 1851, the government abrogated the "transit tax" for Jewish merchants from Russian Poland.

The tide turned quickly, however. Local authorities did not implement the 1849 constitution's equality, claiming that they required explicit directives. The Lemberg authorities used the emperor's 1853 ruling to restrict Jewish settlement in Galician towns. Jewish deputations appealed repeatedly to the kaiser but to no avail. Jews continued to be deprived of rights of landownership, access to state service, and local rights—including municipal citizenship and residence.[63]

Political Participation (1815–1848)

The revolution entailed the "development of political organization and mass political participation on an unprecedented scale."[64] Jews for the first time engaged in national politics in the service of general causes.[65]

As we have seen, Jews had previously been admitted to local and municipal politics: in the Polish-Lithuanian Commonwealth and in some Tuscan towns in the eighteenth century, in Prussia, England, and France in the nineteenth century. They did so as individuals representing their own and other interests yet not those of a Jewish collective.

Jews had also been politically active in the state on their own behalf, as we have repeatedly seen as well. The Damascus Affair's (1840) "blood libel" was a cardinal example. At issue was emancipation itself: if Jews engaged in "ritual murder," killing a monk to use his blood in baking Passover matzah, then Judaism was an immoral and barbaric religion that disqualified Jews from citizenship.

Jews protested the blood libel and the torture of Damascus's Jews using the new public politics of mass meetings, resolutions, delegations, newspaper articles, and alliances with sympathetic Christian groups—in preparation for a delegation sailing to the Middle East. In England Moses Montefiore (1784–1885), head of the Board of Deputies, did so with the government's blessing. In France Adolphe Crémieux (1796–1880), a prominent lawyer who led the struggle against a special legal oath for Jews (chapter 17), did so in opposition to the government, since the Foreign Office (*Quai d'Orsai*) supported the accusation. The new Jewish press across Europe reported extensively on, and advocated aggressively in, the Damascus Affair.[66]

During the era of the French Revolution a few Jews had been elected to national positions in the Batavian Republic yet, as we saw, fleetingly. During the 1848 revolution individual Jews began to play a conspicuous role in national politics. In Vienna the physicians Adolf Fischhof (1816–93) and Joseph Goldmark (b. 1818) delivered rousing speeches and helped organize demonstrations.[67] Two Jews, a student and an artisan, were among the first demonstrators to fall in Vienna. At the public funeral on March 17, 1848, a priest, a pastor, and Vienna's Rabbi Isaac Noah Mannheimer (1793–1865) delivered eulogies.[68] Fischhof and Goldmark later served in the Reichstag alongside two Jewish deputies elected for Galicia, Rabbi Mannheimer, whom the Reichstag chose to serve as second vice president, and Rabbi Meisels.[69]

In the German states numerous Jews served as parliamentarians. Six Jews served in the Frankfurt Pre-Parliament and seven were elected to the German National Assembly. As we have already seen, Gabriel Riesser served as vice president of the Assembly (October 1848). In addition, "Jews were for the first time elected to the Parliaments or Constituent Assemblies of several states of the German Confederation: in Prussia, Bavaria, Brunswick, Mecklenburg-Schwerin, Saxony-Anhalt, Hesse-Homburg, Frankfurt, Hamburg and Lübeck."[70] In France two Jews held appointments as ministers: Adolphe Crémieux at Justice and Michel Goudchaux (1797–1862) at Finance. In Milan three Jews were elected to the National Assembly, while in Venice two Jews were in the cabinet.[71]

Conclusion

The revolution has mixed results. Revolution and counterrevolution temporarily dismantled key components of the confessional and corporate state, paving the way for enduring change. A notable achievement was that most liberals expanded their conception of individual rights and representative government to include equality for members of all confessions and equality of all the confessions.

The revolutionary cauldron helped the various opponents of emancipation begin to shape the potent phenomenon of modern anti-Semitism. They drew on venerable Christian tropes to turn the "Jew" into the symbolic capitalist and religious foe striving to exploit Christians and destroy the church. Some writers turned "emancipation" on its head: they declared the need for "emancipation from the Jews" who were engaged in a vast conspiracy of domination.[72] These tropes would fuel organized political anti-Semitism at century's end (chapter 19).

The revolution unleashed conflicts between nationalities or would-be nationalities, especially in the Habsburg lands. The very term "national minority" emerged during the revolution when the issue of parliamentary democracy collided with that of nationality rights. How could one reconcile "decisions by a parliamentary majority" with "the nationalities' rights" since the latter held a "minority" of votes? The term "minority" jumped from parliamentary discourse to that of national groups.[73]

Jews found themselves caught between competing national claims. Should they identify in Galicia as Poles, Ukrainians (Ruthenians), or Habsburg subjects? In Bohemia as Germans or Czechs?

Opposition to emancipation, the conflicts of nationalities, plus the violence against Jews in the early phase of the revolution combined to make some Jewish leaders look to the state as the one reliable source of emancipation. As Ludwig Philippson (1811–89), a rabbi, prolific author, and editor of the main Jewish newspaper in the German states (*Allgemeine Zeitung des Judentums*) wrote:

> All in all, we Jews recognize with gratitude that among all elements of the modern age it is the State, and above all and in particular the bureaucratic State, that has been and still is most open-minded towards us, since in every period of storm and stress the people rose up against us, and in every period of reaction it was the nobility and the upper bourgeoisie who did the same. Thus it is only the State . . . that grants us tranquility, justice and freedom, and in it alone lie our hopes for the future.[74]

CHAPTER FOURTEEN

Central Europe, 1850–1871

IT TOOK A THIRD SEISMIC EVENT to enact full emancipation in central Europe. Within a little over two decades the creation of the Dual Monarchy and the unifications of Germany and Italy completed what the two previous revolutions had begun: they sufficiently dismantled the corporate and confessional state to begin creating civil societies and constitutional monarchies, however imperfect.

The three developments were intimately related. Piedmont and Prussia both took to the battlefield to overcome Habsburg opposition to unification; Piedmont's success guided Prussia's ambitions. In turn, the Habsburg Empire's shattering defeats forced its restructuring.

The very nature of those three developments entailed new complications. Unification and restructuring left multiple forms of inequality intact and created new ones. The struggle for equality continued in a "post-emancipation" guise. The German Empire introduced a new dualism between the federal constitution and state laws that left aspects of the Jews' status in contention and inherited forms of discrimination in place. The new Kingdom of Italy had seized the Papal States; the Church opposed its very foundation. As one of the kingdom's beneficiaries, Jews became targets of intense Church opposition. The new Dual Monarchy unleashed competing nationalisms. Jews were caught in the conflict between various recognized "peoples" without the advantage of being one.

Italy

Piedmont was Italian unification's postilion. It was the only state on the peninsula free of Habsburg domination that possessed a potent state—indigenous monarchy, powerful army, and increasingly professional bureaucracy, combined with a moderate constitution (*Statuto*)—an elected parliament, and free right of association.[1]

In a decade (1850–60) of frenzied political activity Count Camillo di Cavour (1810–61) turned Piedmont into the peninsula's economically most advanced polity. He abrogated feudal tax exemptions and facilitated free trade, created a central bank and oversaw the foundation of a stock exchange, and upgraded infrastructure (railways, ports, irrigation, roads).[2]

To unify Italy under Piedmont's leadership, Cavour brought liberalism and the Savoyard monarchy into an anti-Habsburg alliance.[3] The first step came with Piedmont's 1859 military victories over the Habsburgs (Magenta, Solferino) that enabled the creation of a northern Italian kingdom: Piedmont annexed Tuscany and Emilia—though at the cost of ceding Savoy and Nice to France in exchange for its support. The next step was in the south. With the Bourbon Kingdom of the Two Sicilies in a decade-long crisis heightened by the monarch's (Ferdinand II) death in May 1859, Garibaldi and his 1,000 Red Shirts successfully invaded. As a nominal officer of Piedmont's army, Garibaldi gifted his conquest to Victor Emmanuel. Finally, with Garibaldi occupying the south, Piedmont invaded the Papal States, swiftly occupying some two-thirds of its territory.[4]

Cavour organized plebiscites for annexation. By early 1861 he could proceed to unify the territories, hold elections for Parliament, and see Victor Emmanuel crowned king of Italy. To resolve the administrative challenges of unification, Cavour extended Piedmont's legal system to the rest of the country. The "Piedmontization" of Italy was the expeditious, although in the long term perhaps not the best, answer to a baffling situation.[5]

As integral members of Piedmont's bourgeoisie, Jews were auspiciously located to participate in unification. After 1815 Piedmont's Jews largely retained the properties and businesses they had gained under Napoleonic equality. Piedmont's government did not fully and consistently apply the laws (Regie Patenti) that aimed to restore the ancien régime economy.[6] Jews were important in maritime trade and agriculture, textiles and real estate. Like Jews in the German states, they understood their status and Italy's fragmentation to be inextricably linked. They participated disproportionately in blood and treasure in the Risorgimento. As proud Piedmontese, they fancied themselves to be "cofounders" of unified Italy.[7]

By 1861 Jews had gained equality everywhere on the peninsula except for Venice, Mantua, Trieste, and Rome.[8] In Sicily a royal decree of February 12, 1861, granted non-Catholics full political and civil rights. The Neapolitan Provinces abolished all differences based on religion. The Kingdom of Italy extended to Venice the laws granting civil and political equality (August 4, 1866). In 1867, as part of a legislative package secularizing Church property and marriage, non-Catholics gained access to all positions in state and society.[9]

The reduced Papal States were the last to be incorporated. Pope Pius IX scandalized liberal Europe by colluding in the kidnapping of Edgardo Mortara (1858), a Jewish boy in Bologna whose nursemaid had allegedly baptized him as a sick infant. The incident could only have happened in the Papal States in which the Inquisition was active, the Church controlled the police, and Jews lacked rights. Rome's Jews, living on sufferance, conducted private diplomacy; Piedmont's Jews, as citizens, orchestrated a public, European-wide campaign. Neither effort succeeded.[10]

In Livorno Jews followed an exceptional path to equality. The *nazione ebrea* retained its corporate privileges (Livornina, 1593) until emancipation, except for two brief intervals. When Napoleon occupied the port, he granted equality. With the restoration, Jewish leaders successfully petitioned Grand Duke Ferdinand III to have the Livornina reinstated, albeit shorn of civil jurisdiction, which they found onerous. Some members of the community dissented, requesting equality.[11] Jewish leaders did indeed request equality in 1847–48, which the 1848 Tuscan constitution granted. With the constitution's 1852 repeal, the Livornina was restored.[12] Finally, Sardinia's 1860 annexation of Tuscany brought Livorno's Jews under Piedmont's constitution, giving them full rights.[13]

The Kingdom of Italy seized Rome in 1870 when France withdrew its troops. France did so in large part because of its impending war with the German states, although the ongoing Mortara scandal had discredited the pope. The pope excommunicated Victor Emmanuel and forbade Italians to vote in national elections with a policy of "neither elected nor electors [*non expedit*]."[14] With Victor Emmanuel II's extension of the law of March 19, 1848, to Rome on October 13, 1870, Jews throughout the peninsula had equal rights.[15] The unification process had pitted the Church and Catholicism against the temporal polity and its Jewish citizens.[16]

Judaism gained equality only after unification. Under Piedmont's "tolerance" of religions (1848), non-Catholic religions were regarded as "protected" or having a "quasi-privileged" status. The Supreme Court in Turin confirmed this construction of the law (September 6, 1871).[17] In contrast, Tuscany had awarded financial support to Jewish communities on January 23, 1860.[18] The Criminal Court (*Codice Zanardelli*; 1889) finally erased distinctions between religions by recognizing all of them as "freely admitted denominations."[19]

Jews erected edifices to their equality. Jews in Florence laid plans for a grand synagogue when that city was the capital (1864–70). The imposing Moorish-style synagogue they inaugurated in 1882 had a prominent place in a fashionable neighborhood.[20] In Rome the Jewish community bought one site in 1888 but renegotiated for a better riverside site in 1896. The Tempio Israelitico (1904), a monumental building in an eclectic style, was second in height only to St. Peter's.[21] In Turin the community launched plans in 1863 for an imposing synagogue. The architect-engineer hijacked the project, building the spire to such a fantastic height that the community could not afford to complete it. The Turin municipality took possession of the building, turned it into a museum to the Risorgimento, and gave Turin's Jews a sum to build an alternative synagogue. The resulting twin-towered Moorish-style building (1884) was imposing yet not grandiose.[22]

Jews integrated swiftly into the new state, gaining elected and appointed office. For example, General Count Giuseppe Ottolenghi (1838–1904), who had served in Garibaldi's militia, served as Minister of War (1902). Luigi Luzzatti (1841–1927), who sat in Parliament for half a century and was thrice Minister of the Treasury, held the office of prime minister (1910) twice.[23]

Opponents aimed to reverse Jewish equality. The Vatican and the Catholic press attacked Jews and Freemasons as the source of the kingdom's anticlericalism.[24] The Catholic press and Catholic politicians called for abolition of the Jews' equality while broadcasting accusations of world conspiracy and ritual murder. They merged their ideas with racism: some claimed that Italy was "a kingdom of Jews."[25] Moreover, on at least two occasions government ministers vehemently opposed appointing Jews to ministerial positions. Some candidates for Parliament faced opponents who declared them unfit because they were Jews.[26] In educational institutions Jews faced antagonism to their appointment as teachers and administrators as well as admission as students.[27] High levels of hostility accompanied high levels of integration.

German States

Bismarck's campaign of "blood and iron" achieved unification by following Piedmont's model: he first removed the Habsburg obstacle so he could create a primarily northern, Protestant Germany (*Kleindeutsch*).[28] Prussia's 1866 victory at Königgratz enabled it to establish hegemony by dissolving the German Confederation (1815–66) and founding the North German Confederation (1867). The victory against France at Sedan (1870) made it possible to proclaim a unified Germany.

The resulting Imperial Constitution (April 16, 1871) was in fact "a *treaty* among the sovereign territories," that is, a "confederation of sovereign principalities" (*Fürstenbund*) that Prussia dominated.[29] The larger German states continued to have ambassadors in each other's capitals, while foreign countries deputed ambassadors to multiple German states, for example, Berlin, Munich, and Dresden. William I was not, as he had wished, "Emperor of Germany": he wore the lesser crown of "German Emperor."[30]

The North German Confederation's constitution of July 1, 1867 (Article 3), had not fully established uniform rights for members of all religions: questions remained about Catholic minorities in Protestant states as well as Jews. Therefore the North German Confederation Parliament voted the Law of July 3, 1869, that abolished curtailment of "civil and citizenship" rights because of difference of creed.[31] Like Riesser in 1849, Eduard Lasker (1829–84), a Jewish lawyer and leading liberal who served in the Prussian House of Representatives and then in the German Parliament, intervened in the debate to oppose special laws, even those favoring Jews, since they would contradict the constitution's principle of equality before the law. Jews in numerous states submitted petitions.[32]

The Jews' equality became a "constitutional" issue subject to a new dualism. From the late 1850s states began to legislate occupational freedom by abolishing the guilds and local residence rights (*Heimatrecht*), thus putting an end to the dualism of state and local citizenship.[33] In the North German Confederation and unified Germany there were, however, fundamental tensions between the largely secular federal constitution and the still Christian state constitutions, not to mention inconsistencies in those state constitutions and their application.[34] Thus a new dualism of federal versus state law and administration arose in which equality was as fragmented and multiform as the emancipation process and unification.

Prussia

Prussia's conservative government exploited the 1850 constitution's fundamental ambiguity to limit Jews' rights and specifically to exclude them from state positions: officials regularly cited the Article (14) recognizing the "Christian state" rather than the Article (12) confirming equality irrespective of religion.[35]

With William I's accession to the throne in 1859, a liberal government reclaimed the Frankfurt Parliament's legacy by emphasizing Article 12. In some ministries, the discussion of the Jews' political status now turned on the question of equality before the law rather than the Christian state.[36]

In February 1859, the Interior Ministry enabled Jewish estate owners to exercise their corporate privilege to participate in regional and provincial diets. The government thereby incorporated a handful of wealthy Jews "into" an estate.[37] That same year Jewish municipal delegates received permission to participate in the election of provincial diets.[38] In February 1860 Minister of Interior Count Maximilian von Schwerin allowed Jews to exercise police authority and serve as mayors.[39] Jewish petitioners' sustained pressure propelled these reforms.[40]

In contrast, Ministers of Education remained adamant in excluding Jews from teaching positions. The Ministry of Justice similarly excluded Jews from the judiciary until 1869.[41] Despite the Prussian Diet's 1863 vote to overturn these policies, the ministries held firm.[42]

After unification, in defiance of the federal constitution and abusing the ambiguity of its own, Prussia continued to exclude Jews from positions in the judiciary, the army, schools, and universities: "Prussia was *de facto* a Christian state."[43] In the judiciary this meant that Jewish lawyers had difficulty being appointed to lower offices. It took a Jewish lawyer an average of eighteen years to be appointed a public notary; a Christian lawyer averaged eight years.[44] Higher offices such as courts clerks (*Assessoren*) remained largely unobtainable. When called to account, Prussian officials denied discrimination.[45]

Catholic politicians also lodged complaints, asserting that the number of Catholic jurists was far lower than the Catholic population warranted. Jewish leaders advocated appointments based on merit; Catholics desired quotas based on the principle of "parity," even if these were contrary to the 1869 Confederation law.[46]

A prestigious reserve officer commission was critical in fashioning an upper bourgeois career. The appointment required graduation from a gymnasium, one year of volunteer military service, and, during that year, superb performance in demanding courses as well as promotion first to the rank of lance corporal or corporal and then officer candidate. This selection process ensured that the reserve officers were a homogeneous "social elite" imbued with a "fierce *esprit de corps*." Since the army was under the kaiser's personal command (*Kommandogewalt*), he had to confirm all reserve officer appointments.

A few Jews did secure such appointments in the halcyon years after unification (1870–80). Although 20,000 to 30,000 Jews served as one-year volunteers by 1910, they failed to obtain such appointments after 1885. An increasingly conservative army officer corps deliberately rejected Jewish applicants. Jewish organizations, with the help of various political parties, protested vigorously and repeatedly against this discriminatory policy in print and in Parliament, claiming that it contravened the constitution.[47]

Prussia emancipated its Jews but not Judaism. Under the law of July 23, 1847, Prussia continued to recognize Judaism as a "tolerated sect" and Jewish communities as private associations. It denied Judaism the status of a privileged corporation under public law accorded to the Protestant and Catholic churches.[48]

Judaism's inferior status brought manifold liabilities. The 1847 law gave state authorities inordinate control over internal community affairs, such as approval of elections to the communal board as well as appointments of rabbis, cantors, teachers, and slaughterers (Articles 35–67). The law deprived the community of state subsidies for buildings and teachers and the ability to sue for libel. The law denied clergy the status of public servants and thus eligibility for state subsidies, exemptions from municipal taxation, and the right to supervise public schools.[49]

Still worse, the 1847 law applied only to the old Prussian provinces. The territories acquired after 1866 retained their existing laws. Prussia thereby replicated its farrago of laws after 1815.[50] It deliberately maintained an "unclear and disorderly" legal situation that enabled the Jews' "communal affairs to be regulated in contradictory ways by scores of anachronistic ordinances and edicts."[51] Prussian officials rebuffed Jewish leaders' efforts to form a central organization, fearing that it would enable Jews to become even more politically active.[52]

Embodying "a demand for emancipation," Berlin Jewry in 1866 inaugurated a monumental synagogue located on a prominent public street in the center of the main Jewish neighborhood and its panoply of affiliated institutions.[53] The Oranienburgerstrasse Synagogue, the largest in the world with seating for 3,000, was a technological marvel featuring iron construction and gas lighting. Its conspicuous Moorish style, including a gilded cupola, marked it as a decidedly non-Christian ecclesiastical building.[54]

The dualism of federal and state law came to the fore with respect to citizenship and naturalization. The federal constitution established criteria for citizenship and naturalization based largely on residence (jus soli). The individual states' considerable latitude in applying the law led to glaring disparities.

From 1870 to World War I, Germany relied on hundreds of thousands of seasonal industrial and agricultural workers from Russia. At the same time, some two million Jews passed through Germany while emigrating westward, and some 100,000 Jews from Russia and the Dual Monarchy, especially Galicia, migrated to the new Germany.[55]

From May 1881 Prussian Minister of Interior Robert von Puttkamer (1828–1900) adopted an increasingly harsh policy to exclude eastern Jews. He ordered the borders sealed, unnaturalized Jews expelled, and naturalization rigorously enforced. Expulsions included German Jewish women wedded to foreign Jews: the federal constitution deprived women who married foreigners of their citizenship. In 1885 Prussia expelled some 30,000 foreigners, including 10,000 Jews. Puttkamer also revived the 1847 law requiring foreign synagogue functionaries to receive a work permit directly from the Ministry of the Interior prior to employment.[56]

In 1885, dissatisfied with local officials' laxity in handling applications for naturalization, Puttkamer transferred the process to his Ministry. In 1890 the Ministry informed regional administrators that "the naturalization of Polish Jews is to be rejected in conformity with the existing policy." The standard phrase bureaucrats employed was that "the naturalization of foreigners of the Mosaic religion is in itself inadmissible." A later Minister of Interior, Bethmann-Hollweg, summarized the policy.

> The naturalization of immigrant Jews is banned by administrative policies; it is possible for the children of immigrants to acquire citizenship only if they were born in Germany, are militarily fit, and are found unobjectionable by the central authorities.[57]

FIGURE 9. Oranienburgerstrasse Synagogue, Berlin (1866). Monumental Moorish-style synagogue; a public building on a major thoroughfare. Leo Baeck Institute, call number 85.2 PID 1682239; Lithograph, Wilhelm Loeillot and/or Eduard Knoblauch.

Prussian ambassadors lobbied the other German states to enforce its harsh policy since, under the federal constitution (II, #3), individuals naturalized in one state of the Reich were eligible to settle in all the others.[58]

Continuing the trend from the 1840s, increasing numbers of Jews participated in municipal and state politics. The three-tier franchise made the commercial and professional Jewish bourgeoisie an important component of the liberal ascendancy in cities such as Breslau and Königsberg.[59] This political integration resulted from a "convergence of interests" with, and tactical alliance between, Jews and the middle class.[60]

Baden

Baden was the exception that proved the rule: here reform did in fact lead to full emancipation prior to unification. Concerned to stabilize the country following the tumultuous 1848 revolution, the government declined to undertake any measures that might arouse opposition.

With the accession of Prince Regent Frederick in 1852, however, Jews began to be admitted to local citizenship and local offices. In 1854 Jewish teachers began to receive the same subsidies as Christians, in 1855 rabbis and teachers the same exemptions as Christian clergy and teachers.[61] Moreover, by 1860 even a conservative deputy who had previously opposed equality admitted that Jews had become like their neighbors: "rural Israelites . . . are as educated [*gebildet*] as a rural Christian citizen and peasant are educated."[62]

In 1860 Frederick I, now Grand Duke (r. 1856–1907), and his liberal ministers (Stabel, Lamey), who settled a tempestuous conflict with the Catholic Church, were determined to unify Baden's laws, especially by making occupational and residential freedom universal.[63] The government presented a bill to the new Diet on January 20, 1862, for which it advocated on principle. It endorsed the individual's free development in society and employed the language of abstract citizenship, that is, "state membership" (*Staatsangehörige*). It was not a matter of whether Jews deserved rights, although they had successfully passed through the 1809 legislation's half-century "preparatory school." Rather, "humanity" and "civilization," the constitution and justice, demanded it.[64]

Among the Diet's members was Dr. Rudolf Kusel, the first Jewish parliamentarian in Baden, who represented Karlsruhe for nine years. He also argued that removing the Jews' disabilities was a matter of right, not benevolence.[65]

It is notable that the dualism of state versus local rights persisted to the end: local residence was the last barrier to equality. To avert opposition in local communities to admitting Jews to residence, the government had originally proposed a five-year waiting period on access to communal property and welfare. The Lower House extended that waiting period to ten years. Jews had to endure another decade of second-class status.

With the addition of that rider the government easily prevailed. The Grand Duke signed the law on October 4, 1862; it went into effect on October 15.[66] That same year Baden dismantled remnants of the confessional state by creating a central state agency to oversee education and the religious denominations.[67] In 1876 Baden legislated subsidies for rabbis' salaries.[68]

Bavaria

Bavaria confirms that reform alone, without the seismic event of unification, would not have produced full legal equality.

Gesetz,

die bürgerliche Gleichstellung der Israeliten betreffend.

Friedrich, von Gottes Gnaden Großherzog von Baden,
Herzog von Zähringen.

Mit Zustimmung Unserer getreuen Stände haben Wir beschlossen und verordnen, wie folgt:

§. 1.

Der §. 58 (früher §. 54) des Bürgerrechtsgesetzes ist aufgehoben. Von dem Tage an, an welchem dieses Gesetz in Wirksamkeit tritt, finden die Bestimmungen der Gemeindeordnung und des Bürgerrechtsgesetzes auf das Rechtsverhältniß der Israeliten zu den Gemeinden Anwendung.

Den Israeliten stehen darnach die in §. 1, Ziffer 1, 2, 3, 5, 6 des Bürgerrechtsgesetzes erwähnten Rechte der Gemeindebürger zu; in Betreff der Theilnahme an dem Gemeinde- und Almendgut und des Anspruchs auf Armenunterstützung aus den Gemeindemitteln (Bürgerrechtsgesetz §. 1, Ziffer 4 und 7) treten die nachfolgenden Paragraphen dieses Gesetzes in Geltung.

§. 2.

Die seitherigen israelitischen Schutzbürger erhalten von dem in §. 1 erwähnten Tage an das Gemeindebürgerrecht und übernehmen zugleich alle Pflichten und Lasten der Gemeindebürger, unter Vorbehalt der in §. 1, Absatz 2 erwähnten vorübergehenden Bestimmungen.

Von dem gleichen Tage an werden ihre Kinder so angesehen, als wenn ihnen das Bürgerrecht angeboren wäre.

§. 3.

Die seitherigen israelitischen Schutzbürger haben für das ihnen durch das gegenwärtige Gesetz verliehene Gemeindebürgerrecht die im §. 13 (früher §. 12) des Bürgerrechtsgesetzes bestimmten Antrittsgebühren nach Abzug dessen, was sie für ihre Aufnahme als Schutzbürger an die Gemeinde bezahlten, zu entrichten.

§. 4.

Bis zum 1. Januar 1872 hängt es von dem Ermessen der Gemeinden ab, ob und unter welchen Voraussetzungen sie den Israeliten den Bürgergenuß, so weit diese nicht jetzt schon Antheil daran haben, zukommen lassen wollen.

FIGURE 10. Baden's Edict of Emancipation, 1862. Leo Baeck
Institute, Joseph Goldman Collection, AR25802.

The government obtained approval for a bill on June 29, 1851, that removed all differences between Christians and Jews in matters of civil law, for example, marriage, property rights, and inheritance. Unlike the failed 1849 bill, this one passed without opposition because it avoided the sensitive issue of residence rights. It offered an improvement in the Jews' status without either granting full equality or infringing on the privileges of individual communities. The infamous 1813 residence quota (*Matrikel*) remained in place, as did restrictions on owning and operating breweries and taverns.[69]

Despite Jewish advocates' numerous petitions in subsequent years, the government showed little interest in introducing new legislation until 1859, when a group of liberals came to power.[70] A bill to abolish the *Matrikel* and the prohibitions on brewing and taverns elicited a tepid debate in Parliament and little controversy in the press. The bill passed by a virtually unanimous voice vote on November 10, 1861.[71] Fischel Arnheim (1812–64), a lawyer and the Jewish representative for an electoral district without Jews, played a decisive role in passing this law as well as the earlier 1851 bill.[72] In Bavaria as in Baden, the dualism of state and local rights endured: local rights were one of the last obstacles to equality.

Full equality came with further legislation. A law of April 16, 1868, abolished all distinctions of religions with regard to immigration; in 1871 Bavaria joined the Second Empire and accepted the federal constitution's equality. On March 26, 1881, Bavaria abrogated all remaining special Jewish taxes.[73]

Unlike Prussia's army, Bavaria's did give Jews reserve officer commissions, albeit in limited numbers. Jews only began to serve in the Bavarian army after its reform in 1869 did away with proxies (permitted to Jews and Mennonites since 1804). Indeed, since large numbers of Jews served, the army introduced a system of furloughs to enable them to celebrate the major Jewish festivals. After 1869 Jews gained reserve officer commissions. The percentage of eligible candidates admitted was far lower than for Christians and the appointments were to less prestigious units, for example, infantry and service corps and not the elite cavalry.[74]

Like Prussia, Bavaria maintained aspects of the confessional state by emancipating Jews but not Judaism. The edicts of March 24, 1809, and June 10, 1813 (Article 23), had accorded Judaism the lesser status of a private society.[75] Bavaria's Protestants received a similar status in 1809.[76] A ministerial decree of June 29, 1863, reorganized existing communal structures and made provision for new ones in areas where Jews had not previously resided. The decree did not revise the communities' inferior status.[77] In 1872 the Parliament did authorize state subsidies for rabbis' salaries.[78]

Various forms of administrative inequality persisted. Jews faced obstacles in receiving state appointments: whereas Jews accounted for 18 percent of Bavaria's lawyers, they comprised only 2 percent of its judges and notaries.[79]

Bavaria's naturalization policies (May 1871) generally excluded Russian and Galician Jews. As one ministerial official put it: "Russian Jews are normally not naturalized."[80]

Habsburg Lands/Dual Monarchy

The compromise that turned the Habsburg Empire into the Dual Monarchy or Austria-Hungary resulted from military defeat (1859, 1866) and fiscal frailty. After gradually suppressing the 1848 revolution the monarchy had turned to a neo-absolutist policy of authoritarian government and repression (the "Sylvester Patent") that reinstated aspects of the confessional state, embodied in the Concordat of 1855.[81] At the same time, Interior Minister Alexander von Bach (1813–93) dismantled key corporate institutions and introduced the lineaments of civil society and the unitary state (*Gesamtstaat*).

After the defeats in Italy (1859), his successors, representatives of a "new constitutionalism" of a functioning Parliament with legislative powers (1861), continued that policy.[82] Thus the government abolished serfdom in Austria (1849) and Hungary (1853); abrogated the guilds and introduced occupational freedom (1859, *Gewerbeordnung*); granted Protestants equality with Catholics (1861, *Protestantenpatent*); and promulgated a standard commercial law (1862).[83]

The defeat at the battle of Sadowa (1866) led to the compromise of the Dual Monarchy that was predicated upon a parliamentary regime. The "Basic Law" of December 21, 1867, created a quasi-constitutional monarchy. The monarchy's alliance with Austro-German and Magyar liberals ushered in the "liberal era" that held until 1879.[84]

Bach's neo-absolutist regime incrementally improved the Jews' status (one exception, affecting only the wealthy, was the 1853 decree prohibiting Jews from buying landed estates).[85] In 1852 Vienna permitted the Jews to organize a recognized community. By 1861 three Jews were serving in the Vienna city council. In 1852 Prague abolished the ghetto.[86] Freedom of residence in the early 1860s enabled widespread migration, especially to urban areas.[87] On January 10, 1860, the emperor abolished the prohibition on Jews serving as apothecaries and in some Crown lands as distillers and tavern owners. On January 13, 1860, the Ministry of the Interior permitted Jews to reside in Galicia and Bukowina's rural areas.[88] An imperial decree of February 18, 1860, gave Galicia and Bukowina's Jews who had graduated from a recognized secondary or technical school or served as army officers the same rights to possess land as Christians. A second decree that same day allowed Jews to buy agrarian lands and to work them in some territories (Upper Austria, Bohemia, Moravia, Silesia, Hungary) although not others (Carinthia, Tirol, Lower Austria).[89]

Full equality followed the compromise that created the Dual Monarchy. The "Basic Law" (*Staatsgrundgesetz*; December 21, 1867), which revived the 1849 constitution's civic and political rights, abolished all remaining restrictions for Jews (Articles 2, 3, 6, 14, 15, 16).[90]

May 1868's three laws began to erect a non-confessional state in defiance of the 1855 Concordat. The first restored the General Code's marriage laws, reducing the Church's grip. The second gave the state control of education, restricting the Church to oversight of religious instruction. The interconfessional law aimed to establish parity among the confessions, including freedom of choice in religion from age fourteen. The law also gave Jews equality as witnesses. The government repudiated the 1855 Concordat in 1870.[91]

The Jewish community first received full recognition as a religious association on March 31, 1890 (Protestantism had gained equality in 1874). The now unified community obligated all professing Jews to join. Freedom of belief and practice was guaranteed.[92]

The 1867 Basic Law (Article 19) recognized the equality of nationalities (*Volksstamm*): it accorded each the cultural right to defend its nationality and language "in school, office and public life."[93] Hungarians alone among the nationalities gained political rights. The government recognized Jews as a religious group; it expressly denied them the status of a people (*Volksstamm*). It treated Yiddish as a dialect or patois (*Lokalsprache*) rather than a proper language. Jews first received recognition as a "people" in 1918.[94]

The Dual Monarchy's imperial army was the "most important all-monarchical institution"; its multinational officer corps "bonded the empire."[95] The 1868 army law created a reserve officer Corps; the admission requirements were virtually the same as Prussia's. In marked contrast to Prussia, however, there was an "extraordinary overrepresentation of Jews" among Habsburg reserve officers. In 1897 Jews constituted about 18.7 percent of all reserve officers, in 1911 about 17 percent. These percentages were in keeping with their proportion of high school and university students.[96]

The Habsburg monarchs were known for ennobling Jews, the first in 1622, the next in 1789.[97] In the Vormärz (1815–48) it was easier for wealthy Jewish bankers to receive a noble title than equal rights. Even ennobled Jews sometimes had to apply to gain residence rights. Ennoblement did not affect emancipation for the titled individual let alone other Jews.[98]

In the liberal era (1866–84) the monarchy readily ennobled Jews for service to the state, especially those who aided the monarchy's always precarious finances (*Wirtschaftsadel*). Franz Joseph wanted the nobility to reflect the monarchy's national diversity.[99] As nationality conflicts and anti-Semitism mounted, the monarchy grew reluctant to grant Jews titles and awards.

In 1858, Vienna's community, numbering some 6,200, inaugurated a public synagogue (*Tempelgasse*) in the neighborhood in which most Jews lived

FIGURE 11. Dohány Street Synagogue, Budapest (1859). Monumental Moorish-style synagogue in a prominent public location. Tablets of the Law on roof. YIVO Album 1, cat. no. BUDAPE 22; 19th century Negroll 50a GDMAIN 48327.

(Leopoldstadt). Publicly visible, the Moorish-style synagogue became a model throughout central Europe.[100]

Hungary

Hungary's civil society remained imperfect. Prior to 1848 the nobles constituted the nation: they alone possessed active citizenship. After 1867 all male residents gained passive citizenship. The franchise was severely limited; the nobility's status endured. Hungary's parliamentary democracy was a notoriously corrupt noble oligarchy. Moreover, among the kingdom's multiple nationalities (Slovaks, Rumanians, Germans, Croats, Serbs, Ruthenians), Magyars alone constituted the nation (*Einheitsstaat*). The one exception was that, in its own "compromise" (*Nagodba*; 1868), Hungary accorded Croatians a special status.[101] Since the Magyars comprised only a slim majority of the kingdom's population, Magyar leaders pressured Jews to identify as Magyars in the voter rolls.[102] Conservative oligarchical Hungary had a more volatile nationalities conflict than did Austria.[103]

Hungary followed Austria in granting Jews equality. Law XVII (December 28, 1867) gave civil and political rights equal to those of "Christian residents" (Article 1) and abrogated all extant laws limiting rights (Article 2). Hungary thereby restored the civil and political rights it had granted in 1849. On July 10, 1868, the state recognized the civil status of the Jews' registry of births, deaths, and marriages, removing it from the Catholic clergy's oversight.

Like Austria, Hungary accorded Judaism equality only decades later: in 1895 (Law XLII) it recognized Judaism as being a "received religion" (*gesetzlich recipirte Religion*).[104] Hungary elevated Judaism's status concomitantly with introducing key elements of civil society: civil marriage, state registration of birth and deaths, and freedom of religious choice, including non-affiliation.[105]

Budapest's Jewish community inaugurated an enormous Moorish-style synagogue with a conspicuous public façade in 1859. The Dohányi Street Synagogue, with its prominent twin towers, accommodated 3,000 and pioneered the use of brick in Budapest's monumental architecture.[106] In 1872 another highly public, Moorish-style synagogue, seating 1,160 in a polygonal shape perhaps alluding to the Dome of the Rock, opened in Rumbach Street.[107]

Galicia

After the disastrous 1863 insurrection, the Polish gentry leadership opted for a pragmatic politics of accommodation. In exchange for imperial patronage, the Galician Diet declared its loyalty to the throne (1866).[108] From 1867 to 1871 Franz Joseph in fact granted Galicia greater privileges than any other Austrian province: the Poles gained virtual autonomy.[109]

The Poles controlled the provincial Diet and the Galician delegation to the national Parliament (*Reichsrat*) through manipulation and corruption. The Poles systematically suppressed the Ruthenians, who constituted an almost equal share of the population. Polish functionaries pressed Jews into the Polish cause by registering them as Polish speakers. For this specific purpose, the Poles wished to "assimilate" the Jews.[110]

In 1865 the Galician Diet voted against a motion that would have permitted Jews the unrestricted right to buy land and estates; the Ruthenian delegation led the opposition.[111] In 1866 the Galician Diet debated whether to accept the Austrian laws governing communities and cities. The law would grant Jewish institutions municipal funding. Moreover, by not recognizing confessional differences, the laws not only would have given Jews political rights but would have made it theoretically possible for them to influence if not control city governments in which they were often a majority or near majority of the population.[112] The Diet introduced quotas based on an 1866 imperial law stipulating that, to preserve the state's Christian character, two-thirds of representatives must be Christian.

With the support of the liberal faction, Jewish delegates in the Diet vociferously opposed these proposals. A Jewish delegation traveled to Vienna and submitted a lengthy memorandum to protest the legislation.[113]

Before the law could go into effect, the imperial government introduced the 1867 Basic Law that invalidated religion-based restrictions. The Galician Diet recognized that it had to accept imperial legislation; the delegates nevertheless debated the issue for two days. Proponents cited the Jews' equality of privileges in the Polish-Lithuanian Commonwealth and Macaulay's speech in the English House of Commons. Opponents pointed to the Jews' pernicious influence on all classes and, while endorsing the principles of equality, opposed its immediate implementation. After a liberal delegate's rousing concluding speech, the Diet voted overwhelmingly in favor.[114]

Jews entered Galician political life from 1861 to 1867.[115] The Ministry of Commerce established three Chambers of Commerce in Galicia on March 26, 1858, in which membership was independent of religion. Jews participated in Brody and Lemberg's Chambers, which in the 1860s gained the right to elect delegates to the Diet.[116] Jewish notables joined the Polish Election Committee and solicited Jewish votes for the Polish National Party. Three Jews were elected to the Diet in 1861, another in 1867.[117] In 1874, for example, Jews were elected to 261 municipal councils, holding a majority in 45 and over a third in 98, as well as ten mayor's offices.[118]

The 1873 introduction of direct elections to the national Parliament (Reichsrat) complicated Polish control. Only a miniscule percentage of the populace was eligible to vote; Polish bureaucrats manipulated the election apparatus. Jewish notables in Lemberg organized a "Jewish Election Committee" that then opened branches elsewhere in Galicia. This committee, which was aligned with German Liberals against Polish autonomy, entered an alliance with the Ruthenian Council (*Rada Ruska*) to support Ruthenian candidates in rural areas and Jewish candidates in urban ones. Three Jewish candidates were elected who then joined the Liberal faction. After 1879 Jewish delegates aligned with the Polish Club.[119]

Galicia appointed Jews to state positions yet in proportionately low numbers. In the judiciary, for example, most Jews were appointed to inferior positions, few to prestigious ones.[120]

Conclusion

In Italy Jews gained rights as Piedmont extended its rule over the peninsula. The Jews' equality came to symbolize liberalism and unification's triumph; that triumph's opponents attacked the Jews' equality and, where possible, discriminated against them.

Unified Germany developed a new dualism: whereas the federal constitution promulgated equality before the law regardless of religion, the individual states maintained their constitutions. Prussia's constitution defined it as a Christian state, and some state ministries (Justice, Education, Interior) and the army enforced that claim. In keeping, Prussia kept Judaism in a distinctly inferior status. Baden granted Jews rights yet only by deferring access to communal property and welfare. Bavaria abolished the infamous residential quota (*Matrikel*; 1861) and a decade later adopted the federal constitution's equality.

The new Dual Monarchy (1867) gave Jews equality by reviving the 1849 constitution. Judaism gained equality some two decades later (1890). Hungary followed Austria in reviving the 1849 constitution to grant Jews equality. Hungary elevated Judaism's status in 1895. Galicia gave Jews rights by accepting the imperial Basic Law that invalidated inequality. Jews entered Galicia's politics with alacrity.

Italian, German, Austrian, and Hungarian Jews built public synagogues, often monumental, often in a Moorish style distinct from surrounding churches, to mark their equality.

That Jews gained equality in the newly restructured Austro-Hungarian dual monarchy and newly unified Germany and Italy did not put an end to the emancipation process. Forms of inequality and discrimination persisted. Jewish leaders continued to pursue the politics of emancipation. Indeed, at the fin de siècle the defense of rights would enter an acute phase.

CHAPTER FIFTEEN

Russia and the Kingdom of Poland, I

TO MAINTAIN RUSSIA'S STANDING among Europe's "Great Powers," the tsars from Nicholas I (1825–55) to Nicholas II (1894–1917) endeavored to allow limited economic and social change without either diminishing their autocratic power or fundamentally altering society's structure. Reform therefore had tangible limits: as soon as a reform appeared to threaten the status quo, the tsar would restrict or revoke it.[1] This was in keeping with the tsars' practice of granting only revocable privileges: as convinced autocrats they did not recognize let alone promulgate inherent or irrevocable rights for any group.[2]

As the tsars extended the empire southward against the Ottoman Empire and eastward across the steppes, they developed policies toward the newly subjugated peoples. Those policies, in turn, affected their treatment of Jews and others in the European territories.[3]

Following the lead of Catherine and Alexander I (1801–25), the tsars continued to utilize significantly modified German and Habsburg policies. They turned the quid pro quo of regeneration for rights into an exchange of regeneration for privileges. Moreover, they granted privileges not en masse but rather to selected groups of Jews with demonstrated utility to the state.[4]

Whereas the central European states gradually shifted from an ambiguous policy of "into" and "out of" estates to an exclusive policy of the latter (chapter 14), the tsars continued to adhere to Catherine's policy of emancipation "into" estates (*soslovie*). The tsars did so to maintain the estates, even though that system was increasingly in tension with Russia's changing society.[5]

Russia's autocratic state did create and permit the emergence of elements of civil society in the second half of the nineteenth century, but these remained embryonic: an independent judiciary (1864) and local assemblies (*zemstvo*), periodicals and professional organizations, civic associations and the expansion of education.[6]

The estate system's rigidity gave rise to an intractable problem of classification, a "taxonomic muddle."[7] The private market town (shtetl) inherited from the Polish-Lithuanian Commonwealth did not fit Russia's economy and estate system. Whereas most Jews registered as urban dwellers (*meshchantsvo*), they in fact resided in rural areas and villages. Other Jews registered as merchants or agriculturalists.[8]

The government's response ranged along a spectrum, resulting in a "recurrent pattern of harshness alternating with minor concessions."[9] When it regarded Jews as dangerous to the peasantry because of their predominance in the liquor trade, it endeavored to remove them from rural areas, either threatening or actually depriving thousands of their livelihood and dislocating entire communities. After the emancipation of the serfs in the 1860s, the government prohibited Jews from purchasing rural land. From the 1880s the government was concerned to prevent radical Jews from disseminating revolutionary ideas in the countryside.

In contrast, when the government regarded Jews as economically beneficial, or realized that wholesale removal was impractical, it devised administrative expedients to allow them to remain in rural areas on a temporary basis.

The nineteenth century brought an additional factor to the fore. Tsarist governments regarded the Jews' numbers as a serious issue. The first partition had yielded some 50,000 Jews; the second and third partitions had brought the numbers to 290,000; by 1820, with the inclusion of the Kingdom of Poland, the Jewish population reached 1.6 million. As early as 1835, the Council of State advising Nicholas I discounted the possibility of granting Jews more privileges "because of the incomparably larger number of them amongst us."[10] By 1880 the Jews numbered 4 million (about 4.7% of the Russian Empire's population), by 1897, 5.1 million.[11] Migration to Russia from Galicia, Turkey, and other impoverished areas contributed to those numbers.[12]

Finally, in Russia as elsewhere, seismic events propelled fundamental legal changes. The Crimean War brought privileges to specific groups; the 1905 revolution political rights; the February 1917 revolution civil rights.[13] In the Kingdom of Poland the threat of insurrection brought Jews political rights in 1861 and some civic rights in 1862. In contrast to western and central Europe, in Russia and the Kingdom of Poland insurrection and revolution brought Jews political rights prior to civil rights.

Conscription

Nicholas I (1825–55) continued Alexander I's policies, which had drawn on Joseph II's precedents (chapter 10). Nicholas's advisors were cognizant of the German states' regeneration policies that were at their most intense in this period (chapter 12). Nicholas's government considered a variety of reform policies for the Jews: reclassification of status and abrogation of the communal executive (kahal), broadening education and creating rabbinical seminaries, and conscription. Revering the army as the premier imperial institution, Nicholas began with conscription.[14]

In 1827 Nicholas abandoned the policy in which taxpayers in general, Jews included, could buy exemption from military service. The government's "Jewish Committee" fully understood that in Prussia and the Habsburg Empire conscription was a step toward rights. Nicholas regarded conscription as a form of "regeneration" or "improvement" but only for individual Jews who would then qualify for integration "into" an estate. The legislation, following Joseph II, therefore exempted from conscription whoever undertook to regenerate himself by farming, working in a factory, or studying in a Russian school.[15]

However harsh the 1827 conscription law, it was neither motivated by hatred of Jews nor a premeditated plan for conversion. Nicholas had a visceral disdain for Jews, but he regarded them as loyal and capable of absorption into the empire.[16] Nicholas I's conscription offers a cardinal example of how Russia's autocratic regime adulterated the "enlightened spirit" of central European policy.[17]

Jews mobilized to oppose conscription. Leaders raised funds throughout the western borderlands to bribe officials to avert the decree. Once conscription began they submitted petitions to gain freedom of observance. The petitions to the government's Jewish committee in St. Petersburg failed; those to local officials and the emperor succeeded.[18]

Nicholas ordered the army to make provisions for Jewish soldiers to observe Jewish law, including paying "chaplain rabbis" (1827–53). Jewish soldiers organized synagogues; sometimes the War Ministry bore the costs. In some regiments, Jewish soldiers organized confraternities (*havurot*), parallel to those of Russian Orthodox soldiers, to attend to their religious needs and general welfare. Judaism was gaining the status of a recognized religion in the Russian army.[19]

If they had served outside the Pale of Settlement, Jewish soldiers were granted the privilege to retire there. Sometimes these ex-soldiers established new Jewish communities. Mostly artisans, these former soldiers constituted a politically loyal and religiously observant Russian-speaking lower-middle class.[20]

While the ordinances for adult Jews did not depart from the general conscription legislation, the "Cantonist" legislation for underage recruits did. Russia drafted only children of Poles (from age eight) and Jews (from age twelve).[21] The Cantonist battalions to which they were sent served as schools for a variety of children: sons of officers, vagrants, and impoverished nobles, as well as soldiers' illegitimate sons. In the 1840s there were 250,000 children in Cantonist battalions and schools.[22]

FIGURE 12. Jews as Russian soldiers, studio portrait, December 1887.
YIVO Institute, Collection RI, cat. no. Troitsck I, no. 3459.

Nicholas regarded Russian Orthodoxy as an efficacious means to integrate the empire's diverse peoples. The Cantonist schools therefore tried to convert all children—Greek Orthodox, Catholic, Protestant, pagan, and Jewish—to Russian Orthodoxy.

There was no advanced planning in the Jews' case; the schools began to convert Jewish children after they had arrived. Once the conversion effort started, the schools did report up the chain of command, including to the tsar himself. The more isolated the young draftees were from other Jews, including adult soldiers, the higher the percentage of converts.[23] In the 1840s a heightened campaign led some Cantonist commanders to coerce en masse conversions, sometimes through torture.[24] The overall number of Jewish converts was less than 1 percent of all Jewish conscripts, or about 10,000 to 15,000 from 1827 to the 1870s. The majority were Cantonists.[25]

Some converted soldiers reverted to Judaism once they had ceased being Cantonists or were transferred to new regiments. Sometimes the authorities prevented that reversion and meted out punishment since apostasy from Russian Orthodoxy was a crime.[26] The Cantonist schools and battalions produced

Jewish soldiers trained in a craft, literate in Russian, and versed in a broad range of secular subjects.[27]

The conscription policy strained communal solidarity. Leaders preferred not to conscript heads of households because of the economic consequences. They instead sought recruits among the unemployed, the poor, and minors. They thus tended to select children rather than adults. The rich and privileged shielded their sons; the sons of the poor and middling bore the policy's brunt. Freelance and community-hired kidnappers (*khappers*) roamed the roads and village streets, and sometimes even broke into homes, to snatch children. In a few places, rioters retaliated by attacking community leaders.[28] The community's policy of conscripting children swelled the ranks of the Cantonists far beyond the Russian army's expectations; it increased the numbers vulnerable to conversion.[29]

Codification

In 1835 the tsarist government promulgated a new codification of Russian law.[30] Nicholas's government also codified existing laws for the empire's recently annexed provinces, including the western ones, to integrate their inhabitants into the empire's legal system.[31]

The codification of laws for the Jews (April 13, 1835) combined Alexander's 1804 legislation with all later laws. The 1835 law was fundamentally ambiguous. For the first time, Russia recognized Jews as subjects.[32] At the same time, the law classified Jews as "aliens" (*inorodtsy*) alongside Muslims and pagans in Siberia and Central Asia.[33]

The law fixed the Pale of Settlement's boundaries, which theretofore had been fluid and de facto; it allowed Jews to move freely within those provinces. It ended forced resettlements. It allowed Jews to pursue their inherited occupations: buying, working, or leasing land and leasing taverns, inns, and mills. The law also permitted them to participate in municipal self-government, restoring Catherine's policies (1785). To preclude Jews from gaining too much political power, the government, following Prussian legislation, restricted them to one-third of representatives in municipal councils and prohibited them from serving as mayor.[34] The law required rabbis to perform the same civic function as Orthodox priests: keeping a register of births, deaths, and marriages. It thereby attempted to co-opt rabbis to the state's apparatus and bring individual Jews under state purview.[35]

Education

In the 1840s Nicholas I turned to a policy he had considered earlier, education. This emphasis was in keeping with his changed policy toward the Polish nobility after the 1830 uprising. Count P. D. Kiselev (1788–1872), the Minister of

State Domains, headed the Committee for the Determination of Measures for the Fundamental Transformation of the Jews in Russia (1840–63), the most influential and effective of such committees. Many of its members also served as architects of Alexander II's Great Reforms.[36]

Kiselev wanted to remake Russia's Jews in the image of their central European coreligionists: he thought German and Austrian policies could turn them into economically productive and enlightened subjects. He recommended education as the first step: Russia should follow

> the example of other states to begin the fundamental transformation of [the Jewish] nation i.e., the removal of those harmful factors that obstruct its path to the general civil order.[37]

The Minister of Education, Sergei Uvarov, similarly looked to central Europe:

> Believe me, if we had such Jews as I met in the different capitals of Germany, we would treat them with the utmost distinction, but our Jews are entirely different.[38]

Uvarov in general championed education as the key to Russia's "maturation" on its own terms.[39] He believed that education and enlightenment were fully compatible with tsarist autocracy and Russia's social structure.[40] He successfully reformed Russia's schools and universities in the 1830s and 1840s. He thought education could also achieve the gradual and peaceful integration of the various nationalities: Poles and Baltic Germans, Transcaucasians and Siberians, as well as Jews.[41]

In the 1840s Kiselev and Uvarov embarked on a regeneration program through government-sponsored schools and rabbinical seminaries. The committee found models in the *maskilic* schools of Riga, Odessa, and Kishniev.[42] The government forged a formative alliance with the *maskilim* that seemingly pitted them against advocates of orthodoxy, both Rabbinic (*mitnagdic*) and Hasidic. That alliance included co-opting Max Lilienthal (1815–82), the German-educated director of the Riga school, to advocate for the new schools in the Pale. Lilienthal, who was familiar only with the Jews of Riga, failed to win Jewish leaders in the Pale of Settlement for the cause.[43]

To facilitate the reforms, the government first subsumed Jewish schools to Uvarov's Ministry of National Enlightenment and then convened a conference (May 6–August 27, 1843) of prominent Jewish representatives.[44] As a result of the conference, the government issued a law (November 13, 1844) establishing Jewish primary and secondary schools that would teach both secular and Jewish subjects. Students would have the same privileges as students at Christian schools, especially exemption from the draft. The only equivalent schools in the empire were for Central Asian Muslims. The government considered the situation of Muslims and Jews to be comparable: an obscurantist clergy oppressed both.[45]

The schools were perhaps most successful in institutionalizing the Haskalah: the *maskilim* staffed the schools and nurtured the next generation of intelligentsia.[46] The schools attracted few students; the government shuttered most of them in 1873.[47]

The 1844 law also established two seminaries (Vilna, Zhitomir, 1847) to train teachers and rabbis. The rabbis, fluent in the vernacular and versed in secular culture, on the model of rabbis in some of the German states, were to serve the government.[48] This reform had a lasting impact: in many cases a dual rabbinate emerged. Communities hired a so-called seminary-trained "Crown rabbi" to satisfy government requirements; another rabbi attended to the community's actual religious needs.[49] In 1847 the government required Crown rabbis to maintain the registries ("metrical books") of births, deaths, and marriages.[50]

Kiselev's committee recommended another measure: the December 19, 1844, abolition of the kahal, the community's executive agency. Those three to five officials had been responsible for administering taxation and justice as well as internal policing.[51] The city councils were to assume responsibility for these functions, which the government would now closely scrutinize.[52] This action further delegitimized the formal community (Kehillah).

Two years later Kiselev's committee introduced a reclassification (*razbor*; 1846) that distinguished between economically "useful" and "useless" Jews. This classification built on Nicholas's earlier legislation that had borrowed its terminology from Prussia's June 1, 1833, ordinance for Poznań.[53] With the exception of farming, the "productive" occupations were conspicuously urban: guild merchants, licensed artisans, and townspeople possessing permanent residence. The nonproductive occupations clearly belonged to the market town (shtetl): petty trade and the liquor industry, unlicensed artisans and day laborers.[54] The reclassification gave nonproductive Jews five years to qualify as useful; they were to be conscripted at five times the normal rate. The reclassification was scheduled to go into effect on January 1, 1850. Postponed several times (1850, twice in 1852), the law became a dead letter.[55]

The Private Market Town (Shtetl)

This reclassification belonged to the state's assault on the shtetl. In trying to undermine the Polish gentry's power, Nicholas's government took aim at the private market town (Polish: *miastezcko*; Yiddish: *shtetl*) based on leaseholding (*arenda*) and the liquor trade. That organization of commerce originated in the Polish-Lithuanian Commonwealth's magnate-dominated corporate society; it did not fit Russia's economy and state. Indeed, the Russian word (*mestechko*) neither adequately nor accurately described the phenomenon. Perplexed Russian bureaucrats eventually came to employ the Jews' economic activities, that is, market days and the liquor trade, to define the private market town.[56]

The shtetl thrived for almost half a century after the partitions: it was a "servant of two masters," the Polish gentry and the Russian state, but "more often than not . . . [it persisted] in a vacuum of power."[57] From the 1790s the Russian state banned legitimate international trade, forcing Jews to smuggle, sell contraband, and collude with corrupt Russian officials.[58] The government in addition began to seize market towns from rebellious Polish nobles; it encouraged Russian notables and Greek orthodox gentry to purchase them.

The tipping point came in the 1840s. To expropriate the Polish nobility, the tsarist government endeavored to suppress shtetl trade and fairs by creating rival state-administered towns and fairs. To control the liquor trade the government excluded Jews from small-scale brewing and vending. The proposed 1846 reclassification (*razbor*) also fueled a flight of Jews from petty trade to artisanship and handwork.[59]

Great Reforms, Selective Integration

Russia's defeat in the Crimean War—the combined failures of antiquated weapons, inadequate transportation, and insufficient munitions production—called into question its Great Power status. Like Prussia's defeat in 1806, military failure made a major reform of society urgent and unavoidable. Alexander II (1855–81) freed some 22.5 million serfs (1861) and introduced representative assemblies (*zemstvo*) in rural areas to govern them (1864), established an independent judicial system to be staffed by trained judges and lawyers (1864), and reformed municipal self-government (1870). The tsar introduced universal conscription and a reserve system to create an army of would-be citizens (1874).[60]

Alexander II extended his reforms to Jews. This was the very period in which various German states and the Habsburg Empire enacted significant emancipatory legislation (chapter 14). Significantly, Jewish notables set the agenda. The government had attempted to control the liquor trade through a system of tax farming. In 1845 the government permitted Jewish guild merchants to work as liquor tax farmers outside the Pale of Settlement. The result was a group of inordinately wealthy Jewish merchants who appointed themselves Russian Jewry's new leaders.[61]

The merchants interceded with the government. They repeatedly submitted petitions (1854, 1855, 1856, 1859) requesting that the government grant privileges to selected groups of Jews who possessed utility to the state. They proposed that such Jews be integrated "into" estates and have the same privileges as other members.[62]

Alexander II subsequently offered privileges to small numbers of individuals he deemed deserving. In 1856 the government allowed Jewish doctors to be employed in state institutions.[63] In 1859 merchants of the first guild gained free residence throughout the empire; in 1861 Jewish university graduates received the same privilege.[64] In 1864 the government permitted Jews to serve as civil servants, especially as lawyers and judges in the newly established independent judicial system.[65] The 1865 privilege of free residence to certified artisans was perhaps the most significant. It was intended to be the equivalent for Jews of the serfs' emancipation since it potentially applied to large numbers.[66] Finally, in 1879 the government gave free residence to pharmacists, dentists, and midwives.[67]

Alexander's policy obviously continued Nicholas I's and its central European precedents. It also resembled other laws the partitioning powers issued in the second third of the nineteenth century. For example, Franz Joseph's imperial decree of February 18, 1860, gave Jews in Galicia and Bukowina who had graduated from a recognized secondary or technical school or served as an army officer the same rights to possess land as Christians (chapter 14).[68] Alexander's legislation was also in keeping with his extension of privileges to other groups: in 1863–64 the government admitted "Old Believers" into the merchant guilds.[69] In the same period he reformed naturalization laws in order to attract foreign "investors, engineers, merchants and skilled workers."[70]

Alexander II's privileges targeted urban professions. In contrast, his government continued to treat rural Jews as pernicious. In 1862 and 1864 the government prohibited Jews from buying land in the western provinces.[71]

In 1856 Alexander II abolished the Cantonist system. The military nevertheless maintained the system for another fifteen years. Despite parents' petitions that their sons be sent home, the army kept large numbers in service by transferring them to artisan units. The military finally recognized that Jewish Cantonists had the same rights as other Cantonists (September 24, 1871), allowing them to rise in rank or be transferred to a reserve unit.[72]

The 1874 universal conscription law in principle gave Jews parity with other conscripts. The Ministry of War at first attempted to enforce that parity. In contrast, the Ministry of the Interior persisted in introducing restrictions that separated Jews from other conscripts, beginning with the registration process itself. Eventually the War Ministry excluded Jews from military schools and set a quota of 3 percent on applications for promotion.[73] Moreover, in response to accusations of Jews dodging the draft, the Ministry of the Interior closely monitored the conscription process, employing a method of computation applied exclusively to Jews that inflated the number of draft dodgers.[74]

The 1870 Municipal Law granted Jews the privilege of participation. Yet the government revived the proviso in Nicholas I's 1835 codification that echoed legislation for Galicia and Posen: it restricted Jews to one-third of aldermen and barred them from the post of mayor.[75]

Alexander's Great Reforms transformed selected groups of Jews. Some established new communities in Moscow, St. Petersburg, and Kiev.[76] The men who founded the Society for the Promotion of Enlightenment among the Jews of Russia (1863) undertook similar tasks to Jewish organizations in the German states: they gave financial aid to Jewish university students and supported vernacular (Russian) publications, including a Bible translation (1872).[77] Jews in Odessa, St. Petersburg, and Moscow created a press and public sphere, much like Jews in western and central Europe in the first half of the nineteenth century. Initially in two languages (Russian and Hebrew), eventually in three (Yiddish), the press became a political forum and fount of legitimacy for the *maskilim* and other intellectuals.[78]

Kingdom of Poland

To recognize Polish national aspirations, the Congress of Vienna created the Kingdom of Poland as the successor to Napoleon's Duchy of Warsaw. The kingdom was a semiconstitutional state with its own government, legislature, and army. The estate system remained intact: the burghers gained political rights although the nobles retained power. The kingdom was connected to Russia through a dynastic union with the Romanovs.[79]

The kingdom in 1820 had a population of some 400,000 Jews. It perpetuated the Duchy of Warsaw's legal arrangements. Contrary to the Code Napoléon, the duchy had used the pretext of the Infamous Decree to deprive Jews of civil and political rights, including municipal citizenship, as well as prohibiting the purchase of real estate (chapter 10).

The kingdom chose to maintain the Infamous Decree's restrictions in 1818, even though it publicly pronounced the Duchy of Warsaw's laws invalid.[80] The kingdom retained or adopted other forms of inequality as well. Since Jews were not citizens, they were excluded from teaching positions and the civil service, from law and medicine, apothecary and land surveying.[81] Warsaw and fifty-five other towns retained designated Jewish quarters.[82] Jews were exempted from military service in return for payment of a huge recruitment tax.[83] To prevent smuggling, the government in 1823 and 1834 forbade Jews without proper occupations to live in designated border zones.

In 1822 the government abolished the official community (kahal) and replaced it with congregational boards. These boards essentially continued the community's work with the same personnel but diminished authority. The government concomitantly abolished Jewish confraternities, especially burial societies (March 1822).[84]

The 1830 revolt brought some Jews into politics. Three hundred served in the Warsaw National Guard; another fourteen hundred formed a less prestigious civil guard.[85] After the ill-prepared revolt's dismal failure, the kingdom lost the major pillars of independence. Russia abolished the Sejm and the army, replaced the constitution with an Organic Statute (February 14–26, 1832) that maintained the legal status quo, and appointed a Russian viceroy, Ivan Paskevich, who ruled for a quarter century. The tsarist government erected a high tariff barrier that crippled the kingdom's economy.

The kingdom introduced conscription on January 1, 1844, and abolished the community's exemption fee. The initial levy was nine hundred Jewish recruits. Substitutes were allowed, though that privilege was abolished in 1874 when the government established a lottery.[86]

Paskevich's government continued to promulgate discriminatory legislation. It tightened the prohibition on Jews producing and selling alcohol in villages (May 1848); excluded Jews from the slaughter of animals in villages (June/July 1851); and reinstated all the restrictions on Jewish residence in towns (August 1854).[87] In consequence, throughout Paskevich's reign, Jewish leaders applied for collective relief from discrimination while individual Jews appealed for exemptions.[88] In 1850 two Jewish notables gained hereditary citizenship and the privilege to purchase land and transmit it to their heirs.[89]

In July 1846 Paskevich introduced legislation forbidding Jewish clothes, softened by a four-year amnesty. In 1851 the legislation was reinforced, forbidding any clothing other than European and prohibiting women from shaving their heads after marriage. Implementation was episodic. The government gave the fines it collected to various Jewish charities, for example, hospitals, orphanages, and poorhouses. The prohibition for women was canceled in 1862, the one for men in 1880.[90]

Alexander II introduced a new era of reform. He amnestied Poles exiled to Siberia after the insurrection and reopened some shuttered Polish institutions, for example, Medical-Surgical Academy. In 1858, he lifted the tariff barrier. Nevertheless, in November 1857 the kingdom reiterated the ban on Jews purchasing real estate and in 1858–59 (Civil Service law) reinstated all existing restrictions.[91]

Alexander II appointed as viceroy a conservative Polish magnate, Count Wielopolski (1803–77), who rejected insurrection. Wielopolski aimed to promote civil society, industry, and the bourgeoisie as well as reforms in agriculture following the model of Prussian Poland. He introduced legislation liberating the serfs from labor services that Alexander II sanctioned on May 16, 1861.[92]

Wielopolski regarded Jews as a critical element of the bourgeoisie and the restructuring of Polish society through the gradual dissolution of the estates. He endeavored to gain their loyalty.[93] His 1861 reform of the towns admitted Jews to municipal citizenship by granting them political rights in self-governing councils. In those same years key associations began to admit Jews for the first time.[94]

Against a background of demonstrations, revolt, and the imposition of martial law (October 14, 1861), Wielopolski proposed legislation derived from a petition Warsaw Jewish leaders submitted in April 1861.[95] The legislation granted Jews equality with Polish burghers ("into" estates), arguing that this followed from the grant of political rights. With an eye to quelling the mounting insurrection, the tsarist government approved the legislation (June 5, 1862).[96]

Jews now enjoyed some of the burghers' fundamental privileges: freedoms of residence and movement, with the right to buy urban and rural real estate. One communal tax replaced all special taxes. They gained juridical standing: Jews could give testimony in courts and in notarial records.[97]

The law was not a principled grant of equality but rather a conditional emancipation that, by removing restrictions, inserted Jews "into" an estate. The law left intact restrictions on occupations (trade, handicrafts, industry) as well as public positions (lawyers, judges, land surveyors).[98] It resembled early nineteenth-century decrees of partial emancipation in the German states, for example, Baden (1809) and Bavaria (1813). It was fully in keeping with Wielopolski's compromise legislation that liberated peasants from enforced labor without granting them freeholds. It put the Jews in the parlous position of gaining rights at the very moment Poles were losing them.[99]

Greater occupational freedom quickly followed: in 1866 Jews were permitted to be advocates; in 1876 they were admitted to state posts.[100] Yet animus against Jews in rural life persisted: a prohibition on producing and selling alcohol in villages remained on the books, as did a law forbidding Jews from caring for Christian children.[101]

To celebrate its new rights, Warsaw's lay leadership erected a grand public synagogue (Tłomackie Street, 1878), a classicizing building seating some eleven hundred. In Łódź community leaders built a public synagogue in 1883 (Zielona Street).[102]

The failed 1863–64 revolt virtually swept away the Kingdom of Poland. Russia incorporated the area into the empire as the "Vistula region" and subjected it to Russification. The tsarist government appointed a Russian governor-general and bureaucracy and made Russian the language of administration (1867) and the courts (1878). The tsarist government also stationed some 200,000 troops in the area.[103]

Conclusion

Russia and the Kingdom of Poland displayed a specific pattern of emancipation. Significantly modifying central European legislation, tsarist governments held to a policy of regeneration for privileges that placed individuals "into" estates.

Nicholas I employed regenerative policies of conscription and education. His codification of law solidified the Pale of Settlement. His effort to weaken the Polish nobility led to a concerted campaign to destroy the shtetl's economy.

In the era of Great Reforms Alexander II extended privileges to individual Jews considered deserving by integrating them "into" estates. His reform favored urban Jews; he continued to discriminate against rural and shtetl Jews. He abolished the reviled Cantonist system. His reforms gave rise to new urban Jewish communities (Moscow, St. Petersburg, Kiev).

The Kingdom of Poland continued its discriminatory policies (chapter 10). In the first half of the nineteenth century, it renewed the Infamous Decree, enacted occupational and residential restrictions, and tried to obstruct Jews' participation in the rural economy. With Alexander II's reforms, a new viceroy, Count Wielopolski, introduced a conditional emancipation "into" estates.

By the 1860s–1870s the Jews of Russia and the Kingdom of Poland had begun to enjoy forms of equality, however circumscribed. Many Jewish leaders expected that in time the government would expand that equality. The 1880s would complicate those expectations.

CHAPTER SIXTEEN

Russia and the
Kingdom of Poland, II

AS ALEXANDER III (1881–94) AND NICHOLAS II (1894–1917) increasingly rejected the "west" and its reforms to search for an indigenous Russian alternative, they began to limit or abolish the privileges Alexander II's Great Reforms granted to the Jews and to impose ever harsher restrictions. Their policies became anomalous; treatment of the Jews did not cohere with policies toward other groups. Moreover, the Jews became symbolically significant to Russia's struggle for its future: they became central to the effort to forge a reactionary ideology. That central role coincided with the emergence of a new organized political anti-Semitism across Europe (chapter 19).

Pogroms, May Laws, Restrictions

In opposition to his predecessor's Great Reforms, Alexander III (1881–94) embarked on a campaign of counterreforms to preserve the status quo by buttressing the nobility's position.[1] The counterreforms aimed to enhance the privileges of Russians (Russification) by diminishing those of religious minorities (Catholics, Muslims, Jews) and national groups (Poles, Finns, Jews), especially in the western territories.[2]

For some fourteen months after the assassination of Alexander II, pogroms roiled southern and southwestern Russia, for example, in Ukraine and New Russia. The state was not directly responsible for the pogroms. Local authorities—whether from ill will, incompetence, or both—procrastinated in many places in suppressing the pogroms. Many perpetrators of the pogroms probably believed that the new tsar had issued an order "to beat the Jews."[3] Stressing the Jews' alleged merciless exploitation of Russians, Alexander III's government held the victims responsible and introduced punitive measures.

Alexander slowly replaced his predecessor's "selective integration" with a policy of "integral segregation."[4] The laws of May 3, 1882, intensified the Jews' residential concentration, creating a "pale within the pale" by prohibiting settlement outside the Pale's towns. The laws further impoverished the Jews by forbidding the purchase of real estate and, of greater consequence, the leasing of estates. Finally, the laws proscribed trade on Christian holidays. These "Provisional Regulations" were administrative decrees rather than statutory law; they remained in place until the end of tsarist rule.[5]

Alexander's policy toward the Jews veered toward the anomalous: other groups were not subjected to so many administrative acts and laws enforcing such a sustained harsh policy of discrimination promoting segregation.[6]

In 1886 the government deprived Jews of the privilege of participating in rural self-government (*zemstvo*). In 1887 the government transferred two cities (Taganrog, Rostov) from a province in the Pale (Ekaterinoslav) to one outside it forbidden to Jews (Don) and proceeded to expel Jewish residents. The same year the Senate forbade Jews to move from one rural area to another.[7] Segregation of Jewish soldiers increased after the Balkan Wars; it took hold in the 1880s.[8] In 1890–92 the government expelled as many as twenty thousand Jews, primarily artisans, from Moscow and St. Petersburg.[9]

The government began to curtail privileges Jews had gained during the Great Reforms in July 1887 by introducing quotas (*numerus clausus*) in secondary schools and universities (10% in the Pale, 5% outside, 3% in the capitals). This temporary administrative decree exemplified the government's heightening of general policies vis-à-vis Jews.[10] Tsarist governments were fundamentally ambivalent about the lower estates' access to education, fearing it threatened the estate system. For example, once it had emerged that Uvarov's reformed schools had succeeded in graduating a considerable number of students from the lower estates, Nicholas I restricted admissions (1848).[11] Under Alexander II some ministers feared Jews were overcrowding the schools and would overwhelm the estates.[12] Debated extensively by the press and local authorities, Alexander III's quotas aimed to defend the estates but also to prevent Jewish students from dominating the professions and swelling the ranks of revolutionaries.[13]

In November 1889, the government limited admission to the bar by requiring the Minister of Justice to approve each candidate.[14] Local restrictions followed. The Odessa bar expelled thirty-two Jewish apprentice lawyers; the Moscow bar (1890) voted to cease admitting Jews as apprentice lawyers altogether.[15] These restrictions had a significant impact: since the civil service and universities were virtually closed, law was the sole arena of employment for university-educated Jews.[16]

Alexander III's counterreforms propelled Jewish organizations to expand their scope. The Odessa branch of the Society for the Promotion of Enlightenment among the Jews (1863) responded to the quotas, and the continuing influx of Jewish immigrants, by subsidizing existing schools and founding new ones, both academic and vocational. In addition, the society assisted the poor with food, clothing, and housing.[17] A change in the society's central leadership in the 1880s and early 1890s brought a new direction. A cadre of lawyers turned to the courts to defend the Jews' privileges: they used a recently reformed state institution to challenge the state.[18]

Reactionary Utopia

The struggle over state policy that began in the concluding years of Alexander III's reign and dominated the first decade of Nicholas II's (1894–1917) played out in the conflict between two ministries. Serge Witte, the Minister of Finance (1892–1903), endeavored to spur Russia's industrialization by fostering capitalism and civil society. He oversaw the building of the Trans-Siberian railroad and put Russia on the gold standard (1897). Witte favored the Jews' gradual emancipation.[19]

In principled opposition, D. A. Tolstoi and later V. K. Pleve at the Ministry of the Interior aimed to maintain the estate structure and buttress the landholding nobility. They envisioned an agrarian, corporatist, and autocratic "reactionary utopia" self-consciously at odds with "Europe." For these anti-constitutionalists, the Jews personified the twin evils of capitalism and revolution. Tolstoi and Pleve embraced anti-Semitism: they championed repressing the Jews, including the wealthy.[20]

The ministries' struggle yielded contradictory policies. In 1903 the government prohibited Jews belonging to the First Merchant Guild or holding a university degree from buying land outside the Pale of Settlement's towns. That prohibition also applied to joint-stock companies.[21] That same year (May 1903), to relieve overcrowding, the government permitted Jews to reside in 101 formerly restricted villages in the Pale and to purchase real estate, and later added another 57 localities.[22]

The start of the Russo-Japanese War brought a loosening of restrictions. In March 1904, the government prohibited expulsions of Jews from interdicted areas. In June 1904, the government allowed Jews into the previously closed border zone. Moreover, the government appointed five Jewish apprentice lawyers to the bar. At war's end, the government resumed expulsions.[23]

The government began to revive the charge of ritual murder, pursuing cases in 1900 (Blondes), 1903 (Kishniev), and 1911 (Beilis, Kiev). In the last, the jury acquitted the defendant but ominously upheld the validity of ritual murder.[24] The Defense Bureau of the Society for the Promotion of Enlightenment among the Jews provided critical legal assistance in these trials. The society also established a press bureau to disseminate information at home and a branch in Berlin to do the same abroad.[25]

Unlike what had occurred in the 1881–82 pogroms, local officials colluded in those in Kishniev (1903) and before (1904) and during (October 1905) the

FIGURE 13. "Great Synagogue" in Vitebsk, provincial city in northern province of Pale of Settlement. YIVO Record ID 3571, Collection R1, Catalog Vitebs 46 Frame 50644.

revolution. Either officials did not take precautions or they allowed anti-Semitic publications to propagate the blood libel and other allegations, or they instructed troops not to intervene. Central government officials in the Ministry of the Interior may have colluded as well. The population assumed, now correctly, that the government condoned violence against Jews, especially during the Easter season (April 6–8, 1903).[26]

The Defense Bureau of the Society for the Promotion of Enlightenment among the Jews supplied legal assistance to the pogrom victims seeking government reparations. Its lawyers used the courtroom to expose official culpability and collusion.[27]

Some Jewish leaders understood the pogroms to be a direct result of their inferior legal status: the government did not afford them equal protection. The conspicuous handful of inordinately wealthy Jews only inflamed the situation.[28] The Society for the Promotion of Enlightenment among the Jews and the Jewish socialist party, the Bund, encouraged Jewish communities to form self-defense units.[29]

Revolution

Russia's ignominious defeat in the war with Japan aroused widespread unrest. The intelligentsia and middle class mobilized through banquet and petition campaigns and the formation of professional unions, the masses through demonstrations and a general strike. Together they fomented the 1905 revolution. In his manifesto of October 17, 1905, Tsar Nicholas II reluctantly granted constitutional government and civil equality. He deliberately withheld such rights from Jews.[30]

The prospect of an elected legislature encouraged the organization of political parties and the formation of the umbrella Union of Unions. Jews organized their own umbrella Union for the Attainment of Full Equality for the Jewish People in Russia (March 1905) that included all the Jewish parties (Liberals, Zionists, Bundists) and joined the Union of Unions (chapter 20).

The Union for the Attainment of Full Equality for the Jewish People in Russia had to intervene to secure Jews the franchise. A delegation convinced Witte, then prime minister, to delete the paragraph that would have denied Jews voting rights. Witte in turn succeeded in convincing the Council of Ministers and the tsar to approve the change.[31]

The result was a singular situation in the history of emancipation: Jews gained political rights prior to having civil rights.[32] This situation also obtained in the Kingdom of Poland; it was a characteristic of the east European pattern of emancipation.

In November 1905 Witte's government extended a new privilege: it permitted joint-stock companies with Jews as shareholders or senior employees to acquire land outside the Pale of Settlement.[33]

Although the first Duma had minimal power, the tsar and his ministers reduced each succeeding Duma's independence by manipulating its electoral composition and suppressing dissent.[34] The Union of Unions and the first and second Duma supported equality for Jews. The Kadets (Constitutional Democrats) understood that without equality for Jews Russia could not attain full political and civil liberty. They alone spoke in favor of rights for Jews at the Duma and tried to introduce legislation. Muslim groups seeking equality also allied with the Kadets.[35]

The tsar dissolved the first Duma before delegates voted on equality for Jews. The Kadets did not manage to propose similar legislation in the short-lived second Duma.[36] The less democratic third (1907) and fourth Duma (1912) did not consider such legislation. With the outbreak of the world war the Kadets joined the "Progressive bloc" that deferred discussion of rights for Jews. Jews felt betrayed.[37]

The revolution was "the high point of the emancipationist faith."[38] Six thousand Jews signed a petition in 1905 demanding equality as their inherent right

> as men who are aware of their human dignity and are conscientious citizens of a modern state. We do not expect that right to be bestowed upon us as an act of grace or magnanimity or as a matter of political expediency, but as a matter of honor and justice.[39]

The Union for the Attainment of Full Equality for the Jewish People in Russia energetically participated in the elections.[40] Twelve Jews gained seats in the first Duma: nine were Kadets; three belonged to the left-leaning Turdoviki (Labor Group). Maxim Vinaver (1862–1926), a prominent lawyer at the forefront of liberalism and the struggle for Jews' rights, nominally led the Jewish deputies, who did not constitute an official bloc.[41] The Jewish deputies debated whether to ask for Jewish rights separately or as part of a general grant of civil rights.

After the dissolution of the first Duma, Jewish politicians formed the Jewish People's Group (February 1907) to lobby on behalf of emancipation and reform of the Jewish community.[42] In the second Duma the number of Jewish delegates dropped to four. In the third Duma, Jewish deputies collected signatures of 166 deputies on a petition to abolish the Pale of Settlement.[43]

As sustained countermeasures quashed the revolution, the government imposed additional restrictions on Jews. In 1908 the government turned the ordinance that imposed the quota (numerus clausus) in education into an imperial law. In March 1911, the government applied that quota to "externs," autodidacts sitting exams for a high school diploma. In 1909 the government excluded Jews from participation in the rural assemblies of self-government (*zemstvo*) introduced to the western provinces.[44] The government disenfranchised Jews in a variety of places and expelled Jews from some locales (1911).[45]

War

Jews alone among "aliens" (*inorodtsy*) were liable for military service; officers' commissions were prohibited.[46] Altogether the government and military administration expelled some 600,000 Jews from the theater of war, including the April 1915 deportation of 190,000 Jews from Kaunus and Kurland. Those banished from the Pale struggled to gain residence in the interior. Wives lost their residence rights when husbands were called for service.[47]

The massive deportations forced the government to extend the Pale of Settlement (August 15, 1915). In keeping with long-standing policy, the measure opened towns and cities but not the countryside. The measure was temporary: Jews were forbidden to purchase real estate in the new areas.[48] At the same time (August 1915) the government admitted veterans and their children to educational institutions outside the existing quota. New regulations were issued for the legal profession that lifted all restrictions for Muslims and Karaites but imposed quotas for Jews (15% within the Pale; 10% in mixed districts; and 5% outside the Pale). Jews with the requisite five years of experience gained promotion to the rank of certified lawyer. These regulations aided established lawyers but made prospects bleak for aspiring lawyers and law students.[49]

Jews finally gained full civil rights with the tsar's abdication. The provisional government dismantled the estate (*soslovie*) system dating from Catherine's reign. On March 20, 1917, it issued the decree, "On the Revocation of Religious and National Disabilities," that abolished all restrictive legislation, including a list of 150 laws applied to Jews.[50]

In the period after 1905–7 Jewish activists had shifted their attention from the Duma, under conservative control, to communal organizations. They helped to develop, albeit modestly, the sinews of a civil society in opposition to a state that persisted in withholding civil rights. Wartime gave these organizations unprecedented opportunities: the tsarist government reluctantly came to rely on civilian organizations for services it could not provide.[51] The Central Jewish Committee for the Relief of Victims of War (*Evreiskii komitet pomoshchi zhertvam voiny* [EKOPO]) took responsibility for Jewish refugees. Existing organizations agreed to a division of labor in the face of the refugees' overwhelming numbers and ramified needs.[52] These efforts democratized communal institutions.[53]

Kingdom of Poland

After the 1880s the legal situation of the kingdom's 1.1 million Jews did not undergo significant change. In 1882 Governor-General Hurka considered introducing the May Laws but refrained.[54] To block a subsequent effort to introduce a version of the May Laws in 1886, the Warsaw Stock Exchange prepared a lengthy memorandum detailing the Jews' crucial role in the kingdom's economy.[55] In 1891 the government did imitate the May Laws by prohibiting Jews from buying rural farmland.[56]

The 1905 revolution mobilized the kingdom as it did Russia. Jews organized political parties, including the Union of Poles of the Jewish Faith, and ran candidates in elections. Even with the revolution's collapse, the October manifesto's freedoms remained in place: voting rights and freedom for associations, trade unions, and the press.[57] A daily press flourished in Yiddish, Hebrew, and Polish. As in Russia, Jews in Congress Poland gained political rights first.

In the Duma election of October 1912, the limited suffrage gave the Jewish bourgeoisie in Warsaw preponderance.[58] Jews held a majority of electors (46 or 40%). The Jewish electors voted for a Socialist candidate, evoking widespread hostility including boycotts and some violence.[59]

Conclusion

Alexander III enacted a policy of "integral segregation" that differentiated the Jews from other minority and national groups. Nicholas II's government propagated an ideology of "reactionary utopia" in which Jews were central, yet there were fundamental ambiguities. For example, his ministries were at odds (Finance versus Interior) and pursued contradictory policies. The government promoted anti-Semitic literature, pogroms, and blood libel trials.

In response to insurrections and the 1905 revolution, the autocratic tsars granted Jews political rights prior to civil rights, though Jewish leaders had to intercede to secure those rights.

The tightening vise of tsarist repression resulted in endemic immiseration. Millions of Jews sought to escape grinding poverty, and to attain greater equality, by emigrating (chapter 19).

CHAPTER SEVENTEEN

Western Europe

THE ACHIEVEMENT OF FULL RIGHTS in western Europe was protracted and complex although narrow in scope. In England, full emancipation meant removal of the disabilities that prohibited officeholding and kept community institutions in an uncertain, inferior status. A few notables initiated and led the process; the organized community engaged toward the end.

In France, emancipation meant removing infringements on rights: the lapsing of Napoleon's Infamous Decree (1818), the state's assumption of rabbis' salaries (1830) and Consistorial funding, and discarding the demeaning Jews' oath (*more judaïco*; 1809–46). Concomitant with this process was Algeria's four-decade replay of emancipation (1830–70). The French state was the main actor throughout. The Consistory played a central political role in all cases, not least in Algeria.

England

In England, the achievement of equality meant the ability to hold office—local, municipal, and national—by swearing the requisite oaths as well as equalizing the status of communal institutions. Among England's approximately 30,000 or so Jews, these issues at first motivated only the elite who were eligible for office and, as communal leaders, were cognizant of their institutions' precarious status. Only a tiny minority who acutely felt the "degrading stigma" of disabilities initially mounted a campaign.[1]

The Jewish elite achieved these goals as part of a major political transformation in the country. England continued to dismantle the confessional state.[2] It removed the disabilities that had kept dissenting Protestants from political and state offices with the abrogation of the Test and Corporation Acts in 1828.[3] The Catholic Emancipation Act (1829) averted a constitutional crisis by allowing Catholics to hold office, and especially the Irish Catholics who had been forcibly incorporated with the unification of 1800 (designed to prevent a Napoleonic invasion through Ireland). Formidable opposition to further erosion of the confessional state took the form of a defense of the "Christian" (rather than the "Protestant" or "Anglican") state.[4] With the First Reform Act (1832) England increased the size of the electorate and redistributed seats from "rotten boroughs" to new cities.[5]

The Irish had mobilized to pressure Parliament, which simultaneously limited the Irish Catholic electorate by raising the property requirement. Daniel O'Connell recommended the same strategy to Jewish leaders: "you must . . . *force* your question on the Parliament."[6]

The Jews' frontal assault failed. The first bill brought to Parliament in 1830 did not pass the Commons. That of 1833 passed the reformed House of Commons but failed in the House of Lords. Twelve successive bills suffered the same fate.[7]

As part of the transformation of England's politics, the Jewish elite collaborated with disparate social groups, fashioning significant alliances. The various political groups that supported these bills—Whigs, progressive and evangelical Tories, Radicals, and Nonconformists—did so in the name of property owners, the rights of Englishmen, and the Constitution.[8] Tories, High Churchmen, and some Liberals opposed them to defend the nation's Christian character.[9]

Through their alliances Jewish leaders supplemented the frontal assault with a step-by-step abolition of disabilities that also, ultimately, recast it as a legal and constitutional issue. They thereby circumvented the question of the Jews' place in a Christian state as well as the parallel issue of whether Jews were a separate nation harboring hopes for messianic restoration.[10] In this way they "forced" the issue.

The first breakthrough came in 1830 when the City of London removed the required oath and granted Jews freedom of the City, permitting them to open retail businesses. In 1833 one of the Inns of Court (Lincoln's Inn) modified its oath to permit the first Jew, Francis Henry Goldsmid (1808–78), who had studied law at the new secular University College, London, to be called to the bar.[11] In 1835 Parliament passed the Sheriff's Declaration Act allowing David Salomons (1797–1873) to become a sheriff of London. In holding that office Salomons significantly followed a Dissenter and a Catholic.[12] In 1845 Parliament approved the Jewish Municipal Relief Act that opened municipal offices to Jews.[13] In 1846 Parliament passed the Religious Opinions Relief Act giving Jewish institutions (synagogues, schools, charities) the same status as those of Nonconformists.[14]

The effort to gain equality became a true campaign in its final stage of admission to Parliament. The Board of Deputies, the association representing most of England's synagogues, and a wider range of Jews now participated.[15] In fact, the Board of Deputies gained statutory recognition, becoming the exclusive body with access to the government, to pursue the struggle for emancipation (1836).[16]

In 1847 the Liberal party put forward five Jewish candidates for Parliament. One of the five, Lionel de Rothschild (1808–79), was elected. In September 1847 Lord George Bentinck, then leader of the Tory party, wrote about Rothschild's election:

> It is like Clare electing O'Connell, Yorkshire Wilberforce. Clare settled the Catholic question, Yorkshire the slave trade, and now the City of London has settled the Jew question.[17]

Rothschild was, of course, unable to take his seat because of the required abjuration oath that included the phrase "on the true faith of a Christian."[18] Over a quarter of a million individuals signed petitions supporting Rothschild.[19] Rothschild resigned his seat, a new election was called, and the process was repeated: the City of London returned Rothschild to Parliament in five consecutive elections. In 1851 Greenwich elected Sir David Salomons in a by-election. He tried to take his seat several times without swearing the oath of abjuration and was evicted.[20]

Finally, in 1858 Parliament, perhaps because the weak Conservative government feared losing a vote, engineered a compromise: each House could administer its own oath.[21] At this point the debate in Parliament turned on the right of electors to seat the representative of their choice, specifically, the City of London's right to select its MP. The repeated refusal to seat Rothschild threatened to foment a constitutional crisis. The explicit issue was the electoral system, the implicit issue the nation's composition. Who comprised the nation, the electorate or the House of Lords?[22] As the Chief Justice, Lord Campbell, put it, he wanted the issue's "constitutional and legal consummation."[23]

The oath Rothschild took on July 26, 1858, significantly used the same formulation as the Plantation Act of 1740.[24] By 1860 four of the original five Jewish candidates had seats in the House of Commons; in 1865 six Jews gained seats.[25] Since the original compromise was limited to that one session, Parliament in 1860 passed the Jews' Act Amendment Bill, making it permanent. The Parliamentary Oaths Acts of 1866 replaced the exclusionary "on the true faith of a Christian" with the neutral "so help me God."[26]

The attainment of full emancipation in England drew on a combination of alliances. Jewish leaders held numerous meetings and corresponded with the highest government officials.[27] At the same time, they gained the support of various associations and political parties, writers and newspapers who advocated on their behalf. They also had the backing of the electors who voted Goldsmid, Rothschild, and other Jewish candidates into various offices.[28]

France

Emancipation in France was not a matter solely of the Revolution or a one-time state decree: it unfolded throughout the nineteenth and twentieth centuries.[29] The process was circumscribed: it concerned either vestiges of the corporate order restricting rights or forms of discrimination dating to Napoleon's reign. In contrast, in Algeria the full range of the Jews' civil and political rights were at issue.

INFAMOUS DECREE

The collapse of Napoleon's empire initiated a four-year conflict over the Infamous Decree (1814–18) that played out under the auspices of Louis XVIII's government and especially its foundational 1814 Charter (*Charte*). The Charter was a hastily composed compromise that attempted to balance between the previous quarter century's competing revolutionary and conservative principles. Whereas the Charter guaranteed individual rights and equality before the law, Louis XVIII himself issued it as a king by divine right. Whereas Article 5 guaranteed freedom of religion and worship, Article 6 declared Catholicism the state religion.[30]

As soon as Napoleon's government fell, the Consistory submitted a memorandum requesting the decree's abrogation.[31] The Consistory submitted numerous petitions to the restored Bourbon government contesting a decree "dictated by . . . caprice and injustice."[32] After the Hundred Days and the second Bourbon restoration the Consistory questioned the decree as being contrary to the Civil Code, which the Charter confirmed, and for effectively turning Jews into foreigners. Subsequent memoranda questioned the decree's legality since it conflicted with the Charter's guarantee of equality.[33]

In opposition, the Council of the Department of Colmar in Alsace (1814) complained that the decree had failed: the Jews did not treat the French as fellow citizens but rather continued to exploit them. The Council of the Department of Haut-Rhin (Alsace) repeated the same diatribe in 1816–17. Later in 1817 the two councils submitted a joint complaint, hoping that the threat of renewal would at least encourage Jewish creditors to extend favorable settlements to debtors. The Ministry of the Interior took notice.[34]

In the meantime, an obscure individual, the Marquis de Lattier (Department of the Drôme), submitted a petition to the two legislative chambers, which he also placed in the press, requesting the decree's renewal. The Chamber of Peers discussed the issue on February 23, the Chamber of Deputies on February 26, 1818. The Chamber of Deputies voted to refer the matter to the Minister of the Interior.[35]

An alarmed Central Consistory leaped into action. It requested an audience with the Minister of the Interior and submitted a letter defending Jews' behavior in the Departments of the Haut and Bas Rhin.[36] It rallied various Consistories (Nancy, Metz, Strasbourg, Marseille) and convened an emergency meeting (March 1).[37]

As the expiration date approached, the Central Consistory submitted a blistering critique of the law's form and content.[38]

> A decree . . . that concomitantly usurped judicial and legislative authority, and usurped them to carry out the most appalling abuse, pronounced the ruin of a large number of Israelites in France, and placed an even greater number for ten years beyond common law [*droit commun*], and also returned them to a state of debasement and banishment from which the progress of enlightenment had freed them in the century's concluding years.[39]

The petition further characterized the decree as "one of the most odious acts of despotism, a true atrocity."[40]

The petitioners objected to renewal as inimical to the 1814 Charter's guarantee of equality before the law.

> Is it just, is it reasonable to conclude that the entire Jewish population be placed beyond the common law [*droit commun*]; that one can refuse the protection and the liberty that the law accords to all citizens; to write on their brow a stamp of opprobrium, and to treat them anew as slaves and outcasts after they have entered as equals and brothers the grand family's bosom?[41]

Renewal would violate the principle that "*all citizens are equal before the law*" (italics in original) by introducing distinctions based on religion:

> it would be the difference of religion that would produce the difference in punishment [for usury]! The Charter [of 1814] guarantees to all religions, just as to all citizens, equal protection; and it is precisely because they observe the laws of Moses that a considerable number of the French will be ruined . . . ![42]

Finally, the Consistory argued that the 1791 law had made Jews French unconditionally. To impose conditions, as did the "preceding government," would be "a monstrous monument of arbitrariness and tyranny."[43]

The Consistory's plea succeeded. Nevertheless, as late as 1823 two Alsatian departments considered trying to renew the decree.[44]

RABBIS' SALARIES

State payment of clerical salaries was another way in which Napoleon had perpetuated discrimination. In exchange for secularizing Church properties the revolutionary state had assumed responsibility for Catholic priests' salaries and pensions. Napoleon did the same for Protestant ministers with the "Organic Articles" (1802).[45] During the Assembly of Notables Jewish leaders had requested the same treatment for rabbis. Napoleon refused, leaving Jewish clergy in an inferior position (chapter 9).[46] The 1814 Charter (Article 7) confirmed this arrangement by guaranteeing state salaries to Catholic and Christian clergy.[47]

Louis Philippe's government overturned the Restoration's privileging of Catholicism by declaring it the religion "professed by the majority."[48] The Consistory approached the government on the issue of rabbis' salaries in August 1830.[49] The government decided to proceed. It appointed a committee and Joseph-Marie Portalis (1778–1858), a distinguished jurist who headed the Supreme Court (*Cour de Cassation*), wrote a favorable report.[50]

Portalis's narrow legal argument was that whereas the Charter of 1814 announced that the state would pay the salaries of Catholic and Christian clergy, the Charter of 1830 did not preclude treating other religions similarly. The broad political argument was that society requires religion for its well-being and thus the state should adopt a policy of "wise tolerance": "If [the legislator] tolerates all religions out of respect for individual liberty, he protects the religions out of the general interest of society." Giving voice to France's religious revival after 1815, Portalis invoked the threat of indifference: "In the century in which we live the evil that threatens society is not the diversity of religious doctrines but their abandonment."[51]

Portalis posited that for a religion to qualify for toleration it had to promote social virtues and display social utility. It was incontrovertible that Judaism, with its many affinities to Christianity, possessed those characteristics. Finally, the Assembly of Notables had imposed on Jews the religious obligation to submit to the state on civil and political issues. In addition, the "Israelites of France" have been regenerated: consider "their progress in our fatherland." Thus rabbis will serve the state, disseminating "enlightenment" (*lumières*) and the "true principles of sociability."[52]

Portalis emphasized that the committee had voted unanimously in favor of the motion and that the cost was negligible.[53] The Chamber of Deputies adopted the measure on December 4, 1830, the Chamber of Peers on February 1, 1831. The state promulgated the law on February 8, 1831.[54]

Consistorial Funding and Communal Debt

The state's assumption of rabbis' salaries was the thin edge of the wedge: the state now became responsible for the Consistory's overall finances. From its inception the Consistory was an anomalous institution since Napoleon's ministers endowed it with the power to levy and collect taxes (Article 12), a key characteristic of an ancien régime corporation. The Consistory was the administrative equivalent of the Infamous Decree: it violated the "principles of liberty and civic equality."[55]

Under Napoleon the Jews were powerless to challenge this arrangement; later they were reluctant to acknowledge its full implications. "If the Jews acknowledged that prior to 1831 they had been less than equal, they would have destroyed the myth of the revolution and emancipation."[56]

A system of obligatory taxation remained in place until 1831. State officials determined the sum to be collected, and the Consistories apportioned taxes according to wealth (*répartition*), a difficult and imprecise procedure. These taxes yielded insufficient funds; the Consistories regularly failed to meet their expenses. For this reason, between 1810 and the 1820s the Consistories of Bordeaux (1810) and Paris introduced the new financial instrument of interest-bearing bonds, mimicking French state practice, to raise funds to build new synagogues. Significantly, in 1841 the French state assumed the remaining debt from bonds issued to fund construction of a Paris synagogue. The state retired the debt by 1846. In 1849 the Paris Consistory donated the building to the Paris municipality.[57]

In 1831 the government took responsibility for the Consistories' budget yet, again, the funds were insufficient.[58] Consistories supplemented that funding with "voluntary" taxation (*cotisation*) on ritual matters: synagogue honors, kosher meat, circumcision. The Consistory enforced these "voluntary" contributions with the threat of exclusion from ritual life.[59]

The state treated the Jews' communal debts as anomalously as rabbis' salaries and the Consistory's budget. The revolutionary government nationalized the debts of the corporations it dissolved; it did not do so for the Jews. The Jewish communities repeatedly, and unsuccessfully, petitioned the revolutionary and Napoleonic governments for equal treatment.[60] The communal debts from the ancien régime (Metz, Alsace, Comtats) therefore remained the responsibility of community members and their heirs.[61] In the case of Alsace, heirs continued to pay their share of those debts as late as 1870, "a commemorative stigma of their ancient servitude." The German occupation voided the debts.[62]

Oaths

Some Jewish leaders publicly asserted that the state's assumption of rabbinic salaries and Consistory budgets had removed the last vestige of inequality.[63] Others contended that one obstacle to full emancipation remained, namely, the *more judaïco* oath, which a court in Alsace (Colmar) had introduced shortly after Napoleon's Infamous Decree. In this instance, the state did not definitively resolve the matter with a single decree: instead, a series of court rulings discredited the oath.

The Revolution's conferral of rights abolished all oaths specific to Jews. On January 10, 1792, the Minister of Justice terminated the practice of special oaths as contrary to equality: "The law does not distinguish between Jew and Christian, Protestant and Catholic, Conformist and Dissident." The simple "I swear" required of all Frenchmen suffices.[64]

Whether Napoleon's government actively promoted the introduction of the *more judaïco* oath remains to be determined. The Infamous Decree did, however, foster an atmosphere that encouraged local authorities to attempt to erode the Jews' equality.[65]

In Colmar, Alsace's "judicial capital" since 1679 and again under Napoleon, the Court of Appeals on February 10, 1809, required a Jewish lender to swear the *more judaïco* on the basis of ancien régime precedents.[66] This effort contradicted the emancipation decree (September 1791) and the Napoleonic Code. Asserting that the Jews of the Department of Rhin were of German origin, the court cited the 1784 *lettres patentes* that permitted Jews to swear an oath according to German usage (Article 18), that is, in a synagogue on a Torah scroll. The ruling further cited a 1530 decree of the Holy Roman Empire describing the elaborate manner for the ceremony: swearing on a Torah scroll, in a synagogue, before ten male witnesses.[67]

French Jewish leaders vehemently attacked this ancien régime procedure. The Central Consistory protested to the Ministry of Justice on August 21, 1809, that the Colmar Court's ruling represented a "new line of demarcation" that prescribed "the most outrageous procedures without example even in the centuries of barbarity." After referring to the relevant decisions of the Sanhedrin (Articles 4, 5, 9), the letter averred: "One does not regenerate through insults and vexations, and one does not elevate man by debasing him."[68] The Central Consistory lodged a similar protest with the Ministry of Cults.[69]

The Chief Rabbi of Witzenheim protested vehemently, yet then acquiesced, when the Colmar Court of Appeals ordered him to administer the oath (July 19, 1809). The Consistory of Haut-Rhin protested again on August 8, 1809, demanding that this "abuse not become a custom."[70]

The Chief Rabbi of Witzenheim's acquiescence did not set a precedent. Most rabbis refused to administer the oath to impede its dissemination. Moreover, the Consistories, both Central (Paris) and local, supported the rabbis' recalcitrance. The first to refuse was Rabbi Jacob Mayer of Strasbourg (1810).[71] The next year the rabbi of Haut-Rhin did the same. The multiplying cases of refusal constituted a concerted defense of emancipation.[72]

The rabbis' stance led to paradoxical court cases: Jews who needed an oath to conduct business sued rabbis who refused to administer it.[73] A case that had come before the Commercial Court of Mayence was referred to the Minister of Cults. He ruled against the *more judaïco* (May 13, 1811) arguing first, that swearing the standard oath ("I swear"; *Je jure*) on a printed Bible as Napoleon had prescribed (October 19, 1808) sufficed; and second, that swearing on a Torah scroll in a synagogue profaned a religious ritual.[74]

The *more judaïco* survived Napoleon's fall. The practice spread to Metz after 1816.[75] That same year the two Chief Rabbis of the Central Consistory issued a declaration that the oath all Frenchmen were required to swear was binding for Jews and therefore sufficient.[76]

After the lapse of the Infamous Decree the oath became the chief means for the courts, especially in Alsace, to subvert the Jews' equality. It was the Royal

Court of Colmar that invented the oath, requested the renewal of the Infamous Decree, and continued to require the oath into the 1840s. Only by making the oath a cause did French Jewish leaders succeed in removing it. Significantly, oaths were a live issue in France at the time: in 1830–31, for example, judges had to decide whether to swear the oath of loyalty to Louis Philippe's government.[77]

An 1827 case in Nîmes turned that city's brilliant young attorney, Adolphe Crémieux (1796–1880), into the cause's champion. He argued that an oath that was not the same for all Frenchmen violated the 1814 Charter's guarantee of equality (Article 1): "there exists in the eyes of the law only citizens, as equal citizens"; "every special measure for a class of individuals violates the Charter"; "all titles, all statuses, all denominations disappear before the majesty of the law."[78]

Crémieux further asserted that a religious oath violated liberty of religion by coercing an individual to make public his private beliefs. Indeed, having the court determine the form and procedure of the oath fundamentally violated religious liberty. Legal cases are between Frenchmen: "the law recognizes neither Jew, nor Protestant, nor Catholic; it recognizes only the French." In this regard as well the *more judaïco* violated the 1814 Charter (Article 5: "Each professes his religion with equal liberty, and obtains for his religion the same protection"). No magistrate has the right arbitrarily to determine the formula of an oath.[79]

The Royal Court of Nîmes accepted Crémieux's arguments: it dismissed the imposition of the *more judaïco* as an arbitrary abuse of power (June 1827).[80]

Colmar was a bastion of the Catholic revival under the Restoration. The Colmar Court (January 18, 1828) reversed the Nîmes ruling by asserting that the *more judaïco* preserved religious freedom: Alsatian Jews followed different religious prescriptions than southern Jews. In support of its position the court again cited the 1784 *lettres patentes*.[81] The *more judaïco* thus survived in its Alsatian birthplace.

In 1839 Crémieux pleaded against the oath in Saverne (Bas Rhin), after the local rabbi refused to administer the oath. Crémieux prevailed. Other cases appeared in 1840 in Alsace (Marmoutier) and in Metz (1843). In both cases the rabbi refused to administer the oath. In the latter case the Chief Rabbi and the Consistory protested to the Ministry of Justice and Cults. Despite the minister's ruling against the oath, local courts continued to use it.[82]

Another case in Saverne (March 1839) began to bring matters to a head. The court required a widow to take the oath to recover the capital on a loan from a Jewish debtor. The rabbi, Lazare Isidor, refused to administer the oath. The widow requested permission to prosecute the rabbi for not fulfilling his duty. The case went to the Council of State (*Conseil d'État*); the Minister of Justice consulted with the Central Consistory and local Consistory. The Consistorial rabbis unanimously opposed the oath, and Crémieux, now president of the Central Consistory, submitted a report opposing any version of the oath, even one sworn on a printed Bible in the courtroom: all Frenchmen should swear the same oath in the same manner. After emphasizing that the oath originated during the period of Napoleon's Infamous Decree, he declared the oath "irreligious," "useless," and "contrary to the law of equality governing all the recognized cults in France."[83]

On January 18 and August 27, 1845, the Council of State ruled the rabbi had the right to refuse to administer the oath since he was not a government agent.[84] The ruling voided the oath in administrative law.

In 1846, the Supreme Court for civil matters (*Cour de Cassation*) judged a case that the Court of Colmar had handled.[85] The Supreme Court ruled that the litigant could not be forced to take the oath *more judaïco*. One oath and one procedure applied to all Frenchmen. The Court held that the pertinent legislation was: the 1791 emancipation decree, the 1808 law organizing the Consistory, the 1831 law making the state responsible for rabbis' salaries, and the 1830 Charter's reassertion of equality before the law and the liberty of religion. Ancien régime precedents were invalid. Furthermore, even if the oath was legal during the exceptional years of the Infamous Decree, once that decree expired the oath should have as well. The Court declared the Royal Court of Colmar's use of the oath illegal and in violation of the Charter, the Civil Code, and the Code of Procedure.[86] The following year (1847) the same Court ruled that in criminal cases witnesses also could not be forced to take the oath.[87] Despite these clear rulings, the Court of Saverne tried, unsuccessfully, to impose the oath in 1848.[88]

To discredit the *more judaïco* oath rabbis and Consistories mounted organized opposition. Crémieux was, to be sure, the most conspicuous proponent, yet one of many. Actively engaged lay and clerical leaders collectively succeeded in rallying the state to disarm local authorities.[89]

Like the National Assembly that issued the emancipation decree in 1791, the two supreme courts ruled on constitutional grounds. The *Conseil d'État* (administrative law) and the *Cour de Cassation* (civil and criminal law) did not pass judgment on the Jews themselves. That debate, whether Jews were successfully regenerated or incorrigibly degenerate, continued throughout the Restoration period.[90] The courts simply declared the Jews to be citizens entitled to equal treatment before the law. In both cases the opposition centered in Alsace. Significant alliances with republican and anticlerical groups enabled that engagement with the state.[91] Similar alliances were critical in Algeria.

Algeria

With the invasion of Algeria (1830), France again had Jews without rights. The emancipation process repeated itself, albeit now with the Central Consistory leading the way. Emancipation in Algeria paralleled that in Alsace. Like

Alsace under the ancien régime, Algeria and its Jews lived under military administration (1830–70). Central Consistory leaders felt their own emancipation was at stake in Alsace and Algeria: they subjected Alsace's and Algeria's Jews to a regime of "regeneration," especially through education.[92]

As early as 1833 the Central Consistory requested the creation of a Consistory for Algeria's approximately 16,000 Jews.[93] At the Central Consistory's behest, two Consistory leaders traveled to Algeria in 1842 to study the situation. In their report, they advocated the creation of a Consistory, the imposition of French civil law and granting of civil rights, and the establishment of schools staffed by French Jewish teachers.[94]

Algeria's military administration followed the metropolitan model by gradually dissolving the Jews' courts. The military first required Jewish judges to obtain authorization to serve and subjected their decisions to appeal in French courts (1832); then deprived the courts of jurisdiction over criminal cases (1834); and finally disbanded the Jews' courts and restricted rabbis to a consultative role in French courts on matters of marriage and divorce (1841).[95]

The military administration made the Jews' legal situation problematic yet concomitantly insisted that the Jews were not ready for full equality.[96] In 1840 the administration submitted a list of twenty-three questions to Jewish leaders that recapitulated the twelve Napoleon's ministers had presented to the Assembly of Notables in 1806.[97] Throughout its forty years the military administration consistently opposed emancipation.[98]

After a papal bull created a diocese in 1838, and the military administration established a Protestant Consistory in 1839, the Jews' continued requests for a Consistory succeeded. On November 9, 1845, the government abolished the former communal institutions and established a Consistory (Algiers, Constantine, Oran).[99] At his formal installation (Algiers; January 31, 1847) the new Grand Rabbi Weil, imported from France, spoke of "a religious and civilizing mission."[100] The French government understood the Consistories as the most efficacious means to introduce French education.[101] European Jewish colonists and the French rabbis appointed as Grand Rabbis initially controlled the consistories.[102] In 1867 the Algerian Consistories came under the Parisian Central Consistory's direct authority.[103]

The establishment of the Consistory and abrogation of prior institutions did not resolve Algerian Jewry's legal status. An 1851 decree reiterated the subjection of contracts of marriage and property to French courts, which were to utilize Jewish law. Yet the courts required litigants to provide proper birth certificates, which most Jews did not possess. Most Jews, meaning those who retained the status of "indigenous Israelites," were left without the means to marry.[104] Few Jews, perhaps less than three hundred, took advantage of the 1865 regulation (*Senatus Consulte*) that Napoleon III introduced after his visit that year, which allowed Jews and Muslims to renounce their "personal status" and naturalize as French citizens.[105]

"Colonial jurists and metropolitan policy makers" understood that only collective equality would resolve the Jews' complex legal status.[106] Napoleon III's government had invested considerable effort in drafting the legislation. Jewish notables in Algiers continued to petition for naturalization.[107] When Crémieux, as Minister of Justice, enacted the 1870 emancipation decree at Tours during the Franco-Prussian War, he merely adapted the existing draft to the radically new circumstances: Algeria passed from military to civilian rule. Settlers gained French citizenship and political rights. France annexed the colony and divided it into administrative departments. For Algeria's Jews, Crémieux adopted the Sanhedrin's principle: if the French state imposed civil law, then Jewish law (*halakha*) obligated them to acquiesce.[108]

The Muslim majority did not attain citizenship. Similarly, the several thousand Mzabi Jews of the Sahara also did not. Southern Algeria first became a French protectorate in 1853; the French occupied the area in 1882 and it remained under military administration until 1957. The French did not apply the "civilizing mission" to the area's residents whose personal status, governed by Mosaic law, permitted polygamy into the 1950s.[109]

The attainment of citizenship had the unexpected consequence of placing the Jews in a parlous position: they now played a crucial role in elections. The 33,000 Jews comprised some 15 percent of the overall electorate but, because of their urban concentration, an even higher percentage in the towns and cities.[110] The Jews' outsized electoral role resulted in a pronounced anti-Jewish (*anti-juif*) opposition that only grew with the naturalization of all European migrants in 1889.[111] Algerian Jews' electoral predicament more closely resembled that of their brethren in Galicia, for example, than in metropolitan France.

Crémieux understood the *anti-juif* movement's calls for the abrogation of emancipation, or at least of the Jews' political rights, as a recapitulation of metropolitan French Jewish history: "They are saying . . . the same things against Algerian Jews that they said in 1790, 1807 and again in 1818 against the Jews of France."[112]

Alliance Israélite Universelle

The founding of the Alliance Israélite Universelle (1860) marked a high point of confidence in emancipation: the Jews of France, the Revolution's beneficiaries, would now strive to bring emancipation to Jews everywhere.

The Alliance supplemented the Consistory. The Consistory, as we have seen, engaged two types of political issues. First, it dealt with those that directly affected French Jews, for example, the Infamous Decree, rabbis' salaries, Consistory budgets, and oaths. Second, it wrestled with those urgent issues in which French and Consistory interests converged, for example, Algeria's Jews. In these cases, the Consistory cooperated with Jewish leaders elsewhere, especially the London Board of Deputies.[113]

The Alliance had a broader purview and deeper commitment than the Consistory: it was concerned with Jews throughout the world and, in addition to issues of the moment, with sustained transformation. The Alliance was the "first permanent and self-contained institution" dedicated to promoting "emancipation" and "moral progress," namely regeneration, for Jews everywhere.[114] Whereas the Consistory largely engaged in private advocacy with government ministers and ministries, only on occasion resorting to the public sphere, the Alliance's leaders employed the strategies of "publicity" and "moral argumentation" to gain the backing of the Great Powers, especially France. They wanted to promote a state policy defending Jews and other religious minorities.[115]

The Alliance's founders, mostly professionals who had been educated in French schools and universities, were staunch republicans who embraced the ideals of "progress and civilization" as a form of secular messianism.[116] Adherents of the ideas of 1789, they wanted France to follow a foreign policy inspired by the secular, republican "civilizing mission" (*mission civilisatrice*) rather than Catholic or ultramontane ideas. For that reason, the Alliance's first public cause was the plight of Syrian Christians.[117]

The proximate cause for the organization's founding was the Mortara case (1858). Church authorities had seized a Jewish child in Bologna, whom a nursemaid had secretly baptized, and refused to release him despite intense domestic and international pressure. The founders' sense of solidarity with Jews everywhere was informed by the traumatic Damascus Affair (1840): the French government refused to repudiate the blood libel and the consul promoting it. They were acutely aware of the extensive public discussions during the Crimean War (1853–56) about Jews' status in the Ottoman Empire as well as the yet unresolved situation of Jews under France's military administration in Algeria.[118]

Despite its patently political agenda, the Alliance took the form of a philanthropic organization or missionary society.[119] The Alliance aimed to promote "emancipation through education."[120] Beginning with a boys school in Tetuan, Morocco (1862), it established a network of schools (1914: 183 schools enrolling 43,700 students), for girls as well as boys, that cultivated conversion to French culture and the civilizing mission. These were the Jewish equivalent of the missionary schools that proliferated in the Maghreb and Mashreq.[121] Through these schools the Alliance's members hoped "that the emancipated Occident will have paid its debt to the regenerated Orient."[122]

Conclusion

The achievement of equality in western Europe was limited in scope. In England it turned on removing the disabilities that prevented Jews from exercising political rights. In France it entailed removing vestiges of inequality that qualified the Jews' supposedly full and unconditional emancipation. In Algeria emancipation recapitulated the experience of Alsace: the full scope of rights was at stake.

Jewish leaders mounted concerted political campaigns that constituted an emancipation politics. The Alliance's founders thought that to secure their own status it was necessary to bring emancipation to Jews everywhere.

CHAPTER EIGHTEEN

The Atlantic World

THE ATLANTIC WORLD of Dutch and British colonies followed the west European pattern of emancipation.[1] Jews were spread across numerous colonies. The thirteen British colonies were not preponderant: each of the communities of "Curaçao, Surinam and Jamaica ... had more Jews in the mid-eighteenth century than all of the North American colonies combined."[2] Jews gained civil rights through either the terms of settlement or an accretion of rights over time. In contrast, to gain political rights they engaged in a concerted campaign, articulating characteristic arguments for emancipation. In this respect the early American republic did not diverge from the other colonies.

Thirteen Colonies

The thirteen colonies exhibited a consistent legal pattern of Jewish settlement in keeping with England's. In the aftermath of the Glorious Revolution and Act of Toleration, the colonies gradually introduced a broad practice of "toleration" of dissenting Protestants and, to a lesser extent, and with major exceptions, of Catholics. By the 1770s and 1780s, after a major shift in politics and public opinion, this became a practice of Protestant pluralism. Protestant pluralism enabled the admission and toleration of Jews.[3]

Protestant pluralism accommodated intimate ties between church and government, including established churches. Virginia, the Carolinas, Maryland, and Georgia established the Church of England and taxed residents to support it. The Congregationalists, who had been dissenters in England, were the established Church in Massachusetts and Connecticut. Delaware, New Jersey, Pennsylvania, and Rhode Island had no established religion.[4] The Jews' emancipation occurred as part of the dismantling of the structures of establishment and Protestant pluralism, a process that unfolded virtually concomitantly in England.

The Sephardic Jewish merchants who from 1654 settled mainly in Charleston, Newport, New York, Philadelphia, and Savannah belonged to the Port Jewish diaspora.[5] Ashkenazim were probably the majority by 1720. The Jews in the colonies lived on sufferance alongside other dissenters from the established churches, for example, Baptists and Quakers. All were saddled with "a wide range of disabilities."[6]

Jews in general enjoyed the right of residence, freedom of occupations (by 1700), and the right to private worship (in the language of the West India Company: to "exercise in all quietness their religion within their houses"). They were denied the right of public worship; Judaism was not recognized. Oaths excluded them from political office. The Plantation Act of 1740, by waiving the oath "on the true faith of a Christian," allowed Jews to become subjects of His Majesty's Government after seven years of uninterrupted residence, a privilege ("naturalization") Jews in England were denied with the repeal of the "Jew Bill" (1753; chapter 5). Few Jews in the American colonies took advantage of the Act.[7]

There was a gap between the de jure and the de facto situation. Though Jews were denied public worship in New York, they had a purpose-built synagogue in the 1690s. Though prohibited from retail trade in New York, as in London, Jews engaged in it as the distinction between retail and wholesale blurred. Thus in the colonial period Jews gradually acquired almost the full range of civil rights under the aegis of Protestant pluralism. Individual colonies removed "disabilities" on an ad hoc basis. As colonial society emerged, Jews attained civil rights in a piecemeal fashion, without legislation.[8]

EARLY REPUBLIC

The Constitution and First Amendment declared equality for all citizens, or at least all white males; Article VI abolished all Test Acts for federal office (1789). During the revolutionary period and beyond, many states preserved Protestant pluralism, including established churches. The Jews' attempt to gain emancipation, acquiring political rights and Judaism's equality, unfolded in the states.[9] Legislatures and newspapers debated the issues, while legislatures and courts removed the Jews' disabilities case by case, state by state.

Numbering perhaps 2,500 in 1776, Jews propelled the process by submitting petitions, organizing meetings, lobbying politicians, publishing articles in the press, and initiating court cases. They enunciated arguments for their inherent or natural rights as guaranteed by the U.S. or state constitutions; they also pressed their claim to having earned their rights as upstanding citizens and taxpayers, officeholders and soldiers.

Virginia's famous proclamation of the "free exercise of religion" (1776) set a high bar that few states followed. Even Virginia took a decade of fierce debate to abolish test oaths and make religion entirely voluntary.[10] Rhode Island did prohibit religious discrimination for officeholding.

Most states delayed and made significant exceptions. New York's constitution was the first to disestablish religion and introduce political equality for Jews (1777); at the same time New York imposed a test act for Catholics that remained in force for almost three decades (1806).[11] In its first constitution (1778) South Carolina made Protestantism the state's established religion and restricted elected office to Protestants. In its second constitution (1790) South Carolina abolished establishment and religious restrictions on officeholding. In 1791 Jews in Charleston incorporated Beth Elohim congregation. In 1776 North Carolina's constitution rejected religious establishment yet limited officeholding to Protestants; North Carolina admitted Catholics to office in 1835, Jews in 1868. Pennsylvania's 1776 constitution included a Test Act for officeholders: belief in God and the Old and New Testaments. Pennsylvania's 1790 constitution embraced a deist definition, requiring belief in God and a future life.[12]

By maintaining an established church or an intimate connection between church and state, including disabilities for dissenters, most states denied Jews political rights. New Jersey (1776) restricted political rights to Protestants less than a week after Virginia passed its constitution. Delaware's constitution required a Trinitarian oath from state officers (1776). Georgia (1777) required that representatives be "of the Protestant religion," though it dropped this provision in its constitution of 1789. In 1780 the Massachusetts constitution provided public support for Protestant ministers (Article III) and limited officeholding to Protestants. The state annulled religious qualifications for officeholders in 1821. It was not until 1833 that Massachusetts abrogated public support for ministers, separated church and state, and made other religions equal under the law. Connecticut disestablished the Congregational Church in 1818 yet continued to recognize only Christian "societies." The first Jewish congregation was incorporated in 1843.[13] Maryland (1776) continued to uphold the established Episcopal Church: it extended religious liberty and the right to hold office to Christians alone, and the legislature passed "vestry acts" (1779, 1798) that defined Church governance, including the selection of ministers.[14] New Hampshire passed a Toleration Act in 1819 that applied only to Protestants; it first allowed non-Protestants to hold office in 1876.

Jews responded to these developments with the same strategies as their brethren in western Europe: they argued from right and worthiness for rights. They laid claim to political rights through the equality federal and state law guaranteed.[15] They trumpeted their records as upstanding citizens who had served the Revolution. They argued that the quid pro quo of "regeneration" for rights did not apply. On the contrary: like the Jews of Bordeaux or London,

Jews in the United States eagerly proclaimed that, because of the generous conditions under which they lived, regeneration was a fait accompli.[16]

Jews of the Philadelphia Synagogue submitted a petition in 1783 to the Council of Censors of Pennsylvania protesting Pennsylvania's religious test: it "deprives Jews of the most eminent rights of freemen." The petitioners deemed the religious test a "stigma upon their nation and religion" that contradicted the Pennsylvania Declaration of Rights.[17] As conscientious taxpaying property owners and merchants who had rendered service to the Revolution in blood and treasure, they insisted that they had earned their rights. One of the two Philadelphia newspapers that printed the petition, the *Independent Gazette*, echoed the petition in combining the two arguments.

> The Jews on this continent have ever demeaned themselves as good and worthy subjects, and have been peculiarly firm and united in the great cause of America; and therefore are, of right, entitled to all the privileges and immunities of her mild and equal government, in common with every other order of people.[18]

Jacob Henry similarly protested when the North Carolina legislature refused to seat him after his election in 1809. He argued for consistency in principle: the state constitution cannot override or contradict the state's 1776 Declaration of Rights that proclaimed freedom of conscience for all. He also asserted his worthiness based on the character of Judaism: it patently "enjoins upon its votaries the practice of every virtue, and the detestation of every vice." Judaism's strict morality dictated his irreproachable "conduct."[19]

The bitter struggle for political rights in Maryland involved similar arguments. Maryland's 1776 constitution, in granting religious liberties to all who professed the Christian religion, intended to include Catholics and sectarian Protestants (Mennonites, Quakers, etc.). Since few if any Jews legally resided there at the time, the constitution did not intend to exclude them.[20] The Jews who subsequently settled in Maryland were prohibited from political office, military commissions, and being called to the bar.

Jews petitioned the Maryland legislature individually and collectively to remove the discriminatory legislation.[21] The "Jew Bill" to remove the remaining disabilities was defeated in 1802, 1804, and twice in 1819. The legislature and the press subsequently debated the issue repeatedly. The press compared Maryland's treatment of its few Jews to current persecutions in Germany, Austria, Turkey, and Russia. The legislature passed the bill once in 1822 but not the required second time. It finally voted the bill through in 1824–25; it went into effect in 1826.

In the public debate from 1818 onward, advocates of equality pointed to the Jews' contributions to the state, past and future. Advocates regarded them as trustworthy and enterprising, as well as bringing to the state much-needed wealth and expertise, especially in Baltimore. Jews made the same arguments.[22]

"EQUAL FOOTING"

The attainment of full equality in the states was not limited to officeholding. It involved additional issues that, as a contemporary phrased it, entailed putting Jews and Judaism on "equal footing": the status of missionaries, Sunday laws, the proposed amendment to the Constitution declaring the United States a "Christian" country, and the nature of public schools.[23] These issues gained importance as the Jewish population grew through immigration and spread across the continent: from some 3,000 in the 1820s to a quarter million by 1880.[24]

Missionaries directly threatened emancipation, especially if they managed to incorporate as legal associations. Missionaries perpetuated negative stereotypes of Judaism as an inferior, superseded religion and of Jews as an immoral people unfit for emancipation. The associations vitiated the idea that equality was a matter of either right or worthiness. They claimed that it was a gift Christians gave Jews to promote conversion.[25]

"Sunday laws" prohibiting work and trade posed the question whether America was a Christian or religiously neutral polity. From as early as 1816, Jews began to challenge Sunday laws in numerous states: Virginia, South Carolina, Maryland, Massachusetts, Nebraska, Ohio, Iowa, Pennsylvania, Alabama, and Louisiana.[26]

A particularly salient case occurred in Richmond, Virginia (1845), when Jews petitioned for the repeal of the municipal ordinance (August 11) that added penalties to the state's. The petitioners asserted their worthiness for rights: their "honesty, fair-dealing, and moral deportment," indeed their "sterling character" as "merchants and citizens," as well as their readiness to take up arms to defend the state. They argued that "the policy of the State of Virginia was never intended to favour any religious dogmas" and that they "see with sorrow the manifestation of the sectarian spirit" in this legislation, which they called a "revolution backwards . . . in contravention of the Constitution and Bill of Rights of this State."[27] The continued opposition succeeded; seventeen months later the ordinance was repealed.

Some Jews turned to the courts for redress. The courts generally upheld the Sunday laws, often by deeming the law a secular ordinance and America a Christian nation.[28]

Since the period of the Constitution's ratification some fringe Protestants had endeavored to recognize the United States as a Christian state by legally acknowledging Jesus' supremacy and restricting officeholding to Protestants.

At midcentury, some Protestant groups held that the failure to include God in the Constitution had caused the Civil War. The National Reform Association's goal was to amend the Constitution's Preamble to acknowledge "Lord Jesus Christ as the Governor among the nations, His revealed will as the supreme law of the land" and the government's purpose to be "to constitute a Christian government." The National Reform Association's efforts stalled when Congress tabled the motion and Lincoln chose not to act; gained new life when William Strong, the association's president (1867–73), was appointed to the U.S. Supreme Court (1870); and then languished after some Protestant denominations voiced opposition. The Board of Delegates of American Israelites mounted a countercampaign, lobbying key political and religious figures.[29]

Schools were another important arena of equality. If schools were denominational or even nondenominationally Protestant, what Daniel Webster called "general tolerant Christianity," they impaired the Jews' claim to equality in the short term and, by institutionalizing and teaching inequality, further diminished it over time. If, in contrast, schools were truly religiously neutral, they became, in the words of Julius Freiberg, true "temples of liberty."[30]

The process of establishing religiously neutral public schools took most of the nineteenth century. Jews tilted decisively toward public schools by the 1860s, making it a virtual article of faith by 1870. Indeed, the second Cleveland Conference of rabbis passed a resolution to that effect almost without debate.[31] Once Jews had opted for the public schools, leaders and organizations remained vigilant to ensure the schools' secular and non-sectarian character.[32]

Curaçao

Jews first attained extensive privileges in Dutch colonies; the British colonies emulated them.[33] The Jews of Curaçao received extensive privileges in 1659: "free exercise of their religion here, [the right] to be protected [by the authorities], the privilege of building houses, and other privileges," including freedom of trade.[34]

Curaçao's Jews consistently defended those privileges through protests to local authorities and the West India Company in Holland. Amsterdam's Jewish stockholders often intervened with the West India Company on their behalf.[35] In 1816 the island came under The Hague's direct rule. Royal decree gave Jews political equality in 1825.[36]

Jamaica

While Jamaica naturalized some 151 Jews through the Plantation Act, its Assembly subjected them to extraordinary taxation and prohibited them from voting and holding office (1711 and 1750).[37] Jews actively campaigned for political rights in the eight decades from 1750 to 1828 but especially in the years 1820–26, virtually concomitant with the debates in Maryland. Jewish activists organized an "effective long-term strategy," which consisted in placing articles in the newspapers, convincing fellow Jews who met the property requirement to go to the polls, and pursuing a lawsuit against an official who had prevented a prominent Jew from voting in 1820.[38]

Jamaica's Assembly passed three statutes removing the Jews' disabilities by altering the required oaths between 1826 and 1830; British officials annulled them since Jews still suffered such disabilities in England. The governor approved the fourth statute of 1831 that amended the oath of abjuration's wording; that year a Jew, Alexander Bravo, took a seat in the Assembly.[39] Jamaica was the first British colony in the Americas successfully to remove all disabilities for Jews. Jews received full rights six months after free blacks and free coloreds.[40]

Canada

Rights in Canada turned on the ability to swear the required oaths. The imperial administration tied the colonies to England's practices, including the order of religious precedence in removing or amending oaths: first Protestant dissenters, then Catholics, and finally Jews.[41] In Canada disabilities were removed colony by colony. That Canada, like Jamaica, remained a colony meant that the process often pitted an elected Assembly favoring equal rights against colonial administrators defending the English status quo. In addition, the colonial administration exercised arbitrary power through royal instructions issued in London.[42]

In the earliest settlements, and especially Quebec Colony, Jews gained various freedoms as a matter of privilege or royal prerogative.[43] Jews arrived as early as 1749 in Halifax; individuals received land from the government and served as jurors. That settlement survived less than a decade. In Quebec Colony, the British administration excluded the majority French Catholic population from the civil administration. Since there were so few Protestants, the administration deemed Jews eligible for office. In the words of a Jewish leader, "A Jew is a Protestant" and "therefore is Entitled to Enjoy all offices."[44] In 1763 a Jew was appointed postmaster; in 1766 another gained the office of notary; and in 1768 a Jew swore an amended oath ("upon the true faith of a Jew") to take office.[45]

The British administration reversed course around 1765. Previously it had encouraged a religiously diverse population to settle its colonies by granting greater freedom than in England itself. Now it attempted to impose its home practices on the colonies, including an Established Church and Test Acts. The

1769 Imperial Act for Altering the Oath of Abjuration introduced the Test Act in all colonies, restricting officeholding to Anglicans.[46] In the new maritime colonies of Nova Scotia, Newfoundland, and Prince Edward Island, the colonial administration enforced the Test Act for officeholding and established the Church of England.

The one exception was Quebec Colony because of its preponderant majority of French Catholics. The Quebec Act of 1774 granted some 70,000 French Catholics civil equality by exempting them from oaths. The colonial administration steadfastly refused, however, to create an Assembly in which French Catholics could exercise their political rights. Quebec Colony was alone in offering "almost equal" civil and political rights to Catholics, Protestant dissenters, and Jews.[47]

An important example of the imperial authorities' retreat to mere toleration for Jews and Protestant dissenters in the former Old Province of Quebec—the 1791 Constitutional Act divided it into Upper and Lower Canada—was land grants. The Plantation Act (1740) had authorized land grants to Jews, who had received them since 1749 (Halifax). In 1798 the Chief Justice of Upper Canada prohibited such grants because of a 1792 proclamation requiring grantees to take Christian oaths. Refused a grant, a Jewish applicant petitioned and succeeded in gaining one by purchasing someone else's claim (1799). Grants to other Jews followed. In addition, Jews gained officer commissions in the militia and appointments to government office (in the last the appointee posted a bond in lieu of swearing the oaths). All these cases depended on government discretion: these were not instances of equality by right but rather by practice, often in response to protest.[48]

In Lower Canada shifting political alliances brought Jews a declaration of equal rights. The French Catholic majority used the 1808 election of a Jew to the Assembly as a stick with which to beat the English, Anglican minority in power. Presumably Ezekiel Hart (1770–1843) would have joined the English faction. The French Catholic majority voted against seating him on the grounds that he did not take the requisite oaths. Reelected in the subsequent election, Hart was again deprived of his seat.[49]

By the late 1820s French Canadian politicians shifted position, allying with the dissenting religions against English-Anglican hegemony: the Assembly had already regularized the Church of Scotland's status.[50] In response to petitions from some Jews, the Assembly passed a Relief Bill permitting them to use the legal register (births, deaths, marriages) as well as according them the right to own land for places of worship and burial. The bill was promulgated on January 18, 1831. Jews submitted two additional petitions requesting the removal of all disabilities to hold office.[51] The Assembly approved a bill in March 1831 that gained royal assent on April 12, 1832:

that all persons professing the Jewish Religion being natural born British subjects inhabiting and residing in this Province, are entitled ... to the full rights and privileges of the other subjects of His Majesty.

This was a "declaratory act"; the various oaths remained in place. In fact, the act merely restored to Jews the equal rights they had enjoyed in the Old Province of Quebec.[52] In response to questions surrounding the implementation of the oath, the Kimber Commission declared that any oath a Jew chose to swear was admissible.[53]

In the new Maritime colonies (Newfoundland, New Brunswick, Prince Edward Island, Nova Scotia) the imperial administration imposed English standards. It accorded Catholics the same inferior status as in Britain itself: public worship (1791, Roman Catholic Relief Act) but no political rights. In 1822 a Catholic was elected to the Assembly but denied his seat because he refused to take the oath against transubstantiation. The Assembly voted full equality for Catholics. The Legislative Council wanted merely to enhance the scope of toleration. Finally, an exception was made permitting the candidate to take his seat.

The turning point came with England's 1828 Repeal of the Test Act and its 1829 Roman Catholic Relief Act that brought equality to Protestant Dissenters and Catholics. The Assemblies of Nova Scotia, Prince Edward Island, and New Brunswick swiftly passed Catholic emancipation acts.[54]

Upper Canada was the first of the Canadian colonies fully to dispense with the requirement of taking the sacrament and making the declaration against transubstantiation for officeholding. The Upper Canada Oaths Act that received royal assent on February 13, 1833, substituted a secular oath of allegiance. The other colonies did not immediately follow Upper Canada's lead. Moreover, the imperial administration refused to allow the colonies to pass legislation abrogating the oaths; it instead enforced the Imperial Act of 1766 that required them. Instructions to colonial governors insisted on this point.

At this stage colonial legislatures vied with the imperial administration. New Brunswick finally took the lead in 1846 by successfully petitioning the imperial administration to abolish all extant oaths in favor of a single oath of allegiance. The lasts oaths in place were those the imperial instructions required the governor of a colony to take on assuming office. These were abolished in 1858 following the Jewish Relief Act in England.[55]

The Plantation Act served as the basis for the Jews' equality, culminating in the confirmation of citizenship rights in 1867 at the time of Confederation (British North America Act).[56] At that time the Jewish population of Canada was approximately 1,100. The struggle for civil rights continued, for example, in the battle to find a place for Jews in Quebec province's confessional school system that was either Protestant or Catholic. That struggle began with Confederation and flared for three decades (1903 to 1930).[57]

Conclusion

In the British colonies of Canada, Jamaica, and the thirteen colonies, Jews achieved civil rights largely without controversy or conflict. In contrast, Jews organized and campaigned for political rights. In the early American republic Jews received rights state by state, in Canada colony by colony. In the United States and Canada political rights were linked to disestablishment of the church and the enactment of religious equality.[58] In Jamaica it was entwined with race relations.

CHAPTER NINETEEN

Mass Society, I

EUROPE BECAME A MASS SOCIETY in the fin de siècle (1870–1914). Explosive population growth gave rise to major metropolises whose residents were divided by rank and religion, gender and class. The torrid pace of industrial development spawned a working class, labor unions, and the intractable "social question." The growth of constitutional government and democracy broadened the franchise and the political spectrum beyond the inherited liberal-conservative divide: socialism emerged at one extreme, reactionary conservatism at the other. Organized political parties and interest groups proliferated; nationalism pervaded political life. Despite these changes, old elites and elite institutions continued to exercise formidable power.[1]

The ostensible achievement of emancipation across western and central Europe ushered in the "post-emancipation" period. To be sure, emancipation remained a work in progress: Jews continued to contend with various forms of inequality, some trivial, some fundamental. The rise of political anti-Semitism aggravated existing forms of discrimination while also introducing new ones.

A threefold mass migration shaped the period. Jews moved up the urban pyramid in their own countries, from villages and towns to provincial and metropolitan cities. They moved westward across the continent, especially from areas of poverty, inequality, and persecution, to countries seemingly offering equality and economic opportunity. Finally, they moved overseas, especially to North and South America. In the period, some 2.5 million Jews emigrated from their native countries.[2]

In response to mass migration and political anti-Semitism, Jewish leaders developed new institutions of social welfare and civil defense as well as a new diplomacy.

Organizations

Emancipation ("out of" estates) in western and central Europe created new community organizations. These organizations varied radically in structure (voluntary vs. compulsory), scope (local/municipal vs. regional/national), and relationship to the state (state sanctioned vs. state created).[3] All were, first and foremost, dedicated to administering internal religious and communal affairs. Whereas some had actively advocated for rights and defended Jewish interests, none were equipped to face the new challenges of the fin de siècle.

New leaders devised a range of new secular organizations to respond to mass migration and political anti-Semitism.[4] The Alliance Israélite Universelle (1860) was the "mother" organization (chapter 17). Founded prior to the advent of mass migration and organized anti-Semitism, it anticipated by a generation two new types of secular, privately funded, national organizations.[5]

The first were national sister organizations, usually begun as an Alliance branch, which honored the commitment to emancipation and regeneration and, in response to migration, developed mass philanthropy and social welfare on an unprecedented scale.[6] The chronology of their founding recapitulated emancipation's: first England (Anglo-Jewish Association, 1871), then the Dual Monarchy (Allianz zu Wien, 1873), followed by Germany (Hilfsverein der deutschen Juden, 1901). The America Hebrew Immigrant Aid and Sheltering Society (1909) responded to similar needs.

The second type was the "civil rights organization" expressly designed to defend emancipation at home against the new political anti-Semitism. Their establishment also followed emancipation's course (Austrian-Israelite Union, 1886; Central Association of German Citizens of the Jewish Persuasion, 1893; Society for the Promotion of Enlightenment among the Jews of Russia's Legal Bureau, 1893).[7] Infringement of rights in the United States provoked Jews to engage in organized civil defense as well (American Jewish Committee, 1906; Anti-Defamation League of B'nai B'rith, 1913).

SOCIAL WELFARE

Beginning in the late 1860s, the mass migration of eastern Europe's Jews (Russia, Galicia, Rumania) transformed Jewish philanthropy across western and central Europe from local charity into a national, professionally administered social welfare. Because of the migration's very dimensions, since millions of others were migrating as well, it ceased to be an "internal" or exclusively Jewish issue.[8]

Following the Alliance, philanthropic organizations in western and central Europe adopted a three-pronged approach to migration. They promoted emancipation, negotiating with governments, and bringing pressure through the press. They funded schools to remedy poverty and underemployment. Finally, they organized the migration to protect the migrants and to minimize their impact on the countries through which they passed.[9] "Jewish charity had come very near to organize world Jewry into a curious sort of body politic."[10]

In the 1860s the Alliance attempted to address the situation in tsarist Russia by opening branches and establishing schools. The Russian government prohibited both. The Alliance also tried to organize mass emigration to the United States: Jewish organizations there objected. In response to these obstacles, the Alliance shifted focus to the Maghreb and the Mashreq.[11]

Nevertheless, the Alliance did take the lead in organizing relief for the first wave of migrants in 1868–69; at the time, no national organization existed in central Europe. In conjunction with the Alliance, Ludwig Philippson, a rabbi and editor of the *Allgemeine Zeitung des Judentums*, convened a conference in Berlin on migration (October 11, 1869). The conference called for emancipation, improved education, and freedom to migrate from the overpopulated Pale of Settlement to Russia's interior. The conference was, however, unable to devise a common strategy. In April 1882, in response to a second wave of migrants (1881–82; Brody), a second conference on migration was held in Berlin whose outcome was similarly inconclusive.[12]

ANGLO-JEWISH ASSOCIATION

Originating as a branch of the Alliance (1870), the Anglo-Jewish Association declared independence (1871) because its leaders thought the Franco-Prussian War and Paris Commune had impaired the Alliance's ability to function. It subsequently worked closely with the Alliance to address shared concerns, as propounded in its original constitution:

> To make every practical effort to remove any disabilities under which the Jews may labour, and to promote, wherever needful, the moral, social and intellectual advancement of our people . . .
>
> To give efficient aid to those who may suffer in consequence of being a member of the Jewish community. . . .
>
> To promote the publication of works calculated to advance these purposes.[13]

Even though it had a clear political mission and interceded regularly with the government, the Anglo-Jewish Association regarded itself, as did the Alliance, as a philanthropic association. It disavowed politics by asserting the identity of its concerns with British national sentiment.[14] On diplomatic issues the Anglo-Jewish Association collaborated with the Board of Deputies of British Jews (establishing a Conjoint Committee in 1878). The organizations interceded together on behalf of Jews in Ottoman Palestine and Romania, Morocco and Turkey, Bulgaria and Russia. They endeavored to discredit blood libels wherever they appeared.

The Anglo-Jewish Association established some fifteen schools, primarily in the Mashreq, for example, Baghdad, Jerusalem, Basra, and Aden, enrolling some nine thousand students by 1905.[15]

ALLIANZ IN VIENNA (1873)

The earliest efforts to establish a Vienna branch of the Alliance failed because the Habsburg government considered the organization subversive. Only after emancipation (1867) and in response to Romanian Jewry's dire situation (1872–73) did Vienna's Jewish elite take action.[16] The Vienna organization explicitly recognized Paris's preeminence and accordingly adopted an exclusively national mission. The Allianz shared its outlook and leaders, lay and rabbinic, with Vienna's organized Jewish community (IKG).[17] From the organization's inception the founders felt compelled to rebut anti-Semites' claims that it was proof of an international Jewish conspiracy.[18]

The Allianz embraced a national mission because of the challenges of migration generally and migration to Vienna specifically. To aid emigrants, especially from Galicia and the Bukowina, Vienna employed professional staff in hospitals, orphanages, and sanatoria, as well as provided cash handouts. It assisted emigrants to America, beginning with those who gathered in Brody, though it restricted aid to Jews from Russia, scrupulously excluding Jews from the Dual Monarchy or Germany. The Allianz engaged diplomatically on behalf of Jews in Romania, Bulgaria, Morocco, and Persia.[19]

From 1883 the Allianz established schools in Galicia. The schools aimed to turn children "into men and to educate them to work."[20] The Baron Hirsch Foundation (1891) assumed financial responsibility for the entire network of schools in Galicia and Bukowina: by 1900 there were fifty schools teaching ten thousand children.[21] The Allianz trained teachers in an institute in Vienna.[22]

The Allianz had more of an uphill battle in Galicia than the Alliance faced in the Maghreb and Mashreq: it lacked government sponsorship and faced opposition on two fronts: Orthodox and Hasidic Jews objected for religious reasons, Poles for nationalist ones.[23] Under pressure from Polish politicians, the Baron Hirsch Foundation recognized Polish as a "school language" even though German remained the language of instruction. In trying to bring the "light" of education to Galicia's Jews, the Baron Hirsch Foundation claimed religious and cultural neutrality. The schools, which taught religious subjects, manifestly propagated Habsburg German language and culture.[24]

JEWISH COLONIZATION ASSOCIATION (1891)

Baron Maurice de Hirsch (1831–96), the scion of a Bavarian Jewish banking family, made his own fortune in building railroads, especially in the Ottoman Empire. He founded the Jewish Colonization Association (JCA; 1891) in response to the Great Migration.[25] The JCA proposed emigration as an antidote to a withheld emancipation, aiming to regenerate Russia's and Romania's Jewish masses through the establishment of agricultural colonies:

to assist and promote the emigration of Jews from any part of Europe or Asia, and principally from countries in which they were being subjected to special taxes or political or other disabilities, to any other parts of the world, and to form and establish colonies in various parts of North and South America and other countries for agricultural, commercial and other purposes.[26]

The JCA first founded agricultural colonies in Argentina, then Brazil, Canada, and the United States, and finally Turkey, Cyprus, and Palestine.[27] In tsarist Russia the JCA supported agriculture, vocational schools, and credit cooperatives.[28]

The JCA was capable of undertaking such far-flung and ambitious projects because the Baron's fabulous munificence made it "probably the greatest charitable trust in the world."[29] The Baron had donated enormous sums to the Alliance Israélite Universelle, including an endowment that generated a huge annual income, founded the Baron Hirsch Stiftung in Vienna, and funded the Baron de Hirsch Fund in New York for relief and resettlement.[30]

HILFSVEREIN DER DEUTSCHEN JUDEN (1901)

Although the Alliance's Central Committee opposed an independent organization in Germany, nationalist competition in the 1890s made such an organization inescapable.[31] In 1903 the journalist and community activist Paul Nathan succeeded in obtaining approval for an independent organization from the German Foreign Office.[32]

The Hilfsverein provided massive aid to Russian Jews after the Kishniev pogrom (1903). In response to the pogroms, the organization adopted the idea of mass migration. Following the model of the Berlin conferences (1869, 1882), the Hilfsverein convened an international conference on migration (Frankfurt; 1904) that resulted in the founding of a Central Office for Jewish Emigration. Under the Hilfsverein's aegis, the organization's goal was "to bring order and purpose to an unplanned Jewish emigration."[33]

The Central Office transcended the pattern of local aid by establishing frontier stations and communication centers to assist east European Jews transiting through Germany to the ports of Hamburg and Bremen. Those stations and centers tried to offer legal safeguards to the migrants: many were stateless and at the mercy of shipping agents and scoundrels. Paul Nathan successfully used the press to convince the major shipping line's director to permit Hilfsverein representatives to be present at the border stations to protect the emigrants' rights as well as to provide better services, including kosher food.[34]

Nathan traveled to Russia to negotiate with the government over discrimination and the Jews' political status (1905–6). He traveled to Romania the next year (1907) for negotiations as well as to provide aid. He did the same in Bulgaria during the Balkan Wars (1913).[35]

JEWISH WOMEN'S LEAGUE
(JÜDISCHER FRAUENBUND; 1904)

Bourgeois Jewish women in Germany organized a social work and welfare organization after their Protestant and Catholic counterparts had done the same. Initially concerned to aid poor and working-class east European Jewish women, they addressed a selected group of issues: white slavery among the migrants, aid to working women and women's education for those settled in Germany, a home for unwed mothers. In time, they added such issues as equal pay for equal work, women's poverty, and women's equality in Judaism. Through the struggle for women's equality the organization hoped to strengthen Judaism and counter anti-Semitism. By 1912 the organization had 32,000 members associated with some 160 affiliates.[36]

HEBREW IMMIGRANT AID AND
SHELTERING SOCIETY (HIAS)

The Hebrew Immigrant Aid and Sheltering Society arose from a merger (1909) between an organization founded to provide a proper Jewish burial for immigrants from eastern Europe who died at Ellis Island with one that provided immigrants with food and lodging.[37] Its stated aim combined the absorption of Jewish immigrants with emancipationist regeneration, for example, financial independence alongside the promotion of agriculture and patriotism.

> To facilitate the lawful entry of Jewish immigrants into the various ports of the United States; to provide those in need with temporary shelter, food, clothing and such other aid as may be found necessary; to guide the immigrants to their destination; to help them obtain employment and prevent them from becoming public charges; to discourage their settling in congested cities; to maintain bureaus of information and to publish literature on the industrial, agricultural and commercial status of the country; to encourage them to follow agricultural pursuits; to take proper measures to prevent ineligible persons from emigration to the United States; to foster American ideals among the newcomers and to instill in them through a knowledge of American history and institutions a true patriotism and love for their adopted country; to make better known to people of the United States the many advantages of desirable immigration and to promote these objects by means of meetings, lectures, and publications.[38]

HIAS provided multiple services to the flood of immigrants: information in Yiddish on what to expect in the United States; representatives who intervened with the shipping companies to improve conditions in steerage; finding the immigrants' relatives in the United States; an Employment Bureau with up-to-date information; a kosher kitchen at Ellis Island. In addition, HIAS funded a representative at Ellis Island who intervened to assist those slated for deportation and employed lawyers to prevent or delay deportation, with significant success.[39]

By 1914 HIAS had become a national organization with a membership of 46,357 individuals; many affiliated organizations; branches in the major ports of embarkation (Baltimore, Boston, Philadelphia); and an office in Washington, D.C.[40] HIAS limited its cooperation with the European social welfare agencies to avoid appearing to encourage immigration.[41] HIAS lobbied against efforts to limit immigration through national quotas, a bill (Burnett-Dillingham) that Congress passed but President Taft vetoed (1913).[42]

The New "Anti-Semitism"

The new phenomenon of organized political "anti-Semitism" emerged after 1870 to oppose or negate emancipation. Wilhelm Marr, an obscure German journalist, coined the term in 1879 to differentiate the older animus toward Jews as adherents of a religion from a new hostility to Jews as a nation or "race" now endowed with equal rights. "Anti-Semitism" was a means to separate Jews from their fellow citizens and demote them.[43]

Anti-Semitism coalesced most older forms of opposition to Judaism, Jews, and emancipation. It drew on Christian antipathy to the "deicide" people who continued to observe an allegedly superseded, superstitious cult; on Christian and secular hostility to the Jews' relationship to money, especially their putative avarice and parasitic business practices; on the Romantic notion of the Christian state; and on the widely diffused idea that European "civilization" was fundamentally and inalterably Christian. These diverse sources meant that anti-Semitism was always a heterogeneous bundle of contradictory positions: Christian and anti-Christian; left-wing and right-wing; anticapitalist and antisocialist.[44]

Anti-Semitism added the significant ingredient of race to fashion a new political ideology. Many anti-Semites treated race as the defining criterion of history and society. They embraced a biological determinism that rendered race definitive. The individual disappeared: race not just predicted but in fact dictated personal characteristics. Some anti-Semites went so far as to link biological determinism to Social Darwinism's notion of the "survival of the fittest." History thereby became an ineluctable war between the races, for example, Aryans versus Jews.[45]

Most anti-Semites abhorred the political structure that had enacted emancipation. They rejected not just the liberal parties' dominance but the very
existence of constitutional government and civil society. They were wedded to
a radical, reactionary critique of the status quo. They combined a general an-
timodernism and hostility to urban life with extreme nationalism, colonial
expansionism, authoritarianism, and corporatism. Anti-Semitism became a
kind of "cultural code" signaling the rejection of democracy, civil society, and
the Jews' emancipation.[46] Anti-Semitism served many as the bridge to post-
liberal politics. It gave coherence and concreteness to reactionary right-wing
ideology and proto-fascist politics.

For anti-Semites emancipation was the great evil that they wished to limit
or abolish.[47] Anti-Semites held Jews to be not just the beneficiaries of the
new order but its very creators. In their eyes equality did not allow Jews to
join state, economy, and culture; rather, it enabled Jews to dominate, corrupt, and "Judaize" state, economy, and culture. Anti-Semites held that Jews
exerted, or were about to exert, absolute control through an overweening
press, an irresistible capitalism, and a corrosive socialism. Anti-Semites
propagated the myth that Jews engaged in a nefarious conspiracy of world
domination.

For anti-Semites Jews undermined the "nation": they were nationalism's
sworn adversary, the hostile "other."[48] For that reason anti-Semites wanted to
roll back or abolish Jews' rights, limit or eliminate their appointments to state
positions, curb their economic participation, and restrict or ban their immigration and naturalization.[49]

Political anti-Semitism swiftly found a following across the continent. Anti-
Semites formed organizations, political parties, and newspapers. They wrote
manifestos and party platforms, circulated petitions and ran for office, organized demonstrations and agitation, and attacked Jews and their property.

Anti-Semitism had some notable successes. Karl Lueger was its poster poli-
tician. A consummate orator, he used anti-Semitism to mobilize a wide swath
of Viennese society to become the highest elected official in the Dual Monarchy, Lord Mayor of Vienna (1897–1910).[50]

In French Algeria, anti-Semitism enjoyed its greatest political success.
Anti-Semitism pervaded the European settlers' political spectrum, uniting socialists, radicals, and clericals. With the election of 1897, avowed anti-Semites
gained control of all municipal governments. For European settlers, whose
numbers increased from some 25,000 in 1840 to 376,000 in 1886, anti-
Semitism gave coherence to a nascent movement for independence. Algeria's
potent anti-Semitism fueled metropolitan France's.[51]

France's Dreyfus Affair (1894–1906) was initially one of anti-Semitism's
signal victories. The anti-Semitic press had paved the way by promoting the
idea that Jewish soldiers were inherently traitorous. The anti-Semitic agitation

that continued throughout the affair's dozen years questioned the Third Republic's legitimacy and divided the nation.[52]

Anti-Semites revived the blood libel and staged trials in Tiszaeszlár (Hungary, 1882); Polná (Bohemia, 1899–1901); Konitz (Germany, 1900); and Kishniev and the infamous Beilis trial (Russia, 1903 and 1911).[53]

In western and central Europe anti-Semitism did not succeed in gaining sufficient political power to implement its program.[54] At the same time, Russia and Romania's discriminatory legislation and violence, while inspiring anti-Semites, continued to shock governments and public opinion across Europe.

Prior to 1914 organized political anti-Semitism had two enduring achievements. First, it gained legitimacy in political discourse and the public sphere. It was not just politicians and parties on the margins that espoused it; mainstream politicians and political parties exploited its political potential.[55] Second, it penetrated civil society. Some secondary associations excluded Jews. Various kinds of associations either felt an affinity for, or expressly adopted, anti-Semitism.[56]

Civil Rights Organizations

In response to organized political anti-Semitism, Jewish emancipationists took advantage of the fin de siècle's new forms of civil and political life: civic associations and political interest groups.[57] Those two models enabled Jews to organize to defend civil rights without founding a political party or forming a voting bloc.

AUSTRIAN-ISRAELITE UNION

The founders of the Austrian-Israelite Union (Österreichisch-Israelitische Union [ÖIU]; 1886) aimed to establish an alternative to the nonpolitical, oligarchic religious community (*Kultusgemeinde*).[58] These upwardly mobile doctors and lawyers, merchants and bankers, mostly new to Vienna, initially conceived of a "civic association" designed to respond to anti-Semitism by pursuing "collective, systematic political activity on all issues related to Jews and Judaism [*Judentum*]."[59]

To gain official approval as a civic association, and perhaps to satisfy less aggressive members, the founders diluted the original program. The approved statutes omitted any mention of combatting anti-Semitism. They instead spoke euphemistically of countering all efforts to "aggravate denominational and racial differences." The original political program gave way to a general statement of concern with "all matters under consultation in the Parliament that concern Jews and Judaism."[60]

Some of the "maximalist" members tried to reclaim the initial impetus. They formed a group named Equality of Rights (1888) that proclaimed the goal of "fighting antisemitism and its deleterious influences" while resisting "any encroachment on, and infringement of, constitutional rights and liberties."[61] The new president in 1901, Maximilian Paul-Schiff, echoed this view when he declared that "I see the Union . . . as the first and sole representative of the political rights of the Jews in Austria."[62] Moreover, the organization revised its statutes in 1902 to define its goal as "protecting the general and political rights of the Jews and aiding those who belong to Judaism in utilizing those rights."[63]

The Austrian-Israelite Union scored a major victory in response to pogroms in Galicia in 1898: its president (Wilhelm Anninger) interceded with the prime minister to request the dispatch of troops and a declaration of martial law. The prime minister complied; the authorities quelled the riots.[64]

The Austrian-Israelite Union significantly established a Legal Defense Committee (1895) that metamorphosed into a full-fledged Legal Defense Bureau (1897).[65] The Legal Defense Bureau's stated task was to provide "legal aid without cost in all cases where the constitutional rights of the Jews as such are discriminated against."[66] The Legal Defense Bureau became so integral that the Austrian-Israelite Union added a clause to its statutes (1903):

> The organization sees its task as safeguarding the general and political rights of the Jews and helping [to guarantee] those rights to those practicing the Jewish religion.[67]

To support the Defense Bureau's growing budget the leaders turned the Viennese club into a national organization. Leaders traveled throughout Austria, Bohemia, and Moravia to recruit dues-paying members, eventually bringing the total to some seven thousand. Most of the legal cases occurred in the provinces where Jews were more vulnerable.[68]

One obstacle the Defense Bureau faced was Austrian law: "a Jewish individual, a Jewish association, nay even the IKG itself, had no right to appear as plaintiffs in cases of offense against Jewry as a whole."[69] In cases in which individuals were not named the Defense Bureau lacked legal standing: it had to persuade a public prosecutor to institute proceedings. Successful libel suits against anti-Semitic newspapers faced a similar problem: newspapers continued to make the same claims but ceased naming individuals. Another obstacle was parliamentary immunity. Anti-Semitic politicians, especially in the Lower Austrian House, could defame the Jews and then publish their remarks with impunity.[70]

The Defense Bureau was especially active in cases of blood libel and forced baptism of minors. The bureau acted expeditiously to avert the Christian Social Party's initiative at the Vienna Municipal School Board (1899) to segregate Jews in separate denominational schools. It was similarly successful, this time with the aid of Jewish representatives in Parliament, in blocking a Christian-Social parliamentarian's 1908 effort to introduce a quota for Jewish pupils in secondary schools. The Defense Bureau vehemently denounced this "first attempt by parliamentary legislation to abrogate Jewish citizens' full rights."[71]

The Austrian-Israelite Union engaged in party politics, though with limited success. As early as 1891–92 political candidates came to the organization seeking endorsement, claiming that they would lead the struggle against anti-Semitism. The Austrian-Israelite Union's members were too politically divided to act in unison.[72] Another factor that hampered the organization was its members' ingrained reluctance to vote for Social Democratic candidates even though, with the Liberals' decline, they presented the strongest alternative to anti-Semitic candidates. In the first election after the introduction of universal male suffrage (1907), the organization split over which Jewish candidates to endorse.[73]

Wilhelmine Germany

Jews in Germany were as fragmented as the Second Empire itself: they had no empire-wide organization. The first attempt to establish a central organization, the German-Israelite Community League (*Deutsch-Israelitscher Gemeindebund*; 1869), foundered for over a decade. The organization's purview was limited to the administration of communities: it was designed to advocate for the equality of "Judaism" and subsidize smaller and medium-sized communities.[74]

With the rise of anti-Semitism the organization tried to bring cases of libel and defamation (from 1875), yet faced the same obstacle as the Austrian-Israelite Union: the public prosecutor had to be convinced to file suit.[75] The Community League found the public prosecutor's repeated rejections insuperable. The organization issued apologetic literature about Judaism and Jews for a German audience; for Jews it produced literature prescribing proper behavior, especially in response to overt anti-Semitism.[76] It lobbied vigorously, albeit unsuccessfully, for revisions of the Prussian Law for the Maintenance of Public Elementary Schools (July 28, 1906) that eroded the principle of equal rights by not properly allocating funds for Jewish schools, not funding religious instruction for Jewish children in interdenominational schools, and not according teachers of Judaism equal standing with teachers of Christianity.[77]

In response to organized anti-Semitism, a group of Liberal Christian politicians founded the Association for Defense Against Anti-Semitism (*Verein zur Abwehr des Antisemitismus*; 1891). They did so to defend the constitution and the rule of law (*Rechtsstaat*). By endeavoring to limit or abolish emancipation, anti-Semites threatened the foundational principle of equality before the law. Similarly, the state's refusal to hire Jews for civil service positions allowed prejudiced bureaucrats to subvert the rule of law. The association primarily engaged in propaganda (posters, pamphlets, speakers) and supported candidates opposed to anti-Semitism.[78]

German Jews in the 1880s experimented with mass politics to counter anti-Semitism. For example, Professor Moritz Lazarus (1824–1903) founded the Jewish Committee (*Das jüdische Comité*) in December 1880: a gathering of notables, it aimed to fight anti-Semitism in public as an issue for all Germans.[79] Beginning in 1886, a number of community organizations and rabbinical associations joined to defend kosher slaughtering against anti-Semites' efforts to outlaw it. These organizations engaged in the new methods of mass mailings to solicit letters and petitions. Some of the groups also produced professionally edited propaganda. These efforts yielded a "network of Jewish political activity."[80]

The Central Association of German Citizens of the Jewish Persuasion (*Centralverein deutscher Staatsbürger jüdischen Glaubens*) was founded (1893) in response to a further wave of anti-Semitism that included the ritual murder trial in Xanten and the Conservative Party's adoption of an anti-Semitic platform (Tivoli convention; 1892).[81] It paralleled the Austrian-Israelite Union and the new German interest groups.[82]

The Central Association's founders believed that since anti-Semites threatened to revoke emancipation, Jews as citizens needed to mount a public campaign to defend their legal equality with all available legal means: "As citizens we neither need nor demand any protection beyond our legal rights."[83] Its founders designed a mass citizens organization: by 1916 the organization had enlisted 40,000 individual members and, through affiliated bodies, more than 200,000 total members.[84] Like other mass organizations, the Central Association engaged in propaganda and published a monthly journal. *Im deutschen Reich* ("In the German Empire"; 1895) became the most widely circulated German Jewish periodical.[85]

The association, many of whose founders were lawyers, opened a Legal Defense Department (*Rechtsschutzkommission*) that aimed to force the judicial system to afford Jews equal protection in cases for which there were clear constitutional safeguards: blasphemy, libel, "disturbing the peace," and "inciting to violence."[86] The Central Association at first encountered the same problem as had the Austrian-Israelite Union and the German-Israelite Community League: public prosecutors refused to file charges. The Central Association succeeded in defeating the arbitrary application of the law by convincing public prosecutors to recognize Jews' collective standing as a plaintiff and bring suits. In contrast, the Defense Bureau usually failed in collective libel suits.[87]

The Central Association's founders gradually realized that legal means were insufficient to uphold equality and state law (*Rechtsstaat*). From 1898 they began to engage in politics, working to defeat anti-Semites running for office in municipal, state, and national elections. The Central Association funneled funds to opposing liberal candidates or their parties. Run-off elections often complicated this effort: the liberal parties (Progressives) sometimes refused to endorse Social Democratic candidates, the liberals' direct competitors, and instead endorsed or allied with a conservative or explicitly anti-Semitic candidate.[88] The Central Association also pressed the liberal parties to nominate Jewish candidates. While the Central Association did not align itself with one political party, it tended to prefer the liberal parties. By 1911 it began to support Socialist candidates as well.

In 1911 the Central Association started to cooperate with the Association for Defense Against Anti-Semitism to pool funds in political campaigns.[89] The Central Association also pressed liberal representatives to question government ministers in the Reichstag about violations of the constitution, for example, discrimination in judicial and reserve officer appointments.[90]

THE RECHTSSTAAT AND CIVIL RIGHTS

Jews established civil rights organizations at virtually the same time in the three empires that aspired to be "states of law" (*Rechtsstaat*): Germany, the Dual Monarchy, and tsarist Russia. In the concluding decades of the century, the Legal Bureau of the Society for the Promotion of Enlightenment among the Jews of Russia, the Austrian-Israelite Union, and the Central Association began to employ legal defense to uphold the *Rechtsstaat* or the promise of one. In the three empires Jews utilized existing legal means to the fullest to defend equality.[91]

Moreover, in the three empires Jews collectively engaged in politics. In Russia the Union for the Attainment of Full Equality for the Jewish People in Russia (1905) and the Jewish People's Group (1907) advocated for full civil rights in the Duma (they also advocated for national minority rights). The Austrian-Israelite Union and the Central Association similarly participated in elections. Notwithstanding the differences in the three empires, Jews developed an emancipation politics that employed similar strategies to defend, or in the Russian case to pursue, emancipation.

AMERICAN JEWISH COMMITTEE (1906)

At the turn of the twentieth century American Jewish leaders were acutely aware of lacking a national organization capable of responding to east European Jewry's persecution and mass migration. In response, an elite group of businessmen, lawyers, and rabbis founded a version of Europe's civil defense organizations. Like the Alliance, the autocratic American Jewish Committee (AJC) billed itself as a philanthropic organization while adopting an emancipationist agenda: it aimed "to prevent infringement of the civil and religious rights of Jews, and to alleviate the consequences of persecution," as well as to strive to gain emancipation for Jews everywhere.[92]

The AJC lobbied discreetly against the enactment of restrictive immigration laws, whether literacy tests or national quotas. To have exact knowledge about American Jews, and especially the recent immigrants, it founded the Bureau of Jewish Social Research and Statistics and published a statistical almanac, the *American Jewish Year Book*. The AJC eschewed litigation and politics, neither supporting Jewish candidates nor requesting Jewish office-holders to lobby on its behalf. It preferred to influence public opinion through community relations and education.[93] The AJC collected funds for social welfare organizations abroad, cooperating with its European counterparts—the British Joint Foreign Committee, the Hilfsverein, and the Alliance.[94]

ANTI-DEFAMATION LEAGUE (ADL)
OF B'NAI B'RITH (1913)

In the mid-nineteenth century, Jewish men excluded from Masons and Odd Fellows lodges had founded B'nai B'rith, a fraternal order (1843). In the early twentieth century, after France's Dreyfus Affair and Russia's Beiliss case, members considered establishing an organization to counter disparaging characterizations of Jews on stage and in dime novels, the press, and movies.[95]

The widespread defamation of Jews in America during the Leo Frank case in Atlanta (1913) moved those men to action. The ADL deemed anti-Semitism a "pernicious and un-American tendency." It adopted a public approach to offensive treatment, announcing its opposition to entertainers, newspapers, and advertisers. It also organized consumer boycotts and mass protests. Like the AJC, the ADL eschewed litigation in favor of influencing public opinion.[96] In keeping with its emancipationist agenda, the ADL endeavored to regenerate the east European immigrants by directing them away from such allegedly unethical occupations as pawnbroking.[97]

NEW DIPLOMACY

Romania and the emerging Balkan states provided the occasion for a new diplomacy: the Congress of Berlin (1878) was the acme of the Alliance's efforts to achieve emancipation for Jews everywhere.[98] International Jewish leaders had commenced efforts on behalf of Romania's Jews when the two principalities gained self-governance (Congress of Paris, 1856) and Romania began a pattern of defying Jewish and Great Power intervention (chapter 21).[99]

Jewish advocates resumed their efforts toward Romania in the early 1870s. On October 29–30, 1872, thirty-five delegates from eight countries (France, England, Germany, Austria, Belgium, Holland, United States, and Romania) convened in Brussels to address Romanian Jewry's distressing situation. The conference established an Executive Committee located in Vienna and enlisted Adolphe Crémieux as honorary president.[100] The conference embraced the Alliance's usual program of promoting emancipation and education; it rejected proposals either of mass emigration to the United States or of boycotting Romanian state loans.[101]

After Serbia and Montenegro's unsuccessful war against the Ottoman Empire, sixty-five Jewish leaders convened in Paris on December 15, 1876, to try to guarantee that Jews would gain the same rights as Christians in the Balkan states and Romania. The Paris meeting submitted a démarche to the German government; it in turn guaranteed its support at the upcoming Constantinople conference. In the event, the conference did not convene.[102]

At the Congress of Berlin, England, France, and Austria's primary aim was to limit Russia's acquisitions; their secondary aim was to protect the region's mixed populations.[103] In preparation for the Berlin Congress the various Jewish organizations (e.g., Alliance, Anglo-Jewish Association, Committee for Romania) concerted their efforts to obtain "clear and unambiguous written declarations that guarantee the civil and political rights of the Jews."[104] To bring domestic pressure on the delegates to the conference, the Romania Committee asked politicians to raise the issue in advance in the parliaments of Hungary, Italy, France, England, and Austria.[105] At the Congress itself the various leaders drafted a memorandum calling for equal rights for members of all the region's faiths. The leaders made virtually daily visits to Congress delegates.[106]

At Bismarck's behest, the Congress first guaranteed Jews' rights in Bulgaria (June 24, 1878), the least controversial case. The French foreign minister (Waddington) insisted on equality for members of all creeds "without differentiation." In the case of Serbia, whose treatment of Jews was on a par with Romania's, the Russian foreign minister (Gorchakov) raised serious objections to equality. In consequence, the Congress (June 29) made Serbian independence conditional on a vague clause guaranteeing religious freedom.[107]

The Congress finally turned to Romania: it adopted a general clause precluding discrimination and securing religious freedom (Article 44). Bismarck vetoed an additional sentence specifically addressing the Jews' status ("The Jews of Romania who do not belong to a foreign nationality have the right to acquire Romanian citizenship"). Bismarck was more concerned to secure German investments in Romania's railroads, including his own, than with the Jews' equality. In fact, he exploited the Jewish issue to extract a favorable settlement on the railroads.[108]

The Congress's intervention was a paper victory; the Romanian government defied it. Romania's new constitution (Article 7) treated all Jews in the country as foreigners and established a torturous naturalization process. Only a few Jews could meet the stringent criteria to gain equal rights (1,500 by 1914). The Romanian government pointed to the disastrous example of Algeria, arguing that emancipation enabled 30,000 Jews to gain power over millions of Arabs and hundreds of thousands of European colonists.[109]

The Alliance and other organizations' first foray into international diplomacy had failed: Romania's defiance nullified the paper rights.[110]

Conclusion

The new conditions of the fin-de-siècle, mass migration from eastern Europe and the rise of the new organized political anti-Semitism propelled Jews across Europe and in the United States to establish social welfare and civil defense organizations. The former practiced solidarity on a grand scale; the latter intervened to protect equality. The organizations' promotion of emancipation was predicated on Jews being a confession or religious group: by functioning under the guise of "welfare" and "civil defense," they deliberately eschewed political claims. From the 1890s new forms of mass Jewish politics emerged that contested that basic assumption.

CHAPTER TWENTY

Mass Society, II

THE NEW POLITICS THAT EMERGED in fin-de-siècle Europe challenged liberal democracy and bourgeois society. The Jewish versions challenged emancipation. Emancipationists held Jews to constitute a religion; the new politics defiantly proclaimed them a nation. At one extreme Zionists dismissed Europe's emancipation as an abject failure and proposed a national alternative to be realized elsewhere. Autonomists or diaspora nationalists espoused "national rights": they deemed civil and political rights insufficient and, in consequence, "western" Europe's emancipation a calamity. Socialists recognized the necessity of rights—civil, political, and national—yet spurned capitalist society and bourgeois politics. At the other extreme Orthodox Jews rejected all secular Jewish politics yet emulated its methods to mobilize a "Torah-true" constituency. They subordinated emancipation to eternal religious goals. The competing ideologies created a complex political matrix.[1]

The new ideologies generated a new language to depict emancipation's allegedly pernicious impact. They coined and cultivated the term "assimilation" to denigrate emancipation's putative destruction of religious and communal life.[2] They deemed emancipation a twofold failure. Within, it ruined Judaism and the Jews ("assimilation"); without, it evoked the new adversary of anti-Semitism.[3] They gave assimilation geographical coordinates, turning the alleged differences across Europe into an ideological code. "West" (western Europe) was the site of emancipation and assimilation, "east" (eastern Europe) the home of an unemancipated and unassimilated Jewry capable of generating a new solution.[4]

In principle, the new ideologies adamantly opposed emancipation. In practice, emancipation remained so critical that defending or striving to attain it bridged seemingly insuperable divisions. In central Europe, the fledgling nationalist movements sought legitimacy by cooperating with emancipationist organizations and leaders. In Russia, all parties recognized that civil rights, especially freedom of residence, were imperative to release the masses from the Pale of Settlement's impoverishing congestion.

Zionism

Zionism was a late nineteenth-century, post-emancipation version of nationalism.[5] Its founders and leaders denounced emancipation as a colossal failure. Herzl thought it the cause of anti-Semitism: "In the principal countries where Anti-Semitism prevails, it does so as a result of the emancipation of the Jews." Emancipation was therefore self-defeating: the anti-Semitism it provoked rendered equality a "dead letter."[6]

Moreover, in Zionists' eyes emancipation destroyed Jewish nationhood by forcibly reducing Judaism to a mere confession. In consequence, "assimilation" triumphed in the form of defection and conversion, indifference and ignorance. Under the constant scrutiny of governments and public opinion, emancipated Jewry's life was tantamount to "slavery within freedom."[7]

> The moral spine of the Jews was in danger of being broken by the so-called emancipation, which in many cases had alienated them from their heritage, and yet had not given them anything more than merely formal equality.[8]

For Zionists the "negation of the Diaspora" became an absolute imperative.[9]

Jews could realize emancipation's promise of true equality through collective "auto-emancipation" in their own land.[10] They would regenerate through occupational diversification ("the conquest of labor"), especially agriculture and manual labor. They would stage a cultural renaissance in the Hebrew language. In contrast to the "assimilated" diaspora Jew, Zionism would produce a healthy and muscular, proud and self-confident "Hebrew." While Zionism drew symbolically on Judaism's messianic tradition, it borrowed much of its substance from emancipation's discourse of regeneration.[11]

From its inception as a movement (First Congress; Basel, 1897), Zionism was a variegated big tent: its adherents were religious and secular, socialist and capitalist, autocratic and democratic. The "politicals" (Herzl) were committed to obtaining an internationally recognized charter. The "practicals" ("Lovers of Zion"; *Hovevei Zion*) were devoted to colonizing Palestine by building settlements. The "culturals" (Ahad Ha-Am; Martin Buber) aimed to build a spiritual and cultural center to reanimate all Jewish life, including the diaspora. Religious believers (*Mizrahi*) aspired to form an observant community that could practice the commandments specific to the Land of Israel. Finally, some Zionists departed the Zionist Congress over the issue of Uganda to search for other possible territories, establishing the Jewish Territorial Organization (ITO; 1905–25); they prioritized rescuing the east European Jewish masses over an exclusive attachment to Zion ("a land for a people, not a people for a land").[12]

Despite condemning emancipation and assimilation, Zionists often cooperated with emancipationist organizations. In Germany, for example, the first generation of Zionists cooperated with the Central Association to defend equality. Collaboration gave way to divisive polemics first when Zionists began to campaign in community elections (1910) and then a radical younger cohort passed the Posen Resolution (1912) requiring each Zionist to commit to emigrating to Palestine.[13]

Although German Zionists derided the founders of the Hilfsverein as "assimilationists" and "plutocrats," they tried to participate in its activities. Zionist representatives attended the Frankfurt (1904) and Brussels (1906) conferences on Russian Jewish emigration.[14] The Hilfsverein and the Zionist movement cooperated for almost a decade in founding Hebrew-language schools in Palestine, including the first Hebrew-speaking kindergarten.[15]

Cooperation foundered over the proposed Technical College's language of instruction. The Hilfsverein wanted Hebrew to be the language of instruction for all subjects except the most technical: mathematics and natural sciences would be taught in German. Members of the second aliyah, the cultural Zionists, and the Hebrew Teachers' Union insisted that Hebrew should be the sole language of instruction.[16]

The Helsingfors conference of Russian Zionists in December 1906 adopted a platform known as "work in the present" (*Gegenwartsarbeit*) that endorsed striving for "complete democracy" in the Diaspora, for example, a democratic constitution, civil rights, and autonomy for minorities. This version of evolutionary or "synthetic" Zionism recognized that, given the unlikelihood of an imminent Zionist revolution "there" (Palestine), adherents should work first for emancipation and minority rights "here" (in their diaspora homes).[17]

Autonomism

At the end of the nineteenth century the multinational Dual Monarchy and tsarist empire confronted pervasive conflicts with and among nationalities. To neutralize those fissiparous conflicts, thinkers began to envision forms of federalism based on the cultural and even political autonomy of national minorities. Such autonomy could be institutionalized through local government.[18]

This idea of national autonomy came to dominate Jewish politics in eastern Europe. In the 1890s the historian and political activist Simon Dubnow (1860–1941) began to enunciate ideas of Jewish autonomy by advocating a bundle of collective rights ranging from language and education to a national assembly with taxing powers. This was an "affirmation of the diaspora" intended to avoid the "national suicide" of "assimilation" induced by the "west's" emancipation through individual rights. "The emancipated Jews of western Europe of that time demanded their liberty not as free men but as slaves."[19]

Dubnow believed that gaining national minority rights alongside civil and political rights would empower eastern European Jews to promote their own language, culture, and limited self-government: "true emancipation means not only liberation of the individual human being, but also of the individual nationality." Dubnow's bottom line was that there should be no sacrifice of "national rights" for "civil rights."[20]

Dubnow's program came to fruition in Russia as civic and national rights became inextricably linked. During the 1905 revolution Dubnow energetically advocated civil rights, joining with a wide range of parties in the umbrella Union for the Attainment of Full Equality for the Jewish People in Russia (March 1905). After 1905 all the major Jewish political parties espoused national rights: all agreed to rights of education, language, and culture. Only national political rights remained an issue. Liberals and Zionists wanted an elected assembly with the power of taxation as a bulwark against the state; socialists objected.[21]

In Vienna, national minority rights struggled as Zionism's "stepchild." The idea emerged in the 1890s with the Jewish People's Association (*Jüdischer Volksverein*; 1897), soon followed by the Jewish People's Party (*Jüdischer Volkspartei*; 1902). Between 1904 and 1906 socialists (Bund) and socialist Zionists (*Poalei Zion*) also embraced autonomy.[22]

Autonomism thrived in Galicia as a form of provincial politics. In the 1880s Galician nationalists, including proto-Zionists, developed ideas that in the 1890s became a program of domestic politics (*Landespolitik*) aspiring to full equality as well as national minority rights. Proponents demanded that the state officially recognize Jews as a nationality. In the 1890s, a public sphere of Yiddish newspapers appeared that, loosely affiliated with Zionism, propagated the idea that Jews were a nationality and Yiddish their national language.

After the publication of *The Jews' State* (1896) and the First Zionist Congress (1897), Herzl's purely political Zionism swiftly dominated the scene: the 1901 Congress expressly prohibited domestic politics (*Landespolitik*). Galician Zionists bridled at this restriction. After Herzl's death (1904) they reclaimed their program of diaspora politics for minority rights. Franz Joseph's introduction of universal male suffrage (1905) enabled the mobilization of Jewish voters, who elected four Jewish representatives to the Austrian Parliament (*Reichsrat*). The four in turn formed a Jewish Club (1907), a historic milestone in national minority representation. To wrest control from the dominant Poles, Zionists allied with a Ruthenian faction.[23]

Socialism

Jewish socialists attributed the Jews' plight, including anti-Semitism and the masses' impoverishment, to the evils of capitalism. Their maxim was: dismantle capitalism, build a socialist society, and the resulting universal equality would eliminate all prejudice and animosity, including toward Jews. The socialists' rejection of capitalism and autocratic tsarism went hand in hand. The strategy was to mobilize the workers through strikes to lead them to revolution against the tsar.

Organized Jewish socialism arose from an alliance between elements of the Russified Jewish intelligentsia and the Jewish proletariat in the Pale of Settlement's northwest provinces where the Jewish artisan proletariat was most numerous and concentrated.[24] The early socialists initially endeavored to educate "circles" (*kruzhok*) of Jewish workers (Russian language, science, political economy) to fashion a worker elite who would, in turn, mobilize the working masses. That approach failed as the now educated workers opted either to continue their education or to improve their own condition.

The socialists then turned to agitation. They organized an underground trade union movement (*kassa*) conducted in Yiddish by the Yeshiva-educated, Yiddish-speaking intelligentsia (*polu-intelligentsiia*), who led workers' strikes yet also boycotts of goods produced by exploitative employers. The strike campaigns enjoyed only temporary success. Employers quickly learned to organize resistance and exploit economic downturns to reverse the workers' gains.[25]

Socialism offered workers a new way of life in its conspiratorial organization. It invested the workers with pride, high ethical standards, and the self-importance of being "subjects" rather than "objects" of history. Socialist libraries introduced them to a broad culture of Yiddish fiction and Yiddish translations of Russian and European literature as well as historical and political works. In short, socialism created a new Jewish man and woman.[26]

Founded in 1897, the General Jewish Labor Union in Lithuania, Poland, and Russia (*Bund*), a Marxist Social Democratic Party, was initially not nationalist. It endorsed the acquisition of civil rights as early as its Third Party Convention (1899). With its leadership competing with Zionists and Autonomists abroad as well as at home, the Bund first adopted the idea of national rights (Fourth Congress; 1901) and four years later demanded full autonomy as well as full civil and political equality (Sixth Congress; 1905). The Bund rejected Zionism as serving the interests of the Jewish bourgeoisie. To Zionism's emigration it counterpoised the legitimacy of "hereness" (*doikayt*).[27]

Orthodoxy

The Agudat Yisrael (Union of Israel, 1912) coalesced from a number of attempts across central and eastern Europe to establish an Orthodox political organization. Orthodox leaders aspired to gain representation to the government (Russia, Germany) and to vie with such secular organizations as the Zionist Congress and the Central Association.

In response to the establishment of the German-Israelite Community League (*Deutsch-Israelitscher Gemeindebund*; 1869) (chapter 19), Orthodox Jews in Frankfurt's separatist community created the Free Association for the Interests of Orthodox Jewry (*Freie Vereinigung für die Interessen des Orthodoxen Judentums*; 1886)." Samson Raphael Hirsch (1808–88) set the organiza-

FIGURE 14. Eighth National Conference of the Bund, Petrograd, 1917.
YIVO Record ID 1050, Collection R1, cat. no. Petrog5 Frame 46389.

tion's agenda of supporting Orthodox Jewish life (students and teachers, circumcision and Kashrut) as well as providing representation to government
agencies.[28]

To have an Orthodox alternative to the ineffective Community League and
the secular Central Association, a new leader, Jacob Rosenheim (from 1906),
tried to unite all of the Orthodox Jewish communities in Germany through the
Free Association. Although his effort failed, it did lead to the convocation of a
conference of Orthodox leaders (Bad Homburg, 1909) from across central and
eastern Europe. That conference probably would have failed as well were it not
for the Zionist Congress's adoption of a cultural program (10th Congress,
Basel, 1911) that propelled the Orthodox to concerted opposition. Lay leaders
convened in Frankfurt in October 1911 and adopted a resolution to create a
"world organization standing on the ground of Torah."[29]

In Galicia, Orthodox and Ultra-orthodox rabbis took almost a decade to
respond to the liberals' establishment of a cultural association (*Shomer Israel*,
1867). In vehement opposition to reports of a plan to erect a teachers' and rabbinical seminary, Orthodox rabbis and Hasidic rebbes received a charter to
establish an organization called Stalwarts of Belief (*Mahzikei Ha-Dat*; 1878).
Its signal achievement was to use religious appeals to mobilize the Orthodox
masses for political purposes: it helped Rabbi Simon Sofer (1820–83) of Cracow gain election to the Austrian Diet (1879).[30]

In Russia, Orthodox and Hasidic leaders first organized to create an alliance with Stolypin's government, which at the time was seeking conservative support. They aimed to use the neglected Rabbinic Commission to gain government recognition for the "spiritual rabbis" in opposition to the official "Crown rabbis." In the Kingdom of Poland 110 Orthodox activists and rabbis convened in Warsaw (December 30, 1908 to January 1, 1909). In Russia proper, a rabbinic assembly met in Vilna (April 20–28, 1909). To alleviate the Jews' poverty representatives called for lifting residential and occupational restrictions, that is, emancipation. Orthodox politics reached its apogee in the Rabbinic Commission of March 1910 during which its leaders had a brief, if dismal, audience with Stolypin (March 16, 1910). The government's support for the Beilis ritual murder trial dashed Orthodox hopes for a rapprochement with the tsarist government.[31]

The leaders who met in Kattowicz (May 27–28, 1912) created the *Aguda*. The leaders' first priority was to maintain an observant community, "to unify, collect and conserve on the basis of our ancient program." Leaders delineated six issues: four concerned exclusively observant Jews (#1 organization, #2 education, #5 press and literature, #6 forum), while two concerned the material life of all Jews (#3 economic conditions, #4 emergency aid). Emancipation did not appear; it at best figured implicitly in the call "to improve the economic conditions of the Jewish masses" (#3).

Conclusion

The spectrum of Jewish politics broadened at the fin de siècle. Zionists and Autonomists espoused the idea that Jews were a nation entitled to its own national life either as a majority in Palestine or a national minority in Europe. Both developed the concept of "assimilation" to denigrate emancipation's pernicious effects. In eastern Europe all the Jews' political parties—emancipationists, Zionists, Autonomists, Bundist Socialists—embraced a version of national minority rights.

The Bund represented a Jewish socialism that dreamed of a classless society to solve the Jewish Question. Orthodox Jews mobilized to press their own causes and to counter the multiple threats of the organized secular political parties.

The developments of the fin de siècle were to shape Jewish life in the first four decades of the twentieth century. Internally emancipation played out in relationship to the network of social welfare and civil defense organizations as well as the matrix of political parties and movements. Externally emancipation would face its gravest test.

PART IV

The Fourth Region

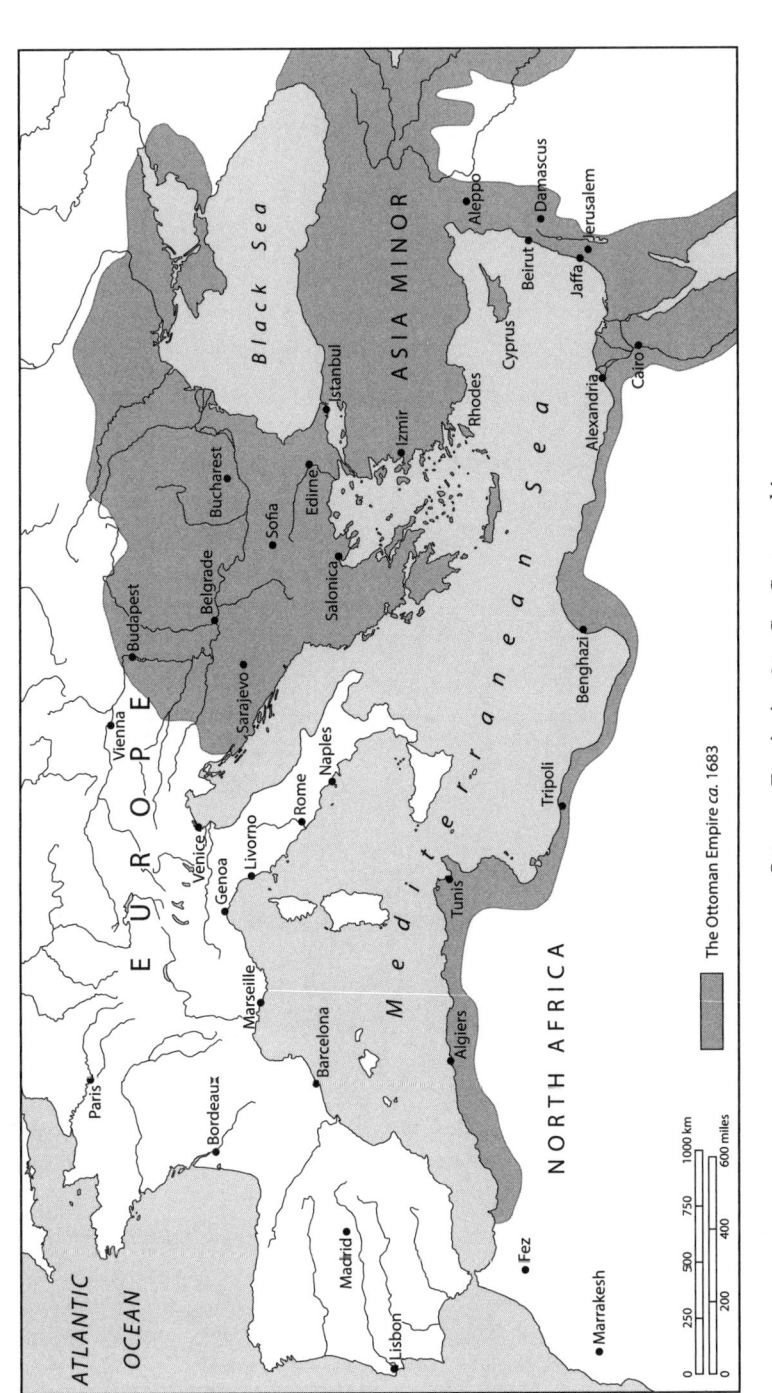

ATLANTIC
OCEAN

EUROPE

Paris

Bordeaux

Madrid

Lisbon

Marrakesh

Fez

NORTH AFRICA

Barcelona

Marseille

Genoa
Venice
Livorno
Rome
Naples

Algiers

Tunis

Tripoli

Mediterranean Sea

Sarajevo

Vienna

Budapest

Belgrade

Sofia

Bucharest

Black Sea

Edirne

Salonica

Istanbul

Izmir

ASIA MINOR

Rhodes

Cyprus

Aleppo

Damascus

Beirut

Jaffa
Jerusalem

Benghazi

Alexandria

Cairo

The Ottoman Empire *ca.* 1683

0   250   500   750   1000 km

0   200   400   600 miles

MAP VIII. Ottoman Empire in 1683. Cox Cartographic.

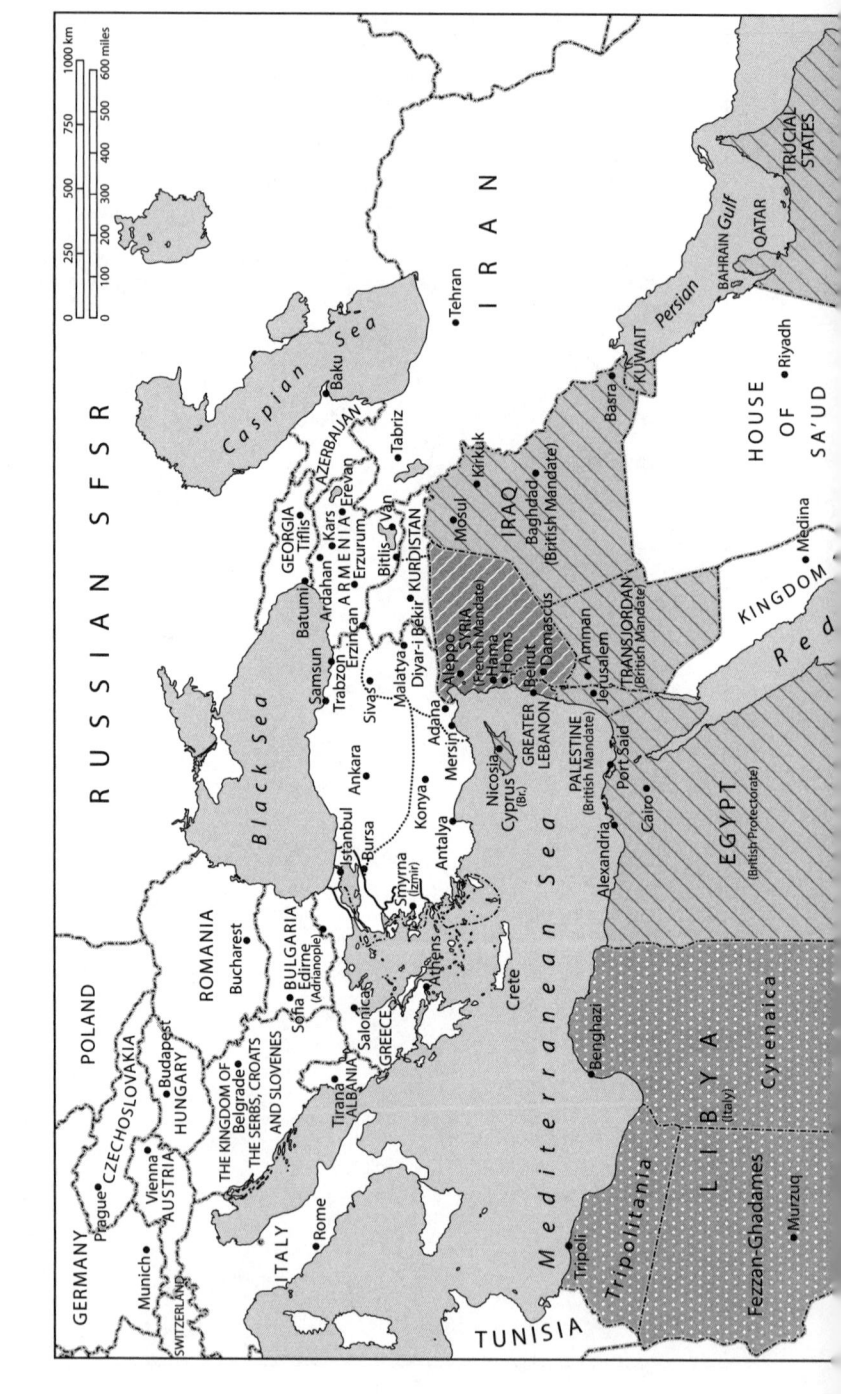

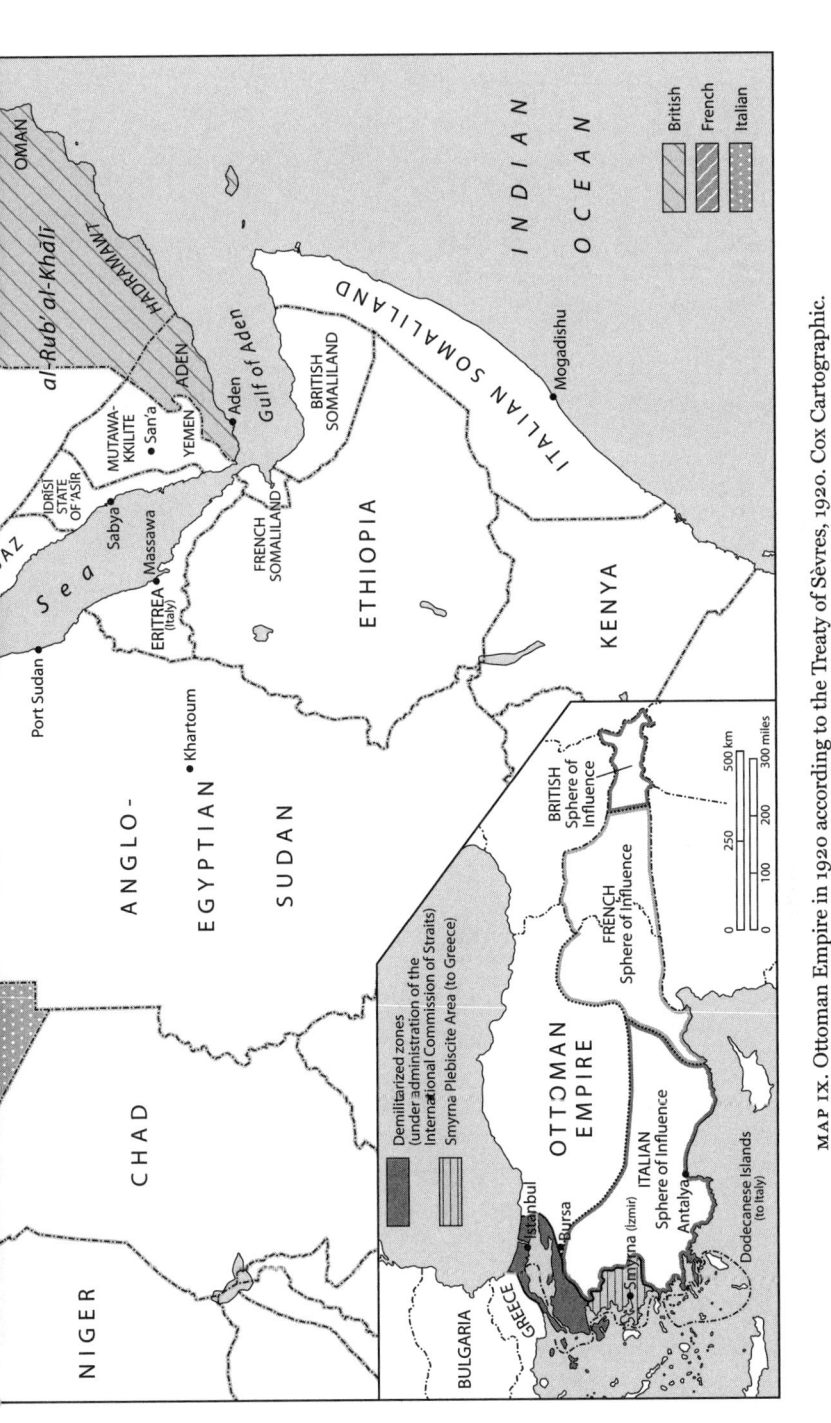

MAP IX. Ottoman Empire in 1920 according to the Treaty of Sèvres, 1920. Cox Cartographic.

OMAN

al-Rub' al-Khālī

HADRAMAWT

INDIAN

OCEAN

British
French
Italian

Aden
Gulf of Aden

BRITISH
SOMALILAND

ITALIAN SOMALILAND

Mogadishu

MUTAWA-
KKILITE
San'a
YEMEN

IDRISI
STATE
OF 'ASĪR

Sabya
Massawa

ERITREA
(Italy)

FRENCH
SOMALILAND

ETHIOPIA

KENYA

HIJAZ

Sea

Port Sudan

ANGLO-

EGYPTIAN

SUDAN

Khartoum

CHAD

NIGER

BRITISH
Sphere of
Influence

FRENCH
Sphere of Influence

500 km

0   100 200 300 miles
0   250

Demilitarized zones
(under administration of the
International Commission of Straits)

Smyrna Plebiscite Area (to Greece)

OTTOMAN
EMPIRE

Istanbul
Bursa

ITALIAN
Sphere of Influence
Antalya

Smyrna (Izmir)

Dodecanese Islands
(to Italy)

BULGARIA

GREECE

Ottoman Empire and Danubian Provinces

THE OTTOMAN EMPIRE comprised the fourth region of emancipation. It granted individuals equal rights while preserving a society organized through legally constituted religious communities that exercised substantial authority. In consequence the Ottoman Empire granted, avant la lettre, a version of national minority rights in the form of cultural rights.

From its formation to the eighteenth century, the Ottoman Empire excelled in its ability to include multiple ethnic and religious groups in a vertical structure built on complex negotiations and accommodation of diverse elites. That structure of toleration included Jews. In the nineteenth and early twentieth centuries that structure of carefully managed vertical relations disintegrated. By increasingly embracing centralization, standardized reform, and an exclusivist and nationalist ideology, while its population became ever more homogeneous, the empire transformed itself into a nation-state.[1]

Origins to Eighteenth Century

The Ottoman territories included multiple Jewries. First, there were the Greek-speaking Jews who had lived continuously in the area under Roman and Byzantine rule (Romaniots). Jews welcomed the Ottoman's expansion, especially in northwestern Anatolia, as an alternative to Byzantine's rule discrimination and growing anarchy. In the fourteenth century Edirne (Adrianople) was, for example, among the largest Jewish communities in Europe.[2]

Second, the Ottoman lands were a refuge for Jews fleeing persecution and expulsion in Europe from the twelfth century but especially from the fourteenth to the sixteenth century (Ashkenazim). Ottoman rulers offered toleration, occupational freedom, and property ownership. With the conquest of Constantinople, Sultan Mehmed II forcefully transported (*sürgün*) some Jews, and induced others with incentives, to repopulate the largely vacant capital. He even allowed the transplants to build new synagogues on existing foundations.[3] Jews soon constituted some 10 percent of the city's population. Mehmed II and Jewish leaders actively tried to attract Jews from Europe.[4]

Third, many of Spain's (1492) and later Portugal's exiled Jews went east or south into the Ottoman Empire (Sephardim). Bayezid II (1481–1512) made a concerted effort to draw the exiles to his realm. He is reported to have said: "you call Ferdinand a wise king, he who impoverishes his country and enriches our own."[5] Some Jews brought professions and crafts, others capital and knowledge of languages and markets.[6]

Fourth, the Ottoman's sixteenth-century conquests of Syria, Egypt, Iraq, and the Holy Land brought venerable Jewish communities under the empire's rule (*Musta'rab*).[7] By the end of the sixteenth century the Ottoman Jewish population had perhaps reached one hundred fifty to two hundred thousand. For some two centuries (1500–1700) the Ottoman Empire's Jews comprised the largest and most prosperous Jewry in the world.[8]

The Ottomans utilized a Byzantine model of rule: they relied on the organized religious community (*ta'ife, cema'at*) to rule non-Muslim populations. This pattern started with the Greek Orthodox and the Armenians, both of whom had an empire-wide ecclesiastical hierarchy. In contrast, Jews had only local authority: a chief rabbi for each city.[9] Moreover, in the cities (Istanbul, Izmir, Salonica, Edirne) that contained large numbers of Jews of diverse origins, each group usually established a separate organization (kahal).[10]

The Byzantine model established religious hierarchy as the empire's primary organizing principle. At the apex were Muslims living under sharia law. Next were Christians and Jews, designated *dhimmis* or peoples of Scripture, who paid a tribute for the privilege of being tolerated in an inferior status under Muslim rule. In personal matters *dhimmis* could choose to use their own courts or sharia courts. Finally, *musta'mins* were "non-Muslim foreigners residing in the empire."[11]

There were regulations of "dress, housing and transportation" for the various religious communities.[12] Each group in principle was assigned a distinct costume, with prescribed cut, colors, and cloth. In practice costumes varied widely across the vast empire as the authorities displayed flexibility and venality. Jews' and Christians' houses had to be lower than Muslims'; they were prohibited from building new synagogues and churches. Jews and Christians were forbidden to ride horses.[13]

From the sixteenth century the Ottomans devised a system of "Capitulations," or "charters of fiscal and commercial privilege," for foreigners.[14] Capitulations were an important instrument in maintaining peaceful relations with non-Muslim powers.[15] At first Genoese merchants formed autonomous colonies at Galata (1453); Venetians later achieved the same (1454) at Naxos. France gained capitulations first for Egypt (1517) and later for all the Ottoman dominions (1569) based on those granted to Venice. The Ottomans required reciprocity for their own merchants. Later, France gained the privilege of representing all Europeans and all Catholics and Catholic institutions (1604, 1618, 1740). The English (1580) and Dutch (1612) received their own capitulations. In the seventeenth century other nations negotiated capitulations as well (Habsburg Empire, 1718; Sweden, 1737; Denmark, 1746; Prussia, 1761; Russia, 1774). Consuls usually governed these foreign enclaves.[16]

Stagnation and Decline

The Ottoman Empire suffered from general stagnation in the early seventeenth century due to the rising costs of war and inflation, exorbitant taxation, and growing anarchy and insecurity. Coupled with the incursion of the European powers and merchants, trade routes and markets shifted.

This stagnation and the accompanying changes had a profound impact on the empire's Jews. Capitulations enabled Europeans and their Ottoman assistants, especially Christians, to replace native competitors, especially Muslims and Jews, as the empire's dominant merchants. The rise of European and Ottoman Christians (Greek Orthodox, Armenians) accelerated the Jews' economic decline.[17]

Moreover, the converted Christian recruits to the Ottoman elite (*devşirme*) displaced the Turkish aristocracy in controlling the empire. These powerful authorities favored Christians: they employed Greeks and Armenians as translators, agents, and tax farmers. Similarly, many European merchants, especially the dominant French, preferred to circumvent Jewish agents. Jews lost their previously favored position.[18]

Some Jews became the Europeans' *protégés* to take advantage of the capitulations' privileges, especially evading the taxation that became ever more onerous. Jews who hoped to gain *protégé* status or foreign citizenship looked to Holland, Prussia, and Denmark. Jewish merchants from Europe regularly used local Jews as agents, thereby giving them protection.[19] Many of the separate communities (kahal) tried to unify to confront the challenges of economic decline that took the form of mounting debts and the increasing inability to provide basic services. In response to Ottoman Jewry's decline, the majority of Jews who fled Spain and Portugal in the seventeenth and eighteenth centuries chose destinations in northwest Europe (chapter 1).[20]

Nineteenth Century

To compete with the European powers that threatened its far-flung territories, the Ottoman Empire began to undertake major reforms at the turn of the nineteenth century.[21] The Ottomans looked to various European countries for

models of reform, including Russia (Peter the Great), France, and the Habsburg lands (Metternich).

At the same time, the empire became enmeshed in Europe's Great Power
struggle as it defended itself through alliances that pitted the powers against
one another.[22] Such alliances turned on the treatment of the various Christian
minorities: European public opinion regularly addressed the Christian minorities, and the powers regularly intervened on their behalf, on occasion genuinely, usually as a fig leaf for self-interest: "moral sentiments" and "imperialistic
designs" were "inextricably linked."[23] Thus the Ottoman Empire's foreign
policy and internal reforms became indissolubly intertwined with the status of
its Christian minorities.

The Ottoman rulers faced such monumental challenges that they essentially "reinvented" the state. Beginning in 1808, the Ottomans aimed to create
a single, centralized military; turn the Grand Vizier's residence (*Sublime Porte*)
into a functioning bureaucracy with new ministries; reorganize taxation based
on a census (1830–31); and reform the postal service.[24]

The three and a half decades of Tanzimat reform (1839–76) initiated a fundamental transformation of Ottoman society by revising the religious hierarchy that had theretofore been society's primary organizing principle.

The Tanzimat commenced with the Imperial Rose Chamber Edict (November 3, 1839; *Khatti-I Sherif*) that proclaimed forthcoming legislation. The
laws would guarantee individual rights of life and property. The government
would also ensure proper judicial proceedings, regularized taxation, and an
equitable draft. The legislation would be uniform, applying to all subjects regardless of religion.

> These imperial concessions are extended to all Our subjects. They will
> enjoy them irrespective of the religion or sect to which they may belong.
> We are according, therefore, complete security to the inhabitants of the
> Empire with regard to their lives, their honor, and their fortunes even
> as it is required by the sacred text of our law.[25]

The edict heralded the civic equality of Christians and Jews. The state introduced the new legal category of "Ottoman" in lieu of religious distinctions;
it replaced *dhimmi* status with the category "non-Muslim Ottoman."[26] The
edict presented an effort at internal reform; it broadcast a clear message that
the empire aimed to join Europe in its treatment of religious minorities.[27]

The reforms were not successfully implemented: in the heartland they were
at best partially introduced, in the more distant provinces not at all. The sultan
and Sublime Porte felt the need for reiteration and elaboration.

The Crimean War (1853–56) provided the occasion. The war's ostensible
cause was competing French and Russian claims to holy sites and protection
of Christians. The real cause was Russia's imperial ambitions. In conversation
with the British ambassador in Moscow tsar Nicholas I called the Ottoman

Empire "the sick man of Europe" and broached the idea of partition. France and England aligned more to thwart Russia than to defend the Ottoman Empire.[28]

The sultan issued the Reform Edict (*Khatti-I Humayun*) on February 18, 1856. The edict confirmed and reinforced the 1839 Imperial Rose Chamber Edict, explicitly claiming membership in Europe and the European powers' influence.

> It is Our desire today to renew and expand still further the newly insti-
> tuted regulations with the aim of arriving at a state of affairs conform-
> ing to the dignity of my Empire and the position which it occupies
> among the civilized nations. We have today, through the fidelity and the
> praiseworthy efforts of all my subjects and with the benevolent and
> friendly concurrence of my noble allies, the Great Powers, received a
> ratification of what ought to be the beginning of a new era.[29]

The edict opened to Christians and Jews the newly founded secular schools as well as the civil service. In addition, they gained the right to public office and to membership in representative assemblies.[30] Christians and Jews gained political as well as civil rights.[31]

Some Muslims criticized the edict for depriving them of "the sacred right" of being "the ruling *millet*." Other groups, such as the Greeks, considered the new equality a demotion: "The government has put us together with the Jews. We were content with the supremacy of Islam."[32]

The Ottoman Empire presents a singular version of emancipation into a society organized into legally constituted confessional communities. Individuals received equal rights; the religious communities or *millets* remained in place. There was no possibility of existing as a "non-Muslim Ottoman" outside of a *millet*. No civil society existed into which members of different religions could integrate.[33] In fact, under foreign pressure after the 1856 decree, the state established new *millets* for hitherto unrepresented religious groups.[34] Thus religion continued to define social organization.

The state reorganized the *millets*' governance in favor of lay elites. In consequence, the *millets* of equal citizens became as much ethnic-national as religious entities.[35] The reorganization of the *millets* displayed the same order of religious precedence as in Europe: Christians first, Jews last. The Ottoman government issued new laws governing self-administration first for the Greek Orthodox (1862), then for Armenians (Apostolic Church; 1863), and finally for Jews (1865).[36]

The reform of the Jewish *millet* had begun with the Grand Rabbinate (1835). The Organic Statute made the Grand Rabbi the administrative leader of the Jewish *millet*. Actual power concentrated, however, in the hands of the laymen who composed a General Council and an Executive Secular Council.[37] In the case of Istanbul, for example, reforming lay leaders ousted a recalcitrant rabbi so they could establish a Jewish school with a mixed secular and religious curriculum.[38]

From the outbreak of the war (1853) Jewish leaders in Britain, France, and the German states had lobbied to ensure that any edict granting equality to non-Muslims would apply to Jews. They were fully aware of the relationship between their emancipation and Ottoman Jewry's. As the editor of the German-language Jewish newspaper put it:

> If the Turkish Jews are passed over . . . then OUR doom is also sealed. . . . Should the Sultan, on the contrary, pronounce the equalization of the Jews with the Christian population, it must sooner or later affect also those Christian states which hitherto yet deny us that equality. We ourselves are therefore immediately concerned thereby.[39]

The British government successfully took the lead.[40] The Reform Edict came one month before the conclusion of the Treaty of Paris in which the Great Powers guaranteed the Ottoman Empire's territorial "integrity."[41]

Did Ottoman Jews briefly enjoy a version of national minority rights avant la lettre? As we have seen (chapter 20), at the nineteenth century's end Jewish "autonomists" or "diaspora nationalists" in multinational tsarist Russia and Austria-Hungary would request collective, national rights in addition to individual civil and political rights. One version of those national rights, namely, cultural rights, meant the ability to administer schools and public institutions, such as courts, in the group's language. At midcentury, prior to the theory's articulation, Ottoman Jewry had apparently attained a version of precisely such rights.

Ottomanization and Turkification

In the four decades prior to its dissolution, the empire fitfully dismantled the *millets* in the name of a unified state serving "Islamic Ottomanism" or "Turkification." The 1869 Citizenship Law gave citizenship to everyone born in the Ottoman Empire. Rights and obligations between state and individual were unmediated; religious bodies had no role in citizenship.[42] The law "merged the principles governing Islamic religious heredity with political affiliation by residence and birth (effectively jus soli and jus sanguinis via paternal descent)."[43]

With the Public Education Law (1869) the Ottoman authorities began to develop a new civil school system. Moreover, after 1886 a new Inspectorate for non-Muslim schools began to inspect Alliance institutions regularly. Nevertheless, non-Muslims maintained separate school systems until 1918.[44]

Between 1877–88 and World War I the Ottoman Empire's population became increasingly Muslim. This change resulted from its loss of European territories (1877–78) followed by the unprecedented population transfers of the

Balkan Wars (1912–13).[45] The result was that "the problem of religious plural-ism had ceased and the question of ethnic minorities had begun."[46]

The demographic and geographic shift caused a clash during the reign of Sultan Abdulhamid II (1876–1909) between two notions of citizenship. "Civic Ottomanism" implied cooperation between the empire's confessions whose members would act patriotically by learning Turkish, serving in the civil guard and army, and publicly celebrating loyalty to the empire and the *millet*. A net-work of new Jewish associations supported this effort.[47] "Islamic Ottomanism," in contrast, emphasized the sultan's role as "caliph" and challenged the non-Muslim minorities to prove their fealty. It often pitted the non-Muslim minori-ties against one another in vying for the state's favor.[48]

The Young Turks (1908) and General Kemal (Attatürk) recast the citizen-ship debate. They rejected "civic Ottomanism" or an inclusive multiethnic, multilingual "Ottomanization." They instead espoused "Turkification," an ex-clusive nation-state identity. The 1908 Young Turk Revolution reinstated the 1876 constitution and Parliament. It ended inequalities by abolishing the tax that released non-Muslims from military duty and introducing universal con-scription.[49] The 1914 abrogation of all capitulations treaties brought numerous Jews under Ottoman jurisdiction and leveled the field between Christian and Jewish merchants.[50]

On the eve of and during the war (1913–15), Ottoman authorities took a further step in "Turkification" or constructing a nation-state by consolidating a uniform judicial system. The government began to dismantle the indepen-dent *millet* courts. It required religious court judges to meet government stan-dards; subjected their decisions to Ottoman courts; brought them under the direct control of the Ministry of Justice; and, finally, made them salaried civil servants under government supervision. The Code of Family Law (November 7, 1917) turned matters of personal status (marriage, divorce) into secular contracts.[51]

Moldavia and Wallachia

In its treatment of religious minorities, the Ottoman Empire endeavored to comply with the European powers. Romania did everything it could to defy them. Romania made it state policy to deny Jews rights: it invented exclusion-ary legislation, condoned expulsions and riots, and engaged in outright pre-varication and deception.[52]

Moldavia and Wallachia were two autonomous principalities that had been under Ottoman suzerainty since 1541. The Congress of Paris (1856) recognized the two as self-governing principalities under the European powers' protec-tion.[53] Prince Alexander Ioan Cuza joined them through personal union in 1859. Romania's constitution of 1866, modeled on Belgium's, established a con-stitutional monarchy, a parliament, and the separation of powers. In practice, the executive dominated the Parliament through frequent dissolutions and manipulation of elections.[54]

Early Wallachian and Moldavian civil codes (1817) recognized Jews as natives. In contrast, during its occupation (1829–34) the Russian administration introduced the Organic Regulations (*Règlement Organique*; 1831) that abrogated native Jews' privileges and deemed all Jews foreigners. The Organic Regulations effaced all distinction between recent immigrants and long-term or native residents. The Moldavian Organic Regulation (Article 94, Chapter 3) introduced the category of the "vagabond Jew": whoever lacked authorization, did not have a fixed occupation, and preyed on the native population could be expelled. In 1856 Moldavia declared itself a Christian state.[55]

Under Prince Cuza's government (1859–66) native Jews briefly enjoyed civic rights.[56] The 1864 Civil Code included two forms of citizenship. The legitimate child of a Romanian man (jus sanguinis) gained automatic citizenship. Anyone born and raised in Romania could claim citizenship a year after reaching maturity (jus soli). Non-Christian inhabitants could request naturalization after ten years of residence; the prince and Parliament would have to approve each request.[57]

Under Prince Charles (from 1866), Romania began to adopt exclusionary legislation.[58] In the parliamentary debates over the 1866 constitution, the conservative opposition succeeded in omitting the Civil Code's provisions for naturalization (jus soli). Descent (jus sanguinis) became virtually the exclusive means to citizenship.[59] Furthermore, an 1866 governmental decree declared all Jews foreigners. Moreover, the 1866 constitution (Article 7) made it impossible for Jews to acquire citizenship: "Only foreigners of the Christian religion may become Romanians."[60]

In the 1899 census 1.6 percent of Jews were citizens; 2.2 percent were foreigners dependent upon the state; and 96.2 percent were foreigners under state protection.[61] Political rights included ownership of rural land and access to civil service positions as well as voting and holding office. Conscription did not lead to citizenship, except for those who fought in wars, yet even they were denied access to officers' commissions. Romania had the second highest proportion of non-citizen residents in Europe.[62]

A further complicating factor in the Jews' status was that the Ottoman capitulations system applied to Romania until independence (1878). Prominent individuals, especially successful merchants and manufacturers, gained protection from foreign powers. Such *sudiți* (*protégés*) enjoyed diplomatic protection and tax privileges, juridical immunity, and exemption from conscription. They were constantly in conflict with the government. As the Romanian government adopted ever harsher laws toward Jews, those who could gained foreign protection.[63]

From 1866 to 1918 the Romanian government promulgated over two hundred administrative regulations restricting Jews' residence in the countryside, rural property ownership, and the practice of professions and occupations.[64] Romania repeatedly expelled Jews by invoking the category of the "vagabond Jew" from Moldavia's Organic Regulations (1831). Officials administered these expulsions arbitrarily, frequently as a pretext for extortion, and often violently.[65]

Beginning in 1855–56 Jews mounted a campaign for emancipation that included petitions, delegations, registering as electors, and establishing a press.[66] Romanian politicians adamantly resisted. Jewish leaders therefore turned to Jews abroad and to the European powers, but to no avail.[67] Jewish leaders across Europe, especially Britain and France, did not intercede on behalf of Romanian Jews in 1858.[68] In contrast, as the situation deteriorated after 1866, Jews abroad began to intercede directly with the Romanian government and indirectly through the Great Powers.[69]

Beginning with Greece (1829) and Belgium (1831), the Great Powers had made independence contingent upon guarantees of religious freedom and equality. In requiring the same of Romania, the Great Powers made the Jews' status a problem for European diplomacy.

In response to Great Power and foreign Jewish interventions, Romania's government lied about its policies and practices.[70] Great Power intervention continued intermittently; it became most forceful at the Congress of Berlin (1878).[71] The European powers stipulated that Romania modify Article 7 of the 1866 constitution that had restricted citizenship to Christians. Romania did so, but once again in a deceptive manner. The new law required a petition to the prince, ten years of residence, and incontrovertible proof of being "useful to the country." Former *sudiți* were disqualified. These requirements made it impossible for the vast majority of Jews to gain citizenship.[72]

Romania gained final independence from the Ottoman Empire after joining Russia in its war against the Ottomans (Turko-Russian War; 1877–78). The treaties of San Stefano and Berlin conferred full independence. In defiance of the Great Powers, Romania declared itself a kingdom, and Charles king, on March 26, 1881.

Conclusion

Diverse Jews assembled in the Ottoman Empire as a result of conquest and migration: Romaniots, Ashkenazim, Sephardim, and Arabic-speaking Jews of the Middle East (*Musta'rab*). Living as a tolerated, inferior religious community (*dhimmis*), Ottoman Jewry became the largest and most prosperous in the world (1500–1700). After a period of economic decline in the eighteenth century, Ottoman Jews gained rights while retaining their religious community in the nineteenth century. Rights conjoined with the *millet* system comprised the Ottoman Empire's own version of emancipation.

In the late nineteenth and early twentieth centuries, the multireligious empire grappled with how to transform itself, especially in light of the loss of its

European territories and Christian populations. Should it be an inclusive polity ("civic Ottomanism") or more of a unified and homogeneous nation-state ("Islamic Ottomanism")? The Young Turks opted for "Turkification" and the erection of a secular nation-state.

Romania's approach to the Jews' citizenship was probably closest to Russia's—despite the fact that it was a dependent state whereas Russia was one of the Great Powers. Romania seemed to emulate Russia's policies: after a brief period of inclusion it engaged in a prolonged campaign of exclusion, discrimination, and outright persecution. Romania defied the intervention of the Great Powers and Jewish diplomacy through prevarication and deception.

PART V

Twentieth-Century Tribulations

MAP X. Europe in 1923 (postwar partitions) and in 1942 at
the height of Hitler's empire. Cox Cartographic.

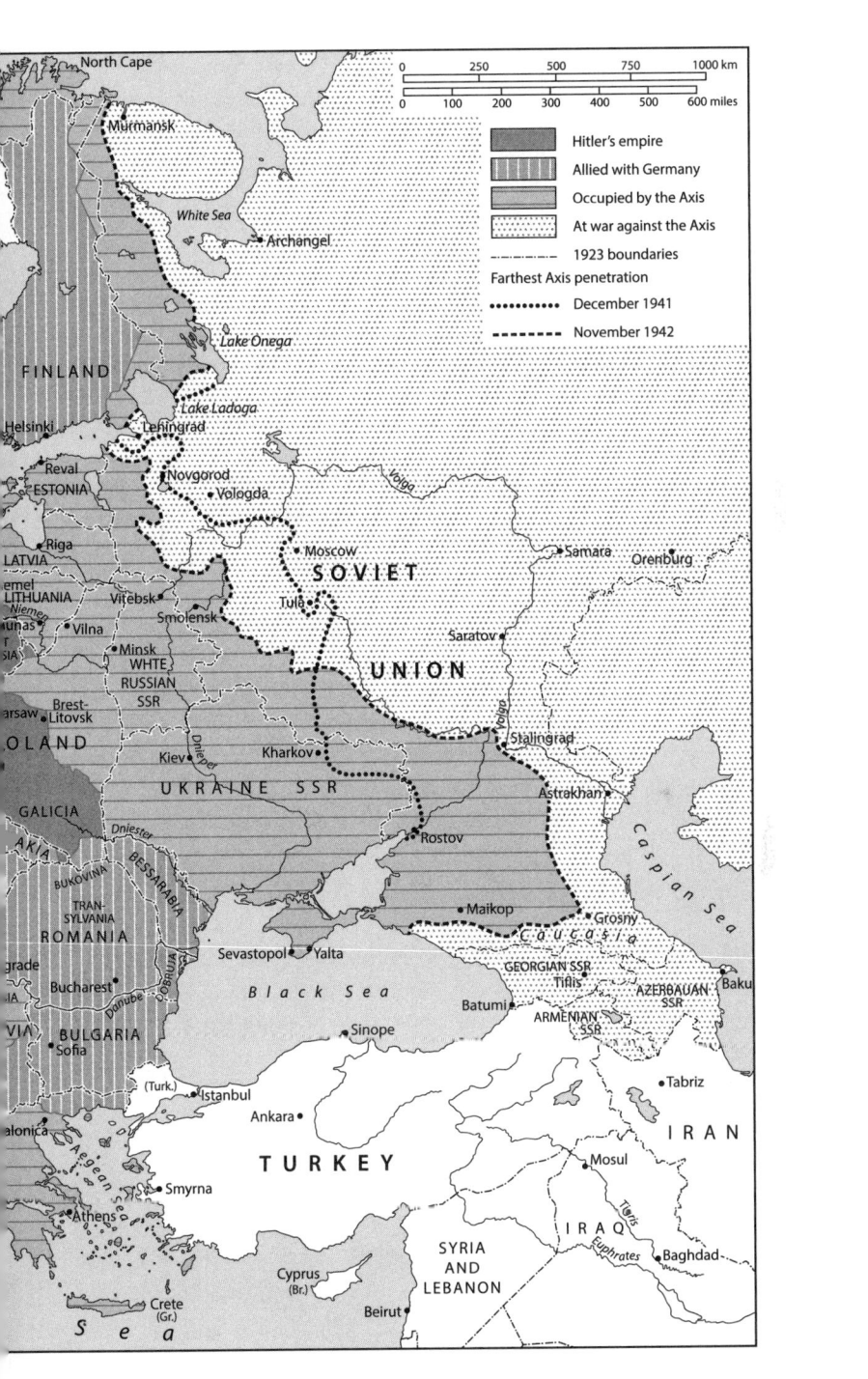

		Hitler's empire
		Allied with Germany
		Occupied by the Axis
		At war against the Axis
–·–·–		1923 boundaries

Farthest Axis penetration

••••••••	December 1941
- - - - -	November 1942

North Cape

Murmansk

White Sea

Archangel

FINLAND

Lake Onega

Helsinki

Lake Ladoga

Leningrad

Reval

Novgorod

Vologda

ESTONIA

Volga

Moscow

Samara

Orenburg

Riga

SOVIET

LATVIA

Vitebsk

Tula

emel

LITHUANIA

Smolensk

Saratov

unas

Vilna

Minsk

UNION

SIA

WHITE

RUSSIAN

Brest-

SSR

Volga

arsaw

Litovsk

Stalingrad

OLAND

Kiev

Kharkov

Dnieper

UKRAINE SSR

Astrakhan

GALICIA

Dniester

Caspian Sea

AKIA

Rostov

BUKOVINA

BESSARABIA

TRAN-

Maikop

SYLVANIA

Grosny

grade

ROMANIA

Sevastopol

Yalta

Caucasia

Bucharest

GEORGIAN SSR

Baku

IA

Danube

Tiflis

AZERBAIJAN

Black   Sea

Batumi

SSR

VIA

BULGARIA

Sinope

ARMENIAN

Sofia

SSR

(Turk.)

Istanbul

Tabriz

alonica

Ankara

IRAN

TURKEY

Mosul

Smyrna

IRAQ

Tigris

Athens

Euphrates

Baghdad

SYRIA

Cyprus

AND

(Br.)

LEBANON

Crete

Beirut

(Gr.)

S

e

a

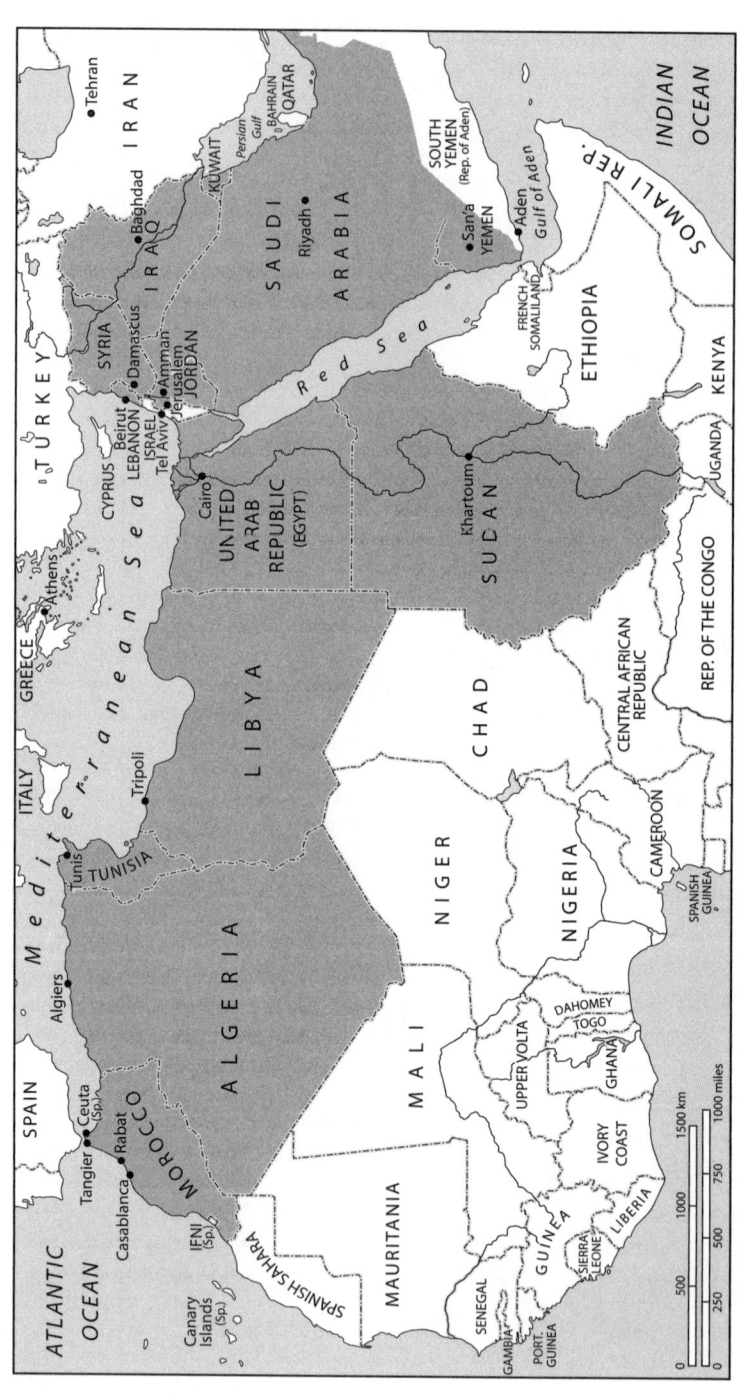

MAP XI. North Africa and Middle East 1967 including
the State of Israel. Cox Cartographic.

Minority Rights

WORLD WAR I was the twentieth century's "seminal catastrophe."[1] The war toppled four empires: the Dual Monarchy, Romanov Russia, the German Reich, and the Ottoman Empire. It destroyed millions of lives through horrific violence that, during the wars and revolutions that followed, migrated from the battlefield to civil society. The war eviscerated the bourgeois liberal order, empowering mass society's radical politics. Unlike the Congress of Vienna's settlement that held for almost a century, the Versailles Peace Treaty lasted less than two decades.

The radical politics that came to power heralded a new era. In some locales, the existing system transformed from within: universal manhood suffrage (1918) helped bring England's Labour Party a parliamentary majority (1924). In other locales, a new democratic order relied upon it: Germany's Social Democrats (1919) quashed communist revolutions to help erect the Weimar Republic. Finally, elsewhere a historically new regime emerged ominously committed to reengineering society and reordering Europe: communism in Russia (1917), fascism in Italy (1922).

World War I and its aftermath brought Jews major triumphs and devastating destruction. The main Jewish political parties reaped substantial success. Russia's February revolution (1917) and the Weimar Republic (1919) delivered full rights. The Versailles Peace Treaty enacted a version of the national minority rights (1919) to which all the Jewish political parties in eastern Europe had subscribed. Zionism gained the international charter Herzl had sought in the Balfour Declaration (1917) and Britain's League of Nations Mandate to implement it (1922). Russia's November Bolshevik revolution (1917) promised Bundists and other leftists a socialist society.

Jews participated in the war as citizen-soldiers in unprecedented numbers: over one million in the Allied forces, some 450,000 among the Central Powers. Individual Jews took prominent roles in their country's war effort, for example,

Walther Rathenau in organizing Germany's wartime economy, Chaim Weizmann in aiding England's munitions industry.[2]

The war and postwar wreaked unprecedented destruction on Jews and other minorities in eastern and east-central Europe: the war displaced some one million Jews.[3] Early in the war tsarist military authorities deported some 600,000 Jews from the Pale of Settlement's western borders without adequate provisions for housing, food, or employment (by December 1915 Russia had an estimated 2.7 million refugees, by 1916 some 5 million).[4] Forced to allow some of the refugees into Russia's interior, the government began de facto to dismantle the Pale of Settlement.[5]

Russian, German, and Dual Monarchy armies traversed Galicia multiple times, during which they destroyed people and property and created some 450,000 refugees.[6] Vienna alone became home to some 100,000 Galician Jewish refugees.[7]

Jewish relief and welfare agencies leaped to the rescue, albeit in keeping with wartime alliances. British Jews could support brethren in Russia, though not Galicia (Fund for the Relief of the Jewish Victims of the War in Russia). The American Joint Distribution Committee, founded in 1914, disbursed enormous funds across eastern Europe while the United States was neutral. After the United States entered the war, it did so primarily in allied Russia.[8]

The postwar's destruction rivaled the war's. The Russo-Polish war dragged on for two years, the Russian Civil War for at least three. Violence against Jews became integral to postwar Poland's nation building and Russia's civil war.[9] In Russia and Ukraine half a million Jews became homeless while some thirty thousand were killed.[10] In the early 1920s east European Jews experienced another "refugee crisis of major proportions."[11] Jewish relief organizations coordinated their efforts and in some cases merged to cope with the dire situation.[12]

The crisis impinged directly on citizenship. The Austrian military's brutal treatment of civilians impelled Viennese Jewish leaders to found an organization to safeguard the rights of Polish Jews under occupation.[13] The collapse of the Habsburg and tsarist empires turned masses of Jews into stateless refugees: a half million from Galicia and a half million in Poland and Rumania.[14] Many contemporaries regarded the White army's pogroms in Russia as a "reaction to Jewish equality" that aimed to restore "disenfranchisement."[15]

National Minority Rights

The Paris Peace Conference introduced a new era of national minority rights among the successor states. While the presumptive successor states fought over borders and population, including minorities, the Great Powers debated the peace in Paris. At the conference, Jewish leaders from America, England, and central Europe served as the major proponents of minority rights since the "Expert Committees" did not invite minority delegations from the affected regions to testify.[16]

All the Jewish parties and leaders advocated equality of civil and political rights; they differed on national minority rights, including their scope. The Alliance Israélite Universelle opposed any form of collective recognition. Lucien Wolf, Anglo-Jewry's foreign minister, reluctantly assented to collective cultural rights (language, schools). Louis Marshall (American Jewish Congress) aspired to political minority rights (national assembly). The nationalist *Comité des délégations juives auprès de la Conférence de la Paix* vigorously advocated a maximalist agenda.[17]

The Great Powers debated three options. First, impose universal standards applicable to themselves and the successor states. Second, enact blanket requirements for all the successor states. Third, negotiate separate treaties with the individual successor states. Following Britain's lead, the powers opted for the last option. That was a modest choice that effectively continued the Congress of Berlin's practices, the major innovation being that the League of Nations, rather than the Great Powers, would administer the treaties.[18]

The treaties were a patent compromise: they included only cultural rights and gave exclusive power to sovereign states.[19] The treaty with Poland served as the template. It guaranteed equality and citizenship (civil and political rights) by making these irrevocable in the successor states' constitutions (Article 1). It guaranteed citizenship ipso facto to all those "habitually resident" in Poland regardless of their previous national affiliation (e.g., German, Austrian, Hungarian, Russian) and gave them the right to opt for a different national citizenship provided they left within one year (Articles 2–6). The treaties limited minority rights to language and education ("culture"; Articles 7 and 8). The treaties did not make state funding mandatory for minority schools; rather, they stipulated that possibility although restricted it to primary education (Article 9). There was no provision for any form of national representation; the treaty permitted exclusively local Jewish organizations (Article 10).[20] Moreover, national minorities had no representation at the League to enforce the treaties: sovereign states were the League's sole constituents.[21]

The eight signatory states—Poland, Czechoslovakia, Yugoslavia, Romania, Greece, Austria, Bulgaria, and Hungary—resented the treaties as infringements on their sovereignty.[22] They aspired to abrogate "Little Versailles" as much as Germany did "Big Versailles." East-central Europe's interwar politics, which pitted the right against the extreme right, militated against realization of the promised rights.[23]

UKRAINE

The short-lived Ukrainian polity (June 1917–July 1918) enthroned national minority rights. It gave 30 percent of representation in the national assembly

(*Rada*) to Russians, Poles, and Jews. The government appointed a "vice-secretary" to the General Secretariat to represent each of the national minorities. The vice-secretary for Jewish Affairs, M. Zilberfarb, treated the post as an "organ of national autonomy." A Jewish National Council formed in October 1917.

After the Bolshevik revolution Ukraine declared itself a "People's Republic" and on January 9, 1918, adopted the law of national-personal autonomy. It stipulated that each nationality was to have a democratically elected National Assembly with legislative and administrative power. The National Assembly would receive funding from the central government as well as levy taxes on its members. Here was the zenith of national minority rights. The German-sponsored Hetman's (Skoropadski) government repealed the national-personal autonomy law in July 1918.[24]

POLAND

The independent Poland (1921) that emerged from the wreckage of the Romanov and Habsburg empires contained the world's second largest Jewish population: some 2,850,000 in 1921 of the state's population (24,000,000). Although aspiring to be a nation-state, Poland was in fact a nationalities-state: Jews and Germans, Belarusians and Ukrainians comprised a third of its population.[25]

Independent Poland violated the Jews' civil rights by not abolishing the partitioning powers' laws. From its inception until 1931, the new state consistently exploited the partitioning powers' laws and administrative mechanisms to either deny Jews citizenship or subvert their rights.[26]

Even before the state's establishment, the debate over the Jews' exercise of electoral rights in municipal elections echoed the partitioning powers' policies. In consequence of the Jews' preponderant numbers in towns and cities, the partitioning powers had restricted, or attempted to restrict, their role in municipal politics as early as Catherine the Great, but the most recent and probably relevant effort had been the 1870 tsarist law that set a limit of one-third of aldermen and prohibited Jews from the mayor's office.[27]

During negotiations for the political structure of a projected independent Poland under the supervision of the German administration (1917–18), the Polish political parties proposed limiting the percentage of Jewish representatives in municipal politics to their overall population in the country rather than the much higher percentage in a specific city. Jewish political leaders acquiesced to this proposal as an act of solidarity and to ensure representation. The agreement also denied the franchise to Jews born outside Polish territory. The actual electoral law (November 28, 1918) did not implement this agreement; rather, it gerrymandered electoral districts to decrease Jewish representation.[28]

From the outset, Poland attempted to deprive Jews of citizenship in violation of the Minority Treaty (clause #1). The Citizenship Law of January 20, 1920, established two systems: descent (jus sanguinis) for ethnic Poles, residence (jus soli) for minorities. An ethnic Pole gained citizenship simply by returning to Poland, showing proof of being Polish, claiming Polish citizenship, and renouncing citizenship elsewhere. Jews or members of other minorities had to demonstrate "permanent residence" from the former partitioning powers' population registries. That was a formidable challenge. The registries were notoriously incomplete: in some cases, registration had been voluntary or in fact ceased (Congress Poland), in other cases it was expensive, cumbersome, and frequently avoided (tsarist Russia).[29] The criterion of "permanent residence" was an invention that did not appear in the Minorities Treaty.[30] Furthermore, the Treaty of Riga (March 18, 1921) that ended the Russo-Polish war denied Jews in the affected eastern territories the option of Polish citizenship (Article 6).[31]

Jewish leaders were acutely aware that the authorities would and did exploit the partitioning powers' laws to deny citizenship and rights. Three Jewish delegates to the Legislative Sejm (May 23, 1919) first proposed a blanket repeal of all the partitioning powers' laws. The Sejm failed to pass the law. The three repeated this effort numerous times (1919–23) without success.[32]

During a visit to Poland in June 1925, Lucien Wolf (1857–1930), Anglo-Jewry's unofficial foreign minister and tireless advocate for Jewish rights, initiated negotiations to reach an overall agreement.[33] That effort at first seemed to succeed. It failed when the Jewish parties insisted the agreement included forty-two clauses that covered the full ranges of rights whereas the government claimed it contained only twelve clauses addressing cultural and religious matters.[34]

Once the Polish state had been constituted, competing state agencies arbitrarily applied the extant laws. For example, it took over three years of inter-agency debate (1921–24) to reach a decision about the costs of medical care for indigent Jews: should the Jewish community bear the costs, as under the partitioning powers, or should a government agency assume the costs, as for other Poles? The government finally agreed to bear the costs (March 19, 1925).[35]

In 1923 the General Prosecutor's Office used Austrian legal provisions to prohibit the use of Yiddish as a public language. In contradiction to the Minority Rights Treaty, this ruling provoked a controversy in the Sejm that continued for many years. In 1928 and 1929 Polish courts resurrected an Austrian law (1814) and a tsarist decree (April 17, 1905) to prohibit Jews from leasing and purchasing land.[36]

The new Polish state consistently excluded Jews from state employment. State institutions did not hire Jewish doctors and lawyers. The number of Jewish teachers in elementary and high schools was disproportionately low.

In former Galicia, the state pensioned off the former Dual Monarchy's Jewish civil servants. University faculties de facto reduced the numbers of Jewish students.[37]

The Minority Rights Treaty did not include the issue of Sunday work. The Sejm passed a law prohibiting Sunday work (1919) designed to emphasize Poland's Catholic faith as well as to hobble Jewish businesses by enforcing a two-day weekend. The authorities did not fully implement the law.[38]

The Piłsudski regime (1926–35), which in general endeavored to ease relations with the national minorities, gradually lifted some restrictions. In 1927 the Minister of Religious Denominations released a circular opposed to quotas in institutions of higher education, which was meant to counter nationalist students' agitation at the universities. The Minister of the Interior permitted the use of Yiddish in public meetings and granted citizenship to some 33,000 Jews who had returned from Russia.[39] Finally, Piłsudski's government enacted a blanket abrogation of all partition-era legislation (April 10, 1931).[40]

HUNGARY

Hungary was the first of the democratic successor states to violate the Jews' civil rights through legislation: following tsarist precedents, it introduced a 1920 quota (Act XXV) on admissions to educational institutions.[41]

Trianon Hungary, a nation-state that had lost over half of its population, underwent a traumatic double revolution (1918–19): first Communist (Béla Kun) with a "red terror," then, after Romanian military intervention, a right-wing reaction with a devastating "white terror." Since Béla Kun and an inordinate number of the revolutionary leaders were Jews, the revolution identified Hungary's 473,355 Jews (1920), who largely constituted the urban industrial and commercial classes, with socialism as well as capitalism.[42]

The numerus clausus was connected to "the post-revolutionary" purge of the left; it linked "university admissions" to "'patriotism and moral uprightness.'"[43] Moreover, the numerus clausus ominously used the criterion of race or nationality rather than religion or language.[44] In theory, the quota applied to all nationalities (percentage of students equal to percentage of population). In practice, it affected only Jews. Before 1918 Jews constituted some 6 percent of the population but sometimes as high as 36 percent of students. It was thus "a Jewish quota hidden within a nationality quota system."[45] Although the government wanted the League of Nations to think otherwise, it strictly enforced the quota.[46]

The British Board of Deputies and the Alliance Israélite Universelle repeatedly protested (1921, 1925, 1927) the numerus clausus to the League of Nations as an infringement on the Minorities Treaty. Hungary's Jewish leaders opposed those protests as interference in Hungary's internal affairs; they appealed to the constitution's equality rather than Minority Rights.[47] In order to avoid further League of Nations scrutiny, the Bethlen government in 1928 replaced the nationality quota with a quota based on father's occupation. That quota was equally effective and did not violate the Minorities Treaty.[48]

The 1920 quota marked the official start of the Magyar-Jewish alliance's unraveling. In the Dual Monarchy, the Magyars had needed Jews to identify with them to maintain their slim political majority. Similarly, the Magyar elite allowed Jews to develop the economy while retaining political power and social prestige. With the loss of territory and population, the Magyar elite no longer needed the Jews' votes. In the new Hungary, the Magyars effectively excluded Jews from the bureaucracy and army officer corps.[49]

AUSTRIA

The Austrian Republic (October 21, 1919) was the first of the successor states and signatories to the Minority Treaties to attempt to employ the criterion of race to deny Jews citizenship. In addition, one of its prestigious universities introduced a quota for Jews.

The country, at first named the Republic of German Austria (November 12, 1918), was a small landlocked state of 6,500,000 bereft of its economic hinterland, much of its German population, and its imperial status and empire.[50] Ninety percent (176,000) of Austria's 191,000 Jews lived in Vienna.[51]

During the war Vienna faced a massive influx of refugees from Galicia and other parts of the empire. A second wave arrived after the war. The new republic thus had to confront the issue of whether to grant Austrian citizenship to the refugees, who were former Austro-Hungarian citizens.

The Treaty of St. Germain (Article 80) authorized persons to "opt for Austrian citizenship if they, according to their race and speech, belong to the German majority of the people of Austria."[52] The treaty employed the terms "race and speech" according to Austro-Hungarian usage: they designated nationality and culture. An Austrian administrative court (June 9, 1921) construed them, however, in a racial, biological sense. On that basis, the nationalist Minister of the Interior (Leopold Walter) commenced rejecting citizenship applications from virtually all Jews.[53]

The Austrian-Israelite Union, Lucien Wolf, and the Alliance Israélite Universelle lodged protests at the League of Nations. The Austrian government initially tried to dodge the issue. It relented when another Austrian Administrative Court (April 1922) repudiated the earlier racial definition and endorsed nationality's conventional acceptation.[54]

Austrian law maintained the dualism of "state citizenship" (*Staatsbürgerschaft*) and "local citizenship" (*Heimatrecht*). One could possess state citizenship without local citizenship, though not vice versa. Former citizens of the Austro-Hungarian monarchy were required to obtain the right of domicile (*Heimatrecht*) in the new Austria in addition to state citizenship.[55]

Many Polish and Hungarian Jewish students either excluded from, or mistreated at, universities in their own countries migrated to Vienna. In March 1923, Vienna's Technical University (*Technische Hochschule*), where Jews constituted some 40 percent of the student body, imposed a quota of 10 percent "for Jewish applicants from abroad," especially from Hungary and Poland.[56] This was the first time since the 1867 emancipation that an institution of higher education introduced a distinction between Jews and non-Jews.[57]

ROMANIA

In Romania, a new chapter in the issue of emancipation had opened since the Congress of Berlin (1878) and its aftermath. Then the question was whether Jews gained citizenship; now the question was which Jews did. This situation resulted from the fact that Romania gained significant territory in the postwar settlement.

In consequence of opportunely joining the victorious powers in World War I, Romania received territories from four other countries: Bessarabia (from Russia), Bukovina (from Austria), Dobrogea (from Bulgaria), and Transylvania (from Hungary). While these territories contained substantial Romanian populations, they also included other groups: Hungarians, Germans, Russians, Ukrainians, and Jews. Minorities constituted about one-third of Romania so that, like Poland, it was a reluctant nation-state.[58]

Romania made multiple attempts at emancipation legislation. The government of M. Marghiloman promulgated a law on naturalization of foreigners (August 27, 1918) that would have included veterans of the Bulgarian campaign and the world war as well as "those born in Romania of parents also born in Romania."[59] When that government fell, Ion I. Bratianu's government annulled the decree and introduced a new one (December 20, 1918; Decree #3902). It was more generous in not requiring proof that parents had been born in Romania, yet more onerous in requiring a court hearing for each case.

As part of the negotiations in Paris, the Romanian government issued a law (May 22, 1919) that omitted the court procedure. Parliament did not vote on the decree so it remained provisional. Finally, the constitution of 1923 (Article 133), which incorporated the Minority Treaty's terms, granted Jews in old Romania (the *Regat*) full rights.[60]

As in Poland, Jews in the new territories had to prove continuous residence since before the war. Those who could not were rendered stateless. The Law Regarding the Acquisition and Loss of Romanian Citizenship (February 24, 1924) defined residence in terms of Austro-Hungarian law, that is, *Heimatrecht*. In the Bukovina Austrian law had required a ten-year residence; in

Transylvania Hungarian law (1886) stipulated four years; in Bessarabia Russian law had not defined criteria for domicile. The law rendered thousands of Jews stateless.[61]

The Romanian state discriminated against Jews in the civil service and the army.[62] Ultranationalist students called for the imposition of a numerus clausus and held frequent, violent, and sometimes murderous demonstrations against Jewish students' admission.[63]

RUSSIA/SOVIET UNION

Late tsarist Russia had been the "prison house of nations"; the Soviet Union aspired to be the "incubator of nations." The Bolsheviks espoused Minority Rights as an organizing principle in the form of "territorialized nationality."[64]

The Provisional Government (April 2, 1917) emancipated the Jews: it granted all individuals equal rights regardless of religion and canceled all existing restrictions. The Soviet government on November 15, 1917, proclaimed a "Declaration of the Rights of the Peoples of Russia" whose fourth principle was "free development for the national minorities and ethnic groups among the population residing on Russian territory."[65] The various Soviet republics similarly promulgated national minority rights. On August 1, 1920, for example, the Republic of Belorussia declared the equality of all national minorities and their languages.[66]

The USSR promised exclusively cultural rights with the aim of the "bolshevization of nationals."[67] The 1925 constitution guaranteed citizens "the right to use their native language freely in meetings, in the courts, in administrative bodies and in public affairs," as well as "to receive education in their native tongue."[68] The Bolshevik government aimed to extend solely cultural rights; it did not devolve political or economic power.[69]

A fundamental tension beset the national rights of Soviet Jews, then the third largest Jewish community in the world (1926: 2,600,000).[70] Prior to the revolution Lenin and Stalin had advocated recognized rights for territorial minorities. They considered the Jews to be a nonterritorial or extraterritorial group that did not qualify for such rights. In fact, Lenin and Stalin understood the Jews' survival as capitalism's handiwork; they posited that in a socialist society the Jews would disappear through assimilation.[71]

Jews initially gained national rights as Soviet bureaucrats made provisions for extraterritorial minorities (Germans, Latvians, Poles, Jews). Two agencies undertook the Jews' Sovietization. In the government, under the aegis of the Peoples' Commissariat for Nationality Affairs, the Commissariat for Jewish National Affairs (*Evkom*; 1918–24) abolished extant Jewish institutions and seized their property and assets. In the Communist Party, the Jewish Sections (*Yevsektsia*) (1918–30), heavily staffed with former Bundists, reeducated Jews to socialism in their own language (Yiddish): they aimed to establish "the dictatorship of the proletariat on the Jewish street." The Jewish sections suppressed all forms of Jewish life inimical to Sovietization, for example, religious practice and Zionism, and fostered new compatible institutions.[72]

From 1923 to approximately the mid-1930s Jewish institutions flourished alongside those of other national minorities. The basic organization of the "soviet," which required a minimum of one thousand people, regulated and promoted community, finance, and social-cultural affairs by erecting a network of courts, schools (1923–24: 366; 1929–30: 1,100), and administrative bodies. In areas of dense Jewish settlement Soviets used Yiddish: at their height there were 168 Jewish soviets in the Ukraine (1932) and 27 in Belorussia (1931).[73]

In 1933 Stalin adopted a policy of a single Soviet nation speaking Russian. The government subsequently began to undermine and dismantle the nationality institutions. The 1936 Stalin constitution guaranteed national language use in schools but not in meetings, courts, and administrative bodies.[74] There were two notable periods in which the Soviet government destroyed Jewish institutions: 1937–38, along with those of other extraterritorial minorities, and 1948–49.[75]

Soviet policy realized the long-standing tsarist goal of destroying the shtetl economy by depriving individual Jews of rights. The Soviet government labeled the small merchants and artisans of the shtetl, often 70 to 80 percent of adult Jews, as "petit-bourgeois," "unproductive," and "enemies of socialism" (*lishchentsy*). It disenfranchised them, relieving them of civil and political rights, including access to ration cards, apartments, health care, employment, and education for their children.[76] In Ukraine in 1926 as many as 68 percent of Jewish adults were traders "deprived of civic rights"; perhaps one-third of all Jews were classified as *lishchentsy*.[77] "Jews were clearly overrepresented among the disfranchised."[78] Just as the state villainized prosperous Ukrainian peasant landowners (*kulaks*), so too did it stigmatize shtetl dwellers. For the masses of Jews labeled *lishchentsy*, the 1917 emancipation was short-lived.[79]

The shtetl dwellers and their children resorted to drastic measures to escape the stigma's lethal implications. Many shtetl denizens migrated within the USSR to shed their identity, especially from Ukraine and Belorussia to the Russian Republic. The move to the cities was the largest migration since the Great Migration abroad (1870–1914): by 1939 87 percent of Jews were living in cities.[80] Others escaped by gaining education and then employment in the state apparatus. Jews comprised an inordinately high percentage of clerical workers, state officials, and members of the intelligentsia. They helped implement the Soviet system—much as ethnic Germans had tsarism.[81] Jews also took industrial jobs in much higher numbers than previously.[82] Some successfully petitioned for the restoration of rights.[83] Finally, through the paving of roads, electrification, and collectivization, a new Soviet industrial and agricultural shtetl emerged.[84] Thus by 1929 the old shtetl economy of small traders had virtually disappeared.[85]

FIGURE 15. Youth parade celebrating tenth anniversary of Bolshevik revolution with banners in Yiddish and Russian (Minsk, 1927). YIVO Collection R1 Minsk 56.

Some twenty thousand Jewish families in Ukraine and some ten thousand in Belarus took up collective agriculture. The Soviet Committee for the Rural Placement of Jewish Workers (*Komzet*) encouraged this endeavor, and the American Jewish Agro-Joint (1924) funded it. By 1928 there were 160 Jewish rural councils in Ukraine and 27 in Crimea. Ukraine had three "Jewish national districts," the highest administrative designation for a nonterritorial minority.[86]

Small numbers of Jews, especially from the impoverished Ukraine, tried their luck in Stalin's radical socialist solution to the "Jewish question," Birobidzhan.[87] A sparsely settled area in the far east of the Soviet Union near the Chinese border (located between the Biro and Bidzhan rivers), Birobidzhan was communism's alternative to Palestine, which Stalin and his government deemed the product of a retrograde bourgeois nationalism.

Birobidzhan endeavored to transform Jews into a territorial minority fully qualified for national rights. It was to have a solid base of agricultural workers who would lead in building a socialist society. Mikhail Kalinin, the ceremonial president of the Soviet state, championed Birobidzhan as early as 1924 and announced its elevation to an "autonomous region" (May 7, 1934).[88]

As early as July 1918 the Bolshevik government legally prohibited anti-Semitism and later made "agitation and propaganda arousing national enmities" a criminal offense (1922, 1927).[89] Yet in the 1930s Stalin's government changed course, introducing widespread discrimination against Jews and other national minorities. In the 1930s and 1940s the government began to discriminate against hiring Jews in state administration. The percentage of Jews dropped precipitously (from over 10% in 1927), as the government deliberately promoted other nationalities, especially Russians and Ukrainians. Moreover, Jews began to disappear from prominent political positions, both local and national. Unofficial yet highly effective educational quotas, especially at universities (where Jews constituted some 11% of students in 1939), were perhaps most damaging.[90]

Passports (December 1932) enabled discrimination. The Soviet government initially introduced passports to control population flight from the starving countryside into cities lacking housing. Passports made nationality unmistakable: it appeared prominently after the date and place of birth. A person born of Jewish parents was automatically designated a Jew. Moreover, the government required the designation of Jewish nationality from 1932.[91]

Conclusion

The Paris Peace Conference introduced national minority rights thereby guaranteeing Jews equality under the League of Nations' supervision. Yet the signatory successor states pursued nationalist policies that in multiple ways subverted the Minority Rights Treaties.

Some tried to deprive Jews of citizenship. Poland introduced a dual system of citizenship law (jus sanguinis for Poles, jus soli for national minorities); Austria tried to use racial categories; and Romania differentiated between Jews from the heartland and its newly acquired territories. All these states continued to use local citizenship law (*Heimatrecht*).

Some states discriminated in still other ways. Hungary introduced quotas in education. Poland exploited the former partitioning powers' discriminatory legislation. Romania excluded Jews from the civil service.

The Soviet Union began by recognizing individual equality and extending minority rights, yet those auspicious developments did not hold. In the 1920s the Soviet Union deprived inordinate numbers of individual Jews of rights and destroyed the shtetl economy. In the 1930s it undermined the Jews' minority rights even as it failed to transform them into a territorial minority.

Worse was to come in east-central and eastern Europe with Nazism's rise and democracy's demise.

Repudiation

DEMOCRATIC GOVERNMENT AND LIBERAL POLITICS had brought emancipation. Their totalitarian repudiation produced the monumental tragedy of 1933–45. The Nazis put the revocation of emancipation front and center.[1] Careful to maintain a semblance of legality, the Nazis abrogated citizenship as the requisite first step to exclusion from the economy, confiscation of property, expropriation of labor, and, finally, with war, deportation and murder. The Nazi template inspired right-wing and fascist governments across Europe: for the authoritarian regimes, abolishing emancipation was foundational. Nazi Germany served as the "laboratory" to 1939; with the war, it spread its methods across Europe.[2]

Governments in Hungary, Romania, Italy, and France also employed citizenship as a criterion to distinguish among Jews. They separated long-established citizens or citizens of the geographical heartland from the recently naturalized, the residents of recently acquired territories, or stateless refugees. Some governments protected the former while condemning the latter to deportation and death.[3]

Germany

When the Nazis came to power in 1933 the sole document that outlined Jewish policy focused squarely on emancipation.

> Should the NSDAP receive an absolute majority, Jews will be deprived of their rights by legal process. If, however, the NSDAP receives power only through a coalition, the rights of German Jews will be undermined through administrative means.[4]

The Nazis chose the option of "legal process." The Third Reich deprived Jews of their citizenship with hundreds of legislative acts. The Nazis peeled away the Jews' rights layer after layer in an almost exact reversal of the emancipation process. Dis-emancipation inverted emancipation's structure.[5]

The Nazis first attacked the political rights that Jews had acquired most recently (1870): access to the civil service and the franchise. Since 1870 Jews had faced formidable discrimination in trying to attain civil service positions (chapter 14). The Law for the Restoration of the Professional Civil Service (*Gesetz zur Wiederherstellung des Berufsbeamtentums*; April 7, 1933) aimed to purge political opponents (Article 4) and "civil servants of non-Aryan descent" (Article 3, Clause 1).[6] The law granted exemptions to civil servants hired before August 1, 1914, or who fought during the world war, or who were fathers or sons of those who "died in action" (Article 3, Clause 2). The Nazis presumed first, that since Jews were "shirkers," few of them had fought in the war; and second, that most Jews had gained civil service positions during the Weimar Republic. Neither was true, so the law was less effective than planned. Nonetheless, about half of the 5,000 Jews in the civil service lost their positions.[7]

Subsequent enactments affected doctors employed in "state supported health insurance programs" as well as patent attorneys and lawyers (April 22, 1933); government employees lacking civil service status (April 24, 1933) and notaries, teachers, and university staff (May 6, 1933).[8] Nazi professional associations such as the League of National Socialist German Lawyers and the League of National Socialist German Physicians vigilantly enforced these prohibitions. Within a few months over half of the Jewish physicians had abandoned practicing. Overall some 12,000 to 13,000 Jewish professionals lost their jobs.[9]

The two Nuremberg laws were the next installment in depriving Jews of political rights. The Reich Citizenship Law (*Reichsbürgergesetz*; September 15, 1935) denied Jews the status of "citizen" by demoting them to a newly invented inferior status. The Nazis introduced a racial dualism that distinguished between the Aryan "Reich citizen" (*Reichsbürger*) who possessed full citizenship, including political rights, and the non-Aryan "state member" (*Staatsangehöriger*) whose rights, if any, were undetermined. The First Decree to the Reich Citizenship Law (*Verordnung zum Reichsbürgergesetz*; November 14, 1935) partially clarified the law by delineating citizenship's prerogatives as holding public office and exercising the franchise. It defined a Jew as "anyone who is descended from at least three full Jewish grandparents."[10]

These laws restored the dualisms that had kept Jews in an inferior status. They recalled both the two levels of citizenship, local (*Stadtsbürgerschaft*) and state (*Staatsbürgerschaft*) that existed from the first emancipation decrees until 1870 (chapter 12), and the tension between state and federal law characteristic of the Wilhelminian era (chapter 14). The difference now was that the subordinate status of "state member" (*Staatsangehöriger*) had not previously existed: the Nazis created it expressly for Jews.[11]

The other Nuremberg law, the Law for the Protection of the German Blood and German Honor (*Gesetz zum Schutze des deutschen Blutes und der deutschen Ehre*), introduced racial segregation. It prohibited Jews from marrying or having extramarital relations with Aryans and from employing "female domestic help . . . under 45 years."[12] The Nazis subsequently segregated public facilities, for example, park benches and housing, using the model of America's Jim Crow laws.[13]

The Nuremberg laws deprived Jews of political rights and segregated them; the laws did not render them stateless. Nazi Germany turned Jews into a "minority" whose inferior status and persecution, at least in theory, should have come under the League of Nations' purview.[14]

The Nazis next peeled away the various civil rights that Jews had acquired during the nineteenth century: freedom of occupation, property ownership, and residence. The Nazis accomplished this by restricting Jews' economic activity continuously from 1933 and engaging in a concerted campaign of legal and extralegal, often violent, expropriation. There was never a lull or "grace period."[15]

Retail trade was the backbone of Jewish economic life in Germany. In 1932 Jews owned some 50,000 businesses; by 1938 only 9,000 were left. The Nazis destroyed this sector through a combination of legal and extralegal methods. Early efforts such as the boycott of April 1, 1933, impinged most on "medium-size[d] and small Jewish shops" as well as those owned by east European Jews. Banks and loan institutions dutifully canceled existing loans and mortgages and refused to extend new credit. Nazi "district economic advisors" (*Gauwirtschaftsberater*) encouraged local Nazi functionaries and other individuals to intimidate and pressure Jewish owners to sell their businesses ("aryanization"), usually for a fraction of their value. Individuals and small firms, banks and large firms, took advantage of aryanization to make quick profits and eliminate or absorb competitors.[16]

Jewish white-collar and blue-collar workers found themselves excluded from employment. In some instances, their employers dismissed them. In other instances, Nazi workers staged "disturbances," showing "Aryans'" refusal to work alongside Jews, and then demanded the Jews' exclusion.[17]

After Germany reached full employment (1936), fueled in part by rearmament, the Nazis accelerated the pace of the assault through a relentless series of decrees.[18] The goal was twofold. First, the Decree for the Elimination of the Jews from German Economic Life (*Verordnung zur Ausschaltung der Juden aus dem deutschen Wirtschaftsleben*; November 12, 1938) excluded Jews entirely from economic activity by closing the full range of businesses (e.g., retail stores, mail-order houses, and fairs), prohibiting ownership of a business, terminating executives, and ejecting members of trades and artisan cooperatives.[19]

The Nazis shifted, second, from "aryanization" to "confiscation" (1938). "Aryanization" had aimed to deny Jews participation in the economy and to

FIGURE 16. Two Nazi stormtroopers enforce boycott of Jewish business (Heimann store, Oberdorf); April 1, 1933. Leo Baeck Institute, call number F 21345; PID 819172.

benefit individuals and companies. It had produced rampant corruption that the authorities now endeavored to impede.[20] "Confiscation" designated state expropriation, that is, state theft.[21] The Nazis developed the confiscation program in Vienna and in Bohemia/Moravia and then introduced it in Germany. The program consisted of five linked procedures.[22]

First, Jews were required to provide a detailed register of all their assets (April 26, 1938).[23] Second was the "universal imposition of blocked [bank] accounts"; funds could not be withdrawn without express government permission.[24] Third came special taxes or levies, such as the billion mark fine, imputing guilt to the Jews, for the Nazis' destruction of property on Kristallnacht (November 12, 1938).[25] Fourth, the Nazis required Jews to convert property and securities into government bonds and low-interest pensions: the funds went directly to the state.[26] Fifth, the Nazis imposed restrictions on the sale or transfer of property and exacted increasingly higher percentages on the transfer of capital abroad, reaching an extortionate 95 percent by 1939.[27]

The Nazis extended the Nuremberg laws by prohibiting Jews from entering public facilities and then made it a new form of expropriation by introducing segregated housing (Police President of Berlin; December 5, 1938).[28] The "Law on Renting Arrangements" of April 30, 1939, removed Jews from the tenant protection system so that they could be evicted from their apartments. The Nazis then crowded Jews into specific buildings in designated neighborhoods

FIGURE 17. Interior view of the destroyed Fasanenstrasse Synagogue, Berlin, Kristallnacht November 1938. Leo Baeck Institute, call number F 21324; PID 84795l.

(*Judenhäuser*).[29] Full segregation also excluded all Jewish children from schools (*numerus nullus*; November 15, 1938).[30]

The Nazis de-emancipated Judaism by demoting Jewish organizations from tax-exempt "publicly incorporated legal bodies" (*Körperschaften des öffentlichen Rechts*) to mere associations (*Vereine des bürgerlichen Rechts*) (March 28, 1938) subject to taxation. The demotion allowed the state to seize a portion of the organizations' assets.[31] The Nazis eventually disbanded all Jewish organizations and seized the remaining assets (June 9, 1943).[32]

The Nazis began to treat the Jews' potential labor as an exploitable asset as well. The first effort (December 20, 1938) was to conscript the labor of Jews whom the Nazis had made indigent.[33] Less than three months later (March 4, 1939) the Nazis subjected all Jews, "state members" and the "stateless," to forced labor. Jews worked in segregated brigades in "building construction" and "soil amelioration" in egregiously unsafe and degrading conditions.[34] By 1941 30,000 or more Jews were engaged in forced manual labor at starvation wages.[35]

From January 1933 to October 1941 the Nazis aimed to encourage or coerce German Jews to emigrate and, with increasing attention from 1936, to strip them of their assets.[36] By 1938 one-quarter of German Jews had left Germany, by 1941 fully three-fifths (270,000 to 300,000 of some 520,000).[37]

The decision for mass murder of all Europe's Jews came in 1941 in conjunction with the invasion of the Soviet Union.[38] Deportations to east European ghettos, concentration camps, and, eventually, death camps began in October 1941. In preparation for deportation, the Nazis enacted a "denaturalization" law that legalized confiscation of the deportees' property. The Nazis had first enacted such a law (July 14, 1933) to expropriate political opponents who had emigrated.[39] The so-called "Eleventh Decree" (November 11, 1941) stripped deported Jews of their citizenship as they crossed the border, permitting confiscation of their property.[40]

The Nazis were so scrupulous as to distinguish between Jews deported "within" the Reich (Theresienstadt, Łódź, Auschwitz, for example, were in territories incorporated into the Reich) and those outside it. The Nazis applied the law of July 14, 1933, to Jews deported within the Reich; they applied the "Eleventh Decree" to those deported outside it. As a staff member at the U.S. embassy in Berlin telegrammed to the secretary of state at the time:

> the many thousands of Jews now being deported into . . . [the Occupied Eastern Territories] each week will soon be de jure as well as de facto deprived of their citizenship and their worldly goods.[41]

In this final act of deportation and abrogating "state membership," the Nazis completed peeling away the Jews' rights. In the end, the Nazis deprived Jews of the right of residence they had gained during the protracted emancipation process or even earlier as a privilege in corporate society.

Poland

In contrast to Germany and such successor states as Hungary and Romania, Poland did not enact blanket legislation depriving Jews of citizenship or excluding them from the economy. This restraint was not due to the Minorities Treaty: Poland repudiated it in 1934. The Polish government adopted measures pertaining to specific occupations and professions.

Until 1931 the Polish authorities relied on the partitioning powers' old laws to infringe the Jews' rights (chapter 22). At the same time, the state relentlessly excluded Jews from the economy.

The fact that Poland had a state-regulated economy eased the task. In 1930–31 the state owned 22.5 percent of commercial and industrial wealth; the percentage continued to grow. The state employed a minimal number of Jews in the extended public sector. As the state took over the formerly Jewish-owned tobacco industry it dismissed Jewish workers. As it took over workmen's insurance clinics it dismissed Jewish doctors. The railroad employed few Jews, the postal service and the municipalities, despite the preponderance of urban Jews, virtually none. Educated Jews clustered in the liberal professions.[42]

In the private sector, the state also encouraged the "elimination of Jews from the fields of commerce and trade." The number of Jewish-owned businesses rapidly declined because of boycotts, discriminatory state regulations, and the refusal to grant credits for mechanization and other improvements. Industrialization did not incorporate Jewish artisans.[43]

Toward the end of Piłsudski's reign, Poland began to lay the groundwork for a more aggressive policy. In January 1934 Poland signed a nonaggression pact with Hitler: with Germany's revanchist threat seemingly eliminated, Poland was free to emulate its exclusion of Jews.[44] On September 13, 1934, Poland withdrew from the League of Nations' enforcement of the Minority Treaties.[45]

After Piłsudski's death (May 1935), the new regime, under a constitution (April 1935) that enhanced authoritarian rule, enacted new laws to infringe on rights.[46] The aim was to promote Poland's "economic self-sufficiency" by ostracizing Jews from the economy, with the proviso, as the prime minister put it (1936), of "economic struggle by all means—but without force."[47] The Polish government never passed an equivalent to the Nuremberg laws formally abrogating Jewish equality: "there was no law passed that applied universally to all Jews. Restrictions specified certain groups and certain spheres of activity," often without actual legislation.[48]

The government actively encouraged emigration, though without offering an actual destination. In 1936 the government proposed Madagascar as an option. The government lobbied vigorously for a destination at the Evian Conference but left empty-handed.[49]

With the ulterior motive of excluding Jews from the meat trade, the Sejm (April 17, 1936) passed a notorious law banning kosher slaughtering. After a storm of domestic and international protest the government amended this "anti-shechita" law to allow some ritual slaughtering in areas where Jews comprised at least 3 percent of the population.[50] From December 1935 various universities, beginning with the Lwów Polytechnic, segregated Jewish students onto so-called "ghetto benches."[51] In September 1937 the Minister of Education authorized universities to pursue this policy. After the government convened an assembly in Warsaw (November 1937), the boycott of Jewish businesses became "a systematic, well-planned and institutionalized campaign."[52]

From 1937 various white-collar associations adopted an "Aryan paragraph" to exclude Jews.[53] A bill guaranteed "the Polish element a predominant position" among lawyers (May 4, 1938). It gave the government full control over the list of barristers as well as appointments to required clerkships and apprenticeships. Some local bar councils required Jews to display their exact names on their birth certificates to highlight their origins.[54]

Government authorities tried to ostracize Jewish physicians and to seize Jewish hospitals, often condemning buildings or suspending annual subsidies. The Union of Polish Physicians adopted a clause limiting membership to "Polish citizens of Christian birth." The government excluded Jewish engineers from apprenticeships while government and private enterprises dismissed Jewish engineers who had positions. Authorities closed Jewish schools ("Sabbath schools") and replaced Jewish teachers with Christians. With the exception of the law for barristers, the Polish authorities implemented these discriminatory measures without introducing legislation.[55]

Partition

The "fourth" partition of Poland inaugurated World War II. Just as three autocratic powers partitioned the Polish-Lithuanian Commonwealth in the eighteenth century, now two totalitarian states divided the Republic of Poland. Nazi Germany and the Soviet Union signed a pact (Molotov-Ribbentrop; August 23, 1939), invaded the country (the Nazis on September 1, 1939; the Soviets on September 17), and began to murder the intelligentsia and reengineer society.[56]

NAZI-OCCUPIED WESTERN POLAND

The Nazis engaged in "economic plunder on an unprecedented scale."[57] Characteristically, the Nazis maintained a semblance of legality, enacting legal measures that recapitulated the process of expropriation in Germany. They first required the incarceration of "Jewish men of Polish state membership" (*polnischer Staatsangehörigkeit*)—using the same term as in the Nuremberg laws—and also required the registration of Jewish property.[58] Subsequent orders prohibited movement or sale of Jewish property (September 12, 1939); blocked bank accounts (September 18, 1939); excluded Jews from numerous economic sectors (December 1939); confiscated and exported enormous quantities of furs; and, finally, shifted from "plunder" to "systematic seizure" with the establishment of centralized Trustee Offices (*Treuhandstellen*).[59] With ghettoization the Nazis deprived the Jews of whatever property remained.[60]

The Nazis treated Polish Jews as stateless. They issued (September 17, 1940) a blanket authorization confiscating the property of "Jews, state members of the former Polish state [*Juden, Staatsangehörigen des ehemals polnischen Staates*]" for the German Reich's benefit.[61] In addition, they ordered (November 15, 1941) the confiscation of all real estate, even if it had been previously sold (so long as it was not entered in the land registry).[62]

SOVIET-OCCUPIED EASTERN POLAND

The Soviets annexed territories containing some 13 million, including 1.5 million Jews (1.2 million residents plus 300,000 refugees from the German occupation). The Soviets integrated eastern Poland into the Soviet system: they systematically murdered political opponents, deported masses (800,000, including some 250,000 Jews), and nationalized the economy.[63]

The Soviet authorities gave all residents Soviet citizenship (November 29, 1939); many Jews felt themselves to be equal citizens for the first time.[64] As part of imposing the Soviet system, the authorities issued passports (March 1940). Because of their politics or occupation, for example, "unproductive" (*lishchentsy*), many Jews received passports valid for less than the usual five years that also included a "criminal paragraph." Many who held these passports were forced to relocate from border areas or major cities. Jewish leaders of all kinds—religious, political, communal—were incarcerated, deported, or fled.[65] In keeping with Soviet policies of the late 1930s, the authorities refused to recognize Jews as a national minority and relentlessly shuttered Jewish institutions.[66]

The Soviet authorities offered citizenship to the 300,000 Jewish refugees. An overwhelming majority refused since they hoped to return home or emigrate; many in fact registered to return to Nazi-occupied western Poland. The Soviets considered these refugees disloyal and a security risk. In June 1940, the authorities instituted mass roundups and deported the refugees to labor camps in Siberia and northern Russia.[67]

Nationalization and collectivization fell into two phases. There was a "pseudo-New Economic Policy" (September 1939–January 1940) in which the authorities nationalized large businesses (banks, factories, state enterprises) and reallocated large estates to peasants while permitting small-scale businesses to function. Full nationalization and collectivization followed (summer

1940 to June 1941).[68] As in the USSR itself, collectivization destroyed the shtetl economy: small shops and businesses closed while independent artisans joined collective artels.[69]

The abolition without warning of Polish currency as legal tender (January 1, 1940) destroyed savings and business capital, turning much of the middle and lower-middle classes into proletarians. The promise of jobs lured some of the unemployed to the USSR's interior.[70] Many Jews were recruited to the lower ranks of the bureaucracy; professionals (agronomists, accountants, engineers, doctors) found jobs in state enterprises; artisans joined producers' cooperatives; and students enrolled in the schools and universities now freed from Poland's numerus clausus.[71]

Hungary

Hungary had been the first of the successor states to infringe on the Jews' rights and the Minority Treaties with a quota in educational institutions (1920) (chapter 22). On May 24, 1938, Hungary promulgated the first "Jewish law" among the successor states, thoroughly violating its constitution and the Minority Treaty.[72]

Hungary was one of Nazi Germany's "opportunistic satellites."[73] It benefited directly from Nazi expansionism: in 1938 it regained parts of Slovakia and Subcarpathian Rus. The Magyar elite wanted to have the best of all possible worlds: to regain territories lost after 1918, enjoy the economic benefits of rearming, and appease the radical right by emulating Nazi Germany, yet also avoid substantial social and economic reform. The Magyar elite therefore opted to sacrifice Hungary's Jews.[74]

The "First Jew Law" (Law for the More Efficient Protection of the Social and Economic Balance; June 28, 1938) aimed to reduce the Jews' participation in Hungary's economy by introducing quotas of 20 percent in business, the professions, and education. These targets were generally to be attained within five years (June 30, 1943), with some exceptions ten years (June 30, 1948). In general Jews were to be hired in business or admitted to practice (law, medicine, engineering) at the reduced rate of 5 percent until the 20 percent quota was reached, although other means were also to be employed.[75]

The Union of Hungarian Jews protested this infringement on equality. Various liberal groups, intellectuals, and politicians joined in rejecting this violation of the constitution. Crucially, all the churches (Lutheran, Calvinist, Catholic) supported the legislation.[76]

In 1939 Hungary joined the Anti-Comintern Pact (January 13), completed its occupation of Carpatho-Ruthenia (March 18), and withdrew from the League of Nations (April 11). Now firmly within the Nazi orbit and bolstered by the spread of dis-emancipation across Europe (Italy, Romania, Austria),

Hungary's government adopted a "Second Jewish Law" (Law to Restrict Jewish Participation in Public and Economic Life; May 4, 1939).

The law significantly shifted from a religious to a racial definition of a Jew. Moreover, the law lowered the quotas from 20 to 6 percent; dismissed professors, teachers, and notaries (by January 1, 1943); withdrew licenses for sale of articles governed by state monopolies; restricted trade licenses to 6 percent; set a limit of 12 percent in "industrial concerns, mines, banks, money exchanges and insurance companies"; and required Jews to obtain permission to buy or sell land and required them to sell land if the authorities so ordered (establishing conditions for expropriation; Articles 15, 16).[77]

The Second Jewish Law further stipulated that no Jew in the future could obtain citizenship through "naturalization, marriage or legitimization" (Article 3).[78] The government reserved the right to annul any Jew's naturalization acquired after July 1, 1914. The state withdrew the right of Jews to be elected to the Upper House of Parliament. "Parliamentary and municipal suffrage" depended upon family residence in Hungary since 1867.[79] The state excluded Jews from "state, county or municipal" civil service positions (Article 5). Finally, the state promoted "Jewish emigration," though it reserved the right to decree regulations "for the protection of the national wealth" (Article 22).

Hungary withheld passports from the 150,000 Jews in the recently acquired territories of Slovakia and Subcarpathian-Rus unless they could produce three witnesses to prove that they had been loyal Hungarians even when under Czechoslovak rule.[80]

The "Third Jewish Law" (August 2, 1941), enacted after the acquisition of additional territory (Northern Transylvania, Délvidék), adopted an even more racist definition of who was a Jew while prohibiting marriage, and extramarital sexual relations, between Jews and non-Jews.[81]

During the war, the Hungarian governments radicalized measures against the Jews. In 1942 the government demoted Judaism from an "established" to a "recognized" cult.[82] The Kállay government (1942–44) extended the expropriation of Jewish businesses and property. In 1942 that government began to draft Jews for unarmed labor battalions ("auxiliary service") that worked at the eastern front. Perhaps as many as half the men died. Hungary sent some six thousand Jews to work as slave laborers in Serbian copper mines.[83] There were massacres. Hungarian authorities handed Jews from the newly acquired territories to the Nazis in Ukraine; mobile killing units (*Einsatzgruppen*) murdered them.[84]

Yet only the Nazi occupation (March 12, 1944) brought mass roundups and deportations to death camps. Moreover, during the deportations, the regent, Horthy, resolutely defended the distinction between the long-settled Jews of the heartland and the recently arrived or newly acquired "eastern" Jews: he ordered a halt to the deportation of Budapest's Jews.[85]

ROMANIA

Like Hungary, Romania was one of Nazi Germany's "opportunistic satellites." Its experience was, however, the reverse of Hungary's.[86] Romania had won significant territory after World War I; with the start of the new war it lost territory. The USSR (June 26, 1940) claimed northern Bukovina and Bessarabia; Hungary took Transylvania (August 30, 1940); Bulgaria occupied southern Dobrudja (September 7, 1940). Romania feared that it would share Poland's fate and disappear altogether. It avoided that outcome, regaining northern Bukovina and Bessarabia in 1941, although with calamitous consequences for the area's Jews.

Romania's government relentlessly attacked the Jews' citizenship from the mid-1930s. The "Law for the Protection of National Labor" (July 16, 1934) restricted Jews to 20 percent of workers in industry and commerce and 50 percent of management.[87] On December 28, 1937, a far-right wing government (Octavian Goga-Alexandru Cuza) came to power. Dedicated to rule by the Romanian "race," the Goga-Cuza government suspended democracy, ruled by decree, and further excluded Jews. The government closed Jewish institutions (newspapers, libraries) and imposed quotas throughout the economy with the aim of the "Romanization of labor." Professional associations began to expel Jews.[88]

On January 21, 1938, the government enacted the "Decree Concerning the Revision of Citizenship": Jews in the annexed provinces had to re-prove their claim to citizenship within twenty days. Jews naturalized in the Old Kingdom had to show basic documents. The burden of proof lay with the individual. Exorbitant fees at every step barred the way, especially for the poor. Moreover, while an individual's status was being examined, his/her citizenship was suspended, which had economic consequences: all licenses and permits were canceled.[89]

King Carol dismissed the Goga-Cuza government on February 10, 1938, suspended the constitution, and took power as a royal dictator. King Carol announced that citizenship was the heart of the Jewish question:

> The measure to be taken to deal [with the question of the Jews in Romania] is on the principle of revision of citizenship for those Jews who entered the country after the war. . . . Those Jews who lived in Romania before the war will remain untouched. But those who came after the war are without legal rights, except as refugees. About them we shall consider what to do.[90]

King Carol's new constitution (February 27, 1938) separated Romanians by race (jus sanguinis) from mere citizens by residence (jus soli).[91]

Carol's government made the process of proving citizenship far more difficult (Supplementary Condition to the March 9, 1938, "Decree Concerning the Revision of Citizenship") by stipulating that only original documents were admissible. Obtaining original documents in a region in which war had destroyed records and borders had repeatedly shifted was often impossible. The Minister of Justice reported that by November 14, 1939, one-third of Romania's Jews (some 270,000), the vast majority in the acquired territories, had lost citizenship and were stateless.[92] As foreigners, the government prohibited them from practicing professions, for example, law, journalism, and publishing, and from employment in many occupations, for example, selling alcohol and tobacco, owning rural property or shops.[93] In addition, the government imposed (December 3, 1938) a special graduated income tax on such "foreigners," that is, Jews. Those unable to pay the tax were assigned to public work projects.[94]

The royal dictatorship began to enact legislation ostracizing Jews from the professions and encouraged the respective professional associations to do the same, even though Romania depended on such experts: accountants (February 8, 1938), pharmacists (March 17, 1938), bankers (May 25, 1938), those holding diplomas from foreign universities (June 9, 1938), technicians (August 1938), and architects (November 27, 1938).[95]

Like Poland, the Romanian government hoped that mass emigration would be the solution, though it also hoped to turn a profit: it wanted a per capita ransom for emigration. The government negotiated with the Zionist movement and explored options at the Evian Conference (July 6–15, 1938).[96]

On August 8, 1940, Prime Minister Gigurtu's government enacted two laws that, resembling Hungary's, for the first time adopted a racial definition and definitively undermined emancipation. First, the laws designated some baptized individuals as Jews. Second, the government outlawed intermarriage and revoked name changes. The laws excluded Jews from the civil service, the professions, and liquor sales and prohibited purchase of rural real estate and industrial enterprises.

The laws established a tripartite hierarchy that punished Jews in the annexed territories. The small group who possessed Romanian citizenship before December 30, 1918, were exempted from the law. Those who had been residents of Old Romania before December 30, 1918, were subject to some of the laws. The residents of the provinces annexed after 1918 were subject to all the laws. The laws' classification spelled the end of equality.[97]

At the same time, the government dismissed Jews from all branches of the civil service. The government ousted Jewish teachers and pupils from schools (August 30, 1940).[98]

In September 1940 Ion Antonescu brought to power a government, at first filled with Iron Guard leaders, that lasted four years (until August 1944). That government quickly enacted laws that aimed at the "Romanization" of the economy. Laws of September 13, 1940, and October 5, 1940, created a system of commissars in factories that gave the Iron Guard control of the economy, and a further law of November 16, 1940, required that Jewish employees be dismissed. These decrees were a significant step toward Romanization.[99]

Three laws removed Jews from the rural economy. The first (October 5, 1940) authorized the government to expropriate Jewish-owned arable land; the second (November 17) nationalized rural industries (granaries, lumberyards, distilleries, mills) and nonarable land (e.g., forests); the third (December 4) confiscated boats and barges.

On March 27, 1941, the government approved the expropriation of Jews' real estate for which, following German practice, they were to be reimbursed in negotiable bonds. Two decrees (May 3, 1941; March 6, 1942) established a "National Center for Romanization" with the Ministry of Finance guaranteeing special credit to Romanians to purchase Jewish businesses and factories.[100]

For the Legionaries "Romanization" spelled plunder and self-aggrandizement, often through terror, especially of "businesses, shops, apartments blocks, and other buildings." Police and other local authorities joined in the criminal looting.[101]

With the start of war with Russia (June 1941), Romania began a campaign of ethnic cleansing through mass murder in its eastern territories.[102] Romania deported thousands of Jews from border areas to the interior in freight cars without any provisions.[103] Most importantly, Romania created its own killing center: Marshal Antonescu sent 185,000 Jews from Bessarabia and northern Bukovina to its eastern territory of Transnistria (Soviet Ukraine).[104] "Besides Germany itself, Romania was the only country which implemented all the steps of the destruction process, from definitions to killings."[105]

To end the Legionaries' plundering, Antonescu's government implemented state confiscation of Jewish wealth in Old Romania. The state seized the Jewish community's property as well as enormous quantities of clothing to send to its soldiers in Russia. It imposed a large tax (two billion lei).[106] A lack of trained Romanians stymied some confiscations: Jews continued to play an important role in industry and especially war production, though often working as virtual slave labor.[107] Enforced labor service applied largely to poor, unemployed Jews.[108]

Despite signing protocols with the Nazi government, the Antonescu government decided during the second half of 1942 not to deport the Jews from Old Romania (Regat). Antonescu changed his mind in the face of the Nazis' major military defeats; protests by various religious and political leaders and foreign diplomats; and fears for Romania's future.[109] At the same time, the Romanian authorities continued to confiscate real estate and arable land, passed laws authorizing expropriation of apartments, and imposed another huge tax (four billion lei).[110]

Italy

Italy did not import its racial laws from Germany, although they did help cement Mussolini's alliance with Hitler.[111] They were indigenous to Fascism's effort to create religious and racial homogeneity integral to a planned second Fascist revolution.

With the Concordat (1929), Mussolini elevated the Catholic Church to a position of supremacy and re-Catholicized the schools. In consequence, he deprived Judaism, as well as other religions, of the equality they had enjoyed since unification.[112] In building an African empire, Mussolini's Italy began to adopt racial laws to protect the "white race." Concomitantly, his government promoted policies to increase Italy's population. With the proclamation of an Italian Empire (May 9, 1936), Italy fully espoused racism.[113]

Fascism had a definite strain of anti-Semitism in its opposition to socialism and capitalism: many fascists identified Jews with both. Mussolini expressed hostility to Jews before taking office and, once in power, questioned the loyalty of Zionists to Italy and the fascist state; he also tried to exclude Jews from appointment to government positions and fascist academies. In April 1934 Mussolini ordered the discrete removal of Jews from state and municipal offices.[114] In September 1938 Mussolini declared all Jews to be Fascism's enemies.[115]

Mussolini's racial laws (1938) were key to a second Fascist revolution. The first revolution (1920s) was the consolidation of authoritarian rule; the second (1930s) was shaping a homogeneous nation to support an imperial totalitarian state. Mussolini aspired to transform Italians from a "race of slaves" into a "race of lords"—imperial citizens who were consummate workers and warriors. The antitheses of the new empire and the new fascist man (*uoma fascista*) were the liberal state and the bourgeois spirit: the Jews personified both.[116] Mussolini wanted Jews to emigrate.[117]

In preparation for the new racial laws the Ministry of the Interior ominously transformed the Central Demography Office into the Office of Demography and Race. In August 1938 that office conducted a census of Italy's Jews (of some 45,200, 37,000 were Italian citizens, 7,000 foreigners).[118]

The 1938 racial laws ejected Jews from the professions and from schools and deprived naturalized Jews of citizenship. The royal decree of September 5, 1938, ostracized Jews from the educational system: pupils from classrooms, teachers from schools, professors from universities and academies.[119] Two days later (September 7, 1938) a law deprived of citizenship Jews who had been naturalized, and banished all foreign Jews who had taken up residence, after January 1, 1919.[120]

The racial legislation (November 17, 1938) combined racial segregation with exclusion from the civil service and the economy. Like the Nuremberg laws, it introduced a new inferior category of state membership: "Italian citizens of the Jewish race" (Article 10). The decree prohibited marriage between an "Italian citizen" and a "person of foreign nationality" (Article 2). It imposed penalties of "loss of salary and rank" for government or party officials violating the prohibition and fines for clergymen officiating at such ceremonies (Article 3). The decree defined who is a Jew (Article 8).

Jews were excluded from the military and companies concerned "with the defense of the nation" (Article 10, a, c) and from banks, insurance companies, and all civil service positions (Article 13). They were prohibited from owning enterprises employing "100 or more persons" and from owning valuable land or urban buildings (Article 10, d, e).[121] The military retired all Jewish officers (December 22, 1938).[122]

A further decree (February 9, 1939) made provision for confiscation of property by establishing the Institute for the Administration and Liquidation of Immovable Property (*Ente di Gestione e Liquidazione Immobiliare*).[123] The government's express purpose was to bring "Jewish capital under stringent Aryan control in the service of the nation."[124] Between 1938 and 1943 the government "aryanized" over a third of Jewish firms.[125] A decree of January 1944 ordered that all Jewish property be confiscated.[126] Despite Mussolini's Second Revolution's express hostility to the "bourgeois spirit," the Jews' exclusion from the economy benefited the Italian bourgeoisie, from shopkeepers to professionals.[127]

With the declaration of war (June 1940), the Italian government began to round up and intern foreign Jewish men in some fifteen camps. The government also began a policy of detention through enforced residence in the countryside or villages. A decree of May 6, 1942, instituted forced labor for all Italian Jews (ages 18–55).[128] With mounting defeats, the government in November 1943 declared Jews "enemy aliens" and the next month began internment.[129]

Mussolini's government went no farther than this. His racial laws deprived Jews of equal citizenship, excluded them from employment, and confiscated their property and businesses. The result was widespread impoverishment.[130] He then began to intern foreign Jews and subject Italian Jews to forced labor. His goal remained to rid Italy of its Jews through emigration.

As in Hungary, it was the Nazis who, after occupying the north of the country (September 8, 1943), commenced hunting Jews to deport them to death camps.[131]

France

Vichy France's "national revolution" radicalized the late Third Republic's increasingly hostile policies toward immigrants. Vichy implemented its own indigenous anti-Semitic legislation. Its Jewish policy was a "rival" to that of, not an import from, Nazi Germany.

France was altogether unique among occupied western European nations in having adopted indigenous anti-Semitic policies. No other occupied country in Western Europe took even the most tentative step in
this direction on its own.[132]

Vichy's "state anti-Semitism" (*antisémitisme d'État*) aimed to use the rule of
law and juridical procedures to abolish the equality of 1791: the state would
regulate Jews for the benefit of all Frenchmen.[133] The government placed
anti-Semitic activists in positions of power, especially at the Commissariat-
General for Jewish Affairs (March 29, 1941).

France had welcomed immigrants, especially men, after its staggering
losses in World War I (1,400,000 men). The government enacted a lenient
naturalization law (August 10, 1927) that granted citizenship after three years
of residence, whereas the previous law had required ten years.[134] During the
1920s and 1930s France became Europe's refugee center: Italians fleeing Fascism (700,000), central Europeans fleeing Hitler, including Jews (300,000),
and Spanish Republicans escaping Franco (400,000).[135] In 1940 there were
between 300,000 and 350,000 Jews in France, about half foreign born.[136]

The political right inflamed anti-immigrant sentiment by exploiting the
Depression's high levels of unemployment and the overwhelming number of
refugees, some of whom received state support. One result was a tightening of
immigration laws. The government subjected foreigners to repatriation, forced
residence in remote rural areas (May 1938), and stripped naturalization from
those deemed undesirable (November 12, 1938). The latter enactment also created the legal basis for establishing concentration camps. Right-wing calls for
legislation restricting Jewish refugees and Jews in France reached an all-time
crescendo.[137]

With France's lightning defeat anti-immigrant and anti-Jewish politics became a reality. The French army expelled Jewish soldiers in summer and fall
1940. Many of the 30,000 foreign Jews who had volunteered became stateless
and consequently were interned or shipped to labor camps.[138] The law of July
22, 1940, allowed Vichy to review all naturalizations since 1927 but especially
those after 1936 when the Popular Front, the right's bête noire, gained power:
15,154 persons lost their citizenship, including some 6,000 Jews.[139]

Vichy began its legislative onslaught with the "Statute on the Jews" (*Statut
des Juifs*; October 3, 1940) that defined a Jew as having two Jewish grandparents. The statute excluded Jews from high civil service positions, the officer
corps, and professions capable of influencing public opinion (teaching, press,
radio, film, theater).[140] A law of October 4, 1940, empowered prefects to intern
foreign Jews.[141]

Eight months later the second "Statute on the Jews" (*Statut des Juifs*; June
2, 1941) concluded the task of excluding Jews from public positions (Articles
2, 3) and commenced purging them from the economy (Articles 5–7). The

legislation also required an ominous census that detailed all personal (family, education, military service, occupations) and economic data (property, income, debts).[142]

Utilizing the census data, the law of July 22, 1941, introduced the "aryanization" of Jewish property and enterprises with the aim of removing "*all Jewish influence* from the national economy" (*toute influence juive dans l'économie nationale*). The law established a bureaucratic procedure for expropriation by authorizing the appointment of trustees to manage or liquidate property and businesses. The law was extended to Algeria, Morocco, and the French Empire's extremities (Guiana, West Indies).[143]

A raft of further decrees from June through December 1941 introduced quotas for the professions (2%) and institutions of higher education (3%). Some exemptions applied to Jews who were war veterans, had notably served the nation, or had lived in France for five generations.[144]

There was nothing clandestine about Vichy's anti-Jewish laws. Numerous ministries across the Vichy government wrote and implemented the legislation. Prefects, courts, and police enforced it.[145]

Vichy authorities at first tried to distinguish in roundups and deportations between established (*Israélites*) and recent immigrants (*Juifs*).[146] The law of June 2, 1941 ("administrative internment"), collapsed that distinction. The German police who arrested 743 Parisian professionals and businessmen on December 14, 1941, simply ignored it.[147] The law of December 11, 1942, that required inscribing the word *Juif* in identity cards, ration cards, and work permits further blurred the distinction.[148] Internment became standard practice for the stateless and foreigners. Internment and forced labor battalions (*groupement de travailleurs étrangers*) prepared the way for the deportations that began on March 27, 1942.[149]

After May 6, 1942, the Commissariat-General for Jewish Affairs abandoned all semblance of legality and participated wholeheartedly in the German program of mass murder.[150] The Vichy government gave the Nazis blanket approval for deportations (July 4, 1942). Vichy tried to fill the quotas for deportations with stateless and foreign Jews; it allowed denaturalization for those who had attained citizenship after 1933.[151] At this point, when the Nazi war machine still seemed invincible, the Vichy government did not defend French Jewish citizens from deportation. Laval and Petain did, however, block wholesale denaturalization (from 1927).[152]

The Nazi government decided to deport all French Jews in the summer of 1942. Moreover, the Nazis wanted to strip all deportees of citizenship. The French police carried out the roundups and deportations.[153]

From the summer of 1943 the Germans accelerated the pace of deportations and ignored all distinctions among Jews. Only at that late date, when Germany appeared headed to defeat, did Vichy try to block the deportation of French citizens.[154] Furthermore, the French police declined to deport French

Jewish citizens from the Drancy internment camp. By spring 1944 the Gestapo was acting independently with only the help of the French paramilitary (Milice).[155] Approximately 75,721 Jews were deported; roughly two-thirds were refugees, one-third French citizens. Only some 3 percent returned.

In Algeria, the Vichy government abrogated the Crémieux Decree in September 1940, reducing Jews to subjects. After the Allied occupation of Algeria, the Free French authorities delayed for over a year before restoring the Jews' citizenship.[156]

Conclusion

Nazi Germany stripped Jews of rights in a reversal of the emancipation process: first political rights, then the freedoms of occupation and property ownership, and finally residence itself. With deportation the Nazis carefully deprived Jews of their inferior form of "state membership" as well as expropriating all remaining property.

Nazi de-emancipation inspired governments across Europe to infringe on Jews' equality or demote them to a lesser status. The governments first expropriated Jews' property and then their labor.

Poland did not pass blanket legislation: it excluded Jews from the economy in a piecemeal fashion. The government encouraged Jews to emigrate. The Nazi and Soviet invasion of Poland led to systematic expropriation of property. The Nazis declared Jews "stateless." The Soviets granted Jews citizenship yet ostracized the "unproductive." Soviet nationalization and collectivization destroyed the shtetl economy and forced Jews to find new forms of employment.

Hungary enacted a series of "Jew Laws." The first (1938) used religious criteria to reduce their economic role. The second (1939) used racial criteria to continue that process and to deprive many of citizenship. The third (1941) enforced racial segregation.

Romania attacked Jews' citizenship from the mid-1930s, requiring a high standard of documentary proof within a dual legal system: jus sanguinis for Romanians, jus soli for minorities. By 1939 fully one-third of Romania's Jews were stateless, liable to lose employment, and subject to exorbitant taxation. In 1938 King Carol's government started to exclude Jews from the professions and a range of occupations, while Antonescu's government (from 1940) aimed at total "Romanization of labor" by excluding Jews and expropriating their property. In general Romania encouraged Jews to emigrate.

Mussolini's 1938 racial laws were integral to his second Fascist revolution, the building of an empire through racial homogeneity. The laws relegated Jews to a newly invented inferior form of citizenship, began to exclude them from the civil service and the economy, and began to lay the groundwork for expropriation of property. Mussolini wanted Italy's Jews to emigrate.

Vichy France aimed to reverse the equality of 1791. The first "Statute" (1940) excluded Jews from the civil service and positions of influence on public opinion. The second "Statute" (1941) extended that effort and began to exclude Jews from the economy and to prepare for expropriation. Vichy began "aryanization" of property in 1941.

Many governments were complicit in the roundups and deportations that ended in mass murder. In contrast, only Romania joined Germany in organizing systematic mass murder.

Reinstatement

RESTORING EMANCIPATION entailed the reinstatement of citizenship, the restitution of property and reparations for resettlement, rehabilitation, forced labor, and "heirless property." In general states promptly reversed denaturalizations and reinstated citizenship as part of their own reestablishment. In contrast, restitution of property and reparations entailed prolonged and contentious processes, in many cases continuing into the twenty-first century.

That the issues of restitution and reparations lingered was in part due to the way governments and populations explained the war to themselves. How did they make sense of unprecedented civilian death, destruction, and despoliation? Among the war's infinite and incomprehensible horrors, could they acknowledge Jews as victims of a special horror? Did governments subsume Jews to some general category such as "victims of fascism" or "victims of occupation"? Or were governments able to recognize a specific Jewish suffering?[1] Jews faced a virtually ubiquitous struggle for recognition that played out in the Displaced Persons camps as well as in their countries of origin.[2]

The war had unexpected results that complicated the Jews' return, especially to east-central Europe. The war and the Soviet postwar settlement turned many of the interwar nationalities-states into virtual nation-states. The Allies redrew borders to create highly homogeneous national populations; they wiped "little Versailles" and the Minority Treaties from the map. Poland, Czechoslovakia, Romania, Hungary, and Germany were more nation-states than before the war. Tragically and ironically, Wilson's principle of national self-determination came to fruition following thirty million deaths, massive population transfers, and untold suffering. East-central Europe had become even less hospitable to Jews.[3]

Rights

The restoration of rights was high on the agenda of most governments in exile and upon their return. With few exceptions, declaring equality proceeded apace.

On the 150th anniversary of Jewish emancipation in France (October 4, 1941), De Gaulle had declared that "Free France . . . is determined to reestablish, after its victory, the equality, in dignity as in duties, of all citizens everywhere on French territory."[4] Three years later the French National Liberation Committee (*Comité Français de Libération*) issued a decree (May 24, 1944) that abrogated the law of July 22, 1940, permitting denaturalizations. Back on French soil, the committee issued a further decree (August 9, 1944) that abolished all racial laws and restored the legal situation ante bellum.[5] In December 1945 Jews regained their positions as civil servants. Foreign Jews who had served in the French army received citizenship; a law of February 3, 1945, legalized "all foreigners present in France."[6]

In Algeria, in contrast, the Free French Government of General Giraud delayed for almost a year before restoring the Crémieux Decree. In March 1943 Giraud reestablished republican institutions and repealed race laws. Only under Allied pressure did his government reinstate the Jews' citizenship (October 20, 1943).[7]

The Allies had pressed Italy to abrogate the racial laws with the Malta armistice (September 29, 1943; Article 31).[8] A royal decree (#25; January 20, 1944) annulled the racial laws and gave to "Italian and foreign citizens declared or considered of the Jewish race" civil and political rights. The new constitution (January 1, 1948) restored full civil and political rights to all who had suffered persecution.

Italy's constitution did, however, enact an ambiguous status for non-Catholic religions, Judaism included. The constitution recognized Mussolini's 1929 Concordat that vouchsafed Catholicism's supremacy (Article 7) while proclaiming equal freedom for all religions (Article 8).[9] Moreover, Mussolini's law of 1930 that created the "Union of Italian Jewish Communities," in which membership was compulsory, remained in force until 1987.[10]

The Dutch government restored Jews' rights by revoking all Nazi laws pertaining to them (September 17, 1944).[11] Nevertheless, the Dutch government's aim to restore order after five years of Nazi occupation did not explicitly acknowledge Jews. The authorities did not recognize stateless Jews as a group: the government incarcerated Jews returning from Bergen-Belsen with Dutch collaborators, for example.[12] A large share of the few survivors in Holland chose to emigrate: most felt that their swift exclusion from the larger society and subsequent persecution had created an irreparable divide. Moreover, they found themselves unable to rebuild a community.[13] As a report of October 1, 1945, put it: "they do not want to be second class citizens *de facto*."[14]

In Germany, the American occupation restored citizenship on September 20, 1945. The "Basic Law of the Federal Republic of Germany" (May 23, 1949) restored rights to all regardless of religion.[15]

Eastern Bloc

The war deepened and accelerated Stalin's efforts to institute an ethnic hierarchy in which great Russians were highest and nonterritorial minorities, especially Jews, lowest. The Cadres Administration (1939) and Central Committee Propaganda and Agitation Administration systematically, albeit unofficially, purged government administration and the arts of Jewish officials during the war and immediately thereafter.

In 1949–50 Stalin transformed this policy into a true campaign, albeit disseminated orally, which resulted in a mass dismissal of Jews from the state machinery (1949–53) as well as the arrest and in some cases execution of those accused of "Jewish bourgeois nationalism."[16] Stalin directed his anti-Western, "anti-cosmopolitan campaign" against Jews, murdering the leaders of the wartime Jewish Anti-Fascist Committee (1952), arresting Birobidzhan's leaders, and further dismissing Jews from state agencies during the alleged "Doctors' Plot" (January 13, 1953).[17] Stalin also destroyed the last vestiges of Jewish national minority culture.[18] Once in power, Khrushchev continued ostracizing Jews, to the point that they became "effectively second class citizens."[19]

The Communist seizure of power in Hungary (1947–49) resulted in Jews experiencing a second "reverse emancipation." Moreover, the government adopted a "silent *numerus clausus*" to limit the number of Jews in state administration. Finally, when the government banished "bourgeois classes" from the cities (1951), sending them to the countryside where they had difficulty finding employment, almost a third were Jews.[20]

Romania's government continued two interwar-period policies that diminished the Jews' rights. First, it tried to appoint exclusively Romanians to the party and state apparatus, expressly excluding Jews. Second, it realized the policy earlier governments had broached in the 1930s of allowing Jews to emigrate in exchange for hard currency (chapter 23). The Israeli government paid a per capita ransom so Jews could emigrate to Israel. Moreover, when the Communists seized power and eliminated all competing political parties and organizations (1947), the government endeavored to co-opt and destroy Jewish institutions using the model of the Soviet "communist sections" (*Yevsektsia*) of the 1920s (chapter 22).[21]

In the new Polish state, Jews were de jure equal citizens.[22] The postwar communist state's employment of Jews began to erode their prewar occupational distinctiveness.[23] Poland encouraged Jews to emigrate until 1947.[24] With the Communists' seizure of power that year, the government began to nationalize all Jewish institutions.[25] Jews remained in prominent positions in the party and security apparatus until 1956 when the Stalinist-Soviet inspired attack on alleged "Polish nationalism" gave way to a campaign against putative "Jewish nationalism."[26]

Restitution

Governments laid the legal foundation for restitution during the war.[27] The Dutch government in exile prohibited agreements to transfer property to the enemy without prior permission from its "Committee for Legal Transactions" (Decree A6; June 7, 1940).[28] The Belgian government in exile nullified all "aryanizations" (January 10, 1941). The Czech government in exile invalidated the German and Czech enactments against Jews since 1938 and threatened "aryanizers" with criminal proceedings (November and December 1941).[29] The Free French invalidated sales of Jewish property (September 15, 1942).[30] Eighteen governments proclaimed their intention to restitute plundered property ("Inter-Allied Declaration Against Acts of Dispossession Committed in Territories Under Enemy Occupation or Control"; January 1943).[31]

Restitution's success depended upon the process of confiscation. Jews stood a better chance of regaining their plundered property if the process had been orderly and "legal": if detailed records were kept; if funds sat in blocked bank accounts; if contracts were drawn up; if notaries registered transfers of property. In contrast, if confiscation consisted of "wild aryanizations," if there were no records, or if goods were simply stolen without registration or reliable witnesses, then claimants struggled to qualify for legal recourse.

The bureaucracy's role was crucial. If the same officials who had enforced confiscation oversaw restitution, as in Germany, Austria, and Italy, then they likely impeded the process at every step (not to mention the victims' humiliation and anger at having to deal with them). Moreover, in some cases the beneficiaries of confiscation mobilized to oppose restitution.

As early as September 25, 1943, the beneficiaries of Vichy's laws organized a "French Association of Owners of Aryanized Property" to "defend their rights."[32] Related organizations emerged in 1944; the government dissolved them.[33] After the liberation some 25,000 Parisian Jews lacked apartments and the associated ration cards, coal cards, and access to benefits. A law of November 14, 1944, restored Jewish property and reinstated Jews in their apartments.[34]

In January 1945 the government founded the Office for the Restitution of Property of the Victims of Statutory and other Expropriation Measures (*Service de restitution des biens des victims des lois et mesures de spoliation*). In association with the Finance Ministry, the office restituted property for over thirty years.[35] Its work depended on Vichy's files, which were incomplete or in some cases missing. In one scholar's estimation:

In terms of value, restitution was made with respect to 90 percent of the total value of businesses, real estate, shares, and bank accounts. . . . In terms of numbers, . . . at least 70 percent of businesses and real estate properties and between 50 and 100 percent of the deposit accounts and stock accounts were returned. The larger the assets, the more likely . . . that restitution was made.[36]

German looting in France, for example, the contents of some 38,000 apartments, was harder to restitute since there were no files. In contrast, for works of art and precious metals there were registries. By the 1970s the German government (Regional State Finance Office, Berlin; *Oberfinanzdirektion*) processed some forty thousand claims for looted art and restituted some 450–500 million DM.[37]

Italy's second royal decree of January 20, 1944, authorized claims to property ("patrimonial rights"). The decree's promulgation was delayed (October 20, 1944) to prevent the Germans from harming Jews in the Republic of Salò. The law of May 5, 1946, authorized the return of Jews' assets. The law did, however, allow credit institutions to charge management fees for the years of confiscation. The government did not resolve this scandalous situation until May 1958 when it officially recognized the Jews' persecution and canceled the charges.[38] Furthermore, the notorious authority that had confiscated Jewish property (EGELI) was put in charge of restoring it, with many of the same bureaucrats still at their desks. In general Italy's legislation on restitution was late, was inadequate, and gave undue legitimacy to forced property transfers.[39]

The Dutch government enacted two decrees that created a legal basis for restituting property. The "Legal Right Decree" (E100; 1944) established a council that delegated tasks to various departments of the government. The "Occupation Measures Decree" (E93; 1944) invalidated some 423 German regulations.[40] Actual restitution encountered the formidable challenge of partially destroyed, incomplete, and muddled records as well as missing property. Since the Nazis murdered the preponderance of Dutch Jews (some 107,000 of 135,000 were deported; only 5,000 returned), few filed claims (some 23,000 by 1950). A 1949 law eased the process by providing death certificates for missing persons.[41]

Since the Second Austrian Republic treated the *Anschluß* as an illegal occupation, it refused to accept liability for the *Anschluß*'s results. The Austrian government deemed itself Nazism's "first victim" (in accord with the 1943 Moscow Declaration). Austria passed seven inordinately complex interlocking restitution laws (1946–49) that made it difficult for Jews to reclaim property. Moreover, former Nazis staffed the restitution agencies.[42] Austria did not create a program to compensate Jews for forcibly expropriated property until 1961 (Claims Fund, *Abgeltungsfond*; Collection Agency Fund, *Sammelstellen*).[43]

The Swiss government did enact restitution legislation to reintegrate into the postwar world. Using wartime emergency powers, the government enacted two decrees ("Decrees on Looted Assets"; *Raubgutbeschlüsse*; December 1945/ February 1946).[44] The subsequent Washington Accord (May 22, 1946) lifted wartime restrictions and in return stipulated Swiss obligations, for example, assigning 50 percent of frozen German assets to the fund for rehabilitation of stateless victims and returning one-sixth of gold transactions.

Despite its legislation, Switzerland invoked its status as a "neutral" country to resist paying restitution. Swiss authorities argued that they had acted in self-defense against an indomitable foe. Moreover, they invoked national independence and the right of business to function unregulated by government. The Swiss banks did nothing to restitute Jewish assets.[45] A 1962 statement summarized the Swiss position: "Switzerland has nothing to make amends for, either to the victims of Nazi persecution or to Jewish or other organizations, and certainly not to the State of Israel."[46]

Thuringia was the first German government to enact restitution legislation (October 1945; *Wiedergutmachungsgesetz*). Although this was in the Soviet zone, it served as a precedent for the Allies.[47] Nevertheless, in the emerging east bloc nationalization of property prevented restitution: it in fact constituted a second state confiscation that reinstated the first, or, in the case of eastern Poland, the first and the second.[48] State nationalization permitted neither private property nor individual claims.

In East Germany, for example, the state seized private property; it returned only Jewish communal property.[49] With the Communist seizure of power, the Czechoslovak government seized Jewish property as state assets. Moreover, the state forced emigrants to Israel to renounce all claims to restitution and inheritance.[50] Romania delayed restituting houses and businesses and then nationalized commerce and industry.[51] The Polish government passed decrees (1945–46) setting requirements for "heirs" that made it difficult for Jews to claim property. Moreover, the communist authorities declared much property abandoned and nationalized it.[52] Poland similarly refused to restore communal property: it withheld recognition from successor organizations and claimed properties for government use.[53] Governments across Eastern Europe refused to recognize specific Jewish suffering.[54]

In Germany's American zone the Military Government promulgated "Law No. 59: The Restitution of Identifiable Property" (November 1947), which authorized owners or their heirs to claim property. The Allies created a legal basis for Jewish organizations to recover unclaimed or heirless property. In the American zone, the Jewish Restitution Successor Organization gained the right to claim heirless property (June 1948). In the British (May 1949) and French (March 1952) zones, the Jewish Trust Corporation held that right.[55]

West Germany's democracy and civil society did not embrace restitution.[56] There was no consensus that the Federal Republic was legally responsible for the Third Reich's confiscations. In fact, owners of Jewish property, primarily of retail trade and real estate, organized voluntary associations and then amalgamated into the Federal Association for Fair Restitution (1950) to oppose Allied restitution legislation and, having failed, then lobbied for compensation.[57] The fact that the personnel in many government financial agencies had carried out the confiscations only made restitution more difficult.[58] The Allies exerted the decisive pressure for restitution.[59]

As the Allied occupation ended, the Federal Republic first took responsibility to restitute property ("Transitional Treaty"; *Überleitungsvertrag*; May 26, 1952). The agreed sum was 1.5 billion DM, which was far below experts' assessments. The "Federal Restitution Law" (*Bundesrückerstattungsgesetz*; July 15, 1957) authorized payment on both restitution claims the courts had upheld and claims on assets whose whereabouts were unknown. Claims from across Europe were now possible, although with two provisos. First, claimants had to have lived in Germany in the period 1933–45 or in the Western Zone in 1945–52. Second, payments could be made only to countries that had diplomatic relations with the Federal Republic—thus excluding claimants in Eastern Europe.[60] Restitution based on the Allied laws (1947–49) reached 3.5 billion DM; under the Federal Republic's laws an additional 4 billion DM was paid. The political issue of restitution appeared to have been laid to rest by 1965. By 1975 the courts had adjudicated 1.2 million individual trials.[61]

The unification of East and West Germany revived the issue of restitution. There were new claims for property in former East Germany as West Germany's restitution laws came into effect. There were also new claimants in the East whom the earlier restitution law (1957) had excluded. The courts resolved many of these cases in the 1990s. In addition, Germany paid another 1.6 billion DM to the Claims Conference for "heirless" property.[62]

In 2000 the German government established a foundation (Remembrance, Responsibility, and the Future) that made available funds for property claims (1 billion DM) in East Germany as well as for those who could not prove their property had been moved to the Federal Republic's former territory (200 million DM).[63]

Reparations

There were two periods of reparations.[64] Jewish organizations and the State of Israel successfully conducted groundbreaking negotiations with the German government in the immediate postwar era (1945–67).[65] In the 1990s a more developed sense of the Holocaust's magnitude and significance, combined with the opening of archives in Eastern Europe, resulted in renewed claims targeting entities that had resisted or escaped the earlier negotiations: Swiss banks, insurance companies, German industry, and the Austrian government.[66]

POSTWAR

At war's end, there were multiple justifications for reparations. First came the costs of resettling, rehabilitating, and supporting survivors (who were known as "Displaced Persons" [DPs] or, legally, as "Non-Repatriable Victims of Nazism"). Next were the victims and their "heirless property." Then came the enormous funds Jewish organizations, especially the American Joint Distribution Committee, had expended on behalf of the Nazis' victims since 1933.[67]

"Stateless refugees" had no nation to represent them in reclaiming property. The Allies devised a legal basis for indemnification of the stateless with the "Final Act on Reparations" (Paris, 1945) and the "Five Power Agreement on Reparations for the Non-Repatriable Victims of Nazism" (Paris, 1946).[68]

Germany's chancellor Konrad Adenauer laid the grounds for reparations in his declaration to the Bundestag (September 1951): "unspeakable crimes have been committed in the name of the German people. . . . The Federal Government are prepared . . . to bring about a solution of the material indemnity problem."[69] The Wassenaar Protocols (August 22, 1952) provided the basis for reparations to individuals and to Jewish successor organizations. The German Federal Indemnification Law (1953) authorized payments.[70]

Leaders of twenty-three Jewish organizations created the Conference on Jewish Material Claims Against Germany to serve as a negotiating entity.[71] The negotiation's success introduced innovations to international relations: a private organization was party to a settlement with a state, individuals were to gain reparations, and the damages were not limited to those caused by war.[72]

Once the conference had successfully negotiated the Wassenaar Protocols, it then (1953–54) became the permanent distribution agency. The Claims Conference channeled the bulk of funds to two other agencies that were already active: the American Joint Distribution Committee serviced survivors in the diaspora, the Jewish Agency survivors in Israel.[73] Headquartered in New York, the Claims Conference evaluated applications for the remaining funds, most of which were earmarked for commemoration, research, and reconstruction of Jewish life.[74]

SECOND PERIOD: 1990S

The Holocaust claims of the 1990s belong to a "much greater phenomenon" of concern for human rights as well as "truth commissions, international criminal trials, and claims to justice for historic wrongs." The "movement for accountability" had succeeded in founding the International Criminal Court (1998). Reparations became standard consequences of such truth commissions and trials.[75]

These larger developments coincided with: the end of the Cold War that made claims possible in post-communist Eastern Europe; the opening of archives in Eastern Europe that made available new documentary evidence; and American "class action" lawsuits that, when combined with political leverage and media attention, brought international banks and corporations to heel.[76]

In Holland in the 1980s–1990s, as the Holocaust gained renewed importance, Jews came to be regarded as eyewitnesses rather than just as victims. That new role yielded new concern with restitution of property.[77]

A government commission (Scholten Commission) quickly discovered that the Amsterdam Stock Exchange, which had traded in stolen Jewish securities during the war, had favored stock traders in the 1950s: the traders in fact organized a strike (1952) to impede restitution.[78] Initial negotiations with the banks (1999) yielded a restitution offer of fifty million guilders. The banks also owned the Stock Exchange. Further negotiations, accompanied by overt threats from the United States to block Dutch banks from conducting business, brought an offer many times the original sum (314 million guilders).[79]

France had restituted property for three decades; reparations began only in 1997. The government-appointed Mattéoli Commission (Study Mission on the Spoliation of the Jews in France; *Mission d'étude sur la spoliation des Juifs de France*; 1997) estimated that in 2000 there was a maximum of 2.3 billion francs of unclaimed property. The government founded an agency to compensate individuals (1999; Commission for the Compensation of Victims of Spoliation; *Commission pour l'indemisation des victims de spoliation*). In addition, it established an academic and educational agency (Foundation for the Remembrance of the Shoah; *Fondation pour la mémoire de la Shoah*) with an endowment of 2.5 billion francs.[80]

Adverse publicity from class action lawsuits by former forced and slave laborers in the United States in the 1990s forced major German firms (Siemens, Degussa) and the German government to fund the Remembrance, Responsibility and the Future foundation. The German government and German corporations each provided five billion DM that was used to compensate forced and slave laborers as well as Holocaust victims, and in addition to defray insurance claims.[81]

Switzerland had resisted restitution let alone indemnification after the war.[82] Starting in 1996, however, Swiss banks trying to enter the American market faced class action lawsuits from survivors and their heirs.[83] The Swiss were forced to examine their role in Germany's war economy.

The Volcker Committee's study revealed deep, complex, and fantastically lucrative collaboration with the Nazis that amounted to "economic . . . integration" in Axis-controlled Europe. The Swiss had realigned trade policy toward Germany (summer 1940): during the war the Swiss government granted Germany credits that reached 1 billion francs (1945).[84] The Swiss had laundered gold and securities and provided a market for looted goods, including art. Swiss companies had taken Nazi contracts and used forced and slave labor to fulfill them. The Volcker Committee found evidence of approximately 50,000 accounts possibly linked to victims.

Confronted with incontrovertible and overwhelming evidence, Swiss banks agreed to pay $1.25 billion against all future claims. The Swiss government refrained from official participation.[85] The case of the Swiss banks served as a precedent for claims against other banks.[86]

Subjected to similar legal processes and political pressures, insurance companies engaged in a settlement procedure that yielded over $306 million to survivors and heirs who owned insurance policies prior to the war. Some claimants received awards without being able to name the precise company; others received awards despite the companies having been nationalized or liquidated; still others received "humanitarian awards" based on a "high level of anecdotal information." The companies also contributed to various programs supporting survivors.[87]

In response to international pressure, the Austrian government adopted a series of stopgap measures from 1961 to 1999 that it labeled "assistance" rather than indemnification.[88] In 2001 Austria began to restitute thousands of works of arts. In a foundation funded jointly by government and business, on the German model, Austria began to disburse "$1.4 billion in per capita payments to Austrian Holocaust survivors worldwide, ... to former forced and slave laborers, pensions for Jews driven from Austria or their children, and settlements of assorted property claims."[89]

The 1990s brought litigation in American courts to recover stolen works of art. These cases were inordinately complex. In the intervening five decades many works of art had changed hands multiple times. Many private buyers were legally "innocent": they had no idea, or claimed to have no idea, of a prior theft. Moreover, there was often a basic question of which laws were applicable, since the original owner or heirs might file suit in one country, often the United States, while the current owners were resident in another. Claims were easier to pursue when a public museum owned the art and there were clear lines of transmission. A conference convened in Washington, D.C. (December 1998), produced a set of guidelines.[90]

Conclusion

The reclamation of citizenship, the restitution of property, and negotiations for reparations stretched across postwar Europe, with some activities continuing into the twenty-first century.

In Western and Central Europe Jews quickly regained citizenship. France, Italy, and Holland abrogated Nazi decrees to restore Jews' citizenship. Germany granted citizenship irrespective of religion.

In east-central and Eastern Europe, in contrast, Jews struggled to regain or retain rights. Stalin's and Khrushchev's governments discriminated against

Jews throughout Soviet society; they effectively turned Jews into second-class citizens. In Hungary Jews experienced a second "reverse emancipation." Romania purged the state apparatus and arranged for Israel to ransom Jews for hard currency. Poland gave Jews citizenship de jure yet began to discriminate against them.

The governments of Holland, Belgium, Czechoslovakia, and France laid the legal foundation for restitution during the war by declaring Nazi expropriations illegal. Eighteen governments signed a declaration to restore property.

Actual restitution was complex and prolonged. France created an agency that restituted property for some thirty years. Italy's inadequate measures were put in the hands of the same agency that had confiscated property. Few Jews survived to reclaim property in Holland. Austria erected legal obstacles and charged the same bureaucrats who had confiscated property with restoring it. Switzerland refused to accept responsibility and restore property. In the east bloc state nationalization of property confirmed the wartime confiscation(s).

In Germany Allied pressure initially was decisive in imposing restitution. The Federal Republic then took responsibility in a process that was restricted to its own borders. After 1989 it extended that effort to the former East German territories.

Reparations fell into two phases. In 1953 the Federal Republic of Germany agreed to pay reparations in a "protocol" that broke new ground in international relations. In a second wave of reparations that began in the 1990s the Amsterdam Stock Exchange, German firms, Swiss banks, and the French and Austrian governments agreed to pay large sums in response to public pressure and class action lawsuits. Reclamation of purloined art works continued into the twenty-first century.

Maghreb and Mashreq

WORLD WAR I was as much a "seminal catastrophe" for the Maghreb (North Africa) and Mashreq (Middle East) as for Europe. The results of the Ottoman Empire's collapse paralleled the Habsburg Empire's, albeit with one principal and portentous difference. In east-central Europe's successor states, the principle of self-determination prevailed, as sovereignty coupled with Minority Rights (chapter 22). In the Maghreb and Mashreq, in contrast, the European powers completed the colonial process that France began with its occupation of Algeria (1830): they now imposed direct rule or protectorate status everywhere.[1]

The interwar and post–World War II period in consequence turned on "decolonization," that is, the quest for self-determination through the foundation of new or newly independent polities.[2] The European powers left the region with the conflicting promises they had made, the borders they had inflicted, and the political divisions they had fomented.[3]

The Jews' status in these states was complex. Jews had numbered among colonialism's beneficiaries. Some had gained citizenship under European auspices individually, some collectively. Under the capitulations treaties prominent individuals had gained the perquisites of European or American protection (*protégés*).[4] Largely urban residents, some Jews participated in the economic boom driven by European commerce; the Alliance's schools had taught the requisite languages and skills.

Zionism complicated the Jews' status. By aspiring to transform Jews from a religious into a territorial national group, Zionism stimulated, and collided with, Arab or pan-Arab nationalism. Zionism reinforced the Jews' apparent links to colonialism in Britain's Balfour Declaration and Palestine Mandate. For fledgling polities, Zionism and the State of Israel raised the specter of disloyalty.

The 1929 Jerusalem or Western Wall riots were a watershed in bringing to the Arab world's attention that conflict as well as the Jews' relationship to

Britain. The Arab Revolt in Palestine (1936–39) brought further attention as well as some active support. Fascist Italy and Nazi Germany provided some sectors of the Arab world with an attractive rival to British and French rule.

World War II turned the two regions into a war zone. The three French Maghrebi lands imposed their own versions of Vichy's "Statute on the Jews" (chapter 23). Tunisia's Jews came under Nazi control (November 1942–May 1943). During the short war with Iraq British authorities refused to intervene to end a Baghdad pogrom.

Many Jews across the two regions felt the Western powers had betrayed them. Others proudly celebrated the postwar restoration of citizenship or the status quo ante.

Each of Israel's wars further eroded the Jews' position. From 1948 onward, Arab states displayed a marked proclivity to identify all Jews with, and to hold them responsible for, Zionism. Arab polities frequently used the occasion of wars to exclude Jews from the economy and diminish or abolish their rights.

After Israel's Declaration of Independence and the ensuing war there was mass emigration from the Mashreq. By 1955 half of the Jews in Arab countries had left. The Sinai War (1956) encouraged Egypt's Jews to flee. With the end of France's colonial rule many Jews abandoned the Maghreb. By 1965 the preponderance of Jews had emigrated from the Maghreb and Mashreq.[5]

Maghreb (North Africa)

French North Africa, where Jews were the only indigenous minority, contained nearly half of Arabic-speaking Jewry at the end of the nineteenth century, approximately two-thirds in 1939. The region was largely under France's direct, and apparently permanent, colonial rule.[6] Attempting to build on experience, French colonial authorities devised three different modes of governing, each with a distinct status for Jews. France annexed Algeria (1830) and gave Jews citizenship collectively (1870). France made Tunisia (1882) a protectorate and enabled Jews to naturalize individually (1910s). France made Morocco (1912) a protectorate and left Jews de jure in their *dhimmi* status.

ALGERIA

After a brutal occupation (1830) and pacification, France annexed Algeria. As military administration gave way to civil government, Jews received citizenship collectively (1870; Crémieux Decree), except for Mzabi Saharan Jews (chapter 17). The Jews' eligibility to vote, combined with their concentration in the cities, provoked the European colonists' (*colons*) resentment, making Algeria a hothouse of organized political anti-Semitism (chapter 19). Vichy authorities revoked the Crémieux Decree, stripping 100,000 Algerian Jews of citizenship (October 7, 1940). They then imposed the "Statutes on the Jews," excluding them from numerous professions and introducing a numerus clausus on students (chapter 23). To Algerian Jews' dismay, the Free French authorities delayed in reinstating the Crémieux Decree (chapter 24).

Algerian Jewish leaders established a civil defense organization (1915) to protect their rights. The Algerian Jewish Committee for Social Studies (*Le Comité Juif Algérien d'Etudes Sociales*; CJAES) avowed "to be on alert that the free exercise of the Jews' rights as citizens not be violated or ignored." In fact, Algerian Jews felt themselves to be second-class citizens because of political anti-Semitism's effects. In 1938–39, for example, Oran's mayor had purged some three hundred Jews from the voting lists; the CJAES succeeded in reinstating them.[7]

In response to Vichy's racist statutes, Algerian Jews founded a new organization (*Comité d'Aide et d'Assistance*) that created a school system for the children expelled from public schools and helped those deprived of jobs to find alternative employment. A secret group of Jewish veterans (Geo-Gras Group) played a crucial role in helping the American and British invasion during its early hours in Algiers (Operation Torch; November 8, 1942). Whether wittingly or unwittingly, American authorities betrayed those conspirators by reinstating Vichy officials who continued to withhold Jews' rights.[8]

After the war (1947), Algerian Jewish leaders established a centralized Federation of the Israelite Communities of Algeria (*Fédération des Communautés Israélites d'Algérie*; FCIA) for the country's 140,000 Jews. The federation supported a rabbinical seminary (*École Rabbinique*; 1948) and promoted Jewish education.[9]

As the civil war began (1954), Jewish leaders tried to walk the tightrope of being loyal to France and neutral toward the independence struggle. The CJAES accordingly declared (1956) that, since the Jews did not constitute a political bloc and the *Consistoire* was a religious organization, Jews would express their opinions as individuals.[10]

There were three turning points amid the accelerating violence. In Constantine (May 12, 1956) Jewish self-defense units trained by Israeli agents repulsed an attack at the end of Ramadan that began with a grenade thrown into a café. That the well-armed Jews killed a score of Muslims aroused tension with the independence movement.[11] The desecration of the Jewish cemetery in Oran (December 1960) convinced some Jews to join the colonists' resistance, including the proto-fascist terrorists (*Organisation de l'Armée Secrète*).[12] During the spiraling terror in spring 1961, Jewish neighborhoods, often located at the crossroads, for example, Constantine, became targets for both sides.[13]

As the independence struggle continued into the late 1950s, Jews began leaving the country. By 1960 the Independence Movement (FLN) pressured

Jewish leaders to abandon their tightrope walk. The CJAES again professed its loyalty to France and the Crémieux Decree.

> The *Comité Juif Algérien d'Etudes Sociales* . . . points out again that the Jewish community of Algeria is not a political, judicial or even geographic entity, and that there exists no Jewish political party or political organization entitled to speak in the name of all the Jews of Algeria. The Jewish community is composed of French citizens who . . . will in common with other French citizens use the rights inherent in that status . . . the Comité thinks that the Jewish community would "live in humiliation" if it renounced a citizenship for the preservation of which it always fought, to which it remains attached with a faithfulness that deserves respect, and which inspired it with its dignity and honor.[14]

The Evian Peace (March 19, 1962) made Algerian independence inevitable; Algeria proclaimed independence on July 3, 1962. From April to September 1962 close to one million colonists (*pied noir*) exited Algeria for metropolitan France.[15] Some 100,000 Algerian Jews were part of that "repatriate" exodus.[16] To cope with the flood of immigrants, the French government created a special "Ministry of Repatriation."[17]

The issue of French citizenship lingered for the Saharan Mzabi Jews. The 1943 renewal of the Crémieux Decree did not include them. The law of September 20, 1947, granting electoral rights affirmed their status as indigenous people (*indigénés*) comparable to Muslims. In 1951 the CJAES advocated for French citizenship; international Jewish organizations (Alliance, World Jewish Congress, Joint Distribution Committee) joined that effort. A marriage law of 1959 still treated them as indigenous people. France finally granted them citizenship in 1961 (Law 61-805), allowing them to join the emigration to the metropole.[18]

France significantly regarded all Christian and Jewish Europeans as citizens returning to the motherland as "repatriates." In stark contrast, it treated Muslims as "refugees." In its effort to deflate the independence movement, de Gaulle's new government (1958) had granted "Muslim French from Algeria" political rights or citizenship coupled with local personal status as Muslims. France revoked that offer after Algeria's independence (July 21, 1962). France required individual Muslims to apply for citizenship within six months (January 1, 1963).[19]

From 1943 to 1963 some 15,000 Algerian Jews emigrated to Israel. In the early years Saharan Mzabi Jews predominated.[20] French authorities actively opposed Israel's efforts to lure Algerian Jews, denying Jewish Agency representatives entrance to the country.[21] Ahmed Ben Bella's imposition of a socialist economy after 1964 encouraged still more Jews to leave. By 1970 some one thousand Jews lived in Algeria.[22]

TUNISIA

Although Tunisia was a nominal Ottoman province since the sixteenth century, the Husaynid dynasty ruled it autonomously. A French protectorate from 1882 to 1956, Tunisia gained internal autonomy in 1954, independence in 1956.

The Ottoman Tanzimat reforms affected Tunisia. The bey enacted the *Pact Fondamental* (September 10, 1857) that offered indigenous Jews ("Tousana") equality before the law and, without abolishing *dhimmi* status, granted them new rights such as acquiring immovable property and exemption from forced labor.[23] Though a rebellion forced the next bey to repeal the constitution (August 30, 1864), the Jews' newly gained rights remained in place.[24]

Italian Jews ("Grana"), many from Livorno, who resided in Tunisia from the late seventeenth century, were subjects of various Italian states and thus exempt from *dhimmi* status. They lived in the European quarter, spoke Italian and Arabic, and gave their children European educations, sometimes by sending them to Italy.[25]

In 1872 the bey limited the Jewish courts' jurisdiction to matrimonial matters.[26] The Alliance established its first school in Tunisia in 1878. Although the bey opposed the school, French pressure prevailed.[27]

The French protectorate (1882) offered new economic and social opportunities; Tunisia's 25,000–30,000 Jews became closely linked to it. In time, the protectorate offered Jews the option of individual naturalization. To warrant French citizenship (1900), Jews initially had to demonstrate exceptional service to France, for example, three years' service, military or civil. None qualified. After leaders of the Jewish group La Justice remonstrated with the authorities, France (1910) loosened requirements and over the next thirteen years 299 Jews gained French citizenship.[28] Decrees of 1920–23 (Morinaud Law) eased individual naturalization. In the decade 1923–33, some 6,460 Jews gained naturalization. At the time of independence (1956), a third of Tunisia's 105,000 Jews were French citizens.[29]

After World War I, Jews began to participate in politics. The regency assigned three seats of the Grand Council's eighteen to Jews (1922). The Tunis Municipal Council reserved a place for one Jew. Jews with French citizenship voted for the dominant French Section.[30] In 1921 the French created a centralized and taxpayer-elected Israelite Community Council (*Conseil de la Communauté Israélite*) in which the various Jewish political groups competed.[31]

Tunisia's Jews suffered discrimination and persecution during the war. At first the Tunisian authorities softened Vichy's Jewish statutes (November 30, 1940) on legal status, education, and the economy either by partial application or by helping Jews circumvent them.[32]

For six months (November 1942 to May 1943) Tunisia's 80,000–90,000 Jews came under direct Nazi control. The Nazis began by arresting leaders; the Tunisian authorities intervened since that action violated the agreement with

Vichy. The Nazis organized labor gangs and engaged in extortion, terror, and abuse. The Nazis did fly some leaders to Europe, where they were murdered. There was no mass murder.[33]

Tunisia had a Jewish population of about 100,000 in 1948.[34] Independent Tunisia (March 20, 1956) granted Jews full citizenship. By the time Tunisia achieved independence, some 22,000 Jews had emigrated to Israel. By June 1967 Tunisia's Jewish population had decreased to 23,000. After rioting in Tunis after the 1967 war, some 15,000–16,000 Jews emigrated, mostly to France.[35] Jews who held French citizenship could take their possessions. Jews with Tunisian citizenship were permitted to take pocket money and their clothes. By 1980, 1,500 Jews lived in Tunisia.[36]

MOROCCO

The Alawite Sharifian dynasty and local warlords had ruled Morocco since the seventeenth century.[37] Jews were the only indigenous minority.[38] Morocco contained the "largest Jewish population in the entire Arab world."[39] The Jewish population in 1912 has been estimated at 110,000; by 1952 it had reached some 240,000–250,000.[40]

The nineteenth-century Ottoman decrees had no impact in Morocco; the Jews' legal status (*dhimmi*) remained unchanged. The French protectorate (1912) abolished demeaning attributes of the Jews' status, for example, tax, clothing, and limitations on synagogue buildings, yet not the juridical classification. Thus "Jews in Morocco remained dhimmis de facto until 1912, and de jure until Moroccan independence in 1956."[41] The French authorities categorized them, alongside Muslims, as natives (*indigènes*). French colonial authorities wanted to avoid what they considered to have been their predecessors' mistake in Algeria where the "granting of citizenship to Jews had been premature."[42]

While professing to keep Morocco's governing institutions intact, French colonial authorities in fact reformed them. They centralized the legal system, thereby hardening religious boundaries. Prior to the colonial occupation, Jews and Muslims, or at least well-informed ones, used the system of multiple courts (e.g., Muslim, Jewish, state, consular) to their advantage, crossing religious boundaries to locate the most advantageous forum. The French authorities ended that system, "reifying" religious differences by introducing "rigid jurisdictional boundaries": Islamic law for Muslims, Jewish law for Jews.[43]

The authorities introduced reforms of Jewish institutions that, by imposing "extremely discreet control," were expressly designed to link them to the colonial system and avoid granting emancipation.[44] The decree of May 22, 1918, required Jews to use their own courts for matters of personal status and inheritance. For commercial issues, they had to use state (*Makhzan*) courts that, employing sharia law, did not recognize Jews as witnesses. The authorities ended the system of consular courts for protected natives (*protégés*). The authorities placed the Jewish court (*beit din*) under a French Inspectorate and required monthly reports.[45] They introduced a parallel administration for European settlers that included a separate legal system.[46]

The Alliance gained control of, and received subsidies from, the French colonial authorities for their own schools as well as French-protectorate schools for Jews (*Écoles franco-israélites*) (1924). This arrangement gave Jews a distinct advantage in competing for jobs in business and the administration. By increasing proximity to the colonizers, it stirred resentment among Muslims.[47] The French authorities hoped that Alliance schools would prevent an "irresponsible" assimilation that would propel Jews to demand French citizenship. The Alliance's leaders in fact waged a constant if unsuccessful campaign for naturalization.[48]

The years of Vichy rule (1940–42) brought the metropole's "Statute on the Jews" to Morocco (October 31, 1940; August 5, 1941) either excluding them from, or limiting their numbers in, numerous professions as well as occupations (chapter 22). The Vichy authorities herded Jewish refugees from Germany, Austria, and Poland into labor and detention camps.[49]

After the war, the French deepened colonial authority by creating two new national institutions. A representative assembly (1945) successfully united all of Morocco's Jews for the first time. A Council of the Rabbis of Morocco (1947) was empowered to issue legally binding ordinances (*takanot*) for religious practice and personal status.[50]

Emigration virtually emptied Morocco of Jews: from 1948 to 1970 some 230,000 went to Israel. The emigration began illegally after 1945. Disappointed with France because of Vichy, some community leaders encouraged impoverished Jews to emigrate. After 1948, and especially after France's de facto recognition of Israel (January 24, 1949), the French authorities allowed a semilegal emigration. Some 70,000 Jews left for Israel between 1948 and 1956.[51]

In the early 1950s Israel delayed further immigration by introducing a policy of "selective immigration" that excluded the indigent and less able-bodied. That policy, which "applied exclusively to North Africans," divided families and produced consternation and resentment.[52] Once the Israeli authorities realized their mistake in deferring emigration when it had been possible, they lifted the policy.

After the struggle against French rule (1953–56), independent Morocco increasingly aligned itself with the Arab states: it joined the Arab League in 1958. At the same time, the government was careful to include Jews.[53] The 1962 constitution granted Jews' citizenship. From the 1960s to the 1990s, some Jewish elites continued either to serve in the government or to play a conspicuous role as advisors.[54]

Morocco banned organized emigration in 1957: some 18,000 emigrated through underground routes between 1957 and 1960. In 1961 King Muhammad

V opened the door to emigration: some 80,000 Jews left under the auspices of the Hebrew Immigrant Aid Society (1961–64).[55]

After the Six Day War (1967) mostly affluent Jews headed to France, Belgium, Spain, and Canada. At the end of 1967 some 50,000 Jews remained in Morocco. The 1973 Yom Kippur War brought another exodus. In 1975 some 22,000 remained; by 2015 some 3,000–4,000 Jews lived in Morocco.[56]

Mashreq (Middle East)

The status of the 460,000 Jews who inhabited the Mashreq in 1947 deteriorated for an ensemble of reasons.[57] Jews were economically conspicuous. In the past, they competed with other minorities in business and for employment; now they competed against the aspiring majority middle class.[58] The emerging Arab nations grew increasingly intolerant of national minorities. Zionism and Israel transformed Jews from a religious into a national minority. The conflict with Israel brought accusations of disloyalty.[59]

EGYPT

Muhammad Ali Pasha, originally the Ottoman commander, created his own reign (1805) and a dynasty that ruled until 1952. Egypt's economy had expanded exponentially by supplying cotton during the American Civil War, leading to rapid growth in Cairo and Alexandria and the building of the Suez Canal. That boom ended in a bust. Britain occupied Egypt in 1882 to ensure repayment to British creditors.[60]

In 1914 Britain declared Egypt a protectorate. A 1919 revolt forced Britain to retreat, yet it retained control of communications, defense, and minorities. The constitution of 1923 (Article 3) guaranteed equal rights regardless of race or religion.[61] The Anglo-Egyptian Treaty gave Egypt independence in 1936.

From the late nineteenth century, most Jews resided in Alexandria and Cairo. The Jewish middle and upper classes quickly embraced European education from the 1860s, sending their children to a range of schools (private; missionary; Alliance, 1896) taught in a variety of languages (French, English, Italian, Greek, German). The children of the poor, who comprised as much as a quarter of the Jewish population, attended free community schools. After World War I many Jews left Egypt's rural areas and other towns to concentrate in the two main urban areas.[62]

The organized Jewish community and its leaders resisted political involvement, kept a low profile, and professed loyalty to the monarchy. In contrast, individual Jews were politically active, publishing journals, serving in the government, and playing a prominent role in founding parties, ranging from liberal to communist. Some supported Egyptian independence.[63]

The Jews' political status became increasingly problematic as Egypt gradually tightened its citizenship laws and nationalized the economy. In the 1927 census, which counted 63,550 Jews, only one-third held Egyptian citizenship (21,944); 25 percent were foreign nationals or protected; and 45–50 percent were stateless.[64]

The 1929 Nationality Law offered Egyptian citizenship on grounds of residence (jus soli) and descent (jus sanguinis). Citizenship automatically accrued to those who resided in Egypt prior to Britain's declaration of war against the Ottoman Empire (November 5, 1914; Articles 1, 3) or had qualified according to a previous law (June 29, 1900; Articles 1, 2). Resident minors could apply for naturalization after they reached their majority (Article 7). Others could apply for naturalization after ten years' residence and proof of good conduct, adequate means of support, and knowledge of Arabic (Article 8). Those with Egyptian parentage, primarily paternal but in some cases maternal, were regarded as Egyptian (Article 6).[65]

Few lower- and middle-class Jews who needed citizenship applied: they lacked documentation, found the fees prohibitive, and were deterred by hostile bureaucrats who allowed applications to linger for years and, under the changing politics of the 1930s and 1940s, excluded non-Muslims.[66] Large numbers of Jews were rendered stateless.[67]

The Montreux Convention of May 8, 1937, abolished the capitulations system; after a twelve-year transition period, the government dissolved the consular courts (1949).[68] The Egyptian Company Law (July 29, 1947), which was aimed at all the foreign business communities, introduced nationality quotas for boards of directors and employees and the proportion of overall salaries they were to receive.[69] Since few Jews were Egyptian nationals, many lost their positions. Jews who applied for Egyptian citizenship to salvage their employment largely failed to obtain it.[70]

Combined with tightened citizenship laws and nationalization of the economy, hostility to Zionism and the State of Israel undermined Egyptian Jewry. On Balfour Declaration Day (November 2, 1945) there was rioting against Jews in Cairo; it spilled over to other non-Muslims—Coptics, Greek Orthodox, Catholics.[71] On November 27, 1947, before the vote on Palestine's partition, Haykal Pasha, the Egyptian representative to the United Nations, voiced a threat.

> The Arab governments will do all in their power to defend the Jewish citizens of their countries, but we all know that an excited crowd is sometimes stronger than the police. Unintentionally, you are about to spark an anti-Semitic fire in the Middle East which will be more difficult to extinguish than it was in Germany.[72]

After the 1948 Arab-Israeli War the government incarcerated some one thousand Jews for alleged Zionist activity and seized some Jewish businesses' assets.[73] There were bombings of Jews' department stores and homes. The government required that brokers on the Egyptian stock exchange be Egyptian nationals (August 1948) and permitted only Egyptian nationals to practice medicine (September 1948).[74] Between June and September 1948 there were multiple bombings and riots. As a result, from 1949 to 1952 some 25,000–30,000 Jews left Egypt, of whom some 15,000–20,000 emigrated to Israel. Many were from the lower or lower-middle classes and stateless.[75] A law of September 24, 1955, abolished Muslim, Christian, and Jewish religious courts, transferring matters of personal status to state courts.[76]

Whereas the 1952 revolution calmed the situation, Nasser's 1956 national-ization of the Suez Canal and other parts of the economy and the ensuing war (against Israel, Britain, and France) exploded it: he expelled Jews wholesale.[77] The government engaged in mass arrests, seized property, and issued orders to leave the country. On November 1, 1956, it issued Proclamation No. 4 that froze bank accounts and sequestered property. The new Nationality Law (No-vember 1956) allowed "Zionists" to be stripped of citizenship.[78]

In the year following the war (October 1956), some 30,000 Jews left Egypt. Many had lost all possessions, many were stateless: those holding Egyptian citizenship were required to relinquish their passports, giving them no choice but to emigrate to Israel.[79] Further legislation in the late 1950s and early 1960s excluded Jews from the economy and required everyone to carry a work card listing religion. By June 1967, 3,000 Jews lived in Egypt, by 2001 three dozen.[80]

IRAQ

Although the region had been under Ottoman rule since 1517, the Turks first established centralized control during the nineteenth-century Tanzimat re-forms (chapter 18). In the last third of the nineteenth century Ottoman pro-vincial governors rebuilt Baghdad's infrastructure (water, transportation), in-troduced new institutions, for example, schools, hospitals, and factories, and connected the area's economy to the empire's.[81]

Ottoman laws applied to the Jews, so with the Tanzimat reforms they became citizens freed of the poll tax (*jizya*). They instead paid a tax to be ex-empted from military service; that tax was abolished in 1909 when universal conscription became mandatory. The Ottomans introduced the structure of a Chief Rabbi (*hakham bashi*) supported by rabbinic and lay councils (chapter 21).[82]

Britain conquered the region in 1917, received the United Nations' mandate to rule it, imported a loyal king (Faisal ibn Hussein, August 1921), whom the French had ousted from Syria, and installed democratic institutions. Iraq served as Britain's laboratory for new ways to govern its empire: maintaining economic and military interests while relinquishing political control. Britain granted Iraq independence in 1932.[83]

The 1924 constitution established an Islamic state (Article 13) in which Jews and Christians were equal citizens, eligible for government appointments (Article 18), with recognized minority rights: they had their own councils and a guaranteed number of seats in Parliament.[84] The 1931 Jewish Community Law kept the Ottoman structure largely in place.

Jews gained education in Alliance schools: the first schools for boys opened in 1864, for girls in 1893. The community also opened Turkish-language schools prior to World War I. The new state opened schools at all levels that Muslims, Jews, and Christians attended together. Jewish teachers taught at state schools, Muslim teachers taught at Jewish schools.[85] Under King Faisal, Jews served in high civil service positions and the cabinet.[86] Moreover, many Jews felt they had a place in Iraq's emerging Arab-language culture alongside other minorities, for example, Sunni Muslims, Christians, Kurds, and Turkmen. Many Jews regarded "the nation-state of Iraq as the political construct most able to meet their demands for citizenship rights and equality."[87]

After the 1929 riots in Palestine, the government banned Zionism, Palestinian newspapers, and Jewish teachers from Palestine.[88] After Faisal's death (1933) the government began to replace Jewish civil servants with Muslims (September 1934). Moreover, in the mid-1930s the government started to impede emigration to Palestine. The Arab Revolt in Palestine encouraged attacks on Jews in Baghdad. Community leaders publicly disavowed Zionism.[89]

During World War II, an anti-British regime took power (April–May 1941), declared war against Britain (May–June 1941), and, openly hostile to Jews, attacked them as the enemy within. For two days (June 1–2, 1941) soldiers, police, youth gangs, and others conducted a pogrom in Baghdad (*Farhud*). The British and loyalist Iraqi forces poised on the city's outskirts refused to intervene.[90]

A pro-British regime remained in power until 1958. After 1945 the government continued to replace Jewish civil servants with Muslim graduates of the country's high schools and universities.[91]

The Iraqi government sent troops to fight in the Arab-Israeli War (1948). Fearing unrest after the troops' defeat, the government imposed martial law. The government began to harass Jews: it detained some wealthy Jews, martial law courts imposed fines and sentences, the government introduced quotas on university admissions and civil service positions, made business transactions difficult, and closed the borders. Parliament outlawed support for Zionism as a crime (July 1948).[92] After the state lifted martial law in December 1949, some 10,000 Jews left the country.

On March 4, 1950, the Iraqi government promulgated a law permitting Jews to leave on the condition that they renounce Iraqi citizenship (Cancellation of Iraqi National Law No. 62 of 1933). The law allowed the emigrants to take only a nominal sum of money. In March 1951, the government froze emigrants' assets.[93] By the end of 1951 some 120,000 Iraqi Jews had left; some 6,000 remained. By 1972, 400 Jews lived in Iraq.[94]

TURKEY

Jews in the new Turkish Republic had been citizens of a multireligious, multi-ethnic empire (chapter 21). Much like their brethren in the Dual Monarchy's successor states, they (1927: 81,872) now belonged to a nation-state that, relatively homogeneous, was increasingly suspicious of its minorities.

The Treaty of Lausanne (July 24, 1923) that recognized the independent Turkish Republic obligated it to Minority Rights (Articles 38–44).[95] In the fledgling republic's eyes, the treaty impeded the formation of a secular state by making Jews and Christians protected minorities: *millet*-like religious courts blocked the formation of a unified legal system and threatened to direct the minorities' loyalty to the religious community rather than the state. The government and the press pressured Jews and the other minorities to renounce those rights. Jewish leaders renounced minority rights (February 1925) as did Greek and Armenian Christians. As a result, Jews and the other minorities were restored de jure to legal equality as Turkish citizens.[96]

The Turkish Republic became resolutely secular. It abolished the empire's Muslim structures, that is, the sultanate (1922) and the caliphate (1924). It promulgated a new legal code, based on Switzerland's, that introduced civil marriage and prohibited religious marriages. The legal code and courts abolished the *millets*; they now governed citizens of all religions. The religious communities became strictly voluntary organizations. In 1928 the republic declared that Islam was no longer the state religion.[97]

The Alliance Israélite Universelle had maintained political independence for six decades (1860–1920). Although the organization clearly identified with France's imperial interests and its civilizing mission, it did not receive official French recognition or subsidies. As Zionism gained in popularity and strength in the Balkans and Ottoman Empire from the fin de siècle, France's foreign office (*Quai d'Orsay*) became increasingly aware of the Alliance's valuable contributions to French interests. It was only in 1920, however, that France first began to subsidize Alliance schools in Turkey.[98]

In 1914 the Ottoman Empire had declared the Alliance's schools Ottoman organizations to allow them to function throughout the war years. In contrast, the Turkish Republic prohibited the schools from having links with "foreign organizations" (1924) and imposed a state curriculum that required instruction in either Turkish or Hebrew. The schools opted for Turkish. Between 1925 and 1929 the republic effectively nationalized Alliance schools.[99]

The republic prohibited international movements it deemed subversive: communism and Islamic movements such as the Muslim Brotherhood (1928) that aimed to restore the caliphate. The law also applied to such organizations as the World Zionist Congress and the World Jewish Congress. Some Zionist groups nonetheless continued to function publicly, others clandestinely. Turkey first lifted that ban at the end of the century (1990s).[100]

In the 1920s some Jews replaced Greeks and Armenians in commerce as the government, more suspicious of Christian minorities, favored them with commercial licenses.[101] The 1930s saw deterioration in the Jews' status as the government dismissed some Jews from civil service positions while some private businesses replaced minority members with Muslim Turks. A pogrom in Edirne (1934) led the Jews of Thrace to migrate to Istanbul or Izmir or to emigrate.[102] During the 1930s and World War II Jews served in the army. They were often placed in unarmed support units; they were not allowed to become officers.[103]

During the war, the government imposed a special capital levy (*Varlık Vergisi*; November 1942) designed to oust non-Muslim minorities from the economy. The levy imposed extortionate assessments on businesses and taxpayers, forcing many owners to sell. The government punished with forced labor those who were unable or unwilling to pay.[104]

In contrast, Turkey resolutely defended its Jewish citizens in France (some 10,000). It renewed lapsed citizenship, provided temporary papers, and intervened to prevent deportation. It refused to accede to German demands to surrender Jewish refugees in its borders. It allowed Zionist representatives to operate in Istanbul to transport Jews to Palestine.[105]

In contrast to Egypt and Iraq, after Israel's establishment Turkey neither expelled its Jews nor deprived them of citizenship. In fact, Turkey recognized Israel early; it was the sole Muslim state to do so.[106] Some 35,000 Turkish Jews emigrated to Israel between 1948 and 1955, especially the poor, those living in smaller communities, and European refugees. Subsequent emigration waxed (after the 1967 war; Turkey's turmoil) and waned (1990s) with Israel's and Turkey's respective fortunes. In 1965, 38,267 Jews lived in Turkey.[107]

Conclusion

The effective end of Jewish life in the Maghreb and Mashreq constituted not only the demise of a distinctive diaspora and a major demographic shift but also the collapse of a political status. For over a millennium Jews had lived under Islam as an inferior yet protected minority (*dhimmi*). Equal citizenship in the nineteenth and twentieth centuries did not prove as durable.

Most Algerian Jews emigrated with the "repatriate exodus" following independence (1962). The majority of Tunisia's Jews left in the eleven years between independence (1956) and the aftermath of the 1967 Six Day War. Morocco had had the largest Jewish community in the Arab world. Jews fled in four waves: 1948–56, 1961–64 with free emigration, 1967, and 1973.

Most of Egypt's Jews departed after either the 1948 war (1949–52) or Nasser's nationalist revolution (1956). The majority of Iraq's Jews emigrated in the period 1948–51. Many Jews left Turkey in the period 1948–55 and after 1967, yet a substantial number remained.

The twentieth century's challenges to the region, especially the rise of exclusionary nationalism during decolonization and afterward as well as its collision with Jewish nationalism, put on full display not just a minority's vulnerability but also the abiding fragility of equal rights.

Israel

ISRAEL'S DECLARATION OF INDEPENDENCE (MAY 14, 1948) twice proclaimed equality. The new state first promised to "uphold the full social and political equality of all its citizens, without distinction of race, creed or sex." The founders then directly addressed Arab citizens, asking them "to play their part in the development of the state, with full and equal citizenship and representation in all its bodies and institutions, provisional and permanent."[1]

Israel introduced two distinct citizenship laws that qualified the promise of equality. The Law of Return (July 5, 1950) accorded Jews citizenship by descent (jus sanguinis). Prime Minister David Ben-Gurion asserted that this right preceded and indeed propelled the state:

> it comprises the central mission of our state, namely, the ingathering of exiles [*kibbutz galuyot*]. This law determines that it is not the state that grants the Jew from abroad the right to settle in the state. Rather, this right is inherent in him by the very fact that he is a Jew.[2]

The Law of Return was one of the state's "Basic Laws."[3] In contrast, the Nationality Law (1952) granted non-Jews citizenship through residence or naturalization (jus soli).[4]

The challenges of war and mass migration understandably consumed the new government's attention. Israel received 340,000 Jewish immigrants in its first eighteen months; its Jewish population doubled in its first five years (May 15, 1948–June 30, 1953).[5] The May 1961 census revealed that nearly half of the Jewish population (1,932,357) had immigrated since 1948.[6]

Whether officially acknowledged or not, the question of citizenship bedeviled Israel from the outset because of its highly heterogeneous populace. First, the Jews themselves were inordinately diverse: in culture and geographical origin, education and religious commitment, as well as political orientation. Second, Israel was a nationalities-state: Arabs, Druze, and Bedouins comprised almost one-fifth of the population. For a national movement predicated on emancipation's "failure," Zionism faced an emancipation issue of its own.

The new state integrated its heterogeneous population through stratification: it created a de facto hierarchy of citizenships based on the exercise of political rights and access to social rights, that is, housing, employment, education, and health care.[7] The hierarchy privileged the formative group in the waves of immigration (aliya). The Ashkenazi settlers who were celebrated as having created the institutions of Jewish settlement (Yishuv; 1882–1948) comprised a republic of pioneers (halutzim) possessing complete citizenship rights. The Jews who came from the Maghreb and Mashreq (Mizrahim) after the state's founding were second-class citizens who had to earn their social rights. Palestinian Israelis were third-class citizens. Governed by martial law and military administration for the state's first nineteen years, they faced comprehensive government discrimination and struggled to exercise political rights. Many were deprived of citizenship. Finally, by investing Orthodox Judaism with exclusive control of personal status (marriage, divorce, burial), the state imposed disabilities on the other "Judaisms" and diminished women's rights. The "ingathering of exiles" became an ingathering of inequalities.[8]

The subordinate groups challenged these inequalities from the start: as a democratic society, Israel spawned civil rights movements from its inception. The government had to contend with various groups staging protests and engaging in civil disobedience to gain recognition and negotiate amelioration.[9]

Republic of Pioneers

The Zionist movement called for the creation of institutions and, eventually, a state that would promote the Hebrew language and a Hebrew-language culture, reverse the Jews' peculiar diasporic occupational pattern ("invert the pyramid"), and attract all Jews who wished to leave the Diaspora, especially the impoverished, oppressed, and ideologically committed. Zionism was to fashion a new Jew and a new Jewish people (chapter 20).[10]

The left-wing Zionist Labor movement came to dominate that effort. The Labor movement fashioned the new ideal of the pioneer (halutz) whose "conquest of [manual] labor" (kibush ha-avoda) and armed defense became the new settlement's (Yishuv) myth of origin. The ideal pioneer wielded a plow with one hand, a rifle with the other.[11] Pioneering constituted the new republican virtue, the collective agricultural settlement (kibbutz) the new polis. Contribution and service became the key to social rights.[12] The Labor movement was the crucial element in "an alliance between organized Zionism, a settlement movement without settlers, and the self-styled pioneers, a workers' movement without work."[13] New institutions were to empower Jews to achieve in their own land the regeneration that emancipation had failed to bring in the diaspora.[14]

The Trade Union Federation (Histadrut; 1920) institutionalized the pioneer ideal.[15] Funded by the World Zionist Organization, the Histadrut was at the heart of "an elaborate, centralized, coherent and bureaucratized network of social institutions" composed of "publicly owned land, cooperative settlement and financial subsidies."[16] The Histadrut controlled land, labor, and capital; it provided employment and housing, health care and unemployment benefits.[17] The "labor economy" (*hevrat ha-ovdim*) put expansion and employment before profit.[18]

The Labor movement gained a dominant position in the period 1927–37: the newly established Labor Party (*Mapai*; 1930) seized control of the four major institutions of Zionism and the Yishuv. With Ben-Gurion leading, the Histadrut owned a large portion of the Jewish economy and functioned as "the executive arm of a . . . party machine."[19] Funding was in the hands of the Jewish Agency, created to cooperate with the Mandatory Authority to implement the Balfour Declaration and expanded (1929) to include non-Zionists in the Diaspora. The National Council (*Va'ad Leumi*) represented the Yishuv politically. Labor became the World Zionist Organization's largest party: it gained control of the executive and elected Ben-Gurion as president (1935).[20]

To be sure, there were competing forms of Zionism that established their own parallel and rival institutions. The so-called "old Yishuv" that preceded Zionist settlement included Sephardi merchants and wage earners who populated Jerusalem and developed Jaffa and Haifa as well as pious Ashkenazi Jews living on the religious dole (*haluka*) in Jerusalem, Tiberias, and Safed.[21] Capitalist agriculture had a salient presence.[22] Despite Zionism's agrarian bias, Israel was "a fully urbanized society" (85% of the population) at its establishment.[23] The new Jewish city of Tel Aviv (1906/7) symbolized the alternative of privately funded urban life, although the city also had prominent socialist components.[24] Religious Zionists (Mizrahi) and the Revisionist political party (1925) established their own institutions.[25]

The Labor Party (Mapai) dominated the state politically for three decades, institutionally for four. Ben-Gurion championed a policy of "statism" or "étatism" (*mamlachtiyut*) that combined the imposition of comprehensive control buttressed by a comprehensive value system expressed in rituals and symbols. Ben-Gurion wanted the state to replace the working class as the embodiment of the pioneering spirit (*halutziyut*) as well as serve as the nation's absolute guardian. Moreover, he invested the state with messianic pretensions linked to the "ingathering of exiles."[26]

The state first and foremost exerted a monopoly on military force by merging the right (*Irgun* and *Stern Gang*) and left's (*Haganah* and *Palmah*) armed units into a unitary army (Israel Defense Forces). The army was also to serve as a principal means of absorbing immigrants into the state. The state exercised exclusive control on foreign affairs and diplomacy. The state then integrated public services, including education (State Education Law, 1953), labor exchanges (State Employment Service Law, 1958), civil courts, and civil law.[27] Significantly, health care (*kupat holim*) remained the Histadrut's domain.

Protests about civil rights were heard almost from the state's inception: bourgeois citizens resisted state restrictions on the right to travel abroad. The "State of Emergency Regulations" (August 1948; November 19, 1948) required an exit permit for foreign travel. The government in addition imposed an exit tax to raise funds and restrict numbers.[28] The government subordinated individual liberties to the "public interest": to secure an exit visa, one had to demonstrate past service to the Zionist project.[29] In response to citizens' unrelenting pressure against this "iron curtain," the government finally recognized the right to foreign travel (1953).[30]

Mizrahim

From 1948 to 1956 some 810,000 immigrants arrived in Israel; the majority, some 450,000, came from the Maghreb and Mashreq.[31] The very terms state agencies used to identify them, "eastern communities" (*edot ha-mizrah*), presumed an inferior alterity.[32] The state classified them neither as actual nor as potential pioneers (*halutzim*). Rather, they were immigrants (*olim*) who, through a policy known as the "blending of exiles" (*mizug ha-galuyot*), were to be reeducated for the new polity.[33] In 1951 the government introduced a policy of "Selective Immigration" (*selektsia*) that was designed to exclude families who were indigent or had a disabled member. That policy was applied exclusively to North African and especially Moroccan Jews.[34]

In the eighteenth to twentieth centuries, western and central European Jews had endeavored to regenerate their east European brethren for emancipation. After 1948, former East European Jews aimed to "Europeanize" oriental Jews to qualify for the Zionist project. Israel practiced its own version of emancipatory regeneration.[35]

The tidal wave of immigrants overwhelmed the new state. Housing, food, employment, and health care were in short supply. Many of the earliest immigrants after the War of Independence were settled in abandoned Arab housing. Later newcomers were sent to immigrant camps, where the average stay was three to six months. The camps had soup kitchens and housed multiple families in a single dwelling.

Transit camps (*ma'abarot*) offered separate accommodation for each family but required them to purchase and prepare their own food. In the transit camps, of which there were 129 in May 1952, employment was episodic and menial, food scarce, sanitation inadequate, education paltry, and the morbidity rate high.[36] Transit camps continued to exist throughout the 1960s.[37] Ben-Gurion characterized the immigrants as a "second nation" (1949).[38]

Under the Law of Return the Maghreb and Mashreq immigrants were de jure citizens.[39] Yet their economic and social marginalization curtailed their civil rights. Fully one-quarter to one-third of the immigrants were settled in development towns that offered inferior housing, poor transportation, and insufficient employment, especially in the low-wage textile industry. On average, some 75 percent of development town residents were Mizrahim.[40] Their children suffered from segregated education: Mizrahi children were directed into the religious stream of schools to which the state devoted fewer resources in development towns. Moreover, a tracking system directed many Mizrahi students to vocational rather than academic studies.[41]

The government directed substantial numbers of Mizrahim to agriculture, settling them in cooperative farming villages (*moshavim*). In the *moshavim* marketing and purchasing were organized collectively while production and consumption were private. Between 1949 and 1958 the authorities established 251 *moshavim* (11,350 households); in 2012 some 300,000 Jews lived in 442 *moshavim*. Educational opportunities for children of the *moshavim* were limited. The kibbutz was a predominantly Ashkenazi institution, the *moshav* a predominantly Mizrahi one.[42]

These policies had long-term consequences. In 1969, Mizrahim earned 70 percent of the average income among foreign-born Israelis but only 58 percent of the Israeli born. That same year only 12 percent of Ashkenazim qualified as living below the poverty line; 30 percent of Mizrahim did. Mizrahim were overrepresented in less prestigious and lower-paying occupations in the first decade of the twenty-first century.[43] While statistics from the 1990s demonstrate that Mizrahi children made significant gains in attaining high school certificates (*bagrut*), the "ethnic hierarchy" remained: Mizrahim trailed Ashkenazim. Moreover, children in development towns continued to have the lowest level of education.[44]

To be sure, the Mizrahim had been stratified from the outset: some arrived with capital, professions, or vocational training, others were indigent and unskilled. Yet the settlement process itself amplified stratification. Mashreq Jews (Iraq, Yemen) who came in the 1950s were settled in former Arab homes in central areas. Their apartments and houses subsequently became valuable real estate that gave them capital for the family's future. In contrast, Maghreb Jews (Moroccans, Tunisians, Libyans) who came in the late 1950s and early 1960s were settled in development towns in public housing that either did not substantially appreciate or in fact depreciated.[45]

Immigrants used all available means to struggle for recognition and protest their grievances. Almost immediately after the War of Independence (February 1949), many Mizrahim started to assert their rights as citizens to resist the manifest injustices.[46]

> Riots, demonstrations, strikes, petitions, letters, appeals to newspapers, and violence were all means the immigrants used to respond to their lack of work and other problems throughout Israel's first decade.[47]

Since the immigrants understood themselves to be engaged in a struggle for "rights," some Mizrahi intellectuals compared their efforts to the Afro-American civil rights movement and to anticolonial struggles throughout the Third World.[48]

Government officials responded by trying to conciliate and negotiate with the immigrants. They often met with a delegation, made promises of redress, and then failed to fulfill the promises. The process then repeated itself.[49] Officials increasingly called on the police to repress the protests.[50] The first government commission convened in response to a decade of demonstrations and riots (Etzioni Commission, 1959) categorically denied the existence of discrimination and encouraged further immigration.[51]

During the 1950s the police recruited Mizrahim to the ranks to regenerate them for the Zionist project. Yet Mizrahim faced overt discrimination: although by 1960 they constituted the majority of policemen, the higher ranks remained predominantly Ashkenazi. Officers deliberately assigned Mizrahi policemen to enforce order at Mizrahi demonstrations, protests, and riots.[52]

Mizrahim experienced the system's blatant discrimination when recently arrived Romanian Jews (1959) received priority for better housing and jobs.[53] In 1971 Mizrahi youths from Jerusalem, who came to be known as the Black Panthers, protested their lamentable conditions.[54] The preferential treatment accorded to Russian Jews after 1989 reinforced the Mizrahim's abiding sense of discrimination. Backed by an enormous loan from the United States ($10 billion; October 1992), the Israeli government gave each Russian family an "absorption basket," including a grant and access to a mortgage, to start life in the country.[55]

Palestinian Israelis

After the War of Independence, the state imposed martial law on the country's approximately 156,000 Palestinian Israelis, curtailing their civil rights for almost two decades (1948–66).[56] The citizenship law (1953) deprived almost two-thirds of Palestinians (100,000) of automatic citizenship, requiring them to apply and swear an oath of allegiance to the state.[57] The state pursued a "divide and rule" policy: it politicized Druze, Bedouins, and Christians, depoliticized Muslims. and criminalized political behavior.[58] The state consistently discriminated against Palestinian Israelis across the broad range of social services, including municipal funding, planning permits, education, health care, and child allowances. The Orr Commission (September 1, 2003) officially recognized state discrimination.[59]

Government policies systematically deprived Palestinian Israelis of land. In 1949 Jews owned 13.5 percent of the land; by 1960 the state and the Jewish National Fund owned 93 percent. By 2000 Palestinian Israelis, who constituted almost 20 percent of the population, owned 3.5 percent of the state's land. They faced major difficulties in establishing new settlements and in receiving building permits in existing ones. From 1975 to 2000 less than 0.3 percent of the public housing units built were designated for the Palestinian Israeli population (fewer than 1,000 of 337,000 units).[60]

Palestinian Israeli municipalities received less funding for infrastructure (water, roads, sewage, electricity) and human services (welfare, education, health) than all types of Jewish municipalities. Funds for public education of Arab children were about one-third lower than in Jewish municipalities. The government exercised strict control over curriculum and the hiring and promotion of teachers.[61] The government first extended the children's allowance (1959) to Palestinian Israelis in 1993.[62]

Palestinian Israelis were consistently the poorest group in Israel. Martial law (1948–66) prevented them from competing in the labor market.[63] A high degree of regional concentration and residential segregation continued to limit employment opportunities, educational options, and health care.[64] In 2010 more than half lived below the poverty line. Arab men earned 60 percent of the average national wage, Arab women 70 percent.[65] Although educational attainment rose substantially for all Israelis, Palestinian Israelis remained at the bottom of the "ethnic hierarchy."[66] Educated Palestinian Israelis largely found suitable employment in their own labor market. As their numbers increased, they faced discrimination in finding jobs commensurate with their qualifications.[67]

Some 15 to 20 percent of the Palestinian Israelis are in fact "internally displaced persons" or "present absentees" (*nifkadim nohahim*): people who left, or were forced from, their original homes (1948) and then resettled elsewhere in Israel.[68] Most of the present absentees wished to return to their original villages. The Law of Absentee Property (1950) deprived them of their land and legal recourse. The Citizenship Law (1953) required them to apply for citizenship. Israel confiscated much of their land and awarded it to Jewish settlements.[69] The Land Acquisition Law (1953) validated the transfer of ownership to the state.[70] The present absentees who received housing in new villages had to renounce claims to assets in their villages of origin.

Despite the Declaration of Independence's promise of "full and equal citizenship and representation in all [the state's] bodies and institutions," Palestinian Israelis have never had full political representation. No Palestinian Israeli political party has been included in a government coalition; no Palestinian Israeli has held a ministerial portfolio.[71]

In the 1950s Palestinian Israelis protested their loss of citizenship through demonstrations and a half-day national strike. An Arab member of the Knesset (Rustum Bustani; Mapam; 1952) denounced "national discrimination."[72] Palestinian Israelis built houses, indeed entire neighborhoods, without permits; they helped some twenty thousand of their brethren return to Israel and gain citizenship.[73] The courts ruled against the incorporation of Palestinian Israeli associations and the standing of political parties.[74] The army violently suppressed demonstrations against land expropriations, including the infamous strike (March 30, 1976; subsequently "Land Day") at which the police killed six Palestinian Israelis.[75]

Palestinian Israelis experienced a political "golden age" for three years under Prime Minister Yitzhak Rabin (1992–95) when their representatives' votes were crucial to maintaining the parliamentary coalition that supported the Oslo Accords.[76] In 1995 the present absentees organized the Association for the Defense of the Rights of the Internally Displaced in Israel.[77]

In the 1990s and the first decade of the twenty-first century, Palestinian Arabs began a campaign for "equality for all citizens" that eventually included national minority rights understood as political equality, cultural autonomy, and the right of present absentees to return to their villages.[78] The fact that Israel had Basic Laws rather than a constitution meant that Palestinian Arabs had less legal protection and fewer means to combat discrimination.[79]

In October 2000, when Palestinian Israelis protested in solidarity with Palestinians in the West Bank and Gaza, the police killed thirteen and wounded scores. In May 2002, the Knesset amended the "Basic Law: The Knesset" and the "Law of Political Parties" to ban individuals and parties that contested Israel's status as a "Jewish and democratic state," and in July 2002 removed the immunity of any Knesset member who did the same.[80] The "Citizenship and Entry to Israel Law" (2003) prohibited reunification of families divided between Israel and the territories Israel has occupied since 1967.[81]

It has become a commonplace to observe that Israel's politics reproduce those of interwar east European Jewry.[82] It is ironic that it would be a fundamental amelioration for Palestinian Israelis were they to attain the status Jews had as a legally recognized minority in interwar eastern Europe (chapter 22).[83]

Unequal "Judaisms"

In 1947 Ben-Gurion pledged that "we have no intention of establishing a theocratic state" and guaranteed "the absence of coercion or discrimination in religious affairs."[84] He violated that pledge; its validity has further diminished over time.[85] Israel adopted key Ottoman laws of personal status. It is legally a Jewish state in two ways. Orthodox Judaism is one of eighteen recognized religions yet functions as if it were the official state religion, receiving a preponderance of the Ministry of Religious Affairs' funding. Moreover, the state ostracized non-Orthodox Judaism.[86] The Law of Return enforces a nationalist definition.[87]

The British Mandatory government incorporated the Ottoman *millet* system (Palestine Order in Council, 1922). It authorized the election of a Rabbinical Council that, consisting of two Chief Rabbis (one Sephardi, one Ashkenazi), other rabbis, and some lay advisors, appointed the rabbinical courts.[88]

Through the Rabbinical Council and the rabbinical courts, Orthodox Judaism controlled matters of personal status, that is, marriage, divorce, and burial.[89]

On the eve of statehood Ben-Gurion agreed not to alter this situation in his so-called "status quo letter" (June 19, 1947) to the main religious party, Agudat Yisrael.[90] The Law and Administration Ordinance (May 1948) maintained the *millet* system for matters of personal status.[91] The Ministry of Religion controlled the registry of marriages and divorces.[92] Ben-Gurion's arrogation of authority to the Orthodox rabbinate became official with the Rabbinical Courts Jurisdiction Law (1953).[93]

Israel followed the Ottoman Empire in not introducing civil marriage: there was no separation between marriage as consecration and marriage as contract.[94] Israel did not follow the Assembly of Notables and Sanhedrin's recognition of the supremacy of civil to religious law in matters of personal status (chapter 9).

Israel instead established two parallel court systems. The civil courts represent Israel as a "democratic" state, the rabbinic courts as a "Jewish" state.[95] In matters of personal status all Jews are forced to submit to the rabbinic courts. Under the Mandate one could opt out; Israel prohibits that. Moreover, the Knesset gave the rabbinic courts coercive power (1995).[96]

The courts are one part of an "elaborate interlocking network":[97]

> a *de facto* hierarchy has been established, with the chief rabbis at the apex. They are followed by the members of the Rabbinic Supreme Court and Council of the Chief Rabbinate, the big city rabbis, and, on a lower level, the district court rabbinic judges. After them come the rabbis of the small settlements, with the synagogue rabbis bringing up the rear.[98]

Since 1955, the one hundred judges who staff the rabbinic courts are equal in status to civil judges, earn the same salaries, and preside in state-owned buildings.[99]

By giving the Orthodox rabbinate exclusive control of personal status (1947), Ben-Gurion pledged "to prevent a rift in the Jewish People." His compromise opened that very rift.[100] Other forms of Judaism (Reform, Conservative, Modern Orthodox) were and are unequal. They have no legal standing; their rabbis cannot officiate at marriages and divorces. By withholding recognition, the state has effectively imposed disabilities, turning these rabbis and their congregants into dissenters.[101] By empowering the Orthodox establishment to conduct life's most important rites of passage, the state authorized a Jewish minority to dictate to the Jewish majority.[102]

Women

Women were and remain second-class citizens because of the Orthodox rabbinate's control of family law. Woman gained political equality during the

Mandate with the granting of the franchise (1926). Yet the Orthodox rabbinate's control of marriage and divorce enforced a normative patriarchal family that limited the impact of the Women's Equal Rights Law (1951).[103] To marry, a woman is required to present certification from the rabbinic authorities of having undergone ritual purification (*mikveh*).[104] In divorce proceedings women have inferior legal standing; the rabbinic courts enforce male dominance.[105]

In the economy women experienced "horizontal and vertical segregation": they were restricted in the kinds of employment available ("mommy jobs") and in their ability to rise in those positions.[106] The 1988 Employment Service Law, which prohibited discrimination on grounds of sex (alongside age, race, religion, or ethnic or national group), had no enforcement mechanism.[107] Moreover, the major institutions of society reinforced gender inequality: the military, political parties, corporations, and even the avowedly egalitarian kibbutz. In fact, gender inequality eclipsed ethnic inequality.[108]

The early civil rights movements included a debate over women's age of marriage. Mandate Palestine's Criminal Code (1936) had set the age of marriage at fifteen. Both rabbinical and Islamic courts resisted this incursion of civil law by insisting on the right to permit younger girls to marry.

After 1948, state authorities and women's advocates campaigned for a higher age. They aimed to ensure that Yemenite girls specifically, and Mizrahi girls generally, would enjoy childhood and education; that as mothers they would be emotionally and culturally mature to raise children; and that they be treated as autonomous individuals freely choosing marriage. The press prominently featured cases of older husbands and their families abusing recalcitrant young brides.

The Knesset passed the Age of Marriage Law (August 1, 1950) that established seventeen as the minimum age. The Chief Rabbinate and religious parties opposed the law. Families, community leaders, and the rabbinate actively resisted it: they lied about girls' ages, forged identity cards, and issued exemptions.[109]

Capitalism, Constitutional Change, and Civil Society

The decade of the mid-1970s to mid-1980s altered the character of citizenship. The state began to make social rights available directly to citizens rather than through the Labor Party and the Histadrut. Israel promulgated two "Basic Laws" that solidified individual rights. It empowered an array of institutions that shaped a citizenship suitable to an increasingly capitalist society.[110]

Labor's hegemony ended between 1977 and 1985. Menachem Begin won election (1977) as the first right-wing (Herut Party) prime minister. Large segments of the Mizrahi, Palestinian, and middle-class electorate—especially the second and third generations—defected from Labor.[111]

Following an economic crisis of the 1980s, Labor lost its grip on the economy and ability to command loyalty across classes.[112] The Likud government forced the Histadrut's hand by depriving it of inexpensive guaranteed credit (1980).[113] The Histadrut began to privatize its variegated industries, creating companies subject to capital markets and committed to profit rather than employment.[114] By the mid-1990s the Histadrut had shed its enterprises. Most importantly, in 1994 the state nationalized health care (Health Insurance Law), making it directly available to all citizens rather than through Histadrut membership. In the process of becoming a conventional union federation, the Histadrut lost two-thirds of its members.[115] The Labor republic had ended.

At the same time, the government tried to rescue the economy from inflation and depression by reducing state intervention and freeing capital markets (Emergency Economic Stabilization Plan, 1985). The Bank of Israel began to set the economy's general direction, removing administrative controls while opening the capital market to domestic and foreign investment. The Tel Aviv Stock Market grew immensely: in five years (1989–94) it twice doubled in value. Israeli companies began to be traded on the New York Stock Exchange. The country was awash with capital.[116]

In lieu of a constitution, the Knesset enacted two Basic Laws (1992) that, in establishing individual rights, aimed "to anchor the . . . State of Israel's values as a Jewish and democratic state." The Basic Law of Human Dignity and Freedom guaranteed the individual's honor, life, liberty, body, property, privacy, and right to travel. The Basic Law of Freedom of Occupation endeavored to secure the individual's "worth, the sanctity of his life and his freedom" through his right to work at any occupation.[117]

The Supreme Court, ensconced in its own building (1992), issued major decisions.[118] The court's decisions on labor tended to favor property over labor, employers over employees. Unions' rights and the right to strike were called into question.[119] The Supreme Court regularly came into conflict with the Orthodox rabbinical courts and Ministry of Religion.[120]

The "status quo" compromise on Judaism's place in society collapsed. With the emergence of competing political blocs, the religious parties negotiated new privileges and funding streams.[121] Mizrahi leaders founded new political parties (TAMI, 1981; Shas, 1983). Shas, overtly religious, succeeded in establishing an alternative network of "welfare services in a religious framework" to service its Mizrahi constituency, for example, schools, synagogues, and ritual baths alongside support for large families, improved housing, and rehabilitation for delinquents and drug addicts.[122]

Nevertheless, the "ethnic hierarchy" remained in place. The Ashkenazi elite maintained control through non-elected institutions such as the Bank of Israel and the Supreme Court.[123] The privatization of enterprises and growth of capital markets magnified inequality, making Israel's the worst of all Western countries aside from the United States. Public sector wages eroded. State expenditures on education, health care, and housing declined; efforts at introducing privatization and market-driven models proliferated. In 1999, 20 percent of the population qualified as poor and 25 percent of children grew up in such families.[124]

Conclusion

In its first half century Israel shaped one citizenship regime and transitioned to a second. The Labor Party and Histadrut had introduced and institutionalized a system of stratification: Ashkenazim as first-class citizens, Mizrahim and women as second-class citizens, Palestinian Israelis as third-class citizens, and the inequality of non-Orthodox Judaism. The advent of unfettered capitalism, a burgeoning civil society, and a nascent constitution in the form of Basic Laws reinforced, rather than removed, the "ethnic hierarchy." Similarly, the inequality of women and non-Orthodox Judaism persisted.

The Israel that initially had tried to regenerate immigrants for the Zionist project was in fact engaged in a larger and even more challenging emancipation process. Indeed, Israel now found itself in desperate need of the "auto-emancipation" that had been Zionism's raison d'être. For Israel's success sovereignty was necessary but not sufficient; equality was also a sine qua non. To become a state of equal citizens, Israel had to free itself from an entrenched structure of inequalities and disabilities, of second- and third-class citizens, of an official or established religion and unrecognized, inferior forms of Judaism.

United States

THE GREAT MIGRATION (1881–1924) from eastern Europe made the United States a center of world Jewry. The Nazis' murder of most of European Jewry magnified that status. While the migrants and their children were citizens, their rights were restricted.

Proponents of an America of "White Anglo-Saxon Protestant origin" erected a structure of inequality in education and housing, employment and secondary associations directed at eastern and southern European immigrants and especially Jews, as well as African Americans. For five or more decades, federal and state governments permitted, and American society sanctioned, overt discrimination. For a half century (1920–70), the Great Migration lived with pervasive infringements on civil rights.[1]

In the period after World War II, American Jewry's civil defense organizations engaged in a concerted emancipation campaign. Jews collaborated with African Americans, Catholics, and other minorities to end inequality.[2] That campaign succeeded: from the 1940s to the 1960s state and federal civil rights laws, and court rulings prohibiting discrimination, dismantled the structure of inequality. Those events constituted American Jews' second emancipation: it positioned the immigrant's children and grandchildren to realize the promise of American equality.

Exclusion

Exclusion of Jews had begun prior to, or at the very onset of, the Great Migration: social tension and competition heightened in the Gilded Age.[3] Resorts (Grand Union Hotel, Saratoga Springs, New York; 1877), real estate developers (Manhattan Beach Corporation, Coney Island, New York; 1879), and college fraternities and societies chose to exclude Jews: Jewish students began to found their own fraternities.[4] The American Catholic press and pulpit disseminated European anti-Semitism.[5]

The massive influx of east European Jews met with massive resistance: "virtually the whole system of anti-Semitic discriminations was worked out by 1917."[6] Numerous organizations and political groups attempted to enact restrictive legislation that would stem the flow of supposedly undesirable immigrants from eastern and southern Europe. The Boston Brahmin Immigration Restriction League (1894), among the most influential, advocated a literacy test for immigrants: Congress approved such legislation in 1897 but President Grover Cleveland vetoed it.[7] The anti-immigrant, agrarian Populist Party lost the campaign for the presidency (1892) yet affected federal and state legislation on immigration for the next thirty years.[8]

Neighborhood violence forced Jewish immigrants in Detroit, Cleveland, Cincinnati, and Brooklyn to organize self-defense units.[9] Jewish leaders founded two civil defense organizations: the American Jewish Committee (1906) and the Anti-Defamation League (1913) (chapter 19): their earliest legislative successes were state civil rights bills prohibiting summer resorts ("places of public accommodation") from excluding prospective patrons "because of race, creed or color."[10]

Opponents of immigration had their first success with the Chinese Exclusion Act (1882). The vetoes of Presidents Grover Cleveland, William Taft, and Woodrow Wilson had repeatedly quashed Congress's efforts to introduce similar quotas for European immigrants. With isolationism's growth after World War I, the opponents of immigration finally succeeded in ending mass European, and especially Jewish, immigration with the adoption of the National Origins Act (1921–24).[11] Immigration's critics similarly succeeded in erecting barriers across American society.

Colleges and universities began to adopt quotas.[12] Harvard president A. Lawrence Lowell, a founder of the Immigration Restriction League, led the way by announcing the need for restrictions. Harvard's admissions office introduced the strategy of "geographical diversity" to reduce the number of Jews, who were largely concentrated in a handful of cities. Numerous institutions limited admission of Jews (quotas ranged from 3 to 16%), whether by introducing "geographical diversity" or including a question on "religious preference" on the application form.[13] The same institutions barred Jews from faculty positions.[14]

Anti-immigrant and anti-Jewish sentiment combined to close, or virtually close, entire sectors of the economy to Jews:

> Utilities, banks, insurance companies, publishing houses, engineering and architectural firms, advertising agencies, school districts, major industrial companies, civic bodies for art and music, hospitals, universities, and law firms were among the major culprits.[15]

When employers advertised positions, they were free to state that they would not consider Jews or members of other groups, for example, Catholics, blacks, and women.[16] Medical schools rigorously limited the number of Jews admitted. Moreover, those who did acquire medical training were often excluded from hospital staffs. To practice, some Jewish doctors were forced to establish hospitals of their own.[17]

Among lawyers, Jews "bore the brunt of elite hostility."[18] Excluded from established "WASP" firms, Jewish lawyers founded solo practices or worked for small Jewish firms in immigrant neighborhoods. In New York City, they largely belonged to the less prestigious of the state's two bar associations.[19] Pennsylvania introduced a system of preceptorship and registration that severely reduced the number of Jews admitted to law school and the bar. Where possible Jewish lawyers entered government service: the New Deal in fact created numerous positions in Washington, D.C., for skilled lawyers.[20]

The private men's clubs that flourished since the middle of the nineteenth century were crucial for business contacts. Some clubs that had previously admitted Jews banned them in the 1920s.[21] Increasingly popular family and country clubs similarly excluded Jews. In response, Jews founded their own, so that in many cities there were parallel Jewish country clubs. The same held for vacation sites: the famous Borscht Belt in Sullivan County, New York, was a parallel Jewish vacation destination.[22]

Immigrants and their children attempting to leave their neighborhoods of first residence for improved housing faced barriers. "Restrictive covenants" often barred Jews, Catholics, blacks, and Asians.[23] Excluded from certain neighborhoods, Jews concentrated elsewhere. In New York City, for example, Park Slope and Brooklyn Heights rejected Jews. Jews instead congregated along the Grand Concourse (Bronx), Eastern Parkway and Ocean Avenue (Brooklyn), Central Park West, West End Avenue and Riverside Drive (Manhattan). Jews lived on "'Jewish' avenues, built by Jewish developers for a Jewish clientele."[24] The pattern was one of "concentrated dispersal": as immigrants and their children moved to middle-class neighborhoods, "Jewish ethnic segregation" increased.[25]

War and Postwar

The three major Jewish civil defense organizations—the American Jewish Committee, the American Jewish Congress, and the Anti-Defamation League—took the lead to combat infringements on "the civil rights of all citizens," aiming at the "firm establishment of equal rights and opportunities for all."[26] They shifted from narrowly defined self-defense to a broad engagement with American pluralism and egalitarianism.[27] They cooperated with a wide spectrum of organizations: religious groups such as the National Council of Churches, National Catholic Welfare Conference, and National Conference of Christians and Jews; racial or ethnic groups, especially African American organizations such as the National Association for the Advancement of Colored

People and National Urban League; and secular organizations such as the CIO unions and the American Civil Liberties Union.[28]

One effort of this broad coalition was "community relations" or "intergroup relations," in which the American Jewish Committee and the Anti-Defamation League were at the forefront.[29] The organizations employed social scientists, especially social psychologists, to conduct research on the problem of discrimination. The organizations then empowered social activists to use mass media to counteract it.

This research and activism defined the issue in psychological terms ("prejudice") of individual identity and group membership. It posited the "unity" of prejudice, asserting that "prejudice" directed at all groups was fundamentally similar and that discrimination harmed all and benefited none.[30] As Rabbi Stephen S. Wise, president of the American Jewish Congress, told a Senate subcommittee on fair employment practices in 1947:

> We regard ethnic discrimination, whether directed against Jews, Negroes, Chinese, Mexicans or any other group, as a single and indivisible problem and as one of the most urgent problems of democratic society.[31]

The American Jewish Committee enunciated a commitment to "join with other groups in the protection of the civil rights of the members of all groups irrespective of race, religion, color or national origin."[32] The organizations produced films, posters, and pamphlets to educate the American public against prejudice. Underlying this production of propaganda was the premise that it was utterly harmonious to be both "American" and "Jewish" since both emphasized "equality, the rule of law and individual rights."[33]

The American Jewish Congress's Commission on Law and Social Action (CLAS; 1945) forged alliances with liberal and minority group organizations to wage an innovative legal campaign to eliminate all discriminatory practices. The aim was to achieve "full equality in a free society."[34] These activists believed that discrimination in the form of "overt social and public practice" was the main source of prejudice.[35] The legal approach addressed "structural inequality" and "the economics of prejudice." Its practitioners dissented from the sociopsychological approach that avoided economics and politics. As one of the leading lawyers put it: they regarded "law itself [as] an educational device."[36]

The American Jewish Congress engaged in intensive "coalition politics" during its peak period of legal activity from 1948 to 1964. The legal staff used "the drafting of legislation, the filing of briefs in major test cases before the courts, testimony before governmental and public commissions and agencies, and the organization of social action on the national, state and municipal levels."[37] For example, eleven states passed fair employment practice laws between 1945 and 1955.[38] The Commission on Law and Social Action also advocated for states establishing commissions to enforce civil rights; by 1957 thirteen states had founded such agencies.[39]

Some of the American Jewish Congress's leading lawyers had worked on the New Deal; they regarded this new campaign as continuing their previous work by further expanding the state's purview.[40] Their activity presumed that "private" entities such as businesses and clubs, neighborhood associations and universities, were the major violators of civil rights. It was thus imperative to extend constitutional protection to the seemingly "private" sphere of "employment, housing, education and accommodation."[41]

In 1948 New York passed the Quinn-Olliffe Bill enforcing fairness in educational practices. In 1950 New York and New Jersey passed laws prohibiting discrimination in private housing projects that enjoyed public assistance. In 1949 New Jersey passed the Freeman Law establishing a new commission, the New Jersey State Division Against Discrimination, to investigate discrimination in the four key spheres of employment, housing, education, and public accommodation.[42] In fact, multiple states and municipalities adopted fair employment practice laws in the decade 1945–55.[43]

In 1957 President Eisenhower signed the Civil Rights Act that established the Commission on Civil Rights. This was a positive but limited step.[44] When President Johnson signed the Civil Rights Act in 1964 and the Voting Rights Act in 1965 the campaign had reached its goal.

Jews began to find open doors to areas of the economy previously closed to them.[45] Jewish lawyers, for example, began to be recruited to elite law firms to the point that they were "virtually indistinguishable from their Protestant counterparts." Some were recruited directly out of the most selective law schools. Other lawyers' New Deal government careers had enabled them to acquire indispensable knowledge of public policy. Some utilized that knowledge to open elite firms in Washington, D.C., and New York.[46]

These efforts at civil rights aimed at legal equality. Legal equality alone was, however, a demonstrable retreat from the New Deal's ambitions of a social welfare that comprised full employment, housing, and education. The Cold War "anti-Communist" attack on the New Deal traduced such programs as "communism": to deflect that charge, Cold War liberals took economic equality off the table. In consequence, the abolition of discrimination did not benefit the truly impoverished. The true beneficiaries were "members of the middle class" who had been subject to religious or ethnic discrimination. The new civil rights tended to benefit Jews and Catholics more than their African American allies.[47]

Inward Turn

With the acquisition of full rights in housing, employment, and education, organized American Jewry ceased to have a coherent and compelling domestic agenda. The breakdown of alliances with other religious and ethnic groups propelled this shift. The concerted opposition of Jewish organizations (American Jewish Committee, American Jewish Congress, Anti-Defamation League) to quotas if not to affirmative action legislation (1972), in the workplace and in educational institutions, ended cooperation with African Americans and a broadly defined domestic agenda.[48] What Jewish leaders perceived to be the allied organizations' disappointing level of concern for Israel (1967), if not outright hostility, further stoked the collapse of domestic alliances.[49]

With desegregation and busing the number of Jewish parents abandoning urban areas and public urban education increased dramatically. Many Jews escaped integrated cities for the residential segregation of the suburbs, for example, Jews left Cleveland for Cleveland Heights and Shaker Heights, Detroit for Oak Park. "Other ethnic groups moved; the Jews fled."[50] Many Jews moved to new regions of the country. Los Angeles and Miami replaced Chicago and Philadelphia as having the second and third largest concentrations of Jewish population.[51]

Many Jewish parents abandoned public education rather than allow their children to attend, or be bused to, integrated schools.[52] The day school movement began as a form of religiously legitimized "white flight" from desegregation equivalent to the South's "white academies." From their inception day schools faced a serious lack of funding and qualified personnel. Day school advocates joined other groups who supported the idea of government "vouchers" to fund parochial schools' secular curriculum.[53]

Lacking compelling domestic issues, many American Jewish organizations in the 1960s grew increasingly concerned with the corrosive impact of America's "open society" on Jewish cohesion and Jewish youth. To counteract an alleged looming "assimilation," Jewish organizations "turned inward." Paradoxically that meant looking to two phenomena abroad: the Holocaust and the State of Israel.[54]

The proposed foci for internal renewal were fundamentally vicarious. The Holocaust and the State of Israel together formed a salvific narrative of destruction and redemption, martyrdom and heroism, yet one that occurred to Jews elsewhere. That narrative reinforced the idea of American Jewish exceptionalism. The extremes of Jewish history were foreign: American Jewry epitomized the happily normal. The inspiration for American Jewry's "civil religion" was to be found abroad.[55]

Synagogues, community centers, and other institutions had commemorated the Holocaust in the 1950s and 1960s.[56] Spurred by the Eichmann trial and the threat of a repetition of the "Holocaust" with the Six Day War, as well as the irruption of ethnic identities in America, Jews began to endow the Holocaust with new significance. Community Holocaust memorials proliferated; Holocaust tourism ("march of the living") attracted ever larger numbers.[57]

The United States Holocaust Memorial Museum (1993) epitomized the linkage between the Holocaust and Israel. The Carter White House first broached the idea of a Holocaust Memorial to assuage American Jews critical of the administration's policies toward Israel.[58] Commission members understood Israel as the countermemorial: "the real memorial was already being built . . . a truly permanent, living memorial—and that is Israel itself."[59]

American Jewish organizations slowly but ineluctably turned their attention to rallying support for Israel. The Six Day War (1967) was a watershed: the United States replaced France as Israel's main ally and supplier of military hardware and aid. The shift took a few decades but was unmistakable. Philanthropic organizations sent the bulk of their funds to Israel. Organizations whose primary focus was domestic saw their revenue shrink and their membership tumble. The agencies lobbying for Israel grew exponentially in size and revenue. American Jewish institutions began to fly the Israeli flag alongside the American and state flags.[60]

The campaign for the free emigration of Soviet Jewry, the continuation after a half-century delay of the Great Migration, similarly belonged to the inward turn. Soviet Jewry became a "new focus of communal purpose."[61] The politically effective publicity campaign, which began in the 1960s but gained momentum after 1971, drew on methods of the civil rights and antiwar (Vietnam) movements. It was a politically efficacious use of "proxy power," in which Jewish organizations found powerful sponsors in Congress who had grave reservations about détente with the Soviet Union.[62] Yet the issue at bottom complemented the growing concern with the Holocaust. It was about "never again": not failing a second time to rescue European Jews. In fact, it was in part about expiating guilt for American Jewry's alleged failure in the 1930s–1940s.[63]

The inward turn produced the development of "Jewish Studies" at American colleges and universities. There was a strong "communalist agenda" behind the proliferating endowments for academic positions. Donors, community organizations, and many academics saw undergraduate courses as the way to build identity to counter "assimilation," an open society's corrosive effects. The timing was propitious: this was the era in which the university curriculum expanded to encompass various forms of ethnic studies. The academics themselves were divided. Some made Jewish survival their primary concern. Others professed a primary loyalty to a discipline and freedom of inquiry.[64]

Conclusion

With the enactment of the 1960s' civil rights laws, American Jewry had waged a successful campaign to dismantle the legal structures that had infringed on the equality of the members of the Great Migration and their children. American Jews had thus attained the privileged position of full equality. Jews born in the postwar period ("baby boomers") entered a world of unimpeded opportunity in a robust economy. Indeed, Jews came to be considered the "model minority" for their affluence and high level of education.[65]

Now counted "among the primary beneficiaries of the American promise," Jews had to resolve the fundamental dilemma of their relationship to the status quo: Should they defend that privileged position at whatever the cost to other groups or advocate a capacious and inclusive America that could bring those privileges to all its members?[66] How would organized American Jewry and especially their leaders construe the perennial question, "is it good for the Jews"? Would they understand it as a parochial question exclusively about Jews and their favorable position in society? Or would they understand it broadly as a query about promoting a society concerned with the welfare of all its members, Jews included?

The dilemma facing American Jewry is, then, not unlike that facing Israelis who enjoy first-class citizenship. With their own rights apparently in place, do they remain concerned for the equality of all members of society? Do they understand emancipation as a finished process, a fait accompli that has a past yet not a future? Or do they regard emancipation as an ongoing challenge that demands strenuous exertion?

Ten Theses on Emancipation

One. Emancipation is the principal event of modern Jewish history. The process of gaining and retaining, exercising and defending, losing and recovering rights has been at the heart of the Jews' experience over the past four and a half centuries.

Two. The term "emancipation" was historically polysemous: it referred to the liberation or elevation of numerous groups. The application of the term to Jews is directly linked to the release of adherents of dissenting or minority religions from persecution or an inferior status. European states defined citizenship vis-à-vis religion. Jews followed other dissenting and minority religions in gaining rights. The Jews' emancipation was an integral aspect of the creation of citizenship across Europe.

The states employed two legal traditions: citizenship by residence (jus soli) and citizenship by descent (jus sanguinis). These laws could be deployed in an inclusive or exclusive manner.

Civil rights denote the freedoms of residence, occupation, property, and worship; political rights denote the franchise, elected and appointed office, and civil service positions.

Three. The emancipation process commenced around 1550 when Jews began to receive extensive privileges in eastern and western Europe and in some instances rights in a nascent civil society. After the first partition of the Polish-Lithuanian Commonwealth (1772), Russia (Catherine II's "Charter for the Towns," 1785) and the Habsburg Empire (Joseph II's edict for Galicia, 1789) attempted but failed to make a transition to rights. Subsequently, the partitioning powers (Russia, Habsburg Empire, Prussia), each in its own way, attempted to dismantle the private market town and the Jewish-gentry alliance that had generated the Jews' privileges. In western Europe there were diverse transitions from privileges and rights to equal rights.

Four. There were two legislative models of emancipation.

Joseph II promulgated a conditional, partial emancipation by reform in which numerous restrictions, many onerous, remained in force. Jews gained rights by moving both "into" estates, for example, admission to guilds, and "out of" estates, for example, dismantling the corporate Jewish community. Joseph II's legislation was the model for states undertaking reform until the mid-nineteenth century.

The French Revolution offered a model of unconditional, full emancipation by revolution—even though the reality was ambiguous. Jews were extracted "out of" estates as part of the Revolution's attempt to dissolve all corporations. The revolutionary option emerged with seismic events such as revolution, national unification, and the restructuring of empires.

Five. There were three regions of emancipation. The "east-west" binary, an ideological construct, neither explains the process nor fits the facts.

A. In western Europe Jews gained civil rights through the circumstances of settlement. They mobilized to gain political rights. This pattern obtained in the Atlantic world as well.

B. In central Europe civil and political rights were at issue. The states granted conditional emancipation contingent upon a regeneration that they legislated and supervised. The states moved Jews both "into" and "out of" estates. A complicating factor was the region's dualism of local and state citizenship. That dualism assumed new forms in imperial Germany (federal vs. state law) and the Third Reich (Aryan citizens vs. non-Aryan "state members").

C. In eastern Europe civil and political rights were at stake. Tsarist Russia adapted to its own needs central Europe's legislation of conditional emancipation. Its quid pro quo was one of regeneration for privileges, albeit for individuals. Emancipation was always about inserting individuals "into" the state-instituted estates. Russia and Congress Poland granted political rights prior to civil rights.

Six. The Ottoman Empire comprised a fourth region of emancipation. It granted equality to adherents of minority religions as individuals while solidifying the religious communities (*millets*). The Ottoman state accorded those communities authority over education and jurisdiction over personal status law.

Seven. The equality of Judaism was fundamental to the Jews' equality. Emancipating the Jews entailed emancipating Judaism. The status of Judaism vis-à-vis other religions was therefore of the utmost importance. States legislated that status; it was written into law. It was also built into synagogues in their status as either "private" or "public" ecclesiastical buildings.

Eight. Emancipation mobilized Jews politically. Jews actively engaged in the emancipation process at all points in gaining and defending, retaining and recovering rights. Jews established an array of voluntary societies—welfare organizations, civil defense organizations—as well as political parties to gain and protect rights.

Nine. Emancipation was ambiguous and interminable. It was neither a one-time, chronologically discrete event nor a linear one. It was recurring. Jews gained and lost and regained and re-lost rights. Emancipation was also fundamentally ambiguous. There were discrepancies between laws and their implementation, between appearance and actuality. There were triumphs and tragedies, progressions and retrogressions.

Ten. Emancipation was at the heart of the twentieth century's colossal events. Organized political anti-Semitism's primary goal was to restrict or abrogate emancipation. The Nazis' destruction of emancipation was the first step toward the Holocaust. The invention of Zionism and the establishment of the State of Israel were predicated on emancipation's abject failure in principle and in practice. In the late twentieth century Jews in the United States and Israel struggled to achieve equality. That process endures. Jews everywhere continue to live in the age of emancipation.

ACKNOWLEDGMENTS

WHEN I BEGAN WRITING THIS BOOK in 2013, I wondered whether it would speak to anyone beyond the narrow audience of specialists who teach and research the subject. Finishing in 2018 I am sadly persuaded of the book's urgent address to a broad audience. Current developments have brought issues of equality and rights to the fore. The fragility of citizenship and democracy is shockingly visible. I have two fervent wishes: that future historians will not have to write about the present as another period that witnessed the dismantling of democracy and rights in Europe and, indeed, the United States and that future historians will not have to identify this as the fateful moment in which the Jews' own state began to implode by renouncing the practices of democracy and the principle of equality.

I am fully aware that this book's basic conceptualization of emancipation, not to mention its conclusions, is highly controversial. I assume many will resist renouncing the fin-de-siècle categories that for over a century have dominated the discourse about emancipation in particular and Jewish life and politics in general. I hope that by suggesting a new set of categories this book will stimulate a forthright and honest discussion rather than the polemics and invective, censorship and ostracism that are the self-inflicted malediction of public Jewish life. Jews everywhere are desperately in need of a new perspective.

I have wanted to write a book about emancipation for over thirty years. Happily, other projects prevented me from doing so. Those decades afforded me an opportunity to learn more history, Jewish and general. I have substantially revised my ideas about the topic. This book is entirely different from the one I had in mind in 1990 when I signed a contract to write it. At that time, and for many years thereafter, I had searching conversations about modern Jewish history and especially about emancipation with my colleague and friend Heinz-Dietrich Löwe. Those conversations have remained a source of inspiration.

I would like to thank the University of Pennsylvania's Herbert Katz Center for Advanced Judaic Studies and its former director, David Ruderman, for a productive and enjoyable semester (2008) in which I first began to conceive this book. I am grateful to Bernie Cooperman and Adam Teller for guiding me in rethinking the early modern period.

David Engel's book, *The Historians of the Jews and the Holocaust* (2010), hit me like a bolt of lightning: it convinced me of the imperative of crossing the chronological barrier of 1933–45. Thank you, David.

I began writing this book while teaching at the Graduate Center of the City University of New York. I would like to thank the Department of History's erstwhile executive officer, Helena Rosenblatt, and erstwhile provost, Chase Robinson, for bringing me to New York. Thank you, Helena, for many illuminating conversations.

I am grateful to my friend and esteemed colleague Mary Gluck and Brown Judaic Studies for the invitation to be a Visiting Scholar in the fall of 2016. That appointment allowed me to present some of the materials on France in this book. Thank you, Mary, for being a gracious host and, as always, a truly wise and incisive critic. Ken Sacks kindly met me repeatedly at the Providence train station, so we could have leisurely chats.

I would like to thank Professors Daniel Menozzi and Ilaria Pavan for generously inviting me to present the essence of this book in four lectures at the Scuola Normale Superiore (May 2018). I am grateful for their warm hospitality and friendship. In Pisa's two-millennium bricolage, its continuous rebuilding through the constant reuse of materials, I discerned a metaphor for emancipation. Thank you, too, Ilaria, for helping me procure a scan of the first page of the Livornina from the Florence State Archive.

Yale's Whitney Humanities Center was a congenial venue in which first to present an overview of the project. I am grateful to Gary Tomlinson for a two-year appointment. Nanette Stahl graciously invited me to present this project at the Sterling Library Judaic Studies Colloquium.

Martin Goodman kindly invited me to deliver the Alfred Lehmann Memorial Lecture (2017) at the Oxford Centre for Hebrew and Jewish Studies. Nehama Aschkenasy provided a friendly forum at the University of Connecticut–Stamford.

Many colleagues have generously helped me with this project. I apologize in advance if I have forgotten anyone.

At the University of Wisconsin–Madison, I would like to thank Laird Boswell, Suzanne Desan, David McDonald, Tony Michels, Jennifer Ratner-Rosenhagen, and Lou Roberts. I am grateful to the University of Wisconsin's Department of History for the privilege of spending nineteen years among able and amiable colleagues.

At Yale, I am grateful to Leslie Brisman, Paul Bushkovitch, Christine Hayes, Hannan Hever, Jennifer Klein, John Merriman, Alan Mikhail, Maurice Samuel, Eliyahu Stern, and Francesca Trivellato. The students in my History 598 (Spring 2017) helped me find my way in studying the twentieth century: Hayk Esaghoulyan, Charlotte Kiechel, and Maya Sweedler.

For kind assistance I would also like to thank Hasia Diner, Chad Goldberg, Marion Kaplan, Ethan Katz, David Kretzmer, Derek Penslar, Till van Rahden, Marsha Rozenblit, Anthony James Steinhoff, and David Troyansky.

The Department of History's office staff have provided invaluable technical assistance: my thanks to Dana Lee and Denise Scott for tolerating my monotonous ineptitude with a smile.

At Princeton University Press it has been a pleasure and a privilege to work with Brigitta van Rheinberg, whose enthusiasm for this project buoyed my spirits during the marathon of research and writing. Amanda Peery conducted an outstanding editorial process for which I am deeply grateful. Two anonymous readers provided excellent suggestions that have improved the book in multiple ways. Eric Crahan, Pamela Weidman, and Debbie Tegarden have expertly guided me through the production process. Jennifer Backer has been a model copyeditor.

My thanks to Vital Zajka for his efficient assistance in procuring illustrations from YIVO. At the Leo Baeck Institute it was a pleasure to work with Renate Evers. My thanks as well to the Amsterdam City Archives and the State Archive of Florence.

David Cox at Cox Cartographic produced beautiful maps quickly and efficiently. Thank you, David.

Introduction. Ambiguous and Interminable Emancipation

1. Mussolini rejected formal democracy: "Fascism trains its guns on the whole block of democratic ideologies and rejects their premises and their practical applications." He instead extolled Fascism as the "purest form of democracy." See *Fascism: Doctrine and Institutions* (Rome: Ardita, 1935), 11–12, 21.

2. Nahum Goldmann, *The Autobiography of Nahum Goldmann: Sixty Years of Jewish Life*, trans. Helen Sebba (New York: Holt, Rinehart & Winston, 1969), 154–63, quotation at 162. Goldmann represented the Planning Committee for the World Jewish Congress (1936), the Comité des Délégations Juives auprès de la Conférence de la Paix (1919), and the Jewish Agency for Palestine (1929). He raised three issues of emancipation with Mussolini: protection of the Jews' rights in the Saar and Austria and Poland's violations of the Minority Rights treaties. Before the quoted sentence, Goldmann said: "Persecuted peoples always tend to be revolutionary, libertarian and democratic." Shlomo Avineri lauded Goldmann as "the epitome of Jewish pre-state diplomacy." See "Statecraft without a State: A Jewish Contribution to Political History?" in Gabriella Gelardini, ed., *Kontexte der Schrift: Ekkehard W. Stegemann zum 60. Geburtstag*, 2 vols. (Stuttgart: Kohlhammer, 2005), 1:418. Cf. Mark A. Raider, ed., *Nahum Goldmann: Statesman without a State* (Albany: State University of New York Press, 2009).

3. Jacob Katz, "The Term 'Jewish Emancipation': Its Origins and Historical Impact," in Alexander Altmann, ed., *Studies in Nineteenth-Century Jewish Intellectual History* (Cambridge, MA: Harvard University Press, 1964), 1–25; Reinhard Rürup, "Emanzipation: Anmerkungen zur Begriffsgeschichte," in *Emanzipation und Antisemitismus: Studien zur "Judenfrage" der bürgerlichen Gesellschaft* (Göttingen: Vandenhoeck and Ruprecht, 1975), 126–32; Karl Martin Grass and Reinhart Koselleck, "Emanzipation," in Otto Brunner, Werner Conze, and Reinhart Koselleck, eds., *Geschichtliche Grundbegriffe: Historisches Lexikon zur politisch-sozialen Sprache in Deutschland*, 8 vols. (Stuttgart: Klett-Cotta, 2004), 2:153–97.

Emancipation has been associated with a triumphalist Protestant reading of European history: Protestants created the Enlightenment and Jewish emancipation was one of its key by-products. In fact, Catholic polities may well have been at the forefront of granting Jews extensive privileges (Polish-Lithuanian Commonwealth, Italian states) as well as rights (Habsburg Empire, France). For the cross-confessional Enlightenment, see David Sorkin, *The Religious Enlightenment: Protestants, Jews and Catholics from London to Vienna* (Princeton: Princeton University Press, 2008).

4. Salo Baron, "Ghetto and Emancipation: Shall We Revise the Traditional View?" *Menorah Journal* 14, no. 6 (June 1928): 515. Baron held the Miller Chair at Columbia from 1930 to 1963.

5. David Vital, *A People Apart: A Political History of the Jews in Europe, 1789–1939* (Oxford: Oxford University Press, 1999), 29.

6. The one extant single-author account appeared over four decades ago. See Jacob Katz, *Out of the Ghetto: The Social Background of Jewish Emancipation, 1770–1870* (Cambridge, MA: Harvard University Press, 1973; 2nd ed., New York: Schocken, 1978). The one collection of documents appeared in 1944. See Raphael Mahler, *Jewish Emancipation: A*

Selection of Documents (New York: American Jewish Committee, 1944). Paul Mendes-Flohr and Jehuda Reinharz, eds., *The Jew in the Modern World: A Documentary History*, 3rd ed. (New York: Oxford University Press, 2011), 121–76 largely followed Mahler. There is no volume on emancipation in New York University Press's influential Essential Papers series.

In the past two decades a few multiauthor volumes have appeared. Pierre Birnbaum and Ira Katznelson, eds., *Paths of Emancipation: Jews, States and Citizenship* (Princeton: Princeton University Press, 1995); Michael Brenner, Vicki Caron, and Uri R. Kaufmann, eds., *Jewish Emancipation Reconsidered: The French and German Models* (Tübingen: Mohr Siebeck, 2003). For a pioneering comparative volume, see Rainer Liedtke and Stephan Wendehorst, eds., *The Emancipation of Catholics, Jews and Protestants: Minorities and the Nation State in Nineteenth-Century Europe* (Manchester: Manchester University Press, 1999). A brief overview is Ulrich Wyrwa, "Die Emanzipation der Juden in Europa," in Elka-Vera Kotowski, Julius H. Schoeps, and Hiltrud Wallenborn, eds., *Handbuch zur Geschichte der Juden in Europa*, 2 vols. (Darmstadt: Primus Verlag, 2001), 2:336–52.

7. Salo Baron memorably called that view the "lachrymose theory of pre-revolutionary woe." See "Ghetto and Emancipation," 526. Baron himself emphasized the loss of internal autonomy (519). For the classic statement of the lachrymose view, see Heinrich Graetz, *History of the Jews*, 6 vols. (Philadelphia: Jewish Publication Society, 1967), especially vol. 5; Graetz, *The Structure of Jewish History and Other Essays*, ed. Ismar Schorsch (New York: Jewish Theological Seminary, 1975). For the origins of the lachrymose view, see David Sorkin, *The Transformation of German Jewry, 1780–1840* (New York: Oxford University Press, 1987).

8. For the east European school that propagated these views, see Jonathan Frankel, "Assimilation and the Jews in Nineteenth-Century Europe: Towards a New Historiography?" in Jonathan Frankel and Steven Zipperstein, eds., *Assimilation and Community: The Jews in Nineteenth-Century Europe* (Cambridge: Cambridge University Press, 1992). For the idealization of the autonomous community, see Jacob Katz, *Tradition and Crisis: Jewish Society at the End of the Middle Ages*, trans. Bernard Dov Cooperman (New York: New York University Press, 1993). For nostalgia for the autonomous community, see, e.g., H. Sacher, *Jewish Emancipation: The Contract Myth* (London: English Zionist Federation, 1917); Jacob Staub, "A Reconstructionist Perspective on the Enlightenment and the Emancipation," *Judaism* 38, no. 4 (Fall 1989): 427–36; Walter S. Wurzburger, "The Enlightenment, the Emancipation and the Jewish Religion," *Judaism* 38, no. 4 (Fall 1989): 401; and Ruth R. Wisse, *Jews and Power* (New York: Schocken, 2007), 33–34, 37–38. For a thoughtful discussion of such nostalgia, see Steven Poppel, "State Building and Jewish Community Organization in Germany," *Contemporary Jewry* 5, no. 2 (Fall 1980): 13.

The touchstone of this view was a misinterpretation of the Count Clermont-Tonnerre's pronouncement during the French Revolution's debates: "to the Jews as individuals everything, to the Jews as a nation nothing." See David Sorkin, *The Count Stanislas de Clermont-Tonnerre's "To the Jews as a Nation . . .": The Career of a Quotation*, Jacob Katz Memorial Lecture, 2011 (Jerusalem: Leo Baeck Institute, 2012).

9. *Resolutions of the 18th Zionist Congress, Prague, Aug. 31–Sept. 3, 1933* (London: Central Office of the Zionist Organisation, 1934), 11: "The events in Germany have sealed the final collapse of all those illusion that beheld a solution to the Jewish question in civil emancipation alone. . . ." See, e.g., A. Z. Eshkoli, *Ha-Emanzipazia Ha-Yehudit: Ha-Mahapeicha Ha-Tsarfatit ve-Malchut Napoleon* (Jerusalem: Kiryat Sefer, 1952), 3–7. My thanks to Hannan Hever and Shmuel Feiner.

10. Rabbi Elmer Berger made this point, albeit polemically, at the end of the war. See his *Emancipation: The Rediscovered Ideal* (Philadelphia: American Council for Judaism, 1945). Robert Gordis noticed this irony in 1965: "We are told in some quarters that the

century and a half of Jewish history extending from the French Revolution in 1789, to the Nuremberg Laws in 1935, has been a tragic aberration. . . . It is noteworthy that there have been few applications by the eloquent *laudatores temporis acti* for reghettoisation and for the surrender of their civic, political and economic positions in Western Society." See "Jewish Tradition in the Modern World: Conservation and Renewal," in A. Leland Jamison, ed., *Tradition and Change in Jewish Experience* (Syracuse: Syracuse University Press, 1978), 146–47. Among numerous examples of those who reject emancipation, see Sacher, *Jewish Emancipation*; Moshe Aberbach, "The Failure of Jewish Emancipation in Europe," in Jack Fruchtman Jr., ed., *A Life in Jewish Education: Essays in Honor of Louis L. Kaplan*, Studies and Texts in Jewish History and Culture, vol. 4 (Bethesda: University of Maryland Press, 1997), 99–137; and Wisse, *Jews and Power*. For an emphasis on emancipation's ambiguities, see Horace Kallen, "The Bearing of Emancipation on Jewish Survival," *YIVO Annual of Jewish Social Science* 12 (1958–59): 9–35 and Paul Mendes-Flohr, "The Emancipation of European Jewry: Why Was It Not Self-evident?" *Studia Rosenthaliana* 30, no. 1 (1996): 7–20. For spirited defenses, see Israel Abrahams, *Jewish Life under Emancipation* (London: St. Clements Press, 1917) and Berger, *Emancipation: The Rediscovered Ideal*; for rehabilitations, see Jakob J. Petuchowski, "The Case for Clermont-Tonnerre," *Judaism* 31, no. 4 (1982): 472–77 and Robert Liberles, "The Implications of Jewish Emancipation," in Haim Marantz, ed., *Judaism and Education: Essays in Honor of Walter I. Ackerman* (Beer-Sheva, Israel: Ben Gurion University of the Negev Press, 1998), 157–69.

11. Michael Marrus, *Lessons of the Holocaust* (Toronto: University of Toronto Press, 2016). "My principal lesson of the Holocaust is . . . beware of lessons" (160).

12. Messianic hopes found expression in the prayer for the State of Israel that Shmuel Yosef Agnon wrote at the request of the Ashkenazi Chief Rabbi Isaac Herzog. The original formulation was: "the commencement of our redemption" (*reshit geulateinu*). Some have adopted a tempered version: "the commencement of the flowering of our redemption" (*reshit tsmihat geulateinu*). See Jacob Katz, "Israel and the Messiah," in Marc Saperstein, ed., *Essential Papers on Messianic Movements* (New York: New York University Press, 1992), 475. More generally, see Aviezer Ravitzky, *Messianism, Zionism, and Jewish Religious Radicalism*, trans. Michael Swirsky and Jonathan Chipman (Chicago: University of Chicago Press, 1993).

13. In a book of twelve chapters Katz (*Out of the Ghetto*) devoted four to causes, three to religious consequences, two to social and demographic results, and one to the legal process.

14. Katz, *Out of the Ghetto*, dates emancipation from 1770 to 1870. Mendes-Flohr and Reinharz, *The Jew in the Modern World*, give the dates 1789–1871. Paula Hyman, "Emancipation," in Arthur A. Cohen and Paul Mendes-Flohr, eds., *Contemporary Jewish Religious Thought: Original Essays on Critical Concepts, Movements, and Beliefs* (New York: Scribner, 1987), 165–70, cites 1790 to 1917. Birnbaum and Katznelson, *Paths of Emancipation*, date emancipation to the long nineteenth century, i.e., from the French to the Russian revolution.

15. Gianfranco Poggi, *The Development of the Modern State: A Sociological Introduction* (Stanford: Stanford University Press, 1978); Andreas Fahrmeir, *Citizenship: The Rise and Fall of a Modern Concept* (New Haven: Yale University Press, 2007), 9 55.

16. Katz, *Tradition and Crisis*, 8. Katz's book was singularly influential in establishing the ideal of the autonomous community. For critiques, see Elisheva Carlebach, "Early Modern Ashkenaz in the Writings of Jacob Katz," 65–83 and Paula E. Hyman, "Jacob Katz as Social Historian," in Jay M. Harris, ed., *Pride of Jacob: Essays on Jacob Katz and His Work* (Cambridge, MA: Harvard University Center for Jewish Studies, 2002), 85–96. For an alternative view, see David B. Ruderman, *Early Modern Jewry: A New Cultural History* (Princeton: Princeton University Press, 2010), 57–98.

17. Historians' long-standing identification of Jewish modernity with the Berlin Haskalah and Moses Mendelssohn made events before the eighteenth century "harbingers" and "precursors." Mahler, *Jewish Emancipation*, treats developments to 1782 as "forerunners." Katz, in "The Term 'Jewish Emancipation,'" treats seventeenth- and eighteenth-century advocates as "forerunners." See Alexander Altmann, ed., *Studies in Nineteenth Century Jewish Intellectual History* (Cambridge, MA: Harvard University Press, 1964), 9. Mendes-Flohr and Reinharz, *The Jew in the Modern World*, call the years 1655–1789 "harbingers of political and economic change" (7–58).

18. Inis L. Claude, *National Minorities: An International Problem* (Cambridge, MA: Harvard University Press, 1955), 7: "As the spirit of nationalism took hold, guaranteed *rights* continued to be primarily religious ones, but the protected *groups* tended to assume the character of national minorities."

19. Scholarship on citizenship tends to marginalize or neglect religion. See David Sorkin, "Religious Minorities and Citizenship in the Long Nineteenth Century: Some Contexts of Emancipation," in Winnifred Fallers Sullivan, Elizabeth Shakman Hurd, Saba Mahmood, and Peter G. Danchin, eds., *Politics of Religious Freedom* (Chicago: University of Chicago Press, 2015), 115–26.

20. Benjamin J. Kaplan, *Divided by Faith: Religious Conflict and the Practice of Toleration in Early Modern Europe* (Cambridge, MA: Harvard University Press, 2007), 194. The Peace of Westphalia (1648), which aimed to end a century of devastating war over religion, promulgated these distinctions. See Clive Parry, ed., *The Consolidated Treaty Series*, 231 vols. (Dobbs Ferry, NY: Oceana Publications, 1969–81), 1:228–29.

21. Rolf Grawert, *Staat und Staatsangehörigkeit: Verfassungsgeschichtliche Untersuchung zur Entstehung der Staatsangehörigkeit* (Berlin: Duncker & Humblot, 1973), 123, 146.

22. Patrick Weil, *How to Be French: Nationality in the Making since 1789*, trans. Catherine Porter (Durham: Duke University Press, 2008).

23. David Sorkin, "Beyond the East-West Divide: Rethinking the Narrative of the Jews' Political Status in Europe, 1600–1750," *Jewish History* 24 (2010): 247–56; Steven E. Aschheim, *Brothers and Strangers: The East European Jew in German and German Jewish Consciousness, 1800–1923* (Madison: University of Wisconsin Press, 1982).

24. For the Germano-centric view, see Katz, *Out of the Ghetto*; Jacob Katz, ed., *Toward Modernity: The European Jewish Model* (New Brunswick, NJ: Transaction Books, 1987); Michael Meyer, *The Origins of the Modern Jew* (Detroit: Wayne State University Press, 1967); Reinhard Rürup, "Jewish Emancipation and Bourgeois Society," *Leo Baeck Institute Yearbook* 14 (1969): 67–91; and Rürup, "The Tortuous and Thorny Path to Legal Equality: 'Jew Laws' and the Emancipatory Legislation in Germany from the Late Eighteenth Century," *Leo Baeck Institute Yearbook* 31 (1986): 3–33.

25. Birnbaum and Katznelson, *Paths of Emancipation*, 3, 17. I have deliberately avoided the topic of ennoblement, which had little if any impact on emancipation, with the possible exception of England. See Kai Drewes, *Jüdischer Adel: Nobilitierungen von Juden im Europa des 19. Jahrhunderts* (Frankfurt: Campus, 2013), 172–73, 186–91, 269. On the contrary, emancipation made ennoblement possible: the vast majority of ennoblements followed emancipation. See Huibert Schijf, "Titled Outsiders: Jewish Nobility in the Nineteenth and Early Twentieth Centuries," in Yme Kuiper, Nikolaj Bijleveld, and Jaap Dronkers, eds., *Nobilities in Europe in the Twentieth Century: Reconversion Strategies, Memory Culture and Elite Formation* (Leuven: Peeters, 2015), 69. Schijf argues that "the elevation of Jews became a sign of the modernization of the ennoblement process itself" (70).

26. For the term, see Mona Ozouf, "Regeneration," in François Furet and Mona Ozouf, eds., *A Critical Dictionary of the French Revolution* (Cambridge, MA: Harvard University

Press, 1989), 781–91. For German-speaking central Europe, see Christian Wilhelm von Dohm, *Über die bürgerliche Verbesserung der Juden*, 2 vols. (Berlin and Stettin: Friedrich Nicolai, 1781–83). For an influential French example, see Abbé Henri Gregoire, *Essai sur la régénération physique, morale et politique des Juifs* (Metz, 1789).

27. Salo Baron, "Newer Approaches to Jewish Emancipation," *Diogenes* 29 (Spring 1960): 57. See also Baron, "Ghetto and Emancipation," 524.

28. Rürup, "Jewish Emancipation and Bourgeois Society."

29. Goldmann, *The Autobiography of Nahum Goldmann*, 138.

30. David Vital, "European Jewry 1860–1919: Political Organisation and Trans-state Political Action," in Paul Smith, ed., *Ethnic Groups in International Relations: Comparative Studies on Governments and Non-Dominant Ethnic Groups in Europe, 1850–1940* (New York: New York University Press, 1991), 5:39–57; Vital, "Diplomacy in the Jewish Interest," in Ada Rapoport-Albert and Steven J. Zipperstein, eds., *Jewish History: Essays in Honour of Chimen Abramsky* (London: Peter Halban, 1988), 683–95; Ezra Mendelsohn, *On Modern Jewish Politics* (New York: Oxford University Press, 1993). For a contrasting view, see David Biale, *Power and Powerlessness in Jewish History* (New York: Schocken, 1986).

31. Leo Pinsker, *"Autoemanzipation!" Mahnruf an seine Stammesgenossen von einem russischen Juden* (Berlin: Issleib, 1882).

32. There are only a handful of theories of emancipation. Hannah Arendt emphasized the Jews' financial relationship to the nation-state: emancipation was an extension of Jewish bankers' privileges, i.e., a quid pro quo of rights for financial services rather than rights for regeneration. See *The Origins of Totalitarianism* (New York: Harcourt Brace, 1951). Salo Baron adopted an eclectic approach by invoking the "totality of forces": capitalism, individualism, state formation, nationalism. See "Newer Approaches to Jewish Emancipation." Jacob Katz emphasized the social consequences of ideological change: the Enlightenment gave rise to a "semi-neutral" society in which Jews and Christians could interact as equals. See *Out of the Ghetto* (1973). Pierre Birnbaum and Ira Katznelson followed Arendt in stressing the state's pivotal role yet recognized multiple state formations and thus multiple emancipation processes. See *Paths of Emancipation*. Jonathan Israel has claimed the "radical Enlightenment" as emancipation's source. See "Jewish Emancipation in the Western World (1780–1860): What Kind of Enlightenment Made It Possible?" *Israel Academy of Sciences and Humanities Proceedings* 9, no. 6 (2018).

Chapter One. Merchant Colonies

1. On Jews as municipal citizens across medieval Europe, see Salo Baron, "Meaning of Citizenship," in *A Social and Religious History of the Jews*, 17 vols. (New York: Columbia University Press, 1952–93), 11:14–17; for Italy, see Cecil Roth, *The Jews of Italy* (Philadelphia: Jewish Publication Society, 1946), 82, 229 (Messina), 120 (Perugia), 124 (Trieste), 132 (Pisa), 138, 156 (Rome), 211–12, 276 (Naples); for central Europe, see Guido Kisch, *The Jews in Medieval Germany: A Study of Their Legal and Social Status* (Chicago: University of Chicago Press, 1949), 139; for Worms, where Jews were burghers as late as the fourteenth century, see Fritz Reuter, *Warmaisa: 1000 Jahre Juden in Worms* (Worms: Verlag Stadtarchiv Worms, 1984), 57.

2. Lois Dubin, "Subjects into Citizens: Jewish Autonomy and Inclusion in Early Modern Livorno and Trieste," *Simon Dubnow Institute Yearbook* 5 (2006): 51–81.

3. Jonathan Israel, *European Jewry in the Age of Mercantilism* (Oxford: Clarendon, 1989), 2–3; Marcus Arkin, "West European Jewry in the Age of Mercantilism: An Economic Interpretation," *Historia Judaica* 22, no. 2 (October 1960): 85–104. On mercantilist

thought, see Charles Wilson, "Trade, Society and the State," in Wilson and E. E. Rich, eds., *Cambridge Economic History of Europe*, 8 vols. (Cambridge: Cambridge University Press, 1967), 4:487–575.

4. M. E. Bratchel, "Alien Merchant Colonies in Sixteenth-Century England: Community Organization and Social Mores," *Journal of Medieval and Renaissance Studies* 14, no. 1 (Spring 1984): 40–41. In the Roman Empire "nation" (*natio*) designated foreigners and especially foreign merchants in ports and cities. In the Middle Ages it designated unions of foreign students at universities, e.g., the four nations at the University of Paris, and groupings of foreign representatives at ecclesiastical councils. See Guido Zermatto, "Nation: The History of a Word," *Review of Politics* 6, no. 3 (1944): 351–66.

5. Frédéric Mauro, "Merchant Communities, 1350–1750," in James D. Tracy, ed., *The Rise of Merchant Empires: Long-Distance Trade in the Early Modern World, 1350–1750* (Cambridge: Cambridge University Press, 1995), 261–66; J. A. Goris, *Étude sur les Colonies marchandes méridionales (portugais, espagnols, italiens) à Anvers de 1488 à 1567*, 2 vols., 2nd ed. (New York: B. Franklin, 1971); Alexander Cowan, "Foreigners and the City: The Case of the Immigrant Merchant," in Cowan, ed., *Mediterranean Urban Culture, 1400–1700* (Exeter: University of Exeter Press, 2000), 45–55.

6. Goris, *Étude sur les Colonies marchandes méridionales*, 32.

7. Ibid., 48–49. Some scholars have recently emphasized the broad variations in the arrangements of merchant colonies. See Regina Grafe and Oscar Gelderblom, "The Rise and Fall of the Merchants Guilds: Re-thinking the Comparative Study of Commercial Institutions in Premodern Europe," *Journal of Interdisciplinary History* 40, no. 4 (Spring 2010): 477–511.

8. Bratchel, "Merchant Colonies," 41.

9. Salo Baron termed this the "vanguard of marranos" in emigration and settlement. See "Modern Capitalism and Jewish Fate," *Menorah Journal* 30 (Summer 1942): 122. On the predominance of lay over rabbinic authority, see David Ruderman, *Early Modern Jewry: A New Cultural History* (Princeton: Princeton University Press, 2010), 57–98.

10. Lois Dubin, *The Port Jews of Habsburg Trieste: Absolutist Politics and Enlightenment Culture* (Stanford: Stanford University Press, 1999); Dubin, "Port Jews Revisited: Commerce and Culture in the Age of European Expansion," in Jonathan Karp and Adam Sutcliffe, eds., *The Cambridge History of Judaism*, vol. 7: *The Early Modern World* (Cambridge: Cambridge University Press, 2017), 550–75; David Sorkin, "The Port Jew: Notes towards a Social Type," *Journal of Jewish Studies* 50 (Spring 1999): 87–97; David Cesarani, ed., *Port Jews: Jewish Communities in Cosmopolitan Maritime Trading Centres, 1550–1950* (London: Frank Cass, 2002); David Cesarani and Gemma Romain, eds., *Jews and Port Cities, 1590–1990: Commerce, Community and Cosmopolitanism* (London: Vallentine Mitchell, 2006). For a critique, see C. S. Monaco, "Port Jews or a People of the Diaspora? A Critique of the Port Jew Concept," *Jewish Social Studies* n.s. 15 (Winter 2009): 137–66.

11. Karel Davids and Jan Lucassen, introduction to Davids and Lucassen, eds., *A Miracle Mirrored: The Dutch Republic in European Perspective* (Cambridge: Cambridge University Press, 1995), 11–12; Otto Brunner, "Stadt und Bürgertum in der europäischen Geschichte," in *Neue Wege der Sozialgeschichte* (Göttingen: Vandenhoeck, 1956), 89–91.

12. Davids and Lucassen, conclusion to *A Miracle Mirrored*, 438–39.

13. Benjamin Arbel, "Jews in International Trade: The Emergence of the Levantines and Ponentines," in Robert C. Davis and Benjamin Ravid, eds., *The Jews of Early Modern Venice* (Baltimore: Johns Hopkins University Press, 2001), 76.

14. Bernard Cooperman, "Venetian Policy towards Levantine Jews in Its Broader Italian Context," in G. Cozzi, ed., *Gil Ebrei e Venezia, Secoli XIV–XVIII* (Milan: Edizioni Comunità,

1987), 65–84; Jonathan Israel, *Diasporas within a Diaspora: Jews, Crypto-Jews and the World Maritime Empires (1540-1740)* (Boston: Brill, 2002), 3, 8–9.

15. Benjamin Ravid, "A Tale of Three Cities and Their *Raison d'État*: Ancona, Venice Livorno and the Competition for Jewish Merchants in the Sixteenth Century," in Alisa Meyuhas Ginio, ed., *Jews, Christians and Muslims in the Mediterranean World after 1492* (London: Frank Cass, 1992), 143. For the charter of 1535, see Max Radin, "A Charter of Privileges of the Jews in Ancona of the Year 1535," *Jewish Quarterly Review* n.s. 4, no. 2 (October 1913): 225–48. Jonathan Israel would locate the shift in attitude toward the Jews to Prague in Rudolf II's charter of 1577. See *European Jewry in the Age of Mercantilism*, 39–40.

16. Bernard Dov Cooperman, "Portuguese Conversos in Ancona: Jewish Political Activity in Early Modern Italy," in Cooperman, ed., *In Iberia and Beyond: Hispanic Jews between Cultures* (Newark: University of Delaware Press, 1998), 305–11.

17. Ibid., 312. It could be that the Kingdom of Aragon anticipated these developments in its charter of 1498 that invited "Jews and New Christians" to settle. See Vincenzo Selleri, "The Juridical Communities of the Aragonese Kingdom of Naples: Municipal Belonging in Renaissance Southern Italy (1442–1503)" (PhD diss., Graduate Center, City University of New York, 2017).

18. Cooperman, "Portuguese Conversos in Ancona," 299, 327–29.

19. Ibid., 333–36.

20. Benjamin Ravid, "An Autobiographical Memorandum by Daniel Rodriga, *Inventore* of the *Scala* of *Spalato*," in Ariel Toaff and Simon Schwarzfuchs, eds., *The Mediterranean and the Jews: Banking, Finance and International Trade (XVI-XVIII Centuries)* (Ramat-Gan: Bar-Ilan University Press, 1989), 189–213, quotation at 208.

21. Arbel, "Jews in International Trade," 90.

22. Ravid suggests that Daniel Rodriga invented the euphemism "Ponentine." See Benjamin Ravid, "The Venetian Government and the Jews," in Davis and Ravid, eds., *The Jews of Early Modern Venice*, 16–20.

23. Arbel, "Jews in International Trade," 87.

24. Charters of 1528 and 1548 had also allowed for synagogues. See Benjamin Ravid, "Cum Nimis Absurdum and the Ancona Auto-da-Fé Revisited: Their Impact on Venice and Some Wider Reflections," *Jewish History* 26 (2012): 89. For an analysis of Venice's differences from other port Jewries, see Benjamin Ravid, "The Sephardic Jewish Merchants of Venice, Port Jews and the Road to Modernity," in F. Francesconi, S. Mirvis, and B. Smollett, eds., *From Catalonia to the Caribbean: The Sephardic Orbit from Medieval to Modern Times: Essays in Honor of Jane S. Gerber* (Leiden: Brill, 2018), 117–35.

25. Carol Herselle Krinsky, *Synagogues of Europe: Architecture, History, Meaning*, 2nd ed. (New York: Dover, 1996), 381.

26. Benjamin Ravid, "An Introduction to the Charters of the Jewish Merchants of Venice," in Elliott Horowitz and Moses Orfali, eds., *The Mediterranean and the Jews: Society, Culture and Economy in Early Modern Times* (Ramat-Gan: Bar-Ilan University Press, 2002), 209–11. For the trade rights of non-Venetians, see Benjamin Ravid, "Venice and Its Minorities," in Eric R. Dursteler, ed., *A Companion to Venetian History, 1400-1797* (Leiden: Brill, 2013), 449–85.

27. David J. Malkiel, "The Ghetto Republic," in Davis and Ravid, eds., *The Jews of Early Modern Venice*, 130.

28. Ibid., 125.

29. Ravid, "The Venetian Government and the Jews," 20.

30. Malkiel, "The Ghetto Republic," 129.

31. *Discorso circa il stato de gl'hebrei et in particolar dimoranti nell'inclita città di*

Ventia (1638). There is an obscure English translation: Lester Walter Roubey, "The Discorso Circa Il Stato Degli Hebrei of the Italian Rabbi Simeone (Simha ben Isaac) Luzzatto with an Introduction on the Life and Works of the Author" (Master of Hebrew Letters thesis, Hebrew Union College, 1947). A different translator published excerpts in *Commentary*: 3 (1947): 371–77, 474–78; 13 (1952): 589–93. For the tract, see Benjamin C. I. Ravid, *Economics and Toleration in Seventeenth-Century Venice: The Background and Context of the Discorso of Simone Luzzatto* (Jerusalem: American Academy for Jewish Research, 1978); Jonathan Karp, *The Politics of Jewish Commerce: Economic Thought and Emancipation in Europe, 1638–1848* (New York: Cambridge University Press, 2008), 21–27.

32. Francesca Trivellato, *The Familiarity of Strangers: The Sephardic Diaspora, Livorno, and Cross-Cultural Trade in the Early Modern Period* (New Haven: Yale University Press, 2009), 127; Samuel Fettah, "Livourne: Cité du Prince, cité marchande (XIVe–XIXe)," in Jean Boutier, Sandro Landi, and Olivier Rouchon, *Florence et la Toscane: XIVe–XIXe siècles: Les dynamiques d'un État italien* (Rennes: Presses Universitaires de Rennes, 2004), 179–80. Fettah emphasizes Livorno as a model, fortified port city that, superseding the medieval city-state, served the Medici dynasty. See also 182.

33. Dubin, "Subjects into Citizens," 60; Trivellato, *The Familiarity of Strangers*, 79.

34. Dubin, "Subjects into Citizens," 60–61.

35. Ibid., 62–63.

36. Jean Pierre Filippini, "Les Nations à Livourne (XVIIe–XVIIIe siècles)," in Simonetta Cavaciocchi, ed., *I Porti Come Impresa Economica* (Prato: Le Monnier, 1988), 584–55; Lucia Frattarelli Fischer, "Urban Forms of Jewish Settlement in Tuscan Cities (Florence, Pisa, Leghorn) during the 17th Century," in Uziel O. Schmelz and Sergio DellaPergalo, eds., *Papers in Jewish Demography 1989*, Jewish Population Studies no. 25 (Jerusalem: World Union of Jewish Studies, 1993), 56. Livorno's Jewish population was: 1601: 124; 1642: 1,145; 1738: 3,476; 1833: 4,948.

37. Dubin, "Subjects into Citizens," 60–61; Bernard D. Cooperman, "Amsterdam from an International Perspective: Tolerance and Kehillah in the Portuguese Diaspora," in Yosef Kaplan, ed., *The Dutch Intersection: The Jews and the Netherlands in Modern History* (Leiden: Brill, 2008), 18.

38. Trivellato, *The Familiarity of Strangers*, 76.

39. Ibid., 93.

40. Ibid., 80–82.

41. Quotation from "La Livornina," Article 29. I am grateful to Professor Bernard Cooperman for permitting me to use his translation. Ravid, "A Tale of Three Cities and Their *Raison d'État*," 138–62.

42. Kenneth Stow, *Catholic Thought and Papal Jewry Policy, 1555–1593* (New York: Jewish Theological Seminary, 1976).

43. Fischer, "Urban Forms of Jewish Settlement in Tuscan Cities," 49–56, quotation at 56.

44. Cecil Roth, *The History of the Jews of Italy* (Philadelphia: Jewish Publication Society, 1946), 309.

45. Ibid., 306.

46. Ravid, "Cum Nimis Absurdum and the Ancona Auto-da-Fé Revisited," 95; Israel, *European Jewry in the Age of Mercantilism*, 46–47.

47. Roth, *The History of the Jews of Italy*, 314.

48. Ibid., 322.

49. Israel, *Diasporas within a Diaspora*, 93: "the Ponentine-Levantine milieu created in Venice in the 1570s and 1580s was pivotal in transforming the north-west European Portuguese New Christian diaspora into an organized Sephardic Jewish trans-Atlantic as

well as trans-European and trans-Near Eastern network." For the western Sephardi diaspora, see Yosef Kaplan, *Ha-Pezura ha-Sefardit ha-Maaravit* (Tel Aviv: Ministry of Defense, 1994).

50. The spokesman was André Govea, professor at the College of Guyenne. See Frances Malino, *The Sephardic Jews of Bordeaux: Assimilation and Emancipation in Revolutionary and Napoleonic France* (University: University of Alabama Press, 1978), 2.

51. Gérard Nahon, "From New Christians to the Portuguese Jewish Nation in France," in Haim Beinart, ed., *Moreshet Sepharad: The Sephardi Legacy*, 2 vols. (Jerusalem: Magnes Press, 1992), 2:337–38.

52. Ibid., 2:338.

53. The Jews were one "nation" alongside the German, Dutch, Flemish, Irish, English, Swiss, and Russian "nations," who had syndics and consuls. See Genevieve Charpentier, *Les relations économiques entre Bordeaux et les Antilles au XVIIIe siècle* (Bordeaux: Bière, 1937), 22–23. See also Malino, *The Sephardic Jews of Bordeaux*, 1–26. For the relevant documents, see Gérard Nahon, ed., *Les "Nations" Juives Portugaises du Sud-Ouest de la France (1684–1791): Documents* (Paris: Fundação Calouste Gulbenkian, 1981), 3–44. For one prominent family, see Richard Menkis, "Patriarchs and Patricians: The Gradis Family of Eighteenth-Century Bordeaux," in Frances Malino and David Sorkin, eds., *Profiles in Diversity: Jews in a Changing Europe, 1750–1870* (Detroit: Wayne State University Press, 1998), 11–45.

54. Günter Böhm, "Die Sephardim in Hamburg," in Arno Herzig, ed., *Die Juden in Hamburg, 1590–1990* (Hamburg: Dölling & Galitz, 1991), 23. The expert opinion was called a "theologisches Gutachten."

55. Hermann Kellenbenz, *Sephardim an der unteren Elbe: Ihre Wirtschaftliche und Politische Bedeutung vom Ende des 16. bis zum Beginn des 18. Jahrhunderts* (Wiesbaden: Steiner, 1958), 99–101, quotation at 31.

56. The exception was for Rodrigo de Castro. See Joachim Whaley, *Religious Toleration and Social Change in Hamburg* (Cambridge: Cambridge University Press, 1985), 75; Kellenbenz, *Sephardim an der unteren Elbe*, 273–75.

57. Kellenbenz, *Sephardim an der unteren Elbe*, 45–50; Whaley, *Religious Toleration and Social Change in Hamburg*, 77.

58. Kellenbenz, *Sephardim an der unteren Elbe*, 49; Böhm, "Die Sephardim in Hamburg," 25.

59. Böhm, "Die Sephardim in Hamburg," 32.

60. Ibid.

61. Ibid., 24, 26.

62. Benjamin Ravid pointed to this difference between Venice and Amsterdam in "'How Profitable the Nation of the Jewes Are': The *Humble Addresses* of Menasseh ben Israel and the *Discorso* of Simone Luzzatto," in Jehuda Reinharz and Daniel Swetschinski, eds., *Mystics, Philosophers and Politicians: Essays in Jewish Intellectual History in Honor of Alexander Altmann* (Durham: Duke University Press, 1982), 170.

63. Krinsky, *Synagogues of Europe*, 391–94. The Beth-Israel Portuguese Synagogue (1639), though in a prominent public space, had the appearance of an opulent mansion. The Ashkenazic Grote Sjoel (1670–71) was a public building in a planned city square that was also unmistakably ecclesiastical. See Barry Stiefel, "The Architectural Origins of the Great Early Modern Urban Synagogue," *Leo Baeck Institute Yearbook* 56 (2011): 119–27.

64. Daniel M. Swetschinski, *Reluctant Cosmopolitans: The Portuguese Jews of Seventeenth-Century Amsterdam* (London: Littman Library, 2000), 187.

65. Yosef Kaplan, "The Sephardim in North-Western Europe and the New World," in Haim Beinart, ed., *Moreshet Sepharad: The Sephardi Legacy*, 2 vols. (Jerusalem: Magnes,

1992), 2:249. Amsterdam refused to issue charters of privilege to the various merchant groups that applied for them: "the urban government made every effort to secure the freedom of individual merchants to trade in the products and markets of their choice. A separate legal status clearly did not fit this policy. Instead, the city magistrate determined that the person and goods of all merchants should be treated equally in equal circumstances." See Oscar Gelderblom, *Cities of Commerce: The Institutional Foundations of International Trade in the Low Countries, 1250–1650* (Princeton: Princeton University Press, 2013), 40. Cities that issued charters were: Alkmaar, 1604; Haarlem, 1605; Rotterdam, 1610.

66. Cooperman, "Amsterdam from an International Perspective," 1–18; Miriam Bodian, *Hebrews of the Portuguese Nation: Conversos and Community in Early Modern Amsterdam* (Bloomington: Indiana University Press, 1997), 60–61; Arent H. Huussen, "The Legal Position of the Jews in the Dutch Republic c. 1590–1796," in Jonathan Israel and Reinier Salverda, eds., *Dutch Jewry: Its History and Secular Culture (1500–2000)* (Leiden: Brill, 2002), 25–41; Swetschinski, *Reluctant Cosmopolitans*, 8–25.

67. Swetschinski, *Reluctant Cosmopolitans*, 13.

68. Ibid., 24–25.

69. Ibid., 25. On Catholics in Amsterdam, see Benjamin J. Kaplan, *Divided by Faith: Religious Conflict and the Practice of Toleration in Early Modern Europe* (Cambridge, MA: Harvard University Press, 2007), 172–74, 180–82.

70. Gershom Scholem argued that the freer and more secure the legal status of the community, the less inhibited the response to Sabbateanism. Consequently, Jews in Amsterdam of all classes, including the rabbis, became enthusiastic adherents. See *Sabbatai Sevi: The Mystical Messiah* (Princeton: Princeton University Press, 1973), 519.

71. Swetschinski, *Reluctant Cosmopolitans*, 221.

72. Ibid., 197.

73. Ibid., 18.

74. Ibid., 196.

75. Ibid., 20.

76. Ibid., 48.

77. Peter van Rooden, "Jews and Religious Toleration in the Dutch Republic," in R. Po-Chia Hsia and H. F. K. van Nierop, eds., *Calvinism and Religious Toleration in the Dutch Golden Age* (Cambridge: Cambridge University Press, 2002), 132–47.

78. Swetschinski, *Reluctant Cosmopolitans*, 182–85.

79. Jonathan Israel, "Religious Toleration in Dutch Brazil (1624–1654)," in Israel and Stuart B. Schwartz, *The Expansion of Tolerance: Religion in Dutch Brazil (1624–1654)* (Amsterdam: Amsterdam University Press, 2007), 14–18.

80. Yosef Hayim Yerushalmi, "Between Amsterdam and New Amsterdam: The Place of Curaçao and the Caribbean in Early Modern Jewish History," *American Jewish History* 2 (1982): 182–83.

81. "General Privilege," August 17, 1665. See Jacob R. Marcus and Stanley F. Chyet, eds., *Historical Essay on the Colony of Surinam, 1788* (Cincinnati: American Jewish Archives, 1974), 188–89.

82. Yerushalmi, "Between Amsterdam and New Amsterdam," 187–88.

83. Jonathan Israel, *The Dutch Republic: Its Rise, Greatness and Fall, 1477–1806* (Oxford: Oxford University Press, 1995), 658.

84. Israel, *Diasporas within a Diaspora*, 392–96; Lucien Wolf, "The First Stage of Anglo-Jewish Emancipation," in Cecil Roth, ed., *Essays in Jewish History* (London: Jewish Historical Society, 1934), 130. The number of immigrants swelled because of the loss of Brazil, the Venetian war with the Ottomans over Crete, and the Spanish Crown's suspension of payments on debts (1647).

85. *Menasseh ben Israel's Mission to Oliver Cromwell: Being a reprint of the Pamphlets published by Menasseh ben Israel to promote the Re-admission of the Jew to England, 1649–1656*, ed. Lucien Wolf (London: Macmillan, 1901). For his mission, see Jonathan Israel, "Menasseh ben Israel and the Dutch Sephardi," in *Diasporas within a Diaspora*, 385–414. Menasseh derived his entire argument for commerce from Luzzatto. See Ravid, "'How Profitable the Nation of the Jewes Are,'" 159–80.

86. David S. Katz, *The Jews in the History of England, 1485–1850* (Oxford: Oxford University Press, 1994), 119–40.

87. "Denizen" was an inferior status: he was subject to "alien duties" and did not have secure property rights. He was not permitted to own or will freehold real estate. At death his property was liable to Crown confiscation (escheat). See J. M. Ross, "Naturalisation of the Jews in England," *Transactions of the Jewish Historical Society of England* 24 (1975): 59–61.

88. Katz, *The Jews in the History of England*, 242; Todd Endelman, *The Jews of Georgian England, 1714–1830: Tradition and Change in a Liberal Society* (Philadelphia: Jewish Publication Society, 1979), 20–25; Lionel Kochan, *The Making of Western Jewry, 1600–1819* (Houndmills, Basingstoke: Palgrave Macmillan, 2004), 78. Issuing a charter to Jewish merchants would have been out of keeping with general policy since "by 1600 all concessions to foreign merchants had been abolished." See Oliver C. Cox, *The Foundations of Capitalism* (New York: Philosophical Library, 1959), 291. For the suppression since 1550 of foreign merchants in support of the growing coalition of merchants and government, which led to "government-backed monopolies" and a "revolution in royal finances," see Robert Brenner, *Merchants and Revolution: Commercial Change, Political Conflict, and London's Overseas Traders, 1550–1653* (Princeton: Princeton University Press, 1993), 53–57.

89. Todd Endelman, *The Jews of Britain, 1656–2000* (Berkeley: University of California Press, 2002), 36.

90. Endelman, *Jews of Georgian England*, 23.

91. Wolf, "The First Stage of Anglo-Jewish Emancipation," 133–35.

92. Kochan, *The Making of Western Jewry*, 83.

93. Katz, *The Jews in the History of England*, 188.

94. H. S. Q. Henriques, *The Jews and the English Law* (London: J. Jacobs, 1908), 173.

95. Kochan, *The Making of Western Jewry*, 80.

96. Ibid., 84.

97. Krinsky, *Synagogues of Europe*, 413; Sharman Kadish, *The Synagogues of Britain and Ireland* (New Haven: Yale University Press, 2011), 5–6.

98. Cecil Roth, *The Great Synagogue, London, 1690–1940* (London: E. Goldston, 1950), 52. The quotation is from D'Blossiers Tovey, *Anglia Judaica* (1738).

99. Yerushalmi, "Between Amsterdam and New Amsterdam," 188. An edited version of the "Act of Suriname (August 17, 1665)" is in Paul Mendes-Flohr and Jehuda Reinharz, *The Jew in the Modern World: A Documentary History*, 3rd ed. (New York: Oxford University Press, 2011), 16–17.

100. Jacob Rader Marcus, *The Colonial American Jew, 1492–1776*, 3 vols. (Detroit: Wayne State University Press, 1970), 1:308, 404–6.

101. Ibid., 1:138–39.

Chapter Two. Burgher Estate

1. Antonio Maria Gratiani, *La vie du cardinal Jean-François Commendon*, trans. Fléchier (Paris, 1614), quoted in Gershon Hundert, *The Jews in Poland-Lithuania in the Eighteenth Century: A Genealogy of Modernity* (Berkeley: University of California Press, 2004), 7.

2. W. Coxe, *Travels into Poland, Sweden and Denmark*, 5 vols. (Dublin, 1784), 3:163, cited in Jacob Goldberg, "The Privileges Granted to the Jewish Communities of the Polish Commonwealth as a Stabilizing Factor in Jewish Support," in Chimen Abramsky, Maciej Jachimczyk, and Antony Polonsky, eds., *The Jews in Poland* (Oxford: Blackwell, 1986), 54.

3. Antony Polonsky, *The Jews in Poland and Russia*, 3 vols. (Oxford: Littman Library, 2010–12), 1:14.

4. For the Austrian charter of 1244, see Jacob Rader Marcus, *The Jew in the Medieval World: A Source Book, 315–1791*, 2nd ed. (Cincinnati: Hebrew Union College Press, 1990), 28–33.

5. Polonsky, *The Jews in Poland and Russia*, 1:42–43.

6. Gershon Hundert, "The Implications of Jewish Economic Activities for Christian-Jewish Relations in the Polish Commonwealth," in Abramsky, Jachimczyk, and Polonsky, eds., *The Jews in Poland*, 57.

7. Polonsky, *The Jews in Poland and Russia*, 1:45–46.

8. Gershon Hundert, "On the Jewish Community in Poland during the Seventeenth Century: Some Comparative Perspectives," *Revue des Études juives* 142 (1983): 362.

9. Ibid.; Gershon Hundert, *The Jews in a Polish Private Town: The Case of Opatów in the Eighteenth Century* (Baltimore: Johns Hopkins University Press, 1992), 68.

10. Hundert, "On the Jewish Community in Poland during the Seventeenth Century," 363–70.

11. A useful survey is Maria Bogucka, "The Jews in the Polish Cities in the 16th–18th Centuries," in Adam Teller, ed., *Studies in the History of the Jews of Old Poland. Scripta Hierosolymitana* 38 (1998): 51–57.

12. Hundert, *The Jews in Poland-Lithuania in the Eighteenth Century*, 29.

13. Goldberg, "The Privileges Granted to the Jewish Communities of the Polish Commonwealth," 33.

14. Ibid., 34–35.

15. Shmuel Ettinger, "The Legal and Social Status of the Jews of Ukraine from the Fifteenth Century to the Cossack Uprising of 1648," *Journal of Ukrainian Studies* 17, no. 1–2 (Summer/Winter 1992): 111–15.

16. Polonsky, *The Jews in Poland and Russia*, 1:96.

17. Shmuel Ettinger, "Jewish Participation in the Settlement of the Ukraine in the Sixteenth and Seventeenth Centuries," in Peter J. Potichnyj and Howard Aster, eds., *Ukrainian-Jewish Relations in Historical Perspective* (Edmonton: Canadian Institute of Ukrainian Studies, University of Alberta, 1988), 27.

18. M. J. Rosman, *The Lords' Jews: Magnate-Jewish Relations in the Polish-Lithuanian Commonwealth during the Eighteenth Century* (Cambridge, MA: Harvard University Press, 1990), 37.

19. The Jews' alliance with the nobles also made them a "token of the power conflict between the Church and the nobles." The Church used the Jews as a symbol to attack the nobles and other groups that resisted its authority. See Magda Teter, *Jews and Heretics in Catholic Poland: A Beleaguered Church in the Post-Reformation Era* (New York: Cambridge University Press, 2006), 80.

20. Rosman, *The Lords' Jews*, 10.

21. Polonsky, *The Jews in Poland and Russia*, 1:100–101.

22. Ibid., 1:101–13, quotation at 110. For the example of the Radziwiłł estates in the period 1689–1764, see Adam Teller, *Kesef, Koah ve-Hashpa'ah: Ha-Yehudim be'Ahuzot Beit Radziwiłł be-Lita be-Meah ha-YH* (Jerusalem: Merkaz Zalman Shazar, 2006), 182–240.

23. Andrzej Wyrobisz, "Power and Towns in the Polish Gentry Commonwealth: The

Polish-Lithuanian State in the Sixteenth and Seventeenth Centuries," in Charles Tilly and Wim P. Blockman, eds., *Cities and the Rise of States in Europe A.D. 1000 to 1800* (Boulder, CO: Westview, 1994), 152. For the eighteenth century Daniel Stone argued that "private cities comprised 66 percent of all cities in the Polish provinces (88 percent in Ukrainian provinces)." See *The Polish-Lithuanian State, 1386–1795* (Seattle: University of Washington Press, 2001), 298.

24. Hundert, *The Jews in a Polish Private Town*, 47.

25. Ibid., 47–68.

26. Nathan Notte Hannover, a contemporary, analyzed the Cossack leader Bogdan Chmielnicki's massacres in 1648–49. Hannover demonstrated that the colonization of the Ukraine rested on the double oppression of the Ukrainian peasants: the Polish nobility exploited their labor while Catholic priests abused their Greek Orthodox belief. By serving as tax farmers and estate managers for the nobility, Jews were a public face of oppression. The rebels consequently targeted Jews, Polish nobles, and Catholic priests. See *Sefer Yavein Metsulah* (Tel Aviv: HaKibbutz Ha-Meuchad, 1966); *Abyss of Despair (Yeven Metzulah): The Famous 17th Century Chronicle Depicting Jewish Life in Russia and Poland during the Chmielnicki Massacres of 1648–1649*, trans. Abraham J. Mesch (New Brunswick, NJ: Transaction Publishers, 1983). For Hannover as a source of history, see Gershon Bacon, " 'The House of Hannover': *Gezeirot Tah* in Modern Jewish Historical Writing," *Jewish History* 17 (2003): 179–206. For a historical and literary analysis, see Adam Teller, "Jewish Literary Responses to the Events of 1648–49 and the Creation of a Polish-Jewish Consciousness," *Culture Front* (2008): 17–45.

27. Ettinger, "Jewish Participation in the Settlement of the Ukraine in the Sixteenth and Seventeenth Centuries," 26.

28. Polonsky, *The Jews in Poland and Russia*, 1:35; Goldberg, "The Privileges Granted to the Jewish Communities of the Polish Commonwealth," 35; Ettinger, "The Legal and Social Status of the Jews of Ukraine," 119–22.

29. Goldberg, "The Privileges Granted to the Jewish Communities of the Polish Commonwealth," 33–36, 43–44; Hundert, *The Jews in Poland-Lithuania in the Eighteenth Century*, 47.

30. Adam Teller, "Telling the Difference: Some Comparative Perspectives on the Jews' Legal Status in the Polish-Lithuanian Commonwealth and the Holy Roman Empire," *Polin* 22 (2009): 109–41; Hundert, *The Jews in a Polish Private Town*, 135; Rosman, *The Lords' Jews*, 74.

31. Hundert, *The Jews in a Polish Private Town*, xiv.

32. Ibid., 17–18.

33. Ibid., 135.

34. Jacob Goldberg, *Jewish Privileges in the Polish Commonwealth: Charters of Rights Granted to Jewish Communities in Poland-Lithuania in the Sixteenth to Eighteenth Centuries*, 2 vols. (Jerusalem: Israel Academy of Sciences and Humanities, 1985–2001), 2:66–68, trans. Adam Teller in "Early Modern Workshop: Jewish History Resources," http://www.earlymodern.org/workshops/2004/teller/text02/intro.php.

35. Carol Herselle Krinsky, *Synagogues of Europe: Architecture, History, Meaning*, 2nd ed. (New York: Dover, 1996), 55; Rachel Wischnitzer, *The Architecture of the European Synagogue* (Philadelphia: Jewish Publication Society, 1964), xxviii, 110; Barry Stiefel, "The Architectural Origins of the Great Early Modern Urban Synagogue," *Leo Baeck Institute Yearbook* 56 (2011): 113–19.

36. The first is Kazimierz (1537). Others are Brest-Litovsk (1657), Premyśl (early seventeenth century), Rzeszów (1762), and Lwow (1772). See Maria Piechotka, "Architecture of Synagogues in the Lands of the Former Polish-Lithuanian Commonwealth, 15th–Early 19th

Century," in Jerzy Malinowski, Renata Piatkowska, and Tamara Sztyma-Knasiecka, *Jewish Artists and Central-Eastern Europe* (Warsaw: DIG, 2010), 34–35.

37. Rosman, *The Lords' Jews*, 194.

38. Hundert, *The Jews in Poland-Lithuania in the Eighteenth Century*, 108–9; Adam Teller, "The Legal Status of the Jews on the Magnate Estates of Poland-Lithuania in the Eighteenth Century," *Gal-ed* 15–16 (1997): 56–60; Teller, "Radziwill, Rabinowicz and the Rabbi of Swierz: The Magnates' Attitude towards Jewish Regional Autonomy in 18th Century Poland-Lithuania," in Teller, ed., *Studies in the History of the Jews in Old Poland: In Honor of Jacob Goldberg* (Jerusalem: Magnes Press, 1998), 246–76.

39. Hundert, "On the Jewish Community in Poland during the Seventeenth Century," 354.

40. François Guesnet, "Agreements between Neighbors: The 'Ugody' as a Source on Jewish-Christian Relations in Early Modern Poland," *Jewish History* 24 (2010): 260–62.

41. Ettinger, "The Legal and Social Status of the Jews of Ukraine," 127–28.

42. Guesnet, "Agreements between Neighbors," 261.

43. Hundert, *The Jews in Poland-Lithuania in the Eighteenth Century*, 25, 45.

44. For the Radziwiłł estates, see Teller, *Kesef, Koah ve-Hashpa'ah*, 43–54.

45. Jacob Goldberg, "*De Non Tolerandis Judaeis*: On the Introduction of the Anti-Jewish Laws into Polish Towns and the Struggle against Them," in Shmuel Yevin, ed., *Studies in Jewish History Presented to Professor Raphael Mahler on His Seventy-Fifth Birthday* (Merhavia, Israel: Sifriyat Po'alim, 1974), 39–52.

46. Ettinger, "The Legal and Social Status of the Jews of Ukraine," 129–30.

47. Goldberg, "*De Non Tolerandis Judaeis*," 42–52.

Chapter Three. Juridical Equality

1. Joachim Whaley, *Germany and the Holy Roman Empire*, 2 vols. (Oxford: Oxford University Press, 2012), 1:2; Whaley describes these two functions as a "defensive alliance of the Estates against external aggression" and a "legal system for the maintenance of public peace." Cf. R. Po-chia Hsia, "Between State and Community: Religious and Ethnic Minorities in Early Modern Germany," in Andrew C. Fix and Susan C. Karant-Nunn, eds., *Germania Illustrata: Essays on Early Modern Germany Presented to Gerald Strauss*, Sixteenth Century Essays and Studies, 18 (Kirksville, MO: Sixteenth Century Journal Publishers, 1992), 180.

2. Whaley, *Germany and the Holy Roman Empire*, 1:38–39.

3. Ibid., 1:2, 13. "Holy Roman Empire of the German Nation" first appeared in 1474 and was formalized in 1512. See 1:17.

4. Mordechai Breuer, "The Jewish Middle Ages," in Michael A. Meyer, ed., *German-Jewish History in Modern Times*, 4 vols. (New York: Columbia University Press, 1996–98), 1:7–14, 41.

5. J. F. Battenberg, "Des Kaisers Kammerknechte: Gedanken zur rechtlich-sozialen Situation der Juden in Spätmittelalter und früher Neuzeit," *Historische Zeitschrift* 245, no. 3 (1987): 559.

6. Ibid., 568–69.

7. Ibid., 571; Breuer, "The Jewish Middle Ages," 41, 44; Adam Teller, "Telling the Difference: Some Comparative Perspectives on the Jews' Legal Status in the Polish-Lithuanian Commonwealth and the Holy Roman Empire," *Polin* 22 (2009): 111–13; Wilhelm Güde, *Die rechtliche Stellung der Juden in den Schriften deutscher Juristen des 16. und 17. Jahrhunderts* (Sigmaringen: Thorbecke, 1981), 44–47.

8. Battenberg, "Des Kaisers Kammerknechte," 557, 569; J. F. Battenberg, "Rechtliche

Rahmenbegingungen jüdischer Existenz in der Frühneuzeit zwischen Reich und Territorium," in *Judengemeinden in Schwaben im Kontext des alten Reiches* (Berlin: Akademie Verlag, 1994), 69–72.

9. Jacob Rader Marcus, *The Jew in the Medieval World: A Source Book, 315–1791*, 3rd ed. (Cincinnati: Hebrew Union College Press, 1990), 28–33.

10. Battenberg, "Des Kaisers Kammerknechte," 573; Sabine Frey, *Rechtsschutz der Juden gegen Ausweisungen im 16. Jahrhundert* (Frankfurt am Main: P. Lang, 1983), 19–21. For letters of protection (*Schutzbriefe*) issued to individual Jews in Kleve in the fourteenth and fifteenth centuries, see Fritz Baer, *Das Protokollbuch der Landjudenschaft des Herzogtums Kleve* (Berlin, 1922), 6–7. For "Schutz- und Schirmbriefen" in Hanau, see Ludwig Rosenthal, *Zur Geschichte der Juden im Gebiet der ehemaligen Grafschaft Hanau*, Veröffentlichungen des Hanauer Geschichtsvereins, vol. 19 (Hanau, 1963), 26–27.

11. Breuer, "The Jewish Middle Ages," 1:51–53. For rural dispersion as a cumulative multigenerational process, see J. Friedrich Battenberg, "Aus der Stadt auf das Land? Zur Vertreibung und Neuansiedlung der Juden im Heiligen Römischen Reich," in Monika Richarz and Reinhard Rürup, eds., *Jüdisches Leben auf dem Land: Studien zur deutsch-jüdischen Geschichte* (Tübingen: Mohr Siebeck, 1997), 9–35. For another assessment, see Michael Toch, "Aspects of Stratification of Early Modern Jewry: Population History and Village Jews," in R. Po-chia Hsia and Hartmut Lehman, eds., *In and Out of the Ghetto: Jewish-Gentile Relations in Late Medieval and Early Modern Germany* (Cambridge: Cambridge University Press, 1995), 77–89.

12. Jonathan Israel, *European Jewry in the Age of Mercantilism, 1550–1750* (Oxford: Clarendon, 1989), 8–14.

13. Whaley, *Germany and the Holy Roman Empire*, 1:1.

14. Ibid., 1:32–33; Gerhard Oestreich, *Verfassungsgeschichte vom Ende des Mittelalters bis zum Ende des alten Reichs* (Munich: DTV, 1970), 21–24; Stephan Wendehorst, "Imperial Spaces as Jewish Spaces: The Holy Roman Empire, the Emperor and the Jews in the Early Modern Period. Some Preliminary Observations," *Simon Dubnow Institute Yearbook* 2 (2003): 442–53.

15. Augsburg (1500) established six administrative regional associations (*Kreise*) that became a crucial infrastructure, organizing military contingents and taxation. The implications of these for the Jews of the HRE are not clear.

16. Frey, *Rechtsschutz der Juden gegen Ausweisungen im 16. Jahrhundert*; Battenberg, "Rechtliche Rahmenbegingungen jüdischer Existenz in der Frühneuzeit zwischen Reich und Territorium," 66–69; Güde, *Die rechtliche Stellung*, 47–67. Whether the Jews were citizens played a major role in the debate over the treatment of Hebrew books between Johannes Reuchlin and Jacob Hoogstraeten. See J. Friedrich Battenberg, "Juden als 'Bürger' des Heiligen Römischen Reichs im 16. Jahrhundert: Zu einem Paradigmenwechsel im 'Judenrecht' in der Reformationszeit," in Rold Decot and Matthieu Arnold, eds., *Christen und Juden im Reformationszeitalter* (Mainz: von Zabern, 2006), 175–97 and Battenberg, "Von der Kammerknechtschaft zum Judenregal: Reflexionen zur Rechtsstellung der Judenschaft im Heiligen Römischen Reich am Beispiel Johannes Reuchlins," in Sabine Hödl, Peter Rauscher, Barbara Staudinger, and Michael Toch, eds., *Hofjuden und Landjuden: Jüdisches Leben in der Frühen Neuzeit* (Berlin: Philo, 2004), 65–90.

17. Johannes Reuchlin, *Recommendation Whether to Confiscate, Destroy and Burn All Jewish Books*, ed. and trans. P. Wortsman (New York: Paulist Press, 2000), 36–37.

18. Stefan Ehrenpreis, "Legal Spaces for Jews as Subjects of the Holy Roman Empire," *Simon Dubnow Institute Yearbook* 2 (2003): 480–85.

19. Frey, *Rechtsschutz der Juden gegen Ausweisungen im 16. Jahrhundert*. Seven of the nine cases brought before the Imperial Court Chamber were successful (133). To which

Court Jews turned depended on the legal status of the entity that was trying to expel them (125). Few cases were brought by individuals (135–36). For a useful overview, see R. Po-chia Hsia, "The Jews and the Emperors," in Charles Ingrao, ed., *State and Society in Early Modern Austria* (West Lafayette, IN: Purdue University Press, 1994), 71–80. For Jewish participation in the politics of imperial cities, especially multiconfessional ones under Lutheran oligarchies, see Christopher B. Friedrichs, "Jews in the Imperial Cities: A Political Perspective," in Hsia and Lehman, eds., *In and Out of the Ghetto*, 275–88.

20. Güde, *Die rechtliche Stellung*, 64–65. The suit concerned the exclusion of Jews from fairs.

21. Wendehorst, "Imperial Spaces as Jewish Spaces," 470.

22. J. Friedrich Battenberg argues that these laws, which competed with and complemented one another, were "supplementary" to the larger legal system rather than a separate system. See "Rechtliche Rahmenbegingungen jüdischer Existenz in der Frühneuzeit zwischen Reich und Territorium," 53–56.

23. Breuer, "The Jewish Middle Ages," 1:65.

24. Israel, *European Jewry in the Age of Mercantilism*, 39–40.

25. Hillel Kieval, *Languages of Community: The Jewish Experience in the Czech Lands* (Berkeley: University of California Press, 2000), 13–14, 18–19, 24–25; Anna M. Drabek, "Das Judentum der böhmischen Länder vor der Emanzipation," in *Der österreichische Staat und die Juden vom Zeitalter des Absolutismus bis zum Ende der Monarchie*, Studia Judaica Austriaca, vol. 10 (Eisenstadt: Roetzer, 1984) 7–9.

26. Rotraud Ries, "German Territorial Princes and the Jews," in Hsia and Lehman, eds., *In and Out of the Ghetto*, 236.

27. Breuer, "The Jewish Middle Ages," 1:66.

28. Frey, *Rechtsschutz der Juden gegen Ausweisungen im 16. Jahrhundert*, 26. The power of the territorial states remained limited in the seventeenth century since they largely relied upon the old corporate order to enforce policy. Corporate entities resisted change by defending their privileges in the imperial courts. Moreover, the states' "all-pervasive fiscalism," the urgent need to raise revenues to finance armies and courts, precluded major economic reforms. Only in the eighteenth century did the states succeed in creating a limited bureaucracy separate from the estates and abolishing corporate privileges that were concomitantly being weakened by an increasingly monetized economy. See Richard Gawthrop, "The Social Role of Seventeenth-Century German Territorial States," in Fix and Karant-Nunn, eds., *Germania Illustrata*, 243–58.

29. V. Press understands the synod's failure as marking the "conclusion of the middle ages for the Jews of the Empire." See "Kaiser Rudolf II und der Zusammenschluß der deutschen Judenheit: Die sogenannte Frankfurter Rabbinerverschwörung von 1603 und ihre Folgen," in A. Haverkamp, ed., *Zur Geschichte der Juden im Deutschland des späten Mittelalters und frühen Neuzeit* (Stuttgart: Hiersemann, 1981), 243–93; Teller, "Telling the Difference," 125–26. For the internal conflicts that perhaps initiated and drove the controversy, see Birgit E. Klein, "The 1603 Assembly in Frankfurt: Prehistory, Ordinances, Effects," *Jewish Culture and History* 10, no. 2–3 (Autumn/Winter 2008): 111–24. For a translation of the synod's proceedings, see Louis Finkelstein, *Jewish Self-Government in the Middle Ages* (New York: Jewish Theological Seminary, 1924), 257–64.

30. While the *Landjudenschaften* had roots reaching back to the fifteenth century, they developed from the second half of the sixteenth century and the early seventeenth century. See Daniel Cohen, "Die Landjudenschaften der brandenburgisch-preußischen Statten im 17. Und 18. Jahrhundert; Ihre Beziehungen untereinander aufgrund neuerschlossener jüdischer Quellen," in P. Baumgart, ed., *Ständetum und Staatsbildung in Brandenburg-Preußen* (1983): 210–11; and Cohen, "Die Entwicklung der Landesrabbinate in den

deutschen Territorien bis zur Emanzipation," in Haverkamp, ed., *Zur Geschichte der Juden im Deutschland des späten Mittelalters und frühen Neuzeit*, 221–42. For the vicissitudes of Jewish life in these areas, and especially educational disarray, see Robert Liberles, "On the Threshold of Modernity: 1618–1780," in Marion A. Kaplan, ed., *Jewish Daily Life in Germany, 1618–1945* (New York: Oxford University Press, 2005), 47, 52, 73.

31. Battenberg, "Rechtliche Rahmenbegingungen jüdischer Existenz in der Frühneuzeit zwischen Reich und Territorium," 72–76.

32. Jonathan Israel, "Central European Jewry during the Thirty Years' War," *Central European History* 16 (1983): 3–30; Breuer, "The Jewish Middle Ages," 1:65; Teller, "Telling the Difference." For the growth of Jewish settlement in Hanau under Philipp Ludwig II (1595–1612), see Rosenthal, *Zur Geschichte der Juden im Gebiet der ehemaligen Grafschaft Hanau*, 49–53.

33. Liberles, "On the Threshold of Modernity," 54; Mordechai Breuer, "The Early Modern Period," in Michael A. Meyer, ed., *German-Jewish History in Modern Times*, 4 vols. (New York: Columbia University Press, 1996), 1:133.

34. Isidore Kracauer, *Geschichte der Juden in Frankfurt a.M. (1150–1824)*, 2 vols. (Frankfurt: Kommission bei Kauffmann, 1925–27), 2:108–13; Gerald Lyman Soliday, *A Community in Conflict: Frankfurt Society in the Seventeenth and Early Eighteenth Centuries* (Hanover, NH: Brandeis University Press, 1974), 180–81.

35. Baer, *Das Protokollbuch der Landjudenschaft des Herzogtums Kleve*, 67.

36. Michael Graetz, "Court Jews in Economics and Politics," in Vivian B. Mann and Richard I. Cohen, eds., *From Court Jews to the Rothschilds: Art, Patronage, and Power, 1600–1800* (Munich: Prestel, 1996), 35–36. For an example of improved legal status, see Mayer Reiss in Berlin (1724), who was "equal in rank with Christian merchants." See also Bernd Schedlitz, *Leffmann Behrens: Untersuchungen zum Hofjudentum im Zeitalter des Absolutismus* (Hildesheim: Lax, 1984).

37. For Moses Wulff in Dessau, see Ernst Walter, *Die Rechtstellung der israelitischen Kultusgemeinden in Anhalt* (Dessau: R. Lehmann, 1934), 3–10; for Breslau, see Bernhard Brilling, *Geschichte der Juden in Breslau von 1454–1702* (Stuttgart: Kohlhammer, 1960), 72; for Kleve, see Baer, *Das Protokollbuch der Landjudenschaft des Herzogtums Kleve*, 19–21; for Vienna, see the "Schutz und Schirm" privilege issued to Abraham Brodt in 1615 reprinted in Gerson Wolf, *Geschichte der Juden in Wien (1156–1876)* (Vienna: Hölder, 1876), 260–61.

38. Baer, *Das Protokollbuch der Landjudenschaft des Herzogtums Kleve*, 19–21.

39. Ibid., 31.

40. Guido Kisch, *Rechts- und Sozialgeschichte der Juden in Halle, 1686–1730* (Berlin: de Gruyter, 1970), 129–33, 146–51. On such "collective general letters," issued after government officials had checked each person, see Breuer, "The Early Modern Period," 1:136.

41. Brilling, *Geschichte der Juden in Breslau*, 43.

42. Ibid., 12.

43. Ibid., 27.

44. Ibid., 37–41. The agents represented such areas as Prague and the Bohemian Lands, Moravia, Large Poland, and Little Poland; and such cities as Lemberg, Rzeszo, Glogau, Zülzer, Posen, and Lissa.

45. Ibid., 48–55.

46. Ibid., 72.

47. Breuer, "The Early Modern Period," 1:102.

48. Ibid., 1:145. The Great Elector, whose model was Holland, admitted Jews to stimulate commerce. In contrast, Frederick Wilhelm I and Frederick II saw the Jews as pernicious, restricted their commercial activities, and exploited them by levying additional forms

of taxation for which they were collectively responsible (*solidarische Haftung*). See Ismar Freund, *Die Emanzipation der Juden in Preußen unter besonderer Berücksichtigung des Gesetzes vom 11. März 1812*, 2 vols. (Berlin: Poppelauer, 1912), 1:7–15, 20–30.

49. Breuer, "The Early Modern Period," 1:148–49. The original admission had been limited to fifty families. Legislation of 1714, 1730, and 1750 introduced additional and increasingly complex means to restrict the number of families. See Freund, *Die Emanzipation der Juden in Preußen*, 1:16–17. For the hierarchy of five classes in Breslau, see Stefi Wenzel, *Jüdische Bürger und kommunale Selbstverwaltung in preussischen Städten, 1808–1848* (Berlin: de Gruyter, 1967), 75–76.

50. Breuer, "The Early Modern Period," 1:101, 151, 245–47; Rudolf Glanz, *Geschichte des niederen jüdischen Volkes in Deutschland: Eine Studie über historisches Gaunertum, Bettelwesen und Vagantentum* (New York: Waldon Press, 1968), 128–71; Jacob Toury, "Der Eintritt der Juden ins deutsche Bürgertum," in Hans Liebeschütz and Arnold Paucker, eds., *Das Judentum in der Deutschen Umwelt, 1800–1850* (Tübingen: Mohr, 1977), 139ff.; Baer, *Das Protokollbuch der Landjudenschaft des Herzogtums Kleve*, 65–78; Kracauer, *Geschichte der Juden in Frankfurt a.M.*, 2:31–33, 145; Karl E. Demandt, *Bevölkerungs- und Sozialgeschichte der jüdischen Gemeinde Niedenstein, 1653–1866* (Wiesbaden: Kommission für die Geschichte der Juden in Hessen, 1980), 43–45; Hermann Arnold, "Bemerkungen über die soziale Grundschicht des deutschen Judentums im 18. und frühen 19. Jahrhundert (mit besonderer Berücksichtigung der Verhältnise im Mittelrheingebiet)," in Brigitta Benzing, Otto Böcher, and Günter Mayer, eds., *Wort und Wirklichkeit: Studien zur Afrikanistik und Orientalistik* (Meisenheim am Gloan: Hain, 1976), 132–52.

51. Breuer, "The Early Modern Period," 1:153.

52. Gerhard Mühlinghaus, "Der Synagogenbau des 17. und 18. Jahrhunderts," in Hans-Peter Schwarz, ed., *Die Architektur der Synagoge* (Stuttgart: Klett-Cotta, 1988), 125–26, 137.

53. Barry Stiefel, "The Architectural Origins of the Great Early Modern Urban Synagogue," *Leo Baeck Institute Yearbook* 56 (2011): 107–12.

54. Mühlinghaus, "Der Synagogenbau des 17. und 18. Jahrhunderts," 148; Breuer, "The Early Modern Period," 1:138.

55. Liberles, "On the Threshold of Modernity," 70–71.

56. Hsia, "Between State and Community," 180.

Chapter Four. Bureaucrat, Laboratory, Emperor

1. Ole Peter Grell and Roy Porter, eds., *Toleration in Enlightenment Europe* (Cambridge: Cambridge University Press, 2000); W. R. Ward, *Christianity under the Ancien Régime, 1648–1789* (Cambridge: Cambridge University Press, 1999).

2. David Sorkin, *The Transformation of German Jewry, 1780–1840* (New York: Oxford University Press, 1987), 23–28. Jonathan Karp emphasizes Dohm's economic ideas and use of history. See *The Politics of Jewish Commerce: Economic Thought and Emancipation in Europe, 1638–1848* (Cambridge: Cambridge University Press, 2008), 94–122. For a penetrating overview, see Hans Erich Bödeker, " 'Aber ich strebe nach einer weitren Sphäre als bloß litterarischer Thätigkeit'; Intentionen, Haltungen und Wirkungsfelder Christian Wilhelm von Dohm," *Zeitschrift für Religions- und Geistesgeschichte* 54, no. 4 (2002): 305–25.

3. Alexander Altmann, *Moses Mendelssohn: A Biographical Study* (Philadelphia: Jewish Publication Society, 1973), 449–54. A leader of Alsatian Jewry, Cerf Berr (1726–94), had approached Moses Mendelssohn to intercede on behalf of his community. Mendelssohn turned to Dohm. See David Sorkin, *Moses Mendelssohn and the Religious Enlightenment* (Berkeley: University of California Press, 1996), 95–119.

4. *Historical Essay on the Colony of Surinam, 1788*, trans. Simon Cohen (American

Jewish Archives) (New York: Ktav, 1974), 6. A committee of Surinam Jews wrote the essay at Dohm's request.

5. For conditional emancipation, see the response of Pastor Schwager in Christian Wilhelm von Dohm, *Über die bürgerliche Verbesserung der Juden*, 2 vols. (Berlin and Stettin: Friedrich Nicolai, 1781–83), 2:89–111. For complete opposition to emancipation, see Johann David Michaelis (1717–91) at 2:31–71.

6. Dohm, *Über die bürgerliche Verbesserung*, 2:152.

7. Ibid., 1:109, 1:92.

8. Ibid., 1:28.

9. Ibid., 1:87.

10. Ibid., 1:99–101, 105–7, 121–22.

11. Ibid., 1:118–20.

12. Ibid., 1:135–50, 2:222–46.

13. Ibid., 1:124–27.

14. Franz Reuss, *Christian Wilhelm Dohms Schrift, "Über die bürgerliche Verbesserung der Juden," und deren Einwirkung auf die gebildeten Stände Deutschlands* (Kaiserslautern, 1891), 35. See also Horst Möller, "Aufklärung, Juenemanzipation und Staat: Urprung und Wirkung von Dohms Schrift Über die bürgerliche Verbesserung der Juden," *Jahrbuch des Instituts für deutsche Geschichte, Beiheft* 3 (1980): 119–49.

15. Reinhard Rürup, "Die Emanzipation der Juden in Baden," in *Emanzipation und Antisemitismus: Studien zur "Judenfrage" der bürgerlichen Gesellschaft* (Göttingen: Vandenhoeck & Ruprecht, 1975), 39–42. There is no comprehensive study of Dohm's impact on legislation.

16. Gregory Hanlon, *Early Modern Italy: 1550–1800; Three Seasons in European History* (Houndmills, Basingstoke: Macmillan, 2000), 269, 283–95.

17. Ibid., 357.

18. Alexander Grab, "Enlightened Despotism and State Building: The Case of Austrian Lombardy," *Austrian History Yearbook* 19, no. 2 (1983–84): 47–48. In 1749 a unified body (*Magistrato Camerale*) was created to handle all financial matters. In 1765 the Austrians further endeavored to centralize policy in a single body (*Supremo Consiglio d'economia*), which was largely staffed by non-Milanese bureaucrats loyal to the Habsburgs. This effort failed. See also 57ff.

19. Verri, *Carteggio*, IV, 332, quoted in Grab, "Enlightened Despotism and State Building," 62.

20. Grab, "Enlightened Despotism and State Building," 67–68.

21. Cecil Roth, *The History of the Jews of Italy* (Philadelphia: Jewish Publication Society, 1946), 423.

22. Carlo Capra, "Habsburg Italy in the Age of Reform," *Journal of Modern Italian Studies* 10, no. 2 (2005): 226.

23. Ibid., 227.

24. Davide Mano, "Towards Jewish Emancipation in the Grand-Duchy of Tuscany: The Case of Pitigliano through the Emblematic Figure of David Consiglio," in Shlomo Simonsohn and Joseph Schatzmiller, eds., *The Italia Judaica Jubilee Conference* (Leiden: Brill, 2013), 107–8.

25. Gerda Graf, *Der Verfassungsentwurf aus dem Jahre 1787 des Granduca Pietro Leopoldo di Toscana* (Berlin: Duncker & Humblot, 1998), 234–45.

26. For the assertion that Jews did occupy seats on the municipal council but were not allowed to fill higher office, see Roberto G. Salvadori, *The Jews of Florence: From the Origins of the Community up to the Present*, trans. Ann Curiel (Florence: La Giuntina, 2001), 52–53.

27. Mano, "Towards Jewish Emancipation in the Grand-Duchy of Tuscany," 115–25.

28. His edict superseded Maria Theresa's *Religionspatent* (1778) that had reiterated all the existing prohibitions for non-Catholics. Joseph appeared to follow the Peace of Westphalia that recognized Lutherans, Calvinists, and Catholics but not dissenting Protestants. See Derek Beales, *Joseph II*, 2 vols. (Cambridge: Cambridge University Press, 1987–2009), 2:168–213.

29. Beales, *Joseph II*, 2:168ff.

30. Joseph Karniel stressed the impact of foreign considerations on domestic policy. See *Die Toleranzpolitik Kaiser Josephs II*, Schriftenreihe des Instituts für Deutsche Geschichte der Universität Tel Aviv, vol. 9 (Stuttgart: Bleicher, 1986).

31. Beales, *Joseph II*, 2:307–32.

32. Rolf Grawert, *Staat und Staatsangehörigkeit: Verfassungsgeschichtliche Untersuchung zur Entstehung der Staatsangehörigkeit* (Berlin: Duncker, 1973), 123, 146–56; Henry E. Strakosch, *State Absolutism and the Rule of Law: The Struggle for the Codification of Civil Law in Austria, 1753–1811* (Sydney: Sydney University Press, 1967), 46–47.

33. Beales, *Joseph II*, 2:201–13.

34. Wolfdieter Bihl, "Zur Entstehungsgeschichte des josephinischen Patents für die Juden Ungarns vom 31. März 1783," in Heinrich Fichtenau and Erich Zöllner, eds., *Beiträge zur neueren Geschichte Österreichs* (Vienna: Böhlau, 1974), 284, 287–88.

35. Beales, *Joseph II*, 2:208–9.

36. Ibid., 2:593. Central were his empire-wide land survey and new taxation system of 1785.

37. Edward Goldstücker, "Jews between Czechs and Germans around 1848," *Leo Baeck Institute Yearbook* 17 (1972): 62–64.

38. Michael Silber, "Equality before Égalité: Joseph II's Policy towards the Jews (1781–1790)," *Tenth World Congress of Jewish Studies* (August 1989): 6; Strakosch, *State Absolutism and the Rule of Law*, 123, 133–34.

39. Karniel, *Die Toleranzpolitik Kaiser Josephs II*, 399; Ruth Kestenberg-Gladstein, *Neuere Geschichte der Juden in den böhmischen Ländern*, 2 vols. (Tübingen: JCB Mohr, 1969), 1:1.

40. Karniel, *Die Toleranzpolitik Kaiser Josephs II*, 400–401; Goldstücker, "Jews between Czechs and Germans around 1848," 62–63.

41. Karniel, *Die Toleranzpolitik Kaiser Josephs II*, 401–2.

42. Ibid., 412.

43. Karniel emphasizes the division between wealthy/desirable and impoverished/undesirable Jews. See ibid., 411.

44. The edict is reprinted in Willibald Müller, ed., *Urkundliche Beiträge zur Geschichte der mähr. Judenschaft in 17. und 18. Jahrhundert* (Olmütz: Laurenz Kullil, 1903), 185–89. There is an English translation in Wilma Abeles Iggers, ed., *The Jews of Bohemia and Moravia: A Historical Reader* (Detroit: Wayne State University Press, 1992), 48–52. For analyses, see Michael Laurence Miller, *Rabbis and Revolution: The Jews of Moravia in the Age of Emancipation* (Stanford: Stanford University Press, 2011), 46–52 and Karniel, *Die Toleranzpolitik Kaiser Josephs II*, 416–18.

45. Bihl, "Zur Entstehungsgeschichte des josephinischen Patents für die Juden Ungarns," 288–90.

46. Two versions of the edict are reprinted in Karniel, *Die Toleranzpolitik Kaiser Josephs II*, 576–85. For his discussion, see 430–35.

47. Beales, *Joseph II*, 2:243–44.

48. Ibid., 2:204–5.

49. Michael Silber, "From Tolerated Aliens to Citizen-Soldiers: Jewish Military Service

in the Era of Joseph II," in Pieter M. Judson and Marsha L. Rozenblit, eds., *Constructing Nationalities in East Central Europe* (New York: Berghahn Books, 2004), 19–36, quotation at 25. For an overview, see Michael Hochedlinger, "'Verbesserung' und 'Nutzbarmachung'? Zur Einführung der Militärpflicht für Juden in der Habsburgermonarchie, 1788–89," in Michael Kaiser and Stefan Kroll, eds., *Militär und Religiosität in der Frühen Neuzeit* (Münster: Lit Verlag, 2004), 97–120. For Protestants as officers, see Beales, *Joseph II*, 2:184. One exception was the formerly Ottoman territory of the Bukovina. Although the Habsburg administration incorporated the Bukovina into Galicia in 1786, it did not impose conscription until 1830. See David Rechter, *Becoming Habsburg: The Jews of Austrian Bukovina, 1774–1918* (Oxford: Littman Library, 2013), 56. On the Habsburg draft and rabbis' and intellectuals' responses, see Derek J. Penslar, *Jews and the Military: A History* (Princeton: Princeton University Press, 2013), 41–47.

50. The three winners of the Metz Academy prize competition pointed to him in their tracts. Abbé Grégoire, *Essai sur la régénération physique, morale et politique des Juifs* (1789), 138, 156, 193; Claude-Antoine Thiéry, *Dissertation sur cette question: Est-il des moyens de render les Juifs plus heureux et plus utiles en France?* 8 vols. (Paris: Editions d'histoire sociale, 1968), 2:82; Zalkind Hourwitz, *Apologie des juifs en réponse à la question: Est-il des moyens de render les Juifs plus heureux & plus utiles en France?* 8 vols. (Paris: Editions d'histoire sociale, 1968), 4:70.

51. Michael Silber, "Josephinian Reforms," *YIVO Encyclopedia of Jews in Eastern Europe*, 2 vols. (New Haven: Yale University Press, 2008), 1:833.

52. Charles Ingrao, *The Habsburg Monarchy, 1618–1815* (Cambridge: Cambridge University Press, 1994), 199. Frederick II of Prussia may have been the first to suggest it (or "King of Jerusalem").

53. Lois Dubin, "Subjects into Citizens: Jewish Autonomy and Inclusion in Early Modern Livorno and Trieste," *Simon Dubnow Institute Yearbook* 5 (2006): 64–67; Francesca Bregoli, *Mediterranean Enlightenment: Livornese Jews, Tuscan Culture, and Eighteenth-Century Reform* (Stanford: Stanford University Press, 2014), 225–32.

54. Lois Dubin, *The Port Jews of Habsburg Trieste: Absolutist Politics and Enlightenment Culture* (Stanford: Stanford University Press, 1999), 61–63.

55. Ibid., 49–50; Dubin, "Subjects into Citizens," 71. Dubin has translated the "Privilege and Statute." See "Privilege and Statute of Maria Theresia for the Jews of Trieste (1771)," Wesleyan University, Middletown, CT, August 2004.

56. Dubin, "Subjects into Citizens," 73–75.

57. Dubin, *The Port Jews of Habsburg Trieste*, 201–2. As late as the 1780s Jews were still unable to gain membership in the Bordeaux Chamber of Commerce.

58. Dubin, "Subjects into Citizens," 76.

Chapter Five. Civic Rights in Western Europe

1. J. M. Ross, "Naturalisation of the Jews in England," *Transactions of the Jewish Historical Society of England* 24 (1975): 59–61.

2. *Great Britain: Collection of Public Statutes. George II. 13 1739/40*, Hansard, *The Parliamentary History of England*, 36 vols. (London: T. C. Hansard, 1806–20), 167–71.

3. Sheldon J. Godfrey and Judith C. Godfrey, *Search Out the Land: The Jews and the Growth of Equality in British Colonia America, 1740–1867* (Montreal: McGill-Queen's University Press, 1995), 40.

4. James H. Kettner, *The Development of American Citizenship, 1608–1870* (Chapel Hill: University of North Carolina Press, 1978), 78. The colonies' authority to grant naturalization was often dubious.

5. Godfrey and Godfrey, *Search Out the Land*, 37, 54.

6. "He [George III] has endeavoured to prevent the population of these states; for that purpose obstructing the laws for the naturalization of foreigners." For colonial naturalization, see Edward A. Hoyt, "Naturalization under the American Colonies: Signs of New Community," *Political Science Quarterly* 67, no. 2 (June 1952): 248–66 and Kettner, *The Development of American Citizenship*, 65–128.

7. Godfrey and Godfrey, *Search Out the Land*, 56.

8. Hoyt, "Naturalization under the American Colonies," 255–56. Hoyt mistakenly lists Rhode Island and Georgia as colonies that naturalized Jews. For evidence of local naturalization, see Jacob Rader Marcus, *The Colonial American Jew, 1492-1776*, 3 vols. (Detroit: Wayne State University Press, 1970); New York in 1715, 1718, 1723, and 1763: 1:405–6, 438; Massachusetts in 1762: 1:437–48.

9. Holly Snyder, "Rules, Rights and Redemption: The Negotiation of Jewish Status in British Atlantic Port Towns," *Jewish History* 20 (2006): 147–70.

10. Stanley Chyet, "The Political Rights of the Jews in the United States, 1776–1840," in Jacob Rader Marcus, ed., *Critical Studies in American Jewish History* (Cincinnati: American Jewish Archives, 1971), 2:39–40, 44–45.

11. Hoyt, "Naturalization under the American Colonies," 253.

12. Kettner, *The Development of American Citizenship*, 75.

13. Godfrey and Godfrey, *Search Out the Land*, 19.

14. Thomas W. Perry, *Public Opinion, Propaganda, and Politics in Eighteenth-Century England: A Study of the Jew Bill of 1753* (Cambridge, MA: Harvard University Press, 1962), 17–20; Maurice Woolf, "Joseph Salvador, 1716-1786," *Jewish Historical Society of England Transactions* 21 (1968): 104–37. For Salvador's letter to the Duke of Newcastle (January 14, 1753) proposing the mechanism and reasons for naturalization, see Cecil Roth, ed., *Anglo-Jewish Letters (1158-1917)* (London: Soncino, 1938), 129–30.

15. Perry, *Public Opinion, Propaganda, and Politics in Eighteenth-Century England*, 46. Salvador's letter emphasizes the wealthy: "Because the Rich among them have by Experience been found to be true Friends to the Government in all its Parts . . . 6th . . . and therefore the Question now lies, whether the Rich Jews ought not to be encouraged and will not be highly useful." Roth, *Anglo-Jewish Letters*, 130. Todd M. Endelman argues that the "ministry's only intention was to free foreign-born Jewish magnates from commercial discrimination." See *The Jews of Georgian England, 1714-1830: Tradition and Change in a Liberal Society* (Philadelphia: Jewish Publication Society, 1979), 25–28.

16. Perry, *Public Opinion, Propaganda, and Politics in Eighteenth-Century England*, 14–15. For the issue of property, see Robert Liberles, "The Jews and Their Bill: Jewish Motivations in the Controversy of 1753," *Jewish History* 2, no. 2 (1987): 29–36. The bill overturned a statute of 1609 that required both an oath containing the phrase "are of the Religion now established in this realm" and taking Anglican communion to be eligible for naturalization by a private act of Parliament. See Perry, *Public Opinion, Propaganda, and Politics in Eighteenth-Century England*, 1, 15 and Kettner, *The Development of American Citizenship*, 67.

17. Perry, *Public Opinion, Propaganda, and Politics in Eighteenth-Century England*, 31–37. Perry emphasizes that immigration and naturalization were perhaps the last issues that could arouse the old Whig-Tory contention. For an analysis of one key newspaper during the "clamor," see G. A. Cranfield, "The 'London Evening-Post' and the Jew Bill of 1753," *Historical Journal* 8, no. 1 (1965): 16–30.

18. Perry, *Public Opinion, Propaganda, and Politics in Eighteenth-Century England*, 46, 69–70. Endelman emphasizes the Whig advocates' conversionary designs. See *Jews of Georgian England*, 60–64.

19. Kettner, *The Development of American Citizenship*, 76.

20. Godfrey and Godfrey, *Search Out the Land*, 10–11.

21. Hansard, *The Parliamentary History of England*, November 15, 1753, xv; 1753–65, 103, 102, cited in Godfrey and Godfrey, *Search Out the Land*, 54.

22. J. H. Blom, R. G. Fuks-Mansfeld, and I. Schöffer, *The History of the Jews in the Netherlands* (Oxford: Littman, 2002), 167. Jews tended to identify politically with the House of Orange. See p. 169.

23. Of 1,204 inhabitants in 1722, 21 were Jews. They built a synagogue in 1737. See Isaac S. Emmanuel and Suzanne Emmanuel, *History of the Jews of the Netherlands Antilles*, 2 vols. (Cincinnati: American Jewish Archives, 1970), 1:518–19. Cf. Godfrey and Godfrey, *Search Out the Land*, 37, 54.

24. Cited in Emmanuel and Emmanuel, *History of the Jews of the Netherlands Antilles*, 1:525.

25. For a convenient summary, see P. M. Jones, *Reform and Revolution in France: The Politics of Transition, 1774–1791* (Cambridge: Cambridge University Press, 1995), 107–38 and Keith Michael Baker, "French Political Thought at the Accession of Louis XVI," *Journal of Modern History* 50 (1978): 279–303.

26. Decree reproduced in Gerard Nahon, ed., *Les "Nations" Juives Portugaises du Sud-Ouest de la France (1684–1791)* (Paris: Fundação Gulbenkian, 1981), 41–44. On the decree, see Arthur Hertzberg, *The French Enlightenment and the Jews: The Origins of Modern Anti-Semitism* (New York: Schocken, 1970), 63–68.

27. For the Paris Parlement's repeated refusal to register the decree (1776, 1783, 1784, 1785), see Paul Hildenfinger, *Documents sur les juifs à Paris au XVIIIe siècle* (Paris, 1913), 41–42 and Zosa Szajkowski, "The Jewish Status in Eighteenth-Century France and the 'Droit d'Aubaine,'" *Historia Judaica* 19 (1957): 148. For Péreire's efforts to extend the privilege to Paris and the colonies, see Evelyne Oliel-Grausz, "Droit et espace Séfarade: Jacob Rodrigues Péreire et l'extension des privilèges du royaume à la nation," *Archives juives* 37, no. 1 (2004): 28–46. For Bordeaux and the islands, see Hertzberg, *The French Enlightenment and the Jews*, 63n28.

Such corporate privileges aroused envy and competition from other Jews. In particular, impoverished Jews from the papal state of Avignon came to Bordeaux to make their way in commerce, selling calico and other goods. The resident merchants objected, as did the leaders of Bordeaux Jewry. In 1759 six Avignonnais families received *lettres patentes* equal to those of the Portuguese. In 1760 the king approved an ordinance (*Règlement de la nation des Juifs Portugais de Bordeaux*) that gave the "nation" the ability to expel a member by a two-thirds vote. The community promptly expelled 152 poor Jews, mostly from Avignon. See Hertzberg, *The French Enlightenment and the Jews*, 95–97.

28. For the "unique" situation of Protestants and Jews, see François Burckard, *Le Conseil Souverain d'Alsace au XVIIIe siècle* (Strasbourg: Société savant d'Alsace, 1995), 29–30.

29. Franklin L. Ford, *Strasbourg in Transition, 1648–1789*, 2nd ed. (New York: W. W. Norton, 1966), 8; Ford, review of Georges Livet, *L'Intendance d'Alsace sous Louis XIV, 1648–1715, American Historical Review* 63 (October 1957): 105. Ford also argued that Strasbourg was "in no sense the capital of Alsace, which was not a defined area capable of having a capital," but Louis XIV attempted to "hammer Alsace into a province" with Strasbourg as the capital. See *Strasbourg in Transition*, 7, 39–40. For an illuminating discussion of France's "natural" boundaries or frontier, including the Rhine, see Peter Sahlins, "Natural Frontiers Revisited: France's Boundaries since the Seventeenth Century," *American Historical Review* 95, no. 5 (1990): 1423–51.

30. France admitted Jewish families to the garrison town of Metz as early as 1567 to

advance credit to soldiers and the bourgeoisie. Residency there was permanent and secure since the king, rather than a local ruler, granted it. See Hertzberg, *The French Enlightenment and the Jews*, 321, 18–19, 125. Treating Alsace and Lorraine as the hyphenated entity "Alsace-Lorraine" was a product of the return to German rule (1871–1918). It is anachronistic to consider them in tandem in the seventeenth and eighteenth centuries. See Laird Boswell, "Alsace-Lorraine," in John Merriman and Jay Winter, eds., *Europe 1789–1914: Encyclopedia of the Age of Industry and Empire*, 5 vols. (Detroit: Scribner's Sons, 2006), 1:50–52.

31. For the correspondence between the military commander and the war minister (1701 and 1713) as well as petitions from various communities wishing to reduce the number of Jews, see Élie Scheid, *Histoire des Juifs d'Alsace* (Paris: Durlacher, 1887), 155–66. For the Duc de Mazarin's failed effort to expel the Jews in 1671, see Robert Weyl and Freddy Raphaël, "Organisation civile et religieuse des juifs en Alsace (1648–1793)," *Revue des sciences sociales de la France de l'Est* 6 (1977): 74. For royal policy, see Georges Livet, *L'Intendance d'Alsace sous Louis XIV, 1648–1715* (Paris: Les Belles Lettres, 1956). For royal efforts to expel Anabaptists, see Rebecca McCoy, "Religious Accommodation and Political Authority in an Alsatian Community, 1648–1715," *Journal of Ecclesiastical History* 52 (2001): 270. For the general situation of Jews, see Zosa Szajkowski, *The Economic Status of the Jews in Alsace, Metz and Lorraine (1648–1789)* (New York: Editions Historiques Franco-Juives, 1954), 20–30 and Simon Schwarzfuchs, "Alsace and Southern Germany: The Creation of a Border," in Michael Brenner, Vicki Caron, and Uri R. Kaufmann, eds., *Jewish Emancipation Reconsidered: The French and German Models* (Tübingen: Mohr Siebeck, 2003), 5–17.

32. McCoy, "Religious Accommodation and Political Authority in an Alsatian Community," 244. Dohm compared the oppressive situation for the Jews in Alsace to that in the German states. See Christian Wilhelm von Dohm, *Über die bürgerliche Verbesserung der Juden*, 2 vols. (Berlin and Stettin: Friedrich Nicolai, 1781–83), 1:79–80. Unlike Alsace, the French interior was not subject to the Peace of Westphalia's regulations governing religious privileges.

33. Ford, *Strasbourg in Transition*, 83, 116, 132; Szajkowski, *The Economic Status of the Jews in Alsace, Metz and Lorraine*, 20, 127. The official designation in the tariff system was *provinces à l'instar de l'étranger effectif*. For the impact of Catholic migration in one village, see McCoy, "Religious Accommodation and Political Authority in an Alsatian Community," 256ff.

34. Szajkowski, *The Economic Status of the Jews in Alsace, Metz and Lorraine*, 25. Strasbourg and Colmar notably held privileges prohibiting Jewish settlement. For details, see Scheid, *Histoire des Juifs d'Alsace*, 131–319.

35. The Metz Parlement repeatedly (1656, 1718) tried to restrict the occupations that royal *lettres patentes* extended to the Jews. See Szajkowski, *The Economic Status of the Jews in Alsace, Metz and Lorraine*, 34–35. For the Jews' extensive knowledge and use of the courts, see Jay Berkovitz, "Acculturation and Integration in Eighteenth-Century Metz," *Jewish History* 24 (2010): 271–94.

36. Szajkowski, *The Economic Status of the Jews in Alsace, Metz and Lorraine*, 5–17. For the decreasing role of Jews in moneylending from midcentury, see Robert Weyl and Jean Daltroff, "Le Cahier de doleance des juifs d'Alsace," *Revue d'Alsace* 109 (1983): 73–75. For a systematic survey demonstrating the Jews did not predominate in moneylending but rather were heavily concentrated in some geographic regions, see Jean Daltroff, *Le pret d'argent des juifs de Basse-Alsace (1750-1791)* (Strasbourg: Publications de la société savant d'Alsace et des regions de l'est, 1993).

37. For the petitions of 1715–17, see Hertzberg, *The French Enlightenment and the*

Jews, 52–55 and Szajkowski, *The Economic Status of the Jews in Alsace, Metz and Lorraine*, 52–53, 64.

38. Robert Weyl, "Synagogues d'Alsace," in Freddy Raphaël and Robert Weyl, *Juifs en Alsace: Culture, société, histoire*, vol. 5: *Franco-Judaïca* (Toulouse: Privat, 1977), 133–34. There may have been public synagogues in Ribeauvillé and Westhoffen, though Weyl offers no evidence. See 140. In three villages (Biesheim, Hagenthal, Wintzenheim) circa 1725 Jews clandestinely moved, restored, or enlarged existing synagogue buildings. The central government (*Conseil Souverain*) ordered them destroyed and the proceeds from the sale of the building materials transferred to the Catholic Church. In contrast, in Biesheim in 1752 Jews requested permission in advance to restore a decrepit synagogue building and were authorized to do so. See 135–38.

39. On Cerf Berr, see M. Ginsburger, *Cerf Berr et son Époque* (Guebwiller: Dreyfus, 1908) and Georges Weill, "Cerf Berr de Medelsheim: Militant de l'émancipation," *Les Nouveaux cahiers* 45 (1975): 30–42. Cerf Berr received personal naturalization in 1775 for his service as an army purveyor. See Peter Sahlins, "Fictions of a Catholic France: The Naturalization of Foreigners, 1685–1787," *Representations* 47 (Summer 1994): 85–110, esp. 101.

40. For the affair, see Szajkowski, *The Economic Status of the Jews in Alsace, Metz and Lorraine*, 123–40. For a portrait of François-Joseph-Antoine Hell (1731–94), Bailiff of Landser (Upper Alsace), who may have been the instigator, see 130–35. For the counterfeiters who were sentenced to death or life in the galleys, see 129. Cerf Berr, "Mémoire sur l'état des juifs en Alsace," in Christian Konrad Wilhelm von Dohm, *Über die bürgerliche Verbesserung der Juden*, 2 vols. (Hildesheim: Georg Olms, 1973), 1:155–200. See Alexander Altmann, *Moses Mendelssohn: A Biographical Study* (Philadelphia: Jewish Publication Society, 1973), 421–61 and David Sorkin, *Moses Mendelssohn and the Religious Enlightenment* (Berkeley: University of California Press, 1996), 95–119.

41. "Mémoire sur l'état des juifs en Alsace," 1:160, 163–64, 174, 186–87, 199. Cerf Berr requested: "legislation that would grant them a free existence and at the same time assure them the legal means to support themselves" (163–64).

42. Ibid., 1:170–73. Colbert imposed the *péage corporel* for foreign Jews in 1663, but by 1672 it was extended to resident Jews as well. See Scheid, *Histoire des Juifs d'Alsace*, 132. For a detailed account, see David Feuerwerker, *L'émancipation des Juifs en France: De l'Ancien Régime à la fin du Second Empire* (Paris: Albin Michel, 1976), 3–48. Feuerwerker emphasizes the impact of Joseph II's 1782 edict on Cerf Berr, who had it translated. See p. 15.

43. "Mémoire sur l'état des juifs en Alsace," 1:190–94. Cerf Berr was trying to rectify a problem. The previous royal *lettres patentes* (February 3, 1777) aimed to secure the community's jurisdiction over civil cases between Jews. In registering the decree, the Metz Parlement changed its meaning by making it voluntary to turn to the Jewish court. See Hertzberg, *The French Enlightenment and the Jews*, 242. For Cerf Berr's ambition to centralize authority in the hands of the leading *parnas* and the rabbis, see Weill, "Cerf Berr de Medelsheim," 37. For a major reinterpretation, see Jay R. Berkovitz, *Protocols of Justice: The Pinkas of Metz Rabbinic Court, 1771-1789* (Leiden: Brill, 2014).

44. "Mémoire sur l'état des juifs en Alsace," 1:199.

45. *Édit du Roi, portant Exemption des Droits de péage corporels sur les Juifs. Du mois Janvier 1784* (Jewish Theological Seminary Library), 2. Feuerwerker reproduces this document. See *L'émancipation des Juifs en France*, 34–35. This language does not appear in the law as published in the standard collection. See Athanase-Jean-Léger Jourdan et al., eds., *Recueil général des anciennes lois françaises, depuis l'an 420 jusqu'à la Revolution de 1789*, 29 vols. (Paris: Belin-Leprieur, 1821–33), 27:360. The privilege acknowledged that certain entities may require indemnification. The city of Strasbourg made such a claim and Cerf

Berr helped finance it. See Hertzberg, *The French Enlightenment and the Jews*, 319; Weill, "Cerf Berr de Medelsheim," 32; and Scheid, *Histoire des Juifs d'Alsace*, 186.

46. Rina Neher-Bernheim, "Aspects démographiques de la préparation des lettres patentes de 1784," in Myriam Yardeni, ed., *Les Juifs dans l'histoire de France* (Leiden: Brill, 1980), 111; Hertzberg, *The French Enlightenment and the Jews*, 321.

47. Sahlins, "Fictions of a Catholic France," 85–110. The fifteen (101–2) included six families from Carpentras, the army supplier Calmer Liefman (1769), the merchant and advocate Valabrègue (1770), the son of Moise Castro Soler (1776), Cerf Berr (1775), the merchant brothers from Havre du Grace Homberg and Lallement (1775), and the Parisian merchants Ruben and Israel Moise (1786).

48. Hannah Arendt, *The Origins of Totalitarianism* (New York: Harcourt Brace, 1951), 12, linked the privileges of these individuals to the later grant of equality to all Jews. She provided no evidence to support this claim.

49. Jourdan et al., *Recueil général des anciennes lois françaises*, 28:472–82, quotation at 474 (clause 3). For an abbreviated English translation, see J. F. Maclear, ed., *Church and State in the Modern Age: A Documentary History* (New York: Oxford University Press, 1995), 7–10. For the edict, see G. Adams, *The Huguenots and French Opinion, 1685–1787: The Enlightenment Debate on Toleration* (Waterloo, Ontario: Wilfrid Laurier University Press, 1991), esp. 295–306; for Louis XIV's declaration of 1715, the edict, and its equivocal implementation, see R. C. Poland, *French Protestantism and the French Revolution, 1684–1815* (Princeton: Princeton University Press, 1957), 25, 77–95. Recalling the Edict of Nantes' consequences ("a state within a state"), the 1787 edict prohibited the formation of a "corps, a community or a particular society." The Parlement of Metz registered the edict with the proviso that it did not apply to the Jews. See Frances Malino, *A Jew in the French Revolution: The Life of Zalkind Hourwitz* (Oxford: Blackwell, 1996), 37–38.

50. Frances Malino, "Les communautés juives et l'Edit de 1787," *Bulletin de la Société de l'Histoire du Protestantisme Français* 134 (1988): 311–28, esp. 314–15. Feuerwerker argues that Malesherbes understood the edict to apply to the Jews. See *L'émancipation des Juifs en France*, 145–58. The Abbé Grégoire mentioned the confusion whether Jews had received "civil liberty" as a result of the 1787 edict in his "Motion en faveur des Juifs" of August 3, 1789, reprinted in *La revolution française et l'Emancipation des Juifs*, 8 vols. (Paris: EDHIS, 1968), 6:5.

51. *Journal de Paris* XXIV, An VII, 22 Frimaire, cited in Malino, "Les communautés juives et l'Edit de 1787," 315.

52. Malesherbes could not reconcile his vision (the abolition of communal autonomy as a precondition for citizenship) with those of Bordeaux Jewry (autonomy plus citizenship) and Alsatian Jewry (priority of autonomy to citizenship). See Malino, "Les communautés juives et l'Edit de 1787," 318–21; Frances Malino, *The Sephardic Jews of Bordeaux: Assimilation and Emancipation in Revolutionary and Napoleonic France* (University: University of Alabama Press, 1978), 27–39; Feuerwerker, *L'émancipation des Juifs en France*, 158–86; and Zosa Sjakowski, "Mishlahoteihem shel Yehudei Bordeaux el Va'adat Malsherbes ve'el ha-Aseifa ha-Leumit," *Zion* 18 (1953): 31–64.

Chapter Six. Partition and Parity

1. The Peace of Utrecht (1713) resulted in a "balance of power" that subverted the extant system of sovereign polities. It divided Europe between partitioners and the potentially partitioned. See Karl Otmar Freiherr von Aretin, "Tausch, Teilung und Länderschacher als Folgen des Gleichgewichtssystems der europäischen Grossmächte: Die polnischen Teilun-

gen als europäisches Schicksal," in Klaus Zernack, ed., *Polen und die polnische Frage in der Geschichte der Hohenzollernmonarchie, 1701–1871* (Berlin: Colloquium, 1982), 56–66; Michael G. Müller, *Die Teilungen Polens, 1772, 1793, 1795* (Munich: Beck, 1984); and Norman Davies, *God's Playground: A History of Poland*, 2 vols. (New York: Columbia University Press, 1982), 1:511–26, quotation from Jacques Mallet-du-Pin at 525. For the pre-history of the partitions, see Jerzy Lukowksi, *The Partitions of Poland: 1772, 1793, 1795* (London: Longman, 1999), 11–18.

2. Israel Bartal, *The Jews of Eastern Europe, 1772–1881*, trans. Chaya Naor (Philadelphia: University of Pennsylvania Press, 2005), 1.

3. Richard Butterwick, "The Enlightened Monarchy of Stanislaw August Poniatowski (1764–1795)," in Butterwick, ed., *The Polish-Lithuanian Monarchy in European Context, c. 1500–1795* (Houndmills, Basingstoke: Palgrave, 2001), 193–218.

4. Lukowksi, *The Partitions of Poland*, 20–24, 34–38.

5. Artur Eisenbach, *The Emancipation of the Jews in Poland, 1780–1870* (Oxford: Blackwell, 1991), 26–27, 35.

6. Raphael Mahler, *A History of Modern Jewry, 1780–1815* (New York: Schocken, 1971), 299.

7. Eisenbach, *The Emancipation of the Jews in Poland*, 35–36; Antony Polonsky, *The Jews in Poland and Russia*, 3 vols. (Oxford: Littman Library, 2010–12), 1:208–9.

8. Daniel Stone, *The Polish-Lithuanian State, 1386–1795* (Seattle: University of Washington Press, 2001), 274–75. For example, a reformist law code of 1778, which would have made Jews subject to municipalities and expelled the indigent, was shouted down before it could be discussed in the Sejm. See p. 276.

9. For a near contemporary characterization, see Michael Stöger, *Darstellung der gesetzlichen Verfassung der galizischen Judenschaft*, 2 vols. (Lemberg: Kuhn & Millikowski, 1833), 1:140.

10. Arnold Springer, "Enlightened Absolutism and Jewish Reform: Prussia, Austria and Russia," *California Slavic Studies* 11 (1980): 258.

11. William Hagen, *Germans, Poles and Jews: The Nationality Conflict in the Prussian East, 1772–1914* (Chicago: University of Chicago Press, 1980), 38–47.

12. Manfred Jehle, " 'Relocations' in South Prussia and New East Prussia: Prussia's Demographic Policy towards the Jews in Occupied Poland, 1772–1806," *Leo Baeck Institute Yearbook* 52 (2007): 24. For a contemporary account of a community employee who, since he spoke German, dealt with the excise officials, see Mosche Wasserzug, "Korot Mosche Wasserzug u-Nedivat Lev Aviv ha-Manoah R. Isserel," *Jahrbuch der jüdisch-literarischen Gesellschaft* 8 (1910): 101ff. Wasserzug acknowledged that the prohibitions on imported goods drove Jews to smuggle contraband. See pp. 97–98.

13. Jehle, " 'Relocations' in South Prussia and New East Prussia," 23–28; Sophia Kemlein, *Die Posener Juden, 1815–1848: Entwicklungsprozesse einer polnischen Judenheit unter preußischer Herrschaft* (Hamburg: Dölling und Galitz, 1997), 45–48; Polonsky, *The Jews in Poland and Russia* 1:226. Wasserzug had difficulty getting official permission to move between regions (from Südpreußen to Neuostpreußen). See "Korot Mosche Wasserzug u-Nedivat Lev Aviv ha-Manoah R. Isserel," 105.

14. Horst Glassl, *Das Österreichische Einrichtungswerk in Galizien (1772–1790)* (Wiesbaden: Otto Harrassowitz, 1975), 12; Svjatoslav Pacholkiv, "Social Implications of the Incorporation of Galicia into the Habsburg Realm," in Harald Heppner, Peter Urbanitsch, and Renate Zedinger, eds., *Social Change in the Habsburg Monarchy*, Eighteenth Century and the Habsburg Monarchy, International Series, vol. 3 (Bochum: Winkler, 2011), 68. Cf. Larry Wolff, *The Idea of Galicia: History and Fantasy in Habsburg Political Culture* (Stanford:

Stanford University Press, 2010), 20: "Galicia, as an invented entity, could be considered to possess no proper history, and was therefore the perfect target for systematic enlightened transformation."

15. Karniel, *Die Toleranzpolitik Kaiser Josephs II*, 441; Wolff, *The Idea of Galicia*, 13–14; Pacholkiv, "Social Implications of the Incorporation of Galicia into the Habsburg Realm," 61–81.

16. Derek Beales, *Joseph II*, 2 vols. (Cambridge: Cambridge University Press, 1987–2009), 2:596–97; Springer, "Enlightened Absolutism and Jewish Reform," 255. Pacholkiv surveys the impact of Habsburg legislation, emphasizing the szlachta's loss of income and authority and the improvement of the peasants' situation. See "Social Implications of the Incorporation of Galicia into the Habsburg Realm," 68–77.

17. Glassl, *Das Österreichische Einrichtungswerk in Galizien*, 15. Most historians agree that the Habsburg military's census was flawed; the numbers were in fact higher.

18. Mahler, *A History of Modern Jewry*, 324.

19. Glassl, *Das Österreichische Einrichtungswerk in Galizien*, 83–85, 89–90, 108–9.

20. Joseph Karniel, *Die Toleranzpolitik Kaiser Josephs II* (Stuttgart: Bleicher, 1986), 438–39; Wolff, *The Idea of Galicia*, 31. In 1778 the Habsburg military administration expelled indigent Jews from the Bukovina, which had been Ottoman territory. See David Rechter, *Becoming Habsburg: The Jews of Austrian Bukovina, 1774–1918* (Oxford: Littman Library, 2013), 33–58.

21. Glassl, *Das Österreichische Einrichtungswerk in Galizien*, 215.

22. "Circularia Imperia," 19.2.1787, cited in Karniel, *Die Toleranzpolitik Kaiser Josephs II*, 443–44. For a brief account, see Beales, *Joseph II*, 2:600.

23. Joseph Karniel has reprinted the full text: "Das Toleranpatent Kaiser Joseph II," *Jahrbuch des Instituts für deutsche Geschichte* 11 (1982): 55–89. The translation in Paul Mendes-Flohr and Jehuda Reinharz, *The Jew in the Modern World: A Documentary History*, 3rd ed. (New York: Oxford University Press, 2011), 46, is incorrect. It translates "christliche und jüdische Untertanen" as "Christian subjects and the Jews."

24. Polonsky, *The Jews in Poland and Russia*, 1:253–57. On the relationship of Jews to the liquor trade in eastern Europe, see Glenn Dynner, *Yankel's Tavern: Jews, Liquor, & Life in the Kingdom of Poland* (New York: Oxford University Press, 2014).

25. Glassl, *Das Österreichische Einrichtungswerk in Galizien*, 219.

26. Polonsky, *The Jews in Poland and Russia*, 1:256.

27. H. R. v. Kopetz, *Versuch einer systematischen Darstellung der in Böhmen bezüglich der Juden bestehenden Gesetze und Verordnungen* (Prague: Gottlieb Haase Söhne, 1846).

28. Michael Silber, "Josephinian Reforms," in Gershon Hundert, ed., *YIVO Encyclopedia of Jews in Eastern Europe* 2 vols. (New Haven: Yale University Press, 2008), 1:833.

29. Edward C. Thaden, *Russia's Western Borderlands, 1710–1870* (Princeton: Princeton University Press, 1984), 44–45; John Doyle Klier, *Russia Gathers Her Jews: The Origins of the "Jewish Question" in Russia, 1772–1825* (DeKalb: Northern Illinois University Press, 1986), 55. For the emergence of the Byelorussian borderland town of Shklov as a center of Jewish commerce, culture, and politics between 1772 and 1795, see David E. Fishman, *Russia's First Modern Jews: The Jews of Shklov* (New York: New York University Press, 1995).

30. Elizabeth had expelled the few Jews in Riga and elsewhere in the empire in 1742–43; that expulsion order remained in force during Catherine's reign. See Richard Pipes, "Catherine II and the Jews," *Soviet Jewish Affairs* 5, no. 2 (1975): 5–6.

31. Polonsky, *The Jews in Poland and Russia*, 1:322, 329–30.

32. John Klier, "The Ambiguous Legal Status of Russian Jewry in the Reign of Catherine II," *Slavic Review* 35, no. 3 (September 1976): 504–17.

33. Gregory Freeze, "The *Soslovie* (Estate) Paradigm and Russian Social History," *American Historical Review* 91, no. 1 (February 1986): 11–36; Isabel de Madariaga, *Russia in the Age of Catherine the Great* (New Haven: Yale University Press, 1981), 277–307; Marc Raeff, *The Well-Ordered Police State: Social and Institutional Change through Law in the Germanies and Russia, 1600–1800* (New Haven: Yale University Press, 1983), 237–44; Elise Kimerling Wirtschafter, *Social Identity in Imperial Russia* (DeKalb: Northern Illinois University Press, 1997), 62–99, 130–40. Freeze notes (p. 18) that Catherine's legislation did not use the term *soslovie*; the term only came into use in the first decades of the nineteenth century.

34. John Klier, "The Concept of 'Jewish Emancipation' in a Russian Context," in Olga Crisp and Linda Edmondson, eds., *Civil Rights in Imperial Russia* (Oxford: Clarendon, 1989), 124.

35. Freeze, "The *Soslovie* (Estate) Paradigm and Russian Social History," argues that the *sosloviia* were not a "systematic policy to create a western order of estates in Russia" (20). Russia had a "polymorphic social structure" (34) in which the poll tax registry served as a crucial dividing line between the privileged and unprivileged (21). Nevertheless, the *sosloviia* persisted until 1917, surviving the Great Reforms and gaining ideological importance after 1870 (26–27).

36. For this image in the first Russian bureaucrat's report on the Jews (M. V. Kakhovskii, 1773), see Klier, *Russia Gathers Her Jews*, 62–64. Like the Jews, Tartars also did not fit the Russian system. For a long-term comparison, see Heinz-Dietrich Löwe, "Poles, Jews, and Tartars: Religion, Ethnicity, and Social Structure in Tsarist Nationality Policies," *Jewish Social Studies* 6, no. 3 (2000): 52–96. It was also Russian policy to remove Orthodox peasants from the rule of non-Christians. See Frank Nesemann, "Aufgeklärter Absolutismus und religiöse Toleranz: Juden und Muslime unter Katharina II," *Leipziger Beiträge zur jüdischen Geschichte und Kultur* 2 (2004): 94.

37. Klier, "The Ambiguous Legal Status of Russian Jewry in the Reign of Catherine II," 507.

38. Ibid. On provincial governors as a small elite connected by marriage and patronage, see John P. LeDonne, "Frontier Governors General, 1772–1825: The Western Frontier," *Jahrbücher für Geschichte Osteuropas* 47, no. 1 (1999): 56–88.

39. Pipes, "Catherine II and the Jews," 9.

40. Klier, "The Ambiguous Legal Status of Russian Jewry in the Reign of Catherine II," 508.

41. Pipes, "Catherine II and the Jews," 10.

42. Ibid., 9. The Russian original with a facing English translation are available in *Catherine II's Charters of 1785 to the Nobility and the Towns*, trans. and ed. David Griffiths and George E. Munro (Bakersfield, CA: Charles Schlacks Jr., 1991), 22–60.

43. Pipes, "Catherine II and the Jews," 11.

44. Polonsky, *The Jews in Poland and Russia*, 1:333; Klier, *Russia Gathers Her Jews*, 69–70.

45. Pipes, "Catherine II and the Jews," 10.

46. Polonsky, *The Jews in Poland and Russia*, 1:333. Merchant petitions would continue to play a role in securing the Jews' political status in Russia (chapter 15).

47. Klier, *Russia Gathers Her Jews*, 71–72.

48. Pipes, "Catherine II and the Jews," 12–13.

49. For this issue in the first half of the nineteenth century, see Yohanan Petrovsky-Shtern, *The Golden Age Shtetl: A New History of Jewish Life in Eastern Europe* (Princeton: Princeton University Press, 2014).

50. Polonsky, *The Jews in Poland and Russia*, 1:193–95.

51. Krystyna Zienkowska, "Citizens or Inhabitants? The Attempt to Reform the Status of the Polish Jews during the Four Years' Sejm," *Acta Poloniae Historica* 76 (1997): 31–52; Daniel Stone, "Jews and the Urban Question in Late Eighteenth Century Poland," *Slavic Review* 50, no. 3 (Autumn 1991): 531–41.

52. Krystyna Zienkowska, "Reforms Relating to the Third Estate," in Samuel Fiszman, ed., *Constitution and Reform in Eighteenth-Century Poland: The Constitution of 3 May 1791* (Bloomington: Indiana University Press, 1997), 344–47.

53. Polonsky, *The Jews in Poland and Russia*, 1:200–204; Eisenbach, *The Emancipation of the Jews in Poland*, 67–82.

54. Eisenbach, *The Emancipation of the Jews in Poland*, 31.

55. Zienkowska, "Reforms Relating to the Third Estate," 347–50.

56. Scott Ury, "The Shtadlan of the Polish-Lithuanian Commonwealth: Noble Advocate or Unbridled Opportunist?" *Polin* 15 (2002): 267–99.

57. Jacob Goldberg, "Mi-Shtadlanut le-Mediniut: Netsigei ha-Kehilot be-Tekufat Sejm Arba ha-Shanim (1788–1792)," in Goldberg, *He-Hevra ha-Yehudit be-Mamlekhet Polin-Lita*, trans. Sophia Lasman (Jerusalem: Zalman Shazar, 1999), 217–18.

58. Eisenbach, *The Emancipation of the Jews in Poland*, 82–91. For the argument that the Jewish representatives should have negotiated with the burghers rather than approaching the Sejm, see Zienkowska, "Citizens or Inhabitants?" 38–39.

59. Eisenbach, *The Emancipation of the Jews in Poland*, 84–85, 103.

60. Ibid., 108.

61. Zienkowska, "Reforms Relating to the Third Estate," 343.

Chapter Seven. Revolution

1. In the vast scholarship on Jews and the Revolution most scholars have concentrated on the December 23–24, 1789, debate and the edict of September 1791. I concentrate on the separate edicts for the Sephardim and Ashkenazim and the qualitative difference between them. It is incontrovertible that the Jews' status raised basic issues of principle laden with symbolic value; it would be a mistake, however, to claim that the Revolution was preoccupied with the Jews: the National Assembly devoted a miniscule amount of its time to their status. For a sustained claim of centrality, see Ronald Schechter, *Obstinate Hebrews: Representations of Jews in France, 1715–1815* (Berkeley: University of California Press, 2003).

2. Robert Weyl and Jean Daltroff, "Le Cahier de Doléances des Juifs d'Alsace," *Revue d'Alsace* 109 (1983): 65–66; David Feuerwerker, *L'émancipation des Juifs en France: De l'Ancien Régime à la fin du Second Empire* (Paris: Albin Michel, 1976), 241–61. The Abbé Grégoire reviewed these events in the "Notice historique" preceding his August 3, 1789, "Motion en faveur des Juifs," *La revolution française et l'Emancipation des Juifs*, 8 vols. (Paris: EDHIS, 1968), 7:iv–v.

3. Eight of 307 *cahiers* endorsed civic rights. See David Feuerwerker, "Anatomie de 307 cahiers de doléances de 1789," *Annales. Économies, Sociétés, Civilisations* 20, no. 1 (1965): 45–61, esp. 56 and Feuerwerker, *L'émancipation des Juifs en France*, 262–85. See also Frances Malino, *A Jew in the French Revolution: The Life of Zalkind Hourwitz* (Oxford: Blackwell, 1996), 70. For an older yet still useful study, see Maurice Liber, *Les Juifs et la convocation des États généraux* (1789) (Louvain-Paris: E. Peeters, 1989).

4. Weyl and Daltroff, "Le Cahier de Doléances des Juifs d'Alsace," 65–80. For the oligarchical process, see p. 71. Cf. Malino, *A Jew in the French Revolution*, 70.

5. "Le Cahier de Doléances des Juifs d'Alsace," paras. 9, 70, 76. For Grégoire's summary of these documents, see "Motion en faveur des Juifs," 7:v–ix.

6. Patrick Weil, *How to Be French: Nationality in the Making since 1789*, trans. Catherine Porter (Durham: Duke University Press, 2008), 13–19.

7. Malino, *A Jew in the French Revolution*, 80.

8. Grégoire, "Motion en faveur des Juifs," 7:1–47. Reportedly 1,000 Jews fled to Mulhouse and Bâle. See Malino, *A Jew in the French Revolution*, 71 and Feuerwerker, *L'émancipation des Juifs en France*, 288–93.

9. Grégoire, "Motion en faveur des Juifs," 7:39. Building on the Jews' memoranda, Grégoire proposed equality through the abrogation of all special taxes (including the Brancas tax in Metz); freedom of residence throughout the kingdom; freedom of religion; the prohibition of insulting terms; and the repeal of all existing laws and privileges contrary to the decree. See also 7:46–47.

10. *Adress présentée a L'Assemblée nationale, le 26 Août 1789, par les Juifs résidans à Paris*, 5:3. The term *état civil* appears on p. 8.

11. Ibid., 5:6–7.

12. Malino, *A Jew in the French Revolution*, 73; Feuerwerker, *L'émancipation des Juifs en France*, 294–97.

13. "Opinion de M. le Comte Stanislas de Clermont-Tonnerre, relativement aux persecutions qui mènacent les Juifes d'Alsace," in *La revolution française et l'Emancipation des Juifs*, 7:2–4. See Feuerwerker, *L'émancipation des Juifs en France*, 304–9.

14. *Archives Parlementaires de 1787 à 1860*, 62 vols. (Paris, 1862–79), 9:201. Gary Kates mistakenly claimed that this motion gave the Jews "passive" or civil rights. Could the king's or the Assembly's protection equal civil rights so long as prior privileges remained in place? Or was the Jews' status simply unresolved? The Jews of Alsace in fact continued to advocate for "passive" as well as "active" political rights. See "Jews into Frenchmen: Nationality and Representation in Revolutionary France," in Ferenc Fehér, ed., *The French Revolution and the Birth of Modernity* (Berkeley: University of California Press, 1990), 103–16, esp. 110. Feuerwerker deems this "the first step of the emancipation of the Jews" but does not clarify whether it equaled civil rights. See *L'émancipation des Juifs en France*, 308–9. For developments in the National Assembly in October and November 1789, see *L'émancipation des Juifs en France*, 311–20.

15. *Archives Parlementaires*, 10:694. Cf. Malino, *A Jew in the French Revolution*, 80; Feuerwerker, *L'émancipation des Juifs en France*, 320–21. Brunet de Latuque was a lawyer from Bordeaux.

16. *Archives Parlementaires*, 10:754.

17. Ibid., 10:756. The translation is from Lynn Hunt, *The French Revolution and Human Rights: A Brief Documentary History* (Boston: Bedford, 1996), 88. This passage, albeit in a garbled version from a contemporary journal, became the emblem of emancipation after 1945. It was virtually unknown until the end of the nineteenth century. For the history of the text and its reception, as well as an account of Clermont-Tonnerre's thought, see David Sorkin, *The Count Stanislas de Clermont-Tonnerre's "To the Jews as a Nation . . .": The Career of a Quotation*, Jacob Katz Memorial Lecture, 2011 (Jerusalem: Leo Baeck Institute, 2012).

18. *Archives Parlementaires*, 10:756. See Feuerwerker, *L'émancipation des Juifs en France*, 323.

19. *Archives Parlementaires*, 10:756–57. Translation in Hunt, *The French Revolution and Human Rights*, 89.

20. *Archives Parlementaires*, 10:757. Translation in Hunt, *The French Revolution and Human Rights*, 89.

21. For the motion the Jews submitted, see "Nouvelle Adresse des Juifs à L'Assemblée nationale, 24 Décembre 1789," in *La revolution française et l'Emancipation des Juifs*, 5:1–4.

The petition reiterated the environmental argument and affirmed the Jews' ability to undertake all the duties of citizenship, including military service. The authors appealed to the Assembly not to contradict its own principles by acquiescing to the opposition.

22. Malino, *A Jew in the French Revolution*, 81–82; Feuerwerker, *L'émancipation des Juifs en France*, 323–27.

23. "Adresse à l'Assemblée nationale," 5:1–8. For an analysis that stresses cooperation between the various communities, see Gérard Nahon, "Séfarades et Ashkenazes en France: La conquête de l'Emancipation (1789–1791)," in Myriam Yardeni, ed., *Les Juifs dans l'Histoire de France* (Leiden: Brill, 1980), 121–45.

24. Nahon, "Séfarades et Ashkenazes en France," 138.

25. "Adresse à l'Assemblée nationale," 5:1–8. Since Simon Dubnow, historians have impugned the Bordeaux Jews for breaking ranks. Nahon argues that the vote of January 28 benefited all the Jews in France and that the Sephardim continued to work with the Ashkenazim. See Nahon, "Séfarades et Ashkenazes en France," 121–22, 137–42.

26. "Adresse à l'Assemblée nationale," 5:2, no. 1.

27. *Archives Parlementaires*, 11:364.

28. Ibid.

29. Ibid., 11:365.

30. "Opinions sur les Juifs d'Alsace," *Recueil des opinions de Stanislas de Clermont-Tonnerre*, 4 vols. (Paris, 1791), 3:37.

31. Ibid., 3:47. This speech does not appear in the *Archives Parlementaires* for January 28, 1790.

32. *Archives Parlementaires*, 11:365. See Feuerwerker, *L'émancipation des Juifs en France*, 338–42.

33. Evelyne Oliel-Grausz noted this in her conclusion to "Droit et espace séfarade: Jacob Rodrigues Péreire et l'extension des privileges du royaume à la Nation," *Archives juives* 37, no. 1 (2004): 43.

34. Nahon, "Séfarades et Ashkenazes en France," 138–39.

35. Malino, *A Jew in the French Revolution*, 92; Feuerwerker, *L'émancipation des Juifs en France*, 332–38, 342–88.

36. Malino, *A Jew in the French Revolution*, 93.

37. Ibid., 95–99.

38. *Chronique de Paris*, January 8, 1791, cited in Malino, *A Jew in the French Revolution*, 102.

39. Yerachmeal Cohen, "Retorikat ha-Emanzipatsiya shel ha-Yehudim u-Temunat he-Atid," in Cohen, ed., *Ha-Mahepekha ha-Tsarfatit ve-Rishuma* (Jerusalem: Zalman Shazar Center, 1991), 168.

40. Kates, "Jews into Frenchmen," 114; *Archives Parlementaires*, 31:372–73.

41. *Archives Parlementaires*, 31:372.

42. Ibid.

43. Ibid., 31:373.

44. Salo Baron, "New Approaches to Jewish Emancipation," *Diogenes* 29 (Spring 1960): 56–81. For the "credibility of France's Constitution," see Malino, *A Jew in the French Revolution*, 113.

45. *Archives Parlementaires*, 31:441–42. For the legislation remaining a dead letter, see Schechter, *Obstinate Hebrews*, 153 and Lionel Kochan, *The Making of Western Jewry, 1600–1819* (Houndmills, Basingstoke: Palgrave, 2004), 259. For the law's promulgation and the Jews' admission to the civic oath, see Feuerwerker, *L'émancipation des Juifs en France*, 401–45.

Chapter Eight. War

1. Stuart Woolf, *Napoleon's Integration of Europe* (London: Routledge, 1991); T. C. W. Blanning, "The Role of Religion in European Counter-revolution, 1789–1815," in Derek Beales and Geoffrey Best, eds., *History, Society and the Churches: Essays in Honour of Owen Chadwick* (Cambridge: Cambridge University Press, 1985), 195–214.

2. Alexander Grab, "From the French Revolution to Napoleon," in John A. Davis, ed., *Italy in the Nineteenth Century, 1796–1900* (New York: Oxford University Press, 2000), 25–26; Michael Boers, "Centre and Periphery in Napoleonic Italy: The Nature of French Rule in the *départements réunis*, 1800–1814," in Michael Rowe, ed., *Collaboration and Resistance in Napoleonic Europe: State-Formation in an Age of Upheaval, c. 1800–1815* (Houndmills, Basingstoke: Palgrave, 2003), 55–73.

3. Geoffrey Symcox, "The Jews of Italy in the *Triennio Giacobino*, 1796–1799," in David Myers et al., eds., *Acculturation and Its Discontents: The Italian Jewish Experience between Exclusion and Inclusion* (Toronto: University of Toronto Press, 2008), 154.

4. Ibid., 156.

5. Grab, "From the French Revolution to Napoleon," 27.

6. Ibid., 28–29. The more radical policies were equality of opportunity, limits on wealth, progressive taxation, free public education, and a welfare system.

7. Mario Rossi, "Emancipation and the Jews of Italy," in Abraham Duker and Meir Ben-Horin, eds., *Emancipation and Counter-Emancipation* (New York: Ktav, 1974), 209.

8. Ibid., 210.

9. Cecil Roth, *The History of the Jews of Italy* (Philadelphia: Jewish Publication Society, 1946), 429. For emancipation decrees in Rome and Padua, see Paul Mendes-Flohr and Jehuda Reinharz, *The Jew in the Modern World: A Documentary History*, 2nd ed. (New York: Oxford University Press, 1995), 121–23. The Cisalpine Constitution of June 30, 1797, is reproduced in Karl Heinrich Ludwig Pölitz, ed., *Die europäischen Verfassungen seit dem Jahre 1789 bis auf die neueste Zeit*, 4 vols. (Leipzig: Brockhaus, 1832–47), 2:350–75. For a chronicle of events in Ancona, see the anonymous "A Miraculous Tale," in Barukh Mevorakh, *Napoleon u-Tekufato* (Jerusalem: Mossad Bialik, 1968), 17–36.

10. Ulrich Wyrwa, *Juden in der Toskana und in Preußen im Vergleich: Aufklärung und Emanzipation in Florenz, Livorno, Berlin und Königsberg i. Pr.* (Tübingen: Mohr, 2003), 167; Carlo Mangio, "La communauté juive de Livorne face à la Révolution Française," in Bernhard Blumenkranz and Albert Soboul, eds., *Les Juifs et la Révolution Française: Problèmes et aspirations* (Toulouse: Privat, 1976), 202–3.

11. Roberto G. Salvadori, *The Jews of Florence: From the Origins of the Community up to the Present*, trans. Ann Curiel (Florence: La Giuntina, 2001), 53.

12. Symcox, "The Jews of Italy in the *Triennio Giacobino*," 159.

13. For the Jews' response to the French occupation of Livorno, see Mangio, "La communauté juive de Livorne face à la Révolution Française," 191–209 and Wyrwa, *Juden in der Toskana und in Preußen im Vergleich*, 157–61.

14. Rossi, "Emancipation and the Jews of Italy," 210; Symcox, "The Jews of Italy in the *Triennio Giacobino*," 158–59; Wyrwa, *Juden in der Toskana und in Preußen im Vergleich*, 167–73; Roth, *The History of the Jews of Italy*, 433–39.

15. Grab, "From the French Revolution to Napoleon," 34.

16. Roth, *The History of the Jews of Italy*, 444.

17. Wyrwa, *Juden in der Toskana und in Preußen im Vergleich*, 183–85.

18. Lois Dubin, *The Port Jews of Habsburg Trieste: Absolutist Politics and Enlightenment Culture* (Stanford: Stanford University Press, 1999), 220.

19. The Patriots' arrest of Princess Wilhelmina, the Prussian king's sister, sparked the

invasion. For the negotiations of the *parnassim* with the various authorities and their exercise of "factual civil authority in the Jewish Quarter" during the revolt, see Jozeph Michman, *Dutch Jewry during the Emancipation Period: Gothic Turrets on a Corinthian Building* (Amsterdam: Amsterdam University Press, 1995), 1–22.

20. Jonathan I. Israel, *The Dutch Republic: Its Rise, Greatness, and Fall, 1477–1806* (Oxford: Clarendon, 1995), 1115.

21. Ibid., 1120–21.

22. The tie to the House of Orange was universally acknowledged. See *Acktenstücke zur Geschichte der Erhebung der Juden zu Bürgern in der Republik Batavien* (Neustrelitz: Michaelis, 1797), 6–8, 63–64. The German translation was intended to promote Jewish emancipation in the German states at the Congress of Rastatt (December 1797). See Michman, *Dutch Jewry during the Emancipation Period*, 87–88.

23. Elchanan Tal, ed., *Ha-Kehilah ha-Ashkenazit be-Amsterdam be-meah ha-18* (Jerusalem: Merkaz Zalman Shazar, 2010), 219–23. For these issues in the polemical pamphlets of the "new community [*naye kille*]," see Jozeph Michman and Marion Aptroot, eds., *Storm in the Community: Yiddish Polemical Pamphlets of Amsterdam Jewry, 1797–98* (Cincinnati: Hebrew Union College Press, 2002), 76, 86, 105–06.

24. Michman, *Dutch Jewry during the Emancipation Period*, 2–29, 77.

25. The decree of March 9, 1632, debarring Jews from retail trade and handicrafts remained in force. See Karina Sonnenberg-Stern, *Emancipation and Poverty: The Ashkenazi Jews of Amsterdam, 1796–1850* (Houndmills, Basingstoke: Macmillan, 2000), 47.

26. For Felix Libertate as an integral element of the "Radicals," see Laurence Charpentier, "Aufklärung und Judenemanzipation in den ersten Jahren der Batavischen Republik (1795–1798)," *Aschkenas: Zeitschrift für Geschichte und Kultur der Juden* 4, no. 1 (1994): 141–52.

27. Michman, *Dutch Jewry during the Emancipation Period*, 188–89.

28. This emphasis probably derived from the multiconfessional nature of Dutch society. See Michman, *Dutch Jewry during the Emancipation Period*, 160; A. Half, "Diyunei ha-Aseifa ha-Leumit shel ha-Republika ha-Batavit bi-dvar ha-Emanzipatsiya la-Yehudim, 1796," in Yosef Michman, ed., *Mekhkarim al toldot Yahadut Holand* (Jerusalem: Magnes Press, 1975), 201–40.

29. *Acktenstücke*, 32.

30. Michman, *Dutch Jewry during the Emancipation Period*, 23. Raphael Mahler argued that the debate turned on "formal acknowledgement of existing facts." See *A History of Modern Jewry, 1780–1815* (New York: Schocken, 1971), 91. David Vital characterized it as "less a dramatic change than a regularization of their status by comprehensive legislation." See *A People Apart: A Political History of the Jews in Europe, 1789–1939* (Oxford: Oxford University Press, 1999), 61. See also *Acktenstücke*, 11. The petition six Jewish members of Felix Libertate submitted to the Batavian National Assembly was limited to political rights: "the uncontested rights of Jews to be considered as active citizens of the Batavian Republic." See *Vorstellung an die Batavische National-Versammlung, welche das Niederländische Volk repräsentirt, übergeben von einer Anzahl in den Batavischen Niederlanden wohnenden Juden zum Beweise des unbestrittenen Rechtes der Juden, als active Bürger der Batavischen Republik behandelt zu warden*, in *Acktenstücke*, 29–89. The Assembly's September 9, 1796, "Admonition" to the various authorities in the Netherlands to enforce the September 2 declaration makes it clear that only political rights were at issue: "it is not a new grant of prerogatives whose recognition was doubtful or controversial; it is merely the clarification that there were no grounds to deny the Jewish residents rights that every member of society can enjoy." Ibid., 96.

31. *Acktenstücke*, 17. J. G. H. Hahn (1761–1823) was Recorder of the Committee the

National Assembly had appointed on March 29, 1796. See Michman, *Dutch Jewry during the Emancipation Period*, 23.

32. *Acktenstücke*, 9–10, 11, 14–15.

33. Ibid., 18–23. Efforts began in 1781 to recruit indigent Amsterdam Jewish males to the Dutch navy, which lacked personnel. Community leaders (*parnassim*) signed a detailed agreement that would guarantee the recruits' ability to observe Jewish law. See Michman, *Dutch Jewry during the Emancipation Period*, 184–87.

34. Arend H. Hussen Jr., "Die Gleichstellung der Juden mit anderen niederländischen Bürgern im Jahre 1796," *Aschkenas* 6, no. 1 (1996): 154.

35. Schimmelpennick made this important point. See Half, "Diyunei ha-Aseifa ha-Leumit shel ha-Republika ha-Batavit bi-dvar ha-Emanzipatsiya la-Yehudim, 1796," 220–21, 234–40. For opponents, see 206–15; for proponents, 215–26. The discussion in the Batavian Republic differed fundamentally from that in France since corporate privilege was not an issue. See ibid., 232. Cf. Hussen, "Die Gleichstellung der Juden mit anderen niederländischen Bürgern im Jahre 1796," 155–60. For an abbreviated version, see "The Debate on Jewish Emancipation (August 22–31, 1796); National Assembly of Batavia," in Paul Mendes-Flohr and Jehuda Reinharz, eds., *The Jew in the Modern World: A Documentary History*, 3rd ed. (New York: Oxford University Press, 2011), 31–44. For the creation of citizenship in the Batavian Republic, see Maarten Prak, "Burghers into Citizens: Urban and National Citizenship in the Netherlands during the Revolutionary Era (c. 1800)," in Michael Hanagan and Charles Tilly, eds., *Extending Citizenship, Reconfiguring States* (New York: Rowman and Littlefield, 1999), 17–35 and Wayne te Brake, "Religious Identities and the Boundaries of Citizenship in the Dutch Republic," in James E. Bradley and Dale K. Van Kley, eds., *Religion and Politics in Enlightenment Europe* (Notre Dame, IN: University of Notre Dame Press, 2001), 254–93.

36. Michman, *Dutch Jewry during the Emancipation Period*, 24; Sonnenberg-Stern, *Emancipation and Poverty*, 50. The first paragraph confirmed active citizenship: it prohibited excluding Jews from "exercising any rights or advantages." The second paragraph, in keeping with the separation of church and state enacted on August 5, 1796, abolished previous laws regulating the "Jewish Church" or "Church Regulations of the Jews." The municipality would no longer employ coercion to enforce the communal authorities' decisions. See Michman and Aptroot, *Storm in the Community*, 6.

37. Michman, *Dutch Jewry during the Emancipation Period*, 25–27.

38. Michman emphasizes the extent to which property qualifications restricted the exercise of the franchise. See ibid., 77–78. For the Radicals' dismissal of the old Ashkenazi Jewish leadership, the instatement of Radicals, and the Radical leaders' failure, see ibid., 81–85.

39. Ibid., 87–89.

40. Ibid., 27–29; Israel, *The Dutch Republic*, 1125.

41. Ernst Rudolf Huber, *Dokumente zur deutschen Verfassungsgeschichte, 1803–1850*, 3rd ed. (Stuttgart: Kohlhammer, 1978), 1:37–38.

42. Joachim Whaley, *Germany and the Holy Roman Empire*, 2 vols. (Oxford: Oxford University Press, 2012), 2:603.

43. German: *Reichsdeputationshauptschluss*. See Huber, *Dokumente zur deutschen Verfassungsgeschichte*, 1:1–28 and Whaley, *Germany and the Holy Roman Empire*, 2:621. Whaley called this "the most extensive redistribution of property in German history prior to 1945" (620). For example, "Baden [received] over seven times the territory that it had lost, Prussia nearly five times, and Württemberg four times" (621).

44. Whaley, *Germany and the Holy Roman Empire*, 2:623: "the *Reichsdeputationshauptschluss* did for the Reich what the revolution had done for France."

45. Ibid., 2:629.

46. Huber, *Dokumente zur deutschen Verfassungsgeschichte*, 1:35–36.

47. Ibid., 1:37–38; Whaley, *Germany and the Holy Roman Empire*, 2:643–44.

48. Whaley, *Germany and the Holy Roman Empire*, 2:559–63.

49. For a typology of the states allied to Napoleon, see Andreas Fahrmeir, "Centralisation versus Particularism in the 'Third Germany,'" in Rowe, ed., *Collaboration and Resistance in Napoleonic Europe*, 107–20.

50. Christopher Clark, "German Jews," in Rainer Liedtke and Stephan Wendehorst, eds., *The Emancipation of Catholics, Jews and Protestants: Minorities and the Nation State in Nineteenth-Century Europe* (Manchester: Manchester University Press, 1999), 126.

51. Jacob Toury, "Types of Jewish Municipal Rights in German Townships: The Problem of Local Emancipation," *Leo Baeck Institute Yearbook* 22 (1977): 55–80. In contrast to Toury's distinction between municipal (*Stadtsrechte*) and state rights (*Staatsrechte*), Baron emphasized the distinction between *privatbürgerliche Gleichberechtigung* (civic rights) and *bürgerliche Gleichberechtigung* (political rights). See Salo Baron, "Newer Approaches to Jewish Emancipation," *Diogenes* 29 (Spring 1960): 70.

52. Shulamit S. Magnus, *Jewish Emancipation in a German City: Cologne, 1798–1871* (Stanford: Stanford University Press, 1997), 25–28.

53. Anton Maria Keim, "Das jüdische Mainz im Zeitalter der Emanzipation und Gleichberechtigung," *Argonautenschiff* 6 (1997): 143.

54. *Code civil des Français* (Paris: F. Didot, 1804); H. A. L. Fisher, "The Codes," in *The Cambridge Modern History*, 13 vols. (Cambridge: Cambridge University Press, 1902–12), 9:148–64; Joseph Goy, "Civil Code," in François Furet and Mona Ozouf, eds., *A Critical Dictionary of the French Revolution* (Cambridge, MA: Harvard University Press, 1989), 437–48.

55. On Westphalia as a model state, see Elisabeth Fehrenbach, *Traditionale Gesellschaft und revolutionäres Recht: Die Einführung des Code Napoléon in den Rheinbundstaaten* (Göttingen: Vandenhoeck, 1974), 14–28, 79–104 and Helmut Berding, "Die Emanzipation der Juden im Königreich Westfalen (1807–1813)," *Archiv für Sozialgeschichte* 23 (1983): 28–34. The kingdom consisted of such territories as the Ecclesiastical Principalities of Paderborn and Münster, the Prussian territories of Mark, Minden, Ravensberg and Tecklenburg, Braunschweig, Kurhessen, and portions of Hannover, as well as the eastern portion of the former Duchy of Westphalia. See Arno Herzig, *Judentum und Emanzipation in Westfalen* (Münster: Aschendorffsche Verlagsbuchhandlung, 1973), 1–4, 12, 14 and Ernst Huber, *Deutsche Verfassungsgeschichte Seit 1789*, 5 vols., 2nd ed. (Stuttgart: Kohlhammer, 1967), 1:77. Some of the former territories had been interested in the Jews solely as a source of revenue; Joseph II's legislation and the public debate around Dohm had no palpable impact. Herzig, *Judentum und Emanzipation in Westfalen*, 10.

56. Fehrenbach, *Traditionale Gesellschaft und revolutionäres Recht*, 79–104.

57. The decree is reprinted in L. Horwitz, *Die Israeliten unter dem Königreich Westfalen* (Berlin: S. Calvary, 1900), 6–7.

58. Herzig, *Judentum und Emanzipation in Westfalen*, 12–13.

59. The Consistory also stirred a controversy by permitting the consumption of legumes during Passover. See Michael A. Meyer, *Response to Modernity: A History of the Reform Movement in Judaism* (New York: Oxford University Press, 1988), 28–43; Jacob Rader Marcus, *Israel Jacobson: The Founder of the Reform Movement in Judaism* (Cincinnati: Hebrew Union College Press, 1972); Felix Lazarus, *Das Königlich Westphälische Konsistorium der Israeliten nach meist unbenützten Quellen* (Pressburg: Alkalay, 1914); and Horwitz, *Die Israeliten unter dem Königreich Westfalen*.

60. Berding, "Die Emanzipation der Juden im Königreich Westfalen," 45.

61. H. A. L. Fisher wrote of Dalberg: "No German had been more pliant or more useful to the Emperor of the French." See *Studies in Napoleonic Statesmanship*, 2nd ed. (New York: Greenwood, 1969), 312. On the equality of Calvinists, see p. 315.

62. Rachel Heuberger and Helga Krohn, *Hinaus aus dem Ghetto: Juden in Frankfurt am Main, 1800–1950* (Frankfurt: Fischer, 1988), 20–22.

63. Ibid., 22–23.

64. Fisher, *Studies in Napoleonic Statesmanship*, 325–29.

65. Fehrenbach, *Traditionale Gesellschaft und revolutionäres Recht*, 114–20.

66. Heuberger and Krohn, *Hinaus aus dem Ghetto*, 23–24.

67. Arno Herzig, "Die Juden in Hamburg, 1780–1860," in Arno Herzig and Saskia Rohde, eds., *Die Juden in Hamburg: 1590 bis 1990; Wissenschaftliche Beiträge der Universität Hamburg zur Ausstellung "Vierhundert Jahre Juden in Hamburg"* (Hamburg: Dölling and Galitz, 1991), 68; Helga Krohn, *Die Juden in Hamburg, 1800–1850: Ihre soziale, kulturelle und politische Enwicklung während der Emanzipationszeit* (Hamburg: Europäische Verlagsanstalt, 1967), 9. Since 1671 Hamburg belonged to a confederation of Hamburg-Altona-Wandsbek. The so-called "three communities" arrangement collapsed with the demise of the Holy Roman Empire. With the law of April 26, 1812, Hamburg was forced to be entirely independent and to organize its own *Consistoire*. See Krohn, *Die Juden in Hamburg*, 18.

68. The memorandum is reproduced in Moses Michael Haarbleicher, *Zwei Epochen aus der Geschichte der Deutsch-Israelitischen Gemeinde in Hamburg* (Hamburg, 1866), 71–77.

69. Krohn, *Die Juden in Hamburg*, 15–17.

70. Herzig, "Die Juden in Hamburg," 68–69.

71. Reinhard Rürup, "Die Emanzipation der Juden in Baden," in *Emanzipation und Antisemitismus: Studien zur "Judenfrage" der bürgerlichen Gesellschaft* (Göttingen: Vandenhoeck & Ruprecht, 1975), 39–44. An early memorandum (1782) explored the lessons to be drawn from Joseph II's edicts, which government bureaucrats continued to discuss for the next decade and a half. From 1797 to 1801 a Privy Council wrote a lengthy memorandum inspired by Dohm's tract in which he summarized all the government's previous deliberations.

72. Fehrenbach, *Traditionale Gesellschaft und revolutionäres Recht*, 104–14.

73. Dagmar Herzog, *Intimacy and Exclusion: Religious Politics in Pre-Revolutionary Baden* (Princeton: Princeton University Press, 1996), 6–7; Fisher, *Studies in Napoleonic Statesmanship*, 45. Baden-Durlach and Baden-Baden were first united in 1771. See Huber, *Deutsche Verfassungsgeschichte seit 1789*, 1:323.

74. Toury, "Types of Jewish Municipal Rights in German Townships," 72, 76.

75. Adolf Lewin, *Geschichte der badischen Juden seit der Regierung Karl Friedrichs (1738–1909)* (Karlsruhe: G. Braun, 1909), 300.

76. Rürup, "Die Emanzipation der Juden in Baden," 47.

77. Ibid., 48–49.

78. Huber, *Deutsche Verfassungsgeschichte Seit 1789*, 1:319–21.

79. The Duchy of Bavaria had expelled its Jews in 1553. See Stefan Schwarz, *Die Juden in Bayern im Wandel der Zeiten* (Munich: G. Olzog, 1963), 57–60 and James F. Harris, *The People Speak! Anti-Semitism and Emancipation in Nineteenth-Century Bavaria* (Ann Arbor: University of Michigan Press, 1994), 9–11. For Protestants, see Gerhard Hirschmann, "Die Evangelische Kirche seit 1800," in Max Spindler, ed., *Handbuch der Bayerischen Geschichte*, 4 vols. (Munich: Beck, 1975), 4, 2: 883–34.

80. Wolfgang Schmidt, "Die Juden in der Bayerischen Armee," in Frank Nägler, ed., *Deutsche Jüdische Soldaten: Von der Epoche der Emanzipation bis zum Zeitalter der Weltkriege* (Hamburg: Mittler, 1996), 64.

81. Schwarz, *Die Juden in Bayern im Wandel der Zeiten*, 96–117; Manfred Treml, "Von der 'Judenmission' zur 'Bürgerlichen Verbesserung': Zur Vorgeschichte und Frühphase der Judenemanzipation in Bayern," in Manfred Treml and Josef Kirmeier, eds., *Geschichte und Kultur der Juden in Bayern: Aufsätze* (Munich: Saur, 1988), 247–65.

82. Fehrenbach, *Traditionale Gesellschaft und revolutionäres Recht*, 133–45.

83. Harris suggests that Bavaria treated its newly acquired Jews as immigrants. See *The People Speak!* 24.

84. Toury, "Types of Jewish Municipal Rights in German Townships."

85. Treml, "Von der 'Judenmission' zur 'Bürgerlichen Verbesserung,' " 256–57.

86. Christopher Clark, *Iron Kingdom: The Rise and Downfall of Prussia, 1600–1947* (Cambridge, MA: Harvard University Press, 2006), 312–13, 327, 340.

87. Ismar Freund, *Die Emanzipation der Juden in Preußen unter besonderer Berücksichtigung des Gesetzes vom 11. März 1812*, 2 vols. (Berlin: Poppelauer, 1912), 1:37ff.

88. *Akten-Stücke, die Reform der Jüdischen Kolonieen in den Preußischen Staaten betreffend* (Berlin, 1793). For this analysis, see Sorkin, *The Transformation of German Jewry*, 73–78.

89. See Freund, *Die Emanzipation der Juden in Preußen*, 1:209–22. The petitions and memoranda are reprinted in ibid., 2:91–96, 99–106, 131–36, 148–50, 207–8, 317, 319, 332–35, 401–4, 406, 407–12, 413–27, 428–53.

90. Albert A. Bruer, *Geschichte der Juden in Preußen (1750–1820)* (Frankfurt: Campus, 1991), 293.

91. Ibid., 274, 280. The persistence of the "body tax" (*Leibzoll*) became an issue of contention with Saxony and France in 1811. See ibid., 294–95.

92. Freund, *Die Emanzipation der Juden in Preußen*, 1:49. The tax was abolished on December 12, 1787, for Jews in Prussia and on July 4, 1788, for foreign Jews traveling to the Frankfurt fair.

93. Bruer, *Geschichte der Juden in Preußen*, 245.

94. Ibid., 266–68; Clark, *Iron Kingdom*, 336. In Berlin Salomon Veit and David Friedländer were elected, in Königsberg Samuel Wulff Friedländer.

95. For the role of Jewish bankers and financiers in the Prussian reform, see Bruer, *Geschichte der Juden in Preußen*, 226–56.

96. For portraits of the major figures, see ibid., 257–64, 271–305.

97. The king personally edited the passages on appointments to state positions and conscription. See ibid., 296–97.

98. Bruer suggests that Schrötter set the tone for conditional emancipation. See ibid., 274–75.

99. Ibid., 269–70; Clark, *Iron Kingdom*, 337.

100. See Jacob Katz, *Out of the Ghetto: The Social Background of Jewish Emancipation, 1770–1870*, 2nd ed. (New York: Schocken, 1978), 169.

101. Mack Walker, *German Home Towns: Community, State, and General Estate, 1648–1871* (Ithaca: Cornell University Press, 1971), 266–67; Heinrich Heffter, *Die deutsche Selbstverwaltung im 19. Jahrhundert: Geschichte der Ideen und Institutionen*, 2nd ed. (Stuttgart: Koehler, 1969), 84–123.

Chapter Nine. Sanhedrin

1. Quoted in Suzanne Desan, *The Family on Trial in Revolutionary France* (Berkeley: University of California Press, 2004), 286. Historians have focused on two issues: first, Napoleon's attitude toward Jews, and especially the Jews of Alsace, and second, the As-

sembly/Sanhedrin's decisions vis-à-vis Jewish law (*halakha*). In contrast, I emphasize the neglected issue of the Assembly's relationship to the Civil Code.

2. For the Jewish communities' disorganization since the Terror, see Robert Anchel, *Napoléon et les Juifs: Essai sur les rapports de l'État français et du culte israélite de 1806 à 1815* (Paris: Presses Universitaires de France, 1928), 42–61. For the Civil Code, see *Code civil des Français* (Paris: F. Didot, 1804).

3. Councillor Beugnot used the phrase in a report to the *Conseil d'État*. Cited in Simon Schwarzfuchs, *Napoleon, the Jews and the Sanhedrin* (London: Routledge and Kegan Paul, 1979), 47. For other accounts that may have reached Napoleon, see Anchel, *Napoléon et les Juifs*, 62–75.

4. Anchel, *Napoléon et les Juifs*, 102–27.

5. Schwarzfuchs, *Napoleon, the Jews and the Sanhedrin*, 27–28, 50–52, 56, 59. A pamphlet that may have influenced Napoleon was Louis Poujol, *Quelques observations concernant les Juifs en général et plus particulièrement ceux d'Alsace* (Paris, 1806).

6. Desan, *The Family on Trial*, 315–16.

7. Ibid., 290–303. Two accounts are H. A. L. Fisher, "The Codes," in *The Cambridge Modern History*, 13 vols. (Cambridge: Cambridge University Press, 1902–12), 9:148–64; and Joseph Goy, "Civil Code," in François Furet and Mona Ozouf, eds., *A Critical Dictionary of the French Revolution* (Cambridge, MA: Harvard University Press, 1989), 437–48. Goy emphasizes the extent to which the Convention's "Committee on Legislation" (1793–94) had established "the broad outlines of the future Civil Code." See 440–41. For an overview of many aspects, see Bernard Schwartz, ed., *The Code Napoleon and the Common-Law World* (Westport, CT: Greenwood, 1956).

8. Quoted in Fisher, "The Codes," 9:155.

9. Patrick Weil, *How to Be French: Nationality in the Making since 1789*, trans. Catherine Porter (Durham: Duke University Press, 2008), 12–29. From 1790 "all foreigners were automatically French if they had been resident in France for five years, had acquired property, had set up a business, or had received a letter of municipal affiliation" (17). Quotation at 20. Napoleon initially favored jus soli to make all males liable to conscription. The jurist François Tronchet favored, and prevailed in introducing, jus sanguinis.

10. Weil, *How to Be French*, 27–29.

11. Schwarzfuchs, *Napoleon, the Jews and the Sanhedrin*, 50; Anchel, *Napoléon et les Juifs*, 95. Schwarzfuchs notes that in a meeting with his ministers Napoleon had denied the Jews' citizenship (49). Napoleon significantly made the Minister of the Interior, rather than the Minister of Cults, responsible for the Assembly: "Napoleon had definitely chosen the political, not the civil, path to deal with the Jews" (52). Ronald Schechter argues that Napoleon convened the Assembly and Sanhedrin to cast himself as liberator of the Jews and a Moses-like legislator to legitimize his illegitimate rule. See *Obstinate Hebrews: Representations of Jews in France, 1715–1815* (Berkeley: University of California Press, 2003), 194–209.

12. *Collection des actes de l'Assemblée des Israélites de France et du royaume d'Italie* (Paris, 1807), 131. English translation in M. Diogene Tama, *Transactions of the Parisian Sanhedrim, or Acts of the Assembly of Israelitish Deputies of France and Italy* (London, 1807), 132.

13. *Collection des actes*, 132. English translation in Tama, *Transactions*, 133. Molé, from the Council of State, probably composed the questions. See Schwarzfuchs, *Napoleon, the Jews and the Sanhedrin*, 54–55.

14. Simon Schwarzfuchs, *Les Juifs d'Algérie et la France (1830–1855)* (Jerusalem: Ben-Zvi, 1981), 36–37, question #18; Joshua Schreier, "Napoléon's Long Shadow: Morality,

Civilization, and Jews in France and Algeria, 1808–1870," *French Historical Studies* 30, no. 1 (Winter 2007): 77–103; Sarah Abrevaya Stein, *Saharan Jews and the Fate of French Algeria* (Chicago: University of Chicago Press, 2014), 17, 99.

15. Desan, *The Family on Trial*, 93–140, 303. Historians estimate that from 1792 to 1803 some 38,000 to 50,000 divorces took place.

16. Schwarzfuchs, *Napoleon, the Jews and the Sanhedrin*, 98.

17. Ibid., 52–53, 69; Anchel, *Napoléon et les Juifs*, 162. Initially no provision was made for the delegates' expenses. Eventually the Jewish communities were forced to defray them (54).

18. Frances Malino, "From Patriot to Israelite: Abraham Furtado in Revolutionary France," in Jehuda Reinharz and Daniel Swetschinski, eds., *Mystics, Philosophers and Politicians: Essays in Jewish Intellectual History in Honor of Alexander Altmann* (Durham: Duke University Press, 1982), 213–48; Alan Forrest, *Society and Politics in Revolutionary Bordeaux* (Oxford: Oxford University Press, 1975), 56, 113, 124, 129–30, 211, 243, 245.

19. Tama, *Transactions*, 136–37.

20. Cerf Berr funded the yeshiva, initially located in Bischheim. See Alexis Blum, "Sinzheim, le porte-parole des Ashkenazim," in Bernhard Blumenkranz and Albert Soboul, eds., *Le Grand Sanhédrin de Napoléon* (Paris: Archives Juives, 1979), 118–31.

21. Schwarzfuchs, *Napoleon, the Jews and the Sanhedrin*, 63–71.

22. Tama, *Transactions*, 150. On "the law of the land is law," see Gil Graff, *Separation of Church and State: Dina de-Malkhuta Dina in Jewish Law, 1750–1848* (Tuscaloosa: University of Alabama Press, 1985).

23. Graff, *Separation of Church and State*, 71–109; Charles Touati, "Le Grand Sanhédrin de 1807 et le droit rabbinique," in Bernhard Blumenkranz and Albert Soboul, eds., *Le Grand Sanhédrin de Napoléon* (Paris: Archives Juives, 1979), 27–48. Eric Smilévitch understands the Assembly's decisions to have authorized the unprecedented incursion of a fundamentally Christian law code into the interior of Jewish life. See "Halakha et code civil: Questions sur le Grand Sanhédrin de Napoléon," *Pardès* 3 (1986): 9–25. Jay Berkovitz emphasizes the importance of Rabbi Aaron Worms of Metz (1754–1836), a delegate to the Assembly and Sanhedrin, who had written a discourse on gentiles' status in Jewish law. See "The Napoleonic Sanhedrin: Halachic Foundations and Rabbinical Legacy," *CCAR Journal* (Winter 2007): 11–34 and *Rites and Passages: The Beginnings of Modern Jewish Culture in France, 1650–1860* (Philadelphia: University of Pennsylvania Press, 2004), 115–43.

24. Tama, *Transactions*, 150–51.

25. Ibid., 152–54.

26. Ibid., 156.

27. The Sanhedrin would omit the first part of the answer, thereby emphasizing that, while civilly binding, Jewish law prohibited mixed marriage. See Berkovitz, "The Napoleonic Sanhedrin," 16–21. On resistance, see Ismar Schorsch, "On the History of the Political Judgment of the Jew," in *From Text to Context: The Turn to History in Modern Judaism* (Hanover, NH: Brandeis University Press, 1994), 125 and Schechter, *Obstinate Hebrews*, 225–26.

28. Schwarzfuchs, *Napoleon, the Jews and the Sanhedrin*, 71.

29. Tama, *Transactions*, 179–80.

30. Schwarzfuchs, *Napoleon, the Jews and the Sanhedrin*, 72.

31. Tama, *Transactions*, 180–81.

32. Ibid., 182.

33. Ibid., 195.

34. Ibid., 197–201.

35. Ibid., 201–7. Ronald Schechter argues that the Assembly was asserting a "primitive

equality" that demonstrated the superiority of Jewish law to Napoleon's new code. See *Obstinate Hebrews*, 224–25.

36. Tama, *Transactions*, 207.

37. Ibid., 246; Schwarzfuchs, *Napoleon, the Jews and the Sanhedrin*, 80. The government enlisted thirty new rabbis to join the fifteen already present (85).

38. Schwarzfuchs, *Napoleon, the Jews and the Sanhedrin*, 93.

39. Ibid., 94–95.

40. The Consistory had no basis in the Reformed Church; it was a pure imposition of state authority. Napoleon included the Lutherans of Alsace as well. For a translation of the "Organic Articles for Protestant Bodies" (April 6, 1802), see J. F. Maclear, ed., *Church and State in the Modern Age: A Documentary History* (New York: Oxford University, 1995), 101–5.

41. For the "Plan d'organisation du culte juif en France," see Schwarzfuchs, *Napoleon, the Jews and the Sanhedrin*, 42–43.

42. Tama, *Transactions*, 285–92.

43. Cited in Schwarzfuchs, *Napoleon, the Jews and the Sanhedrin*, 98–100.

44. Ibid., 111–13.

45. Anchel, *Napoléon et les Juifs*, 285–411.

46. Phyllis Cohen Albert, *The Jewish Oath in Nineteenth-Century France* (Tel Aviv: Tel Aviv University, 1982); Schwarzfuchs, *Napoleon, the Jews and the Sanhedrin*, 142.

47. Berkovitz, *Rites and Passages*, 130. Simon Schwarzfuchs reproduces the Malesherbes Commission's questions in *Du Juif à l'israélite: Histoire d'une mutation (1770–1870)* (Paris: Fayard, 1989), 87–89.

48. *Archives Nationales* F19 11004; Anchel, *Napoléon et les Juifs*, 229; Schwarzfuchs, *Napoleon, the Jews and the Sanhedrin*, 125. For Napoleon's embrace of "regeneration" and "conditional" emancipation, see Alyssa Goldstein Sepinwall, "Napoleon, French Jews, and the Idea of Regeneration," *CCAR Journal* 54, no. 1 (2007): 55–76.

49. Schwarzfuchs, *Napoleon, the Jews and the Sanhedrin*, 123–24.

Chapter Ten. Partitions

1. Jerzy Lukowski, *The Partitions of Poland: 1772, 1793, 1795* (London: Longman, 1999), 128–82.

2. For the tsarist administration's efforts to break the Polish nobility's power by purchasing or expropriating estates and limiting jurisdiction, see Yochanan Petrovsky-Shtern, *The Golden Age Shtetl: A New History of Jewish Life in East Europe* (Princeton: Princeton University Press, 2014). In 1778 the tsarist administration deprived the gentry of jurisdiction over Jews in private towns (a privilege it had held since 1539). The gentry frequently violated the new regulation. See Matthias Rest, *Die Russische Judengesetzgebung von der ersten polnishcen Teilung bis zum "Polozenie dlja Evreev" (1804)* (Wiesbaden: Harrassowitz, 1975), 135.

3. Curtis G. Murphy, "Progress without Consent: Enlightened Centralism vis-à-vis Local Self-Government in the Towns of East Central Europe and Russia, 1764–1840" (PhD diss., Georgetown University, 2011).

4. Petrovsky-Shtern, *The Golden Age Shtetl*, 145.

5. John Doyle Klier, *Russia Gathers Her Jews: The Origins of the "Jewish Question" in Russia, 1772–1825* (DeKalb: Northern Illinois University Press, 1986), 130; Glenn Dynner, *Yankel's Tavern: Jews, Liquor, & Life in the Kingdom of Poland* (New York: Oxford University Press, 2014), 1–102.

6. Karl Otmar Freiherr von Aretin, "Tausch, Teilung und Länderschacher als Folgen des

Gleichgewichtssystems der europäischen Grossmächte: Die polnischen Teilungen als europäisches Schicksal," in Klaus Zernack, ed., *Polen und die polnische Frage in der Geschichte der Hohenzollernmonarchie, 1701–1871* (Berlin: Colloquium, 1982), 60.

7. Sophia Kemlein, *Die Posener Juden, 1815–1848: Entwicklungsprozesse einer polnischen Judenheit unter preußischer Herrschaft* (Hamburg: Dölling und Galitz, 1997), 49.

8. Ibid., 51. The legislation is reprinted in Heinrich Simon and Ludwig von Rönne, *Die früheren und gegenwärtigen Verhältnisse der Juden in den sämmtlichen Landestheilen des Preußischen Staates* (Breslau: Aderholz, 1843), 292–302.

9. Kemlein, *Die Posener Juden*, 52.

10. Antony Polonsky, *The Jews in Poland and Russia*, 3 vols. (Oxford: Littman, 2010–12), 1:227; Artur Eisenbach, *The Emancipation of the Jews in Poland, 1780–1870* (Oxford: Blackwell, 1991), 116.

11. Louis Lewin, "Ein Judentag aus Süd- und Neuostpreußen," *Monatsschrift für Geschichte und Wissenschaft des Judentums* 59 (July/September 1915): 180–92, 59 (October/December): 278–300; here p. 279.

12. Ibid., 281–82.

13. Ibid., 285–86.

14. Cited in ibid., 285.

15. Janet M. Hartley, *Alexander I* (London: Longman, 1994), 49–50.

16. Polonsky, *The Jews in Poland and Russia*, 1:337.

17. Gavriil Romanovich Derzhavin, "An Opinion Regarding the Prevention of Famine in White Russia and the Organization of the Way of Life of the Jews (1800)," trans. Alexander Fried, *Aschkenas–Zeitschrift für Geschichte und Kultur der Juden* 14, no. 2 (2004): 229–312.

18. Derzhavin, "An Opinion," 267. For Prussia as a model, see 293; for Prussia's elimination of Jewish self-government (kahal), see 286. Arnold Springer argued that Derzhavin's proposal belonged to the tradition of enlightened absolutism and was consistent with Catherine's interventionist legislation of the 1790s. See "Gavriil Derzhavin's Jewish Reform Project of 1800," *Canadian-American Slavic Studies* 10, no. 1 (Spring 1976): 1–23. For a comparison of Derzhavin's and I. G. Frizel's (governor of Lithuania province) ideas with the legislation, see Shmuel Ettinger, "Takanat 1804," in *Bein Polin le-Russiya* (Jerusalem: Mossad Bialik, 1992), 234–56.

19. Derzhavin, "An Opinion," 290–91. Derzhavin criticized the organization of the agricultural economy in Belorussia in general, finding fault with the roles of, and the relationship between, the gentry, whom he castigated for being inefficient managers and spendthrifts, the peasants, whom he criticized as inherently lazy, and the Jews. See 243–54.

20. David E. Fishman, *Russia's First Modern Jews: The Jews of Shklov* (New York: New York University Press, 1995), 85–91, quotation at 85. See "The Project of Nota Chaimonovich [Notkin]," *Aschkenas–Zeitschrift für Geschichte und Kultur der Juden* 14, no. 2 (2004): 312. On Notkin, Nevakhovich, and Peretz, see Eisenbach, *The Emancipation of the Jews in Poland*, 125 and Polonsky, *The Jews in Poland and Russia*, 1:344.

21. Cited in Klier, *Russia Gathers Her Jews*, 130.

22. At least three members of the committee (Czartoryski, Potocki, and Kochubei) viewed education as a means of reform as well as being seriously engaged reformers. See Klier, *Russia Gathers Her Jews*, 123.

23. Rest, *Die Russische Judengesetzgebung*, 157.

24. Hartley, *Alexander I*, 52–54.

25. Klier, *Russia Gathers Her Jews*, 141.

26. Rest, *Die Russische Judengesetzgebung*, 179; Klier, *Russia Gathers Her Jews*, 140.

27. Rest, *Die Russische Judengesetzgebung*, 170–71; Klier, *Russia Gathers Her Jews*,

131–33. Perhaps this is less surprising if one considers that even the arch-leveler of corporations, Joseph II, left intact the estates' fiscal function, the *Buchhaltereien*. See Henry E. Strakosch, *State Absolutism and the Rule of Law: The Struggle for the Codification of Civil Law in Austria, 1753–1811* (Sydney: Sydney University Press, 1967), 134.

28. It may have had import for the tiny minority who sought higher education and subsequently formed the nucleus of a Jewish intelligentsia. For Derzhavin's use of Mendelssohn as a model, albeit misconstrued, see "An Opinion," 292.

29. Polonsky, *The Jews in Poland and Russia*, 1:349–50; Klier, *Russia Gathers Her Jews*, 161; Rest, *Die Russische Judengesetzgebung*, 177.

30. Klier, *Russia Gathers Her Jews*, 138.

31. Strakosch, *State Absolutism and the Rule of Law*, 98, 180, 186, 188.

32. The Habsburg government embraced the concept of uniform law as early as 1753 ("The general welfare of all subjects under one God, one sovereign and one law" [*Die gesammten Unterthanen zu allgemeiner Wohlfahrt untern einem Gott, einem Landsfürsten und einerlei Gesetz*]). See Rolf Grawert, *Staat und Staatsangehörigkeit: Verfassungsgeschichtliche Untersuchung zur Entstehung des Staatsangehörigkeit* (Berlin: Duncker & Humblot, 1973), 146. For that very reason, citizenship was "state citizenship" rather than territorial citizenship. The Habsburg government's primary consideration was unifying an empire of multiple peoples and polities; separating its citizens from those of neighboring countries was decidedly secondary. Dieter Gosewinkel, *Einbürgern und Ausschließen: Die Nationalisierung der Staatsangehörigkeit vom Deutschen Bund bis zur Bundesrepublik Deutschland* (Göttingen: Vandehoeck & Ruprecht, 2001), 35.

33. Franz von Zeiller, whose title was Aulic Councillor, played a leading role in the legislation, which he based on Kantian principles and specifically the concept of "strict law" (*strenges Recht*). He superintended the three drafts of the interim period (1801–6, 1807–9, 1809–10). See Zeiller, *Abhandlung über die Principien des allgemeinen bürgerlichen Gesetzbuches*, 2nd ed. (Vienna: Manz, 1986), 10; Waltraud Heindl and Edith Saurer, *Grenze und Staat: Paßwesen, Staatsbürgerschaft, Heimatrecht, und Fremdengesetzgebung in der österreichischen Monarchie, 1750–1867* (Vienna: Böhlau, 2000), 97; and Strakosch, *State Absolutism and the Rule of Law*, 195–215.

34. Strakosch, *State Absolutism and the Rule of Law*, 188.

35. Michael Stöger, *Darstellung der gesetzlichen Verfassung der galizischen Judenschaft*, 2 vols. (Lemberg: Kuhn & Millikowski, 1833), 1:1–9, 2:1–2.

36. Heindl and Saurer, *Grenze und Staat*, 97–98; Ulrike von Hirschhausen, "From Imperial Inclusion to National Exclusion: Citizenship in the Habsburg Monarchy and in Austria, 1867–1923," *European Review of History* 16, no. 4 (August 2009): 552.

37. Stöger, *Darstellung der gesetzlichen Verfassung der galizischen Judenschaft*, 1:22–23; Heindl and Saurer, *Grenze und Staat*, 109.

38. Stöger, *Darstellung der gesetzlichen Verfassung der galizischen Judenschaft*, 1:19.

39. Ibid., 1:31–42.

40. The prescribed book for the examination was Herz Homberg's *Bnei Zion*. For this book, see Rachel Manekin, "The Moral Education of Jewish Youth: The Case of Bne Zion," in Ivo Cerman, Rita Krueger, and Susan Reynolds, eds., *The Enlightenment in Bohemia: Religion, Morality and Multiculturalism* (Oxford: Voltaire Foundation, 2011), 273–93.

41. Stöger, *Darstellung der gesetzlichen Verfassung der galizischen Judenschaft*, 1:17–19.

42. Ibid., 1:49, 51.

43. Ibid., 1:179–88.

44. Ibid., 1:212–16.

45. Ibid., 1:145–55, 193–97.

46. Ibid., 1:169.

47. Ibid., 1:173.

48. Ibid., 1:177.

49. Ibid., 1:117; William O. McCagg Jr., *A History of Habsburg Jews, 1670–1918* (Bloomington: Indiana University Press, 1989), 111–12; Polonsky, *The Jews in Poland and Russia* 1:254–55.

50. Lukowski, *The Partitions of Poland*, 184.

51. John Stanley, "The Adaptation of the Napoleonic Political Structure in the Duchy of Warsaw (1807–1813)," *Canadian Slavonic Papers* 31, no. 2 (June 1989): 128–45; Eisenbach, *The Emancipation of the Jews in Poland*, 128–31. For the Polish leaders, see Jarosław Czubaty, "The Attitudes of the Polish Political Elite towards the State in the Period of the Duchy of Warsaw, 1807–1815," in Michael Rowe, ed., *Collaboration and Resistance in Napoleonic Europe: State-Formation in an Age of Upheaval, c. 1800–1815* (Houndmills, Basingstoke: Palgrave, 2003), 169–85.

52. Stanley, "The Adaptation of the Napoleonic Political Structure in the Duchy of Warsaw," 141; Eisenbach, *The Emancipation of the Jews in Poland*, 137.

Chapter Eleven. Restoration

1. Francois Delpech, "De 1815 à 1894," in Bernhard Blumenkranz, ed., *Histoire des Juifs en France* (Toulouse: Privat, 1972), 306. For the Charter as a compromise between conflicting positions, see James Roberts, *The Counter-Revolution in France, 1787–1830* (Houndmills, Basingstoke: Macmillan, 1990), 84–85.

2. Jozeph Michman, *Dutch Jewry during the Emancipation Period: Gothic Turrets on a Corinthian Building, 1787–1815* (Amsterdam: Amsterdam University Press, 1995), 216–27. The Consistory's controversial innovations were public announcements in Dutch and the use of surnames in awarding synagogue honors.

3. Max Kohler, *Jewish Rights at International Congresses* (Philadelphia: Jewish Publication Society, 1917), 22–23; Emile Cammaerts, *A History of Belgium: From the Roman Invasion to the Present Day* (New York: Appleton, 1921), 278–82.

4. Tim Chapman, *The Congress of Vienna: Origins, Processes and Results* (London: Routledge, 1998), 43.

5. The Habsburgs recovered the area around Ternopil but not the area surrounding Lublin that had been lost to the Duchy of Warsaw. See Antony Polonsky, *The Jews in Poland and Russia*, 3 vols. (Oxford: Littman, 2010–12), 1:249 and Artur Eisenbach, *The Emancipation of the Jews in Poland, 1780–1870* (Oxford: Blackwell, 1991), 149.

6. The area comprised some 30,000 square kilometers and some 800,000 inhabitants. See Sophia Kemlein, *Die Posener Juden, 1815–1848: Entwicklungsprozesse einer polnischen Judenheit unter preußischer Herrschaft* (Hamburg: Dölling and Galitz, 1997), 58 and Polonsky, *The Jews in Poland and Russia*, 1:229.

7. C. A. Macartney, *National States and National Minorities* (New York: Russell & Russell, 1934), 160. The Article read: "*Les Polonais, sujets respectifs des hautes parties contractantes, obtiendront la conservation de leur nationalité, d'après les forms d'existence politique que chacun des gouvernements, auxquels ils appartiennent, jugera convenable de leur accorder.*"

8. Chapman, *The Congress of Vienna*, 49.

9. Ernst Huber, *Deutsche Verfassungsgeschichte Seit 1789*, 5 vols., 2nd ed. (Stuttgart: Kohlhammer, 1967), 1:543–54; James J. Sheehan, *German History, 1770–1866* (Oxford: Oxford University Press, 1989), 393–410.

10. Michael Hundt, *Die Mindermächtigen deutschen Staaten auf dem Wiener Kongress* (Mainz: Zabern, 1996), 339.

11. On Bavaria and Württemberg after 1815, see Huber, *Deutsche Verfassungsgeschichte Seit 1789*, 1:321–22, 329–34.

12. Salo Baron, *Die Judenfrage auf dem Wiener Kongress* (Vienna: Löwit, 1920), 72–85; Edward Timms, "The Pernicious Rift: Metternich and the Debate about Jewish Emancipation at the Congress of Vienna," *Leo Baeck Institute Yearbook* 46 (2001): 8; Christopher Clark, *Iron Kingdom: The Rise and Downfall of Prussia, 1600–1947* (Cambridge, MA: Harvard University Press, 2006), 389.

13. Baron, *Die Judenfrage auf dem Wiener Kongress*, 147.

14. *Actenstükke die Verbesserrung des bürgerlichen Zustandes der Israeliten betreffend* (Stuttgart and Tübingen: J. G. Cotta, 1815), 18. He included the edicts of Prussia, Baden, Bavaria, Denmark, and the Netherlands. See 85–157.

15. Ibid., 51.

16. Ibid., 42–44. For Humboldt's memorandum, see David Sorkin, *The Transformation of German Jewry, 1780–1840* (New York: Oxford University Press, 1987), 31–32. For a translation, see "Regarding the Draft of a New System of Legislation of the Jews" (July 17, 1809), in Max Kohler, *Jewish Rights at the Congresses of Vienna (1814–15) and Aix-La-Chapelle (1818)* (New York: American Jewish Committee, 1918), 71–83.

17. *Actenstükke*, iv, 70, 77.

18. Michael Hundt, "Die Vertretung der jüdischen Gemeinden Lübecks, Bremens und Hamburgs auf dem Wiener Kongreß," *Blätter für deutsche Landesgeschichte* 130 (1994): 143–90. Two memoranda are reproduced at 183–90.

19. The petitions are reproduced in Nathan Michael Gelber, "Aktenstücke zur Judenfrage am Wiener Kongress 1814–15," *Esra* 6 (1919): 172–79. See Baron, *Die Judenfrage auf dem Wiener Kongress*, 117–46 and Hilde Spiel, *Fanny von Arnstein: Daughter of the Enlightenment*, trans. Christine Shuttleworth (New York: New Vessel Press, 2013), 283, 294–96, 311.

20. Hundt, "Die Vertretung der jüdischen Gemeinden Lübecks, Bremens und Hamburgs auf dem Wiener Kongreß," 161–62.

21. Ernst Huber, *Dokumente zur deutschen Verfassungsgeschichte, 1803–1850*, 3rd ed. (Stuttgart: Kohlhammer, 1978), 1:84–90. For the genesis of Article 16, see Renate Penßel, "Der Wiener Kongress und der Rechtsstatus der jüdischen Gemeinden in Deutschland," in Heinz Duchhardt and Johannes Wischmeyer, eds., *Der Wiener Kongress: Eine kirchenpolitische Zäsur?* (Göttingen: Vandenhoeck & Ruprecht, 2013), 232–38.

22. Heinrich de Wall, "Art. 16 I DBA: Individualrecht oder Regelung zu Gunsten der Kirchen? Die Kontroversen zum Fall Kettenberg innerhalb und außerhalb der Bundesversammlung," in Duchhardt and Wischmeyer, eds., *Der Wiener Kongress*, 253–59; Huber, *Deutsche Verfassungsgeschichte Seit 1789*, 1:412–15; Wolfgang Altgeld, "German Catholics," in Rainer Liedtke and Stephan Wendehorst, eds., *The Emancipation of Catholics, Jews and Protestants: Minorities and the Nation State in Nineteenth-Century Europe* (Manchester: Manchester University Press, 1999), 102–7.

23. Anhalt-Dessau, Schwarzburg-Rudolstadt, and Schaumburg-Lippe awarded Catholics equal rights. Sachsen-Gotha-Altenburg, Sachsen-Coburg-Saalfeld, and Mecklenburg Schwerin granted rights with some restrictions. See Michael Hundt, "Die Mindermächtigen und die Kirchenartikel: Das Problem der Rechtstellung der Katholiken in den kleineren deutschen Staaten," in Duchhardt and Wischmeyer, eds., *Der Wiener Kongress*, 155.

24. Ibid., 156–57.

25. I have modified the translation in Raphael Mahler, *Jewish Emancipation: A Selection of Documents* (New York: American Jewish Committee, 1944), 37–38.

26. Penßel, "Der Wiener Kongress und der Rechtsstatus der jüdischen Gemeinden in Deutschland," 235–36. Most historians attribute the redactions to Johann Smidt (1773–1857), a municipal senator who acted as Bremen's foreign minister. Smidt was primarily concerned to protect the small polities' sovereignty against Prussia: he wanted the Confederation to take the place of the Holy Roman Empire. He dominated among the Hanseatic representatives. See Hundt, *Die Mindermächtigen deutschen Staaten auf dem Wiener Kongress*, 203–8.

27. Baron did not specify whether Hardenberg and Metternich realized the implications of the change. See *Die Judenfrage auf dem Wiener Kongress*, 164–70; Penßel contends that they fully grasped the implications. See "Der Wiener Kongress und der Rechtsstatus der jüdischen Gemeinden in Deutschland," 237. For Metternich's and Hardenberg's accounts of the Article, see Hundt, "Die Vertretung der jüdischen Gemeinden Lübecks, Bremens und Hamburgs auf dem Wiener Kongreß," 177–78.

28. Baron, *Die Judenfrage auf dem Wiener Kongress*, 196.

29. Penßel, "Der Wiener Kongress und der Rechtsstatus der jüdischen Gemeinden in Deutschland," 247.

30. Hundt, "Die Vertretung der jüdischen Gemeinden Lübecks, Bremens und Hamburgs auf dem Wiener Kongreß," 152; Baron, *Die Judenfrage auf dem Wiener Kongress*, 196.

31. Baron, *Die Judenfrage auf dem Wiener Kongress*, 186–93; Penßel, "Der Wiener Kongress und der Rechtsstatus der jüdischen Gemeinden in Deutschland," 244–47.

32. Penßel, "Der Wiener Kongress und der Rechtsstatus der jüdischen Gemeinden in Deutschland," 241–42.

33. Heinrich Simon and Ludwig Rönne, *Die früheren und gegenwärtigen Verhältnisse der Juden in den sämmtlichen Landestheilen des Preußischen Staates* (Breslau: Aderholz, 1843), x–xi; Penßel, "Der Wiener Kongress und der Rechtsstatus der jüdischen Gemeinden in Deutschland," 242–44.

34. Mack Walker, *German Home Towns: Community, State, and General Estate, 1648–1871* (Ithaca: Cornell University Press, 1971), 267ff.

35. Hannelore Burger, "Die Staatsbürgerschaft," in Waltraud Heindl and Edith Saurer, eds., *Grenze und Staat: Paßwesen, Staatsbürgerschaft, Heimatrecht und Fremdengesetzgebung in der österreichischen Monarchie, 1750–1867* (Vienna: Böhlau, 2000), 108–9. The criteria for citizenship were: birth to a citizen parent, service to the state, an occupation requiring residence, ten years of residence, certification of moral character.

36. Chapman, *The Congress of Vienna*, 42; David Laven, "The Age of Restoration," in John A. Davis, ed., *Italy in the Nineteenth Century, 1796–1900* (New York: Oxford University Press, 2000), 52.

37. Cecil Roth, *The History of the Jews of Italy* (Philadelphia: Jewish Publication Society, 1946), 445–50; Laven, "The Age of Restoration," 55–59.

Chapter Twelve. Central Europe, 1815–1847

1. In German history, these decades are known as the "Pre-March" (*Vormärz*) or forerunners to the 1848 revolution.

2. Napoleon either had not impinged, or impinged less, upon such north and central German states as Brunswick, Hanover, Saxony, and the two Mecklenburgs. The free cities were Hamburg, Bremen, Lübeck, and Frankfurt am Main.

3. James J. Sheehan, *German History, 1770–1866* (Oxford: Oxford University Press, 1989), 411–25; Mack Walker, *German Home Towns: Community, State, and General Estate, 1648–1871* (Ithaca: Cornell University Press, 1971), 283–353.

4. Sheehan, *German History*, 427. Sheehan calls the period 1800–1830 "the apogee of the *Beamtenstaat*"; powerful representative institutions had yet to emerge. See p. 441.

5. Ibid., 440; Walker, *German Home Towns*, 260–79; Jonathan Sperber, *The European Revolutions, 1848–1851*, 2nd ed. (Cambridge: Cambridge University Press, 2005), 27–32.

6. Rolf Grawert, *Staat und Staatsangehörigkeit: Verfassungsgeschichtliche Untersuchung zur Entstehung der Staatsangehörigkeit* (Berlin: Duncker & Humblot, 1973), 164–65. For the impact of this dualism on Jews, see Jacob Toury, "Probleme Jüdischer Gleichberechtigung auf Lokalbürgerlicher Ebene," *Jahrbuch des Instituts für Deutsche Geschichte* 2 (1973): 267–86 and Toury, "Types of Jewish Municipal Rights in German Townships: The Problem of Local Emancipation," *Leo Baeck Institute Yearbook* 22 (1977): 55–80. For a comparison across Europe, see Artur Eisenbach, *The Emancipation of the Jews in Poland, 1780–1870* (Oxford: Blackwell, 1991), 230–31.

7. Andreas Fahrmeir, *Citizenship: The Rise and Fall of a Modern Concept* (New Haven: Yale University Press, 2007), 64–65, 68; Fahrmeir, "Nineteenth-Century German Citizenships: A Reconsideration," *Historical Journal* 40, no. 3 (1997): 738–39; and Toury, "Probleme Jüdischer Gleichberechtigung auf Lokalbürgerlicher Ebene," 267–86.

8. Fahrmeir, "Nineteenth-Century German Citizenships," 738. Fahrmeir stresses that jus soli prevailed in the multiple German states until the unified German Empire introduced jus sanguinis.

9. Grawert, *Staat und Staatsangehörigkeit*, 164–93.

10. Baden, Bavaria, and Württemberg signed such treaties. See Fahrmeir, "Nineteenth-Century German Citizenships," 733–39 and Grawert, *Staat und Staatsangehörigkeit*, 135. The Frankfurt National Assembly employed the term "Staatsangehörige" (181).

11. Ernst Huber, *Deutsche Verfassungsgeschichte Seit 1789*, 5 vols., 2nd ed. (Stuttgart: Kohlhammer, 1967), 1:412–15.

12. Thomas Nipperdey, "Verein als soziale Struktur in Deutschland im späten 18. und frühen 19. Jahrhundert," in *Gesellschaft, Kultur, Theorie: Gesammelte Aufsätze zur neuren Geschichte* (Göttingen: Vandenhoeck, 1976), 174–205; Klaus Tenfelde, "Civil Society and the Middle Classes in Nineteenth-Century Germany," in Nancy Bermeo and Philip Nord, eds., *Civil Society before Democracy: Lessons from Nineteenth-Century Europe* (Lanham, MD: Rowman & Littlefield, 2000), 83–110.

13. Reinhard Rürup, "The Tortuous and Thorny Path to Legal Equality: 'Jews Laws' and Emancipatory Legislation in Germany from the Late Eighteenth Century," *Leo Baeck Institute Yearbook* 31 (1986): 9.

14. Christopher Clark, "German Jews," in Rainer Liedtke and Stephan Wendehorst, eds., *The Emancipation of Catholics, Jews and Protestants: Minorities and the Nation State in Nineteenth-Century Europe* (Manchester: Manchester University Press, 1999), 123.

15. Rürup, "The Tortuous and Thorny Path to Legal Equality," 21; Volkmar Eichstädt, *Bibliographie zur Geschichte der Judenfrage* (Hamburg: Hanseatische Verlagsanstalt, 1938).

16. For example, Friedrich Rühs, *Über die Ansprüche der Juden an das deutsche Bürgerrecht*, 2nd ed. (Berlin, 1816). On the debate, see Selma Stern-Taubler, "Der literarische Kampf um die Emanzipation in den Jahren 1816–20 und sein ideologischen und soziologischen Voraussetzungen," *Hebrew Union College Annual* 23, pt. 2 (1950–51): 171ff, and David Sorkin, *The Transformation of Germany Jewry, 1780–1840* (New York: Oxford University Press, 1987), 37–40.

17. Johann Ludwig Ewald, *Ideen über die nötige Organisation der Israeliten in Christlichen Staaten* (Karlsruhe, 1816); Alexander Lips, *Über die künftige Stellung der Juden in den deutschen Bundesstaaten* (Erlangen, 1819). Ewald (1747–1822) was a clergyman and civil servant in Baden, Lips a professor of philosophy at the University of Erlangen, Bavaria.

18. Sorkin, *The Transformation of German Jewry, 1780–1840* (New York: Oxford University Press, 1987); Robert Liberles, "Was There a Jewish Movement for Emancipation in Germany?" *Leo Baeck Institute Yearbook* 31 (1986): 35–49.

19. Gabriel Riesser, "Über die Stellung der Bekenner des mosaischen Glaubens in Deutschland: An die Deutschen aller Confessionen," in Uri Kaufmann and Jobst Paul, eds., *Gabriel Riesser: Ausgewählte Werke* (Vienna: Böhlau, 2012), 37–85. On Riesser, see Fritz Friedländer, *Das Leben Gabriel Riessers: Ein Beitrag zur Inneren Geschichte Deutschlands im Neunzehnten Jahrhundert* (Berlin: Philo, 1926) and Arno Herzig, *Gabriel Riesser* (Hamburg: Ellert & Richter, 2008).

20. Ludwig Börne, "Geschichte und Menschen der französischen Revolution," in *Sämtliche Schriften*, 5 vols. (Düsseldorf: Melzer, 1964), 3:1067.

21. The new territories comprised the former Saxony, Hesse-Darmstadt, Nassau, the Kingdom of Westphalia, and the Grand Duchy of Poznań. For the estimate of twenty-one, see Heinrich Simon and Ludwig Rönne, *Die früheren und gegenwärtigen Verhältnisse der Juden in den sämmtlichen Landestheilen des Preußischen Staates* (Breslau: Aderholz, 1843), x–xi. For thirty, see Wilhelm Freund, *Zur Judenfrage in Deutschland* (Berlin, 1843).

22. Rürup, "The Tortuous and Thorny Path to Legal Equality," 17; Ismar Freund, *Die Emanzipation der Juden in Preußen unter besonderer Berücksichtigung des Gesetzes vom 11. Marz 1812*, 2 vols. (Berlin: Poppelauer, 1912), 1:241–46; Annegret H. Brammer, *Judenpolitik und Judengesetzgebung in Preußen, 1812 bis 1847* (Berlin: Schelzky & Jeep, 1987), 100–140. For the Prussian bureaucracy's confused image of the Jews, see Herbert Strauss, "Pre-Emancipation Prussian Policies towards the Jews, 1815–1847," *Leo Baeck Institute Yearbook* 11 (1966): 107–36. For the massive bureaucratic materials, see Manfred Jehle, ed., *Die Juden und die jüdischen Gemeinden Preußens in amtlichen Enquêten des Vormärz*, 4 vols. (Munich: Saur, 1998).

23. Simon and Rönne, *Die früheren und gegenwärtigen Verhältnisse*, 45–50.

24. Volkmar Wittmütz, "Preußen und die Kirchen im Rheinland, 1815–1840," in Georg Mölich, Meinhard Pohl, and Veit Veltzke, eds., *Preußens schwieriger Westen: Rheinischpreußische Beziehungen, Konflikte und Wechselwirkungen* (Duisburg: Mercator, 2003), 134–61; Christopher Clark, *Iron Kingdom: The Rise and Downfall of Prussia, 1600–1947* (Cambridge, MA: Harvard University Press, 2006), 412–27.

25. Clark, *Iron Kingdom*, 401–8. The Rhineland's Napoleonic laws later inspired Prussia's 1848 Code.

26. Ibid., 424–27; Christopher Clark, *The Politics of Conversion: Missionary Protestantism and the Jews in Prussia, 1728–1941* (Oxford: Clarendon, 1995), 124–75.

27. Freund, *Die Emanzipation der Juden in Preußen*, 1:230–33.

28. Rürup, "The Tortuous and Thorny Path to Legal Equality," 18; Freund, *Die Emanzipation der Juden in Preußen*, 1:238–40; Horst Fischer, *Judentum, Staat und Herr in Preußen im frühen 19. Jarhhundert: Zur Geschichte der staatlichen Judenpolitik* (Tübingen: Mohr, 1968), 122–30.

29. Moritz Veit, *Der Entwurf einer Verordnung über die Verhältnisse der Juden und das Edikt vom 11. März 1812* (Berlin, 1847), 19.

30. Stefi Wenzel, *Jüdische Bürger und kommunale Selbstverwaltung in Preussichen Städten*, Veröffentlichungen der Historischen Kommission zu Berlin, vol. 21 (Berlin: de Gruyter, 1967), 19–95; Peter Pulzer, *Jews and the German State: The Political History of a Minority, 1848–1933* (Oxford: Blackwell, 1992), 69–83. Examples were David Friedländer, Salomon Veit, and David Alexander Benda (Berlin).

31. Wenzel, *Jüdische Bürger und kommunale Selbstverwaltung*, 96–151. Examples were Guttentag and Gleiwitz.

32. Ibid., 36, 67, 91, 104, 123; Strauss, "Pre-Emancipation Prussian Policies towards the Jews," 128.

33. Wenzel, *Jüdische Bürger und kommunale Selbstverwaltung*, 65, 106–9, 130–31; Shulamit Volkov, "Die Verbürgerlichung der Juden in Deutschland als Paradigma," in *Jüdisches Leben und Antisemitismus im 19. Und 20. Jahrhundert* (Munich: Beck, 1990), 111–30; Simone Lässig, *Jüdische Wege ins Bürgertum: Kulturelles Kapital und sozialer Aufstieg im 19. Jahrhundert* (Göttingen: Vandenhoeck & Ruprecht, 2004).

34. Poznań did not belong to the German Confederation because of its large Polish population; it was not subject to Article 16 encouraging an "amelioration" of the Jews' status. Sophia Kemlein, *Die Posener Juden, 1815–1848: Entwicklungsprozesse einer polnischen Judenheit unter preußischer Herrschaft* (Hamburg: Dölling and Galitz, 1997), 71–78. Jews were also not subject to conscription; they instead paid a fee (*Rekrutengeld*). See Fischer, *Judentum, Staat und Herr in Preußen*, 140–50.

35. Wenzel, *Jüdische Bürger und kommunale Selbstverwaltung*, 162–64.

36. Kemlein, *Die Posener Juden*, 90–92.

37. Ibid., 94–95.

38. Those peasants in possession of medium or large holdings became enfranchised freeholders; the others became landless cottagers, essentially laborers. See William W. Hagen, *Germans, Poles and Jews: The Nationality Conflict in the Prussian East, 1772–1914* (Chicago: University of Chicago Press, 1980), 81. Hesse had introduced a two-class system for its Jews in 1816. See Rürup, "The Tortuous and Thorny Path to Legal Equality," 18.

39. Kemlein, *Die Posener Juden*, 91, 96–97.

40. Simon and Rönne, *Die früheren und gegenwärtigen Verhältnisse*, 305–9. The preface announced that this was a provisional law; new legislation would supersede it. The law also responded to the 1830 uprising and the government's deteriorating position. See Kemlein, *Die Posener Juden*, 99–100.

41. The January 14, 1834, instruction for implementation of the 1833 ordinance spelled out the treatment of the third group. See Simon and Rönne, *Die früheren und gegenwärtigen Verhältnisse*, 315. Article 19 used the term "letters patent" (*Naturalization-Patenten*). In 1824 the Staatsrat's proposal had rejected this sort of categorization, recommending an extension of the 1812 edict. See Kemlein, *Die Posener Juden*, 93. Hesse-Kassel adopted a similar two-class system on October 29, 1833. See Rürup, "The Tortuous and Thorny Path to Legal Equality," 20.

42. On the naturalization of women, see Kemlein, *Die Posener Juden*, 143.

43. Kemlein argues that all eligible Jews exerted themselves to gain naturalization, with no distinction between the "liberal" and "orthodox." See *Die Posener Juden*, 141–52.

44. Some areas maintained an existing privilege to exclude Jews (*non tolerandis Judaeis*) until 1833 or even until 1848 (Bromberg). See Brammer, *Judenpolitik und Judengesetzgebung in Preußen*, 118.

45. Ismar Freund, *Die Rechtsstellung der Juden im preußischen Volksschulrecht* (Berlin: Guttentag, 1908), 5.

46. Kemlein argues that the ordinance was primarily concerned with the community's organization and debts. See *Die Posener Juden*, 108–28.

47. For the opening of new schools, see ibid., 128–41.

48. Ibid., 167–68.

49. Ibid., 168–79; Hagen, *Germans, Poles and Jews*, 96.

50. Kemlein, *Die Posener Juden*, 183–88. Posen Jews were the first from "Poland" to emigrate to the United States.

51. For the ordinance's deleterious impact on the tolerated, see Kemlein, *Die Posener Juden*, 153–57.

52. Wenzel, *Jüdische Bürger und kommunale Selbstverwaltung*, 155ff.

53. Ibid., 162–64.

54. The governor was Flotwell. See ibid., 164–65.

55. Ibid., 186–99. For percentages, see Kemlein, *Die Posener Juden*, 165.

56. Clark, *Iron Kingdom*, 438.

57. For a pamphlet supporting the introduction of corporations for Jews, see Theodor Brand, *Die Judenfrage in Preußen* (Breslau, 1842).

58. Brammer, *Judenpolitik und Judengesetzgebung in Preußen*, 251–54, 274–94.

59. Ibid., 294–300.

60. Clark, *Iron Kingdom*, 436–46; Brammer, *Judenpolitik und Judengesetzgebung in Preußen*, 251ff. For the Jews' protests, including petitions from various communities, see 255–63.

61. Kemlein, *Die Posener Juden*, 193.

62. At the Diet's opening session, the king asserted his absolute power and rejected a constitution. See Brammer, *Judenpolitik und Judengesetzgebung in Preußen*, 338–39.

63. Veit, *Der Entwurf einer Verordnung über die Verhältnisse der Juden und das Edikt vom 11. März 1812*, 16.

64. "Draft of a Regulation Concerning the Jews' Situation" (*Entwurf einer Verordnung, die Verhältnisse der Juden betreffend*). See Brammer, *Judenpolitik und Judengesetzgebung in Preußen*, 335–72 and Rürup, "The Tortuous and Thorny Path to Legal Equality," 25–26.

65. See Michael A. Meyer, *German-Jewish History in Modern Times*, 4 vols. (New York: Columbia University Press, 1996–98), 1:47.

66. Freund, *Die Emanzipation der Juden in Preußen*, 2:501–6, 510–18; Freund, *Die Rechtsstellung der Juden im preußischen Volksschulrecht*, 9–11. The Prussian government had given that status to schools in Aachen and Gollub in 1845.

67. Freund, *Die Emanzipation der Juden in Preußen*, 2:507–10.

68. Kemlein, *Die Posener Juden*, 195–200. The particular laws governing the Jewish community from 1833 and 1847 remained in place until 1939. The 1847 law was never entirely abolished.

69. Cologne expelled its Jews in 1424. Shulamit Magnus, *Jewish Emancipation in a German City: Cologne, 1798–1871* (Stanford: Stanford University Press, 1997), 4.

70. Ibid., 27–45, 64–70. The Infamous Decree was modified in 1845 and abolished in 1847. The French Consistorial system was in place from 1808 until 1863.

71. Ibid., 71–102.

72. Ibid., 117–35, quotation at 182.

73. Ibid., 118–19, 122, 125, 135.

74. Ernst Rudolf Huber, *Dokumente zur deutschen Verfassungsgeschichte, 1803–1850*, 3rd ed. (Stuttgart: Kohlhammer, 1978), 1:173; Adolf Lewin, *Geschichte der badischen Juden seit der Regierung Karl Friedrichs (1738–1909)* (Karlsruhe: G. Braun, 1909), 185–86; Reinhard Rürup, "Die Emanzipation der Juden in Baden," in *Emanzipation und Antisemitismus: Studien zur "Judenfrage" der bürgerlichen Gesellschaft* (Göttingen: Vandenhoeck and Ruprecht, 1975), 50.

75. Lewin, *Geschichte der badischen Juden*, 197–98; Rürup, "Die Emanzipation der Juden in Baden," 52–54, 59.

76. In the justification for its 1862 law admitting Jews to residence throughout the polity, Baden's government acknowledged the demotion: the law had turned a de facto division between Christians and Jews into a de jure status. See Lewin, *Geschichte der badischen Juden*, 304.

77. Ibid., 243–44, 252–53; Rürup, "Die Emanzipation der Juden in Baden," 58.

78. For extensive lists, see Selma Täubler-Stern, "Die Emanzipation der Juden in Baden," in *Gedenkbuch zum hundertfünfundzwanzigjährigen Bestehen des Oberrats der Israeliten Badens* (Frankfurt: Kauffmann, 1934), 96–97, 101n2.

79. Rürup, "Die Emanzipation der Juden in Baden," 54, 158n180; Rürup, "The Tortuous and Thorny Path to Legal Equality," 21; Lewin, *Geschichte der badischen Juden*, 255–60.

80. Rürup, "Die Emanzipation der Juden in Baden," 56–61; David A. Meola, "German Jews and the Local German Press: The Jewish Struggle for Acceptance in Constance, 1846," *Leo Baeck Institute Yearbook* 59 (2014): 55–72.

81. Rürup, "Die Emanzipation der Juden in Baden," 64; Dagmar Herzog, *Intimacy and Exclusion: Religious Politics in Pre-Revolutionary Baden* (Princeton: Princeton University Press, 1996), 59–84. The Deutschkatholiken were denied the right to organize churches and their political rights. In defense, liberals espoused the principle of religious freedom, rejecting religion as a reason to deny rights. A week after the Lower Chamber debated dissenters it turned to the Jews' status (August 21, 1846). On liberals and Jews, see Reinhard Rürup, "German Liberalism and the Emancipation of the Jews," *Leo Baeck Institute Yearbook* 20 (1975): 59–68.

82. Stefan Schwarz, *Die Juden in Bayern im Wandel der Zeiten* (Munich: Olzog, 1963), 182–83; Manfred Treml, "Von der 'Judenmission' zur 'Bürgerlichen Verbesserung': Zur Vorgeschichte und Frühphase der Judenemanzipation in Bayern," in Manfred Treml and Josef Kirmeier, eds., *Geschichte und Kultur der Juden in Bayern: Aufsätze* (Munich: Saur, 1988), 251–52.

83. Schwarz, *Die Juden in Bayern*, 187–92.

84. Simon and Rönne, *Die früheren und gegenwärtigen Verhältnisse*, 21.

85. Gerhard Hirschmann, "Die evangelische Kirche seit 1800," in Max Spindler, ed., *Handbuch der bayerischen Geschichte*, 4 vols. (Munich: Beck, 19??–1975), 4, 2:890–92.

86. Huber, *Dokumente zur deutschen Verfassungsgeschichte*, 155–71; James F. Harris, *The People Speak!: Anti-Semitism and Emancipation in Nineteenth-Century Bavaria* (Ann Arbor: University of Michigan Press, 1994), 51: although not "democratic," the "Bavarian Parliament was representative and possessed power to approve or deny all forms of legislation." Altgeld, "German Catholics," 104.

87. The representatives left the question of local rights (Article 9) unresolved. The Assembly debated how to implement the prohibition on house-to-house peddling (May 1, 1819; para. 20) and (para. 21) dissolved Jewish corporations, making local communities responsible for all outstanding debts. Schwarz, *Die Juden in Bayern*, 201–13.

88. Schwarz, *Die Juden in Bayern*, 201–13.

89. Samson Rosenfeld, *Denkschrift an die Hohe Stände-Versammlung des Königreichs Baiern, die Lage der Israeliten und ihre bürgerliche Verbesserung betreffend* (Munich, 1819), 17. Rosenfeld petitioned again in 1837. See A. Eckstein, *Der Kampf der Juden um ihre Emanzipation in Bayern* (Fürth: Georg Rosenberg, 1905), 35, 59. For the hardships the restrictions caused, see Treml, "Von der 'Judenmission' zur 'Bürgerlichen Verbesserung,'" 255–56.

90. Rosenfeld, *Denkschrift*, 7.

91. Schwarz, *Die Juden in Bayern*, 215–16.

92. Ibid., 216. For the riots as opposition to emancipation, see Jacob Katz, *Die Hep-Hep-Verfolgungen des Jahres 1819* (Berlin: Metropol, 1994) and Stefan Rohrbacher, "The 'Hep Hep' Riots of 1819: Anti-Jewish Ideology, Agitation and Violence," in Christhard Hoffmann, Werner Bergmann, and Helmut Walser Smith, eds., *Exclusionary Violence: Antisemitic Riots in Modern German History* (Ann Arbor: University of Michigan Press, 2002), 23–42.

93. Schwarz, *Die Juden in Bayern*, 219.

94. Ibid., 221.

95. Harris, *The People Speak!* 51–53.

96. Eckstein, *Der Kampf der Juden um ihre Emanzipation in Bayern*, 40–66.

97. Harris, *The People Speak!* 53–58.

98. Schwarz, *Die Juden in Bayern*, 235–39; Harris, *The People Speak!* 53.

99. Harris, *The People Speak!* 56–58. For the example of a rabbi in Kissingen, see Lazarus Adler, *Die bürgerliche Stellung der Juden in Bayern: Ein Memorandum, der hohen Kammer der Abgeordneten ehrerbietigst vorgelegt* (Munich, 1846).

100. Adler quoted a member of the Bavarian Assembly, Dr. Schwindl, who argued this in the 1831 debate. See Adler, *Die bürgerliche Stellung der Juden in Bayern*, 5–6.

101. Ibid., 6–9. Adler queried how the idea of the "Christian State" justified various restrictions, e.g., residence and marriage (*Matrikel*), oaths, and funding for Jewish institutions. See 9–14. He surveyed Judaism to show that none of its beliefs conflicted with the duties of citizenship. See 14–21.

102. Ibid., 23. The Bavarian government's decade-long deliberation (1826–36) over reorganizing Judaism as an ecclesiastical hierarchy or Consistory in keeping with the Christian religions also failed. See Schwarz, *Die Juden in Bayern*, 242–50.

103. Robin Okey, *The Habsburg Monarchy: From Enlightenment to Eclipse* (New York: St. Martin's, 2001), 68–98; Huber, *Deutsche Verfassungsgeschichte Seit 1789*, 1:414–15. Joseph von Wertheimer, *Die Juden in Österreich: Vom Standpunkte der Geschichte, der Rechts und des Staatsvortheils*, 3 vols. (Leipzig, 1842) draws on regional handbooks (Hieronymus von Scari, *Systematische Darstellung der in Betreff der Juden in Mähren und im k.k. Antheile Schlesiens erlassenen Gesetze und Verordnungen* [Brünn: L. W. Seidel, 1835]; Michael Stöger, *Darstellung der gesetzlichen Verfassung der galizischen Judenschaft*, 2 vols. [Lemberg: Kuhn & Millikowski, 1833]). See 2:268.

The Civil Law Code (*Allgemeines Bürgerliches Gesetzbuch*; 1812; #29–31) implemented jus soli in establishing a ten-year residence and a productive occupation as the basic criteria for citizenship. See Hannelore Burger, "Passwesen und Staatsbürgerschaft," in Waltraud Heindl and Edith Saurer, eds., *Grenze und Staat: Paßwesen, Staatsbürgerschaft, Heimatrecht und Fremdengesetzgebung in der österreichischen Monarchie, 1750–1867* (Vienna: Böhlau, 2000), 109–24.

104. Max Grunwald, *Vienna* (Philadelphia: Jewish Publication Society, 1936), 167–213.

105. Carol Herselle Krinsky, *Synagogues of Europe: Architecture, History, Meaning*, 2nd ed. (New York: Dover, 1996), 186–91; Grunwald, *Vienna*, 214–21. This building became home to the so-called "Vienna rite" (*minhag Wien*), which served as a model for Jews throughout the Habsburg Empire and western Europe. See Marsha Rozenblit, "The Struggle over Religious Reform in Nineteenth-Century Vienna," *Association for Jewish Studies Review* 14, no. 2 (1989): 179–221. Jews first gained authorization to form an organized community in 1852.

106. Heinrich von Kopetz, *Versuch einer systematischen Darstellung der in Böhmen bezüglich der Juden bestehenden Gesetze und Verordnungen* (Prague: Gottlieb Haase Söhne, 1846), 3–14.

107. Scari, *Systematische Darstellung der in Betreff der Juden in Mähren und im k.k. Antheile Schlesiens erlassenen Gesetze und Verordnungen*, 11.

108. Ibid., 17.

109. Ibid., 36, 168 (under general law); 156 (not full subjects).

110. Ibid., 176–78.

111. Ibid., 73, 114–15 (Brünn), 157 (Olmütz).

112. Ibid., 107 for estates, 170–72 for servants.

113. Ibid., 78–79.

114. Stöger, *Darstellung der gesetzlichen Verfassung der galizischen Judenschaft*, 2:1–2.

115. Antony Polonsky, *The Jews in Poland and Russia*, 3 vols. (Oxford: Littman, 2010–

12), 1:256. Biala, Bochnia, Zywiec, Wieliczka, and Jaslo excluded Jews. Other towns maintained Jewish quarters (Lviv, Sambir, Tarnow, and Nowy Sacz).

116. Stöger, *Darstellung*, 2:13–48.

117. Ibid., 2:57–61.

118. R. J. W. Evans, "Progress and Emancipation in Hungary during the Age of Metternich," *Leo Baeck Institute Yearbook* 46 (2001): 55–65; Wolfdieter Bihl, "Das Judentum Ungarns, 1780–1914," in *Studien zum Ungarischen Judentum*, Studia Judaica Austriaca, vol. 3 (Eisenstadt: Roetzer, 1976), 20–21; Michael Silber, "The Entrance of Jews into Hungarian Society in Vormärz: The Case of the 'Casinos,'" in Jonathan Frankel and Steve Zipperstein, eds., *Assimilation and Community: The Jews in Nineteenth-Century Europe* (Cambridge: Cambridge University Press, 1992), 288–91. Jews first gained entrance to the new casinos in provincial cities in alliance with the gentry. Entrance in Budapest came later.

119. Joseph Freiherrn v. Eötvös, *Die Emancipation der Juden*, trans. Hermann Klein, 2nd ed. (Pesth, 1841). See Evans, "Progress and Emancipation in Hungary during the Age of Metternich," 62.

120. Daniel Ehrmann, *Betrachtungen über Jüdische Verhältnisse* (Pest, 1841) 9, 18 (quotation), 23.

Chapter Thirteen. Revolution

1. Salo Baron, "The Impact of the Revolution of 1848 on Jewish Emancipation," in Abraham G. Duker and Meir Ben-Horin, eds., *Emancipation and Counter-Emancipation* (New York: Ktav, 1974), 153.

2. Rights survived in Piedmont and Denmark (Constitution of June 5, 1849). See Ismar Elbogen, *A Century of Jewish Life* (Philadelphia: Jewish Publication Society, 1944), 36–37.

3. Baron, "The Impact of the Revolution of 1848 on Jewish Emancipation," 165.

4. Reinhard Rürup, "The European Revolutions of 1848 and Jewish Emancipation," in Werner E. Mosse, Arnold Paucker, and Reinhard Rürup, eds., *Revolution and Evolution: 1848 in German-Jewish History* (Tübingen: Mohr, 1981), 18, 21; James F. Harris, *The People Speak!: Anti-Semitism and Emancipation in Nineteenth-Century Bavaria* (Ann Arbor: University of Michigan Press, 1994), 76.

5. Jonathan Sperber, *The European Revolutions, 1848–1851*, 2nd ed. (Cambridge: Cambridge University Press, 2005), 109–12.

6. Ibid., 59–63, 112–17.

7. Hardenberg's "State Indebtedness Law" (January 17, 1820) required a "national estates assembly" to approve new loans. See Ernst Rudolf Huber, *Dokumente zur deutschen Verfassungsgeschichte, 1803–1850*, 3rd ed.(Stuttgart: Kohlhammer, 1978), 1:72 and Christopher Clark, *Iron Kingdom: The Rise and Downfall of Prussia, 1600–1947* (Cambridge, MA: Harvard University Press, 2006), 458.

8. Clark, *Iron Kingdom*, 468–75, estimates that 300 protestors and 100 soldiers died.

9. Ibid., 478–81.

10. Huber, *Dokumente*, 1:484–93; Rürup, "The European Revolutions of 1848 and Jewish Emancipation," 19–20.

11. Huber, *Dokumente*, 1:502; Rürup, "The European Revolutions of 1848 and Jewish Emancipation," 22.

12. Annegret H. Brammer, *Judenpolitik und Judengesetzgebung in Preußen, 1812 bis 1847* (Berlin: Schelzky & Jeep, 1987), 375–83.

13. Sophia Kemlein, *Die Posener Juden, 1815–1848: Entwicklungsprozesse einer pol-*

nischen Judenheit unter preußischer Herrschaft (Hamburg: Dölling and Galitz, 1997), 200–201.

14. James J. Sheehan, *German History, 1770-1866* (Oxford: Clarendon, 1989), 659-60.

15. Rioters targeted Christian and Jewish individuals accused of usury and extortion. See Reinhard Rürup, "Die Emanzipation der Juden in Baden," in *Emanzipation und Antisemitismus: Studien zur "Judenfrage" der bürgerlichen Gesellschaft* (Göttingen: Vandenhoeck & Ruprecht, 1975), 35-37.

16. Ibid., 65-67; Elbogen, *A Century of Jewish Life*, 10-11.

17. Harris, *The People Speak!* 63-64.

18. Ibid., 58-63.

19. Ibid., 70.

20. Ibid., 78-80. Communities had lost that right in the edict of 1813 but regained it in 1818.

21. Ibid., 126; 87-122 focuses on Ernst Zander's *Volksbote für den Bürger und Landmann*, 123-57 on petitions.

22. Ibid., 192-93.

23. Huber, *Dokumente*, 1:326-28.

24. Brian E. Vick, *Defining Germany: The 1848 Frankfurt Parliamentarians and National Identity* (Cambridge, MA: Harvard University Press, 2002), 79-80. For non-Germans, see 110-38.

25. Franz Wigard, ed., *Stenographsicher Bericht über die Verhandlungen der deutschen constituirenden Nationalversammlung zu Frankfurt am Main*, 9 vols. (Frankfurt: Sauerländer, 1848), 3:1632. For the Pre-Parliament's Basic Rights (March 31–April 4, 1848), see Huber, *Dokumente*, 1:336.

26. Johann Gustav Droysen, ed., *Die Verhandlung des Verfassungs Ausschusses der deutschen Nationalversammlung* (Leipzig: Weidmann, 1849), 8. I have modified the translations in Rürup, "The European Revolutions of 1848 and Jewish Emancipation," 21n52.

27. See Droysen, *Die Verhandlung des Verfassungs Ausschusses*, 9.

28. Wigard, *Stenographsicher Bericht*, 3:1762.

29. Ibid., 3:1758.

30. Ibid., 3:1754-55. Mohl also claimed that "the Israelite population will always and forever be like a drop of oil swimming on the water of the German nationality."

31. Wigard, *Stenographsicher Bericht*, 3:1759-61.

32. Ibid., 3:1755-57. Riesser emphasized the "marvel of the law."

33. Vick, *Defining Germany*, 95-104. Vick argues that the delegates spoke from a neohumanist "culture of nationhood" that emphasized "progressive dialectical historical change" (19-78). Local rights and poor laws appeared in relation to non-German citizens (115). Increasing intolerance for negative stereotypes diminished their use (106).

34. Rürup, "The European Revolutions of 1848 and Jewish Emancipation," 21.

35. *Orient* 9 (November 16, 1848): 374, quoted in Baron, "The Impact of the Revolution of 1848 on Jewish Emancipation," 196n44.

36. David Laven, "The Age of Restoration," in John A. Davis, ed., *Italy in the Nineteenth Century, 1796-1900* (Oxford: Oxford University Press, 2000), 65-67.

37. The most influential was perhaps Massimo d'Azeglio's "On the Civil Emancipation of the Jews" (*Dell' emancipazione civile degli israeliti*, 1848). See Andrew M. Canepa, "Emancipation and the Jewish Response in Mid-Nineteenth-Century Italy," *European History Quarterly* 16 (1986): 406-19 and Mario Rossi, "Emancipation of the Jews in Italy," *Jewish Social Studies* 15 (1953): 120-23.

38. Canepa, "Emancipation and the Jewish Response," 418-28.

39. Ibid., 415-18.

40. David I. Kertzer, *The Popes against the Jews: The Vatican's Role in the Rise of Modern Anti-Semitism* (New York: Knopf, 2001), 63. In 1823 Leo XII had ordered Jews back into the ghettos "to overcome the evil consequences of the freedom that [they] have enjoyed."

41. Cecil Roth, *The History of the Jews in Italy* (Philadelphia: Jewish Publication Society, 1946), 458–60, 465–66; Kertzer, *The Popes against the Jews*, 108–9.

42. Roth, *The History of the Jews in Italy*, 460–63.

43. Canepa, "Emancipation and the Jewish Response," 409–10; Roth, *The History of the Jews in Italy*, 465–67. After Carlo Alberto abdicated, his son, Vittorio Emanuele II, confirmed the constitution, including equality for members of all faiths.

44. Rossi, "Emancipation of the Jews in Italy," 130; Roth, *The History of the Jews in Italy*, 468.

45. Sheehan, *German History*, 663–65; Robin Okey, *The Habsburg Monarchy: From Enlightenment to Eclipse* (New York: St. Martin's, 2001), 128–29; R. John Rath, *The Viennese Revolution of 1848* (Austin: University of Texas Press, 1957), 57–89; István Deák, *The Lawful Revolution: Louis Kossuth and the Hungarians, 1848-1849* (New York: Columbia University Press, 1979), 63–106.

46. Okey, *The Habsburg Monarchy*, 139.

47. Edmund Bernatzik, *Die österreichischen Verfassungsgesetze* (Leipzig: Hirschfeld, 1906), 73–82; Filip Friedmann, *Die Galizischen Juden im Kampfe um ihre Gleichberechtigung (1848-1868)* (Frankfurt: Kauffmann, 1929), 69. For a penetrating plea for equality invoking legal and humanitarian arguments, as well as a detailed survey of the Jews' legal situation in Lower Austria, see A. Freiherrn von Stifft, *Ein Wort für unsere israelitischen Brüder: An die Vertreter der Provinz Nieder-Oesterreich* (Vienna: Dorfmeister, 1848).

48. Rath, *The Viennese Revolution of 1848*, 179–81. For the Constitutional Committee's deliberations and actions, see Alfred Fischel, *Die Protokolle des Verfassungsausschusses über die Grundrechte: Ein Beitrag zur Geschichte des österreichischen Reichstags vom Jahre 1848* (Vienna: Gerlach & Weidling, 1912).

49. Okey, *The Habsburg Monarchy*, 142. Ten years of residence was the primary criterion for naturalization or citizenship; after 1833 the applicant had to apply to initiate the process. See Hannelore Burger, "Passwesen und Staatsbürgerschaft," in Waltraud Heindl and Edith Saurer, eds., *Grenze und Staat: Paßwesen, Staatsbürgerschaft, Heimatrecht und Fremdengesetzgebung in der österreichischen Monarchie, 1750-1867* (Vienna: Böhlau, 2000), 121–23.

50. Bernatzik, *Die österreichischen Verfassungsgesetze*, 108–9; Burger, "Passwesen und Staatsbürgerschaft," 161–63; Elbogen, *A Century of Jewish Life*, 21.

51. Bernatzik, *Die österreichischen Verfassungsgesetze*, 108–9; Heinrich Jaques, *Denkschrift über die Stellung der Juden in Oesterreich*, 4th ed. (Vienna, 1859), xv–xvii. Equality entailed abolishing the *Familiantengesetz* and special oaths.

52. See Friedmann, *Die Galizischen Juden im Kampfe um ihre Gleichberechtigung*, 73–74.

53. Ibid., 77.

54. Bernatzik, *Die österreichischen Verfassungsgesetze*, 178–85. Historians are divided about the situation. Wolfgang Häusler asserted that the law was only partially restricted, never abrogated. See "Konfessionelle Probleme in der Wiener Revolution von 1848," in *Das Judentum im Revolutionsjahr 1848*, Studia Judaica Austriaca, vol. 1 (Vienna: Herold, 1974), 73–74. Friedmann asserted that the 1848 laws were not withdrawn. See *Die Galizischen Juden im Kampfe um ihre Gleichberechtigung*, 79n2. Baron and Jaques asserted that the law was repealed on December 31, 1851. See "The Impact of the Revolution of 1848 on Jewish Emancipation," 166, and Jaques, *Denkschrift über die Stellung der Juden in Oesterreich*,

xxiii. For the confusion around the final sentence, see Jaques, *Denkschrift über die Stellung der Juden in Oesterreich*, xxxv.

55. Friedmann, *Die Galizischen Juden im Kampfe um ihre Gleichberechtigung*, 79–81.

56. Jaques, *Denkschrift über die Stellung der Juden in Oesterreich*, 5–6, 8–13; Burger, "Passwesen und Staatsbürgerschaft," 164.

57. Wolfgang Häusler, "Assimilation und Emanzipation des ungarischen Judentums um die Mitte des 19. Jahrhunderts," in *Studia Judaica Austriaca*, vol. 3 (Eisenstadt, 1976), 62–70.

58. Ibid., 60, 74; Deák, *The Lawful Revolution*, 314–15; William O. McCagg Jr., *A History of Habsburg Jews, 1670–1918* (Bloomington: Indiana University Press, 1989), 90–91; László Kontler, *A History of Hungary: Millennium in Central Europe* (Houndmills, Basingstoke: Palgrave Macmillan, 2002), 259.

59. Bernatzik, *Die österreichischen Verfassungsgesetze*, 49–73; Rürup, "The European Revolutions of 1848 and Jewish Emancipation," 29; Häusler, "Assimilation und Emanzipation des ungarischen Judentums um die Mitte des 19. Jahrhunderts," 74–76.

60. Antony Polonsky, *The Jews in Poland and Russia*, 3 vols. (Oxford: Littman, 2010–12), 1:162–63. See also Antony Polonsky, "The Revolutionary Crisis of 1846–1849 and Its Place in the Development of Nineteenth-Century Galicia," in Zvi Gitelman, ed., *Culture and Nations of Central and Eastern Europe: Essays in Honor of Roman Szporluk* (Cambridge, MA: Harvard University Press, 2000), 443–69.

61. Okey, *The Habsburg Monarchy*, 139; Friedmann, *Die Galizischen Juden im Kampfe um ihre Gleichberechtigung*, 54.

62. Jaques, *Denkschrift über die Stellung der Juden in Oesterreich*, xiv; Friedmann, *Die Galizischen Juden im Kampfe um ihre Gleichberechtigung*, 71–72.

63. Friedmann, *Die Galizischen Juden im Kampfe um ihre Gleichberechtigung*, 69–83; Polonsky, *The Jews in Poland and Russia*, 1:267.

64. Sperber, *The European Revolutions*, 123.

65. Heinrich Graetz implied that 1848 inaugurated Jewish politics. See *History of the Jews*, 6 vols. (Philadelphia: Jewish Publication Society, 1895), 5:322–23. Salo Baron asserted that 1848 put an end to the "political quietism of the ghetto era": "The Impact of the Revolution of 1848 on Jewish Emancipation," 166–67. See Rürup, "The European Revolutions of 1848 and Jewish Emancipation," 31 and Ulrich Wyrwa, *Juden in der Toskana und in Preußen im Vergleich: Aufklärung und Emanzipation in Florenz, Livorno, Berlin und Königsberg i. Pr.* (Tübingen: Mohr, 2003), 425–26.

66. Jonathan Frankel, *The Damascus Affair: "Ritual Murder," Politics and the Jews in 1840* (Cambridge: Cambridge University Press, 1997); Abigail Green, *Moses Montefiore: Jewish Liberator, Imperial Hero* (Cambridge, MA: Harvard University Press, 2010).

67. Rath, *The Viennese Revolution of 1848*, 103–5. That they were physicians was no accident: "the medical school at the Vienna University was both the only college open to Jews before the 1840s and the only one during the 1840s where freedom of speech was more or less allowed." See McCagg, *A History of Habsburg Jews, 1670–1918*, 94.

68. Rürup, "The European Revolutions of 1848 and Jewish Emancipation," 24; Baron, "The Impact of the Revolution of 1848 on Jewish Emancipation," 160.

69. Friedmann, *Die Galizischen Juden im Kampfe um ihre Gleichberechtigung*, 70–1. Mannheimer gave two influential speeches (September 25 and October 5) justifying cancellation of all special taxes.

70. Rürup, "The European Revolutions of 1848 and Jewish Emancipation," 26; Ernst Hamburger, *Juden im öffentlichen Leben Deutschlands: Regierungsmitglieder, Beamte und Parlamentarier in der monarchischen Zeit* (Tübingen: Mohr, 1968), 170–209; Jacob Toury, *Die politischen Orientierungen der Juden in Deutschland: Von Jena bis Weimar* (Tübingen:

Mohr, 1966), 47–99. In the Pre-Parliament: Berthold Auerbach, Julius Fürst, Johann Jacoby, Ignaz Kuranda, Gabriel Riesser, and Moritz Veit. In the National Assembly: Jacoby, Kuranda, Riesser, and Veit plus Ludwig Bamberger, Moritz Hartmann, and Friedrich Levysohn.

71. Baron, "The Impact of the Revolution of 1848 on Jewish Emancipation," 163. Leone Pincherle was Minister at Agriculture and Commerce and Isaac Maurogonato at Finance. For the estimate of 200 Jews taking up arms in the 1848 revolution, see Tullia Catalan, "Italian Jews and the 1848–49 Revolutions: Patriotism and Multiple Identities," in Silvana Patriarca and Lucy Riall, eds., *The Risorgimento Revisited: Nationalism and Culture in Nineteenth-Century Italy* (Houndmills, Basingstoke: Palgrave Macmillan, 2012), 223. There were also prominent and numerous Jewish conservatives in a number of countries. See Rürup, "The European Revolutions of 1848 and Jewish Emancipation," 30 and Toury, *Politischen Orientierungen*, 68–99.

72. Rürup, "The European Revolutions of 1848 and Jewish Emancipation," 41–51; Häusler, "Konfessionelle Probleme in der Wiener Revolution von 1848," 71–72; Jacob Katz, *From Prejudice to Destruction: Anti-Semitism, 1700–1933* (Cambridge, MA: Harvard University Press, 1980). For the origins of these tropes in responses to the French Revolution, see Michele Battini, *Socialism of Fools: Capitalism and Modern Anti-Semitism* (New York: Columbia University Press, 2016).

73. Kai Struve, "'Nationale Minderheit': Begriffgeschichtliches zu Gleichheit und Differenz," *Leipziger Beiträge zur jüdischen Geschichte und Kultur* 2 (2004): 233–58, quotation at 242. The Habsburg Constitutional Committee, for example, discussed the issue of nations lacking representation (*nicht vertretenen Völker*) in its first session. See Anton Springer, ed., *Protokolle des Verfassungs-Ausschusses im Oesterreichischen Reichstage, 1848–1849* (Leipzig: Hirzel, 1885), 9–11. For the case of Galicia, see Polonsky, "The Revolutionary Crisis of 1846–1849."

74. *Allgemeine Zeitung des Judentums* 18 (1854): 40, cited in Rürup, "The European Revolutions of 1848 and Jewish Emancipation," 41. See Willehad Paul Eckert, "Ludwig Philippson und seine 'Allgemeine Zeitung des Judentums' in den Jahren 1848/49 -Die Revolution im Spiegel der Zeitung," in *Studia Judaica Austriaca*, vol. 1, 112–25.

Chapter Fourteen. Central Europe, 1850–1871

1. Anthony Cardoza, "Cavour and Piedmont," in John A. Davis, ed., *Italy in the Nineteenth Century, 1796–1900* (New York: Oxford University Press, 2000), 109; Alberto Mario Banti, "Public Opinion and Associations in Nineteenth-Century Italy," in Nancy Bermeo and Philip Nord, eds., *Civil Society before Democracy: Lessons from Nineteenth-Century Europe* (Lanham, MD: Rowman and Littlefield, 2000), 47.

2. Cardoza, "Cavour and Piedmont," 117–19. Cavour's efforts to diminish the Church's power were less successful. He did manage to abolish ecclesiastical courts and church sanctuary for criminals (Siccardi Laws, 1850). He did not manage to impose state control over donations of property to the Church. His efforts identified Piedmontese liberalism with anticlericalism.

3. Ibid., 121–22.

4. Cardoza, "Cavour and Piedmont," emphasizes that Cavour did not have a blueprint for unification but rather adroitly seized opportunities.

5. Ibid., 130–31. For Piedmont as the liberal/monarchic rather than the democratic/republican option, see Banti, "Public Opinion and Associations in Nineteenth-Century Italy," 48.

6. Dan V. Segre, "The Emancipation of Jews in Italy," in Pierre Birnbaum and Ira

Katznelson, eds., *Paths of Emancipation: Jews, States, and Citizenship* (Princeton: Princeton University Press, 1995), 217. For economic changes under Napoleon, see John A. Davis, "Economy, Society and the State," in *Italy in the Nineteenth Century*, 237.

7. Segre, "The Emancipation of Jews in Italy," 229. For a prominent example, see Arnaldo Momigliano, *Essays on Ancient and Modern Judaism* (Chicago: University of Chicago Press, 1994), 121–34, 225–26. Jews in other states participated as well. For Tuscany, see Ulrich Wyrwa, "Jewish Experiences in the Italian Risorgimento: Political Practice and National Emotions of Florentine and Leghorn Jewry (1849–1860)," *Journal of Modern Italian Studies* 8, no. 1 (2003): 16–35.

8. Cecil Roth, *The History of the Jews in Italy* (Philadelphia: Jewish Publication Society, 1946), 469–70.

9. David I. Kertzer, "Religion and Society, 1789–1892," in Davis, ed., *Italy in the Nineteenth Century*, 194.

10. David I. Kertzer, *The Kidnapping of Edgardo Mortara* (New York: Knopf, 1997).

11. For the petition and discussion, see Carlotta Ferrara degli Uberti, "The 'Jewish Nation' of Livorno: A Port Jewry on the Road to Emancipation," in David Cesarani and Gemma Romaine, eds., *Jews and Port Cities, 1590–1990: Commerce, Community and Cosmopolitanism* (London: Vallentine Mitchell, 2006), 163–64.

12. Livorno's Jews petitioned jointly with those of Pisa, Florence, Pitigliano, and Siena. See Uberti, "The 'Jewish Nation' of Livorno," 167–68. On the tumultuous events of 1848–49 in Livorno, see David G. LoRomer, *Merchants and Reform in Livorno, 1814–1868* (Berkeley: University of California Press, 1987), 213–43.

13. Francesca Bregoli, *Mediterranean Enlightenment: Livornese Jews, Tuscan Culture, and Eighteenth-Century Reform* (Stanford: Stanford University Press, 2014), 246. Livorno lost its free port status in 1868. On Livorno's Mediterranean diaspora, see Liana E. Funaro, "A Mediterranean Diaspora: Jews from Leghorn in the Second Half of the 19th Century," in Marta Petricioli, ed., *L'Europe méditerranéenne; Mediterranean Europe* (Brussels: Peter Lang, 2008), 95–110.

14. The Kingdom of Italy tried to bridge the divide: the Law of Guarantees (1871) recognized the pope as a sovereign and granted him an annual income. Christopher Duggan, "Politics in the Era of Depretis and Crispi, 1870–96," in Davis, ed., *Italy in the Nineteenth Century*, 155–56. For excommunication, see Kertzer, "Religion and Society," 190.

15. Mario Rossi, "Emancipation of the Jews in Italy," in Abraham Duker and Meir Ben-Horin, eds., *Emancipation and Counter-Emancipation* (New York: Ktav, 1974), 227.

16. David I. Kertzer, *The Popes against the Jews: The Vatican's Role in the Rise of Modern Anti-Semitism* (New York: Knopf, 2001).

17. Article 1: "The Roman Catholic religion is the only religion of the state. The other cults that now exist are tolerated insofar as they conform with the law." See Kertzer, "Religion and Society," 193.

18. Wyrwa, "Jewish Experiences in the Italian Risorgimento," 23.

19. Rossi, "Emancipation of the Jews in Italy," 228. The shift was from "tolerated denominations" (*culti tollerati*) to "accepted denominations" (*culti ammessi*).

20. Carol Herselle Krinsky, *Synagogues of Europe: Architecture, History, Meaning* (New York: Dover, 1985), 348–50; L. Scott Lerner, "The Narrating Architecture of Emancipation," *Jewish Social Studies* 6, no. 3 (Spring/Summer 2000): 1–30.

21. Krinsky, *Synagogues of Europe*, 364–68. The synagogue displayed Roman, Greek, Assyrian, and Egyptian influences.

22. Ibid., 374–78.

23. Segre, "The Emancipation of Jews in Italy," 227; Wyrwa, "Jewish Experiences in the Italian Risorgimento," 26–27.

24. Kertzer, *The Popes against the Jews*, 86–165; Elizabeth Schächter, *The Jews of Italy*,

1848-1915: Between Tradition and Transformation (London: Vallentine Mitchell, 2011). 97–151. For Catholic associations, see Banti, "Public Opinion and Associations in Nineteenth-Century Italy," 54. For an idealized view, see Cecil Roth, *The History of the Jews of Italy*, 474–75: "Jews were accepted freely, naturally and spontaneously as members of the Italian people. . . . Thus there was no part of the world where religious freedom was more real, or religious prejudice was so small."

25. Kertzer, *The Popes against the Jews*, 144. The quotation is from Father Ballerini (1891), an editor of *Civiltà cattolica*, a Jesuit journal that expressed Vatican opinion.

26. Schächter, *The Jews of Italy*, 110–14. The ministerial positions were Enrico Poggi's rejection of Sansone D'Ancona as Minister of Finance, 1861, and Francesco Pasqualigo's rejection of Isacco Maurogonato for the same office, 1873.

27. Ibid., 115–16.

28. Christopher Clark, *Iron Kingdom: The Rise and Downfall of Prussia, 1600–1947* (Cambridge, MA: Harvard University Press, 2006), 511–12.

29. Ibid., 556–57. For the law, see Ernst Huber, *Dokumente zur deutschen Verfassungsgeschichte* (Stuttgart: Kohlhammer, 1964), 2:289–305. The empire incorporated twenty-two monarchs and four kingdoms. See Kai Drewes, *Jüdischer Adel: Nobilitierungen von Juden im Europa des 19. Jahrhunderts* (Frankfurt: Campus, 2013), 13.

30. Clark, *Iron Kingdom*, 587–88.

31. Ibid., 583.

32. Annegret H. Brammer, *Judenpolitik und Judengesetzgebung in Preußen, 1812 bis 1847* (Berlin: Schelzky & Jeep, 1987), 391–95.

33. For the old dualism's demise, see Mack Walker, *German Home Towns: Community, State and General Estate, 1648–1871* (Ithaca: Cornell University Press, 1971), 405–31. Guilds were abolished in Saxony, 1857; Württemberg, 1861; Baden, 1862; and Bavaria, 1862.

34. Peter Pulzer, *Jews and the German State: The Political History of a Minority, 1848–1933* (Oxford: Blackwell, 1992), 34. Jews functioned within a "zone of discretion and improvisation in which Reich or territorial laws were supplemented or qualified by local regulations." See Christopher Clark, "The Jews and the German State in the Wilhelmine Era," in Michael Brenner, Rainer Liedtke, and David Rechter, eds., *Two Nations: British and German Jews in Comparative Perspective* (Tübingen: Mohr Siebeck, 1999), 163.

35. Brammer, *Judenpolitik und Judengesetzgebung in Preußen*, 375–83.

36. Ibid., 383–85; Michael Brenner, "Between Revolution and Legal Equality," in Michael A. Meyer, ed., *German-Jewish History in Modern Times*, 4 vols. (New York: Columbia University Press, 1996–98), 2:292–93.

37. The law of July 23, 1847 (#3), had forbidden Jewish estate owners to exercise "corporate" privileges. See Ismar Freund, *Die Emanzipation der Juden in Preußen*, 2 vols. (Berlin: Poppelauer, 1912), 2:502.

38. Brammer, *Judenpolitik und Judengesetzgebung in Preußen*, 383–84.

39. Ibid., 385; Brenner, "Between Revolution and Legal Equality," 294.

40. Brammer, *Judenpolitik und Judengesetzgebung in Preußen*, 385.

41. Ibid., 386–87. The Ministers of Education were Bethmann-Hollweg and Heinrich v. Mühler. They appointed some Jews to teaching positions when no qualified Christian candidate was available.

42. Ibid., 389.

43. Pulzer, *Jews and the German State*, 48.

44. Ibid., 46.

45. Clark, *Iron Kingdom*, 584. Prussia appointed three Jewish magistrates in 1870. The number of Jewish judges decreased between the 1870s and 1890s. See Pulzer, *Jews and the German State*, 45, 48.

46. Pulzer, *Jews and the German State*, 44–53, 62. Catholics were underrepresented at

the universities, Jews overrepresented: "For every 100,000 males in Prussia between 1887 and 1897 there were 33 Catholic university students, 58 Protestant and 519 Jewish in the three secular faculties. In the law faculty . . . the ratios were 9:17:104" (49).

47. Werner T. Angress, "Prussia's Army and the Jewish Reserve Office Controversy before World War I," *Leo Baeck Institute Yearbook* 17 (1972): 19–42. Some historians argue there were no appointments of Jews after 1878. Of the 1,200–1,500 baptized Jews, some 300 received commissions (32–33). The Reichstag first debated the issue in 1904 and then annually from 1908 to 1914. For a brief account including some officers' memoirs, see Derek J. Penslar, *Jews and the Military: A History* (Princeton: Princeton University Press, 2013), 88–91.

There was a similar brief window around 1870 for ennoblement. Abraham Oppenheim was the first Jew Prussia ennobled (1868). The same high bureaucrats prevented reserve officer appointments and ennoblements. See Drewes, *Jüdischer Adel*, 180, 207–12, 248–52.

48. Marjorie Lamberti, "The Prussian Government and the Jews: Official Behavior and Policy-Making in the Wilhelminian Era," *Leo Baeck Institute Yearbook* 17 (1972): 5–17. The community had the status of a private person (*juristicher Person*) (#37) for fiscal purposes. For the law, see Freund, *Die Emanzipation der Juden in Preußen*, 2:510.

49. Lamberti, "The Prussian Government and the Jews," 7–8.

50. Ibid., 6. The new territories were Hanover, Hesse-Cassel, Nassau, Schleswig-Holstein, and Frankfurt. This situation would continue into the Weimar period when at least twelve different laws were in force. See Ismar Freund, *Die Rechtstellung der Synagogengemeinden in Preußen: Ein Beitrag zur Revision der bisherigen Gesetzgebung* (Berlin: Philo Verlag, 1926), 5.

51. Lamberti, "The Prussian Government and the Jews," 17.

52. Ibid., 14.

53. Saskia Coenen Snyder, *Building a Public Judaism: Synagogues and Jewish Identity in Nineteenth-Century Europe* (Cambridge, MA: Harvard University Press, 2013), 28.

54. Krinsky, *Synagogues of Europe*, 265–70; Snyder, *Building a Public Judaism*, 25–85.

55. Jack Wertheimer, *Unwelcome Strangers: East European Jews in Imperial Germany* (New York: Oxford University Press, 1987), 19. Germany's alien population rose from 270,000 in 1871 to 1.26 million in 1910.

56. Ibid., 44–46.

57. Ibid., 54–55.

58. Ibid., 59.

59. Till van Rahden, *Jews and Other Germans: Civil Society, Religious Diversity and Urban Politics in Breslau, 1860–1925* (Madison: University of Wisconsin Press, 2008); Stefanie Schüler-Springorum, *Die jüdische Minderheit in Königsberg/Preussen, 1871–1945* (Göttingen: Vandenhoeck, 1996), 59–67.

60. Pulzer, *Jews and the German State*, 87: "The aspirations of the Jewish community coincided . . . with that of the professional and commercial middle class in general, and the legislative achievements of the decade 1866–77 seemed to confirm the wisdom of the tactical alliance . . . freedom of movement, uniform legal codes and coinage."

61. Adolf Lewin, *Geschichte der badischen Juden seit der Regierung Karl Friedrichs (1738–1909)* (Karlsruhe: G. Braun, 1909), 296. For Jews gaining state appointments (judiciary, university) in the 1850s, see 297–98.

62. Reinhard Rürup, "Die Emanzipation der Juden in Baden," in *Emanzipation und Antisemitismus: Studien zur "Judenfrage" der bürgerlichen Gesellschaft* (Göttingen: Vandenhoeck & Ruprecht, 1975), 67–69. Lewin, *Geschichte der badischen Juden*, 304–6 reprints the government's justification.

63. Ernst Huber, *Deutsche Verfassungsgeshichte seit 1789*, 5 vols. (Stuttgart: Kohlhammer, 1963), 3:191–98.

64. Lewin, *Geschichte der badischen Juden*, 304–6; Rürup, "Die Emanzipation der Juden in Baden," 69–71. The government received 194 petitions opposing the law. These cited Jewish practices and beliefs. Professor Ludwig Häusser presented counterarguments, citing the Talmud and persecution of the Jews. See Lewin, *Geschichte der badischen Juden*, 306–14.

65. Ernst Hamburger, *Juden im öffentlichen Leben Deutschlands: Regierungsmitglieder, Beamte und Parlamentarier in der monarchischen Zeit* (Tübingen: Mohr, 1968), 235–36. Jews had gained political rights in 1849. Kusel received 70 of 78 votes. See Lewin, *Geschichte der badischen Juden*, 303.

66. Rürup, "Die Emanzipation der Juden in Baden," 71–3.

67. Lewin, *Geschichte der badischen Juden*, 317.

68. Marjorie Lamberti, "The Jewish Struggle for the Legal Equality of Religions in Imperial Germany," *Leo Baeck Institute Yearbook* 23 (1978): 109.

69. James F. Harris, *The People Speak! Anti-Semitism and Emancipation in Nineteenth-Century Bavaria* (Ann Arbor: University of Michigan Press, 1994), 197–98; Stefan Schwarz, *Die Juden in Bayern im Wandel der Zeiten* (Munich: Olzog, 1963), 284–86 reprints the decree.

70. For the petitions, see Schwarz, *Die Juden in Bayern*, 287–92.

71. Harris, *The People Speak!* 201–3.

72. Hamburger, *Juden im öffentlichen Leben Deutschlands*, 210–11. He represented Hof-Müncheberg.

73. Harris, *The People Speak!* 203.

74. Wolfgang Schmidt, "Die Juden in der Bayerischen Armee," in Frank Nägler, ed., *Deutsche Jüdische Soldaten: Von der Epoche der Emanzipation bis zum Zeitalter der Weltkriege* (Hamburg: Mittler, 1996), 63–85. There were 48 Jewish reserve officers in 1907, 129 in 1913.

75. These were ordinances and not laws. See Joseph Heimberger, *Die staatskirchenrechtliche Stellung der Israeliten in Bayern: Ein Beitrag zur Lehre von den Privatkirchengesellschaften* (Freiburg im Breisgau: Mohr, 1893), 30.

76. Gerhard Hirschmann, "Die Evangelische Kirche seit 1800," in Max Spindler, ed., *Handbuch der Bayerischen Geschichte*, 4 vols. (Munich: Beck, 1975), 4, 2:883–901.

77. Schwarz, *Die Juden in Bayern*, 299–301; Heimberger, *Die staatskirchenrechtliche Stellung der Israeliten in Bayern*. Heimberger reproduces the legislation at 187–89. Bavaria did not rectify that status during the Wilhelminian and Weimar periods.

78. Lamberti, "The Jewish Struggle for the Legal Equality of Religions in Imperial Germany," 109.

79. Pulzer, *Jews and the German State*, 60.

80. Wertheimer, *Unwelcome Strangers*, 58.

81. Edmund Bernatzik, *Die österreichischen Verfassungsgesetze* (Leipzig: Hirschfeld, 1906), 177–85; Robin Okey, *The Habsburg Monarchy: From Enlightenment to Eclipse* (New York: St. Martin's, 2001), 161–63; Peter Leisching, "Die römisch-katholische Kirche in Cisleithanien," in Adam Wandruszka and Peter Urbanitsch, eds., *Die Habsburgermonarchie, 1848–1918*, 9 vols. (Vienna: Österreichischen Akademie der Wissenschaften, 1985), 4:25–34; Wilhelm Brauneder, "Die Verfassungsentwicklung in Österreich, 1848 bis 1918," in *Die Habsburgermonarchie, 1848–1918*, 7, 1:138–39. For the Concordat's impact on Protestants, see Friedrich Gottas, "Die Geschichte des Protestantismus in der Habsburgermonarchie," in *Die Habsburgermonarchie, 1848–1918*, 4:551–54.

82. Bernatzik, *Die österreichischen Verfassungsgesetze*, 219–73; Brauneder, "Die Verfassungsentwicklung in Österreich, 1848 bis 1918," 156–58.

83. Okey, *The Habsburg Monarchy*, 166–76; Gottas, "Die Geschichte des Protestantismus in der Habsburgermonarchie," 4:555–56. The patent did not give Protestantism equality with Catholicism. That came in May 1874.

84. Bernatzik, *Die österreichischen Verfassungsgesetze*, 330–447; Okey, *The Habsburg Monarchy*, 187–202.

85. Okey, *The Habsburg Monarchy*, 173.

86. Wolfgang Häusler, "Das österreichische Judentum zwischen Beharrung und Fortschritt," in *Die Habsburgermonarchie, 1848–1918*, 4:656.

87. Bihl, "Die Juden," in *Die Habsburgermonarchie, 1848–1918*, 3, 2:884–87. The migrations were from Galicia to Hungary; from the Carpathians to Bohemia and Lower Austria, especially Vienna; and from Bohemia/Moravia to Vienna.

88. Ibid., 3, 2:893.

89. Ibid., 3, 2:894.

90. Bernatzik, *Die österreichischen Verfassungsgesetze*, 366–71; Hannelore Burger, "Passwesen und Staatsbürgerschaft," in Waltraud Heindl and Edith Saurer, eds., *Grenze und Staat: Paßwesen, Staatsbürgerschaft, Heimatrecht und Fremdengesetzgebung in der österreichischen Monarchie, 1750-1867* (Vienna: Böhlau, 2000), 168–72; Brauneder, "Die Verfassungsentwicklung in Österreich, 1848 bis 1918," 181–82.

91. Bihl, "Die Juden," 3, 2:894; Leisching, "Die römisch-katholische Kirche in Cisleithanien," 4:42–63.

92. Bihl, "Die Juden," 3, 2:897.

93. Bernatzik, *Die österreichischen Verfassungsgesetze*, 370.

94. Bihl, "Die Juden," 3, 2:903–4. There were four failed attempts (1880–1910) to gain Yiddish the status of a language and Jews the status of a nationality. See Gerald Stourzh, "Galten die Juden als Nationalität Altösterreichs? Ein Beitrag zur Geschichte des cisleithanischen Nationalitätenrechts," in *Studia Judaica Austriaca*, vol. 10 (Eisenstadt: Roetzer, 1984), 73–117. For a positive reassessment of the Dual Monarchy, stressing the nationality issue's "centripetal" impact in a developed civil society, see Gary B. Cohen, "Nationalist Politics and the Dynamics of State and Civil Society in the Habsburg Monarchy, 1867–1914," *Central European History* 40 (2007): 241–78.

95. István Deák, *A Social and Political History of the Habsburg Officer Corps, 1848–1918* (New York: Oxford University Press, 1990), ix, 4. 66. Austria had a separate National Guard (*Landwehr*) as did Hungary (*Honvéd*).

96. Ibid., 172. Statistics at 174–75. The monarchy outdid the other European powers in admitting Jews into its officer corps; without it, the process of Jewish integration into business, industry, education, the arts, and the administration would have been decidedly more difficult.

97. Jacob Bassevi (1622), Israel Hönig (1789). See Drewes, *Jüdischer Adel*, 150, 167.

98. Ibid., 186–91, 202. Jews received lesser titles, e.g., "Baron" (*Freiherr*) and not "Earl" (*Graf*).

99. Ibid., 224–34, 291; Huibert Schijf, "Titled Outsiders: Jewish Nobility in the Nineteenth and Early Twentieth Centuries," in Yme Kuiper, Nikolaj Bijleveld, and Jaap Dronkers, eds., *Nobilities in Europe in the Twentieth Century: Reconversion Strategies, Memory Culture and Elite Formation* (Leuven: Peeters, 2015), 59.

100. Krinsky, *Synagogues of Europe*, 191–94.

101. Bernatzik, *Die österreichischen Verfassungsgesetze*, 571–90; László Péter, "Die Verfassungsentwicklung in Ungarn," in *Die Habsburgermonarchie, 1848–1918*, 7, 1:338–66.

102. Robert A. Kann, "Hungarian Jewry during Austria-Hungary's Constitutional Period (1867–1918)," *Jewish Social Studies* 7, no. 4 (1945): 357–86.

103. Cohen, "Nationalist Politics and the Dynamics of State and Civil Society in the Habsburg Monarchy," 275.

104. Wolfdieter Bihl, "Das Judentum Ungarns, 1780–1914," in *Studia Judaica Austriaca*, vol. 3 (Eisenstadt: Roetzer, 1976), 21–22. Croatia granted Jews equality in 1873.

105. László Kontler, *A History of Hungary: Millennium in Central Europe* (Houndmills, Basingstoke: Palgrave Macmillan, 2002), 285, 291.

106. Krinsky, *Synagogues of Europe*, 157–59.

107. Ibid., 159–62. Otto Wagner was the architect.

108. James Shedel, "Austria and Its Polish Subjects, 1866–1914: A Relationship of Interests," *Austrian History Yearbook* 19–20 (1983–84): part 2, 25.

109. Bernatzik, *Die österreichischen Verfassungsgesetze*, 749–51. In 1867 Vienna permitted Poles to dominate the school board, making way for Polonized schools. In 1869 the emperor decreed Polish the language of Galicia's courts and bureaucracy. In 1870–71 Polish became Cracow and Lemberg universities' official language. In 1870 the emperor gave the Poles a monopoly on the viceroyalty and in 1871 created a Polish-controlled cabinet post (*Landesminister*) for Galicia. The municipal government transformed the formerly German city of "Lemberg" into a conspicuously Polish "Lwów." Individual Poles also held high office in Vienna. See Shedel, "Austria and Its Polish Subjects," 24 and Harald Binder, "Making and Defending a Polish Town: 'Lwów' (Lemberg), 1848–1914," *Austrian History Yearbook* 34 (2003): 57–81.

110. Filip Friedmann, *Die Galizischen Juden im Kampfe um ihre Gleichberechtigung (1848–1868)* (Frankfurt: Kauffmann, 1929), 205. In 1862 Galicia contained 2,072,663 Catholics/Poles; 2,077,112 Greek Orthodox/Ruthenians; and 448,973 Jews. See Rachel Manekin, *Yehudei Galitsia veha-Huka ha-Austrit: Reshita shel Politika Yehudit Modernit* (Jerusalem: Zalman Shazar, 2015), 20n9.

111. Friedmann, *Die Galizischen Juden im Kampfe um ihre Gleichberechtigung*, 88, 169–71; Manekin, *Yehudei Galitsia veha-Huka ha-Austrit*, 38. Agenor Goluchowski introduced the motion on landholding.

112. Joshua Shanes, *Diaspora Nationalism and Jewish Identity in Habsburg Galicia* (New York: Cambridge University Press, 2012), 43. For the Viennese government's earlier deliberations, see Manekin, *Yehudei Galitsia veha-Huka ha-Austrit*, 24ff. Jewish representatives raised the issue of equality in the first 1861 Diet; the Diet did not consider it. See Friedmann, *Die Galizischen Juden im Kampfe um ihre Gleichberechtigung*, 167–68.

113. Friedmann, *Die Galizischen Juden im Kampfe um ihre Gleichberechtigung*, 171–79; Manekin, *Yehudei Galitsia veha-Huka ha-Austrit*, 32–43. Joseph Kalchberg was the bureaucrat who proposed restrictions to defend the state's Christian character. He limited restrictions to state offices; Jews were to have full access to local offices (*Gemeindeämte*). See his *Kleine Beiträge zu großen Fragen in Oesterreich*, 2nd ed. (Leipzig: Brockhaus, 1860): "to be excluded from the following state offices: from all offices that have a representative function (*Repräsentation*), from directing an office, from individual judicial offices and from influencing or determining Christian-ecclesiastical issues" (74).

114. *Die Debatten über die Judenfrage in der Session des gallizischen Landtages vom J. 1868* (Lemberg, 1868). Smolka gave the final speech. See Friedmann, *Die Galizischen Juden im Kampfe um ihre Gleichberechtigung*, 179–81; Manekin, *Yehudei Galitsia veha-Huka ha-Austrit*, 47–54. In the next two years Lemberg excluded all restrictions based on religion from its municipal laws.

115. Friedmann, *Die Galizischen Juden im Kampfe um ihre Gleichberechtigung*, 162. Manekin, *Yehudei Galitsia veha-Huka ha-Austrit*, 15–16, sees modern Jewish politics emerging in Galicia in this period. In Galicia Jews created an independent Jewish politics and functioned in the public sphere as representatives of the Jewish public to further an agenda informed by Jewish interests.

116. Friedmann, *Die Galizischen Juden im Kampfe um ihre Gleichberechtigung*, 121.

117. Shanes, *Diaspora Nationalism and Jewish Identity in Habsburg Galicia*, 36–37.

118. Friedmann, *Die Galizischen Juden im Kampfe um ihre Gleichberechtigung*, 182.

119. Bernatzik, *Die österreichischen Verfassungsgesetze*, 751–57; Shanes, *Diaspora Nationalism and Jewish Identity in Habsburg Galicia*, 42–45; Friedmann, *Die Galizischen Juden im Kampfe um ihre Gleichberechtigung*, 185–87.

120. Friedmann, *Die Galizischen Juden im Kampfe um ihre Gleichberechtigung*, 139.

Chapter Fifteen. Russia and the Kingdom of Poland, I

1. W. Bruce Lincoln, *The Great Reforms: Autocracy, Bureaucracy, and the Politics of Change in Imperial Russia* (DeKalb: Northern Illinois University Press, 1990).

2. Raymond Pearson, "Privileges, Rights and Russification," in Olga Crisp and Linda Edmondson, eds., *Civil Rights in Imperial Russia* (Oxford: Clarendon, 1989), 93–102.

3. Jane Burbank has characterized the Russian Empire as a "regime of differentiated, alienable, but nonetheless legal and meaningful rights." The tsars strove for the "completeness" of an "inclusionary legalism" that applied to all the manifold religious and national groups through collective, revocable rights. See "An Imperial Rights Regime: Law and Citizenship in the Russian Empire," *Kritika: Explorations in Russian and Eurasian History* 7, no. 3 (2006): 397–431.

4. Israel Bartal, *The Jews of Eastern Europe, 1772–1881*, trans. Chaya Naor (Philadelphia: University of Pennsylvania Press, 2005), 71; Pearson, "Privileges, Rights and Russification," 93.

5. Paul Bushkovitch, *A Concise History of Russia* (New York: Cambridge University Press, 2012), 222; Benjamin Nathans, *Beyond the Pale: The Jewish Encounter with Late Imperial Russia* (Berkeley: University of California Press, 2002), 72–79.

6. Laura Engelstein, "The Dream of Civil Society in Tsarist Russia: Law, State and Religion," in Nancy Bermeo and Philip Nord, eds., *Civil Society before Democracy: Lessons from Nineteenth-Century Europe* (Lanham, MD: Rowman and Littlefield, 2000), 23–42; Manfred Hildermeier, *Bürgertum und Stadt in Rußland, 1760–1870: Rechtliche Lage und Soziale Struktur* (Cologne: Böhlau, 1986), 307–22.

7. Michael Stanislawski, "Russian Jewry, the Russian State, and the Dynamics of Jewish Emancipation," in Pierre Birnbaum and Ira Katznelson, eds., *Paths of Emancipation: Jews, States, and Citizenship* (Princeton: Princeton University Press, 1995), 266. Nathans calls this an "analytic disorder." See *Beyond the Pale*, 73.

8. Stanislawski, "Russian Jewry, the Russian State, and the Dynamics of Jewish Emancipation," 266–69.

9. Hans Rogger, *Jewish Policies and Right-Wing Politics in Imperial Russia* (Oxford: Macmillan, 1986), 112.

10. Quoted in ibid., 16. For this issue, see John Klier, "The Concept of 'Jewish Emancipation' in a Russian Context," in Crisp and Edmondson, eds., *Civil Rights in Imperial Russia*, 129; Yohanan Petrovsky-Shtern, *Jews in the Russian Army, 1827–1917: Drafted into Modernity* (New York: Cambridge University Press, 2009), 34.

11. Antony Polonsky, *The Jews in Poland and Russia*, 3 vols. (Oxford: Littman, 2010–12), 1:322–23, 2:3.

12. Petrovsky-Shtern, *Jews in the Russian Army*, 40; Bartal, *The Jews of Eastern Europe*, 41; Michael Stanislawski, *Tsar Nicholas I and the Jews: The Transformation of Jewish Society in Russia, 1825–1855* (Philadelphia: Jewish Publication Society, 1983), 57.

13. Nathans, *Beyond the Pale*, 372.

14. Petrovsky-Shtern, *Jews in the Russian Army*, 29.

15. Stanislawski, *Tsar Nicholas I and the Jews*, 19; Petrovsky-Shtern, *Jews in the Russian Army*, 62.

16. Yohanan Petrovsky-Shtern, *The Golden Age Shtetl: A New History of Jewish Life in East Europe* (Princeton: Princeton University Press, 2014), 48. For Nicholas's intention to convert the Jews, see Stanislawski, *Tsar Nicholas I and the Jews*, 15.

17. Petrovsky-Shtern, *Jews in the Russian Army*, 16–18, 24, 29, 34–36, 59, 62; Stanislawski, *Tsar Nicholas I and the Jews*, 17. Only those classified as "merchants" continued to be able to buy exemptions for their sons. See Nathans, *Beyond the Pale*, 27.

18. Petrovsky-Shtern, *Jews in the Russian Army*, 46–54.

19. Ibid., 65–66. The navy was perhaps more vigilant than the army in serving Jewish recruits' needs (67–69).

20. Petrovsky-Shtern, *Jews in the Russian Army*, 69–88; Stanislawski, *Tsar Nicholas I and the Jews*, 169–70.

21. Rogger, *Jewish Policies and Right-Wing Politics in Imperial Russia*, 10; Petrovsky-Shtern, *Jews in the Russian Army*, 63.

22. Petrovsky-Shtern, *Jews in the Russian Army*, 90–95.

23. Ibid., 93–95, 102–3.

24. Stanislawski, *Tsar Nicholas I and the Jews*, 22–25. On Jewish literary sources confusing primitive medical procedures with conversionary torture, see Petrovsky-Shtern, *Jews in the Russian Army*, 106.

25. Stanislawski asserted that half of the Cantonists converted. See *Tsar Nicholas I and the Jews*, 25. As evidence of inconsistent policies, Nicholas in 1848 prohibited Jewish converts from taking Russian names. See Petrovsky-Shtern, *Jews in the Russian Army*, 113.

26. Petrovsky-Shtern, *Jews in the Russian Army*, 113–24. A circular of August 18, 1905, permitted Jews who had converted to revert to Judaism.

27. Ibid., 108–10.

28. Stanislawski, *Tsar Nicholas I and the Jews*, 128–33; David Assaf, ed., *Journey to a Nineteenth-Century Shtetl: The Memoirs of Yekhezkel Kotik* (Detroit: Wayne State University Press, 2002), 175.

29. Stanislawski, *Tsar Nicholas I and the Jews*, 13–34.

30. Michael Speransky, the distinguished bureaucrat and poet, oversaw the codification. The existing code dated from Tsar Alexis (1649). Ten previous commissions over a century had unsuccessfully attempted to codify Russian law. See Marc Raeff, *Michael Speransky: Statesman of Imperial Russia, 1772–1839* (Hague: Nijhoff, 1957), 320–23. Speransky was inspired by natural law theory and Savigny's historical school of jurisprudence. For the introduction to his 1809 proposal, see Marc Raeff, ed., *Plans for Political Reform in Imperial Russian, 1730–1905* (Englewood Cliffs, NJ: Prentice-Hall, 1966), 92–109.

31. Raeff, *Michael Speransky*, 340–42.

32. Stanislawski, "Russian Jewry, the Russian State, and the Dynamics of Jewish Emancipation," 272.

33. Klier, "The Concept of 'Jewish Emancipation' in a Russian Context," 132–33; Rogger, *Jewish Policies and Right-Wing Politics in Imperial Russia*, 26; Heinz-Dietrich Löwe, "Poles, Jews and Tatars: Religion, Ethnicity and Social Structure in Tsarist Nationality Policies," *Jewish Social Studies* 6, no. 3 (2000): 52–96.

34. Stanislawski, *Tsar Nicholas I and the Jews*, 36–37. In Posen (1820s) Prussia limited Jews to one-third of representatives and in 1831 prohibited Jewish mayors (chapter 12).

35. Eugene M. Avrutin, *Jews and the Imperial State: Identification Politics in Tsarist Russia* (Ithaca: Cornell University Press, 2010), 33.

36. Nathans, *Beyond the Pale*, 69.

37. Quoted in Stanislawski, *Tsar Nicholas I and the Jews*, 44; Nathans, *Beyond the Pale*, 31–34. The tsarist government undermined the Polish nobility's remaining legal autonomy, stripped impoverished nobles of their titles and immunity from taxation, and subjected

them to a double rate of conscription. Kiselev looked to Prussia, Austria, Bavaria, and Baden.

38. Quoted in Stanislawski, *Tsar Nicholas I and the Jews*, 45.

39. Cynthia H. Whittaker, *The Origins of Modern Russian Education: An Intellectual Biography of Count Sergei Uvarov, 1786–1855* (DeKalb: Northern Illinois University Press, 1984), 4, 32–40. Uvarov tried to chart a middle course between Slavophiles and Westernizers, advocating "a Russian system and a European education."

40. Whittaker, *The Origins of Modern Russian Education*, 100, 109, 129, 139–40.

41. Ibid., 189–212.

42. Ibid., 203.

43. Stanislawski, *Tsar Nicholas I and the Jews*, 69–96.

44. The rabbis were the leaders of mitnagdic orthodoxy, Yizhak of Volozhin, and Habad Hasidism, Menahem Mendel Schneersohn. Also attending was a financier, Israel Halperin of Berdichev, and the director of the Odessa school, Bezalel Stern. Stanislawski, *Tsar Nicholas I and the Jews*, 77–82.

45. Whittaker, *The Origins of Modern Russian Education*, 211.

46. Stanislawski, *Tsar Nicholas I and the Jews*, 106–9.

47. Nathans, *Beyond the Pale*, 31–38.

48. Some German states required rabbis to apply for certification, which often included a university degree. See Ismar Schorsch, "Emancipation and the Crisis of Religious Authority: The Emergence of the Modern Rabbinate," in *From Text to Context: The Turn to History in Modern Judaism* (Hanover, NH: Brandeis University Press, 1994), 9–50.

49. Azriel Shohat, *Mosad "Ha-Rabbanut mi-Ta'am" be-Rusiyah: Parasha be-Ma'avak ha-Tarbut bein Haradim le-bein Maskilim* (Haifa: Haifa University Press, 1975); Assaf, *Journey to a Nineteenth-Century Shtetl*, 380, 386.

50. Avrutin, *Jews and the Imperial State*, 34.

51. Polonsky, *The Jews in Poland and Russia*, 1:371; Stanislawski, *Tsar Nicholas I and the Jews*, 123–27.

52. Stanislawski, "Russian Jewry, the Russian State, and the Dynamics of Jewish Emancipation," 267; Isaac Levitats, *The Jewish Community in Russia, 1772–1844* (New York: Columbia University Press, 1943), 38–45.

53. Rogger, *Jewish Policies and Right-Wing Politics in Imperial Russia*, 11; Stanislawski, *Tsar Nicholas I and the Jews*, 156.

54. Brian Horowitz, *Jewish Philanthropy and Enlightenment in Late-Tsarist Russia* (Seattle: University of Washington Press, 2009), 27.

55. Stanislawski, *Tsar Nicholas I and the Jews*, 159–60.

56. Petrovsky-Shtern, *The Golden Age Shtetl*, 12–20. For the liquor industry in the Kingdom of Poland, see Glenn Dynner, *Yankel's Tavern: Jews, Liquor, & Life in the Kingdom of Poland* (New York: Oxford University Press, 2014).

57. Petrovsky-Shtern, *The Golden Age Shtetl*, 36.

58. Ibid., 57–89.

59. Ibid., 91–149; Stanislawski, *Tsar Nicholas I and the Jews*, 171–82.

60. Lincoln, *The Great Reforms*, 62.

61. Stanislawski, *Tsar Nicholas I and the Jews*, 172; Assaf, *Journey to a Nineteenth-Century Shtetl*, 218, 334; Nathans, *Beyond the Pale*, 40 gives the date of 1848.

62. Nathans, *Beyond the Pale*, 50–58; Louis Greenberg, *The Jews in Russia*, 2 vols. (New Haven: Yale University Press, 1944–51), 1:91–92.

63. Nathans, *Beyond the Pale*, 61.

64. Ibid., 59, 62. For the example of Kiev, which admitted Jews from 1859, see Natan

M. Meir, *Kiev, Jewish Metropolis: A History, 1859–1914* (Bloomington: Indiana University Press, 2010).

65. Horowitz, *Jewish Philanthropy and Enlightenment*, 25.

66. Ibid., 55.

67. On Alexander II's reforms and the rise of public opinion, which influenced policy, see John Doyle Klier, *Imperial Russia's Jewish Question, 1855–1881* (Cambridge: Cambridge University Press, 1995).

68. Wolfdieter Bihl, "Die Juden," in Adam Wandruszka and Peter Urbanitsch, eds., *Die Habsburgermonarchie, 1848–1918*, 9 vols. (Vienna: Österreichischen Akademie der Wissenschaften, 1985), 3, 2:894.

69. Peter Waldron, "Religious Toleration in Late Imperial Russia," in Crisp and Edmondson, eds., *Civil Rights in Imperial Russia*, 110.

70. Eric Lohr, *Russian Citizenship: From Empire to Soviet Union* (Cambridge, MA: Harvard University Press, 2012), 48–53.

71. Heinz-Dietrich Löwe, *The Tsars and the Jews: Reform, Reaction and Anti-Semitism in Imperial Russia, 1772–1917* (Chur, Switzerland: Harwood, 1993), 45. Löwe quotes the Minister of the Interior at length on 45–46.

72. Petrovsky-Shtern, *Jews in the Russian Army*, 124–27.

73. Ibid., 129–34.

74. Ibid., 136–43; 139: "the draft reports consistently compared the entire draft pool with the number drafted, rather than the number drafted with the number of those selected by lottery."

75. Klier, "The Concept of 'Jewish Emancipation' in a Russian Context," 136.

76. The 1897 census listed some 313,000 Jews in the interior. See Nathans, *Beyond the Pale*, 66. In general: Yvonne Kleinmann, *Neue Orte -neue Menschen: Jüdische Lebensformen in St. Petersburg und Moskau im 19. Jahrhundert* (Göttingen: Vandenhoeck & Ruprecht, 2006). For Kiev, see Meir, *Kiev, Jewish Metropolis*.

77. The Society for the Promotion of Enlightenment among the Jews (OPE) devoted three-eighths of its budget to support university students and one-eighth to promote publications in Russian. Mandelshtam's translation appeared in 1872. See Horowitz, *Jewish Philanthropy and Enlightenment*, 36–45 and Nathans, *Beyond the Pale*, 225–30. For German Jewish organizations dedicated to regeneration, see David Sorkin, *The Transformation of German Jewry, 1780–1840* (New York: Oxford University Press, 1987), 112–23 and Simone Lässig, *Jüdische Wege ins Bürgertum: Kulturelles Kapital und sozialer Aufstieg im 19. Jahrhundert* (Göttingen: Vandenhoeck, 2004), 533–37. For France, see Jay Berkowitz, *The Shaping of Jewish Identity in Nineteenth-Century France* (Detroit: Wayne State University Press, 1989), 105–10.

78. Alexander Orbach, *New Voices of Russian Jewry: A Study of the Russian-Jewish Press of Odessa in the Era of the Great Reforms, 1860–1871* (Leiden: Brill, 1980); Eli Lederhendler, *The Road to Modern Jewish Politics: Political Tradition and Political Reconstruction in the Jewish Community of Tsarist Russia* (New York: Oxford University Press, 1989).

79. Artur Eisenbach, *The Emancipation of the Jews in Poland, 1780–1870* (Oxford: Blackwell, 1991), 153–54.

80. For this contradiction as well as other proposals, see Eisenbach, *The Emancipation of the Jews in Poland*, 168–78.

81. François Guesnet, *Polnische Juden im 19. Jahrhundert: Lebensbedingungen, Rechtsnormen und Organisation im Wandel* (Cologne: Böhlau, 1998), 199.

82. On petitions for exemptions, see Eisenbach, *The Emancipation of the Jews in Poland*, 225–26.

83. Ibid., 250.

84. Guesnet, *Polnische Juden im 19. Jahrhundert*, 190–92, 223; Polonsky, *The Jews in Poland and Russia*, 1:290–92.

85. Polonsky, *The Jews in Poland and Russia*, 1:298. To join the Warsaw National Guard Jews had to shave their beards.

86. Petrovsky-Shtern, *Jews in the Russian Army*, 27–28, 46; Guesnet, *Polnische Juden im 19. Jahrhundert*, 183–84.

87. Eisenbach, *The Emancipation of the Jews in Poland*, 378.

88. Ibid., 299–307. Some sixty Jews gained personal privileges before 1861.

89. Ibid., 377.

90. Guesnet, *Polnische Juden im 19. Jahrhundert*, 193–99.

91. Eisenbach, *The Emancipation of the Jews in Poland*, 377, 386.

92. Ibid., 444.

93. Polonsky, *The Jews in Poland and Russia*, 1:278, 308–9. Two other groups courted the kingdom's Jews. The tsarist government wanted their support to avert another insurrection. The Polish opposition wanted them in the anti-tsarist camp.

94. Eisenbach, *The Emancipation of the Jews in Poland*, 434–35, 445, 450–51. The most important associations were the Merchant Confraternity and the Craftsmen's Assembly. In the election of 1861 Jews were elected in significant numbers: of 615 members of district councils, 27; of 184 municipal councillors, 28; of 184 deputy councillors, 40.

95. Artur Eisenbach, "Le problème des Juifs polonaise en 1861 et les projets de réforme du Marquis Aleksander Wielopolski," *Acta Poloniae Historica* 20 (1969): 142–44. A Jewish delegation met with Wielopolski on April 4, 1861; Jews helped draft laws later that month.

96. The Russians acquiesced to Wielopolski's draft because a senior civil servant reported that the law would not introduce serious differences in the legal situation between Russia and the kingdom. See Eisenbach, *The Emancipation of the Jews in Poland*, 231, 442, 454, 468.

97. Guesnet, *Polnische Juden im 19. Jahrhundert*, 188–92.

98. Eisenbach, "Le problème des Juifs polonaise en 1861," 160–61.

99. Eisenbach, *The Emancipation of the Jews in Poland*, 16, 444, 449; on the general situation, see Piotr S. Wandycz, *The Lands of Partitioned Poland, 1795–1918* (Seattle: University of Washington Press, 1974), 161–72.

100. Klier, "The Concept of 'Jewish Emancipation' in a Russian Context," 135; Greenberg, *The Jews in Russia*, 1:76.

101. Guesnet, *Polnische Juden im 19. Jahrhundert*, 189; Polonsky, *The Jews in Poland and Russia*, 1:311.

102. Carol Herselle Krinsky, *Synagogues of Europe: Architecture, History, Meaning* (New York: Dover, 1985), 230–33; Polonsky, *The Jews in Poland and Russia*, 1:317.

103. Wandycz, *The Lands of Partitioned Poland*, 172–79.

Chapter Sixteen. Russia and the Kingdom of Poland, II

1. Heinz-Dietrich Löwe, *The Tsars and the Jews: Reform, Reaction and Anti-Semitism in Imperial Russia, 1772–1917* (Chur, Switzerland: Harwood, 1993), 62–65.

2. Raymond Pearson, "Privileges, Rights and Russification," in Olga Crisp and Linda Edmondson, eds., *Civil Rights in Imperial Russia* (Oxford: Clarendon, 1989), 95–97.

3. I. M. Aronson, *Troubled Waters: The Origins of the 1881 Anti-Jewish Pogroms in Russia* (Pittsburgh: University of Pittsburgh Press, 1990).

4. Yohanan Petrovsky-Shtern, *Jews in the Russian Army, 1827–1917: Drafted into Mo-*

dernity (New York: Cambridge University Press, 2009), 167. For "selective integration," see Benjamin Nathans, *Beyond the Pale: The Jewish Encounter with Late Imperial Russia* (Berkeley: University of California Press, 2002). There were government commissions (Pahlen) that proposed emancipatory policies that the powerful Finance Ministry consistently supported. See I. M. Aronson, "The Prospects for the Emancipation of Russian Jewry during the 1880s," *Slavonic and East European Review* 55, no. 3 (1977): 348–69 and Löwe, *The Tsars and the Jews*, 55–76, 129.

5. John Klier, "The Concept of 'Jewish Emancipation' in a Russian Context," in Crisp and Edmondson, eds., *Civil Rights in Imperial Russia*, 138. The May Laws were not as extreme as Minister of the Interior Ignatiev's initial proposals.

6. Michael Stanislawski, *Tsar Nicholas I and the Jews: The Transformation of Jewish Society in Russia, 1825–1855* (Philadelphia: Jewish Publication Society, 1983), 4–5; Löwe, *The Tsars and the Jews*, 55–76. A near contemporary account that made this argument was Lucien Wolf, ed., *The Legal Sufferings of the Jews in Russia: A Survey of Their Present Situation, and a Summary of Laws* (London: Fisher Unwin, 1912).

7. Löwe, *The Tsars and the Jews*, 70.

8. Petrovsky-Shtern, *Jews in the Russian Army*, 167.

9. Eugene M. Avrutin, *Jews and the Imperial State: Identification Politics in Tsarist Russia* (Ithaca: Cornell University Press, 2010), 99–108; Löwe, *The Tsars and the Jews*, 71.

10. Löwe, *The Tsars and the Jews*, 75; Pearson, "Privileges, Rights and Russification," 95.

11. Cynthia H. Whittaker, *The Origins of Modern Russian Education: An Intellectual Biography of Count Sergei Uvarov, 1786–1855* (DeKalb: Northern Illinois University Press, 1984), 139–40.

12. Löwe, *The Tsars and the Jews*, 39.

13. Nathans, *Beyond the Pale*, 257–307. By the turn of the century "more Russian Jews were studying in institutions of higher education in Europe . . . than in the Russian Empire" (280). The tsarist government successfully pressed German states (Prussia, Bavaria) to introduce quotas for foreign students.

14. The law applied to Jews, Muslims, and Karaites. The few Muslim and Karaite candidates gained admission. See Salo Baron, *The Russian Jew under Tsars and Soviets* (New York: Macmillan, 1964), 57.

15. Nathans, *Beyond the Pale*, 355.

16. Ibid., 340–66; Löwe, *The Tsars and the Jews*, 75; Pearson, "Privileges, Rights and Russification," 95.

17. Brian Horowitz, *Jewish Philanthropy and Enlightenment in Late-Tsarist Russia* (Seattle: University of Washington Press, 2009), 98–101; Natan M. Meir, *Kiev, Jewish Metropolis: A History, 1859–1914* (Bloomington: Indiana University Press, 2010), 284–90, 297–307.

18. Horowitz, *Jewish Philanthropy and Enlightenment*, 89–90; Nathans, *Beyond the Pale*, 324–34; Louis Greenberg, *The Jews in Russia*, 2 vols. (New Haven: Yale University Press, 1944–51), 2:123–37. The Gintsburgs hired as their secretary in 1893 the lawyer Genrikh Sliozberg (1863–1937). He replaced the *maskil* Emanuel Levin.

19. Hans Rogger, *Jewish Policies and Right-Wing Politics in Imperial Russia* (Oxford: Macmillan, 1986), 84–90.

20. Löwe, *The Tsars and the Jews*, 103–28; the reactionaries and their supporters utilized anti-Semitic rhetoric to discredit Witte. The Interior Ministry came into conflict with the War Ministry over name changes: the War Ministry approved of Jews changing their names, the Interior Ministry prohibited changes. Avrutin, *Jews and the Imperial State*, 152.

21. Löwe, *The Tsars and the Jews*, 139.

22. Ibid., 144; Rogger, *Jewish Policies and Right-Wing Politics in Imperial Russia*, 79–80.

23. Löwe, *The Tsars and the Jews*, 144–45.

24. Rogger, *Jewish Policies and Right-Wing Politics in Imperial Russia*, 40–55; Löwe, *The Tsars and the Jews*, 295–96.

25. Benjamin Nathans, "The Other Modern Jewish Politics: Integration and Modernity in Fin de Siècle Russia," in Zvi Gitelman, ed., *The Emergence of Modern Jewish Politics: Bundism and Zionism in Eastern Europe* (Pittsburgh: University of Pittsburgh Press, 2003), 27–28; Christoph Gassenschmidt, *Jewish Liberal Politics in Tsarist Russia, 1900–1914* (New York: New York University Press, 1995), 8–9. Paul Nathan and Lucien Wolf established journals in Berlin, Paris, and London to publicize the situation.

26. Löwe, *The Tsars and the Jews*, 148–55; Antony Polonsky, *The Jews in Poland and Russia*, 3 vols. (Oxford: Littman, 2010–12), 2:47–59; Abraham Ascher, "Anti-Jewish Pogroms in the First Russian Revolution," in Yaacov Ro'I, ed., *Jews and Jewish Life in Russia and the Soviet Union* (Ilford, Essex: Frank Cass, 1995), 127–45.

27. Gassenschmidt, *Jewish Liberal Politics in Tsarist Russia*, 9–10, 15–18; Samuel Kucherov, "Jews in the Russian Bar," in Jacob Frumkin, ed., *Russian Jewry (1860–1917)*, 2 vols. (New York: Thomas Yoseloff, 1966), 1:219–52.

28. Nathans, *Beyond the Pale*, 321. Some Russians concurred. See the quotation from Vladimir Nabokov in Alexis Goldenweiser, "Legal Status of Jews in Russia," in Frumkin, ed., *Russian Jewry*, 1:90–91.

29. Gassenschmidt, *Jewish Liberal Politics in Tsarist Russia*, 15. For the Bund, self-defense and revolution merged. See Jonathan Frankel, *Jewish Politics and the Russian Revolution of 1905* (Spiegel Lectures) (Tel Aviv: Tel Aviv University Press, 1982), 8.

30. Löwe, *The Tsars and the Jews*, 257.

31. Gassenschmidt, *Jewish Liberal Politics in Tsarist Russia*, 25–26.

32. Michael Stanislawski, "Russian Jewry, the Russian State, and the Dynamics of Jewish Emancipation," in Pierre Birnbaum and Ira Katznelson, eds., *Paths of Emancipation: Jews, States, and Citizenship* (Princeton: Princeton University Press, 1995), 280.

33. Löwe, *The Tsars and the Jews*, 205.

34. Abraham Ascher, *The Revolution of 1905: A Short History* (Stanford: Stanford University Press, 2004), 73–86. The Duma proposed laws, but the Council of State had to approve and the tsar validate them. The tsar controlled foreign policy, the army, and administrative appointments; ministers were responsible to the tsar. The electoral system was curial as well as regional.

35. Greenberg, *The Jews in Russia*, 2:120. For speeches in the first Duma, see Goldenweiser, "Legal Status of Jews in Russia," 94–95.

36. Löwe, *The Tsars and the Jews*, 228–29.

37. Greenberg, *The Jews in Russia*, 2:120; Löwe, *The Tsars and the Jews*, 337–43, 352–65.

38. Frankel, *Jewish Politics and the Russian Revolution of 1905*, 6.

39. *Pravo* (1905): 9, quoted in Greenberg, *The Jews in Russia*, 2:114.

40. Gassenschmidt, *Jewish Liberal Politics in Tsarist Russia*, 22.

41. Vinaver, a leader of the Kadets, lost his right to hold office by signing the Vyborg Appeal (June 22, 1906) that called for passive resistance after the government dissolved the first Duma. See Greenberg, *The Jews in Russia*, 2:114–16 and Nathans, "The Other Modern Jewish Politics," 20–34.

42. Alexander Orbach, "The Jewish People's Group and Jewish Politics in Tsarist Russia, 1906–1914," *Modern Judaism* 10 (1990): 1–15.

43. Greenberg, *The Jews in Russia*, 2:119; Goldenweiser, "Legal Status of Jews in Rus-

sia," 95. Orthodox and Hasidic Jews unsuccessfully tried to create an alliance with Stolypin's government. See Vladimir Levin, "Orthodox Jewry and the Russian Government: An Attempt at Rapprochement, 1907–1914," *East European Jewish Affairs* 39, no. 2 (2009): 187–204.

44. Löwe, *The Tsars and the Jews*, 259–60.

45. Ibid., 261, 290–93.

46. Ibid., 323. For an overview of the Jews' legal situation on the eve of the war, see Goldenweiser, "Legal Status of Jews in Russia," 96–109.

47. Löwe, *The Tsars and the Jews*, 325; Abraham G. Duker, "Jews in the World War: A Brief Historical Sketch," *Contemporary Jewish Record* 2, no. 5 (1939): 9–13.

48. Avrutin, *Jews and the Imperial State*, 183; Löwe, *The Tsars and the Jews*, 329–34.

49. Goldenweiser, "Legal Status of Jews in Russia," 114–15; Löwe, *The Tsars and the Jews*, 328, 345–48.

50. Gregor Aronson, "Jewish Communal Life in 1917–18," in Frumkin, ed., *Russian Jewry*, 2:13–16; Eric Lohr, *Russian Citizenship: From Empire to Soviet Union* (Cambridge, MA: Harvard University Press, 2012), 128–29.

51. Steven J. Zipperstein, "The Politics of Relief: The Transformation of Russian Jewish Communal Life during the First World War," *Studies in Contemporary Jewry* 4 (1988): 22–29; S. Ettinger, "The Jews in Russia at the Outbreak of the Revolution," in Lionel Kochan, ed., *The Jews in Soviet Russia since 1917*, 3rd ed. (Oxford: Oxford University Press, 1978), 26–28.

52. The Society for Manual Work concentrated on labor bureaus; the Society for the Protection of the Jews' Health organized medical and sanitary relief; and the Society for the Spread of Enlightenment among the Jews was responsible for education. Zipperstein, "The Politics of Relief," 30–31; Simon Rabinovitch, *Jewish Rights, National Rites: Nationalism and Autonomy in Late Imperial and Revolutionary Russia* (Stanford: Stanford University Press, 2014), 180–85, 197.

53. The decisive factors were the need to build institutions in new areas or rebuild destroyed institutions in old ones; the fact that a large range of Jews, not just the poor, needed relief; and the participation of a cadre of professionals who pushed a democratic agenda. See Zipperstein, "The Politics of Relief," 32–33.

54. Artur Eisenbach, *The Emancipation of the Jews in Poland, 1780–1870* (Oxford: Blackwell, 1991), 520. For the shifting relations between Poles and Jews, see Theodore R. Weeks, "Poles, Jews and Russians, 1863–1914: The Death of the Ideal of Assimilation in the Kingdom of Poland," *Polin* 12 (1999): 242–56.

55. Polonsky, *The Jews in Poland and Russia*, 2:89.

56. François Guesnet, *Polnische Juden im 19. Jahrhundert: Lebensbedingungen, Rechtsnormen und Organisation im Wandel* (Cologne: Böhlau, 1998), 192.

57. Polonsky, *The Jews in Poland and Russia*, 2:103–4.

58. The 1861 law introducing elective city government did not go into effect because of the insurrection. The administration in place since 1818 remained. Alexander II's municipal reform (1870) did not apply in the Kingdom of Poland. See Theodore R. Weeks, "Nationality and Municipality: Reforming City Government in the Kingdom of Poland, 1904–1915," *Russian History* 21, no. 1 (1994): 23–26.

59. Polonsky, *The Jews in Poland and Russia*, 2:66–67, 107–10.

Chapter Seventeen. Western Europe

1. The phrase is from Isaac Lyon Goldsmid. Quoted in Todd Endelman, *The Jews of Britain, 1656–2000* (Berkeley: University of California Press, 2002), 101. For lack of interest

in emancipation, see Geoffrey Alderman, "English Jews or Jews of the English Persuasion? Reflections on the Emancipation of Anglo-Jewry," in Pierre Birnbaum and Ira Katznelson, eds., *Paths of Emancipation: Jews, States, and Citizenship* (Princeton: Princeton University Press, 1995), 135–36 and U. R. Q. Henriques, "The Jewish Emancipation Controversy in Nineteenth-Century Britain," *Past and Present* 40 (1968): 127–29.

2. Ursula Henriques, *Religious Toleration in England, 1787–1833* (Toronto: University of Toronto Press, 1961).

3. With the repeal of the Test and Corporation Acts Parliament introduced a new declaration that included the words "on the true faith of a Christian." This declaration barred Jews from holding office. See Francis Henry Goldsmid, *Remarks on the Civil Disabilities of British Jews* (London: Colburn & Bentley, 1830), 13–14 and Henriques, *Religious Toleration in England*, 184.

4. For the centrality of the Christian state, see David Feldman, *Englishmen and Jews: Social Relations and Political Culture, 1840–1914* (New Haven: Yale University Press, 1994), 28–47; M. C. N. Salbstein, *The Emancipation of the Jews in Britain: The Question of the Admission of the Jews to Parliament, 1828–1860* (Rutherford, NJ: Fairleigh Dickinson University Press, 1982), 146–61; David Cesarani, "British Jews," in Rainer Liedtke and Stephan Wendehorst, eds., *The Emancipation of Catholics, Jews and Protestants: Minorities and the Nation State in Nineteenth-Century Europe* (Manchester: Manchester University Press, 1999), 37–44; and Henriques, "The Jewish Emancipation Controversy in Nineteenth-Century Britain," 131–33. For a contemporary discussion, see Francis Henry Goldsmid, *The Arguments Advanced against the Enfranchisement of the Jews Considered in a Series of Letters* (London: Bentley, 1833), 3–7. For Goldsmid, see Tony Hammond, "F. H. Goldsmid and Archbishop Whately of Dublin: Their Significance in the Emancipation Debate," *Jewish Historical Studies* 35 (1996–98): 153–66.

5. John A. Phillips and Charles Wetherell, "The Great Reform Act of 1832 and the Political Modernization of England," *American Historical Review* 100, no. 2 (April 1995): 411–36.

6. Feldman, *Englishmen and Jews*, 28: "the Jewish minority was too small to compel Parliament to open its doors." Daniel O'Connell's letter (September 11, 1829) to I. L. Goldsmid is quoted in Salbstein, *The Emancipation of the Jews in Britain*, 123–24.

7. Feldman, *Englishmen and Jews*, 31. Members of Parliament had to swear three oaths: allegiance, supremacy, and abjuration. Only the last (from 1701) contained the words "on the true faith of a Christian." See Salbstein, *The Emancipation of the Jews in Britain*, 51.

8. Feldman, *Englishmen and Jews*, 36–47. The role of conversionists such as the Philo-Judean Society should not be overlooked. See Henriques, *Religious Toleration in England*, 178.

9. Feldman, *Englishmen and Jews*, 28–36; Endelman, *The Jews of Britain*, 102–3.

10. Israel Finestein, "Some Modern Themes in the Emancipation Debate in Early Victorian England," in Jonathan Sacks, ed., *Tradition and Transition: Essays Presented to Chief Rabbi Sir Immanuel Jakobovits to Celebrate Twenty Years in Office* (London: Jews' College Publications, 1986), 131–46; Salbstein, *The Emancipation of the Jews in Britain*, 144–45.

11. H. S. Q. Henriques, *The Jews and the English Law* (London: J. Jacobs, 1908), 203–6. Goldsmid wrote one of the first tracts advocating emancipation. See *Remarks on the Civil Disabilities of British Jews* (London: Colburn & Bentley, 1830).

12. Salbstein, *The Emancipation of the Jews in Britain*, 125. Salomons "had the unanimous electoral support of the City Livery."

13. For David Salomons's efforts to get this legislation passed, see Salbstein, *The Emancipation of the Jews in Britain*, 127–37. Salomons took office as alderman for Cordwainer Ward in 1847 and as Lord Mayor of the City of London in 1855.

14. Henriques, "The Jewish Emancipation Controversy in Nineteenth-Century Britain," 130.

15. The Board of Deputies excluded the Reform West London Synagogue. For the role of the *Jewish Chronicle* and the Jewish Association for the Removal of Civil and Religious Disabilities, see David Cesarani, *The Jewish Chronicle and Anglo-Jewry, 1841–1991* (Cambridge: Cambridge University Press, 1994), 15, 18–22, 35–36 and Endelman, *The Jews of Britain*, 107–8.

16. Aubrey Newman, *The Board of Deputies of British Jews, 1760–1985* (London: Vallentine, Mitchell, 1987), 7–9; Alderman, "English Jews or Jews of the English Persuasion," 130–31.

17. Quoted in Salbstein, *The Emancipation of the Jews in Britain*, 165. Bentinck lost his position as Tory leader because of his December 1847 speech in favor of emancipation. See 166–67.

18. After delaying presenting himself in Parliament, Rothschild was asked to choose between the Protestant and Catholic oath. He answered: "I desire to be sworn upon the Old Testament." He swore the oaths of allegiance and supremacy but not the oath of abjuration. See Salbstein, *The Emancipation of the Jews in Britain*, 177–79.

19. Feldman, *Englishmen and Jews*, 31.

20. Salbstein, *The Emancipation of the Jews in Britain*, 179–86. Salomons's provocative behavior resulted in a court case.

21. Lord Aberdeen suggested the compromise as early as 1853. See Salbstein, *The Emancipation of the Jews in Britain*, 191. For details, see 221–42.

22. Feldman, *Englishmen and Jews*, 43. After Rothschild's first election advocates began to emphasize the constitutional theme. See Salbstein, *The Emancipation of the Jews in Britain*, 176.

23. Salbstein, *The Emancipation of the Jews in Britain*, 226.

24. Contemporaries pointed to the Plantation Act's solution. See, e.g., *Short Statement on Behalf of His Majesty's Subjects Professing the Jewish Religion* (London: Pelham Richardson, 1835), 13–14.

25. Feldman, *Englishmen and Jews*, 46; Cesarani, *The Jewish Chronicle and Anglo-Jewry*, 38.

26. See Salbstein, *The Emancipation of the Jews in Britain*, 241.

27. Ibid., 61–63, 72, 133, 226. For the campaign being conducted "behind closed doors," see Abigail Green, *Moses Montefiore: Jewish Liberator, Imperial Hero* (Cambridge, MA: Harvard University Press, 2010), 85–92.

28. The Reform Act encouraged the rise of organized political parties. See Phillips and Wetherell, "The Great Reform Act of 1832 and the Political Modernization of England," 411–36. The period 1810–50 was an "assertive and expansive phase" for the development of public meetings and open associations. See Robert J. Morris, "Civil Society, Subscriber Democracies and Parliamentary Government in Great Britain," in Nancy Bermeo and Philip Nord, eds., *Civil Society before Democracy: Lessons from Nineteenth-Century Europe* (Lanham, MD: Rowman and Littlefield, 2000), 111–33. For the example of the Liberal London Registration Association first selecting, and then repeatedly backing, Lionel Rothschild, see Salbstein, *The Emancipation of the Jews in Britain*, 141–61. For his characterization of the groups for and against, see 202–3. For newspapers, see Finestein, "Some Modern Themes in the Emancipation Debate in Early Victorian England," 133. For a petition in 1830 from Liverpool carrying 1,000 signatures, see 137. For Montefiore being "at the heart of Britain's philanthropic and abolitionist nexus," see Green, *Moses Montefiore*, 103ff.

29. For this view of France, especially in comparison to the German states, see Reinhard Rürup, "Jewish Emancipation and Bourgeois Society," *Leo Baeck Institute Yearbook* 14 (1969): 67–91. Pierre Birnbaum would have France's Jews emancipated with the Revolution

and Napoleon but not entered "into modernity" or "fully admitted to the state" until the Third Republic. See "Between Social and Political Assimilation: Remarks on the History of Jews in France," in Birnbaum and Katznelson, eds., *Paths of Emancipation*, 94, 110.

30. Frederick B. Artz, *France under the Bourbon Restoration, 1814–1830* (Cambridge, MA: Harvard University Press, 1931), 37–42; Guillaume de Bertier de Sauvigny, *The Bourbon Restoration*, trans. Lynn Case (Philadelphia: University of Pennsylvania Press, 1966), 65–71.

31. Robert Anchel, *Napoléon et les Juifs: Essai sur les rapport de l'État français et du culte israélite de 1806 à 1815* (Paris: Presses Universitaires de France, 1928), 412–13.

32. Ibid., 413. The memoranda were dated May 14, May 30, and June 9, 1814. The quotation is from the last.

33. Ibid., 413–14.

34. Ibid., 414–15. For a response, see Alphonse Théodore Cerfberr, *Observations sur les voeux émis par les conseils généraux des département du Haut- et du Bas-Rhin* (November 1817).

35. Anchel, *Napoléon et les Juifs*, 416–18. The petition is reproduced in Rina Neher-Bernheim, ed., *Documents inédits sur l'entrée des Juifs dans la Société française (1750–1850)*, 3 vols. (Tel Aviv: Diaspora Research Institute, 1977), 2:25–26. For newspaper reports of the chambers' proceedings, see Achille-Edmond Halphen, *Recueil des lois, décrets, ordonnances, avis du conseil d'État, arrêtes et règlements* (Paris: Bureaux des Archives Israélites, 1851), 302–7.

36. Neher-Bernheim, *Documents inédits*, 2:42, 51.

37. Ibid., 2:42–51.

38. Paragraph 18. See Halphen, *Recueil des Lois*, 47. For the Infamous Decree and the *more judaïco* as two encroachments on emancipation, see Jean-Jacques Clère, "Une emancipation tardivement contestée: Les exceptions apportées au principe d'égalité à l'égard des Juifs pendant le XIXe siècle," in *Le droit antisémite de Vichy* (Paris: Seuil, 1996), 57–72.

39. *Requête adressée au Roi par le Consistoire Central des Israélites: Contre la prorogation du Décret du 17 mars 1808, qui soumet les Juifs à une legislation spéciale* (Paris: Ballard, 1818), 1. The Consistory and the two Grand Rabbis signed the petition.

40. Ibid., 2.

41. Ibid., 9–10.

42. Ibid., 11.

43. Ibid. To oppose the decree's renewal Léon Halévy (1802–83) founded the first Jewish newspaper in France, *L'Israélite français*. See Jay R. Berkovitz, *Rites and Passages: The Beginnings of Modern Jewish Culture in France, 1650–1860* (Philadelphia: University of Pennsylvania, 2004), 157 and Aron Rodrigue, "Léon Halévy and Modern French Jewish Historiography," in Elisheva Carlebach, John M Efron, and David N. Myers, eds., *Jewish History and Jewish Memory: Essays in Honor of Yosef Hayim Yerushalmi* (Hanover, NH: Brandeis University Press, 1998), 413.

44. Hyman, *The Emancipation of the Jews of Alsace*, 19. For archival sources, see Neher-Bernheim, *Documents inédits*, 2:84–97. For Protestants as second-class citizens in the Bourbon restoration, see André Encrevé, "French Protestants," in Liedtke and Wendehorst, eds., *The Emancipation of Catholics, Jews and Protestants*, 76.

45. Alfred Cobban, *A History of Modern France*, 3 vols. (Harmondsworth, Middlesex: Penguin, 1968), 1:167–69; Encrevé, "French Protestants," 73.

46. Simon Schwarzfuchs, *Napoleon, the Jews and the Sanhedrin* (London: Routledge, 1979), 121–23, 138–39, 142.

47. Article 7 read: "The ministers of the catholic, apostolic and roman religion and those of the other Christian cults alone receive salaries from the royal treasury."

48. Cobban, *A History of Modern France*, 2:97.

49. The Consistory rejected the idea of asking for a revision of Article 6 and instead voted unanimously to ask for state payment of rabbis' salaries (Article 7). See Neher-Bernheim, *Documents inédits*, 2:267–74. For the background, see Robert Anchel, *Notes sur les frais du Culte Juif en France de 1815 à 1831* (Paris: Hemmerlé, 1928).

50. On Portalis, see Marcel Rousselet, *La Magistrature sous la Monarchie de Juillet* (Paris: Recueil Sirey, 1937), 239–42.

51. *Rapport fait à la Chambre par M. le comte Portalis, au nom d'une Commission spéciale chargée de l'examen du projet de loi qui met à la charge de l'État le traitement des ministres du culte israélite* (Paris, 1831), 1–2, 5, 16.

52. Ibid., 12–13, 15.

53. Ibid., 11, 15.

54. Neher-Bernheim, *Documents inédits*, 2:255. The law read: "As of January 1, 1831 the ministers of the Israelite cult shall receive their salaries from the public treasury."

55. Anchel, *Napoléon et les Juifs*, 501. See also Phyllis Cohen Albert, *The Modernization of French Jewry: Consistory and Community in the Nineteenth Century* (Hanover, NH: Brandeis University Press, 1977), 122 and Lisa Moses Leff, *Sacred Bonds of Solidarity: The Rise of Jewish Internationalism in Nineteenth-Century France* (Stanford: Stanford University Press, 2006), 69.

56. Albert, *The Modernization of French Jewry*, 155.

57. Leff, *Sacred Bonds of Solidarity*, 68.

58. Albert, *The Modernization of French Jewry*, 197.

59. Ibid., 188.

60. The relevant legislation was enacted on July 14, 1791, July 30, 1791, and August 15, 1793. The Council of 500 subsequently dealt with the dissolution of debts in 1797. Despite four favorable reports, the council opted not to include the Jewish communities in the legislation. See Zosa Szajkowski, *Autonomy and Communal Jewish Debts during the French Revolution of 1789* (New York: Kohut Memorial Foundation, 1959), 45–56.

61. Ibid., 73–74, 93–97.

62. Anchel, *Napoléon et les Juifs*, 519–30; Szajkowski, *Autonomy and Communal Jewish Debts*, 102–18.

63. "État politique des Israélites en 1840," *Archives Israélites de France* 1 (1840): 594.

64. David Feuerwerker, *L'Emancipation des juifs en France, de l'ancien régime à la fin du Second Empire* (Paris: Albin Michel, 1976), 565–67. Marguerite-Louis François Du Port-Dutertre circulated the order.

65. Phyllis Cohen Albert, *The Jewish Oath in Nineteenth-Century France* (Spiegel Lectures #3) (Tel Aviv: Tel Aviv University, 1982), 8.

66. Jean-Marie Schmitt, "Centre politique de l'Alsace française," in Georges Livet, ed., *Histoire de Colmar* (Toulouse: Privat, 1983), 128–30, 136.

67. Feuerwerker, *L'Emancipation des juifs en France*, 568–70, 575. The oath invoked Deuteronomy 5:12 on taking God's name in vain.

68. Albert, *The Jewish Oath in Nineteenth-Century France*, 21.

69. Feuerwerker, *L'Emancipation des juifs en France*, 571–72.

70. Ibid., 574–75.

71. Albert, *The Jewish Oath in Nineteenth-Century France*, 17. Jacob Mayer wrote a pamphlet defending his refusal, arguing that the *more judaïco* had no standing in French law and was contrary to historic Jewish practice. See Feuerwerker, *L'Emancipation des juifs en France*, 577–78.

72. Feuerwerker, *L'Emancipation des juifs en France*, 578–81. Rabbis in the German states after 1815 played a leading role in promoting emancipation; in France they fought its

erosion. See Robert Liberles, "Was There a Jewish Movement for Emancipation in Germany," *Leo Baeck Institute Yearbook* 31 (1986): 37–40.

73. Albert, *The Jewish Oath in Nineteenth-Century France*, 9.

74. Feuerwerker, *L'Emancipation des juifs en France*, 587–88.

75. Albert, *The Jewish Oath in Nineteenth-Century France*, 8.

76. Feuerwerker, *L'Emancipation des juifs en France*, 592–93.

77. Rousselet, *La Magistrature sous la Monarchie de Juillet*, 63–75. In contrast to France, Belgium outlawed the *more judaïco* in 1818. See Albert, *The Jewish Oath in Nineteenth-Century France*, 6.

78. Adolphe Crémieux, *Second plaidoyer sur cette question: Le Juif français doit-il être soumis à prêter le serment more judaïco?* (Nîmes: Durand-Belle, 1827), 2, 6, 7.

79. Ibid., 18–22, 29, 30–32; Feuerwerker, *L'Emancipation des juifs en France*, 596–600. See S. Posener, *Adolphe Crémieux: A Biography*, trans. Eugene Golob (Philadelphia: Jewish Publication Society, 1940), 36–48.

80. Feuerwerker, *L'Emancipation des juifs en France*, 600–601.

81. Ibid., 600–606. The Colmar Court also fabricated entirely false histories for German and Portuguese Jews to justify the oath. See 604. For the Colmar Court and Catholic revival, see Gabriel Braeuner, "Culture d'ancien régime et culture élargie (1679–1870)," in Livet, *Histoire de Colmar*, 190.

82. Feuerwerker, *L'Emancipation des juifs en France*, 610–17.

83. Ibid., 624–25.

84. Ibid., 625–28, 639–40. At the same time, in response to an earlier case at Marmoutier, which the Civil Court of Saverne judged, the minister held that a rabbi can be required to administer the oath.

85. The Colmar Court submitted a lengthy judgment that reiterated its fabricated history of the oath as well as its libelous claims about Alsatian Jewry. It asserted that they were German and therefore subject to the laws in place since the Peace of Westphalia. See Feuerwerker, *L'Emancipation des juifs en France*, 630–34. For the composition of the *Cour de Cassation*, see Rousselet, *La Magistrature sous la Monarchie de Juillet*, 249–71.

86. Feuerwerker, *L'Emancipation des juifs en France*, 640–43.

87. Albert, *The Jewish Oath in Nineteenth-Century France*, 11.

88. Feuerwerker, *L'Emancipation des juifs en France*, 645–48.

89. For France as a "strong state" that shaped the way emancipation unfolded, see Pierre Birnbaum and Ira Katznelson, "Emancipation and the Liberal Offer," in *Paths of Emancipation*, 3–36. For the limited development of associations in France, see Raymond Huard, "Political Association in Nineteenth-Century France: Legislation and Practice," in Bermeo and Nord, eds., *Civil Society before Democracy*, 135–42.

90. For the regeneration debate in the Bourbon restoration, see Charles Bail, *Des Juifs au dix-neuvième siècle, ou Considérations sur leur état civil et politique en Europe* (Paris: Treuttel, 1816) and M. Moureau, *De l'incompatibilité entre le Judaïsme et l'exercice des droits de cité* (Paris: Crochard, 1819). On the debate, see Jay R. Berkovitz, *Rites and Passages: The Beginnings of Modern Jewish Culture in France, 1650–1860* (Philadelphia: University of Pennsylvania Press, 2004), 144–57 and Julie Kalman, *Rethinking Antisemitism in Nineteenth-Century France* (New York: Cambridge University Press, 2010), 23–45.

91. Leff, *Sacred Bonds of Solidarity*, 9, 42, 55–56, 118, 131, 138, 152–3, 159, 177, 183, 213; Michael Graetz, *The Jews in Nineteenth-Century France: From the French Revolution to the Alliance Israélite Universelle* (Stanford: Stanford University Press, 1996), 194–248.

92. Including Algeria's emancipation here neither denies the specificity of Algerian society nor deprives Algerians of agency. I merely recognize the fact that when France im-

posed its administration, to be sure forcefully and brutally, the Jews' status became part of French political history. For French Jews' self-image as "saviors of the Jewish world," see Michel Abitbol, "The Encounter between French Jewry and the Jews of North Africa: Analysis of a Discourse (1830–1914)," in Frances Malino and Bernard Wasserstein, eds., *The Jews in Modern France* (Hanover, NH: Brandeis University Press, 1985), 31–38 and Aron Rodrigue, "Comment," in Michael Brenner, Vicki Caron, and Uri R. Kaufmann, eds., *Jewish Emancipation Reconsidered: The French and German Models* (Tübingen: Mohr Siebeck, 2003), 121–28. For Algerian Jews' responses to "regeneration," see Joshua Schreier, *Arabs of the Jewish Faith: The Civilizing Mission in Colonial Algeria* (New Brunswick, NJ: Rutgers University Press, 2010). For a historiographical survey, see Susan Slyomovics and Sarah Abrevaya Stein, "Jews and French Colonialism in Algeria: An Introduction," *Journal of North African Studies* 17, no. 5 (2012): 749–55.

93. Yosef Sharvit, *Toldot Yehudei Algerya be-Edan Ha-Tsarfati, 1830–1962* (Tel Aviv: Misrad Ha-Bitahon, 2010), 13; Simon Schwarzfuchs, *Les Juifs d'Algérie et la France (1830–1855)* (Jerusalem: Ben-Zvi, 1981), 21–29; Zosa Szajkowski, "The Struggle for Jewish Emancipation in Algeria after the French Occupation," *Historia Judaica* 18, no. 1 (April 1956): 28. For a survey, see Morton Rosenstock, "Economic and Social Conditions among the Jews of Algeria, 1790–1848," *Historia Judaica* 18, no. 1 (April 1956): 3–26 and Claude Martin, *Les israélites algériens de 1830 à 1902* (Paris: Herakles, 1936), 23–39. For the background, see Charles-Robert Ageron, *Modern Algeria: A History from 1830 to the Present* (London: Hurst & Co., 1991).

94. The report is reprinted in Schwarzfuchs, *Les Juifs d'Algérie*, 67–201; he discusses it at 42–52. See Szajkowski, "The Struggle for Jewish Emancipation in Algeria after the French Occupation," 30–31 and Martin, *Les israélites algériens*, 59–74. The two leaders were Jacques Altaras (1786–1873) and Joseph Cohen (1817–99).

95. Michael Shurkin, "French Liberal Governance and the Emancipation of Algeria's Jews," *French Historical Studies* 33, no. 2 (2010): 271; Schwarzfuchs, *Les Juifs d'Algérie*, 33–34; Szajkowski, "The Struggle for Jewish Emancipation in Algeria after the French Occupation," 27.

96. Martin, *Les israélites algériens*, 111–13.

97. Schwarzfuchs, *Les Juifs d'Algérie*, 36–37.

98. Sharvit, *Toldot Yehudei Algerya be-Edan Ha-Tsarfati*, 30.

99. Schwarzfuchs, *Les Juifs d'Algérie*, 36; Morton Rosenstock, "The Establishment of the Consistorial System in Algeria," *Jewish Social Studies* 18, no. 1 (1956): 44–50; Sharvit, *Toldot Yehudei Algerya be-Edan Ha-Tsarfati*, 24. Albert Cohn, James Rothschild's emissary, had an audience with King Louis Philippe to advocate the establishment of the Consistory. See Graetz, *The Jews in Nineteenth-Century France*, 105–6.

100. Rosenstock, "The Establishment of the Consistorial System in Algeria," 53.

101. Shurkin, "French Liberal Governance and the Emancipation of Algeria's Jews," 273. On education, see Martin, *Les israélites algériens*, 94–99.

102. Shurkin, "French Liberal Governance and the Emancipation of Algeria's Jews," 275.

103. Albert, *The Modernization of French Jewry*, 46. During 1862–67 the Algiers Consistory served as the intermediary to Paris.

104. Leff, *Sacred Bonds of Solidarity*, 212.

105. Shurkin, "French Liberal Governance and the Emancipation of Algeria's Jews," 277. Even fewer Muslims were willing to renounce their personal status to gain naturalization.

106. Leff, *Sacred Bonds of Solidarity*, 213.

107. Shurkin, "French Liberal Governance and the Emancipation of Algeria's Jews," 279; Martin, *Les israélites algériens*, 119–20, 132–36.

108. Leff, *Sacred Bonds of Solidarity*, 213. For the Crémieux Decree as an "imperialistic" "enforced emancipation . . . that did not allow for individual choice," see Yaron Tsur, "Colonial and Post-Colonial Jewries: The Middle East and North Africa," in Mitchell B. Hart and Tony Michels, eds., *The Cambridge History of Judaism: The Modern World*, 8 vols. (Cambridge: Cambridge University Press, 2017), 8:224–28.

109. Sarah Abrevaya Stein, *Saharan Jews and the Fate of French Algeria* (Chicago: University of Chicago Press, 2014), 16, 42–56, 58, 89.

110. Martin, *Les israélites algériens*, 183–203; Leff, *Sacred Bonds of Solidarity*, 208.

111. Martin, *Les israélites algériens*, 204–366; Sharvit, *Toldot Yehudei Algerya be-Edan Ha-Tsarfati*, 38. The immigrants were largely Maltese, Italians, and Spaniards. Organized anti-Semitism first appeared in colonial Algeria and then reached metropolitan France. As Edouard Drumont wrote: "It is perhaps by way of Algeria that the anti-Semitic campaign in France will begin" (*La France juive*, 2:47). Cited in Leff, *Sacred Bonds of Solidarity*, 218.

112. Adolphe Crémieux, *Gouvernement de la Défense nationale: Actes de la Délégation à Tours et à Bordeaux* (Tours: Ernest Mazereau, 1871), pt. 1, 78, cited in Leff, *Sacred Bonds of Solidarity*, 211.

113. Aron Rodrigue, *French Jews, Turkish Jews: The Alliance Israélite Universelle and the Politics of Jewish Schooling in Turkey, 1860–1925* (Bloomington: Indiana University Press, 1990), 19; Graetz, *The Jews in Nineteenth-Century France*, 108–9.

114. Leff, *Sacred Bonds of Solidarity*, 159. For the close relations between the Alliance and the Consistory, see Graetz, *The Jews in Nineteenth-Century France*, 255–57, 269–82. For the founding appeal and an early report containing the statutes, see Paul Mendes-Flohr and Jehuda Reinharz, *The Jew in the Modern World: A Documentary History*, 3rd ed. (New York: Oxford University Press, 2011), 292–96.

115. Leff, *Sacred Bonds of Solidarity*, 198.

116. Louis Koenigswarter, president of the Provisional Committee (1862), cited in Graetz, *The Jews in Nineteenth-Century France*, 252.

117. Leff, *Sacred Bonds of Solidarity*, 152; Zosa Szajkowski, "Jewish Diplomacy: Notes on the Occasion of the Centenary of the Alliance Israélite Universelle," *Jewish Social Studies* 22, no. 3 (1960): 131–58.

118. The Alliance's ideological roots lay in Saint-Simonism and the republican tradition. See Graetz, *The Jews in Nineteenth-Century France* and Leff, *Sacred Bonds of Solidarity*.

119. The Universal Evangelical Alliance served as a model for the Alliance. See Rodrigue, *French Jews, Turkish Jews*, 21 and Graetz, *The Jews in Nineteenth-Century France*, 259–60. For individuals, see Élisabeth Antébi, *Les missionaires juifs de la France, 1860–1939* (Paris: Calmann-Lévy, 1999).

120. Narcisse Leven, *Cinquante ans d'histoire: L'Alliance Israélite Universelle (1860–1910)*, 2 vols. (Paris: F. Alcan, 1911–20), 2:7–8, "l'émancipation par l'instruction."

121. In Turkey Alliance teachers saw themselves as "missionaries" and competed directly with missionary schools. See Rodrigue, *French Jews, Turkish Jews*, 37, 54, 63–64, 72; Michael M. Laskier, *The Alliance Israélite Universelle and the Jewish Communities of Morocco, 1862–1962* (Albany: State University of New York Press, 1983); and Georges Weill, "The Alliance Israélite Universelle and the Emancipation of Jewish Communities in the Mediterranean," *Jewish Journal of Sociology* 24, no. 2 (1982): 117–34. For the Alliance's inability to function in Russia and Congress Poland, see Zosa Szajkowski, "The Alliance Israélite Universelle and East-European Jewry in the 60s," *Jewish Social Studies* 4, no. 2 (1942): 139–60.

122. Narcisse Leven, May 31, 1864, cited in Rodrigue, *French Jews, Turkish Jews*, 24. Membership in 1861 was 850; in 1885 it was 30,000.

Chapter Eighteen. The Atlantic World

1. For a fuller account, see David Sorkin, "Is American Jewry Exceptional? Comparing Jewish Emancipation in Europe and America," *American Jewish History* 96, no. 3 (2010): 175–200.

2. Jonathan D. Sarna, *American Judaism: A History* (New Haven: Yale University Press, 2004), 28. The Jews of Curaçao sent funds to aid synagogues in New York, Philadelphia, Newport, and Charleston. See Isaac S. Emmanuel and Suzanne A. Emmanuel, *History of the Jews of the Netherland Antilles*, 2 vols. (Cincinnati: American Jewish Archives, 1970), 1:165–69.

3. Thomas J. Curry, *The First Freedoms: Church and State in America to the Passage of the First Amendment* (New York: Oxford University Press, 1986), 78–104; Chris Beneke, *Beyond Toleration: The Religious Origins of American Pluralism* (New York: Oxford University Press, 2006).

4. Stanley F. Chyet, "The Political Rights of the Jews in the United States: 1776–1840," in Jacob R. Marcus, ed., *Critical Studies in American Jewish History*, 3 vols. (Cincinnati: American Jewish Archives, 1971), 2:28–30; Curry, *The First Freedoms*, 105–33.

5. Yosef Kaplan has called this the "western sephardi" diaspora. See *He-Pezura ha-Sefardit ha-Ma'aravit* (Tel Aviv: Misrad Ha-Bitahon, 1994).

6. Oscar Handlin and Mary F. Handlin, "The Acquisition of Political and Social Rights by the Jews in the United States," *American Jewish Yearbook* 56 (1955): 50.

7. David Katz, *The Jews in the History of England, 1485–1850* (Oxford: Oxford University Press, 1994), 242; Sheldon J. Godfrey and Judith C. Godfrey, *Search Out the Land: The Jews and the Growth of Equality in British Colonial America, 1740–1867* (Montreal: McGill-Queen's University Press, 1995), 56.

8. Abram Vossen Goodman, *American Overture: Jewish Rights in Colonial Times* (Philadelphia: Jewish Publication Society, 1947). For civic rights and the disparity between "custom" and "law," see Salo W. Baron, "The Emancipation Movement and American Jewry," in Jeannette Meisel Baron, ed., *Steeled by Adversity: Essays and Addresses on American Jewish Life* (Philadelphia: Jewish Publication Society, 1947), 90–91, 96–97.

9. Hasia Diner, *The Jews of the United States, 1654–2000* (Berkeley: University of California Press, 2004), 40.

10. Curry, *The First Freedoms*, 134–48.

11. Chyet, "The Political Rights of the Jews in the United States," 39–40, 44–45. The phrase aimed at Catholics was the obstacle of loyalty to foreign powers "ecclesiastical as well as civil."

12. Morton Borden, *Jews, Turks and Infidels* (Chapel Hill: University of North Carolina Press, 1984), 11; Curry, *The First Freedoms*, 148–52, 160–61.

13. Chyet, "The Political Rights of the Jews in the United States," 48–50, 53–55, 60–61; Curry, *The First Freedoms*, 163–64.

14. Curry, *The First Freedoms*, 153–58.

15. After independence synagogues changed the prayer for the government to recognize the republic. They replaced the monarch and royal family with a list of the highest offices of government. Congregants no longer stood to show subservience. The 1830 prayer book of the Charleston Reform congregation, for example, explicitly celebrated equality: "this much favoured land . . . where the noble and virtuous mind is the only crown of distinction and equality of rights the only fountain of power." See Jonathan Sarna, "Jewish Prayers for the U.S. Government: A Study in the Liturgy of Politics and the Politics of Liturgy," in Karen Halttunen and Lewis Perry, eds., *Moral Problems in American Life: New Perspectives on Cultural History* (Ithaca: Cornell University Press, 1998), 206–11.

16. Isaac Leeser, *The Claims of the Jews to an Equality of Rights: Illustrated in a Series of Letters to the Editor of the Philadelphia Gazette* (Philadelphia: C. Sherman, 1840).

17. The Declaration of Rights read: "no man who acknowledges the being of a God can be justly deprived or abridged of any civil rights as a citizen on account of his religious sentiments." The Test read: "I do acknowledge the Scriptures of the old and new Testament to be given by divine inspiration."

18. Quoted in Borden, *Jews, Turks and Infidels*, 21. For the petition, see Jonathan D. Sarna and David G. Dalin, *Religion and State in the American Jewish Experience* (Notre Dame, IN: University of Notre Dame Press, 1997), 70–72.

19. Sarna and Dalin, *Religion and State*, 82–85; Borden, *Jews, Turks and Infidels*, 42–44. In North Carolina there was a gap between law and practice. Until 1868 the constitution permitted only Protestants to hold office. In practice Jews and Catholics held significant offices from the early nineteenth century. Jews similarly held offices in England before having the legal right to do so. See Geoffrey Alderman, *Modern British Jewry* (Oxford: Oxford University Press, 1992), 30, 53.

20. Edward Eitches, "Maryland's 'Jew Bill' [1826]," *American Jewish Historical Quarterly* 60, no. 3 (1971): 261: in 1776 Maryland "contained a disenfranchised Catholic population and no [legally recognized] Jewish population."

21. Ibid., 267. The Baltimore merchant Solomon Etting submitted petitions in 1797 and 1802 while the Jews of Maryland presented a collective memorial in 1823.

22. Borden, *Jews, Turks and Infidels*, 36–42; Sarna and Dalin, *Religion and State*, 94–97. During the final debate Etting claimed that the Jews made a significant economic contribution to Maryland and the United States; had served in both the Revolutionary War and the War of 1812; and had faithfully discharged their duties in holding numerous federal offices. Leeser, *The Claims of the Jews to an Equality of Rights*, 50: "in this country, where there exist no legal disqualifications against us, at least not in those states where we are most numerous." Lesser noted Massachusetts's and North Carolina's "disqualifications" (82).

23. Jonas Phillips used this phrase in his letter to the Federal Constitutional Convention (1787).

24. Leeser, *The Claims of the Jews to an Equality of Rights*, 4–5, 20–47; Diner, *The Jews of the United States*, 75–79.

25. Naomi Cohen, *Encounter with Emancipation: The German Jews in the United States, 1830–1914* (Philadelphia: Jewish Publication Society, 1984), 66–72; Eli Faber, *A Time for Planting: The First Migration, 1654–1820* (Baltimore: Johns Hopkins University Press, 1992), 131–32. For a non-Jew's protest on principle, see Sarna and Dalin, *Religion and State*, 92–94. For other early missionary societies, see Diner, *The Jews of the United States*, 58–59.

26. Leeser, *The Claims of the Jews to an Equality of Rights*, 88–91; Albert M. Friedenberg, "The Jews and the American Sunday Laws," *Publications of the American Jewish Historical Society* 11 (1903): 101–15; Borden, *Jews, Turks and Infidels*, 103–27. In 1828 the General Union for Promoting the Observance of the Christian Sabbath was founded in New York City, largely to prohibit the movement and delivery of the mail on Sunday. The General Union failed but marked the start of an evangelical campaign on behalf of Sunday laws. In 1844 a National Lord's Day Convention convened in Baltimore. In England Jews gained the right, through special legislation (1871), to open their factories or workshops on Sunday for Jewish workers if they closed their doors on Saturdays. See Alderman, *Modern British Jewry*, 65.

27. Sarna and Dalin, *Religion and State*, 142–47.

28. Borden, *Jews, Turks and Infidels*, 109–12; Sarna and Dalin, *Religion and State*, 142–47.

29. Borden, *Jews, Turks and Infidels*, 58–74; Sarna and Dalin, *Religion and State*, 167–73. Jews protested Strong's nomination, and prominent rabbis and Jewish organizations, such as the Union of American Hebrew Congregations, promoted the idea of strict separation of church and state. Another manifestation was the occasional Thanksgiving proclamation that asserted the country's Christian character. For the case of South Carolina governor Hammond (1844), see Sarna and Dalin, *Religion and State*, 112–21.

30. Lloyd P. Gartner, "Temple of Liberty Unpolluted: American Jews and Public Schools, 1840–1875," in Bertram W. Korn, ed., *A Bicentennial Festschrift for Jacob Rader Marcus* (New York: Ktav, 1976), 157–89, quotation at 180. Freiberg was a delegate to the Ohio constitutional convention of 1874. See also Cohen, *Encounter with Emancipation*, 93ff. Jews were excluded from schools in England by compulsory prayers or school charters. See Ursula Henriques, *Religious Toleration in England, 1787–1833* (London: Routledge and Kegan Paul, 1961), 180.

31. Resolution #2: "We love and revere this country as our home and fatherland for us and our children; and therefore consider it our paramount duty to sustain and support the government; to favor by all means the system of free education, leaving religious instruction to the care of the different denominations." Gartner, "Temple of Liberty Unpolluted," 177. For the debate in the 1850s, see Sarna and Dalin, *Religion and State*, 185–86.

32. For cases in Cincinnati and San Francisco, see Sarna and Dalin, *Religion and State*, 187–90 and Gartner, "Temple of Liberty Unpolluted," 178–80.

33. When Jews in Brazil protested against harassment by the Dutch Reformed clergy, the Dutch States-General, prodded by Jews in Amsterdam, issued the Honorable Patent (Patenta Onrossa) of 1645, promising Jews equal treatment with "our native-born," essentially civic parity. Similarly, the Dutch West Indies Company, endeavoring to attract colonists to the "Wild Coast" of Guiana in Essequibo, promised on November 12, 1657, "that they would treat the Jews—as their own burghers" and on November 15 further guaranteed "that all Jews shall be accepted as burghers, even as the natives of the Province of Zeeland who take up their residence in the aforementioned places." The 1659 charter for Curaçao, albeit lost, presumably vouchsafed a similar civic parity, since Jews actively defended their "equality" in later periods. See Yosef Hayim Yerushalmi, "Between Amsterdam and New Amsterdam: The Place of Curaçao and the Caribbean in Early Modern Jewish History," *American Jewish History* 2 (1982): 182–87.

34. Emmanuel and Emmanuel, *History of the Jews of the Netherland Antilles*, 1:48. Curaçao possessed an outstanding natural port and the Dutch first used it as a naval base for pirating on the Spanish Main. A commercial hub from the 1660s, Curaçao linked Spanish, British, and French colonies with the Dutch trading network. Jewish traders (1702: 600 Jews; 1748: 1,500) played a major role: in 1759 Jews owned just under one-third of the shares (123 of 400) of the marine insurance consortium. See Jonathan Israel, "Jews of Dutch America," in Paolo Bernardini and Norman Fiering, eds., *The Jews and the Expansion of Europe to the West, 1450–1800* (New York: Berghahn, 2001), 335–46.

35. In 1713, for example, when a French pirate boldly raided Curaçao and held it hostage for ransom, Curaçao's leaders suggested that the Jews pay a collective assessment. The community representatives protested, insisting that the Jews pay as individuals like everyone else. See Emmanuel and Emmanuel, *History of the Jews of the Netherland Antilles*, 1:106. In 1717, in response to the Jews' protests over discrimination in the handling of the mail, the West India Company issued an emphatic directive to the Curaçao authorities that the Jews be treated equally with fellow Christian inhabitants. Ibid., 1:111.

36. Cornelis Ch. Goslinga, *The Dutch in the Caribbean and in Surinam, 1791/5–1942* (Assen/Maastricht: Van Gorcum, 1990), 62, 67. During the revolutionary and Napoleonic era the Dutch West India Company was dissolved (1791); there was a slave rebellion (1795); and Curaçao came under French influence (1796–97) and then English rule (1800–1803,

1807–16). By the time of full emancipation the Jews' numbers were much reduced (1816: 1,021; 1833: 747) as a result of the island's declining role in trade.

37. Jews may have comprised as much as 10 percent of the white population in the eighteenth century. See Thomas G. August, "An Historical Profile of the Jewish Community in Jamaica," *Jewish Social Studies* 49, no. 3–4 (1987): 304.

38. Holly Snyder, "Rules, Rights and Redemption: The Negotiation of Jewish Status in British Atlantic Port Towns, 1740–1831," *Jewish History* 20 (2006): 147–70. The official was a deputy marshal; the prominent Jew was Levy Hyman.

39. Godfrey and Godfrey, *Search Out the Land*, 196. By 1849 Jews accounted for one-sixth of the Assembly's members; as early as 1849 a Jew served as Speaker of the House and in the 1860s another was appointed Finance Minister. See August, "An Historical Profile of the Jewish Community in Jamaica," 306.

40. Swithin Wilmot, "Jewish Politicians in Post-Slavery Jamaica: Electoral Politics in the Parish of St. Dorothy, 1849–1860," in Jane Gerber, ed., *The Jews in the Caribbean* (Oxford: Littman, 2014), 261–62. Twenty-seven Jews sat in the Jamaican Assembly between 1831 and its dissolution in 1866. Some Jews allied with the propertied classes, white and colored, while some Jewish retailers allied with black small landholders.

41. Godfrey and Godfrey, *Search Out the Land*, 204–6.

42. Ibid., xix.

43. Ibid., 140.

44. Some of the Jews in Quebec were army suppliers (ibid., 93–101). The quotation is from Gershom Mendes Seixas.

45. Maxine Jacobson, "Struggles and Successes: The Beginnings of Jewish Life in Canada in the Eighteenth Century," in Ira Robinson, ed., *Canada's Jews: In Time, Space and Spirit* (Boston: Academic Studies Press, 2013), 24.

46. Godfrey and Godfrey, *Search Out the Land*, 133–34.

47. Ibid., 131–38.

48. Ibid., 154–70.

49. Michael Brown, "The Beginning of Jewish Emancipation in Canada: The Hart Affair," *Michael: On the History of the Jews in the Diaspora* 10 (1986): 31–38.

50. Irving Abella, *A Coat of Many Colours: Two Centuries of Jewish Life in Canada* (Toronto: Lester & Orpen Dennys, 1990), 27.

51. Ibid., 28–29.

52. Godfrey and Godfrey, *Search Out the Land*, 171–89.

53. Abella, *A Coat of Many Colours*, 30–32.

54. Godfrey and Godfrey, *Search Out the Land*, 190–96.

55. Ibid., 190–215.

56. Ibid., 231.

57. Gerald Tulchinsky, "The Contours of Canadian Jewish History," in Robert J. Brym, William Shaffir, and Morton Weinfeld, eds., *The Jews in Canada* (Toronto: Oxford University Press, 1993), 6–7.

58. The broad similarities in regard to emancipation should not mask the fundamental differences between Jewish history in Canada and the United States. See ibid., 5–21 and Jonathan Sarna, "The Value of Canadian Jewish History to the American Jewish Historian and Vice-Versa," *Canadian Jewish Historical Society Journal* 5, no. 1 (1981): 17–23.

Chapter Nineteen. Mass Society, I

1. Arno Mayer, *Persistence of the Old Regime: Europe to the Great War* (New York: Pantheon, 1981); Norman Stone, *European Transformed, 1878–1919* (Cambridge, MA: Harvard University Press, 1984).

2. Berlin: from 18,953 (1860) to 144,007 (1910); Vienna: from 6,217 (1860) to 146,926 (1900); Budapest: from 44,747 (1870) to 203,687 (1910); Warsaw: from 89,000 (1870) to 300,000 (1910); Łódź: from 3,000 (1860) to 96,671 (1900); Odessa: from 25,000 (1860) to 138,935 (1900). See Paul Mendes-Flohr and Jehuda Reinharz, eds., *The Jew in the Modern World: A Documentary History*, 3rd ed. (New York: Oxford University Press, 2011), 884. In an enormous scholarship see, e.g., Steven Lowenstein, "The Pace of Modernization of German Jewry in the Nineteenth Century," *Leo Baeck Institute Yearbook* 21 (1976): 41–56; Arcadius Kahan, *Essays in Jewish Social and Economic History*, ed. Roger Weiss (Chicago: University of Chicago Press, 1986), 31–34, 70–81; Marsha L. Rozenblit, *The Jews of Vienna, 1867–1914: Assimilation and Identity* (Albany: State University of New York Press, 1983), 13–45; and Gur Alroey, *Ha-Mahapeikha ha-Shkeita: Ha-Hagira ha-Yehudit mei-ha-Emperiya ha-Russit, 1875–1924* (Jerusalem: Zalman Shazar Center, 2008).

3. Robert Liberles, "Emancipation and the Structure of the Jewish Community in the Nineteenth Century," *Leo Baeck Institute Yearbook* 31 (1986): 51–67; Bart Wallet, "Napoleon's Legacy: National Government and Jewish Community in Western Europe," *Simon Dubnow Institute Yearbook* 6 (2007): 291–309.

4. Evyatar Friesel, "The Centralverein and the America Jewish Committee: A Comparative Study," *Leo Baeck Institute Yearbook* 36 (1991): 98.

5. Tobias Brinkmann, "Zivilgesellschaft transnational: Jüdische Hilfsorganisationen und jüdische Massenmigration aus Osteuropa in Deutschland, 1868–1914," in Rainer Liedtke and Klaus Weber, eds., *Religion und Philanthropie in den europäischen Zivilgesellschaften: Entwicklungen im 19. und 20. Jahrhundert* (Schöningh: Paderborn, 2009), 143; Eli Bar-Chen, *Weder Asiaten noch Orientalen: Internationale jüdische Organisationen und die Europäisierung "rückständiger" Juden* (Würzburg: Ergon, 2005).

6. Derek Penslar, *Shylock's Children: Economics and Jewish Identity in Modern Europe* (Berkeley: University of California Press, 2001), 227; Bar-Chen, *Weder Asiaten noch Orientalen*.

7. Evyatar Friesel, "The Political and Ideological Development of the Centralverein before 1914," *Leo Baeck Institute Yearbook* 31 (1986): 121.

8. This transformation was underway in the larger society as well: a growing consensus came to regard the "social question" as society's responsibility. Penslar, *Shylock's Children*, 174–95; Ingo Haar, "Jüdische Zivilgesellschaft und transnationale Flüchtlingspolitik in Zentraleuropa um 1900: Die 'Allianzen' in Wien und Berlin vom improvisierten Einsatz in Brody bis zur geregelten Amerikamigration," in Ulla Kriebernegg, Gerald Lamprecht, Roberta Maierhofer, and Andrea Strutz, eds., *"Nach Amerika nämlich!" Jüdische Migrationen in die Amerikas im 19. und 20. Jahrhundert* (Göttingen: Wallstein, 2012), 91–109; Brinkmann, "Zivilgesellschaft transnational," 138–57. For a pioneering comparison of social welfare in two cities, see Rainer Liedtke, *Jewish Welfare in Hamburg and Manchester c. 1850–1914* (Oxford: Clarendon Press, 1998).

9. Brinkmann, "Zivilgesellschaft transnational," 139–41. For the east European migrant as the emancipated Jew's "mirror opposite," see Steven E. Aschheim, *Brothers and Strangers: The East European Jew in German and German Jewish Consciousness, 1800–1923* (Madison: University of Wisconsin Press, 1982).

10. Hannah Arendt, "Zionism Reconsidered," in Jerome Kohn and Ron H. Feldman, eds., *The Jewish Writings* (New York: Schocken, 2007), 356.

11. Zosa Szajkowski, "The Alliance Israélite Universelle and East-European Jewry in the 1860s," *Jewish Social Studies* 4, no. 2 (1942): 139–60.

12. Brinkmann, "Zivilgesellschaft transnational," 143–50. In both cases local committees emerged to cooperate with the Alliance. Rabbis played a major role.

13. David Loewe, "The Anglo-Jewish Association: Past and Present," in Alan Stephanie and Ralph Walden, eds., *For the Sake of Humanity: Essays in Honour of Clemens N. Nathan*

(Leiden: Brill, 2006), 203–5; Bar-Chen, *Weder Asiaten noch Orientalen*, 35–36. Reform Jews, whom the Board of Deputies excluded, played a central role in founding the Anglo-Jewish Association.

14. David Feldman, *Englishmen and Jews: Social Relations and Political Culture, 1840–1914* (New Haven: Yale University Press, 1994), 122–23; Bar-Chen, *Weder Asiaten noch Orientalen*, 119–23.

15. Eugene C. Black, *The Social Politics of Anglo-Jewry, 1880–1920* (Oxford: Blackwell, 1988), 44–50; Loewe, "The Anglo-Jewish Association," 207.

16. The initial organization was called the Executive Committee for Rumanian Jews (Executiv-Comités für die rumänischen Juden). Björn Siegel, *Österreichisches Judentum zwischen Ost und West: Die Israelitische Allianz zu Wien, 1873–1938* (Frankfurt: Campus, 2008), 65.

17. Ibid., 30–42, 65–84; Siegel, " 'Das "Es werde Licht" ist gesprochen; . . .' Die Bildungsmissionen der Israelitischen Allianz zu Wien, der Baron Hirsch-Stiftung und Alliance Israélite Universelle im Vergleich, 1860–1914," *Transversal* 12, no. 1–2 (2011): 85–89; Zosa Szajkowski, "Conflicts in the Alliance Israélite Universelle and the Founding of the Anglo-Jewish Association, the Vienna Allianz and the Hilfsverein," *Jewish Social Studies* 19 (1957): 29–50.

18. Szajkowski, "Conflicts in the Alliance Israélite Universelle," 1–2, 37–38; Siegel, *Österreichisches Judentum zwischen Ost und West*, 73.

19. Siegel, *Österreichisches Judentum zwischen Ost und West*, 74; Rozenblit, *The Jews of Vienna*, 149; Haar, "Jüdische Zivilgesellschaft und transnationale Flüchtlingspolitik in Zentraleuropa um 1900," 103–5.

20. M. Friedländer, secretary of the Allianz, in a letter of September 18, 1899, cited in Siegel, " 'Das "Es werde Licht" ist gesprochen,' " 96; Siegel, *Österreichisches Judentum zwischen Ost und West*, 110–34.

21. S. Adler-Rudel, "Moritz Baron Hirsch: Profile of a Great Philanthropist," *Leo Baeck Institute Yearbook* 8 (1963): 40–41; Siegel, *Österreichisches Judentum zwischen Ost und West*, 147–59.

22. Siegel, " 'Das "Es werde Licht" ist gesprochen,' " 99. Vienna's teachers' institute (*Lehranstalt für die Heranbildung von Religionslehrern in Wien*) was modeled on the Alliance's Paris *École Normale Israélite Orientale*.

23. Siegel, *Österreichisches Judentum zwischen Ost und West*, 134–46.

24. Siegel, " 'Das "Es werde Licht" ist gesprochen,' " 94–97, 100–102.

25. Adler-Rudel, "Moritz Baron Hirsch," 29–69.

26. Theodore Norman, *An Outstretched Arm: A History of the Jewish Colonization Association* (London: Routledge and Kegan Paul, 1985), 21. In an interview in the *North American Review* 416 (July 1891), Hirsch defined his goals as "physical and moral regeneration" and the formation of "capable citizens." See Adler-Rudel, "Moritz Baron Hirsch," 62.

27. Yehuda Levin, "Labor and Land at the Start of Jewish Settlement in Argentina," *Jewish History* 21 (2007): 341–59; Yair Seltenreich and Yossi Katz, "Between the Galilee and Its Neighbouring Isle: Jules Rosenheck and the JCA Settlements in Cyprus, 1897–1928," *Middle Eastern Studies* 45, no. 1 (2009): 87–109; Yair Seltenreich, "Cultural Aspects of Philanthropy: Belle Époque Administrators and Jewish Peasants in the Galilee," *Mediterranean Historical Review* 23, no. 1 (2008): 35–51.

28. Norman, *An Outstretched Arm*, 43–44; Adler-Rudel, "Moritz Baron Hirsch," 58–59.

29. *Encyclopaedia Britannica* 13 (1910): 525, quoted in Norman, *An Outstretched Arm*, xvi.

30. Adler-Rudel, "Moritz Baron Hirsch," 39, 43–44.

31. The German and German Jewish press attacked the Alliance for disseminating French propaganda; German Jews complained of a lack of representation on the Paris Central Committee. See Szajkowski, "Conflicts in the Alliance Israélite Universelle," 38–47 and Bar-Chen, *Weder Asiaten noch Orientalen*, 123–28.

32. Ernst Feder, "Paul Nathan, the Man and His Work," *Leo Baeck Institute Yearbook* 3 (1958): 66–67.

33. *Geschäftsbericht* 2 (1903), *Hilfsverein der deutschen Juden* (Berlin, 1904), 30, cited in Brinkmann, "Zivilgesellschaft transnational," 153; Moshe Rinott, "The Zionist Organization and the Hilfsverein," *Leo Baeck Institute Yearbook* 21 (1976): 262; Feder, "Paul Nathan, the Man and His Work," 71.

34. The shipping line was the Hamburg-America (Hamburg-Amerika-Packetfahrt-Aktiengesellschaft [HAPAG]). The director was Albert Ballin. See Brinkmann, "Zivilgesellschaft transnational," 153–55. The Hilfsverein coordinated the Alliance's and Anglo-Jewish Association's efforts on behalf of Russian emigrants. Bar-Chen, *Weder Asiaten noch Orientalen*, 73.

35. Feder, "Paul Nathan, the Man and His Work," 67–70.

36. Marion A. Kaplan, *The Jewish Feminist Movement in Germany: The Campaigns of the Jüdischer Frauenbund, 1904–1938* (Westport, CT: Greenwood Press, 1979), 44, 86–87, 89.

37. Mark Wischnitzer, *Visas to Freedom: The History of HIAS* (Cleveland: World Publishing Company, 1956). For earlier efforts (1870, 1881), see 27–36. For the Hebrew Sheltering House Association (1904–9), see 47–48.

38. Ibid., 50–51.

39. Ibid., 53–55. For Jewish lawyers and immigration law, see Britt Tevis, "'The Hebrew Are Appearing in Court in Great Numbers': Toward a Reassessment of Early Twentieth-Century American Jewish Immigration History," *American Jewish History* 100, no. 3 (July 2016): 319–47 and Tevis, "May It Displease the Court: Jewish Lawyers and the Democratization of American Law, 1890–1932" (PhD diss., University of Wisconsin–Madison, 2016), 64–131.

40. Wischnitzer, *Visas to Freedom*, 52–62.

41. Ibid., 72–73.

42. Ibid., 55–58. President Cleveland vetoed an attempt to limit immigration through literacy tests (1891).

43. Moshe Zimmermann, *Wilhelm Marr: The Patriarch of Anti-Semitism* (New York: Oxford, 1986).

44. For anti-Semitism as anticapitalism opposed to emancipation, see Michele Battini, *Socialism of Fools: Capitalism and Modern Anti-Semitism* (New York: Columbia University Press, 2016). For the Vatican's role, see David I. Kertzer, *The Popes against the Jews: The Vatican's Role in the Rise of Modern Anti-Semitism* (New York: Knopf, 2001). For socialism, see George Lichtheim, "Socialism and the Jews," *Dissent* 15, no. 4 (July–August 1968): 314–41 and Robert Wistrich, *Socialism and the Jews: Dilemmas of Assimilation in Germany and Austria-Hungary* (Rutherford, NJ: Fairleigh Dickinson University Press, 1982).

45. George L. Mosse, *Toward the Final Solution: A History of European Racism* (New York: Harper and Row, 1980).

46. Shulamit Volkov, "Antisemitism as a Cultural Code," *Leo Baeck Institute Yearbook* 23 (1987): 25–45; Volkov, *Germans, Jews, and Antisemites: Trials in Emancipation* (Cambridge: Cambridge University Press, 2006); Zev Sternhell, "The Roots of Popular Anti-Semitism in the Third Republic," in Frances Malino and Bernard Wasserstein, eds., *The Jews in Modern France* (Hanover, NH: Brandeis University Press, 1985), 103–34.

47. Pulzer, *The Rise of Political Anti-Semitism in Germany and Austria*, xiv, xviii–xix,

31–32; Katz, *From Prejudice to Destruction*, 246, 268. Lucien Wolf asserted: "Anti-Semitism is . . . exclusively a question of European politics and its origin is to be found . . . in the social conditions resulting from emancipation of the Jews in the middle of the 19th century." See "Anti-Semitism," *Encyclopedia Britannica*, 11th ed. (1910), 2:134.

48. Julie Kalman, *Rethinking Antisemitism in Nineteenth-Century France* (Cambridge: Cambridge University Press, 2010).

49. Jacob Katz, *From Prejudice to Destruction: Anti-Semitism, 1700–1933* (Cambridge, MA: Harvard University Press, 1980); Peter Pulzer, *The Rise of Political Anti-Semitism in Germany and Austria*, 2nd ed. (London: Peter Halban, 1988); Bruce F. Pauley, *From Prejudice to Persecution: A History of Austrian Anti-Semitism* (Chapel Hill: University of North Carolina Press, 1992); Sternhell, "The Roots of Popular Anti-Semitism in the Third Republic," 103–34; Robert F. Byrnes, *Antisemitism in Modern France: The Prologue to the Dreyfus Affair* (New Brunswick, NJ: Rutgers University Press, 1950); Stephen Wilson, *Ideology and Experience: Antisemitism in France at the Time of the Dreyfus Affair* (Rutherford, NJ: Fairleigh Dickinson University Press, 1982); Pierre Birnbaum, *The Anti-Semitic Moment: A Tour of France in 1898*, trans. Jane Marie Todd (New York: Hill & Wang, 2003).

50. John W. Boyer, *Political Radicalism in Late Imperial Vienna: Origins of the Christian Social Movement, 1848–1897* (Chicago: University of Chicago Press, 1981); Boyer, *Culture and Political Crisis in Vienna: Christian Socialism in Power, 1897–1918* (Chicago: University of Chicago Press, 1995); Brigitte Hamann, *Hitler's Vienna: A Dictator's Apprenticeship*, trans. T. Thornton (Oxford: Oxford University Press, 2001).

51. Yosef Sharvit, *Toldot Yehudei Algerya be-Edan Ha-Tsarfati, 1830–1962* (Tel Aviv: Misrad Ha-Bitahon, 2010), 38–9; Zosa Szajkowski, "Socialists and Radicals in the Development of Antisemitism in Algeria (1884–1900)," *Jewish Social Studies* 10, no. 3 (1948): 257–80; Claude Martin, *Les israélites algériens de 1830 à 1902* (Paris: Herakles, 1936), 169–366. Eduard Drumont represented an Algeria district in Parliament.

52. Michael Burns, *France and the Dreyfus Affair: A Documentary History* (Boston: Bedford/St. Martin's, 1999), 7–13. See Byrnes, *Antisemitism in Modern France*; Wilson, *Ideology and Experience*; and Birnbaum, *The Anti-Semitic Moment*. For the Jews' political activity, see Michael Burns, *Dreyfus: A Family Affair, 1789–1945* (New York: Harper Collins, 1991). For anti-Semitism as individual "performance," see Mary Louise Roberts, *Disruptive Acts: The New Woman in Fin-de-Siècle France* (Chicago: University of Chicago Press, 2002), 131–64. See also Ruth Harris, *Politics, Emotions, and the Scandal of the Century* (New York: Metropolitan Books, 2010). For an incident anti-Semitic propaganda and agitation invented, see Helmut Walser Smith, *The Butcher's Tale: Murder and Anti-Semitism in a German Town* (New York: W. W. Norton, 2002).

53. Smith, *The Butcher's Tale*.

54. Richard S. Levy, *The Downfall of the Anti-Semitic Political Parties in Imperial Germany* (New Haven: Yale University Press, 1975).

55. For Bismarck's opportunistic use of anti-Semitism, see Paul Massing, *Rehearsal for Destruction: A Study of Political Anti-Semitism in Imperial Germany* (New York: Howard Fertig, 1967). For an example of anti-Semitism's failure in municipal politics, see Till van Rahden, "Words and Action: Rethinking the Social History of German Antisemitism, Breslau, 1870–1914," *German History* 18, no. 3 (2000): 413–38.

56. George L. Mosse, *The Crisis of German Ideology: Intellectual Origins of the Third Reich* (New York: Grosset & Dunlap, 1964), 149–233. German and Austrian university fraternities infamously excluded Jews. See Norbert Kampe, *Studenten und "Judenfrage" im Deutschen Kaiserreich: Die Entstehung einer akademischen Trägerschicht des Antisemitismus* (Göttingen: Vandenhoeck, 1988). For Jewish responses, see Tamara Ehs, "Das Extramurale Exil: Vereinsleben als Reaktion auf universitären Antisemitismus," in Evelyn

Adunka, Gerald Lamprecht, and Georg Traska, eds., *Jüdisches Vereinswesen in Österreich im 19. und 20. Jahrhundert* (Innsbruck: StudienVerlag, 2011), 15–29. In contrast to Germany and Austria, Russian students maintained solidarity. See Benjamin Nathans, *Beyond the Pale: The Jewish Encounter with Imperial Russia* (Berkeley: University of California Press, 2002), 239–56.

57. Dirk Stegmann, *Die Erben Bismarcks: Parteien und Verbände in der Spätphase des Wilhelminischen Deutschlands. Sammlungspolitik 1897–1918* (Cologne: Kiepenheuer and Witsch, 1970); Margaret Lavinia Anderson, *Practicing Democracy: Elections and Political Culture in Imperial Germany* (Princeton: Princeton University Press, 2000), 378–89; Pieter M. Judson, *The Habsburg Empire: A New History* (Cambridge, MA: Harvard University Press, 2016), 334–50.

58. Vienna's community organization (*Israelitische Kultusgemeinde* [IKG]; 1852) had emerged after the 1848 revolution's grant of equality. Viennese Jewish leaders submitted a proposal for an organized community in August 1850. The government approved the IKG provisionally in 1852, then permanently in 1867. Designed to administer religious life through a communal tax, the organization had no political brief. Its officers were the community's wealthy elite, many ennobled, who also funded many of Vienna's Jewish charitable institutions, including the Allianz. See Max Grunwald, *Vienna* (Philadelphia: Jewish Publication Society, 1936), 395–97 and Marsha L. Rozenblit, *The Jews of Vienna, 1867–1914: Assimilation and Identity* (Albany: State University of New York Press, 1983), 148–49.

59. *Österreichische Wochenschrift* 14 (1885): 1. Cited in Jacob Toury, "Troubled Beginnings: The Emergence of the Österreichisch-Israelitische Union," *Leo Baeck Institute Yearbook* 30 (1985): 464. The term for "civic association" was *Bürgerverein*. Josef Samuel Bloch (1850–1923) was among the founders. He called for organized Jewish defense to respond to anti-Semitism (Rohling, Tiszaeszlár). He founded a newspaper, *Österreichische Wochenschrift* (1884), dedicated to the defense of Jewish rights through an association (*jüdischen Bürgerverein*). He served as a representative in Parliament. Toury, "Troubled Beginnings," 462, 475. For the ÖIU's place in Habsburg Jewry's "tripartite identity" (politically Habsburg; culturally German, Czech, or Polish; ethnically Jewish), see Marsha L. Rozenblit, *Reconstructing a National Identity: The Jews of Habsburg Austria during World War I* (New York: Oxford University Press, 2001), 3–38.

60. Toury, "Troubled Beginnings," 473; Rozenblit, *The Jews of Vienna*, 156.

61. Jacob Toury, "Years of Strife: The Contest of the Österreichisch-Israelitische Union for the Leadership of Austrian Jewry," *Leo Baeck Institute Yearbook* 33 (1988): 181.

62. Ibid., 197.

63. Ibid., 198.

64. Jacob Toury, "Defense Activities of the Österreichisch-Israelitische Union before 1914," in Jehuda Reinharz, ed., *Living with Antisemitism. Modern Jewish Responses* (Hanover, NH: Brandeis University Press, 1987), 179.

65. Toury, "Years of Strife," 182–83; Rozenblit, *The Jews of Vienna*, 157–58.

66. Toury, "Defense Activities," 170.

67. Rozenblit, *The Jews of Vienna*, 157–58.

68. Toury, "Years of Strife," 196; Toury, "Defense Activities," 170.

69. Toury, "Defense Activities," 173.

70. Ibid., 173–75, 177.

71. Ibid., 185–86; see also 180–85, 188–90.

72. Toury, "Years of Strife," 185–87.

73. Rozenblit, *The Jews of Vienna*, 181–84.

74. For "legislatively encouraged decentralization," see Ismar Schorsch, *Jewish Responses to German Anti-Semitism, 1870–1914* (New York: Columbia University Press, 1972),

18, 23–52 and Jehuda Reinharz, *Fatherland or Promised Land: The Dilemma of the German Jew, 1893–1914* (Ann Arbor: University of Michigan Press, 1975), 11–13. Of some 2,000 communities, only 113 had joined in 1872, in 1879 only 131. By 1893 membership had reached 500. There was also a nationalist agenda of creating a German alternative to the Alliance.

75. Schorsch, *Jewish Responses to German Anti-Semitism*, 40–42; Reinharz, *Fatherland or Promised Land*, 24–27. The public prosecutor gained a near monopoly on criminal cases with the promulgation of the Imperial Code of Criminal Procedure (October 1, 1879).

76. Schorsch, *Jewish Responses to German Anti-Semitism*, 49–52. The Community League was initially located in Leipzig as an unincorporated organization. In 1881 the Saxon government denied an application for incorporation and prohibited its activities. The Community League relocated to Berlin, where it was incorporated in 1898.

77. Marjorie Lamberti, *Jewish Activism in Imperial Germany: The Struggle for Civil Equality* (New Haven: Yale University Press, 1978), 123–75.

78. Schorsch, *Jewish Responses to German Anti-Semitism*, 79–101; Reinharz, *Fatherland or Promised Land*, 35–36. Another short-lived organization of Christians was the *Vereinigung zur Bekämpfung der Rassenhetze* (VBR). See Jacob Borut, "The Rise of Jewish Defence Agitation in Germany, 1890–1895: A Pre-History of the C.V.?" *Leo Baeck Institute Yearbook* 36 (1991): 71–75.

79. Schorsch, *Jewish Responses to German Anti-Semitism*, 59–65; Reinharz, *Fatherland or Promised Land*, 25.

80. Robin Judd, *Contested Rituals: Circumcision, Kosher Butchering, and Jewish Political Life in Germany, 1843–1933* (Ithaca: Cornell University Press, 2007), 156–63. For other individuals and organizations, see Borut, "The Rise of Jewish Defence Agitation in Germany," 68–88.

81. Reinharz, *Fatherland or Promised Land*, 38. After the announcement of the organization's founding, anti-Semitic candidates received 263,000 votes in the 1893 Reichstag election (up from 47,000 in 1890).

82. Farmers' League (*Bund der Landwirte*; 1893); Pan German League (*Alldeutscher Verband*; 1893); German Federation of Commercial Employees (*Deutscher Handlungsgehilfen Verband*; 1893); Central Association of German Industrialists (*Centralverband deutscher Industrieller*; 1876).

83. Reinharz, *Fatherland or Promised Land*, 41.

84. Friesel, "The Political and Ideological Development of the Centralverein before 1914," 124, 143–44; Schorsch, *Jewish Responses to German Anti-Semitism*, 119; Yaakov Borut, "The 1890's as a Turning Point in German Jewish History," *Aschkenas: Zeitschrift für Geschichte und Kultur der Juden* 18/19, no. 1 (2008/2009): 41–58.

85. Schorsch, *Jewish Responses to German Anti-Semitism*, 122.

86. Lawyers utilized these four sections of the 1876 Uniform Criminal Code. See ibid., 123–24.

87. Ibid., 123–32. The *Verband der deutschen Juden* (1904) aspired to be a broader organization with a "public mandate" through representation of major communities and organizations. It supplemented the Central Association by addressing the German government and defending Judaism through scholarly literature (149–77).

88. Lamberti, *Jewish Activism in Imperial Germany*, 7–77; Peter Pulzer, *Jews and the German State: The Political History of a Minority, 1848–1933* (Oxford: Blackwell, 1992), 96–193. This was especially the case in the years of the so-called Bülow Bloc (1907–9), when the liberal parties joined conservatives in a pro-government coalition.

89. Schorsch, *Jewish Responses to German Anti-Semitism*, 132–33.

90. Lamberti, *Jewish Activism in Imperial Germany*; Reinharz, *Fatherland or Promised Land*, 65–70; Friesel, "The Political and Ideological Development of the Centralverein

before 1914," 126–30. The parties were the *Freisinnige Volkspartei* and the *Freisinnige Vereinigung*, which in 1910 combined to form the *Fortschrittliche Volkspartei*.

91. Benjamin Nathans, "The Other Modern Jewish Politics: Integration and Modernity," in Zvi Gitelman, ed., *The Emergence of Modern Jewish Politics* (Pittsburgh: University of Pittsburgh Press, 2003), 25–29.

92. Naomi W. Cohen, *Not Free to Desist: A History of the American Jewish Committee, 1906–1966* (Philadelphia: Jewish Publication Society, 1972), 3–18. At preliminary meetings, prospective members debated whether the organization should be congregation based and democratic or executive committee–based and autocratic (12–13). On the AJC's composition as a philanthropic organization ("what I am trying to avoid more than anything else is, the creation of a political organization"), see Louis Marshall to Rabbi Joseph Stolz, January 12, 1906, in Charles Reznikoff, ed., *Louis Marshall: Champion of Liberty*, 2 vols. (Philadelphia: Jewish Publication Society, 1957), 1:21–22.

93. Gregg Ivers, "The Political Organization of American Jewry, 1906–1947," *Studies in Jewish Civilization* 4 (1993): 120.

94. Cohen, *Not Free to Desist*, 19–36. Prior to World War I the AJC had minimal staff.

95. Deborah Dash Moore, *B'nai B'rith and the Challenge of Ethnic Leadership* (Albany: State University of New York Press, 1981), 5–6. For hostile images and hostility, see Nathan C. Belth, *A Promise to Keep: A Narrative of the American Encounter with Anti-Semitism* (New York: Times Books, 1979), 36–57 and Leonard Dinnerstein, *Antisemitism in America* (New York: Oxford University Press, 1994), 35–77.

96. Ivers, "The Political Organization of American Jewry," 133–35; Moore, *B'nai B'rith and the Challenge of Ethnic Leadership*, 104–13.

97. Moore, *B'nai B'rith and the Challenge of Ethnic Leadership*, 105, 113. The ADL continued these efforts until the 1940s.

98. Carole Fink, *Defending the Rights of Others: The Great Powers, the Jews, and International Minority Protection, 1878–1938* (Cambridge: Cambridge University Press, 2004), 3.

99. Ibid., 15.

100. Siegel, *Österreichisches Judentum zwischen Ost und West*, 52–64; N. M. Gelber, "The Intervention of German Jews at the Berlin Congress 1878," *Leo Baeck Institute Yearbook* 5 (1960): 221–22.

101. Fink, *Defending the Rights of Others*, 15–16; Gelber, "The Intervention of German Jews at the Berlin Congress 1878," 224–25.

102. Gelber, "The Intervention of German Jews at the Berlin Congress 1878," 227–28. The German Reichstag twice (1876, 1878) blocked a German-Romanian trade treaty that would have permitted discrimination against German Jews traveling in Romania. Fritz Stern, *Gold and Iron: Bismarck, Bleichröder, and the Building of the German Empire* (New York: Vintage, 1977), 371–77.

103. Gelber, "The Intervention of German Jews at the Berlin Congress 1878," 221–22.

104. Alliance letter of February 19, 1878, cited in ibid., 230; Carol Iancu, *Jews in Romania, 1866–1919: From Exclusion to Emancipation*, trans. Carvel de Bussy (Boulder, CO: East European Monographs, 1996), 90. For background correspondence, see Carol Iancu, *Bleichröder & Crémieux: Le combat pour l'émancipation des Juifs de Roumanie devant le Congrés de Berlin. Correspondance inédite (1878–1880)* (Montpellier: Centre de recherches et d'études juives et hébraïques, 1987).

105. Iancu, *Jews in Romania*, 91–92; Gelber, "The Intervention of German Jews at the Berlin Congress 1878," 233–34.

106. Gelber, "The Intervention of German Jews at the Berlin Congress 1878," 237–41. Gerson Bleichröder was especially active in lobbying Bismarck and Russia's Count Shuvalov.

107. Fink, *Defending the Rights of Others*, 26–27.

108. Ibid., 24–29; Gelber, "The Intervention of German Jews at the Berlin Congress 1878," 241–42; Stern, *Gold and Iron*, 358–93.

109. Fink, *Defending the Rights of Others*, 30–32; Iancu, *Jews in Romania*, 94–100, 105–9.

110. Bar-Chen, *Weder Asiaten noch Orientalen*, 76.

Chapter Twenty. Mass Society, II

1. For a system of three competing politics—emancipationist, auto-emancipationist, orthodox—see Jonathan Frankel, "Modern Jewish Politics East and West (1840–1939): Utopia, Myth, Reality," in Zvi Gitelman, ed., *The Quest for Utopia: Jewish Political Ideas and Institutions through the Ages* (Armonk, NY: M. E. Sharpe, 1992), 93–95. I prefer the neutral term "nationalist" to the polemical "auto-emancipationist." Some scholars have focused on a shifting youth culture in new urban settings. See Scott Ury, *Barricades and Banners: The Revolution of 1905 and the Transformation of Warsaw Jewry* (Stanford: Stanford University Press, 2012).

2. Jacob Toury, "Emancipation and Assimilation: Concepts and Conditions," (Hebrew) *Yalkut Moreshet* 2, no. 2 (April 1964): 167–82; Phyllis Cohen Albert, "Israelite and Jew: How Did Nineteenth-Century French Jews Understand Assimilation," in Jonathan Frankel and Steven J. Zipperstein, eds., *Assimilation and Community: The Jews in Nineteenth-Century Europe* (Cambridge: Cambridge University Press, 1992), 88–109; Gerson Cohen, "The Blessings of Assimilation in Jewish History," in Steve Israel and Seth Forman, eds., *Great Jewish Speeches Throughout History* (Northvale, NJ: Jason Aronson, 1994), 183–91; Zalman Shazar, *Morning Stars*, trans. Sulamith Schwartz Nardi (Philadelphia: Jewish Publication Society, 1967), 187–88.

3. "Assimilation" was the autonomists' bête noire. See Simon Rabinovitch, *Jewish Rights, National Rites: National and Autonomy in Late Imperial and Revolutionary Russia* (Stanford: Stanford University Press, 2014), 154, 223.

4. Jonathan Frankel, "Assimilation and the Jews in Nineteenth-Century Europe: Towards a New Historiography," in Frankel and Zipperstein, eds., *Assimilation and Community*, 1–37; Steven E. Aschheim, *Brothers and Strangers: The East European Jew in German and German Jewish Consciousness, 1800–1923* (Madison: University of Wisconsin Press, 1982).

5. H. R. Trevor-Roper, *Jewish and Other Nationalism* (London: Weidenfeld & Nicolson, 1962).

6. Theodor Herzl, *Der Judenstaat*, in *Zionistische Schriften*, 3rd ed., 5 vols. (Tel Aviv: Hozaah Ivrith), 1:39, 35, translation in *The Jewish State* (Mineola, NY: Dover, 1988), 89, 85. The title of Herzl's book has usually been mistranslated. One recent edition renders it correctly: *The Jews' State* (Northvale, NJ: Jason Aronson, 1997). The usual Hebrew translation is accurate: "Medinat ha-Yehudim."

7. Ahad Ha-Am, "Avdut be-Tokh Herut," *Kol Kitvei Ahad Ha-Am* (Tel Aviv: Dvir, 1960), 64–69.

8. Leo Strauss, "Letter to the Editor: The State of Israel," in Kenneth Hart Green, ed., *Jewish Philosophy and the Crisis of Modernity: Essays and Lectures in Modern Jewish Thought by Leo Strauss* (Albany: State University of New York Press, 1997), 414.

9. For the phrase "negation of the Diaspora," see Ahad Ha-Am, *Kol Kitvei*, 399–403, translation in Arthur Hertzberg, ed., *The Zionist Idea: A Historical Analysis and Reader*, 2nd ed. (New York: Harper and Row, 1966), 270–77. Gideon Shimoni places Zionism

among the nationalisms of diaspora groups lacking a territory and a single vernacular. See *The Zionist Ideology* (Hanover, NH: Brandeis University Press, 1995), 5–6.

10. Leo Pinsker, *"Autoemanzipation!" Mahnruf an seine Stammesgenossen von einem russischen Juden* (Berlin: Issleib, 1882).

11. Hertzberg, *The Zionist Idea*, 15–100; Arieh Bruce Saposnik, *Becoming Hebrew: The Creation of a Jewish National Culture in Ottoman Palestine* (New York: Oxford University Press, 2008). For Herzl as a "super-emancipationist," see Steven Beller, *Herzl* (London: Peter Halban, 1991).

12. Shimoni, *The Zionist Ideology*; Hertzberg, *The Zionist Idea*; David Vital, *The Origins of Zionism* (Oxford: Clarendon, 1975); Vital, *Zionism: The Formative Years* (Oxford: Clarendon, 1982); Vital, *Zionism: The Crucial Phase* (Oxford: Clarendon, 1987); Gur Alroey, *Zionism without Zion: The Jewish Territorial Organization and Its Conflict with the Zionist Organization* (Detroit: Wayne State University Press, 2016).

13. Schorsch, *Jewish Responses to German Anti-Semitism*, 179–202; Reinharz, *Fatherland or Promised Land*, 171–224; Stephen M. Poppel, *Zionism in Germany, 1897–1933: The Shaping of a Jewish Identity* (Philadelphia: Jewish Publication Society, 1977); Hagit Lavsky, *Before Catastrophe: The Distinctive Path of German Zionism* (Detroit: Wayne State University Press, 1996), 18–31.

14. Moshe Rinott, "The Zionist Organization and the Hilfsverein," *Leo Baeck Institute Yearbook* 21 (1976): 265–66.

15. Ernst Feder, "Paul Nathan, the Man and His Work," *Leo Baeck Institute Yearbook* 3 (1958): 72. The Hilfsverein supported twenty-eight schools in Palestine. Twenty-two used exclusively Hebrew as the language of instruction while six utilized predominantly Hebrew.

16. Rinott, "The Zionist Organization and the Hilfsverein," 268–69. A full exposition is available in Moshe Rinott, *Hevrat ha-Ezra le-Yehudei Germanya* (Jerusalem: Hebrew University Press, 1971). The "language conflict" and World War I delayed the Technion's opening until 1925. In Vienna Herzl first planned to infiltrate the Allianz (1900–1901) and then twice endeavored publicly to convert the organization to Zionism (1899, 1902). In his novel Herzl envisaged Zionism revolutionizing Jewish philanthropy. See *Old-New Land*, trans. Lotta Levensohn (New York: Bloch, 1960), 176. The Zionist newspaper, *Die Welt*, held the Allianz responsible for Romanian Jews' mass emigration. See Björn Siegel, *Österreichisches Judentum zwischen Ost und West: Die Israelitische Allianz zu Wien, 1873–1938* (Frankfurt: Campus, 2008), 209–17.

17. Vital, *Zionism: The Formative Years*, 467–75; Rabinovitch, *Jewish Rights, National Rites*, 104ff.; Oscar Janowsky, *The Jews and Minority Rights (1898–1919)* (New York: Columbia University Press, 1933), 98–113. On some Zionist activists' defense of minority rights and transition to human rights, see James Loeffler, *Rooted Cosmopolitans: Jews and Human Rights in the Twentieth Century* (New Haven: Yale University Press, 2018).

18. Rabinovitch, *Jewish Rights, National Rites*, 52–59, 76–77.

19. Simon Dubnow, *Nationalism and History: Essays on Old and New Judaism* (New York: Atheneum, 1970), 110.

20. Ibid., 113, 134, 137; Rabinovitch, *Jewish Rights, National Rites*, 3, 223.

21. Rabinovitch, *Jewish Rights, National Rites*, 77–78, 104, 110–13, 135.

22. David Rechter, "A Nationalism of Small Things: Jewish Autonomy in Late Habsburg Austria," *Leo Baeck Institute Yearbook* 52 (2007): 87–109. The two primary figures were Hermann Kadisch (1861–1934) and Max Rosenfeld (1884–1919).

23. Joshua Shanes, *Diaspora Nationalism and Jewish Identity in Habsburg Galicia* (New York: Cambridge University Press, 2012); Rechter, "A Nationalism of Small Things,"

87–109. In committing to local diaspora politics, Galicia's Zionists attempted to free themselves from Vienna's domination. They achieved this by formal separation (October 1907; Seventh Galician Provincial Conference).

24. Moshe Mishkinsky, "Regional Factors in the Formation of the Jewish Labor Movement in Czarist Russia," *YIVO Annual of Jewish Social Studies* 14 (1969): 27–52.

25. Ezra Mendelsohn, *Class Struggle in the Pale: The Formative Years of the Jewish Workers' Movement in Tsarist Russia* (Cambridge: Cambridge University Press, 1970); Henry J. Tobias, *The Jewish Bund in Russia: From Its Origins to 1905* (Stanford: Stanford University Press, 1972); Jonathan Frankel, *Prophecy and Politics: Socialism, Nationalism and the Russian Jews, 1862–1917* (Cambridge: Cambridge University Press, 1981).

26. Mendelsohn, *Class Struggle in the Pale*, 153–55.

27. Frankel, *Prophecy and Politics*, 171–257.

28. Alan L. Mittleman, *The Politics of Torah: The Jewish Political Tradition and the Founding of Agudat Israel* (Albany: State University of New York Press, 1996), 103–5.

29. Ibid., 123.

30. See Rachel Manekin, *Yehudei Galitsia veha-Huka ha-Austrit: Reshita shel Politika Yehudit Modernit* (Jerusalem: Zalman Shazar, 2015), 122–62; Gershon C. Bacon, *The Politics of Tradition: Agudat Yisrael in Poland, 1916–1939* (Jerusalem: Magnes Press, 1996), 29–32.

31. See Vladimir Levin, "Orthodox Jewry and the Russian Government: An Attempt at Rapprochement, 1907–1914," *East European Jewish Affairs* 39, no. 2 (2009): 187–204.

Chapter Twenty-One. Ottoman Empire and Danubian Provinces

1. Karen Barkey, *Empire of Difference: The Ottomans in Comparative Perspective* (New York: Cambridge University Press, 2008).

2. Esther Benbassa and Aron Rodrigue, *The Jews of the Balkans: The Judeo-Spanish Community, 15th to 20th Centuries* (Oxford: Blackwell, 1995), 1–10; Minna Rozen, *A History of the Jewish Community in Istanbul: The Formative Years, 1453–1566* (Leiden: Brill, 2002), 45–47; Rozen, "The Jews of Istanbul in the Ottoman Era (1453–1923) from a Romaniot Perspective," in *Studies in the History of Istanbul Jewry, 1453–1923: A Journey through Civilizations* (Turnhout: Brepols, 2015), 7–50.

3. Joseph Hacker, "The Sürgün System and Jewish Society in the Ottoman Empire during the Fifteenth to the Seventeenth Centuries," in Aron Rodrigue, ed., *Ottoman and Turkish Jewry: Community and Leadership* (Bloomington: Indiana Turkish Studies, 1992), 1–65.

4. Halil İnalcık, "Foundations of Ottoman-Jewish Cooperation," in Avigdor Levy, ed., *Jews, Turks, Ottomans: A Shared History, Fifteenth through the Twentieth Century* (Syracuse, NY: Syracuse University Press, 2002), 3–7; Stanford J. Shaw, *The Jews of the Ottoman Empire and the Turkish Republic* (New York: New York University Press, 1991), 1–28.

5. Shaw, *The Jews of the Ottoman Empire and the Turkish Republic*, 33.

6. Rozen, *A History of the Jewish Community in Istanbul*, 47–49.

7. The conquests in the east shifted the empire's orientation from "Islamo-Christian" to "Islamic religiosity." See Barkey, *Empire of Difference*, 102–8.

8. İnalcık, "Foundations of Ottoman-Jewish Cooperation," 8–14; Shaw, *The Jews of the Ottoman Empire and the Turkish Republic*, 40; Daniel Goffman, "Jews in Early Modern Ottoman Commerce," in Levy, ed., *Jews, Turks, Ottomans*, 17–20; Rozen, *A History of the Jewish Community in Istanbul*, 222–43; Aryeh Shmuelevitz, *The Jews of the Ottoman Em-*

pire in the Late Fifteenth and the Sixteenth Centuries: Administrative, Economic, Legal and Social Relations as Reflected in the Responsa (Leiden: Brill, 1984), 128–78; Mark Alan Epstein, *The Ottoman Jewish Communities and Their Role in the Fifteenth and Sixteenth Centuries* (Freiburg: Schwarz, 1980).

9. Leah Bornstein-Makovetsky, "Jewish Lay Leadership and Ottoman Authorities during the Sixteenth and Seventeenth Centuries," in Rodrigue, ed., *Ottoman and Turkish Jewry*, 87–121; Shmuelevitz, *The Jews of the Ottoman Empire in the Late Fifteenth and the Sixteenth Centuries*, 15–30; Barkey, *Empire of Difference*, 137–40.

10. Benbassa and Rodrigue, *The Jews of the Balkans*, 11–35; Shaw, *The Jews of the Ottoman Empire and the Turkish Republic*, 48–56; Rozen, *A History of the Jewish Community in Istanbul*, 64–98.

11. M. Şükrü Hanioğlu, *A Brief History of the Late Ottoman Empire* (Princeton: Princeton University Press, 2008), 19, 25–26; Barkey, *Empire of Difference*, 109–53.

12. Barkey, *Empire of Difference*, 120.

13. Shaw, *The Jews of the Ottoman Empire and the Turkish Republic*, 78–81.

14. Alexander H. De Groot, "The Historical Development of the Capitulatory Regime in the Ottoman Middle East from the Fifteenth to the Nineteenth Centuries," *Oriente Moderno* 22, no. 3 (2003): 579.

15. Ibid., 575–604. "Capitulations" dated to Fatimid rule in Egypt; the first was granted to Pisan merchants (1149). The capitulations nominally belonged to domestic policy since Islamic law did not recognize the existence of non-Islamic states.

16. Maurits H. van den Boogert, *Capitulations and the Ottoman Legal System: Qadis, Consuls and Beratlis in the 18th Century* (Leiden: Brill, 2005), 7–9.

17. Goffman, "Jews in Early Modern Ottoman Commerce," 15–34; Benbassa and Rodrigue, *The Jews of the Balkans*, 44–49; Avigdor Levy, *The Sephardim in the Ottoman Empire* (Princeton: Darwin Press, 1992), 71–89.

18. Goffman, "Jews in Early Modern Ottoman Commerce," 20–34.

19. Minna Rozen, "Strangers in a Strange Land: The Extraterritorial Status of Jews in Italy and the Ottoman Empire in the Sixteenth to the Eighteenth Centuries," in Rodrigue, ed., *Ottoman and Turkish Jewry*, 123–66.

20. Benbassa and Rodrigue, *The Jews of the Balkans*, 45.

21. Around 1800 the empire stretched "from Algeria to Yemen, Bosnia to Caucasus, and Eritrea to Basra" and numbered some 30 million. See Hanioğlu, *A Brief History of the Late Ottoman Empire*, 7. For the role of international trade and life-term tax farming (from 1695) in transforming "intermediate political networks" into non-imperial horizontal alliances in the eighteenth and nineteenth centuries, see Barkey, *Empire of Difference*, 197–263.

22. Hanioğlu, *A Brief History of the Late Ottoman Empire*, 4, 48, 66, 77.

23. Norman A. Stillman, *The Jews of Arab Lands in Modern Times* (Philadelphia: Jewish Publication Society, 1991), 6.

24. Hanioğlu, *A Brief History of the Late Ottoman Empire*, 41, 59–62.

25. Translation in Norman A. Stillman, *The Jews of Arab Lands: A History and Source Book* (Philadelphia: Jewish Publication Society, 1979), 96.

26. The 1869 Ottoman Law of Nationality codified these terms. See Kemal H. Karpat, "Millets and Nationality: The Roots of the Incongruity of Nation and State in the Post-Ottoman Era," in Benjamin Braude and Bernard Lewis, eds., *Christians and Jews in the Ottoman Empire: The Functioning of a Plural Society*, 2 vols. (New York: Holmes & Meier, 1982), 1:162–63; Hanioğlu, *A Brief History of the Late Ottoman Empire*, 74.

27. Stillman, *The Jews of Arab Lands in Modern Times*, 8–9, asserts that the 1839 leg-

islation derived from "European inspiration" whereas that of 1856 derived from "European intervention."

28. Werner E. Mosse, *The Rise and Fall of the Crimean System, 1855–71: The Story of a Peace Settlement* (London: Macmillan, 1963), 1–7.

29. Translation in Stillman, *The Jews of Arab Lands: A History and Source Book*, 357–60. See Winfried Baumgart, *The Peace of Paris, 1856: Studies in War, Diplomacy and Peacemaking*, trans. Ann Pottinger Saab (Santa Barbara, CA: ABC-Clio, 1981), 128–30.

30. Shaw, *The Jews of the Ottoman Empire and the Turkish Republic*, 155–56.

31. The 1876 constitution reiterated these rights. See "The Ottoman Constitution, Promulgated the 7th Zilbridje, 1293 (11/23 December 1876)," *American Journal of International Law* 2, no. 4 (October 1908): 367–87. For individual rights regardless of religion, Articles 8 and 17. For access to civil service position, Article 18.

32. Jevdet Pasha, *Tezakir* (Ankara: Türk Tarih Kurumu Basimevi, 1953), 67–68, translated in Stillman, *The Jews of Arab Lands: A History and Source Book*, 361.

33. Aron Rodrigue, "From *Millet* to Minority: Turkish Jewry," in Pierre Birnbaum and Ira Katznelson, eds., *Paths of Emancipation: Jews, States and Citizenship* (Princeton: Princeton University Press, 1995), 238–61; Daniel J. Schroeter, "The Changing Relationship between the Jews of the Arab Middle East and the Ottoman State in the Nineteenth Century," in Levy, ed., *Jews, Turks, Ottomans*, 88–107.

34. The new *millets* were for Catholics and the Serbian/Bulgarian Orthodox. See Shaw, *The Jews of the Ottoman Empire and the Turkish Republic*, 157. The Reform Era's centralization may have given the *millet* system greater importance than it previously had. Historians may have mistakenly read that new importance back into earlier Ottoman history. See Benjamin Braude, "Foundation Myths of the *Millet* System," in Braude and Lewis, eds., *Christians and Jews in the Ottoman Empire*, 1:69–88.

35. For the ambiguous role of the *millets* in nineteenth-century social change, see Roderic H. Davison, "The *Millets* as Agents of Change in the Nineteenth-Century Ottoman Empire," in Braude and Lewis, eds., *Christians and Jews in the Ottoman Empire*, 1:319–37.

36. Hanioğlu, *A Brief History of the Late Ottoman Empire*, 76.

37. Shaw, *The Jews of the Ottoman Empire and the Turkish Republic*, 149, 166–68; Avigdor Levy, *The Sephardim in the Ottoman Empire* (Princeton: Darwin Press, 1992), 105–8. The office of Grand Rabbi had either been vacant for some three centuries or in fact never existed. Historians debate whether the reforms restored or invented the office.

38. Aron Rodrigue, "Abraham de Camondo of Istanbul: The Transformation of Jewish Philanthropy," in Frances Malino and David Sorkin, eds., *Profiles in Diversity: Jews in a Changing Europe, 1750–1870* (Detroit: Wayne State University Press, 1998), 46–56. For Egypt, see Jacob Landau, "Changing Patterns of Community Structures, with Special Reference to Ottoman Egypt," in Levy, ed., *Jews, Turks, Ottomans*, 77–87.

39. Ludwig Philippson, *Jewish Chronicle* (April 21, 1854), cited in Aron Rodrigue, *French Jews, Turkish Jews: The Alliance Israélite Universelle and the Politics of Jewish Schooling in Turkey, 1860–1925* (Bloomington: Indiana University Press, 1990), 14.

40. Eliyahu Feldman, "The Question of Jewish Emancipation in the Ottoman Empire and the Danubian Principalities after the Crimean War," *Jewish Social Studies* 41, no. 1 (1979): 41–45. French Jewish leaders saw their own status at issue in the way France handled the matter. See Lisa Moses Leff, *Sacred Bonds of Solidarity: The Rise of Jewish Internationalism in Nineteenth-Century France* (Stanford: Stanford University Press, 2006), 148–50.

41. Baumgart, *The Peace of Paris, 1856*, 189–91.

42. Rodrigue, "From *Millet* to Minority: Turkish Jewry," 242; Riva Kastoryano, "From

Millet to Community: The Jews of Istanbul," in Rodrigue, ed., *Ottoman and Turkish Jewry*, 253–77. For the Jewish population, see Kemal H. Karpat, "Jewish Population Movements in the Ottoman Empire, 1862–1914," in Avigdor Levy, ed., *The Jews of the Ottoman Empire* (Princeton: Darwin Press, 1994), 399–421.

43. Ariel Salzmann, "Citizens in Search of a State: The Limits of Political Participation in the Late Ottoman Empire," in Michael Hanagan and Charles Tilly, eds., *Extending Citizenship, Reconfiguring States* (Lanham, MD: Rowman and Littlefield, 1999), 45.

44. Rodrigue, "From *Millet* to Minority: Turkish Jewry," 245; Rodrigue, *French Jews, Turkish Jews*, 157; Julia Phillips Cohen, *Becoming Ottomans: Sephardi Jews and Imperial Citizenship in the Modern Era* (New York: Oxford University Press, 2014), 10.

45. Cohen, *Becoming Ottomans*, 78–80. On population transfers and refugees, see Carole Fink, *Defending the Rights of Others: The Great Powers, the Jews, and International Minority Protection, 1878–1938* (Cambridge: Cambridge University Press, 2004), 39–44, 64–65 and Michael Marrus, *The Unwanted: European Refugees in the Twentieth Century* (New York: Oxford University Press, 1985), 40–50.

46. Salzmann, "Citizens in Search of a State," 50.

47. Cohen, *Becoming Ottomans*; Hasan Kayalı, "Jewish Representation in the Ottoman Parliaments," 507–17; Esther Benbassa, "Associational Strategies in Ottoman Jewish Society in the Nineteenth and Twentieth Centuries," 457–484 and İlber Ortaylı, "Ottomanism and Zionism during the Second Constitutional Period, 1908–1915," 527–37, in Levy, ed., *The Jews of the Ottoman Empire*. The conflict between advocates of the Alliance/Ottomanization versus Zionists played out in the associations.

48. Cohen, *Becoming Ottomans*, 24–80, quotation at 79; Nergis Canefe, "Ottoman Jews to Turkish Citizens: Characters in Search of an Author," in Canefe, ed., *The Jewish Diaspora as a Paradigm: Politics, Religion and Belonging* (Istanbul: Libra Kitapçılık, 2014), 211–67.

49. Rodrigue, *French Jews, Turkish Jews*, 87, 125; Feroz Ahmad, "The Special Relationship: The Committee of Union and Progress and the Ottoman Jewish Political Elite, 1908–1918," in Levy, ed., *Jews, Turks, Ottomans*, 212–30; M. Şükrü Hanioğlu, "Jews in the Young Turk Movement to the 1908 Revolution," in Levy, ed., *The Jews of the Ottoman Empire*, 519–26.

50. Shaw, *The Jews of the Ottoman Empire and the Turkish Republic*, 231–32. On competition between Jewish and Christian merchants, see Jacob M. Landau, "Relations between Jews and Non-Jews in the Late Ottoman Empire: Some Characteristics," in Levy, ed., *The Jews of the Ottoman Empire*, 539–46.

51. Shaw, *The Jews of the Ottoman Empire and the Turkish Republic*, 229–30.

52. Carol Iancu, *Jews in Romania, 1866–1919: From Exclusion to Emancipation* (Boulder, CO: East European Monographs, 1996), 10. For a contemporary collection of documents, see Isidore Loeb, *La situation des Israélites en Turquie, en Serbie et en Roumanie* (Paris: J. Baer, 1877), 197–394.

53. Baumgart, *The Peace of Paris, 1856*, 116–25.

54. Keith Hitchins, *Rumania, 1866–1947* (Oxford: Clarendon, 1994), 19–22; Constantin Iordachi, "The Unyielding Boundaries of Citizenship: The Emancipation of 'Non-Citizens' in Romania, 1866–1918," *European Review of History* 8, no. 2 (2001): 162. The middle and lower boyars (gentry) who dominated the bureaucracy created a "bureaucratic nationalism."

55. W. G. East, *The Union of Moldavia and Wallachia, 1859: An Episode in Diplomatic History* (Cambridge: Cambridge University Press, 1929), 11–17; Iancu, *Jews in Romania*, 23–26. Moldavia invited Jews to settle its sparsely populated territories in the eighteenth and early nineteenth centuries. As in the Polish-Lithuanian Commonwealth, Jews created

small market towns on private estates. Moldavia's Jewish population increased from 30,000 in 1803 to 118,922 in 1859. Some earlier writers treated Romania's anti-Jewish policies as a Russian import. See Joseph Berkowitz, *La question des Israélites en Roumanie: Étude de son histoire et des divers problems de droit qu'elle soulève* (Paris: Jouve and Cie, 1923).

56. Iancu, *Jews in Romania*, 34–35.

57. Iordachi, "The Unyielding Boundaries of Citizenship," 163.

58. Hitchins, *Rumania*, 165.

59. Iordachi, "The Unyielding Boundaries of Citizenship," 163–64.

60. Cited in Iancu, *Jews in Romania*, 39. The clause remained in force until 1879. See Hitchins, *Rumania*, 16–17.

61. Joshua Starr, "Jewish Citizenship in Rumania (1878–1940)," *Jewish Social Studies* 3, no. 1 (January 1941): 62.

62. Iordachi, "The Unyielding Boundaries of Citizenship," 165, 167–68.

63. Ibid., 168–69. In Moldavia in 1860 some 6,164 families qualified as *sudiți*.

64. Iancu, *Jews in Romania*, 110–26; Iordachi, "The Unyielding Boundaries of Citizenship," 169.

65. Hitchins, *Rumania*, 165; Iancu, *Jews in Romania*, 25, 46–67.

66. Feldman, "The Question of Jewish Emancipation in the Ottoman Empire," 51.

67. French and English representatives addressed the issue in the Protocol of the Constantinople Conference (1856); the Peace Congress did not. See Feldman, "The Question of Jewish Emancipation in the Ottoman Empire," 46–48. For Ludwig Philippson's letter to Napoleon III, see N. M. Gelber, "The Intervention of German Jews at the Berlin Congress 1878," *Leo Baeck Institute Yearbook* 5 (1960): 221–22.

68. Feldman, "The Question of Jewish Emancipation in the Ottoman Empire," 57; Iancu, *Jews in Romania*, 30–34. The one exception was Gustave Rothschild, who interceded in the name of his father, Baron James.

69. Crémieux visited Bucharest to intercede in 1866, Moses Montefiore in 1867. See Abigail Green, *Moses Montefiore: Jewish Liberator, Imperial Hero* (Cambridge, MA: Harvard University Press, 2010), 339–58. Benjamin Peixotto came to Romania as the consul of the United States expressly to aid his fellow Jews. See Iancu, *Jews in Romania*, 61–64.

70. Iordachi, "The Unyielding Boundaries of Citizenship," 169.

71. Feldman, "The Question of Jewish Emancipation in the Ottoman Empire," 46–64; Iancu, *Jews in Romania*, 89–105; Fink, *Defending the Rights of Others*, 5–38. For a comparison of Romania (1878) with Morocco (1880) that emphasizes Great Power realpolitik, especially Britain's, see Abigail Green, "The Limits of Intervention: Coercive Diplomacy and the Jewish Question in the Nineteenth Century," *International History Review* 36, no. 3 (2014): 473–92.

72. Iancu, *Jews in Romania*, 105–9; Hitchins, *Rumania*, 52–53, 165. Perhaps 1,000 Jews qualified for citizenship in the period 1879–1914; most had fought in the war of independence.

Chapter Twenty-Two. Minority Rights

1. George F. Kennan, *The Decline of Bismarck's European Order: Franco-Russian Relations, 1875–1890* (Princeton: Princeton University Press, 1979), 3.

2. Derek Penslar, *Jews and the Military: A History* (Princeton: Princeton University Press, 2013), 157; Shulamit Volkov, *Walther Rathenau: Weimar's Fallen Statesman* (New Haven: Yale University Press, 2012), 122–26; Jehuda Reinharz, *Chaim Weizmann: The Making of a Statesman* (New York: Oxford University Press, 1993), 40–72.

3. Panikos Panayi, "Dominant Societies and Minorities in the Two World Wars," in Pan-

ayi, ed., *Minorities in Wartime: National and Racial Groupings in Europe, North America and Australia during the Two World Wars* (Oxford: Berg, 1993), 3–23.

4. Oleg Budnitskii, *Russian Jews between the Reds and the Whites, 1917–1920*, trans. Timothy J. Portice (Philadelphia: University of Pennsylvania Press, 2012), 73; Michael Marrus, *The Unwanted: European Refugees in the Twentieth Century* (New York: Oxford University Press, 1985), 54.

5. Abraham G. Duker, "Jews in the World War: A Brief Historical Sketch," *Contemporary Jewish Record* 2, no. 5 (1939): 9–13; Antony Polonsky, *The Jews in Poland and Russia*, 3 vols. (Oxford: Littman Library, 2010–12), 3:6–7. The August 15, 1915, suspension was temporary. See Eugene M. Avrutin, *Jews and the Imperial State: Identification Politics in Tsarist Russia* (Ithaca: Cornell University Press, 2010), 183.

6. Duker, "Jews in the World War," 13; S. Ansky, *The Enemy at His Pleasure: A Journey through the Jewish Pale of Settlement during World War I*, trans. Joachim Neugroschel (New York: Metropolitan Books, 2002).

7. David Rechter, *The Jews of Vienna and the First World War* (Oxford: Littman Library, 2001), 67–100.

8. Moses A. Leavitt, *The JDC Story, 1914–1952* (New York: American Jewish Joint Distribution Committee, 1953), 4–7. The JDC spent $14,938,000 during the war. In Russia, it distributed its funds through EKOPO (Jewish Committee for Relief of War Sufferers), in Germany through the *Hilfsverein*, and in Austria-Hungary through the *Allianz zu Wien*. Jonathan Frankel, "The Paradoxical Politics of Marginality: Thoughts on the Jewish Situation during the Years 1914–21," *Studies in Contemporary Jewry* 4 (1988): 9–10.

9. For the examples of Kielce, Lemberg, and Pinsk, see Carole Fink, *Defending the Rights of Others: The Great Powers, the Jews, and International Minority Protection, 1878–1938* (Cambridge: Cambridge University Press, 2004), 101–30. For Bolshevik and White pogroms, see Budnitskii, *Russian Jews between the Reds and the Whites*, 90, 116–22, 216–74, 286, 391. Wrangel, unlike Denikin, prevented pogroms. See 167–72.

10. Marrus, *The Unwanted*, 58. "In the years of war, revolution and civil war from 1914 to 1921, half a million Jews were expelled, or fled from their homes, 150,000 to 200,000 were killed or wounded and 300,000 children were orphaned." See Benjamin Pinkus, *The Jews of the Soviet Union: The History of a National Minority* (Cambridge: Cambridge University Press, 1988), 62–63. Budnitskii, *Russian Jews between the Reds and the Whites*, 216–17, estimates 50,000 to 200,000 Jews killed and another 200,000 seriously injured (1918–20).

11. Marrus, *The Unwanted*, 66–68.

12. The JDC expended $22,796,000 in 1919–21. It also began to send its own trained workers into the field. Leavitt, *The JDC Story*, 7–8. Emigdirect = United Committee for Jewish Emigration; HICEM combined HIAS, ICA (Jewish Colonization Association), and Emigdirect.

13. Austrian Central Committee to Protect the Jewish Population's Civil Rights in the Northern War Zones (*Österreichische Zentralkommitee zur Wahrung des staatsbürgerlichen Interesssen der jüdischen Bevölkerung im nördlichen Kriegsgebiete*). See Rechter, *The Jews of Vienna and the First World War*, 86–87.

14. Fink, *Defending the Rights of Others*, 288, 292.

15. N. I. Shtif, *Pogromy na Ukraine* (Berlin, 1922) cited in Budnitskii, *Russian Jews between the Reds and the Whites*, 220. Budnitskii traces a "model" of military pogroms (1915–22) in which the authorities became perpetrators (236, 273). Jews appeared as a hostile group in military textbooks from the late tsarist period onward. See Peter Holquist, "To Count, to Extract and to Exterminate: Population Statistics and Population Politics in Late Imperial and Soviet Russia," in Ronald Grigor Suny and Terry Martin, eds., *A State of*

Nations: Empire and Nation-Making in the Age of Lenin and Stalin (New York: Oxford University Press, 2001), 111–44.

16. Fink, *Defending the Rights of Others*, 148.

17. Oscar I. Janowsky, *The Jews and Minority Rights (1898–1919)* (New York: Columbia University Press, 1933), 264–319; Fink, *Defending the Rights of Others*, 98–99, 128, 194–202; Mark Levene, "Authority and Legitimacy in Jewish Leadership: The Case of Lucien Wolf (1857–1930)," *Jewish Political Studies Review* 4, no. 1 (Spring 1992): 85–110; Eugene C. Black, "Lucien Wolf and the Making of Poland: Paris, 1919," *Polin* 2 (1987): 5–36. Zionist representatives at the conference opposed the application of the principle of self-determination in Palestine. They wanted to delay the formation of a polity until Jews constituted a majority.

18. Fink, *Defending the Rights of Others*, 153–59, 244–46, 261.

19. Fink terms them a "hybrid experiment." See *Defending the Rights of Others*, 264. Cf. Janowsky, *The Jews and Minority Rights*, 360–69. For a sense of triumph, see the letter of Louis Marshall, Cyrus Adler, and Nahum Sokolow (July 11, 1919) to Boris Bogen quoted in ibid., 389–90.

20. *Protection of Linguistic, Racial and Religious Minorities by the League of Nations: Provisions Contained in the Various International Instruments at Present in Force* (Geneva: Publications de la Société des Nations; I. B. Minorités, 1927), 2. National representation was one Article (4) of the American Jewish Congress's "Jewish Bill of Rights" (1918). See Janowsky, *The Jews and Minority Rights*, 266–67.

21. Fink, *Defending the Rights of Others*, 215–16, 244–46.

22. Later signatories were Albania, Finland, Estonia, Latvia, and Lithuania. Ibid., 267, 278.

23. Ezra Mendelsohn, *The Jews of East Central Europe between the World Wars* (Bloomington: Indiana University Press, 1983), 5.

24. Janowsky, *The Jews and Minority Rights*, 230–40.

25. Mendelsohn, *The Jews of East Central Europe*, 23, cites 3.11 million in 1931. Polonsky, *The Jews in Poland and Russia*, 3:60, cites 2.11 million in 1921.

26. Abraham G. Duker, *The Situation of the Jews in Poland* (New York: American Jewish Congress, 1936), 7.

27. Catherine's Charter for the Towns (1785) permitted Jews to participate in municipal elections, yet officials blocked those who won offices by not permitting them to swear the required oath (chapter 6). After the adoption of the 1833 ordinance in Posen, Prussian officials limited Jews to one-third of municipal offices (chapter 12). On the eve of full rights (1866), the Galician Diet tried to introduce legislation stipulating that two-thirds of representatives in municipal government must be Christian (chapter 14).

28. Marcos Silber, "Ambivalent Citizenship: The Construction of Jewish Belonging in Emergent Poland, 1915–1918," *Simon Dubnow Institute Yearbook* 10 (2011): 161–83.

29. For tsarist Russia's notoriously incomplete registries of Jews' births, deaths, and marriages ("metrical books"), see Avrutin, *Jews and the Imperial State*, 58–85.

30. Shlomo Netzer, *Ma'avak Yehudei Polin al Zekhuyoteihem ha-Ezrahiyot veha-Leumiyot* (Tel Aviv: Tel Aviv University Press, 1980), 168–73; David Engel, "Citizenship in the Conceptual World of Polish Zionists," *Journal of Israeli History* 27, no. 2 (2008): 191–99.

31. Netzer, *Ma'avak Yehudei Polin*, 175–76.

32. Szymon Rudnicki, "The Jews' Battle in the Sejm for Equal Rights," in Slawomir Kapralski, ed., *The Jews in Poland*, 2 vols. (Cracow: Jagiellonian University Printing House, 1992–99), 2:148–153; Duker, *The Situation of the Jews in Poland*, 7–11. The three Jewish delegates were Apolinary Hartglass, Yitzchak Grünbaum, and Osias Thon. The attempted

repeals were: June 12, 1919; March 20, 1920; June 16, 1921: laws of Congress Poland; December 14, 1922: tsarist laws; July 27, 1923: Austrian laws; May 15, 1928.

33. Fink, *Defending the Rights of Others*, 283–94; Mark Levene, *War, Jews and the New Europe: The Diplomacy of Lucien Wolf, 1914–1919* (Oxford: Littman Library, 1992).

34. Polonsky, *The Jews in Poland and Russia*, 3:71–72; Netzer, *Ma'avak Yehudei Polin*, 177–78.

35. Rudnicki, "The Jews' Battle in the Sejm for Equal Rights," 154.

36. Szymon Rudnicki, "Anti-Jewish Legislation in Interwar Poland," in Robert Blobaum, ed., *Antisemitism and Its Opponents in Modern Poland* (Ithaca: Cornell University Press, 2005), 150–57; Polonsky, *The Jews in Poland and Russia*, 3:71.

37. Mendelsohn, *The Jews of East Central Europe*, 42–43.

38. Frank Golczewski, "The Problem of Sunday Rest in Interwar Poland," in Yisrael Gutman, Ezra Mendelsohn, Jehuda Reinharz, and Chone Shmeruk eds., *The Jews of Poland between Two World Wars* (Waltham, MA: Brandeis University Press, 1989), 158–72. Where police enforced the law, Jewish proprietors often found ways to circumvent it, e.g., bribery, using only the rear door.

39. Polonsky, *The Jews in Poland and Russia*, 3:73–74.

40. Rudnicki, "Anti-Jewish Legislation in Interwar Poland," 158.

41. Victor Karady and Peter Tibor Nagy, eds., introduction to *The Numerus Clausus in Hungary: Studies on the First Anti-Jewish Law and Academic Anti-Semitism in Modern Central Europe* (Budapest: Centre for Historical Research, 2012), 17; Peter Tibor Nagy, "The First Anti-Jewish Law in Inter-war Europe," in ibid., 56.

42. László Kontler, *A History of Hungary: Millennium in Central Europe* (Houndmills, Basingstoke: Palgrave Macmillan, 2002), 325–44.

43. Mária M. Kovács, "The Hungarian Numerus Clausus: Ideology, Apology and History, 1919–1945," in Karady and Nagy, eds., *The Numerus Clausus in Hungary*, 45; Nagy, "The First Anti-Jewish Law in Inter-war Europe," 60; Andor Ladányi, "On the 1928 Amendment to the Hungarian Numerus Clausus Act," in Karady and Nagy, eds., *The Numerus Clausus in Hungary*, 70.

44. Mendelsohn, *The Jews of East Central Europe*, 105.

45. Kovács, "The Hungarian Numerus Clausus," 28–29. The legislation left it to individual university faculties to decide whether converts should be included in the quota. The medical faculty at Budapest decided affirmatively. The government did not want to take responsibility for the legislation, fearing international repercussions: only a third of Parliament was present to vote on the law (32–33). Nagy, "The First Anti-Jewish Law in Inter-war Europe," 60–61.

46. Kovács, "The Hungarian Numerus Clausus," 46–52. For the flight of Jewish students abroad, see Michael Miller, "From White Terror to Red Vienna," in Frank Stern and Barbara Eichinger, eds., *Wien und die jüdische Erfahrung, 1900–1938* (Vienna: Böhlau, 209), 307–23.

47. Ladányi, "On the 1928 Amendment to the Hungarian Numerus Clausus Act," 74–82; Randolph L. Braham, *The Politics of Genocide: The Holocaust in Hungary*, 2 vols. (New York: Columbia University Press, 1981), 1:31–32; Mendelsohn, *The Jews of East Central Europe*, 109–10. For Vilmos Vázsonyi's speech, see András Kovács, "Hungarian Jewish Politics from the End of the Second World War until the Collapse of Communism," *Studies in Contemporary Jewry* 19 (2003): 127–28.

48. Kovács, "The Hungarian Numerus Clausus," 52; Ladányi, "On the 1928 Amendment to the Hungarian Numerus Clausus Act," 84–111.

49. István Deák, "Hungary and the Jewish Question, 1918–1944," in *The Auschwitz Reports and the Holocaust in Hungary* (Boulder, CO: Social Science Monographs, 2011), 9;

Mendelsohn, *The Jews of East Central Europe*, 106. For the Magyar-Jewish alliance's tense ambiguities, see Mary Gluck, *The Invisible Budapest: Metropolitan Culture at the Fin de siècle* (Madison: University of Wisconsin Press, 2016).

50. Steven Beller, *A Concise History of Austria* (Cambridge: Cambridge University Press, 2006), 197–231.

51. Herwig Wolfram, ed., *Österreichische Geschichte: Geschichte der Juden in Österreich* (Vienna: Ueberreuter, 2006), 497–504.

52. Quoted in Bruce F. Pauley, *From Prejudice to Persecution: A History of Austrian Anti-Semitism* (Chapel Hill: University of North Carolina Press, 1992), 86.

53. Harriet Pass Freidenrich, *Jewish Politics in Vienna, 1918–1938* (Bloomington: Indiana University Press, 1991), 12, 53–54; Fink, *Defending the Rights of Others*, 288.

54. Freidenrich, *Jewish Politics in Vienna*, 26; Pauley, *From Prejudice to Persecution*, 86–88. Between 1920 and 1925 some 20,360 Jews applied for Austrian citizenship.

55. Lukas Langhoff, *Staatsbürgerschaft und Heimatrecht in Österreich* (Vienna: Manzsche, 1920), 1–6. The treaties of St. Germain and Trianon retained local domicile (*Heimatrecht*) as the primary criterion of citizenship in the Austro-Hungarian successor states. R. Graupner, "Statelessness as a Consequence of Sovereignty over Territory after the Last War," in P. Weis and R. Graupner, *The Problem of Statelessness* (London: World Jewish Congress, 1944), 30–36.

56. Quoted in Miller, "From White Terror to Red Vienna," 312.

57. Pauley, *From Prejudice to Persecution*, 95.

58. Mendelsohn, *The Jews of East Central Europe*, 171–73.

59. Carol Iancu, *Jews in Romania, 1866–1919: From Exclusion to Emancipation* (Boulder, CO: East European Monographs, 1996), 179.

60. Ibid., 179–82.

61. Joshua Starr, "Jewish Citizenship in Rumania (1878–1940)," *Jewish Social Studies* 3, no. 1 (January 1941): 67.

62. Mendelsohn, *The Jews of East Central Europe*, 186.

63. Lucian Nastasă, "Anti-Semitism at Universities in Romania (1919–1939)," in Karady and Nagy, eds., *The Numerus Clausus in Hungary*, 219–42. The worst violence occurred in Oradea Mare in Transylvania.

64. Ronald Grigor Suny and Terry Martin, preface to *A State of Nations*, vii. The editors call the USSR "the first state to found its federation on the basis of territorialized nationality" and argue that it became "an empire of national states."

65. As early as 1914 Lenin planned to introduce equality for Jews and to recognize them as a nationality. See William Korey, "The Legal Position of Soviet Jewry: A Historical Enquiry," in Lionel Kochan, ed., *The Jews in Soviet Russia since 1917*, 3rd ed. (Oxford: Oxford University Press, 1978), 78.

66. Pinkus, *The Jews of the Soviet Union*, 53–54. For later constitutions (1925, 1936), see Korey, "The Legal Position of Soviet Jewry," 91.

67. Suny and Martin, introduction to *A State of Nations*, 12.

68. Korey, "The Legal Position of Soviet Jewry," 83–84.

69. Terry Martin, "An Affirmative Action Empire: The Soviet Union as the Highest Form of Imperialism," in Suny and Martin, eds., *A State of Nations*, 75. Lenin and Stalin understood these limited cultural rights as "oblast autonomy."

70. Polonsky, *The Jews in Poland and Russia*, 3:254.

71. Jacob Miller, "Soviet Theory on the Jews," in *The Jews in Soviet Russia since 1917*, 46–63.

72. Zvi Y. Gitelman, *Jewish Nationality and Soviet Politics: The Jewish Sections of the CPSU, 1917–1930* (Princeton: Princeton University Press, 1972).

73. Pinkus, *The Jews of the Soviet Union*, 66–71; Polonsky, *The Jews in Poland and Rus-*

sia, 3:269–70. For flourishing Jewish institutions in a provincial capital, see Elissa Bemporad, *Becoming Soviet Jews: The Bolshevik Experiment in Minsk* (Bloomington: Indiana University Press, 2013).

74. Korey, "The Legal Position of Soviet Jewry," 85.

75. Pinkus, *The Jews of the Soviet Union*, 70, 88, 193, 197.

76. Ibid., 92; Polonsky, *The Jews in Poland and Russia*, 3:283. Stalin abolished the category in his 1936 constitution when he declared the Soviet Union a "classless society." On the *lishchentsy*, see Elise Kimerling, "Civil Rights and Social Policy in Soviet Russia, 1918–1936," *Russian Review* 41, no. 1 (January 1982): 24–46 and Eric Lohr, *Russian Citizenship: From Empire to Soviet Union* (Cambridge, MA: Harvard University Press, 2012), 151–52.

77. Pinkus, *The Jews of the Soviet Union*, 64, 93, 99; Polonsky, *The Jews in Poland and Russia*, 3:243.

78. Kimerling, "Civil Rights and Social Policy in Soviet Russia," 45. Similarly, Golfo Alexopoulos, *Stalin's Outcasts: Aliens, Citizens and the Soviet State, 1926–1936* (Ithaca: Cornell University Press, 2003), 58: "Jewish communities tended to be the hardest hit by disenfranchisement after the government assault on private trade."

79. For petitions requesting restoration of rights that express precisely this sense, see Alexopoulos, *Stalin's Outcasts*, 80–81.

80. C. Abramsky, "The Biro-Bidzhan Project, 1927–1959," in *The Jews in Soviet Russia since 1917*, 67; Pinkus, *The Jews of the Soviet Union*, 181.

81. Yuri Slezkine, *The Jewish Century* (Princeton: Princeton University Press, 2004), 247.

82. Pinkus, *The Jews of the Soviet Union*, 86–87, 90–91, 96–97. For the extent of disenfranchisement in the former Pale of Settlement, see Bemporad, *Becoming Soviet Jews*, 34–38.

83. Alexopoulos, *Stalin's Outcasts*.

84. The population of the shtetl fell from 40% of Russian Jews in 1914 to 20% in 1929. See Polonsky, *The Jews in Poland and Russia*, 3:282–90.

85. Pinkus, *The Jews of the Soviet Union*, 94.

86. Polonsky, *The Jews in Poland and Russia*, 3:290–93.

87. Abramsky, "The Biro-Bidzhan Project," 73–74. By the 1970s Jews were less than 1% of the rural population. See Pinkus, *The Jews of the Soviet Union*, 264.

88. Abramsky, "The Biro-Bidzhan Project," 74–75; Miller, "Soviet Theory on the Jews," 57–58; Korey, "The Legal Position of Soviet Jewry," 81; Pinkus, *The Jews of the Soviet Union*, 74.

89. Korey, "The Legal Position of Soviet Jewry," 97.

90. Ibid., 92–97; Polonsky, *The Jews in Poland and Russia*, 3:257.

91. Korey, "The Legal Position of Soviet Jewry," 80; Pinkus, *The Jews of the Soviet Union*, 57, 212. On passports in the Stalinist system, see David Shearer, "Elements Near and Alien: Passportization, Policing and Identity in the Stalinist State, 1932–1952," *Journal of Modern History* 76 (2004): 835–81, who sees passports as a "demographic and geographic map . . . of Stalinist-style socialism" that served as a major "instrument of governance" (839–40).

Chapter Twenty-Three. Repudiation

1. Reinhard Rürup, "Das Ende der Emanzipation," in Arnold Paucker, ed., *Die Juden im Nationalsozialistischen Deutschland: The Jews in Nazi Germany, 1933–1943* (Tübingen: Mohr, 1986), 97–114; P. Weis, "Statelessness as a Legal-Political Problem," in P. Weis and R. Graupner, *The Problem of Statelessness* (London: World Jewish Congress, 1944), 21.

2. Avraham Barkai, *From Boycott to Annihilation: The Economic Struggle of German*

Jews, 1933–1943, trans. William Templer (Hanover, NH: Brandeis University Press, 1989), 188; Nahum Goldmann, *The Autobiography of Nahum Goldmann: Sixty Years of Jewish Life,* trans. Helen Sebba (New York: Holt, Rinehart & Winston, 1969), 139.

3. István Deák, "Hungary and the Jewish Question, 1918–1944," in *The Auschwitz Reports and the Holocaust in Hungary* (Boulder, CO: Social Science Monographs, 2011), 1.

4. Cited in Karl Schleunes, *The Twisted Road to Auschwitz: Nazi Policy toward German Jews, 1933–1939* (Urbana: University of Illinois Press, 1970), 70.

5. Rürup, "Das Ende der Emanzipation," 104; Peter Pulzer, "The Beginning of the End," in Paucker, ed., *Die Juden im Nationalsozialistischen Deutschland,* 26: "The process of disemancipation and dissimilation was a mirror-image of that of emancipation and assimilation, even if telescoped."

6. Joseph Walk, ed., *Das Sonderrecht für die Juden im NS-Staat: Eine Sammlung der gesetzlichen Maßnahmen und Richtlinien-Inhalt und Bedeutung* (Heidelberg: Müller, 1981), 12, translation in Bernard Dov Weinryb, *Jewish Emancipation under Attack: Its Legal Recession until the Present War* (New York: American Jewish Committee, 1942), 40–41. The law defined a "non-Aryan" as anyone having "one parent or grandparent . . . of Jewish faith."

7. Schleunes, *The Twisted Road to Auschwitz,* 102–6; Barkai, *From Boycott to Annihilation,* 26–27.

8. Barkai, *From Boycott to Annihilation,* 192n32; Walk, *Das Sonderrecht für die Juden,* 16–20.

9. Barkai, *From Boycott to Annihilation,* 28–31.

10. Walk, *Das Sonderrecht für die Juden,* 127; Weinryb, *Jewish Emancipation under Attack,* 45–46. That the Jews were denationalized "in fact, though not in law," see Weis, "Statelessness as a Legal-Political Problem," 9.

11. The term "state member" (*Staatsangehöriger*) was a nineteenth-century coinage (chapter 12).

12. Weinryb, *Jewish Emancipation under Attack,* 45.

13. James Q. Whitman, *Hitler's American Model: The United States and the Making of Nazi Race Law* (Princeton: Princeton University Press, 2017).

14. Carole Fink, *Defending the Rights of Others: The Great Powers, the Jews, and International Minority Protection, 1878–1938* (Cambridge: Cambridge University Press, 2004), 330.

15. Barkai, *From Boycott to Annihilation,* 57.

16. Ibid., 16–19, 34, 63–64, 69–77, 111.

17. Ibid., 33.

18. Ibid., 110.

19. There was an additional clarification on November 23, 1938 (*Verordnung zur Durchführung der Verordnung über die Ausschaltung der Juden aus dem deutschen Wirtschaftsleben*). Walk, *Das Sonderrecht für die Juden,* 254, 258; Weinryb, *Jewish Emancipation under Attack,* 53–54.

20. Martin Dean, *Robbing the Jews: The Confiscation of Jewish Property in the Holocaust, 1933–1945* (New York: Cambridge University Press, 2008), 94–95. Measures included "valuations by external business accountants."

21. Ibid., 2–3; Schleunes, *The Twisted Road to Auschwitz,* 132–68.

22. Dean, *Robbing the Jews,* 259. Dean labels this the "Vienna" or "Austrian model" (11, 108–10).

23. Weinryb, *Jewish Emancipation under Attack,* 49; Walk, *Das Sonderrecht für die Juden,* 223 (*Verordnung über die Anmeldung des Vermögens von Juden*).

24. Dean, *Robbing the Jews,* 136.

25. Ibid., 62, 113–16, 382; Weinryb, *Jewish Emancipation under Attack*, 53; Walk, *Das Sonderrecht für die Juden*, 255 (*Verordnung über eine Sühneleistung der Juden deutscher Staatsangehörigkeit*).

26. Dean, *Robbing the Jews*, 113, 232, 273–76, 355, 381–82; Weinryb, *Jewish Emancipation under Attack*, 49, 55–57; "Second Decree on the Basis of the Decree Regarding the Registration of Jewish Property," November 24, 1938; Walk, *Das Sonderrecht für die Juden*, 258–59 (*Anordnung auf Grund der Verordnung über die Anmeldung des Vermögens von Juden*); "Decree Regarding the Utilization of Jewish Property," December 3, 1938; Walk, *Das Sonderrecht für die Juden*, 262 (*Verordnung über den Einsatz des jüdischen Vermögens*).

27. Barkai, *From Boycott to Annihilation*, 100.

28. Weinryb, *Jewish Emancipation under Attack*, 56; Walk, *Das Sonderrecht für die Juden*, 262 (*Polizeipräsident Berlin*).

29. Barkai, *From Boycott to Annihilation*, 167; Weinryb, *Jewish Emancipation under Attack*, 57: "Law of Leases Contracted with Jews," April 30, 1939; Walk, *Das Sonderrecht für die Juden*, 292 (*Gesetz über Mietverhältnisse mit Juden*).

30. Weinryb, *Jewish Emancipation under Attack*, 54. On children's lives, see Marion A. Kaplan, *Between Dignity and Despair: Jewish Life in Nazi Germany* (New York: Oxford University Press, 1998), 94–118.

31. Barkai, *From Boycott to Annihilation*, 117; Weinryb, *Jewish Emancipation under Attack*, 47–48, "Law Regarding the Legal Status of the Jewish Religious Communities," March 28, 1939; Walk, *Das Sonderrecht für die Juden*, 219 (*Gesetz über die Rechtsverhältnisse der jüdischen Kultusvereinigungen*).

32. Barkai, *From Boycott to Annihilation*, 184; Walk, *Das Sonderrecht für die Juden*, 399 (*Vermögen der Reichsvereinigung*).

33. Barkai, *From Boycott to Annihilation*, 147; Walk, *Das Sonderrecht für die Juden*, 270 (*Arbeitseinsatz arbeitsloser Juden*).

34. Weinryb, *Jewish Emancipation under Attack*, 57–58.

35. Barkai, *From Boycott to Annihilation*, 159–62; Weinryb, *Jewish Emancipation under Attack*, 57–58 (March 4, 1941); Walk, *Das Sonderrecht für die Juden*, 336 (*Arbeitseinsatz von Juden*).

36. Schleunes, *The Twisted Road to Auschwitz*, 169–213; Michael R. Marrus, *The Holocaust in History* (Hanover, NH: Brandeis University Press, 1987), 25–30; Walk, *Das Sonderrecht für die Juden*, 353 (*Verbot der Auswanderung von Juden*).

37. Kaplan, *Between Dignity and Despair*, 73, 132. Abraham Margaliot, "Emigration: Planung und Wirklichkeit," in Paucker, ed., *Die Juden im Nationalsozialistischen Deutschland*, 303, gives the lower figure of 235,000 emigrants from a 1933 population of 520,000. Rürup, "Das Ende der Emanzipation," 113, asserts that two-thirds of German Jewry had left by 1941.

38. Mobile killing units (*Einsatzgruppen*) began mass shootings during the invasion of the Soviet Union. Historians debate whether the Nazis' decision to murder European Jewry stemmed from the elation of victory or the despair of defeat. See Schleunes, *The Twisted Road to Auschwitz*; Marrus, *The Holocaust in History*, 25–30; and Timothy Snyder, *Bloodlands: Europe between Hitler and Stalin* (New York: Basic Books, 2010), 187–223.

39. Dean, *Robbing the Jews*, 18, 161 (Law for Denaturalization and Confiscation of Political Opponents); Walk, *Das Sonderrecht für die Juden*, 36 (*Gesetz über Widerruf von Einbürgerungen und die Aberkennung der deutschen Staatsangehörigkeit*).

40. Dean, *Robbing the Jews*, 226–27; Walk, *Das Sonderrecht für die Juden*, 357 (*Verordnung zum Reichsbürgergesetz*); Weis, "Statelessness as a Legal-Political Problem," 9. The Nazis proposed similar legislation in preparation for the deportation of Romanian Jews.

See Jean Ancel, "Plans for the Deportation of the Rumanian Jews and Their Discontinuation in Light of Documentary Evidence (July–October 1942)," *Yad Vashem Studies* 16 (1984): 382–83.

41. Cited in Dean, *Robbing the Jews*, 226. For lists of the "expatriated," see Michael Hepp, ed., *Die Ausbürgerung deutscher Staatsangehöriger, 1933–1945, nach den in Reichsanzeiger veröffentlichten Listen*, 3 vols. (Munich: KG Saur, 1985–88).

42. Raphael Mahler, "Jews in Public Service and the Liberal Professions in Poland, 1918–39," *Jewish Social Studies* 6, no. 4 (1944): 291–350, esp. 297: "State employment was virtually barred to them; so too . . . was municipal employment."

43. Abraham G. Duker, *The Situation of the Jews in Poland* (New York: American Jewish Congress, 1936).

44. Yisrael Gutman, "Polish Antisemitism between the Wars: An Overview," in Yisrael Gutman, Ezra Mendelsohn, Jehuda Reinharz, and Chone Shmeruk eds., *The Jews of Poland between Two World Wars* (Waltham, MA: Brandeis University Press, 1989), 106–7; Ezra Mendelsohn, *The Jews of East Central Europe between the World Wars* (Bloomington: Indiana University Press, 1983), 69–70; Antony Polonsky, *The Jews in Poland and Russia*, 3 vols. (Oxford: Littman, 2010 –12), 3:78–79.

45. Polonsky, *The Jews in Poland and Russia*, 3:78.

46. For the new electoral laws and Jews' participation, see Joseph Marcus, *Social and Political History of the Jews in Poland, 1919–1939* (Berlin: Mouton, 1983), 349–54.

47. Cited in Mendelsohn, *The Jews of East Central Europe*, 71; Marcus, *Social and Political History of the Jews in Poland*, 364–69.

48. Szymon Rudnicki, "Anti-Jewish Legislation in Interwar Poland," in Robert Blobaum, ed., *Antisemitism and Its Opponents in Modern Poland* (Ithaca: Cornell University Press, 2005), 170; Mahler, "Jews in Public Service and the Liberal Professions in Poland," 309–50.

49. L. Yahil, "Madagascar: Phantom of a Solution for the Jewish Question," in Bela Vago and George L. Mosse, eds., *Jews and Non-Jews in Eastern Europe, 1918–1945* (New York: John Wiley, 1974), 315–34; Marcus, *Social and Political History of the Jews in Poland*, 387–410; Goldmann, *The Autobiography of Nahum Goldmann*, 171–72. For Poland's efforts to gain colonies for general emigration, including applications to the League of Nations, see Tara Zahra, "Zionism, Emigration and East European Colonialism," in Ethan B. Katz, Lisa Moses Leff, and Maud S. Mandel, eds., *Colonialism and the Jews* (Bloomington: Indiana University Press, 2017), 183–84.

50. Duker, *The Situation of the Jews in Poland*, 19–20; Marcus, *Social and Political History of the Jews in Poland*, 357–58.

51. Marcus, *Social and Political History of the Jews in Poland*, 356–57.

52. Emanuel Melzer, "Antisemitism in the Last Years of the Second Polish Republic," in Gutman et al., eds., *The Jews of Poland between Two World Wars*, 133.

53. Melzer, "Antisemitism in the Last Years of the Second Polish Republic," 129–30, 135; Mendelsohn, *The Jews of East Central Europe*, 73; Jerzy Tomaszewski, "The Role of Jews in Polish Commerce, 1918–39," in Gutman et al., eds., *The Jews of Poland between Two World Wars*, 153–54; Mahler, "Jews in Public Service and the Liberal Professions in Poland," 312.

54. Mahler, "Jews in Public Service and the Liberal Professions in Poland," 318–23.

55. Ibid., 327–50.

56. Snyder, *Bloodlands*, 119–54.

57. Dean, *Robbing the Jews*, 383, 177.

58. Walk, *Das Sonderrecht für die Juden*, 304, September 7, 1939, Incarceration of Polish Jews (*Inschutznahme polnischer Juden*).

59. Dean, *Robbing the Jews*, 177–83.

60. Ibid., 187.

61. Walk, *Das Sonderrecht für die Juden*, 327, September 17, 1940 (*Verordnung über das Vermögen von Angehörigen des ehemals polnischen Staates*).

62. Walk, *Das Sonderrecht für die Juden*, 355–56, November 15, 1941 (*Behandlung von Grundstücken im Eigentum von Juden mit ehemals polnischer Staatsangehörigkeit*).

63. Jan Tomasz Gross, "The Sovietisation of Western Ukraine and Western Beylorussia," in Norman Davies and Antony Polonsky, eds., *Jews in Eastern Poland and the USSR, 1939–46* (Houndmills, Basingstoke: Macmillan, 1991), 60–76.

64. Ben-Cion Pinchuk, *Shtetl Jews under Soviet Rule: Eastern Poland on the Eve of the Holocaust* (Oxford: Blackwell, 1990), 6, 97–99, 111, 128–29; Polonsky, *The Jews in Poland and Russia*, 3:387–88; Gross, "The Sovietisation of Western Ukraine and Western Beylorussia," 70–71.

65. Pinchuk, *Shtetl Jews under Soviet Rule*, 35–37, 95. Many of the leaders and intellectuals fled to Vilnius.

66. Ibid., 39–40, 65–79; Polonsky, *The Jews in Poland and Russia*, 3:394–95.

67. Polonsky, *The Jews in Poland and Russia*, 3:382–84, 396–99; Pinchuk, *Shtetl Jews under Soviet Rule*, 102–16; Snyder, *Bloodlands*, 141, 151; Gross, "The Sovietisation of Western Ukraine and Western Beylorussia," 72–73. Jews were deported in the third of four deportations.

68. Polonsky, *The Jews in Poland and Russia*, 3:378; Pinchuk, *Shtetl Jews under Soviet Rule*, 5–11.

69. The Soviet authorities transformed the physical shtetl by replacing or repurposing old buildings. The public celebration of the Jewish holidays and rituals disappeared or went indoors. See Pinchuk, *Shtetl Jews under Soviet Rule*, 92–101, 130–33.

70. Ibid., 44, 46–47.

71. Polonsky, *The Jews in Poland and Russia*, 3:390–91; Pinchuk, *Shtetl Jews under Soviet Rule*, 49–51. Thousands of former middle-class Jews and refugees also participated in the parallel black-market economy, which Soviet personnel patronized (60–64).

72. Mendelsohn, *The Jews of East Central Europe*, 116.

73. Raul Hilberg, *The Destruction of the European Jews*, 2nd ed. (New York: New Viewpoints, 1973), 473.

74. Deák, "Hungary and the Jewish Question," 10–11; Randolph L. Braham, *The Politics of Genocide: The Holocaust in Hungary*, 2 vols. (New York: Columbia University Press, 1981), 1:118–27. Braham reproduces Darányi's infamous speech at Györ justifying the law (121).

75. Israel Cohen, "The Jews in Hungary," *Contemporary Review* 156 (July 1, 1939): 573; Braham, *The Politics of Genocide*, 125–26. For a contemporary justification, see László Ottlik, "The Hungarian Jewish Law," *Hungarian Quarterly* 4, no. 3 (1938): 399–412: "the Nuremberg laws which explicitly exclude the Jews from the ranks of the German nation and deprive them of any public status, and the Hungarian measure which neither interferes with their public rights or [*sic*] their equality in the eyes of the law, but merely tries to make room for Gentile Hungarians in walks of life where they have been hopelessly crowded out by Jewish predominance" (403–4).

76. Braham, *The Politics of Genocide*, 122–23.

77. Cohen, "The Jews in Hungary," 578. For the text of the law, see Weinryb, *Jewish Emancipation under Attack*, 70–80. For its uneven implementation yet devastating impact on "the lower middle class, the intellectuals, and the *lumpenproletariat*," see Yehuda Don, "The Economic Effect of Antisemitic Discrimination: Hungarian Anti-Jewish Legislation, 1938–1944," *Jewish Social Studies* 48 (1986): 63–82 and Hilberg, *The Destruction of the European Jews*, 514–17.

78. Weis, "Statelessness as a Legal-Political Problem," 11.

79. Weinryb, *Jewish Emancipation under Attack*, 72: "only if he himself and his parents—likewise their parents, if his parents were born after December 31, 1867—were born in Hungary and are able to prove authentically, and in addition to other prerequisites stipulated by law, that his parents or—assuming that his parents were born after December 31, 1867—their antecedents have lived continuously on Hungarian territory since December 31, 1867."

80. Cohen, "The Jews in Hungary," 578–79. Hungary was a destination for Jewish refugees from 1918 to 1944. See Livia Rothkirchen, "Hungary: An Asylum for the Refugees of Europe," *Yad Vashem Studies* 7 (1968): 127–42.

81. Braham, *The Politics of Genocide*, 194–95; Hilberg, *The Destruction of the European Jews*, 512–14.

82. Mendelsohn, *The Jews of East Central Europe*, 124–25.

83. Hilberg, *The Destruction of the European Jews*, 517–21.

84. Randolph L. Braham, "The Kamenets Podolsk and Délvidék Massacres: Prelude to the Holocaust in Hungary," *Yad Vashem Studies* 9 (1973): 133–56.

85. Horthy prohibited further deportations on July 7, 1944. See Deák, "Hungary and the Jewish Question," 19–22, who asserts that Szálasi's government deserves credit as well; Hilberg, *The Destruction of the European Jews*, 547–54.

86. Hilberg, *The Destruction of the European Jews*, 485. For a review of scholarship, see Roland Clark, "New Models, New Questions: Historiographical Approaches to the Romanian Holocaust," *European Review of History* 19, no. 2 (2012): 303–20.

87. Mendelsohn, *The Jews of East Central Europe*, 204; Weinryb, *Jewish Emancipation under Attack*, 64–65.

88. Jean Ancel, *The Economic Destruction of Romanian Jewry* (Jerusalem: Yad Vashem, 2007), 38–39; Mendelsohn, *The Jews of East Central Europe*, 206–7.

89. Joshua Starr, "Jewish Citizenship in Rumania (1878–1940)," *Jewish Social Studies* 3, no. 1 (1941): 72; Ancel, *The Economic Destruction of Romanian Jewry*, 41–42; Weis, "Statelessness as a Legal-Political Problem," 12. The decree is reproduced in Romanian and German in Jean Ancel, ed., *Documents Concerning the Fate of Romanian Jewry during the Holocaust*, 12 vols. (New York: Beate Klarsfeld Foundation, 1986), 8:162–77.

90. Quoted in Mendelsohn, *The Jews of East Central Europe*, 205.

91. Radu Ioanid, *The Holocaust in Romania: The Destruction of Jews and Gypsies under the Antonescu Regime, 1940–1944* (Chicago: Ivan R. Dee, 2000), 19.

92. Starr, "Jewish Citizenship in Rumania," 76–77.

93. Ibid., 80.

94. Ibid., 77; Weinryb, *Jewish Emancipation under Attack*, 66; Henry Eaton, *The Origins and Onset of the Romanian Holocaust* (Detroit: Wayne State University Press, 2013), 53.

95. Ancel, *The Economic Destruction of Romanian Jewry*, 56–58.

96. Ibid., 58–59.

97. Ioanid, *The Holocaust in Romania*, 20–21; Eaton, *The Origins and Onset of the Romanian Holocaust*, 49–50; Hilberg, *The Destruction of the European Jews*, 488. For the decree, see Ancel, *Documents Concerning the Fate of Romanian Jewry during the Holocaust*, 8:185–88.

98. Ancel, *The Economic Destruction of Romanian Jewry*, 65–68.

99. Ibid., 77–78.

100. Ioanid, *The Holocaust in Romania*, 24–25; Hilberg, *The Destruction of the European Jews*, 488–91; Ancel, *The Economic Destruction of Romanian Jewry*, 147–53.

101. Ancel, *The Economic Destruction of Romanian Jewry*, 88–132.

102. "The mass murder of Jews was neither a by-product of war nor collateral damage but an integral part and predefined goal of the Eastern campaign." See Simon Geissbühler, "What We Know about Romania and the Holocaust," in Geissbühler, ed., *Romania and the Holocaust: Events-Contexts-Aftermath* (Stuttgart: Ibidem-Verlag, 2016), 249 and Vladimir Solonari, *Purifying the Nation: Population Exchange and Ethnic Cleansing in Nazi-Allied Romania* (Baltimore: Johns Hopkins University Press, 2010). Violence against Jews started prior to the war. Romanian soldiers massacred Jews as they withdrew from Bessarabia and Bukovina in 1940. See Ioanid, *The Holocaust in Romania*, 37–61. Iron Guardists staged lethal pogroms elsewhere. For the example of Iasi, see Radu Ioanid, "The Holocaust in Romania: The Iasi Pogrom of June 1941," *Contemporary European History* 2, no. 2 (1993): 119–48. When Antonescu defeated an Iron Guard putsch (January 20, 1941), the Legionaries staged a pogrom in Bucharest. See Eaton, *The Origins and Onset of the Romanian Holocaust*, 67–68.

103. Eaton, *The Origins and Onset of the Romanian Holocaust*, 73; Hilberg, *The Destruction of the European Jews*, 491–92.

104. Hilberg, *The Destruction of the European Jews*, 494–96. The camps murdered Jews through starvation and mass shootings. Antonescu explicitly approved the murders: "We must not be afraid of going down in history as barbarians." See Th. Lavi, "The Background to the Rescue of Romanian Jewry during the Period of the Holocaust," in Vago and Mosse, eds., *Jews and Non-Jews in Eastern Europe*, 178 and Dennis Deletant, *Hitler's Forgotten Ally: Ion Antonescu and His Regime, Romania, 1940–44* (Houndmills: Palgrave Macmillan, 2006). The Romanian governor had decreed Transnistria a "penal colony for Jews" (November 11, 1941). See Joseph B. Schechtman, "The Transnistria Reservation," *YIVO Annual of Jewish Social Science* 8 (1953): 178–96.

105. Hilberg, *The Destruction of the European Jews*, 485.

106. Ancel, *The Economic Destruction of Romanian Jewry*, xx.

107. Ibid., 160–68.

108. Hilberg, *The Destruction of the European Jews*, 498–99.

109. Ioanid, *The Holocaust in Romania*, 238–58, 271–88; Hilberg, *The Destruction of the European Jews*, 485, 499–503. Antonescu saw the Jews of Bessarabia as hostile Communists; the Jews of Old Romania were merely unwanted aliens. See Stephen Fischer-Galati, "Fascism, Communism and the Jewish Question in Romania," in Vago and Mosse, eds., *Jews and Non-Jews in Eastern Europe*, 157–76, esp. 171. For Antonescu's shifting policies, see Lavi, "The Background to the Rescue of Romanian Jewry during the Period of the Holocaust," 177–86. For the combination of motives, see Ancel, "Plans for the Deportation of the Rumanian Jews," 381–420.

110. Hilberg, *The Destruction of the European Jews*, 503; Ancel, *The Economic Destruction of Romanian Jewry*, 330–32, 345–53.

111. For the emphasis on racism's diplomatic role, see Maurizio Cabona, "Mussolini and the Jews," *Telos* 133 (2006): 95–119; Renzo de Felice, *The Jews in Fascist Italy* (New York: Enigma Books, 2001); and Meir Michaelis, *Mussolini and the Jews: German-Italian Relations and the Jewish Question in Italy, 1922–1945* (Oxford: Oxford University Press, 1978).

112. Ilaria Pavan, "Fascism, Anti-Semitism, and Racism: An Ongoing Debate," *Telos* 164 (Fall 2013): 52–62.

113. Michele Sarfatti, *The Jews in Mussolini's Italy: From Equality to Persecution* (Madison: University of Wisconsin Press, 2006), 42–110.

114. Ibid., 101.

115. Ibid., 138.

116. Franklin Hugh Adler, "Why Mussolini Turned on the Jews," *Patterns of Prejudice* 39, no. 3 (2005): 285–300; Adler, "Jew as Bourgeois, Jew as Enemy, Jew as Victim of Fas-

cism," *Modern Judaism* 28, no. 3 (2008): 306–26; Pavan, "Fascism, Anti-Semitism, and Racism."

117. Adler, "Why Mussolini Turned on the Jews," 298–99; Sarfatti, *The Jews in Mussolini's Italy*, 144–46.

118. Susan Zuccotti, *The Italians and the Holocaust: Persecution, Rescue & Survival*, 2nd ed. (Lincoln: University of Nebraska Press, 1996), xxv, 5, 35–36; Sarfatti, *The Jews in Mussolini's Italy*, 126–27.

119. Sarfatti, *The Jews in Mussolini's Italy*, 155–56; Weinryb, *Jewish Emancipation under Attack*, 81–82.

120. Zuccotti, *The Italians and the Holocaust*, 36; Weinryb, *Jewish Emancipation under Attack*, 81.

121. Weinryb, *Jewish Emancipation under Attack*, 82–86.

122. Zuccotti, *The Italians and the Holocaust*, 38; Sarfatti, *The Jews in Mussolini's Italy*, 151.

123. Sarfatti, *The Jews in Mussolini's Italy*, 153–54.

124. Cited in ibid., 153.

125. Ibid.

126. Dean, *Robbing the Jews*, 353.

127. Adler, "Jew as Bourgeois, Jew as Enemy," 318.

128. Zuccotti, *The Italians and the Holocaust*, 52–61; Sarfatti, *The Jews in Mussolini's Italy*, 147–50.

129. Zuccotti, *The Italians and the Holocaust*, xxvi.

130. Sarfatti, *The Jews in Mussolini's Italy*, 171–73.

131. Ibid., 178–211; Zuccotti, *The Italians and the Holocaust*, 139–65.

132. Michael R. Marrus and Robert O. Paxton, *Vichy France and the Jews*, 2nd ed. (Stanford: Stanford University Press, 1995), 359, see also 12–13, 366, 369. Scholars continue to debate the extent to which France's policies were autonomous. For German pressure and example, see Laurent Joly, "The Genesis of Vichy's Jewish Statute of October 1940," *Holocaust and Genocide Studies* 27, no. 2 (2013): 276–98. For Vichy's autonomy, see Michael Mayer, " 'Die französische Regierung packt die Judenfrage ohne Umschweife an': Vichy-Frankreich, deutsche Besatzungsmacht und der Beginn der 'Judenpolitik' im Sommer/ Herbst 1940," *Vierteljahreshefte für Zeitgeschichte* 58, no. 3 (2010): 329–62.

133. Marrus and Paxton, *Vichy France and the Jews*, 89, 138. Xavier Vallat (1891–1972), Commissariat-General for Jewish Affairs, formulated the initial program.

134. Patrick Weil, *How to Be French: Nationality in the Making since 1789*, trans. Catherine Porter (Durham: Duke University Press, 2008), 67–71.

135. Michael R. Marrus, *The Unwanted: European Refugees in the Twentieth Century* (New York: Oxford University Press, 1985), 67–71. From 1921 to 1926 foreigners increased by 60% (1,532,000 to 2,409,000), comprising 6% of the population. Weil, *How to Be French*, 66.

136. Marrus and Paxton, *Vichy France and the Jews*, xviii.

137. Ibid., 55–56. There were eventually thirty-one camps in the unoccupied zone (165). For the scandalous, often lethal conditions at Gurs, Rivesaltes, Le Vernet, Les Milles, and elsewhere, see 172–76.

138. Ibid., 68–69. For the example of a Polish Jew (Zosa Szajkowski) who was not naturalized, volunteered for the French Foreign Legion, fought in the war, and then became stateless, see Lisa Moses Leff, *The Archive Thief: The Man Who Salvaged French Jewish History in the Wake of the Holocaust* (New York: Oxford University Press, 2015), 51–52.

139. Weil, *How to Be French*, 107–24.

140. Claire Andrieu, ed., *La persecution des Juifs de France, 1940–1944, et le rétablisse-*

ment de la légalité républicaine: Recueil des textes officiels, 1940–1999 (Paris: La Documentation française, 2000), 89. Joly, "The Genesis of Vichy's Jewish Statute of October 1940," 288–91; Mayer, "'Die französische Regierung packt die Judenfrage ohne Umschweife an,'" 338–50; Marrus and Paxton, *Vichy France and the Jews*, 3–4. Six senators and twelve deputies identified as Jews were removed from office (149). The Nazis abolished the citizenship of all German Jews in occupied France (November 15, 1940). See Walk, *Das Sonderrecht für die Juden*, 330 (*Kollektive Ausbürgerung der deutschen Juden im besetzten Frankreich*).

141. Andrieu, *La persecution des Juifs de France*, 90.

142. Ibid., 102–3.

143. Ibid., 108–9; Dean, *Robbing the Jews*, 300–310; Marrus and Paxton, *Vichy France and the Jews*, 104–6. Altogether there were 67 texts with 397 articles governing "aryanization." By May 1, 1944, the Vichy authorities had placed some 42,227 Jewish enterprises in trusteeship (153). Besides enriching individuals, aryanization promoted the concentration of business (159). Endemic from the start, corruption increased dramatically under Darquier (294–96).

144. Marrus and Paxton, *Vichy France and the Jews*, 98–99.

145. Ibid., 125–37, 146.

146. Asher Cohen, "Pétain, Horthy, Antonescu and the Jews, 1942–1944: Toward a Comparative View," *Yad Vashem Studies* 18 (1987): 74–77; Marrus and Paxton, *Vichy France and the Jews*, 85.

147. Marrus and Paxton, *Vichy France and the Jews*, 115, 167. The Germans made it an even thousand with randomly arrested foreign Jews (226).

148. Andrieu, *La persecution des Juifs de France*, 139; Marrus and Paxton, *Vichy France and the Jews*, 148. The Vichy government rejected the German practice of requiring Jews to wear a Star of David (209–10, 236).

149. Marrus and Paxton, *Vichy France and the Jews*, 170, 227–28. Nazi bureaucrats wanted all French deportees to be stripped of citizenship.

150. Ibid., 286–87. Louis Darquier de Pellepoix (1897–1980) was appointed Commissariat-General for Jewish Affairs on May 6, 1942. Vichy's last legislation for Jews was the December 11, 1942, decree requiring that *Juif* be inscribed in all identity papers. Darquier did not subsequently succeed in enacting legislation (291).

151. Ibid., 233, 260. The deportations of summer 1942 aroused public opposition (270–79) and discredited the Vichy regime.

152. Ibid., 321–29.

153. Ibid., 228, 241, 304–9, 324.

154. Weil, *How to Be French*, 121; Marrus and Paxton, *Vichy France and the Jews*, 329–30.

155. Marrus and Paxton, *Vichy France and the Jews*, 323, 334–35.

156. Andrieu, *La persecution des Juifs de France*, 91; Marrus and Paxton, *Vichy France and the Jews*, 193–97.

Chapter Twenty-Four. Reinstatement

1. Pieter Lagrou, "Return to a Vanished World: European Societies and the Remnants of Their Jewish Communities, 1945–47," in David Bankier, ed., *The Jews Are Coming Back: The Return of the Jews to Their Countries of Origin after WWII* (Jerusalem: Yad Vashem, 2005), 14–15. For the "chain of exclusion" in Holland, see Dienke Hondius, "Bitter Homecoming: The Return and Reception of Dutch and Stateless Jews in the Netherlands," in ibid., 108–35.

2. Michael Brenner, *After the Holocaust: Rebuilding Jewish Lives in Postwar Germany*

(Princeton: Princeton University Press, 1997), 16–18. The Jewish Displaced Persons (DPs) increased from 40,000 in 1946 to 182,000 in 1947. The overwhelming majority (167,000) were in the American zone. The British zone had some 12,000, the French zone some 1,200. Earl Harrison's report to President Truman (August 1945) was explosive precisely because it recognized the Jews' specific experience and advocated separate camps. See Atina Grossmann, *Jews, Germans, and Allies: Close Encounters in Occupied Germany* (Princeton: Princeton University Press, 2007), 138–40.

3. Lagrou, "Return to a Vanished World," 5–6. Some twelve million ethnic Germans were expelled or chose to migrate westward. Grossmann, *Jews, Germans, and Allies*, 132.

4. Renée Poznanski, "French Apprehensions, Jewish Expectations: From a Social Imaginary to a Political Practice," in Bankier, ed., *The Jews Are Coming Back*, 34.

5. Patrick Weil, "The Return of Jews in the Nationality or in the Territory of France," in Bankier, ed., *The Jews Are Coming Back*, 69; Poznanski, "French Apprehensions, Jewish Expectations," 34.

6. Weil, "The Return of Jews," 64; Ronald W. Zweig, *German Reparations and the Jewish World: A History of the Claims Conference*, 2nd ed. (London: Frank Cass, 2001), 49. Weil asserted the "egalitarian republicans" triumphed in the postwar battle over citizenship (71).

7. Poznanski, "French Apprehensions, Jewish Expectations," 41–44.

8. Guri Schwarz, *After Mussolini: Jewish Life and Jewish Memories in Post-Fascist Italy* (London: Vallentine Mitchell, 2012), 5.

9. Mario Toscano, "The Abrogation of Racial Laws and the Reintegration of Jews in Italian Society (1943–1948)," in Bankier, ed., *The Jews Are Coming Back*, 150–56. This ambiguity is reminiscent of the Bourbon restoration's 1814 Charter. See chapter 11.

10. Schwarz, *After Mussolini*, 21–24. The Jewish establishment wanted to retain compulsory membership.

11. F. C. Brasz, "After the Second World War: From 'Jewish Church' to Cultural Minority," in J. C. H. Blom, R. G. Fuks-Mansfeld, and I. Schöffer, eds., *The History of Jews in the Netherlands* (Oxford: Littman Library, 2002), 338.

12. Hondius, "Bitter Homecoming," 112–13.

13. Conny Kristel, "Revolution and Reconstruction: Dutch Jewry after the Holocaust," in Bankier, ed., *The Jews Are Coming Back*, 139.

14. Cited in Hondius, "Bitter Homecoming," 119.

15. The Federal Republic remained under Allied supervision until 1955, when it achieved full sovereignty. Grossmann, *Jews, Germans, and Allies*, 252, 267.

16. "On Measures for Eliminating Defects in Selection and Training of Personnel in Connection with Serious Mistakes Revealed in the Work with Cadres in the Ministry of the Automobile and Tractor Industry" (June 21, 1950); Gennadi Kostyrchenko, "The Genesis of Establishment Anti-Semitism in the USSR: The Black Years, 1948–1953," in Zvi Gitelman and Yaacov Ro'I, eds., *Revolution, Repression, and Revival: The Soviet Jewish Experience* (Lanham, MD: Rowman and Littlefield, 2007), 187–88; Benjamin Pinkus, *The Jews of the Soviet Union: The History of a National Minority* (Cambridge: Cambridge University Press, 1988), 139–208.

17. Stalin's policies inspired trials across the east bloc: Rajk in Hungary, Slansky in Czechoslovakia, and Pauker and Luca in Romania. See Antony Polonsky, *The Jews in Poland and Russia*, 3 vols. (Oxford: Littman, 2010–12), 3:601.

18. Kostyrchenko, "The Genesis of Establishment Anti-Semitism," 185–89.

19. Polonsky, *The Jews in Poland and Russia*, 3:658.

20. András Kovács, "Hungarian Jewish Politics from the End of the Second World War until the Collapse of Communism," *Studies in Contemporary Jewry* 19 (2003): 137–38. All Hungarians were deprived of rights.

21. With emigration Romania's Jewish population dropped from 430,000 (1945); to 144,198 (1956); to 100,000 (1965); to 19,000 (1989). Leon Volovici, "Romanian Jewry under Rabbi Moses Rosen during the Ceausescu Regime," *Studies in Contemporary Jewry* 19 (2003): 183–86; Liviu Rotman, "Romanian Jewry: The First Decade after the Holocaust," in Randolph L. Braham, ed., *The Tragedy of Romanian Jewry* (New York: Columbia University Press, 1994), 288. The West German government similarly ransomed ethnic Germans. See Charles Hoffman, *Gray Dawn: The Jews of Eastern Europe in the Post-Communist Era* (New York: HarperCollins, 1992), 127.

22. Irena Hurwic-Nowakowska, *A Social Analysis of Postwar Polish Jewry* (Jerusalem: Shazar Center, 1986), 38.

23. Ibid., 41.

24. Natalia Aleksiun, "The Vicious Circle: Jews in Communist Poland, 1944–1956," *Studies in Contemporary Jewry* 19 (2003): 170. Poland's Jewish population shrank in a decade from 240,000 (1946) to 88,257 (1948) to 25,000–30,000 (1956–57) (159–60). There were perhaps 70,000 to 80,000 Jews in 1952. Cf. Polonsky, *The Jews in Poland and Russia*, 3:607, 646; Hurwic-Nowakowska, *A Social Analysis*, 31.

25. Hurwic-Nowakowska, *A Social Analysis*, 45–50; Polonsky, *The Jews in Poland and Russia*, 3:645.

26. Polonsky, *The Jews in Poland and Russia*, 3:647.

27. In the Netherlands, the return of possessions to the rightful owners was called "restoration of legal rights" (*Rechtsherstel*). Martin Dean, *Robbing the Jews: The Confiscation of Jewish Property in the Holocaust, 1933–1945* (New York: Cambridge University Press, 2008), 4.

28. Gerard Aalders, "A Disgrace? Postwar Restitution of Looted Jewish Property in the Netherlands," in Chaya Brasz and Yosef Kaplan, eds., *Dutch Jews as Perceived by Themselves and by Others* (Leiden: Brill, 2001), 395.

29. David Bankier, introduction to *The Jews Are Coming Back*, viii.

30. Poznanski, "French Apprehensions, Jewish Expectations," 31.

31. Zweig, *German Reparations*, 11; Michael R. Marrus, *Some Measure of Justice: The Holocaust Era Restitution Campaign of the 1990s* (Madison: University of Wisconsin Press, 2009), 68. The Inter-Allied Declaration is reprinted in Nehemiah Robinson, *Indemnification and Reparations: Jewish Aspects* (New York: Institute of Jewish Affairs, 1944), 275–78.

32. Poznanski, "French Apprehensions, Jewish Expectations," 28–29, 29n12.

33. Claire Andrieu, "Two Approaches to Compensation in France: Restitution and Reparation," in Martin Dean, Constantin Goschler, and Philipp Ther, eds., *Robbery and Restitution: The Conflict over Jewish Property in Europe* (New York: Berghahn Books, 2007), 145.

34. Poznanski, "French Apprehensions, Jewish Expectations," 46–47.

35. Andrieu, "Two Approaches to Compensation in France," 134–35.

36. Ibid., 136.

37. Ibid., 137–38.

38. Toscano, "The Abrogation of Racial Laws and the Reintegration of Jews in Italian Society," 150–54.

39. Ilaria Pavan, "Indifference and Forgetting: Italy and Its Jewish Community, 1938–1970," in Dean, Goschler, and Ther, eds., *Robbery and Restitution*, 175, 179; Schwarz, *After Mussolini*, 12.

40. Aalders, "A Disgrace?" 396–97.

41. Ibid., 397–403.

42. Marilyn Henry, *Confronting the Perpetrators: A History of the Claims Conference*

(London: Vallentine Mitchell, 2007), 161–63; Nahum Goldmann, *The Autobiography of Nahum Goldmann: Sixty Years of Jewish Life*, trans. Helen Sebba (New York: Holt, Rinehart & Winston, 1969), 281–82.

43. Robert Knight, "Restitution and Legitimacy in Post-war Austria, 1945–53," *Leo Baeck Institute Yearbook* 36 (1991): 413–41; Henry, *Confronting the Perpetrators*, 151–63.

44. Regula Ludi, "'Why Switzerland?' Remarks on a Neutral's Role in the Nazi Program of Robbery and Allied Postwar Restitution Policy," in Dean, Goschler, and Ther, eds., *Robbery and Restitution*, 196.

45. Ludi, "'Why Switzerland?'" 197–99.

46. Federal Councilor Ludwig von Moos cited in ibid., 195.

47. Zweig, *German Reparations*, 15.

48. Gerald D. Feldman, "Reflections on the Restitution and Compensation of Holocaust Theft: Past, Present, Future," in Dean, Goschler, and Ther, eds., *Robbery and Restitution*, 266–67; Eduard Kubů and Jan Kuklík Jr., "Reluctant Restitution: The Restitution of Jewish Property in the Bohemian Lands after the Second World War," in Dean, Goschler, and Ther, eds., *Robbery and Restitution*, 223–39; Dariusz Stola, "The Polish Debate on the Holocaust and the Restitution of Property," in Dean, Goschler, and Ther, eds., *Robbery and Restitution*, 240–55.

49. Jürgen Lillteicher, "West Germany and the Restitution of Jewish Property in Europe," in Dean, Goschler, and Ther, eds., *Robbery and Restitution*, 103.

50. Kubů and Kuklík, "Reluctant Restitution," 233–34.

51. Volovici, "Romanian Jewry under Rabbi Moses Rosen during the Ceausescu Regime," 183.

52. Stola, "The Polish Debate on the Holocaust," 244.

53. Aleksiun, "The Vicious Circle," 169. Stola claims that Poland did restore some Jewish communal property, as it did for the other religions. See "The Polish Debate on the Holocaust," 249.

54. For Poland's denial of Jewish suffering, see Joanna Michlic, "The Holocaust and Its Aftermath as Perceived in Poland: Voice of Polish Intellectuals, 1945–47," in Bankier, ed., *The Jews Are Coming Back*, 206–30. For the USSR and east bloc, see Timothy Snyder, *Bloodlands: Europe between Hitler and Stalin* (New York: Basic, 2010), 339–77.

55. Zweig, *German Reparations*, 15, 140, 188.

56. For Germans as "victims," see Grossmann, *Jews, Germans, and Allies*, 15–86.

57. Constantin Goschler, "Jewish Property and the Politics of Restitution," in Dean, Goschler, and Ther, eds., *Robbery and Restitution*, 120.

58. Lillteicher, "West Germany and the Restitution of Jewish Property," 102; Grossmann, *Jews, Germans, and Allies*, 174. On the "enigma of German irresponsibility," see Moses Moskowitz, "The Germans and the Jews: Postwar Report," *Commentary* 2 (July 1946): 7–14.

59. Lillteicher, "West Germany and the Restitution of Jewish Property," 103–8; Grossmann, *Jews, Germans, and Allies*, 114; Peter Hayes, "Plunder and Restitution," in Peter Hayes and John K. Roth, eds., *Oxford Handbook of the Holocaust* (New York: Oxford University Press, 2010), 548.

60. Hayes, "Plunder and Restitution," 550.

61. Lillteicher, "West Germany and the Restitution of Jewish Property," 103–6; Goschler, "Jewish Property and the Politics of Restitution," 123–25.

62. Hayes, "Plunder and Restitution," 549; Henry, *Confronting the Perpetrators*, 106.

63. Goschler, "Jewish Property and the Politics of Restitution," 126–29.

64. In international law until 1945, the term "reparations" was applied to "compensation by agreement between former belligerent states for war and occupation damages." The re-

sulting agreement was a "treaty." See Lucy Dawidowicz, "German Collective Indemnity to Israel and the Conference on Jewish Material Claims against Germany," *American Jewish Year Book* 54 (1953): 471, 483. Subsequent usage has widened to include various forms of compensation. See Pablo de Greiff, ed., *The Handbook of Reparations* (Oxford: Oxford University Press, 2006).

65. Feldman, "Reflections on the Restitution and Compensation of Holocaust Theft," 262; Marrus, *Some Measure of Justice*, 73–75.

66. Andrieu, "Two Approaches to Compensation in France"; Zweig, *German Reparations*, vii, 9. Switzerland and its banks had been a major obstacle in postwar negotiations (3).

67. Zweig, *German Reparations*, 33. Jewish aid organizations had spent some $1.1 billion (1933–51).

68. Ibid., 187–88. In Italy, Greece, Holland, Hungary, and Poland "heirless assets" were assigned to the organized Jewish communities (188). For contemporary accounts of statelessness, see P. Weis and R. Graupner, *The Problem of Statelessness* (London: World Jewish Congress, 1944) and Hannah Arendt, "The Stateless People," *Contemporary Jewish Record* 8, no. 2 (April 1, 1945): 137–53.

69. Cited in Zweig, *German Reparations*, 21.

70. Ibid., 106. For the negotiations, see *Documents Relating to the Agreement between the Government of Israel and the Government of the Federal Republic of Germany* (Jerusalem: Ministry for Foreign Affairs, 1953); Nana Sagi, *German Reparations: A History of the Negotiations* (Jerusalem: Magnes Press, 1980); and Goldmann, *The Autobiography of Nahum Goldmann*, 249–82.

71. Zweig, *German Reparations*, 22–23. The American Jewish Committee wanted an official negotiating entity as a counterweight to the State of Israel (69–70).

72. Dariel Colonomos and Andrea Armstrong, "German Reparations to the Jews after WWII: A Turning Point in the History of Reparations," in de Greiff, ed., *The Handbook of Reparations*, 391; Goldmann, *The Autobiography of Nahum Goldmann*, 217–19, 249, 273–76. Goldmann suggested that the innovative struggle for reparations replaced the interwar concern with minority rights. Dawidowicz, "German Collective Indemnity to Israel and the Conference on Jewish Material Claims against Germany," 471, 483 points out that the settlement was designated a "protocol," not a "treaty."

73. Zweig, *German Reparations*, 4, 41, 186. The Jewish organizations were careful to distinguish between "material" claims, for which reparations were appropriate, and "spiritual" claims (31), which required other forms of expiation. Adenauer upheld this distinction in his speech to the Bundestag.

74. The claims conference funded historical commissions in the DP camps; YIVO's archive; the *Centre de Documentation Juive Contemporaine* in Paris and a Memorial (*Le Tombeau du Martyr Juif Inconnu*; the City of Paris gave the site); and the Memorial Foundation for Jewish Culture (1964). Zweig, *German Reparations*, 156–61.

75. William Schabas, foreword to Marrus, *Some Measure of Justice*, xi–xii.

76. Marrus, *Some Measure of Justice*, 3–9, 25–30; Avi Beker, ed., *The Plunder of Jewish Property during the Holocaust: Confronting European History* (New York: New York University Press, 2001).

77. Hondius, "Bitter Homecoming," 108.

78. Manfred Gerstenfeld, "How the Jewish Community Defeated the Banks and Stock Exchange in the 2000 Dutch Restitution Negotiations," *Jewish Political Studies Review* 22, no. 1–2 (Spring 2010): 2/9–3/9.

79. Ibid., 5/9.

80. Andrieu, "Two Approaches to Compensation in France," 135–40.

81. Goschler, "Jewish Property and the Politics of Restitution," 128; Marrus, *Some Measure of Justice*, 20–22.

82. Zweig, *German Reparations*, 3.

83. Marrus, *Some Measure of Justice*, 4. In contrast, the court dismissed the class action lawsuit filed in New York against the Polish state (1999). See Stola, "The Polish Debate on the Holocaust and the Restitution of Property," 251.

84. Ludi, " 'Why Switzerland?' " 187–88.

85. Ibid., 202–3.

86. Marrus, *Some Measure of Justice*, 18–19.

87. Ibid., 22–25.

88. Henry, *Confronting the Perpetrators*, 153.

89. Hayes, "Plunder and Restitution," 554.

90. Marrus, *Some Measure of Justice*, 36–59. For the "Washington Conference Principles on Nazi-Confiscated Art" (December 3, 1998), see 156–57n78.

Chapter Twenty-Five. Maghreb and Mashreq

1. George F. Kennan, *The Decline of Bismarck's European Order: Franco-Russian Relations, 1875–1890* (Princeton: Princeton University Press, 1979), 3. For the world war's impact, see David Fromkin, *A Peace to End All Peace: The Fall of the Ottoman Empire and the Creation of the Modern Middle East* (New York: Avon, 1989) and Susan Pedersen, *The Guardians: The League of Nations and the Crisis of Empire* (Oxford: Oxford University Press, 2015).

2. Todd Shepard, *The Invention of Decolonization: The Algerian War and the Remaking of France* (Ithaca: Cornell University Press, 2006); Martin Shipway, *Decolonization and Its Impact: A Comparative Approach to the End of the Colonial Empires* (Malden, MA: Blackwell, 2008).

3. Fromkin, *A Peace to End All Peace*.

4. For the fate of Jewish *protégés*, see Sarah Abrevaya Stein, *Extraterritorial Dreams: European Citizenship, Sephardi Jews, and the Ottoman Twentieth Century* (Chicago: University of Chicago Press, 2016).

5. Norman Stillman, *The Jews of Arab Lands in Modern Times* (Philadelphia: Jewish Publication Society, 1991), 141. For a comprehensive survey, see Abdelwahab Meddeb and Benjamin Stora, eds., *A History of Jewish-Muslim Relations: From the Origins to the Present Day*, trans. Jane Marie Todd and Michael B. Smith (Princeton: Princeton University Press, 2013), 164–603; Georges Bensoussan, *Juifs en pays arabes: Le grand déracinement, 1850–1975* (Paris: Tallandier, 2012) examines Morocco, Libya, Egypt, Yemen, and Iraq.

6. Stillman, *The Jews of Arab Lands*, 4, 51, 59, 121.

7. Ibid., 62–63; David Cohen, "Algeria," in Reeva Spector Simon, Michael Menachem Laskier, and Sara Reguer, eds., *The Jews of the Middle East and North Africa in Modern Times* (New York: Columbia University Press, 2003), 463–64.

8. Cohen, "Algeria," 464–45.

9. Michael M. Laskier, *North African Jewry in the Twentieth Century: The Jews of Morocco, Tunisia, and Algeria* (New York: New York University Press, 1994), 13, 312–13. The Jewish schools met during the public schools' two recess days: Thursday and Sunday.

10. Laskier, *North African Jewry*, 319.

11. Ibid., 319–22; Cohen, "Algeria," 468.

12. Cohen, "Algeria," 467.

13. Laskier, *North African Jewry*, 332.

14. Ibid., 329–30.

15. Shepard, *The Invention of Decolonization*, 207.

16. Cohen, "Algeria," 469; Shepard, *The Invention of Decolonization*, 182.

17. Shepard, *The Invention of Decolonization*, 223.

18. Sarah Abrevaya Stein, *Saharan Jews and the Fate of French Algeria* (Chicago: University of Chicago Press, 2014), 110–48.

19. Shepard, *The Invention of Decolonization*, 19–20, 220, 271.

20. Laskier, *North African Jewry*, 316; Stein, *Saharan Jews*.

21. Shepard, *The Invention of Decolonization*, 174–77.

22. Cohen, "Algeria," 470.

23. Haim Saadoun, "Tunisia," in Simon, Laskier, and Reguer, eds., *The Jews of the Middle East and North Africa in Modern Times*, 445; Daniel J. Schroeter and Joseph Chetrit, "Emancipation and Its Discontents: Jews at the Formative Period of Colonial Rule in Morocco," *Jewish Social Studies* n.s. 13, no. 1 (2006): 175.

24. H. Z. Hirschberg, *A History of the Jews in North Africa*, 2 vols. (Leiden: Brill, 1981), 2:113–15.

25. Ibid., 2:82–85; Saadoun, "Tunisia," 446.

26. Hirschberg, *A History of the Jews in North Africa*, 2:135.

27. Saadoun, "Tunisia," 446.

28. Ibid., 448.

29. Hirschberg, *A History of the Jews in North Africa*, 2:133–34; Stillman, *The Jews of Arab Lands*, 60. Hirschberg gives the total figure of 7,311 (1910–50).

30. Hirschberg, *A History of the Jews in North Africa*, 2:134–35; Stillman, *The Jews of Arab Lands*, 62.

31. Saadoun, "Tunisia," 449.

32. Laskier, *North African Jewry*, 72–73; Saadoun, "Tunisia," 454.

33. Hirschberg, *A History of the Jews in North Africa*, 2:139–43; Laskier, *North African Jewry*, 73–76; Saadoun, "Tunisia," 454–55.

34. Saadoun, "Tunisia," 444.

35. Ibid., 455–56.

36. Laskier, *North African Jewry*, 265–86; Saadoun, "Tunisia," 456–57.

37. Michael Menachem Laskier and Eliezer Bashan, "Morocco," in Simon, Laskier, and Reguer, eds., *The Jews of the Middle East and North Africa in Modern Times*, 472.

38. Jessica M. Marglin, *Across Legal Lines: Jews and Muslims in Modern Morocco* (New Haven: Yale University Press, 2016), 5, 29.

39. Stillman, *The Jews of Arab Lands*, 14–15.

40. Laskier and Bashan, "Morocco," 486.

41. Marglin, *Across Legal Lines*, 6, 178; Schroeter and Chetrit, "Emancipation and Its Discontents," 180.

42. Marglin, *Across Legal Lines*, 178; Schroeter and Chetrit, "Emancipation and Its Discontents," 179, 188. To justify withholding citizenship the French authorities appealed to Moroccan law that required perpetual allegiance to the sultan (Treaty of Algeciras, 1906; Sharifian decree, 1921) as well as to international treaties (Convention of Madrid, 1880).

43. Marglin, *Across Legal Lines*.

44. Quotation of Resident-General Lyautey cited in Schroeter and Chetrit, "Emancipation and Its Discontents," 190–91.

45. Schroeter and Chetrit, "Emancipation and Its Discontents," 181–95. Marglin, *Across Legal Lines*, 171–96: this rigid system took hold by the 1930s.

46. Laskier and Bashan, "Morocco," 474; Marglin, *Across Legal Lines*, 179. The European colonists resided in new neighborhoods (*nouvelles villes*).

47. Michael M. Laskier, *The Alliance Israélite Universelle and the Jewish Communities*

of Morocco, 1862–1962 (Albany: State University of New York Press, 1983), 159–63; Laskier and Bashan, "Morocco," 488.

48. Laskier, *The Alliance Israélite Universelle*, 163–71; Laskier and Bashan, "Morocco," 492.

49. Laskier, *North African Jewry*, 76–81; Laskier, *The Alliance Israélite Universelle*, 180.

50. Schroeter and Chetrit, "Emancipation and Its Discontents," 195–96.

51. Laskier, *North African Jewry*, 84–113.

52. Stillman, *The Jews of Arab Lands*, 167; Laskier and Bashan, "Morocco," 499.

53. Laskier and Bashan, "Morocco," 500. Leon Benzaquen served as Minister of Post and Telegraph.

54. Ibid., 503.

55. Ibid., 501–2.

56. Marglin, *Across Legal Lines*, 202.

57. Hayyim J. Cohen, *The Jews of the Middle East, 1860–1972* (Jerusalem: Israel Universities Press, 1973), 69. Iraq: 125,000; Iran: 100,000; Turkey: 80,000; Egypt: 66,000; Yemen and Aden: 54,000; Syria and Lebanon: 35,000.

58. Keith David Watenpaugh, *Being Modern in the Middle East: Revolution, Nationalism, Colonialism and the Arab Middle Class* (Princeton: Princeton University Press, 2006).

59. Cohen, *The Jews of the Middle East*, 15; Shimon Shamir, "The Evolution of the Egyptian Nationality Laws and Their Application to the Jews in the Monarchy Period," in Shamir, ed., *The Jews of Egypt: A Mediterranean Society in Modern Times* (Boulder, CO: Westview, 1987), 61–62.

60. E. R. J. Owen, *Cotton and the Egyptian Economy, 1820–1914: A Study in Trade and Development* (Oxford: Clarendon, 1969); Jean-Marc Ran Oppenheim, "Egypt and the Sudan," in Simon, Laskier, and Reguer, eds., *The Jews of the Middle East and North Africa in Modern Times*, 411.

61. Shamir, "The Evolution of the Egyptian Nationality Laws," 33.

62. Jacob Landau, "Changing Patterns of Community Structures, with Special Reference to Ottoman Egypt," in Avigdor Levy, ed., *Jews, Turks, Ottomans: A Shared History, Fifteenth through the Twentieth Century* (Syracuse, NY: Syracuse University Press, 2002), 77–87; Oppenheim, "Egypt and the Sudan," 415, 417, 421–22; Cohen, *The Jews of the Middle East*, 108–12.

63. Oppenheim, "Egypt and the Sudan," 423–24; Gudrun Krämer, "Political Participation of the Jews in Egypt between World War I and the 1952 Revolution," in Shamir, ed., *The Jews of Egypt*, 68–82.

64. Oppenheim, "Egypt and the Sudan," 412; Stillman, *The Jews of Arab Lands*, 54.

65. The law is reprinted in Shamir, ed., *The Jews of Egypt*, 237–42.

66. Shamir, "The Evolution of the Egyptian Nationality Laws," 54–59.

67. Cohen, *The Jews of the Middle East*, 50. For the background to the 1929 law, and especially the competition between jus soli and jus sanguinis, see Shamir, "The Evolution of the Egyptian Nationality Laws," 34–46.

68. Cohen, *The Jews of the Middle East*, 48.

69. Ibid., 88; Michael M. Laskier, *The Jews of Egypt, 1920–1970: In the Midst of Zionism, Anti-Semitism, and the Middle East Conflict* (New York: New York University Press, 1992), 300–301. Shamir suggests that after the 1937 Montreux Convention Egyptians had begun to control previously foreign companies and to expel foreign employees. See "The Evolution of the Egyptian Nationality Laws," 53.

70. Shamir, "The Evolution of the Egyptian Nationality Laws," 59–60.

71. Stillman, *The Jews of Arab Lands*, 142–3.

72. Cited in Cohen, *The Jews of the Middle East*, 49.

73. Shamir, "The Evolution of the Egyptian Nationality Laws," 34. The estimate of the Jewish population for 1948 is 70,000 to 80,000, of whom 5,000 were Egyptian citizens, 30,000 foreign nationals, and 40,000 stateless.

74. Cohen, *The Jews of the Middle East*, 50.

75. Oppenheim, "Egypt and the Sudan," 428.

76. Cohen, *The Jews of the Middle East*, 52–53.

77. Oppenheim, "Egypt and the Sudan," 411.

78. Shamir, "The Evolution of the Egyptian Nationality Laws," 60.

79. Ibid., 60.

80. Oppenheim, "Egypt and the Sudan," 428–29.

81. Reeva Spector Simon, "Iraq," in Simon, Laskier, and Reguer, eds., *The Jews of the Middle East and North Africa in Modern Times*, 348–49; Paul Dumont, "Jews, Muslims, and Cholera: Intercommunal Relations in Baghdad at the End of the Nineteenth Century," in Avigdor Levy, ed., *The Jews of the Ottoman Empire* (Princeton: Darwin Press, 1994), 353–72.

82. Cohen, *The Jews of the Middle East*, 23–24; Simon, "Iraq," 356.

83. Pedersen, *The Guardians*, 41, 262–86.

84. Philip Willard Ireland, *Iraq: A Study in Political Development* (London: J. Cape, 1937) summarizes the constitution at 382–89. From 1925 to 1946 four deputies represented the Jews; from 1946 to 1951 six deputies and one senator. See Cohen, *The Jews of the Middle East*, 27 and Orit Bashkin, *A History of the Jews in Modern Iraq: New Babylonians* (Stanford: Stanford University Press, 2012), 21, 59.

85. Bashkin, *A History of the Jews in Modern Iraq*, 67–84.

86. Simon, "Iraq," 352–53, 357, 360; Bashkin, *A History of the Jews in Modern Iraq*, 60.

87. Bashkin, *A History of the Jews in Modern Iraq*, 15–57, quotation at 57. She emphasizes the distinction, but also compatibility, between a "Pan-Arab" and a "territorial-patriotic" conception of Iraqi nationhood.

88. Cohen, *The Jews of the Middle East*, 26.

89. Bashkin, *A History of the Jews in Modern Iraq*, 34–36, 102–11; Cohen, *The Jews of the Middle East*, 27–28; Simon, "Iraq," 354, 364.

90. Bashkin, *A History of the Jews in Modern Iraq*, 112–40; Cohen, *The Jews of the Middle East*, 29–31. For the officers who created the anti-British regime, see Reeva S. Simon, *Iraq between the Two World Wars: The Creation and Implementation of a Nationalist Ideology* (New York: Columbia University Press, 1986).

91. Simon, "Iraq," 363.

92. Ibid., 365; Cohen, *The Jews of the Middle East*, 32–34. For the "vicious circle" of Iraqi government ineptitude, Israeli opportunism, and Jews' loss of faith in Iraqi democracy, see Bashkin, *A History of the Jews in Modern Iraq*, 183–228.

93. Cohen, *The Jews of the Middle East*, 34–35. For text of the law, see Stillman, *The Jews of Arab Lands*, 525.

94. Simon, "Iraq," 348; Stillman, *The Jews of Arab Lands*, 158–64. Israeli agents' role in provoking emigration, including bombings (April 8, 1950; January 14, March 14, and June 5–6, 1951), remains controversial. See Bashkin, *A History of the Jews in Modern Iraq*, 206–8 and Hannan Hever and Yehouda Shehav, "Alimut Baghdad (1950–1951), alimut archiyonim," *Theoriya u-Bikoret* 49 (Winter 2017): 1–20.

95. J. C. Hurewitz, *Diplomacy in the Near and Middle East. A Documentary Record: 1914–1956*, 2 vols. (Princeton: D. Van Nostrand, 1956), 2:119–27.

96. Stanford J. Shaw, *The Jews of the Ottoman Empire and the Turkish Republic* (New York: New York University Press, 1991), 244–46; Cohen, *The Jews of the Middle East*, 20.

97. Aron Rodrigue, *French Jews, Turkish Jews: The Alliance Israélite Universelle and*

the Politics of Jewish Schooling in Turkey, 1860–1925 (Bloomington: Indiana University Press, 1990), 165; Rodrigue, "From *Millet* to Minority: Turkish Jewry," in Pierre Birnbaum and Ira Katznelson, eds., *Paths of Emancipation: Jews, States and Citizenship* (Princeton: Princeton University Press, 1995), 257; Riva Kastoryano, "From *Millet* to Community: The Jews of Istanbul," in Aron Rodrigue, ed., *Ottoman and Turkish Jewry: Community and Leadership* (Bloomington: Indiana University Turkish Studies, 1992), 266; Shaw, *The Jews of the Ottoman Empire and the Turkish Republic*, 246, 251; Jacob Landau, "Ottoman Turkey," 279 and George E. Gruen, "Turkey," 303–4, 313, in Simon, Laskier, and Reguer, eds., *The Jews of the Middle East and North Africa in Modern Times*; Cohen, *The Jews of the Middle East*, 20.

98. Rodrigue, *French Jews, Turkish Jews*, 145–57.

99. Ibid., 157–66.

100. Shaw, *The Jews of the Ottoman Empire and the Turkish Republic*, 251; Gruen, "Turkey," 305, 313; Cohen, *The Jews of the Middle East*, 23.

101. Cohen, *The Jews of the Middle East*, 97.

102. Shaw, *The Jews of the Ottoman Empire and the Turkish Republic*, 254; Gruen, "Turkey," 306.

103. Cohen, *The Jews of the Middle East*, 20.

104. Shaw, *The Jews of the Ottoman Empire and the Turkish Republic*, 255–56; Gruen, "Turkey," 307–8; Cohen, *The Jews of the Middle East*, 97–98.

105. Stanford J. Shaw, "Turkey and the Jews of Europe during World War II," 246–59 and Frank Tachau, "German Jewish Emigrés in Turkey," 233–45 in Levy, ed., *Jews, Turks, Ottomans*.

106. Shaw, *The Jews of the Ottoman Empire and the Turkish Republic*, 270.

107. Cohen, *The Jews of the Middle East*, 76–78; Gruen, "Turkey," 310. For Istanbul, see Kastoryano, "From *Millet* to Community," 253–77.

Chapter Twenty-Six. Israel

1. Itamar Rabinovich and Jehuda Reinharz, eds., *Israel in the Middle East: Documents and Readings on Society, Politics, and Foreign Relations, 1948–Present* (New York: Oxford University Press, 1984), 14–15. The Supreme Court initially ruled that the Declaration of Independence was not "a constitutional law which determined the validity or invalidity of ordinances and statutes." Subsequent court rulings and the decisions of attorneys general have established the principle of equality by invoking the Declaration. David Kretzmer, *The Legal Status of the Arabs in Israel* (Boulder, CO: Westview, 1990), 7–11, quotation at 8.

2. Paul Mendes-Flohr and Jehuda Reinharz, *The Jew in the Modern World: A Documentary History*, 3rd ed. (New York: Oxford University Press, 2011), 712; Amnon Rubenstein, *Ha-Mishpat ha-Konstitutsioni shel Medinat Yisrael*, 2 vols., 5th ed. (Jerusalem: Schocken, 1996), 1:109–12; Ariel Bin-Nun, *The Law of the State of Israel: An Introduction* (Jerusalem: Rubin Mass, 1990), 15–17. Ben-Gurion rejected a definition based on Jewish law (*halakha*); the original law did not define who was a "Jew." In 1970 the Knesset introduced a definition based on *halakha*, i.e., anyone born of a Jewish mother. At the same time, it introduced an additional track for family members, i.e., gentile spouses, children of mixed marriages, even grandchildren of mixed marriages.

Yad Vashem, the Holocaust research center founded by Israel's Parliament (Knesset; August 1953), proposed its own version of the "ingathering of exiles": to confer retroactive Israeli citizenship on all Holocaust victims to show they had been "gathered to their people." In response to the American Jewish Committee's opposition, Yad Vashem dropped the project. See Ronald W. Zweig, *German Reparations and the Jewish World: A History of the Claims Conference*, 2nd ed. (London: Frank Cass, 2001), 162–66.

3. Rabinovich and Reinharz, eds., *Israel in the Middle East*, 40. Israel opted for "Basic Laws" over a constitution. For the role of the concept of nationality (*le'om*) in the Law of Return, see Don Handelman, "Contradictions Between Citizenship and Nationality: Their Consequences for Ethnicity and Inequality in Israel," *International Journal of Politics, Culture and Society* 7, no. 3 (1994): 441–59.

4. Shulamit Aloni, *Ha-Ezrah u-Medinato: Yesodot be-Torat ha-Ezrahut*, 4th ed. (Tel Aviv: Israel Defense Forces Publications, 1967), 135–40; Rubenstein, *Ha-Mishpat ha-Konstitutsioni*, 1:296–98, 2:877–904. Arab residents who could prove Palestinian citizenship had to register (March 1, 1952) to obtain Israeli citizenship. Their children were citizens by virtue of birth in the country. Non-Jews born in the country who could not prove prior citizenship had to be naturalized (2:888). A 1980 amendment to the Nationality Law awarded citizenship to anyone born in Israel if one parent was an Israeli national, in that instance removing the distinction between Jews and Arabs. See Kretzmer, *The Legal Status of the Arabs in Israel*, 89–90. Palestine had long been a land of migration whose inhabitants implicitly understood citizenship to be based on residence (jus soli). See Hillel Cohen, *Year Zero of the Arab-Israeli Conflict: 1929* (Waltham, MA: Brandeis University Press, 2015), 8, 34–35. The Palestine Citizenship Order (July 24, 1925) defined a Palestinian citizen as a "Turkish subject habitually resident in the territory of Palestine" (jus soli). Cited in Anis F. Kassim, "The Palestinians: From Hyphenated to Integrated Citizenship," in Nils A. Butenschon, Uri David, and Manuel Hassassian, eds., *Citizenship and the State in the Middle East: Approaches and Applications* (Syracuse, NY: Syracuse University Press, 2000), 204.

5. Howard M. Sachar, *A History of Israel: From the Rise of Zionism to Our Time* (New York: Knopf, 1985), 395; Orit Rozin, *A Home for All Jews: Citizenship, Rights, and National Identity in the New Israeli State*, trans. Haim Watzman (Waltham, MA: Brandeis University Press, 2016), 3. There were 690,000 immigrants from 1948 to 1951.

6. Rozin, *A Home for All Jews*, 118.

7. Gershon Shafir and Yoav Peled, *Being Israeli: The Dynamics of Multiple Citizenship* (Cambridge: Cambridge University Press, 2002), 28. In Labor Zionism's terms, integration through stratification constituted a preference for "statist normalization" or "Jewish normalization" over a "revolutionary" or "socialist" society. See Mitchell Cohen, *Zion and State: Nation, Class and the Shaping of Modern Israel*, 2nd ed. (New York: Columbia University Press, 1992), 226.

8. Shafir and Peled, *Being Israeli*.

9. Bryan K. Roby, *The Mizrahi Era of Rebellion: Israel's Forgotten Civil Rights Struggle, 1948-1966* (Syracuse, NY: Syracuse University Press, 2015); Rozin, *A Home for All Jews*, 12. On Israel's ability to "absorb" protest, see Eva Etzioni-Halevy, "Protest Politics in the Israeli Democracy," *Political Science Quarterly* 90, no. 3 (1975): 497–520.

10. Jehuda Reinharz, "The Transition from Yishuv to State: Social and Ideological Changes," in Laurence J. Silberstein, ed., *New Perspectives on Israeli History: The Early Years of the State* (New York: New York University Press, 1991), 28–29; Myron J. Aronoff, "Myths, Symbols, and Rituals of the Emerging State," in Silberstein, ed., *New Perspectives on Israeli History*, 175–92; Arieh Bruce Saposnik, *Becoming Hebrew: The Creation of a Jewish National Culture in Ottoman Palestine* (New York: Oxford University Press, 2008). The first aliyah (1882–1903) brought some 25,000 Jews to Palestine; the second (1904–14) some 40,000 to 55,000. Calvin Goldscheider, *Israeli Society in the 21st Century: Immigration, Inequality and Religious Conflict* (Waltham, MA: Brandeis University Press, 2015), 41.

11. Yael Zerubavel, "New Beginning, Old Past: The Collective Memory of Pioneering in Israeli Culture," in Silberstein, ed., *New Perspectives on Israeli History*, 193–215; Lilly Weiss-

brod, *Israeli Identity: In Search of a Successor to the Pioneer, Tsabar and Settler* (London: Frank Cass, 2002).

12. S. Ilan Troen, *Imagining Zion: Dreams, Designs and Realities in a Century of Jewish Settlement* (New Haven: Yale University Press, 2003); Shafir and Peled, *Being Israeli*, 37–73; Rozin, *A Home for All Jews*, 12.

13. Michael Shalev, "The Political Economy of Labor-Party Dominance and Decline in Israel," in T. J. Pempel, ed., *Uncommon Democracies: The One-Party Dominant Regimes* (Ithaca: Cornell University Press, 1990), 89.

14. Mapai's leadership largely emerged from the second aliyah (1904–14), but the group itself did not constitute a "social or political elite in the thirties." See Yosef Gorny, "Changes in the Social and Political Structure of the Second Aliya between 1904 and 1940," in Jehuda Reinharz and Anita Shapira, eds., *Essential Papers on Zionism* (New York: New York University Press, 1996), 371–421. In 1948, 54,200 Jews lived in 177 kibbutzim (7.6% of the Jewish population). See Goldscheider, *Israeli Society in the 21st Century*, 99.

15. Ze'ev Tzahor, "The Histadrut: From Marginal Organization to 'State-in-the-Making,'" in Reinharz and Shapira, eds., *Essential Papers on Zionism*, 473–508; Cohen, *Zion and State*, 105–33; Yonathan Shapiro, *The Formative Years of the Israeli Labor Party* (Beverly Hills: Sage, 1976).

16. Shafir and Peled, *Being Israeli*, 45–46.

17. Ibid., 62. The Histadrut did not admit Palestinian Arabs as full members until April 1957. See Don Peretz, "Early State Policy towards the Arab Population, 1948–1955," in Silberstein, ed., *New Perspectives on Israeli History*, 98.

18. Yitzhak Greenberg, "The Contribution of the Labor Economy to Immigrant Absorption and Population Dispersal during Israel's First Decade," in S. Ilan Troen and Noah Lucas, eds., *Israel: The First Decade of Independence* (Albany: State University of New York Press, 1995), 279–96. Forty-eight percent of the immigrants between 1922 and 1937 came without resources. Lilly Weissbrod, "Economic Factors and Political Strategies: The Defeat of the Revisionists in Mandatory Palestine," *Middle Eastern Studies* 19, no. 3 (1983): 328.

19. Shalev, "The Political Economy of Labor-Party Dominance and Decline in Israel," 92. The Labor Party had many characteristics of a right-wing party: it combined "nationalism, 'opportunism,' [and] machine politics" while crossing class lines (86, 126). On the Labor Party's internal machinery, see Myron J. Aronoff, *Power and Ritual in the Israel Labor Party: A Study in Political Anthropology*, 2nd ed. (Armonk, NY: M. E. Sharpe, 1993).

20. Shafir and Peled, *Being Israeli*, 68–69. Two labor parties (Ahdut Ha'avoda and HaPoel Ha-Tsair) merged to form Mapai (1930). The parties may have merged in response to Revisionism. Weissbrod, "Economic Factors and Political Strategies," 334. The Histadrut began a campaign in 1927 to take control of the Zionist movement. See Tzahor, "The Histadrut," 501–3 and Shapiro, *The Formative Years of the Israeli Labor Party*, 231–53.

21. Ruth Kark and Joseph B. Glass, "Eretz-Israel/Palestine, 1800–1948," in Reeva Spector Simon, Michael Menachem Laskier, and Sara Reguer eds., *The Jews of the Middle East and North Africa in Modern Times* (New York: Columbia University Press, 2003), 335–46; Tudor Parfitt, *The Jews in Palestine, 1800–1882* (Woodbridge, Suffolk: Royal Historical Society, 1987); Rachel Sharabi, *Ha-Yishuv ha-Seferadi bi-Yerushalyim be-Shilhe ha-Tekufah ha-Otomanit, 1893–1914* (Tel Aviv: Ministry of Defense, 1989); Israel Bartal, "'Old Yishuv' and 'New Yishuv': Image and Reality," *Jerusalem Cathedra* 1 (1981): 215–31 and Bartal, *Galut be-Aretz: Yishuv Eretz-Yisrael be-terem Tsiyonut: Masot u-Mehkarim* (Jerusalem: Hassifria Haziyonit, 1994); Yehoshua Kaniel, "The Terms 'Old Yishuv' and 'New Yishuv': Problems of Definition," *Jerusalem Cathedra* 1 (1981): 232–45; Troen, *Imagining Zion*, 114–28; Walter P. Zenner, "Sephardic Communal Organizations in Israel," *Middle East Journal* 21, no. 2 (Spring 1967): 173–86.

22. Simon Schama, *Two Rothschilds and the Land of Israel* (New York: Knopf, 1978); Nahum Karlinsky, *Perihat he-Hadar: Yazemut Peratit be-Yishuv, 1890–1939* (Jerusalem: Magnes, 2000). For a prominent entrepreneur, see Eli Shaltiel, *Pinhas Rutenberg: Aliyato u-Nefilato shel Ish Hazak be-Eretz Yisrael, 1879–1942*, 2 vols. (Tel Aviv: Am Oved, 1990).

23. Goldscheider, *Israeli Society in the 21st Century*, 84–85. The 1945 population was 49% urban: Muslims (30%), Christians (80%), Jews (74%). See Kark and Glass, "Eretz-Israel/Palestine," 336.

24. Troen, *Imagining Zion*, 85–111; Maoz Azaryahu and S. Ilan Troen, *Tel Aviv, The First Century: Visions, Designs, Actualities* (Bloomington: Indiana University Press, 2012). The fifth aliyah (1933–39), primarily of German Jews, brought an infusion of capital and industry. Sachar, *A History of Israel*, 188–90. Tel Aviv's population in 1939 (150,000) was almost one-third of the Yishuv.

25. Weissbrod, "Economic Factors and Political Strategies," 326–44; Weissbrod, "The Rise and Fall of the Revisionist Party, 1928–1935," *Jerusalem Quarterly* 30 (1984): 80–93. The Revisionists established a rival defense force (1931), trade union (1933), and Zionist Organization (1935). By 1920 the "Mizrahi" nationalist-religious party had 2,000 pupils in some 25 schools. Cohen has called this structure, in which each Zionist stream established its own institutions yet Labor dominated, "hegemonic segmented pluralism." The Revisionists faltered in such institution building. See *Zion and State*, 132, 141.

26. Reinharz, "The Transition from Yishuv to State"; Alan Dowty, "Israel's First Decade: Building a Civic State," in Troen and Lucas, eds., *Israel: The First Decade of Independence*, 31–50; Eliezer Don-Yehiya, "Political Religion in a New State: Ben-Gurion's *Mamlachtiyut*," in Troen and Lucas, eds., *Israel: The First Decade of Independence*, 171–92; Cohen, *Zion and State*, 201–59.

27. From 1933 the Va'ad Leumi administered four independent educational streams: "General" or secular; Mizrahi or religious Zionist; Histadrut or Labor; Agudat Israel or Orthodox. In 1953 the government merged these into two official systems—General and Histadrut into the General State system, Mizrahi into the Religious State system—while the Agudat Israel schools were recognized but unofficial. Cohen, *Zion and State*, 237–45.

28. Rozin, *A Home for All Jews*, 76–77, 87. The State of Emergency remains in place.

29. Ibid., 88, 103.

30. Ibid., 111–13. The 1992 Basic Law of Human Dignity and Freedom (Article 6) enshrined the right to travel abroad.

31. Roby, *The Mizrahi Era of Rebellion*, 1. By 1975 there were some 751,000 Mizrahi immigrants.

32. Ella Shohat, "Sephardim in Israel: Zionism from the Standpoint of Its Jewish Victims," *Social Text* 19–20 (Autumn 1988). 1–35; Shohat, "The Invention of the Mizrahim," *Journal of Palestine Studies* 29, no. 1 (Autumn 1999): 5–20; Derek Penslar, *Israel in History: The Jewish State in Comparative Perspective* (London: Routledge, 2007), 109–10. For the term in Mandatory Palestine, see Abigail Jacobson and Moshe Naor, *Oriental Neighbors: Middle Eastern Jews and Arabs in Mandatory Palestine* (Waltham, MA: Brandeis University Press, 2016).

33. S. N. Eisenstadt, *The Transformation of Israeli Society* (London: Weidenfeld & Nicolson, 1985), 298–99. Penslar, *Israel in History*, 194–95, argues that Israel's state radio (Kol Yisrael) shunned Arabic-language programming while broadcasting in other immigrant languages, e.g., Yiddish, Ladino, European languages.

34. Norman A. Stillman, *The Jews of Arab Lands in Modern Times* (Philadelphia: Jewish Publication Society, 1991), 167.

35. Avraham Abbas, *From Ingathering to Integration* (Jerusalem: World Sephardi Fed-

eration, 1959); Handelman, "Contradictions between Citizenship and Nationality," 451–55; Roby, *The Mizrahi Era of Rebellion*, 1, 37–38.

36. Abbas, *From Ingathering to Integration*, 10–12; Roy Kozlovsky, "Temporal States of Architecture: Mass Immigration and Provisional Housing in Israel," in Sandy Isenstadt and Kishwar Rizvi, eds., *Modernism and the Middle East: Architecture and Politics in the Twentieth Century* (Seattle: University of Washington Press, 2008), 139–60. Housing consisted of tents, canvas huts, wooden shacks, and tin huts.

37. Roby, *The Mizrahi Era of Rebellion*, 136.

38. Rozin, *A Home for All Jews*, 158; Abbas, *From Ingathering to Integration*, 7; Eliezer Schweid, "Judaism in Israeli Culture," in Uzi Rebhun and Chaim I. Waxman, eds., *Jews in Israel: Contemporary Social and Cultural Patterns* (Hanover, NH: Brandeis University Press, 2004), 245–47.

39. Local councils sometimes disenfranchised transit camp residents by preventing them from voting in local elections. See Roby, *The Mizrahi Era of Rebellion*, 56. For complaints of second-class status in the Mandatory period, see Jacobson and Naor, *Oriental Neighbors*, 173, 197.

40. S. Ilan Troen, "New Departures in Zionist Planning: The Development Town," in Troen and Lucas, eds., *Israel: The First Decade of Independence*, 441–60; Goldscheider, *Israeli Society in the 21st Century*, 103–5. The government designed development towns for multiple purposes: fill vacant areas, defend the borders, and disperse Israel's urban population. In 1951 there were fifteen development towns accommodating 120,000; by 1956 there were twenty-two. By the mid-1960s development towns housed 20% of Israel's Jewish population. On the construction of housing and development towns, see Greenberg, "The Contribution of the Labor Economy to Immigrant Absorption and Population Dispersal during Israel's First Decade," 286–94.

41. Abbas, *From Ingathering to Integration*, 12–17; Shafir and Peled, *Being Israeli*, 84–87; Goldscheider, *Israeli Society in the 21st Century*, 164.

42. Goldscheider, *Israeli Society in the 21st Century*, 101–2. *Moshavim* farmed land leased from the state (Israel Lands Administration). See Kretzmer, *The Legal Status of the Arabs in Israel*, 66–68.

43. Goldscheider, *Israeli Society in the 21st Century*, 167. For the earlier period, see Sammy Smooha, *Israel: Pluralism and Conflict* (Berkeley: University of California Press, 1978), 154–56.

44. Goldscheider, *Israeli Society in the 21st Century*, 157–69.

45. Shafir and Peled, *Being Israeli*, 78.

46. Roby, *The Mizrahi Era of Rebellion*, 47; Rozin, *A Home for All Jews*, 144; Tamar Hermann, "New Challenges to New Authority: Israeli Grassroots Activism in the 1950s," in Troen and Lucas, eds., *Israel: The First Decade of Independence*, 105–22.

47. Rozin, *A Home for All Jews*, 138.

48. Roby, *The Mizrahi Era of Rebellion*, 174–76. The Council of the Sephardi Community of Jerusalem published a pamphlet to protest endemic discrimination. See *Danger, Jewish Racialism! Israel's Sephardim: Integration or Disintegration* (Jerusalem, 1965).

49. Roby, *The Mizrahi Era of Rebellion*, 53–54; Etzioni-Halevy, "Protest Politics in the Israeli Democracy," 497–520.

50. Rozin, *A Home for All Jews*, 142.

51. Roby, *The Mizrahi Era of Rebellion*, 139, 150–51.

52. Abbas, *From Ingathering to Integration*, 17; Roby, *The Mizrahi Era of Rebellion*, 22, 28, 32, 37.

53. Roby, *The Mizrahi Era of Rebellion*, 149.

54. Erik Cohen, "The Black Panthers and Israeli Society," *Jewish Journal of Sociology* 14, no. 1 (1972): 93–109; Sachar, *A History of Israel*, 742–43.

55. Elazar Leshem and Moshe Sicron, "The Soviet Immigrant Community in Israel," in Rebhun and Waxman, eds., *Jews in Israel*, 81–117. The 1970s brought 150,000 immigrants from the USSR. By 2000 there were 1.1 million, or 18% of Israel's population.

56. Martial law was based on British Mandatory Emergency Regulations (1945). A Minorities Ministry functioned briefly (May 1948 to June 1949). See Elie Rekhess, "Initial Israeli Policy Guidelines towards the Arab Minority, 1948–1949," in Silberstein, ed., *New Perspectives on Israeli History*, 103–23; Peretz, "Early State Policy towards the Arab Population," 82–100. The General Zionist newspaper *Haboker* proclaimed in 1953: "Citizenship in a democratic country cannot be granted by installments." For the government's debate over martial law, see Ilan Pappé, "An Uneasy Coexistence: Arabs and Jews in the First Decade of Statehood," in Troen and Lucas, eds., *Israel: The First Decade of Independence*, 639–46. The Palestinian Israeli population became increasingly Muslim: from 70% in 1948 to 83% in 2013. It has ranged from 18% of Israel's population (1948) to 21% (2012; 1,647,000). Goldscheider, *Israeli Society in the 21st Century*, 62–65.

57. Pappé, "An Uneasy Coexistence," 621–26; Kassim, "The Palestinians," 204–6. The 100,000 included those living in areas occupied by Israel after 1948 as well as those who fled or were expelled but remained in Israel ("present absentees"). Article 6 detailed the naturalization process. The 1980 amendment to the Nationality Law eased the process of gaining citizenship. See Kretzmer, *The Legal Status of the Arabs in Israel*, 38–40.

58. Ilan Peleg and Dov Waxman, *Israel's Palestinians: The Conflict Within* (New York: Cambridge University Press, 2011), 24–25; Alina Korn, "Crime and Law Enforcement in the Israeli Arab Population under the Military Government," in Troen and Lucas, eds., *Israel: The First Decade of Independence*, 659–79. For control and co-optation, see Ian Lustick, *Arabs in the Jewish State: Israel's Control of a National Minority* (Austin: University of Texas Press, 1980) and Hillel Cohen, *Good Arabs: The Israeli Security Agencies and the Israeli Arabs, 1948–1967*, trans. Haim Watzman (Berkeley: University of California Press, 2010).

59. Peleg and Waxman, *Israel's Palestinians*, 96. For legal discrimination, see Kretzmer, *The Legal Status of the Arabs in Israel*, 77–134.

60. Nadim N. Rouhana and Areej Sabbagh-Khoury, "Palestinian Citizenship in Israel: A Settler Colonial Perspective," in Frederick E. Greenspahn, ed., *Contemporary Israel: New Insights and Scholarship* (New York: New York University Press, 2016), 35–37; Peleg and Waxman, *Israel's Palestinians*, 39–43; Kretzmer, *The Legal Status of the Arabs in Israel*, 49–55, 60–69, 95–98; Zeev Rosenhek and Michael Shalev, "The Contradictions of Palestinian Citizenship in Israel: Inclusion and Exclusion in the Israeli Welfare State," in Butenschon, David, and Hassassian, eds., *Citizenship and the State in the Middle East*, 301–4, 309–12. The Jewish Agency developed new settlements and infrastructure. Its services were mandated exclusively for Jewish settlements.

61. Majid Al-Haj, *Education, Empowerment, and Control: The Case of the Arabs in Israel* (Albany: State University of New York Press, 1995); Peleg and Waxman, *Israel's Palestinians*, 43–54.

62. Shafir and Peled, *Being Israeli*, 289; Goldscheider, *Israeli Society in the 21st Century*, 94; Rosenhek and Shalev, "The Contradictions of Palestinian Citizenship in Israel," 297–301, 307–9.

63. Shafir and Peled, *Being Israeli*, 55.

64. Goldscheider, *Israeli Society in the 21st Century*, 70–72.

65. Peleg and Waxman, *Israel's Palestinians*, 35–38; Goldscheider, *Israeli Society in the 21st Century*, 168.

66. Goldscheider, *Israeli Society in the 21st Century*, 157, 169.

67. Al-Haj, *Education, Empowerment, and Control*, 203–13; Lustick, *Arabs in the Jewish State*, 21–24.

68. For flight within Israel and abroad, see Benny Morris, "The Origins of the Palestinian Refugee Problem," in Silberstein, ed., *New Perspectives on Israeli History*, 42–56 and Morris, *The Birth of the Palestinian Refugee Problem, 1947–1949* (Cambridge: Cambridge University Press, 1988).

69. Arnon Golan, "The Transfer to Jewish Control of Abandoned Arab Lands during the War of Independence," in Troen and Lucas, eds., *Israel: The First Decade of Independence*, 403–40.

70. Hillel Cohen, "The Internal Refugees in the State of Israel: Israeli Citizens, Palestinian Refugees," *Palestine-Israel Journal* 9, no. 2 (2002): 43–51; Cohen, *Ha-Nifkadim ha-Nokhahim: Ha-Plitim he-Palestinayim be-Yisrael me-az 1948* (Jerusalem: Institute for Israeli Arab Studies, 2000); Peretz, "Early State Policy towards the Arab Population," 93–96; Kretzmer, *The Legal Status of the Arabs in Israel*, 55–69. The state also confiscated some Moslem Trust (*Waqf*) lands whose administrators were "absentee." The 1967 Agricultural Settlement Law aimed to prevent Jewish settlements from allowing Arabs to farm portions of their land.

71. Rozin, *A Home for All Jews*, 3–4.

72. Cohen, *Good Arabs*, 39–64, 195–230; Pappé, "An Uneasy Coexistence," 623–24. Tawfiq Tubi, a Communist MK, noted the violation of jus soli: "citizenship is given first of all to the population that was born in the country."

73. Cohen, *Good Arabs*.

74. Kretzmer, *The Legal Status of the Arabs in Israel*, 22–26. The political association was "The Land" (*el-Ard*), the political party the "Socialist List." Mapai received the majority of Palestinian Israeli votes into the 1970s.

75. Pappé, "An Uneasy Coexistence," 626.

76. Peleg and Waxman, *Israel's Palestinians*, 89–90. Rabin's government increased funding in education, health, and welfare and appointed two Arabs as deputy ministers. Rabin's government also depended on the Mizrahi Shas party's lack of opposition to the Oslo Accords. Sami Shalom Chetrit, "Mizrahi Politics in Israel: Between Integration and Alternative," *Journal of Palestine Studies* 29, no. 4 (2000): 58.

77. Peleg and Waxman, *Israel's Palestinians*, 66–67. The "internally displaced" numbered approximately 25,000 in 1948; in 2000 they numbered between 200,000 and 300,000.

78. Rouhana and Sabbagh-Khoury, "Palestinian Citizenship in Israel," 32–61; Peleg and Waxman, *Israel's Palestinians*, 59–66.

79. Peleg and Waxman, *Israel's Palestinians*, 138–39.

80. Ibid., 118.

81. Rouhana and Sabbagh-Khoury, "Palestinian Citizenship in Israel," 40.

82. Ezra Mendelsohn, *On Modern Jewish Politics* (New York: Oxford University Press, 1993), 125.

83. In 1949 Yitzhak ben-Zvi, later Israel's second president, wrote: "We . . . are not like the Poles in Poland and the Arabs are not like the Jews in Poland." Cited in Rekhess, "Initial Israeli Policy Guidelines towards the Arab Minority," 105.

84. Eran Kaplan and Derek J. Penslar, eds., *The Origins of Israel, 1882–1948: A Documentary History* (Madison: University of Wisconsin Press, 2011), 369.

85. Susan M. Weiss and Netty C. Gross-Horowitz, *Marriage and Divorce in the Jewish State: Israel's Civil War* (Waltham, MA: Brandeis University Press, 2013), 17.

86. Martin Edelman, "'Protecting' the Majority: Religious Freedom for Non-Orthodox Jews in Israel," in Frederick A. Lazin and Gregory S. Mahler, eds., *Israel in the Nineties: Development and Conflict* (Gainesville: University Press of Florida, 1996), 14–15; Meir Silverstone, "The Israel Ministry of Religious Affairs and the Chief Rabbinate of Israel," *Public Administration in Israel and Abroad* 14 (1974): 31–44.

87. Rubenstein, *Ha-Mishpat ha-Konstitutsioni*, 1:148; Kretzmer, *The Legal Status of the Arabs in Israel*, 21. After the Chief Rabbinate of Israel Law (1980) and the Prevention of Fraud in Kashrut Law (1983) Kretzmer asserted:

"No laws grant a non-Jewish religious body statutory status similar to that of the Chief Rabbinate . . . the statutory status given to the Chief Rabbinate must be regarded as another of the legal manifestations of the Jewish state."

Weiss and Gross-Horowitz, *Marriage and Divorce*, called it an established "church" (25); an "official state-sanctioned religious court system" (197); and a "theocratic island within an otherwise democratic state" (180). For a "national Church," see Israel Bartal, "The Closeness Which Alienates or the Alienation Which Brings Closer? Jewish Religion and Israeli Culture," in Charles S. Liebman and Elihu Katz, eds., *The Jewishness of Israelis: Responses to the Guttman Report* (Albany: State University of New York Press, 1997), 121–24.

88. Rubenstein, *Ha-Mishpat ha-Konstitutsioni*, 1:149–54; Bin-Nun, *The Law of the State of Israel*, 6–8, 22–27, 57, 144–54; Sachar, *A History of Israel*, 135. The Mandate adopted a framework for civil marriage but left it incomplete. Sharabi, *Ha-Yishuv ha-Seferadi bi-Yerushalyim be-Shilhe ha-Tekufah be-Otomanit.* Under the Ottomans there had been only one Chief Rabbi, the Sephardi "Hakam Bashi."

89. For one group of jurists' failure to create a "national-secular legal system" in Mandatory Palestine, see Ronen Shamir, *The Colonies of Law: Colonialism, Zionism and Law in Early Mandate Palestine* (Cambridge: Cambridge University Press, 2000).

90. Kaplan and Penslar, *The Origins of Israel*, 368–72; Menachem Friedman, "The Structural Foundation for Religio-Political Accommodation in Israel: Fallacy and Reality," in Troen and Lucas, eds., *Israel: The First Decade of Independence*, 51–77, emphasized wartime exigencies.

91. Rubenstein, *Ha-Mishpat ha-Konstitutsioni*, 1:149–53; Weiss and Gross-Horowitz, *Marriage and Divorce*, 11.

92. P. A. Alsberg, "Registration of Births, Deaths and Marriages in European Jewish Communities, in Palestine and in Israel," *Archivum: Revue Internationale des Archives* 9 (1959): 101–19; Goldscheider, *Israeli Society in the 21st Century*, 113–15.

93. Rubenstein, *Ha-Mishpat ha-Konstitutsioni*, 1:151; Weiss and Gross-Horowitz, *Marriage and Divorce*, xi, 2, 12. The law gave rabbinic courts parallel jurisdiction in ancillary matters related to divorce: alimony, child custody, and division of assets.

94. Ben-Gurion explicitly pledged that there would be no civil marriage (#6). Kaplan and Penslar, *The Origins of Israel*, 371; Rubenstein, *Ha-Mishpat ha-Konstitutsioni*, 1:147–49.

95. Rubenstein, *Ha-Mishpat ha-Konstitutsioni*, 1:316; Weiss and Gross-Horowitz, *Marriage and Divorce*, 15. Weiss and Gross-Horowitz call this "legal schizophrenia." Daphna Hacker, "Religious Tribunals in Democratic States: Lessons from the Israeli Rabbinical Courts," *Journal of Law and Religion* 27, no. 1 (2011): 79 labels it a "dual family law regime."

96. Rubenstein, *Ha-Mishpat ha-Konstitutsioni*, 1:316; Weiss and Gross-Horowitz, *Marriage and Divorce*, 26.

97. Rubenstein, *Ha-Mishpat ha-Konstitutsioni*, 1:156–72, 298–300; Hacker, "Religious Tribunals in Democratic States," 59–81; Dowty, "Israel's First Decade," 43. Israel abolished the Ministry of Religious Affairs in 2003 and transferred authority for the rabbinic courts to the Ministry of Justice. For an early Orthodox critique (1959), see Yeshayahu Leibowitz, "A Call for the Separation of Religion and State," in *Judaism, Human Values, and the Jewish State* (Cambridge, MA: Harvard University Press, 1992), 174–84.

> At present, we have a [secular] state . . . which recognizes religious institutions
> as state agencies, supports them with its funds, and, by administrative means,

imposes, not religion, but certain religious provisions chosen arbitrarily by political negotiation. . . . There is no greater degradation of religion than maintenance of its institutions by a secular state. (176)

Leibowitz dismissed the "status quo" arrangement as "mere clerical politics." See "The Crisis of Religion in the State of Israel" (1952), in *Judaism, Human Values, and the Jewish State*, 170.

98. Simon Schwarzfuchs, *A Concise History of the Rabbinate* (Oxford: Blackwell, 1993), 140.

99. Ibid., 137–41; Weiss and Gross-Horowitz, *Marriage and Divorce*, 50. In 2011 the state spent $40 million on the rabbinic courts. On selection of judges, see Sharon Shenhav, "At Issue: Choosing Religious Court Judges in Israel: A Case Study," *Jewish Political Studies Review* 18, no. 3/4 (2006): 141–49.

100. Kaplan and Penslar, *The Origins of Israel*, 370.

101. Rubenstein, *Ha-Mishpat ha-Konstitutsioni*, 1:145–46; Edelman, " 'Protecting' the Majority," 13–33.

102. Ephraim Tabory, "The Israel Reform and Conservative Movements and the Market for Liberal Judaism," in Rebhun and Waxman, eds., *Jews in Israel*, 285–314. For efforts at change since the 1990s, see Adam S. Ferziger, "Religion for the Secular: The New Israeli Rabbinate," *Journal of Modern Jewish Studies* 7, no. 1 (2008): 67–90.

103. Rubenstein, *Ha-Mishpat ha-Konstitutsioni*, 1:315.

104. Weiss and Gross-Horowitz, *Marriage and Divorce*, 44–46, 77, 172.

105. Rubenstein, *Ha-Mishpat ha-Konstitutsioni*, 1:312–26; Weiss and Gross-Horowitz, *Marriage and Divorce*, 167–70.

106. Shafir and Peled, *Being Israeli*, 97–103. Typical jobs, all low paid, were nursing, teaching, clerical work, and services.

107. Kretzmer, *The Legal Status of the Arabs in Israel*, 83.

108. Goldscheider, *Israeli Society in the 21st Century*, 144–52.

109. Rozin, *A Home for All Jews*, 15–66.

110. Asher Arian, *The Second Republic: Politics in Israel* (Chatham, NJ: Chatham House, 1998).

111. Shalev, "The Political Economy of Labor-Party Dominance and Decline in Israel," 118–20; Myron J. Aronoff, "Israel under Labor and the Likud: The Role of Dominance Considered," in Pempel, ed., *Uncommon Democracies*, 267; Yonathan Shapiro, *The Road to Power: Herut Party in Israel*, trans. Ralph Mandel (Albany: State University of New York Press, 1991).

112. Shalev, "The Political Economy of Labor-Party Dominance and Decline in Israel," 115. By the mid-1970s Labor had not only exhausted its success with the politics of nationalism and other sources of popular legitimacy, it also no longer possessed the capacity to manage the political economy effectively. It was in this double sense that Israel had arrived at the end of the era of Mapai hegemony (125).

113. Shafir and Peled, *Being Israeli*, 239.

114. Ibid., 245–48. The outstanding example was Koor, the industrial giant, that metamorphosed into Israel's "first multinational holding company" (1988). To become profitable, Koor laid off 40% of its workers, constituting 4% of the country's civilian labor force.

115. Ibid., 225–29. Membership dropped from 1.6 million (1994) to 600,000 (1998).

116. Ibid., 240–43.

117. Text reprinted in Guy Bechor, *Huka le-Yisrael: Sipuro shel Ma'avak* (Or Yehuda: Ma'ariv Book Guild, 1996), 279–82; Rubenstein, *Ha-Mishpat ha-Konstitutsioni*, 2:907–998, 1134–70. These were the tenth and eleventh Basic Laws. The first nine primarily concerned government functions: Knesset (1958); Israel Land Administration (1960); The

President (1964); The Government (1968); The State Economy (1976); The Armed Forces (1976); Jerusalem, The Capital of Israel (1980); The Judiciary (1984); State Comptroller (1988).

118. Pnina Lahav, "Rights and Democracy: The Court's Performance," in Ehud Sprinzak and Larry Diamond, eds., *Israeli Democracy under Stress* (Boulder, CO: Lynne Rienner, 1993), 125–52, would date the court's activism from the 1970s. The Judges Law of 1953 solidified the court's standing: judges gained tenure and were appointed by committee. Cf. Arian, *The Second Republic*, 265–78.

119. Ruth Ben-Israel, "From Collective Justice to Individual Justice: Changing Employment Relationships in Israel," in J. R. Bellace and M. G. Rood, eds., *Labour Law at the Crossroads: Changing Employment Relationships, Studies in Honour of Benjamin Aaron* (Hague: Kluwer, 1997), 27–55.

120. Martin Edelman, "A Portion of Animosity: The Politics of the Disestablishment of Religion in Israel," *Israel Studies* 5, no. 1 (2000): 204–27.

121. Daphne Barak-Erez, "Law and Religion under the Status Quo Model: Between Past Compromises and Constant Change," *Cardozo Law Review* 30, no. 6 (2009): 2495–2507, asserts the compromise, albeit fluid, largely held until 1977. The subsequent emergence of two competing political blocs enabled the religious parties to negotiate.

122. Chetrit, "Mizrahi Politics in Israel," 58; Lilly Weissbrod, "Shas: An Ethnic Religious Party," *Israel Affairs* 9, no. 4 (2003): 79–104.

123. Shafir and Peled, *Being Israeli*, 269.

124. Ibid., 284.

Chapter Twenty-Seven. United States

1. The claim of American Jewish "exceptionalism" precludes an emancipation process. Many historians of American Jewry appear to accept that claim as an article of faith. They consequently classify these phenomena under the parochial category of "anti-Semitism" that isolates them from the issues of civil rights and citizenship. See, e.g., Nathan C. Belth, *A Promise to Keep: A Narrative of the American Encounter with Anti-Semitism* (New York: Times Books, 1979) and Leonard Dinnerstein, *Antisemitism in America* (New York: Oxford University Press, 1994). An émigré scholar classified them as "racism." See Ismar Elbogen, *A Century of Jewish Life* (Philadelphia: Jewish Publication Society, 1960), 559–70. For the recognition of the United States as a center of Jewish life, see the founding statement of the American Jewish Archives: *American Jewish Archives* 1, no. 1 (June 1948): 2–3. On "exceptionalism," see Tony Michels, "Is America 'Different'? A Critique of American Jewish Exceptionalism," *American Jewish History* 96, no. 3 (2010): 201–24. For citizenship and emancipation, see Rogers M. Smith, *Civic Ideals: Conflicting Visions of Citizenship in U.S. History* (New Haven: Yale University Press, 1997).

2. The Great Migration (1915–75) of African Americans to the North (some six million), refugees from the South's segregation ("Jim Crow") and violence, confronted that same structure of inequality. See Isabel Wilkerson, *The Warmth of Other Suns: The Epic Story of America's Great Migration* (New York: Vintage, 2010); James N. Gregory, *The Southern Diaspora: How the Great Migration of Black and White Southerners Transformed America* (Chapel Hill: University of North Carolina Press, 2005); and Alferdteen Harrison, ed., *Black Exodus: The Great Migration from the American South* (Jackson: University Press of Mississippi, 1991).

3. John Higham, *Send These to Me: Immigrants in Urban America*, rev. ed. (Baltimore: Johns Hopkins University Press, 1984), 95–152.

4. Marianne Rachel Sanua, *Going Greek: Jewish College Fraternities in the United*

States, 1895–1945 (Detroit: Wayne State University Press, 2003); Marcia Graham Synnott, "Anti-Semitism and American Universities: Did Quotas Follow the Jews?" in David A. Gerber, ed., *Anti-Semitism in American History* (Urbana: University of Illinois Press, 1986), 237–38.

5. Dinnerstein, *Antisemitism in America*, 45–48.

6. Higham, *Send These to Me*, 136.

7. Dinnerstein, *Antisemitism in America*, 44–45. For the immigration service's exclusion of Jews, see Britt Tevis, "'The Hebrew Are Appearing in Court in Great Numbers': Toward a Reassessment of Early Twentieth-Century American Jewish Immigration History," *American Jewish History* 100, no. 3 (July 2016): 319–47.

8. Dinnerstein, *Antisemitism in America*, 49–50.

9. John Higham, *Strangers in the Land: Patterns of American Nativism, 1860–1925*, 2nd ed. (New Brunswick, NJ: Rutgers University Press, 1988).

10. John Higham, "Social Discrimination against Jews in America, 1830–1930," *Publications of the American Jewish Historical Society* 47 (1957): 16.

11. Belth, *A Promise to Keep*, 88–96.

12. Following tsarist practice, Poland and Hungary adopted quotas (numerus clausus) in higher education at the same time (chapter 22).

13. Synnott, "Anti-Semitism and American Universities," 233–71; Belth, *A Promise to Keep*, 96–110. For Columbia and Harvard, see Harold S. Wechsler, *The Qualified Student: A History of Selective College Admission in America* (New York: John Wiley & Sons, 1977), 133–75.

14. Susanne Klingenstein, *Jews in the American Academy, 1900–1940: The Dynamics of Assimilation*, 2nd ed. (Syracuse, NY: Syracuse University Press, 1998); Klingenstein, *Enlarging America: The Cultural Work of Jewish Literary Scholars, 1930–1990* (Syracuse, NY: Syracuse University Press, 1998).

15. Dinnerstein, *Antisemitism in America*, 89; Belth, *A Promise to Keep*, 110–14; Higham, *Send These to Me*, 169–70. For executives at large companies, see Abraham K. Korman, *The Outsiders: Jews and Corporate America* (Lexington, MA: Lexington Books, 1988).

16. Dinnerstein, *Antisemitism in America*, 88.

17. For a survey at the time, see Jacob A. Goldberg, "Jews in the Medical Profession: A National Survey," *Jewish Social Studies* 1, no. 3 (1939): 327–36. See Synnott, "Anti-Semitism and American Universities," 251–58.

18. Jerold S. Auerbach, "From Rags to Robes: The Legal Profession, Social Mobility and the American Jewish Experience," *American Jewish Historical Quarterly* 66, no. 2 (1976): 264.

19. Albert I. Goldberg, "Jews in the Legal Profession: A Case of Adjustment to Discrimination," *Jewish Social Studies* 32, no. 2 (1970): 148. The more prestigious was the Association of the Bar of the City of New York, the less so the New York County Lawyers' Association.

20. Auerbach, "From Rags to Robes," 255–65.

21. Dinnerstein, *Antisemitism in America*, 91.

22. Ibid., 92–93.

23. For the Federal Housing Authority (1934) as an engine of discrimination, see Charles Abrams, *Forbidden Neighbors: A Study of Prejudice in Housing* (New York: Harper & Brothers, 1955), 227–43.

24. Marshall Sklare, "Jews, Ethnics and the American City," *Commentary* (April 1972): 72, cited in Deborah Dash Moore, *At Home in America: Second Generation New York Jews* (New York: Columbia University Press, 1981), 18. For a "network of builders and real estate operators," see 234.

25. Moore, *At Home in America*, 30–31. The pattern was of successive areas of "compact settlement" (236).

26. American Jewish Committee resolution of 1947 and *ADL Bulletin* 6, no. 8 (November 1949): 2, cited in Stuart Svonkin, *Jews against Prejudice: American Jews and the Fight for Civil Liberties* (New York: Columbia University Press, 1997), 21, 25.

27. Arthur A. Goren, "A 'Golden Decade' for American Jews: 1945–1955," in Peter Y. Medding, ed., *A New Jewry? America since the Second World War*, Studies in Contemporary Jewry, vol. 8 (New York: Oxford University Press, 1992), 3–20; Svonkin, *Jews against Prejudice*, 11–17.

28. Svonkin, *Jews against Prejudice*. For employment, and the dense network of alliances African Americans created, including Jewish organizations, see Nancy MacLean, *Freedom Is Not Enough: The Opening of the American Workplace* (Cambridge, MA: Harvard University Press, 2006).

29. Svonkin, *Jews against Prejudice*, 3–4.

30. Higham, *Send These to Me*.

31. Quoted in Svonkin, *Jews against Prejudice*, 18.

32. Murray Friedman, *The Utopian Dilemma: New Political Directions for American Jews* (Washington, DC: Ethics and Public Policy Center, 1985), 1–35.

33. Goren, "A 'Golden Decade' for American Jews," 3–20; Svonkin, *Jews against Prejudice*, 6; Jonathan Sarna, "The Cult of Synthesis in American Jewish Culture," *Jewish Social Studies* 5, no. 1–2 (Fall 1998/Winter 1999): 52–79.

34. This was the title of the Commission on Law and Social Action's declaration. Svonkin, *Jews against Prejudice*, 80.

35. Alexander Pekelis, "A Pioneering Approach," *Congress Weekly* 23, no. 14 (April 16, 1956): 3: "the pattern of discrimination itself was proving the most fertile source of prejudice." Stephen S. Wise, 1947, "overt social and public practice," cited in Svonkin, *Jews against Prejudice*, 82. This idea had a long history. Gabriel Riesser had made this argument about the 1819 Hep Hep riots. See "Über die Stellung der Bekenner des Mosaischen Glaubens in Deutschland: An die Deutschen aller Confessionen," in Uri R. Kaufmann and Jobst Paul, eds., *Ausgewählte Werke* (Vienna: Böhlau, 2012), 1:79–80. Jewish lawyers in tsarist Russia, especially those who staffed the Defense Bureau of the Society for the Promotion of Enlightenment among the Jews (OPE), had repeatedly articulated this idea. See Benjamin Nathans, "The Other Modern Jewish Politics: Integration and Modernity in Fin de Siècle Russia," in Zvi Gitelman, ed., *The Emergence of Modern Jewish Politics* (Pittsburgh: University of Pittsburgh Press, 2003), 25–26.

36. Svonkin, *Jews against Prejudice*, 84.

37. Pekelis, "A Pioneering Approach," 3; Svonkin, *Jews against Prejudice*, 88–89.

38. Svonkin, *Jews against Prejudice*, 89: New York, New Jersey, Massachusetts, Connecticut, Rhode Island, Washington, Oregon, New Mexico, Michigan, Minnesota, Pennsylvania.

39. Svonkin, *Jews against Prejudice*, 92–93.

40. Ibid., 81–82.

41. Ibid., 96–97.

42. Ibid., 90–91.

43. Dinnerstein, *Antisemitism in America*, 154; Svonkin, *Jews against Prejudice*, 89.

44. Milton R. Konvitz, *A Century of Civil Rights* (New York: Columbia University Press, 1961), 72–78.

45. Korman, *The Outsiders*, 111–16.

46. Auerbach, "From Rags to Robes," 265–73.

47. Svonkin, *Jews against Prejudice*, 37, 56, 85, 109–10, 177; Stanley Lieberson, *A Piece*

of the Pie: Blacks and White Immigrants since 1880 (Berkeley: University of California Press, 1980); Gavin Wright, *Sharing the Prize: The Economics of the Civil Rights Revolution in the American South* (Cambridge, MA: Harvard University Press, 2013).

48. Michael E. Staub, *Torn at the Roots: The Crisis of Jewish Liberalism in Postwar America* (New York: Columbia University Press, 2002), 76–111; MacLean, *Freedom Is Not Enough*, 185–224; Korman, *The Outsiders*, 140–53.

49. Svonkin, *Jews against Prejudice*, 179–80. Earl Raab, *The Turbulent Decades: Jewish Communal Services in America 1958–78* (New York: Conference of Jewish Communal Service, 1981), 537, identified three periods in Jewish communal services: fighting anti-Semitism (to 1945); attaining civil rights and civil liberties (post–World War II); defense of Israel (from 1960s and especially 1967). Cited in Michael Kotzin, "Local Community Relations and Their National Body," in Alan Mittleman, Jonathan D. Sarna, and Robert Licht, eds., *Jewish Polity and American Civil Society: Communal Agencies and Religious Movements in the American Public Sphere* (Lanham, MD: Rowman and Littlefield, 2002), 83–84.

50. Nathan Glazer, "The American Jewish Urban Experience," in Dana Evan Kaplan, ed., *The Cambridge Companion to American Judaism* (Cambridge: Cambridge University Press, 2005), 273. For the chilling example of Boston, see Hillel Levine and Lawrence Harmon, *The Death of an American Jewish Community: A Tragedy of Good Intentions* (New York: Free Press, 1992): "the promotion of equality as the supreme value has also failed us" (9).

51. Glazer, "The American Jewish Urban Experience," 271–82; Deborah Dash Moore, *To the Golden Cities: Pursuing the American Jewish Dream in Miami and L.A.* (New York: Free Press, 1994).

52. For public education's authority in the interwar period, see Moore, *At Home in America*, 88–121.

53. For an early overview before dramatic growth, see Alvin I. Schiff, "Jewish Day Schools in the United States," *Encyclopedia Judaica Year Book* (1974): 137–47. The percentage of Jewish students in day schools rose from 10% in 1975 to 25% in 2007. Howard Deitcher and Alex Pomson, "Jewish Day Schools Worldwide: Achievements, Challenges, and Aspirations," in David J. Schnall and Moshe Sokolow, eds., *The Azrieli Papers: Dimensions of Orthodox Day School Education* (New York: Yeshiva University Press, 2011), 24–25; Marvin Schick, *A Census of Jewish Day Schools in the United States* (New York: Avi Chai, 2009). For the role of "white flight," see Stuart Kelman, "Why Parents Send Their Children to Non-Orthodox Jewish Day Schools: A Study of Motivation and Goals," *Studies in Jewish Education* 2 (1984): 289–98 and Deitcher and Pomson, "Jewish Day Schools Worldwide," 25–26. For debates at the time, see Michael E. Staub, *Torn at the Roots: The Crisis of Jewish Liberalism in Postwar America* (New York: Columbia University Press, 2002), 76–111. For parents' choice, see Steven M. Cohen and Shaul Kelner, "Why Jewish Parents Send Their Children to Day Schools," in Jack Wertheimer, ed., *Family Matters: Jewish Education in an Age of Choice* (Waltham, MA: Brandeis University Press, 2007), 80–100 and Alex Pomson, " 'Dorks with Yarmulkes': An Ethnographic Inquiry into the Surprised Embrace of Parochial Day Schools by Liberal American Jews," in Zvi Bekerman and Ezra Kopelowitz, eds., *Cultural Education-Cultural Sustainability: Minority, Diaspora, Indigenous and Ethno-Religious Groups in Multicultural Societies* (New York: Routledge, 2008), 305–21. For an advocate, see Jack Wertheimer, "Who's Afraid of Jewish Day Schools?" *Commentary* 108, no. 5 (1999): 49–53.

54. Svonkin, *Jews against Prejudice*, 187–89. For a Federation's turn from the city, working-class Jews, and the problem of equality to suburban life and foreign issues, see Levine and Harmon, *The Death of an American Jewish Community*, 199, 282, 322.

55. Lynn Rapaport, "The Holocaust in American Jewish Life," in Kaplan, ed., *The Cambridge Companion to American Judaism*, 187–208; Jonathan S. Woocher, *Sacred Survival: The Civil Religion of American Jews* (Bloomington: Indiana University Press, 1986). For the projection of Jewish nationhood abroad, see Steven Rosenthal, "Long-distance Nationalism: American Jews, Zionism and Israel," in Kaplan, ed., *The Cambridge Companion to American Judaism*, 209–24 and James Loeffler, "Nationalism without a Nation? On the Invisibility of American Jewish Politics," *Jewish Quarterly Review* 105, no. 3 (2015): 367–98.

56. Hasia Diner, *We Remember with Reverence and Love: American Jews and the Myth of Silence after the Holocaust* (New York: New York University Press, 2009).

57. Jack Kugelmass, "Why We Go to Poland: Holocaust Tourism as Secular Ritual," in James E. Young, ed., *The Art of Memory: Holocaust Memorials in History* (New York: Prestel, 1994), 175–83.

58. Edward T. Linenthal, *Preserving Memory: The Struggle to Create America's Holocaust Museum* (New York: Viking, 1985), 17–20, 47.

59. Hyman Bookbinder, quoted in Linenthal, *Preserving Memory*, 34.

60. For the long history of Zionist lobbying and fundraising, see Martin J. Raffel, "History of Israel Advocacy," in Mittleman, Sarna, and Licht, eds., *Jewish Polity and American Civil Society*, 103–79. For a comparison to Irish fundraising, see Dan Lainer-Vos, *Sinews of the Nation: Constructing Irish and Zionist Bonds in the United States* (Cambridge: Polity Press, 2013). Since the Reagan administration's shift of funding to the states (1980s) there has been a dramatic leap in government funding to Jewish social welfare institutions. See Joel M. Carp, "The Jewish Social Welfare Lobby in the United States," in Mittleman, Sarna, and Licht, eds., *Jewish Polity and American Civil Society*, 181–232, esp. 184–92.

61. Howard M. Sachar, *A History of the Jews in America* (New York: Knopf, 1992), 928; Levine and Harmon, *The Death of an American Jewish Community*, 322.

62. Henry L. Feingold, *"Silent No More": Saving the Jews of Russia, the American Jewish Effort, 1967–1989* (Syracuse, NY: Syracuse University Press, 2007), 296.

63. Ibid., 306; Sachar, *A History of the Jews in America*, 916, 928.

64. Harold S. Wechsler and Paul Ritterband, "Jewish Learning in American Universities: The Literature of a Field," *Modern Judaism* 3, no. 3 (1983): 253–89.

65. Barry Chiswick, "The Postwar Economy of American Jews," in Medding, ed., *A New Jewry? America since the Second World War*, 85–101; Chiswick, "The Occupational Attainment and Earnings of American Jewry, 1890–1990," *Contemporary Jewry* 20, no. 1 (1999): 68–98; Carmel U. Chiswick, "The Economics of American Judaism," in Kaplan, ed., *The Cambridge Companion to American Judaism*, 315–25. For an account of why blacks fared poorly in comparison to southern and eastern European immigrants, see Lieberson, *A Piece of the Pie*.

66. Auerbach, "From Rags to Robes," 283.

INDEX

Note: Page numbers in italic type refer to illustrations.

Abdulhamid II, sultan of Ottoman Empire, 269

actors, 94–95

Adenauer, Konrad, 316

Adler, Lazarus, 159

African Americans, 346, 348, 350–51

Age of Marriage Law (Israel, 1950), 343

agricultural colonies, 237–38

Agudat Yisrael, 342

Ahad Ha-Am, 251

Alexander I, tsar of Russia, 131, 132, 142

Alexander II, tsar of Russia, 5, 194, 196–99, 200, 202

Alexander III, tsar of Russia, 5, 202–4, 208

Alfonso, duke of Este, 25

Algeria, 8, 219–21, 241, 248, 307, 310, 321–23

Algerian Jewish Committee for Social Studies, 322–23

Alliance Israélite Universelle, 221–23, 235–36, 238, 247–49, 279, 282, 283, 320, 323, 324, 326, 330, 331, 438n118, 438n119

Allianz zu Wien, 235, 237, 451n16

Alsace: anti-Jewish sentiment in, 93, 100–101, 118, 213–14; Affair of Counterfeit Receipts, 77;

Jewish debt in, 216; Jews' status in, 9, 62, 70, 75–78, 91, 92, 95–97, 100–101, 104, 118, 126–27, 141, 216–18; self-government in, 77; synagogues in, 76–77

American Civil Liberties Union, 349

American Jewish Agro-Joint, 287

American Jewish Committee, 235, 246–47, 347–48, 351

American Jewish Congress, 348–51; Commission on Law and Social Action, 349–50

American Jewish Year Book (almanac), 247

American Joint Distribution Committee, 278, 316, 323

American War of Independence, 75

Amsterdam: Jews' status in, 19, 29–31; synagogues in, 18, 29–30, 369n63

Amsterdam Stock Exchange, 317

Anabaptists, 75, 105, 113

Ancona, 20–21

Anglo-Egyptian Treaty (1936), 327

Anglo-Jewish Association, 235, 236, 248

Anninger, Wilhelm, 243

Anti-Comintern Pact (1939), 298

Anti-Defamation League of B'nai B'rith, 235, 247, 347–48, 351

anti-Semitism: in Algeria, 241, 321; in Austria, 237, 242–44; Catholic, 346; coining of term, 240; countries hospitable to, 241–42; in education, 243–44; emancipation and equality as targets of, 240–42, 244–45, 356; emancipation blamed as cause of, 251; Fascism and, 303; in France, 241–42, 304–5; in Germany, 244–46; ideas underlying, 240–41; organizations for addressing, 235, 242–46; organizations fueled by, 241–42; political, 4, 240–42, 245; race as factor in, 240, 282, 283; revolutions of 1848 as contributing factor to, 171; in Russia, 204, 242; in Soviet Union, 287–88; in United States, 247, 346–47

Antonescu, Ion, 301–2, 467n104

Arab-Israeli War (1948), 328, 330

Arab League, 326

Arab Revolt (Palestine, 1936–39), 321, 330

arenda (leasing system), 36

Armenians, 264, 265

Arnheim, Fischel, 182

Arnstein, Nathan, 144

art, restitution and reparations involving, 313, 317–18

Aryanization, 291–92, 304, 306, 312

A NOTE ON THE TYPE

{ ≈≈≈✴≈≈≈ }

THIS BOOK has been composed in Miller, a Scotch Roman typeface designed by Matthew Carter and first released by Font Bureau in 1997. It resembles Monticello, the typeface developed for The Papers of Thomas Jefferson in the 1940s by C. H. Griffith and P. J. Conkwright and reinterpreted in digital form by Carter in 2003.

Pleasant Jefferson ("P. J.") Conkwright (1905–1986) was Typographer at Princeton University Press from 1939 to 1970. He was an acclaimed book designer and AIGA Medalist.

The ornament used throughout this book was designed by Pierre Simon Fournier (1712–1768) and was a favorite of Conkwright's, used in his design of the *Princeton University Library Chronicle*.